Social Psychology

Fourth Edition

Social Psychology

Sociological Perspectives

Fourth Edition

David E. Rohall
Ohio University

Melissa A. Milkie
University of Toronto

Jeffrey W. Lucas
University of Maryland

WAVELAND PRESS, INC.
Long Grove, Illinois

For information about this book, contact:
Waveland Press, Inc.
4180 IL Route 83, Suite 101
Long Grove, IL 60047-9580
(847) 634-0081
info@waveland.com
www.waveland.com

10-digit ISBN 1-4786-5226-8
13-digit ISBN 978-1-4786-5226-7

Printed in the United States of America

7 6 5 4 3 2 1

To our mothers, Theresa, Judy, and Patricia,
who helped shape our curiosity about the world.

CONTENTS

PREFACE

It is an exciting time to be a social psychologist! As of this writing, COVID is in the past, giving us the space to reflect on what people around the globe experienced in the 2020s. Since our last edition, there has been a global expansion of the use of technology in everyday life and sociologists have applied social psychological perspectives to help us understand its impact on our lives.

As with all of our updates, we have reviewed hundreds of books and research articles to either expand the topics included in the book or support existing theory and research. We have also updated our biographies for the Cooley-Mead Award recipients with current books related to those write-ups.

This time, we decided to include boxes about careers in social psychology. As many readers know, the field is interesting and exciting but challenging to link to specific jobs. Our goal is to provide some guidance that instructors can use to talk to students about careers. We also hope that students will see the soft skills that they can use from a social psychology course in their work lives. Please keep in mind that these jobs change in time and context—position titles change and have different requirements depending on the location and organization. We are also certain that there are many other positions that we have not considered. The real goal is to inspire readers to consider careers that they may not have even heard of!

Let's take a look at some of the changes we have made in specific chapters.

Chapter 1 Introduction to Sociological Social Psychology

- We start with an emphasis on the role of technology in our day-to-day lives with a new focus on digital sociology, the study of social interactions using digital mediums.
- The textbox, "Human and Animal Interaction" was changed to "Human and Nonhuman Interaction" to expand the idea that social psychology can also include the ways that humans interact with all aspects of the environment, notably computers and other nonhuman objects.
- We include additional, more recent readings on the biographies of Charles Horton Cooley and George Herbert Mead, should students want to have more information on these scholars.
- We start our discussions of careers in social psychology with a primer, giving readers some ideas to consider about finding work related to the field. There

are few jobs with those titles on the undergraduate level, but many jobs that utilize skills from the field. We also encourage students to consider things that they should start doing now to improve their chances of finding employment after they graduate from college.

Chapter 2 Perspectives in Sociological Social Psychology

- In this chapter, we add more information in the symbolic interaction section on the concepts of expressive order and accounts (i.e., Marvin Scott and Stanford Lyman 1968) as a means of understanding social order. Our goal is to demonstrate to students the situational basis of understanding why people do what they do, that people respond to the world around them based on social conditions as much as, or more than, the dispositions of the individuals they are interacting with.
- We also introduce the Center for Research on Interpersonal Behavior (CRIB) to the discussion of the Iowa School of symbolic interaction. The goal is to provide more historical background to the development of the field.
- We start our second career discussion by reviewing the role of graduate school in sociology and psychology. Since most of the chapters will emphasize jobs at the undergraduate level, we wanted students to understand that another set of jobs are available if they choose to do graduate work. We emphasize the goal of becoming a college professor here but also discuss the idea that graduate programs in psychology and social work will allow students to become certified counselors.

Chapter 3 Studying People

- In this chapter, we continue to look for ways to provide tools for readers to use in collecting data in their everyday lives, especially in the digital world. We include a new box about online ethnographies as a way to encourage students to apply research design principles to study online social interaction.
- More information is provided about the social nature of Institutional Review Boards, that they are made up of people who decide on research protocols with the same limitations that all human interactions have, and with the same biases that accompany any group decision process.
- Additional tips are provided at the end of the chapter to encourage students to conduct research, emphasizing the stresses associated with research that involves interacting with people but also excitement about participant observation and any research that helps them to better understand the social world.
- "Online experiments" are now included in our terminology. We also include the concept of grounded theory in our review of ethnographies.
- We highlight access to the free statistical software, R (www.r-project.org) in our review of programs to help students conduct research projects.
- This chapter's focus on careers is the first one to bring real job examples for people related to the chapter topic. We emphasize a number of jobs available to researchers at the undergraduate level.

Chapter 4 The Social Psychology of Stratification

- We include a brief review of Weber's bases of power and authority in society as a way to include new work by Randall Collins on the microsociological basis of inequality in society.
- There is a new box titled "Tay, the Racist Chatbot" that highlights the limits of science and technology in stopping the biases and inequalities created by humans.
- Our career focus here includes jobs specifically designed to deal with issues related to inequality in society. We introduce the US federal office called the Equal Employment Opportunity Commission. We also point out that many colleges and universities have offices specifically designed to address these concerns. There are many other opportunities out there, we just wanted readers to start considering ways to look for similar jobs.

Chapter 5 Self and Identity

- We added a new box titled, "The Digital Self." Our goal is to review theory and research about how individuals create and manage their self-presentations online.
- In our attempts to guide students in learning about careers related to topics of each chapter, we emphasize this use of the literature on how people build their self-concept in practical applications. Here, we focus on psychology technicians and academic success coaches. The first role explicitly emphasizes the use of personality tests to help offenders to rethink their future roles in life. Academic success coaches help students consider ways to use their education in the development of their future selves. In both cases, it requires some understanding of self-processes to be successful.

Chapter 6 Socialization over the Life Course

- We extend our discussion of "other" agents of socialization to more fully examine the role of media and technology in socialization processes. We also expand our discussion of video games and look at the current and potential role of artificial intelligence (AI) in these processes.
- In addition to adding citations for our review of theories and research in socialization, we include a new box on jobs related to the idea of socialization. We discuss how teaching is probably most directly related to socialization. But we also point out that any job that involves training can be thought of as socialization (e.g., human resources).

Chapter 7 The Social Psychology of Deviance

- In this chapter, we expand Box 7.5 on white-collar crime to examine the dark web and other ways people use the internet for deviance.
- We updated statistics for Figure 7.2 on the distribution of crimes in the US from 2003 to present. A similar update was made to Table 7.1 about perspectives of the morality of different behaviors.

- We add Figure 7.3 about the sex offender registry map. This application is important because it illustrates the ways that we track people who are deemed criminals with modern technologies.
- We add Figure 7.4 about school shootings. The goal here is to provide information about some more current forms of crimes and deviance that appear regularly in the media today.
- Like other chapters, we added new citations relevant to our Cooley-Mead Award recipient box. Here, several pieces relevant to Howard Becker are included such as *Zur Aktualitat von Howard S. Becker: Einfuhrung in sein Werk* by Dagmar Danko and Thaddeus Muller's 2014 article: "Chicago, Jazz and Marijuana: Howard Becker on Outsiders" in the journal *Symbolic Interaction*.
- We expand applications of the concept of stigma as a way of showing that it is more than just about having a criminal record. We also include examples of ways that modern technology helps us identify and publicly label people who are labelled deviant (e.g., sex offenders).
- There is also a new box on jobs linked to the study of deviance. Our goal is to go beyond the traditional discussion of law enforcement careers to discuss alternative ways of using theories and research in this chapter in career choices, focusing more on jobs like victim advocates and probation officers.

Chapter 8 Mental Health and Illness

- In this chapter, a new box is used to apply the concept of the stress process to better understand the role of media use and mental health. We also research on the stress associated with the 2020 COVID-19 pandemic.
- There are a number of career ideas we could have included in our new career section of this chapter. We decided to focus on psych techs and substance abuse counselors. As with our inclusion in Chapter 5, psych techs support licensed psychologists in many different types of facilities. This position is a bit different than the one in the previous chapter. Many people do not know that you can be a licensed substance abuse counselor without a graduate degree. It does require some special training, but this training can be done as an undergraduate student.

Chapter 9 Social Attitudes

- We include a new paragraph on Robin DiAngelo's *White Fragility* (2018) and Eduardo Bonilla-Silva's (2022) concept of "racism without racists."
- We also add the concept of myside bias to help bridge the biases associated with groups affiliations to individuals' tendency to be biased toward our own attitudes and opinions.
- We include some research on the role of diversity training on prejudice in the workplace to add another tool for trying to reduce the biases that exist in society.
- Our inclusion of career ideas focuses on data collection related to opinion polls, much like Chapter 3. We also try to show readers how there are jobs that are, in

part, designed to help people consider their attitudes toward the world. Specifically, we use the example of a position as a diversity specialist who is expected to help create a positive culture of diversity in their organization.

Chapter 10 The Sociology of Emotions and Relationships

- As with other chapters, we bring in research to explore ways that relationships develop in the digital world. We also bring in some research related to the importance of touch for human relationships.
- Louis Zurcher's study of ephemeral roles during poker games is applied to playing video games online, a place for people to relax their everyday performances in a non-institutional environment.
- We add the concept of networked individualism as a way to apply the principles of community to online social interactions.
- We include a box that reviews the ways that AI can influence the future of human relationships. First, we discuss how AI can be a partner in and of itself, as the technologies make dialogue more seamless and personal. AI can also help improve existing platforms for individuals to meet, such as online dating and social networking sites. This box is unique because it was written by ChatGPT!
- We also include a new section called, "Relationships, Online" to discuss ways that communication changed as more and more people began connecting online over platforms like Zoom and Teams. How does this change dynamics as reviewed in Chapter 5 on the topic dramaturgy? What do we know about this new way of interacting with one another?
- We titled our box on careers, "Making Emotion Work" as a way of bridging the topic of emotions with specific jobs. One career connected to emotions is human resources where individuals must work with a variety of people in organizations—dealing with very positive situations (e.g., offering people new work!) and negative ones (e.g., dealing with complaints about people). This work requires a lot of emotional intelligence! People in human services must also have a strong sense of self and know how to manage emotions.

Chapter 11 Collective Behavior

- While we have already covered collective memories in our previous work, we decided to add the idea of the sociology of the future to demonstrate how collective imagination can refer to past, present, as well as future. It is not just about how people reimagine the past to suit modern perspectives but also how we believe the future will or should be and the role of this collective thinking in making present day decisions.
- We replace a box reviewing the details of the Stairway to the Stars event with a discussion of the COVID-19 pandemic as collective behavior. The idea is to help see how people's thoughts, feelings, and behaviors during the pandemic may have

been influenced by what was going on in society and how there is awareness among some about living in a global community.

- We provide a few examples of ways that readers can get involved—often for pay—in the social change industry. Our examples include community organizer with a digital version of that job. Of course, there are other organizations that exist to help with community development including the Office of Housing and Urban Development. We could have found many more for specific movements like Greenpeace and programs that put young people into communities to help them address specific issues (e.g., AmeriCorps and Peace Corps in the United States). We hope that these examples will inspire readers to find fulfilling work addressing the kinds of issues that are important to them.

Acknowledgements

We would like to acknowledge the many mentors, students, and colleagues we've engaged with over the years whose ideas, questions, and research have shaped and sharpened our approach to social psychology. A special thanks to Don Rosso, Senior Editor at Waveland Press, who took the time and resources to transition this book to Waveland. We also appreciate his patience in the process! We could not have updated this book without Dakota West, who made editing as painless as possible. Many thanks to Debi Underwood, the designer who revised and prepared all of the figures and photos in this edition. We appreciate all of the staff at Waveland Press for helping bring this project to fruition!

PART 1

Perspectives and Methods

The first section of this book will give you an overview of sociological social psychology, including the ways scholars in the field approach research and link their work to the larger field of sociology. The first chapter will review concepts that sociological social psychologists use in developing theories and research. We will also provide an overview of the three major perspectives in social psychology: symbolic interactionism, social structure and personality, and group processes. Chapter 2 will review these perspectives extensively, providing detailed information about the theories and research within each approach. Chapter 3 will examine the primary methods used by sociological social psychologists to study people.

Early in each chapter, you will find a series of questions to focus on; then, each chapter section will end with a review of how the questions have been addressed. Each chapter closes with a section titled "A Take-Away Message" in which we apply the material to everyday life. We also include a series of discussion questions to provoke additional thinking and learning. Finally, we provide a list of key words used in each chapter and summaries of them. We believe these tools will help you learn the most important concepts, theories, and research in the field of sociological social psychology.

1

Introduction to Sociological Social Psychology

I guess you could say that I became obsessed with figuring the man out. He was so rude to me in the classroom that day, basically telling me that I had no business in college. I had to know what this guy was about. Was he just a jerk? Did he have a bad day? I wanted to know why he was so hurtful to me. I started asking around and everyone said that he was a great guy. Then I wondered if I might have been the problem—maybe I said something to set him off. I tried to ask him, but he did not want to talk about it. The professor later told me that the guy was going through some hard times. Maybe that was it...

—Krystal, sophomore English major

Trying to understand the behaviors of other people can be difficult. Although social psychologists take numerous approaches to examining the social world, we all have an interest in understanding the thoughts, feelings, and behaviors of the people around us. You are probably reading this book because your desire to learn about people led you to take a social psychology class. You have probably even developed your own opinions or "theories" about human behavior. You might have opinions about a particular person—perhaps a theory about why a friend struggles in many of her classes. Or, you may have developed more general explanations that account for the behaviors of many people in different situations, such as theories about what leads people to have more or fewer friends in college. Personal opinions such as these do not fit social scientists' criteria for what constitutes a theory, but the general idea is the same: just as you may theorize about social life, social scientists seek to develop explanations for the often-complex ways that people act, think, or feel.

In the vignette that opens this chapter, we see a student trying to make sense of another student's behavior. Apparently the second student has done something to her that makes her wonder what might have caused the behavior. At first, she relies on the personality of the other person: "Is he just a jerk?" She investigates the matter and discovers that other people think highly of him and realizes that she probably does not have the whole picture. Gradually, she begins to put together a story about the man and how his current life circumstances may have contributed to his behavior.

Most of us engage in efforts to gather and use available information about people to reach conclusions about them. In this way, we are all social scientists, searching the world around us for clues as to how and why people act the ways they do. But two crucial things separate social science from personal theories of human behavior. First, social scientists do not rely on speculation. Rather, they systematically test theories and revise them based on what they learn. Second, social scientists do not develop theories about the behavior of a single individual. Rather, they seek to develop theories that explain how and why different people will tend to behave in similar ways when facing similar situations or when placed in certain roles or settings. Social psychologists develop theories and then test them by using observations, surveys, experiments, and other approaches. They also use various forms of research to develop theories. Whatever the approach, the goal of social psychological research is to explain and predict people's behavior, a powerful tool to unlocking mysteries of the social world.

Social psychology is the systematic study of people's thoughts, feelings, and behaviors in social contexts. Social psychologists approach the study of human behavior in

Photo 1.1 Social psychologists study the social contexts influencing individuals' thoughts, feelings, and behaviors. Can you recall a time when you acted differently in a group than you might have if you had been alone?

Source: blvdone/Shutterstock

different ways, but those trained in sociology will pay attention to factors beyond people's most immediate social environments. Krystal, the student in the opening vignette, could make her investigation more sociological by incorporating additional levels of analysis. She might investigate the larger social conditions that may be exacerbating her classmate's immediate social problems. Maybe he just lost his job in a recession that caused additional stresses in his life that led him to be more irritable. Thus, when sociologists study social psychology, they assess the effects of broad social conditions on people's thoughts, feelings, and behaviors and also emphasize the ways in which society shapes the meanings of social interactions. The goal of this book is to provide you with an extensive review of the theories and research developed by sociological social psychologists. In this chapter, we will offer a brief overview of the field of sociology and the ways in which sociological social psychologists incorporate the larger field of sociology into their work. Specifically, we will address the following questions:

- What is sociology? How does macrosociology differ from microsociology?
- What are the differences in the ways that sociologists and psychologists approach social psychology?
- What are the major perspectives in the field of sociological social psychology?
- What do I need to know to study the effects that social forces have on my day-to-day life?

SOCIOLOGY, PSYCHOLOGY, AND SOCIAL PSYCHOLOGY

> *Sociology first came alive to me after watching the film* Capitalism: A Love Story. *I didn't agree with everything Michael Moore had to say about American society, but his film made me wonder how much power other people had over me. It's amazing that rich people have so much control over our lives. They wrecked the economy and they kept their money. What about the rest of us?*
>
> —Steve, junior political science major

Sociology is the systematic study of society. "Society" is a broad term that includes many levels of social interaction, from those occurring among individuals to complex relations among nations. Sociologists analyze social life across these levels of analysis (Aron 1965; Collins 1985). We usually think of society as a larger entity that exists above and beyond its individual members. Until something negative happens to us, we may not think much about the effects of society on our lives. If a downturn in the economy leads to a job loss, for instance, we may blame the government or get angry at "the direction society is going." But what do we mean by "society" beyond government rules and regulations? In what other ways can society affect our lives? Sociologists try to elaborate the specific ways that societal processes work to influence people's lives.

In the vignette from Steve, the political science major, we see "society" come alive for a student after he watches a controversial film about the American economy. Steve notices that some people in the world have more power than others, and he questions whether those people deserve the power they have. When sociologists study social life, their goals often include examining how people's social positions and statuses—for example, being an owner of a business, being married, being a woman, or living in poverty—affect people's thoughts, feelings, and behaviors, as well as their power in relation to others.

This section of the chapter will review the different levels of analysis used in sociology, including macrosociology and microsociology. It will also discuss differences in how psychologists and sociologists approach the study of social psychology. Finally, we will review the history of sociological social psychology.

Macrosociology and Microsociology

People's societies and cultures affect them in many ways. To understand these influences, sociologists study social phenomena in different ways. Suppose you are interested in studying racial discrimination. One way to explore this interest would be to conduct a field experiment in which employers are presented with identical résumés from fictitious pairs who differ only in their racial status and to assess the number of callbacks from employers for applicants with the same stated backgrounds (see Pager 2003). You might for example find that White applicants receive more callbacks than African American applicants. You also could study racial discrimination on a day-to-day basis, more specifically, in the lives and interactions of people from different racial and ethnic backgrounds (May 2001; Nash 2000). For example, you might find that minority-group members, on average, are treated with more suspicion by others in public spaces than are members of the majority group. Both of these examples demonstrate the same basic social phenomenon—discrimination—that favors majority-group members and disfavors minority-group members. The studies, however, approach the issue from different levels of analysis: one at the level of organizations, and one focused on interpersonal interactions.

Macrosociology focuses on the analysis of large-scale social processes (see Boxes 1.1 and 1.2). Instead of researching individual thoughts, feelings, and behaviors, macrosociology studies larger groups and social institutions (Nolan and Lenski 2004). Macrosociologists use societal-level data to examine phenomena such as poverty rates, incidence of violence, and large-scale social change. For instance, C. Wright Mills (2002, originally 1951) traced patterns of change in the American economy from the late nineteenth century to the early twentieth century, showing the fall of independent farming and the concurrent rise of white-collar professions. He went on to explain the long-term effects of the early American economy on the society and culture of the United States in the 1950s. Mills showed that companies in the bureaucratic age of the 1950s exerted a great deal of control over people's lives, despite the emphasis that U.S. culture placed on independence and freedom. In Mills' view, this converted the American middle classes from independent entrepreneurs to a group alienated from their own labor.

Macrosociologists also conduct comparative studies across societies and cultures. There are currently 193 members of the United Nations, representing almost all the

Box 1.1 Macro-Level Sources of Information

Social psychological information is all around us. Macrosociologists, who use information that applies to whole societies, rely on many sources of data. For example, the United States Census Bureau (www.census.gov) is the hub of widespread demographic information about the United States today. In addition to conducting a count of the US population every 10 years, the Census Bureau maintains current population estimates for the United States and the world. Census data comprise a valuable resource for sociologists interested in studying the US population. It includes detailed information about Americans' income levels, health insurance, education, and housing, among many other topics. Sociologists regularly use census data to track important social issues such as poverty or segregation and to examine broad societal conditions associated with those issues—for example, comparing poverty rates by region, race, or gender (e.g., Roehrkasse 2021).

The United Nations (www.un.org) and the World Bank (www.worldbank.org) provide extensive datasets on nations across the world. Like the Census Bureau, these organizations allow researchers to examine basic demographic information for all the countries on the planet. Researchers can also use these data to study poverty, conflicts, and other important social issues. Macrosociologists use these and other sources of data to track large-scale social processes.

Macro-level data, including population size, literacy, and unemployment rates, provide an understanding of the social and economic contexts of people's lives and the types of problems people face in their daily lives.

Box 1.2 Theoretical Perspectives in Macrosociology

Two major theoretical perspectives in macrosociology are structural functionalism and conflict theory. The structural functionalist perspective emphasizes how elements of society interact in ways that help it maintain order. Important sociologists linked to structural functionalism include Émile Durkheim (1858–1917) and Talcott Parsons (1902–1979). From the functionalist perspective, society resembles a biological organism in which each part of the body has a function that promotes the survival of the whole. In society, similarly, different groups and individuals function to keep society alive—accountants, teachers, and garbage collectors are all needed to keep society working. However, not all parts of this system are of equal value. The heart, for instance, is more important for survival than a big toe. From a functionalist perspective, this specialization leads to differentiation and the establishment of a hierarchy, with some people gaining higher social standing than others. Right or wrong, medical doctors, for example, may be perceived as contributing more to the maintenance and stability of society

(*continued*)

than street cleaners. The result is a class system in which some people gain more money and prestige than others. Change in society occurs when environmental conditions make new roles necessary or more important. In this way, information technology professionals have become an important part of Western economies in just the last 30 or 40 years, leading to high salaries and more prestige than some other professions.

The social conflict perspective focuses on social inequalities, especially those associated with class differences. Important theorists linked to the conflict perspective include Karl Marx (1818–1883) and C. Wright Mills (1916–1962). In contrast to the functionalist emphasis on maintaining overall harmony in a society, conflict theorists see society as made up of members—both individuals and groups—who are constantly battling over limited resources. Conflict theorists differ from functionalists in their view of what keeps society together, and they focus on different elements of society in explaining social phenomena.

Although these perspectives are often applied to understanding macrosociological processes, functional and conflict theorists have also emphasized the social psychological relevance of their ideas (House 1977). For instance, Marx employed the concept of "alienation," a psychological state in which people feel disconnected from their work, to describe one of the effects of capitalist economies on individuals in society. And there are "Radical Interactionists" who utilize conflict theory to focus on themes of dominance and power in symbolic interactionist theory and research (Athens 2009). Hence, macrosociological perspectives can be applied to understand some aspects of microsociological phenomena. Can you think of ways to apply these perspectives to everyday interactions between people?

countries in the world. Sociologists, especially demographers, examine differences in such parameters as fertility, mortality, and immigration rates across the world. For example, when researchers study how resource levels relate to trends in fertility and mortality, they find that some of the richest nations in the world—those with the most resources to raise children—have the lowest fertility rates (Pampel 2001).

The subject of this book is **microsociology**, or the study of the effects of interpersonal interactions, the larger society on social psychological processes, and relationships within and between groups. Microsociologists are also concerned with the ways in which individuals participate in the construction and maintenance of society.

As you can see, both macrosociologists and microsociologists study society, but they do it at different levels and in unique ways. Consider divorce as a social phenomenon. Macrosociologists are typically interested in rates of divorce and in how changing divorce rates affect the institution of the family. They may also compare social policies and divorce rates by region or across nations in an effort to understand the conditions that affect the rate of divorce (Diekmann and Schmidheiny 2004; Wilde 2001; Yi and Deqing 2000). In contrast, microsociologists would be more interested in the perceived causes and outcomes of divorces than in divorce rates. A microsociologist might conduct a study in which a number of divorced men and women talk about the factors that influenced their decisions to divorce their spouses. Or a microsociologist might study the mental health consequences of going through a divorce and whether these consequences are different for women than for men. Both macrosociological and microsociological approaches contribute to our understanding of the social aspects of divorce. One involves societal-level factors, while the other focuses on the ways in which people make sense of divorce and how their lives may change with the end of a marital relationship.

Larger social conditions provide a context for understanding interactions between individuals. In one study, a researcher examined divorce rates across 22 countries, finding that divorce rates are associated with marital equality (Yodanis 2005). That is, countries in which divorce is more common (represented by rates of divorce) also have a more equal distribution of work between men and women in the household than countries with lower divorce rates. Hence, a "divorce culture" may affect men's and women's personal relationships in a direct way, giving women more leverage in their marriages. At the same time, individuals are often not aware of how larger social conditions affect their decision-making processes, making it challenging for people to understand links between macro-level processes and their everyday lives. In another study of people living in 52 different nations, sociologists found that countries that offered greater support systems—those governments that are better at providing security and services—had lower levels of individual-level religiosity, such as the level of importance people attach to God, and the frequency of prayer and church attendance, controlling for individual and other factors (Conway and Spruyt 2018). In other words, growing up in a particular country can have profound effects on some of people's most personal and deeply held values and beliefs.

A bridge between micro- and macro-level phenomena is the meso-level; Gary Alan Fine and Tim Hallett (2023) say, "This is where the action is" (p. 2). **Meso-level** analysis is at the group or organizational level (see Figure 1.1). For example, formal rules often dictate how people in an organization are expected to behave. At the same time, however, informal norms can develop that more strongly determine behavior than do formal rules. Many of these processes are manifested in organizational structures such as work, the courts, and other bureaucracies (see Blok et al. 2019; Turco 2010). Individuals interact and people do have agency but the interactions often reflect rules, policies, and procedures that come from community or societal-level entities. For instance, Hallett and Meanwell (2016) analyzed data from 20 US Congressional hearings about the No Child Left Behind Act. Although a national-level policy, its reauthorization required meso-level hearings in which individuals debated its efficacy. The study showed how individuals came together to determine the ultimate meaning of the No Child Left Behind Act. The important thing from this study was that individuals were involved in both taking something made outside of the group, in this case, the No Child Left Behind law, and reforming it to reflect the values and beliefs of the people in the committee, an organizational structure. Lars Johannessen's (2019) study of "street-level bureaucracy" showed how Norwegian emergency services workers would utilize ambiguities

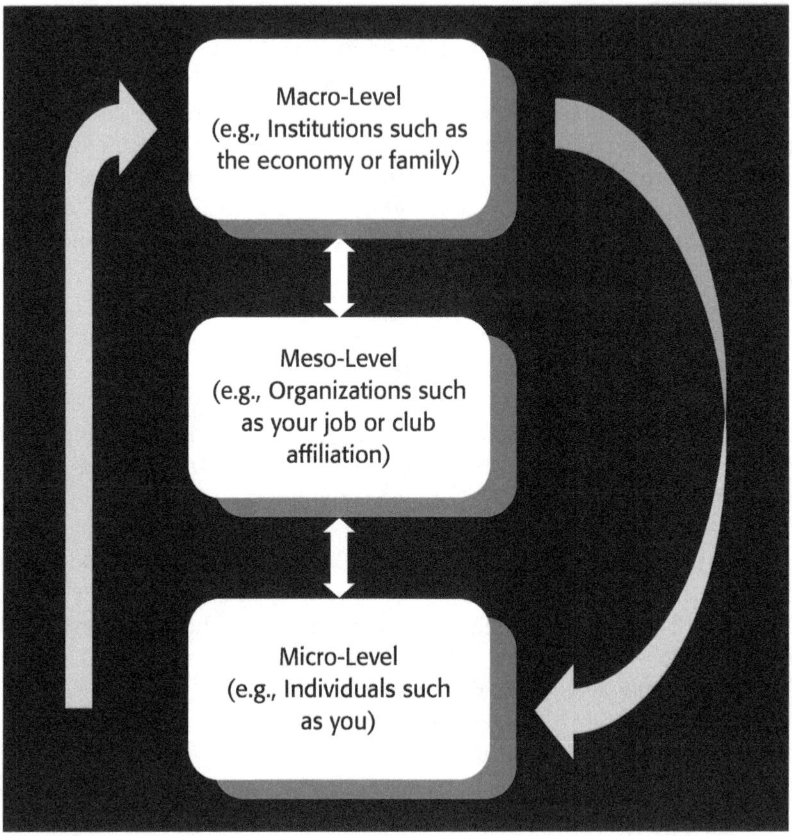

Figure 1.1 The Many Relationships between Macro-, Meso-, and Micro-Levels of Society.

in service policies to reduce crowding in clinics, by encouraging clients with few symptoms to consider other ways of dealing with their ailments. This process was observed in 69 of the 342 observed assessments. Together, these two studies also help to show how individuals are involved in making rules for society and how those rules get filtered into everyday interactions through meso-level social structures.

It is also important to note that macro-level societal conditions can have direct effects on your everyday life, even if you are not aware of it. For instance, where you live can be related to your walking pace! People living in more economically advanced countries, those with colder climates and more individualistic cultures, have faster walking paces than those in more rural, warmer, and communalistic cultures (Levine and Norenzayan 1999). Research also indicates that people feel an increasing sense of time scarcity even though work hours on average have not increased. Digital and other technologies that were designed to make our lives easier and give us more free time have created a scenario in which people feel obligated to multitask and take on more work (Kelland 2007; Wajcman 2015; Wacjcman and Dodd 2017).

Sociological and Psychological Social Psychology

We have defined microsociology as the study of how larger society influences basic social psychological processes. Some social psychologists come from the field of **psychology**, which is the study of human thought processes and behavior. There is some overlap between sociology and psychology. Scholars in sociology, particularly microsociology, like those in psychology, study how the behaviors, thoughts, and emotions of individuals are created and modified by the social conditions in which they live. However, sociological social psychology, as we discussed in this chapter, is an extension of the larger field of sociology that emphasizes effects of societal forces—in addition to immediate social contexts—on individuals' lives.

Social contexts can range from a small group of people to the larger culture and social conditions manifested in a society as a whole. In a sense, social psychology serves as a natural bridge between the fields of sociology (which focuses on the social conditions influencing people) and psychology (which takes the individual as the central concern) (see Figure 1.2). However, sociologists are more likely than psychologists to take into account effects of structural forces and statuses. For instance, sociologists are more likely than psychologists to compare the self-esteem levels of different racial and ethnic groups (Rosenberg 1986; Schieman, Pudrovska, and Milkie 2005). Conversely, psychologists are more likely than sociologists to study the thinking processes associated with self-esteem (Crocker and Park 2003).

As a subfield of sociology, sociological social psychology brings sociological perspectives to the study of social psychology. Early scholars, such as William James (1842–1910), George Herbert Mead (1863–1931), and W. E. B. DuBois (1868–1963), became well-known for their ability to articulate how social forces influence day-to-day interactions, as we will discuss in more detail throughout this book. During the same time period, as seen in Box 1.3, many psychologists were developing some of the prominent research and theories associated with individual behaviors and internal thought processes.

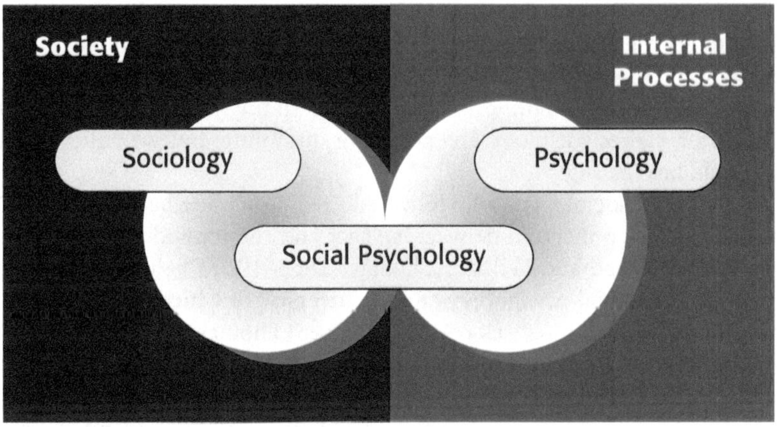

Figure 1.2 Social Psychology Merges Elements of Two Fields.

Box 1.3 Psychoanalysis in Psychology

Psychologists generally are interested in internal processes. The German psychologist Sigmund Freud (1856–1939) popularized the idea of the unconscious mind and the development of personality over time. Freud's psychoanalytic method was designed as a means of gaining access to an individual's subconscious thoughts. Psychoanalysis emphasizes the role of conscious and unconscious processes that manifest themselves in everyday life. The role of the psychoanalyst is to access all these inner thoughts and feelings in an effort to liberate individuals from their problems by resolving the internal conflicts that have evolved over time. Hence, the analyst must often reconstruct life events and childhood experiences—a process that may take years of analysis to accomplish (Cockerham 2003). Effects of larger social conditions do enter into psychoanalytic perspectives, but the analysts tend to focus primarily on internal dynamics. Sociologists, by contrast, are less likely to draw a dividing line between internal and external worlds; rather, we view thoughts and feelings as a continual exchange of information between our internal thinking processes and information we obtain from the external world.

Historical Context of Sociological Social Psychology

The term "sociology" was coined by the French social philosopher Auguste Comte (1798–1857) in 1838. Comte was a staunch proponent of positivism, which is the belief that the scientific method is the best approach to the production of knowledge. Comte attempted to place sociology in the context of more traditional scientific disciplines. In his view, the complexities of social dynamics would make sociology the most challenging scientific field. We as sociologists think about all the factors that influence what people do on a daily basis—the situational, structural, and historical conditions that lead people to do the things that they do. Because of all of these influences on human behavior, some theorists since Comte have argued that social behavior is too complex to understand using the scientific method. It is certainly true that the complexity of human behavior makes sociology a challenging discipline, but we believe that it also makes our field fascinating.

The generation of sociologists who followed Auguste Comte began to make keen observations about the connection between society and the individual. Sociologists such as George Herbert Mead and William Thomas (1863–1947) helped found a uniquely American school of social psychology at the University of Chicago. Mead studied how social conditions affect our senses of self. Thomas (Thomas and Znaniecki 1958) focused on the role of life histories as a way of assessing the effects of social and historical changes on individuals' lives over time. This research led to the classic book *The Polish Peasant in Europe and America* (originally published in intervals between 1918 and 1920). The ideas of these early sociologists helped in the creation of symbolic interactionism, a perspective in sociological social psychology that will be reviewed in detail in this and subsequent chapters.

Other major contributors to the development of sociological social psychology include Charles Horton Cooley (1864–1929) and Georg Simmel (1858–1918). Cooley (1909) contributed to the development of sociological social psychology in part with his theoretical formulation of primary and secondary groups. "Primary groups" refer to small groups of people with whom we have face-to-face contact, such as our friends and family, whereas "secondary groups" are larger and less intimate. Cooley proposed that primary and secondary groups produce fundamentally different types of interactions. Simmel, a German sociologist at the University of Berlin, viewed society as a complex network of interactions between dyads (two-person groups) and triads (three-person groups) (Simmel 1950). W. E. B. Dubois, an American sociologist trained at Harvard and in Germany, elaborated on the social psychological dimensions of racial discrimination in the United States. Harriet Martineau (1802–1876), the "mother of sociology," contributed to early theorizing, to symbolic interactionism, and to methodological approaches in sociology.

These sociological social psychologists helped to lay the foundation for the perspectives and theories that modern social psychologists use to study human behavior in a social context. The next section will elaborate on the perspectives they helped to create.

Charles Horton Cooley and George Herbert Mead are two of the founding sociological social psychologists. Their work inspired generations of sociologists to study social psychology. Their influence led to the development of the Cooley-Mead Award from the Social Psychology Section of the American Sociological Association (ASA) to recognize outstanding contributions to the field of social psychology. All of the persons profiled in biographies in subsequent chapters were recipients of this prestigious award.

Charles Horton Cooley*

Charles Horton Cooley was born on August 17, 1864, in Ann Arbor, Michigan. He was the son of Mary Elizabeth Horton and the renowned law school professor and State Supreme Court Justice Thomas McIntyre Cooley. After attending the University of Michigan, Cooley graduated with a degree in mechanical engineering. After some work and traveling, he returned to the University of Michigan for graduate work in political economy and sociology in 1890. Cooley received his PhD in philosophy in 1894.

Cooley became an assistant professor of sociology and taught the University of Michigan's first sociology course in 1899. Cooley spent a great deal of time speculating and contemplating the subject of self and its relationship to society. He observed the development of his own children, which he used to help construct his theories.

Cooley participated in the founding of the American Sociological Society (now the ASA) in 1905 and served as its eighth president in 1918. In his work *Personal Competition* (1899), he found that as the United States was expanding and becoming more industrialized, and people seemed to be becoming more individualistic and competitive, appearing to exhibit less concern for family and neighborhood. Some of Cooley's other works were inspired by this trend and include *Human Nature and the Social Order* (1902), on symbolism of the self, and *Social Organization* (1909), in which he discusses the importance of primary groups.

George Herbert Mead

George Herbert Mead was born on February 27, 1863, in South Hadley, Massachusetts. Mead's family moved to Oberlin, Ohio, in 1870, where his father, Hiram Mead, became a professor at the Oberlin Theological Seminary. Mead earned his master's degree in philosophy at Harvard University; then he traveled to Leipzig, Germany, with his close friend Henry Castle and Henry's sister, Helen Castle (whom he later married), to pursue graduate work in philosophy and physiological psychology at the University of Leipzig. He later transferred to the University of Berlin to study physiological psychology and economic theory.

Mead's graduate work was interrupted in 1891 by the offer of an instructorship in philosophy and psychology at the University of Michigan. He never completed his PhD. In 1894, Mead took a teaching position at the University of Chicago, where he stayed until he died in 1931. Mead went on to make substantial contributions in both social psychology and philosophy. His major contribution to the field of social psychology was his attempt to show how the human self is revealed in the process of social interaction, especially by way of linguistic communication (later called "symbolic interactionism"). A compilation of some of his best writings can be found in the book *Mind, Self, and Society* (1934).

*Information about Charles Horton Cooley was obtained from the ASA website (www.asanet.org); details about George Herbert Mead's biography come from Baldwin (1986).

Additional Resources:

Charles Horton Cooley: Imagining Social Reality by Glenn Jacobs. Amherst and Boston, MA: University of Massachusetts Press, 2006.

Updating Charles H. Cooley: Contemporary Perspectives on a Sociological Classic by Natalia Ruiz-Junco and Baptiste Brossard. London: Routledge, 2019.

George Herbert Mead in the Twentieth Century by F. Thomas Burke and Krysztof Piotr Skowronski. Lanham, MD: Lexington Books, 2013.

George Herbert Mead's Conception of Society: A Critical Reflection by Jean-Francois Cote. London and New York: Routledge, 2015.

Becoming Mead: The Social Process of Academic Knowledge by Daniel Huebner. Chicago: University of Chicago Press, 2014.

The Timeliness of George Herbert Mead edited by Hans Joas and Daniel R. Huebner. Chicago: University of Chicago Press, 2015.
Mind, Self, and Society: The Definitive Edition by George Herbert Mead (Edited by Charles W. Morris). Chicago: University of Chicago Press.

Section Summary

In this section of the chapter, we answered the following questions: What is sociology? How does macrosociology differ from microsociology? What are the differences in the ways that sociologists and psychologists study social psychology? We defined sociology as the systematic study of society. Some sociologists focus on macro-level processes in society, the study of societies as a whole. Other sociologists focus on micro-level processes, or how society affects people's thoughts, feelings, and behaviors in social contexts and how individuals contribute to the construction of society. Although both sociologists and psychologists study social psychology, sociological social psychologists emphasize effects of large social forces in our lives. Important historical figures in sociological social psychology include George Herbert Mead, Charles Horton Cooley, Georg Simmel, and W. E. B. Dubois, among others.

A Take-Away Message

How can you utilize knowledge from social psychology in your own life? There are several things you can do with this material. First, for your personal use, it may help you to know that larger social forces can affect your life, but how they affect you depends, in part, on the country you live in (macro-level), on the groups to which you belong (meso-level) and on how you and others around you react to these influences (micro-level). Put another way, relationships between individuals and society are complicated and cannot be explained with simple truisms such as "It's all about who you know." These types of statements may have some value, but there are a number of forces acting on us every day (and, of course, we are forces acting on other people too!). You will learn throughout this text that your decisions and actions may not be as independently "your own" as you think. There is value in knowing the history of social psychology because it sets the stage for contemporary work in the field. Theorists and researchers in social psychology and other fields approach the study of people in different ways. If you continue to take courses in the social sciences, especially classes in research methods, these differences will become abundantly clear to you.

PERSPECTIVES IN SOCIOLOGICAL SOCIAL PSYCHOLOGY

Johnny and I got along really well when we worked together at the copy shop. Then he got a promotion—he became my boss. All of a sudden, he started ordering me around and wouldn't joke with me anymore.

> *In fact, he stopped hanging around with me—he got new friends in management, I guess. I say his position went to his head, making him act the way he did. My friends say that it is natural for people to change when they become a manager.*
>
> —Susan, junior management major

There are many different ways to investigate social forces in people's day-to-day lives. You may decide to focus on immediate social surroundings, or you may try to understand the effects of larger social institutions—for example, the economy—on people's lives. In this vignette, Susan is trying to understand how a promotion could lead to such dramatic changes in the behavior of her friend—now her boss. Could a simple promotion really lead a person to such an abrupt change in interaction style?

Susan's friends answer the question somewhat differently than she does. In other words, they analyze Johnny's behavior differently, based on their perspectives. Similarly, sociological social psychologists, who construct general explanations for behaviors across people, times, and places, tend to work within one or more broad perspectives that reflect their orientations. The three perspectives most used to characterize sociological social psychology are symbolic interactionism, social structure and personality, and group processes (House 1977; Smith-Lovin and Molm 2000). We review the basic tenets of each of these perspectives in this chapter and will elaborate on them in Chapter 2. (See also Table 1.1.)

TABLE 1.1 Three Perspectives in Sociological Psychology: A Comparison

Perspective	View of the Role of Individual in Society	Area of Focus
Symbolic interactionism	Individual is an active participant in the construction of society.	Meaning-making processes.
Social structure and personality	The nature of interaction is based on adherence to the roles that people occupy.	Emphasizes process of how larger social structures influence individuals.
Group processes	When individuals form into social groups, certain basic processes emerge.	Processes that occur in group contexts regularly emerge in interactions.

Symbolic Interactionism

Symbolic interactionism is the study of how people negotiate the meaning of social life during their interactions with other people. George Herbert Mead is often credited as the founder of symbolic interactionism. In a compiled volume of his works, *Mind, Self, and Society from the Standpoint of a Social Behaviorist*, Mead (1934) argued that we create meaning through our interactions with the people around us. Once agreed on, that meaning becomes our social reality. The meanings we attach to ourselves, other people, and objects are negotiated over time. We use language to give meaning to everything in our lives and to the world around us.

From the symbolic interactionist perspective, the important connection between society and our inner experiences lies in our interactions with other people. These interactions provide information about the world, which we then accept or modify for our own use (Heise 1999; Mead 1934; Rosenberg 1990).

Photo 1.2 Symbolic interactionism emphasizes the social conditions that influence the development of meaning through people's day-to-day interactions. Have you ever tried to argue against the dominate beliefs of a group? How did it turn out?

Social Structure and Personality

The **social structure and personality** perspective focuses on the connections between larger societal conditions and the individual—specifically, on the influence of social structure on individuals. **Social structure** refers to "persisting patterns of behavior and interaction between people or social positions" (House 1992, p. 526). Because there is stability among relationships and positions, sociologists study these patterns and their effects on individuals' thoughts, feelings, and behaviors.

The social structure and personality perspective can help explain the vignette that opens this section. One of the characters, Johnny, is promoted to a new position and starts acting differently. His new position may require that he tells people what to do, regardless of his feelings toward his coworkers. From the social structure and personality perspective, our positions in society dictate, to some degree, the ways we are expected to think, feel, and behave. Perhaps the change in position caused Johnny to rethink his relationships with his former coworkers. Other elements of social structure that can affect our lives will be reviewed in Chapter 2.

Group Processes

The third face of sociological social psychology, **group processes**, focuses on how basic social processes operate in group contexts (Smith-Lovin and Molm 2000). Groups are an important part of society and reflect a significant area of social psychological research in both sociology and psychology. Because it takes only two people to make a group, and because humans are inherently social, we all spend a considerable amount of time in our lives in group settings, including with family, friends, and coworkers. The group processes perspective focuses on our interactions and positions within and across these groups.

Group processes scholars are particularly interested in processes that come into play when groups form. Status is an example. When you form into groups in your classes, you might notice that some people talk more and have their opinions solicited more often than others. How are these differences that reflect status determined by group members? Power is another group process. When you negotiate the price of a car, certain features of the setting give you or the other person more power to set the final price. What are these situational characteristics that confer power? Justice is another example of a group process. When you decide whether the money you earn at your job is fair, you do so by comparing yourself to other people. What groups do we compare ourselves to in these situations, and how do we come to decide that things are fair or unfair? In short, group processes scholars are interested in answering these sorts of questions by studying the processes—such as status, power, and justice—that occur in group contexts.

Three Perspectives in One

The perspectives reviewed in this section are not mutually exclusive, and the line between one perspective and another will not always be clear throughout this text. But their goals are the same: to understand interactions among individuals, society, and basic social processes (Hausmann and Summers-Effler 2011; Miller 2011; Turner 2011). There are multiple ways to approach the study of human behavior, and each paradigm in sociological social psychology provides a lens to help decide which social dynamics to focus on and which techniques to utilize in a study. In examining gender dynamics related to paid work, a symbolic interactionist, for instance, is more inclined to study the social construction of work identities utilizing in-depth interviews, whereas social structure and personality researchers may conduct surveys to compare distress scores among men and women and try to understand how work conditions lead to differences in mental health across genders. Group processes researchers are more likely to use experiments to test theories about how men and women may be treated differently in work groups even when they have comparable skills. Researchers use different paradigms to study the same or similar social phenomena. These different starting points lead them to focus on different social dynamics and use different methods.

Section Summary

The goal of this section was to answer the question "What are the major perspectives in sociological social psychology?" We defined three major perspectives, or "faces," in social psychology: symbolic interactionism, social structure and personality, and group processes. The symbolic interactionist face examines how people negotiate the meaning of social life through interactions with other people. The social structure and personality face of sociological social psychology focuses on the connections between larger societal conditions and the individual. Finally, the group processes face emphasizes how basic social processes develop in group contexts. These three faces of social psychology will be used to structure how we present research and theories throughout this book.

A Take-Away Message

The three faces of sociological social psychology provide a heuristic device to capture theories and research in the field of sociological psychology. These perspectives may also give you a sense of quite different ways to view the world in your everyday life. For example, can you see yourself as an active member of society, asserting definitions about who you are and changing your world (symbolic interactionism)? Can you also see yourself as a recipient of the forces that come through workplaces, families, or neighborhoods (social structure and personality)? Of course, both of these processes are at work—we affect and are affected by society all of the time—as we will explore more in the next chapter.

YOUR SOCIAL PSYCHOLOGICAL TOOLKIT

> *I remember my first social psychology course. There was so much to know—so many different topics and ideas. I was not really sure how to bring it all together. Human life is so complex, but through my concentration in social psych, I now feel like an expert.*
>
> —Jamal, sophomore sociology major

Jamal's story is probably a familiar one for many students who are just starting to study the social sciences. Understanding the social contexts of human behavior means that you must be able to incorporate elements of both the macro- and micro-levels of society—how the influence of society plays out in social structures, as well as in interactions among individuals. On your journey through social psychology, there are a few essential tools that you can take with you: the concepts and terms that sociologists employ in developing and describing their theories and research. We will be using these concepts throughout this text to help you understand how sociologists develop, carry out, and interpret social psychological research.

The Sociological Imagination

The effects of society on our lives are complex. How do we develop the ability to "see" society in our daily lives? Peter Berger (1973) says that we can see social forces in everyday life through individuals' expressions and behavior. We make choices every day without much deliberation—such as purchasing food or deciding how to spend an evening with friends or family. How do these choices reflect larger cultural values and norms?

An important tool for seeing such forces in your life is the **sociological imagination**—the ability to see our personal lives in the context of the history, culture, and social structure of the larger society within which we live. C. Wright Mills (1959) argued that sociologists must understand the larger cultural, structural, and historical conditions influencing individuals before arriving at any conclusions about the causes of their behaviors, decisions, or experiences. Specifically, Mills said, "The sociological imagination enables its possessor to understand the larger historical scene in terms of its meaning for the inner life and the external career of a variety of individuals" (1959, p. 5).

The sociological imagination gives us, as social psychologists, the vision necessary to assess the social conditions that may influence individuals' thoughts, feelings, and behaviors. If we limit our perspective on the social world to explanations that do not take social factors into consideration, we will miss some of the possible causal explanations for behavior. (See Box 1.4 as an example of how the sociological imagination can extend to human–nonhuman interactions!). In a classic example, Durkheim (1951, originally 1897) questioned the traditional approach to understanding suicide, which focused on the mental health of the individual. He proposed that suicide rates are influenced by societal conditions above and beyond personal problems. Durkheim first examined his ideas by comparing suicide rates over time and in different countries. He found that both time and place affected suicide rates—something that would not be true if suicide simply reflected factors internal to an individual. Durkheim concluded that suicide had to be, in part, a manifestation of social issues as well as personal problems. His research showed that groups that are better integrated into society have lower suicide rates than groups with fewer social connections. For instance, married people, who are presumably better integrated into society as part of a social unit, were less susceptible to suicide than singles.

The sociological imagination is the most important tool in your kit because it can help you decide which of the other tools to bring to your analysis. That is, by seeing all of the factors that are affecting your life (and the lives of people around you), you

Box 1.4 Human–Nonhuman Interactions

If you use your sociological imagination a bit, you come to see that interaction need not be limited to humans. In sociology and anthropology, there is a growing field of study on human–animal interactions or "animals and society" (Jerolmack 2005). Current theory and research includes the insect, and even the material world, as more of our lives involve working with machines and artificial intelligence (see Govorushko 2018 for a focus on human–insect interactions). Some of the roots of this field of study are grounded in the symbolic interactionist perspective, extending analysis of human interactions to those among humans and animals, even emphasizing the development of animal cultures as distinct in and of themselves (Alger and Alger 2003). While there may be some disagreement about animals' abilities to exchange meaning, at least in the ways that humans do, there is no doubt that the meaning of animals in human society is socially constructed. In other words, some animals are considered more or less acceptable than others in human society—and this acceptance changes over time and across different cultures around the world. For example, some animals are more or less acceptable for companionship than others (e.g., cats versus rats). Humans may impart their own personalities onto animals, and people and animals regularly engage each other in both work (e.g., sled or guide dogs) and play (Jerolmack 2009). Dogs and other pets—referred to as "animal companions" in the field of animals and society—may also serve as a source of social support (Cline 2010). The same can be said of interactions among humans and objects. Consider two movies with the actor Tom Hanks. In *Castaway* (2000), he plays a man stranded on an island after an airplane crash but finds comfort in a friend he makes out of a Wilson volleyball. A more recent film, *Finch* (2021) tells a futuristic story in which most humans die of a disease. In this case, Hanks makes another companion but this one is a robot with artificial intelligence (AI). In both cases, objects are given meaning, and once given, they become part of daily lives in a way similar to another human.

are better able to assess the causes of your own behavior. In the book *Wheelchair Warriors: Gangs, Disability, and Basketball*, sociologist Ronald Berger (1973) helps coauthor Melvin Juette employ the sociological imagination to explain how his "private troubles" are associated with "public issues." Juette aspired to play wheelchair basketball after a gunshot wound related to gang activity. Ultimately, by employing the sociological imagination, the authors were able to dissect how social conditions (e.g., neighborhood contexts) influenced personal decisions (i.e., to join a gang), leading to different sets of outcomes (e.g., pursuing a dream of playing wheelchair basketball).

How might you build your sociological imagination skills? Having a good understanding of social history is one part of this equation, to be able to tie what people did 100 years ago to current social conditions. According to Howard Becker (2014), it is also essential that sociologists keep updated on what is going on in the world today.

You must have information about people's behaviors in different roles (e.g., firefighter, priest, or drug addict) in different parts of the world. Having such knowledge provides the information you will need to make connections between the thoughts, feelings, and behaviors of the most disperate sets of people over time and across the world.

Other Tools in Your Kit

The sociological imagination is a tool that social psychologists can use to understand influences of society on individuals. Where do we find society? From a social psychological perspective, society exists both between and within individuals. It also takes the form of our positions in society, which give us different levels of power and access to resources, and links us to those with whom we interact based on those positions. And it also creates internalized expectations associated with those positions. When we try to see the larger influences of society, we must consider our relative positions in groups as well as how our culture views and gives meaning to those relationships and positions. Society, from this perspective, is only as stable as the people, positions, and relationships that make it up. In a sense, society exists amid both stability and change, as people either accept existing rules or try to change them to meet the needs of contemporary life. The following concepts will help you know what to look for as you are trying to identify "society" as an influence in your day-to-day life.

Social Norms and Values

Social norms are behavioral guidelines—the rules that regulate our behavior in relationships. If society exists through our relationships with one another, then it is guided by the rules of conduct that apply to those relationships. One of the first things we learn about a society is its rules of conduct. **Values** differ from social norms in that they refer to deeply held ideals and beliefs. The laws of a given society codify many of its shared values and norms. For example, murder is considered such a destructive behavior that we impose large penalties for committing such an act. Other lesser violations of values, such as doing something inappropriate in front of a crowd, may be met only with public reactions. Someone will not go to jail for cutting in front of other people in line at a store, but they might be the target of ostracism or mocking from others. Society, then, can influence people's behaviors by establishing both formal and informal rules of conduct.

We can discover a society's formal rules by examining its laws. But the process of identifying informal rules is more complex (see Box 1.5). An easy example of the power of norms can be seen each time you enter the college classroom. Students enter the room, take a seat, and face forward as they wait for the class to start. They are expected to be quiet as the professor teaches the class. One of the authors of this text dealt with a situation in which a group of two or three students would not quiet their conversation as the class started. It was clear that other students were perturbed, and those students managed to give subtle (and not-so-subtle) signals for them to quiet down. In this case, the professor did not have to enforce classroom norms because the other students were happy to do it!

Box 1.5 Ethnomethodology

Harold Garfinkel (1917–2011) proposed a method of studying society as reflected in our typical, day-to-day interactions that he called **ethnomethodology** (Garfinkel 1967). Ethnomethodology is both a theory and a method of inquiry. That is, it is a theoretical understanding of the linkages between the individual and society, and it is also a methodological approach to studying the relationship between the individual and society. One way that ethnomethodologists study informal social norms is through breaching experiments.

Breaching experiments include any method of violating social order to assess how people construct social reality (Ritzer 1996). Garfinkel was famous for asking students to perform breaching acts and then report on reactions to these events. In a classic example, students were instructed to engage in a conversation and insist that their partner explain commonplace remarks. The following excerpt comes from Garfinkel's (1967) book, *Studies in Ethnomethodology*.

> SUBJECT: I had a flat tire.
> EXPERIMENTER: What do you mean, you had a flat tire?
> SUBJECT (appears momentarily stunned and then replies in a hostile manner): What do you mean, "What do you mean?" A flat tire is a flat tire. That is what I meant. Nothing special. What a crazy question.

This interaction demonstrates that there are implicit rules that we expect not to be questioned during a simple exchange. When those rules are broken, there is an emotional reaction (note the hostility of the subject), followed by an attempt to restore order (restating the comment about the flat tire) and explain the interruption; in this case, the subject explains the experimenter's question as simply crazy. Implicit rules are essential to the appearance of social order in everyday life. However, we may not be aware of such rules until they are broken in some way. Breaching experiments provide a way of finding and assessing informal norms and values. In a more modern example of studying rule making and sustaining processes, Liberman (2013) describes having students video record themselves playing a new board game, observing how they reference the game rules to guide their play. Through everyday observations, one can see the interplay of formal rule-making structures and negotiations that occur internally and between people about whether and how to follow them.

Additional Resources:

Re-Assembling a Corpus: Garfinkel's Ethnomethodology and Intellectual History by Andrew Carlin. Walnut Creek, CA: Left Coast Press, 2014.

People may follow norms even with different motivations for doing so. In *Tally's Corner*, Elliot Liebow (1967) observed a group of poor men living in Washington, DC, during the 1960s. The men's lives revolved around a corner carryout restaurant, where some men were waiting for work or just "hanging out." Every man had a different reason for hanging out at the corner—some were waiting for someone to offer a part-time job, others were avoiding their families, and still others were just socializing. Despite their different reasons for being on the corner, all of them converged there on a regular basis, and this convergence served as a norm of street-corner life, although the norm-guiding behavior was not driven by the same motivation for everyone. Relationships set up expectations that can operate so that deliberate decision making about where to go or what to do doesn't really happen; rather, norms serve as guidelines for our behaviors.

Photo 1.3 Children learn technical and social skills in their interactions with adults and other children. What social skills are being taught in this environment?

Source: wavebreakmedia/Shutterstock

Statuses and Roles

Another aspect of society consists of the statuses that people occupy. **Status** refers to a person's position in a group or society that is associated with varying levels of prestige and respect. Statuses are often formalized so that the relative standings of group members can be easily identified. In a workplace setting, for instance, a supervisor is paid to manage a group of people and may be given the right to tell people what to do. The power associated with the supervisory position often brings with it respect and prestige. Other times, status develops more informally.

Status includes a set of expectations about how to behave in a group. These expectations refer to **roles** in society. Roles and statuses are related but distinct concepts. For instance, medical doctors hold positions of relatively high status in Western society. Expectations associated with their roles include looking after the health of their patients and overseeing nurses' work. Clergy also have relatively high status in society, but expectations for these persons are quite different, including guiding the spiritual lives of members of their communities, uniting people in marriage, and having warm and caring manners. In other words, clergy and medical doctors may occupy similar status positions, but they hold noticeably different roles in society. Statuses, then, refer to our positions in a group or society, whereas roles refer to the specific expectations about how to behave in those positions.

Organizations and Institutions

Society is also reflected in the regular patterns of behavior and relationships among people. Norms of behavior may include regular work schedules (for example, 9:00 a.m. to 5:00 p.m.) and sleep patterns. Much of this regulation exists within **organizations**—groups that share a common purpose and contain a formal set of rules and authority structure. Our work and school lives revolve around meeting the demands of our superiors within the rules of those organizations. At work, we are paid to produce a product or service, but we must do so within certain guidelines and procedures. At school, we must turn in papers and tests to our teachers to be judged worthy of a passing grade.

When the accumulation of both formal rules and informal norms produces patterns of behavior for an entire group or even a whole society, these norms are often collectively referred to as an "institution." A **social institution** consists of patterns of interaction in which the behavior of a large group is guided by the same norms and roles (Jary and Jary 1991) (see Box 1.6). Traditionally, sociologists have divided society into five major institutions: family, economy, religion, education, and government. Although the norms and rules that govern these institutions may vary by society, almost all human societies have ways of raising children (family), systems of exchange (economy), and educational systems. In addition to being found in most or all of the countries in the world today, these institutions have been found to exist in societies going back thousands of years.

Institutions are different from other sets of relationships because they involve complex sets of rules or laws that serve to guide behaviors. For instance, there are many formal and informal rules governing the family in the United States. Laws restrict the number of spouses that are allowed in a family and other behaviors such as spousal or child abuse. There are also informal rules of conduct in the family. For instance, it is not necessarily illegal to have affairs outside of marriage, but opinion polls continually show that most Americans frown on such behavior (Newport 2009). Parents' behaviors are guided by laws, such as at what age it is OK to leave a child home alone, though

Box 1.6 Major Institutions in Society

Much of people's lives can be studied in the context of social institutions—stable patterns of behavior guided by norms and roles. Institutions provide a context for studying individuals' thoughts, feelings, and behaviors. Most societies around the world contain at least the following five institutions:

- *Economy and work*: Ways of coordinating and facilitating the process of gathering resources and converting them into goods and commodities needed in the society.
- *Politics, government, and the military*: Systems for preserving order in society.
- *Family*: An institution for regulating sexual relations and child rearing.
- *Religion*: Rituals and beliefs regarding sacred things in society.
- *Education*: The institution devoted to the creation and dissemination of knowledge and information about the larger world.

These institutions help define us. For instance, our positions in the economy, defined by our jobs and income, have significant effects on how we live. Our positions also affect the types of people with whom we interact, the ways in which we interact, and our values.

these vary by state or country. Parents may not agree with the laws. One author of this book felt comfortable leaving a mature 7-year-old home alone, though it may have violated laws, given that close-by neighbors were aware the child was inside reading a book for a short time while the parent went to fetch a sibling from school. Other North American parents may have disapproved or even called police to report such behavior. In Japan, however, it is common for very young children, ages 5 or 6, to travel alone through the public sphere to get to school or to shop for the family. Individuals usually learn the rules associated with a given institution through their interactions with other people.

Culture

Each society has its own **culture**—its unique patterns of behavior and beliefs. The norms, roles, and relationships that make up social institutions vary from one society to another, giving each society its own "personality." For example, two societies may have very different sets of expectations associated with being a father. Hence, to study people from different places, we must examine the ways in which these people's lives reflect their cultures. Researchers must also recognize that a given group or society has its own unique set of institutions—different from those that may exist in the researcher's own culture. For example, the higher education system in the United States in terms of access, variety of organizations, and values is different from many others around the world.

The components of culture include language, symbols, values and beliefs, norms, and material artifacts (see Box 1.7). Differences in language are often most immediately apparent between societies. We use different words and symbols to represent some of

Box 1.7 Elements of Culture

As sociological social psychologists, we must be aware of elements of culture that have effects on our thoughts, feelings, and behaviors. These include symbols, values and beliefs, language, norms, and material culture.

- *Symbols*: Anything that carries a particular meaning recognized by people who share the same culture.
- *Values and beliefs*: Standards by which people assess desirability, goodness, and beauty that serve as both guidelines for living (values) and specific statements that people hold to be true (beliefs).
- *Language*: A system of symbols that allows people to communicate.
- *Norms*: Rules and expectations for people's behavior within a society.
- *Material culture*: The tangible artifacts of a culture—for example, cars, clothing, and computers.

The various elements of culture often interact to help us interpret a social situation and decide how to react to other people. People from different cultures may understand the meaning of an action differently and, as a result, may respond with different sets of feelings and actions. To an American, for example, the gesture of raising the middle finger has negative connotations and is likely to produce feelings of anger, perhaps leading to an aggressive response. In England, the same gesture may produce no feelings, whereas a "V" sign may be offensive. Such cultural variations are important to understanding social psychological phenomena.

the same objects and ideas. Even subtle differences in everyday practices between cultures can have large implications for how people live their lives. In "The Body Ritual of the Nacirema," Horace Miner (1956) described a "foreign" culture in which the primary belief is that the body is ugly and has a natural tendency toward disease. As a result, the "tribe members" visit "magical practitioners" for the mouth and body on a regular basis. Eventually, readers discover that the "Nacirema" are simply "Americans" (Nacirema is American spelled backward)!

Miner's point is that it is hard to understand our own culture unless we step outside it enough to see how what we consider "normal" may look to outsiders. Although we can think independently of the people around us, we often make our choices within the boundaries of a culture. For example, when you are thirsty, you may choose to buy bottled water even when tap water is safe and available because water purchased in small plastic bottles is valued as "pure" and has higher status in your culture; however, this may not be something that people would do in a society that is more critical of marketers' claims about pureness. Rather, they might see such a purchase as wasteful of money and contributing to environmental degradation from plastic bottles.

Culture is not something "out there" that affects us. Rather, we engage in culture production through each interaction we have with other people. This perspective can be summarized in this line from the book *Popular Culture as Everyday Life* by Dennis Waskul and Phillip Vannini, "[Culture is] an assemblage of ideas, practices, experiences, representations, material objects and other 'things' and phenomena that comprise the mainstream, ordinary ways of life of large groups of people" (2015; 7). This definition gives us the ability to study culture using empirical methods and can help us dissect social situations, using culture to explain people's behavior in a given situation.

In similar fashion, society provides both formal and informal rules for making more important decisions—for example, about marriage and intimate partnership. Some cultures limit marital relationships to a single man and woman. However, some Western cultures have recently extended legal marriage to couples of the same sex. A small number of societies allow for multiple marriage partners. Sociologists try to understand the societal and cultural guidelines that influence the behavior of individuals in a given society. Consider the findings using data from a Pew Research Center study in Figure 1.3 (Silver 2019). Given what you know about world affairs, why might individuals in these select countries be more or less likely to agree that control over our lives is determined by outside forces—and why might people from these countries have different beliefs about how much of what happens to them is a result of their own doing?

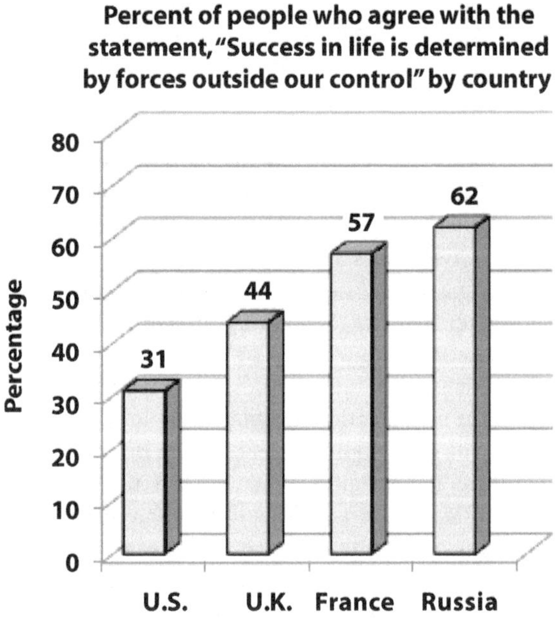

Figure 1.3 The Intersection of Culture and Personal Beliefs.

Source: Silver 2019.

The social psychological study of culture also emphasizes the ways in which individuals contribute to the development and maintenance of culture in everyday life. How are the formal and informal rules that guide behaviors transmitted from one group to another? How do they change over time? These processes can be studied in the context of socialization among small groups of family members and friends. For instance, Gary Alan Fine (1979) studied a group of youth baseball teams by observing the culture of each group and the changes in those cultures over time. He found that the culture of the group changed as new people entered and left the group but that some consistency was maintained as new members learned the ways of the group from older, more senior team members. It is important to emphasize that individuals are contributing to the construction of culture; we are not just passive recipients of it! In this sense, we are both shaped by culture and "architects" of our social worlds (Sheperd and Stephens 2010).

Section Summary

This section answered the question "What do I need to know to study the effects of society in my day-to-day life?" Here, we introduce an important concept in the field of sociology, the sociological imagination, which is a tool to help you see the larger context of people's decisions and behaviors. In addition, we have given you a toolkit to help you develop the sociological imagination, a kit that includes important concepts that sociologists use in research, such as norms, values, statuses, roles, institutions, and culture. All these concepts help to illuminate the effects of society on individuals' thoughts, feelings, and behaviors.

A Take-Away Message

The sociological toolkit can be utilized in your personal, social, and professional lives. Like the three paradigms, concepts such as roles, statuses, and so forth, can help explain the ways people treat you or why you made certain decisions in your life. People act toward us based on their dispositions and personalities, but their behaviors are also affected by the expectations of others (roles and norms). Sometimes people act against those expectations (and when they do they often face social sanctions), but more often they conform to social roles and norms. Consider these factors when you are making your next big decision, for example, about what to major in, or what job to take: how does my role as a daughter or son, parent or future parent affect my decision? How does the region in which I live matter? Do the values of the larger culture or my subculture push me one way or another, by deeming how much respect or status I might have once in the position? In terms of learning sociological social psychology, we need to know the terminology that researchers use in the field if we are to progress. While roles and norms may appear to be common vernacular, they have specific meanings to social scientists. Understanding their full meaning will help you better craft your endeavors in both research and theory building.

OUR DIGITAL WORLD

> *I pretty much stay online. I mean, I go to school, but my real friends are online. When I am not studying or working, I pretty much play League of Legends or Overwatch with my friends. It is a pretty diverse group when you think about it. I have friends from England, Germany, and Japan! Hardly any of my friends at school interact with anyone but the people in our town...*
>
> —Tony, junior history major

No one can deny the growth of the role of the internet, AI, and electronics in our lives. In 2021, one survey found that 97% of American adults had a cellphone and 90% of them had a smartphone (Pew Research Center 2024). We are now connected to one another in a way that has never existed in human history. How does this change human relationships, if at all? **Digital sociology** is the study of the ways that people interact in the digital environment, an environment that relies on converting analog experiences into electronic ones (e.g., speech or pictures). It can include texting or using online platforms such as YouTube. It may include online dating or communicating with family members using electronic devices. In the case of Tony, he has largely taken himself out of in-person physical interactions and embraced an online world, at least for his leisure time. Perhaps this choice will have negative consequences in some ways, but it certainly provides him access to a diversity that does not exist in his physical world.

Anthropologists regularly study material culture; every culture has artifacts that both reflect and are part of a society's culture (see Box 1.7). Society—certainly Western society—is moving to the point in which elements of the electronic world are being infused into everyday life; in this scenario it is not just part of the larger culture, it is imbricated into it, a "sociomaterial" world in which human and nonhuman interactions seamlessly occur and which ultimately shape the people involved in those interactions (Lupton 2015). The ultimate ends of these processes may be the development of cyborgs, a creature that contains elements of human and nonhuman parts. Many interactions already occur digitally and under this schema, and people will start incorporating artificial intelligence (AI) into those interactions. Consider the use of digital assistants such as Siri, Alexa, and Google in your life today and how much has changed since their inception.

There are different ways to study interactions online and through using digital devices. In this text, we decided to infuse the book with research and theory in this area amidst other topics. In our view, the current outlook for digital sociology is not based on the ending of one type of interaction—physical interactions among people—but the addition of digital interactions (Chayko 2017). As such, our digital world is something that people incorporate into their lives. It is more than just a tool, at least for some people. There are online communities and many people rely on the internet to help them get their work done. In other cases, people may simply supplement traditional interactions with the use of a cellphone to make calls or to look up an item for reviews. We will bring up relevant sociological theory and research in digital sociology in each chapter.

Box 1.8 Careers in Social Psychology: A Primer

What can you do with a degree in social psychology? If you are reading this book as part of a sociology or psychology class, it might be moving you toward finishing your degree in one of those fields. There are few specific jobs with the title, "Social Psychologist" or even "Psychologist" or "Sociologist" for people with bachelor's degrees. Nonetheless, social psychology provides tools that can be used in any number of fields. Some tools are more relevant for certain types of jobs than others. In this text, we provide some ideas for finding work after completing an undergraduate degree. We focus on jobs that either require just an undergraduate degree or maybe no degree at all. If something interests you, you should investigate it right away. You will be more competitive in obtaining those positions upon graduation if you do some voluntary or paid internships before you graduate. Consider asking your advisor to supervise an internship or two before you graduate. You can often get college credit for internships too!

Section Summary

The final section of this chapter answered the question "How has social life changed with the introduction of digital technology?" Here, we introduce the idea of digital sociology, a way to assess how people are changing the ways they interact with one another with the inclusion of technology. Digital sociology also examines how people may be changing the ways they relate to the physical world based in advanced technologies.

A Take-Away Message

The sociological toolkit does not change with the inclusion of technology. We still use norms and roles when online, although they can be modified in some ways. Have you ever been frustrated with something that was posted online? Happy to receive positive messages from a friend via texts? We will explore the overlap in our traditional and digital worlds with the idea that digital interactions will likely become "traditional" at some point of human history. For example, cellphone use today has become normal for most people in the Western world.

BRINGING IT ALL TOGETHER

> *There Is so much to study in social psychology. I feel like I can't take it all in sometimes. I look forward to signing up for classes because I know that each one represents another aspect of human life to be studied. I truly wish I had the time to take more classes!*
>
> —Jacky, senior sociology major

Jacky's attitude toward social psychology is understandable given the size and scope of the field. Social psychologists study many aspects of human life—everything from the social factors influencing feelings of love to behaviors in small groups. You will probably find some of those areas more interesting than others, and you may also find that some areas of social life are not covered in this or other textbooks.

Our goal in this book is to provide you with an overview of sociological social psychology—its perspectives, theories, and concepts—along with the skills necessary to evaluate theories and research in the social sciences more broadly. Think of each chapter as a sociological journey into a new area of social life.

As you begin your investigation into sociological social psychology, you should be ready to use your sociological imagination to see how society influences individuals' thoughts, feelings, and behaviors. The theories and research we review in this book should help you develop your imagination. The first part of the book will introduce you to the major perspectives and methods used by sociological social psychologists. The next part applies these perspectives to the studies of self and society, with a discussion of social psychological perspectives and our senses of self and identity. The final part of the text considers applications of social psychological research to the study of different aspects of social life, including deviance, mental health, and emotions.

One primary goal is to make social psychological theories, concepts, and research findings applicable to your daily life. We encourage you to try to apply what you read to your own life; to your interactions at home, at work, and among friends; and to the things you see and hear in the media. Think about this book chapter both as an introduction to the field of sociological social psychology and as the start of a larger journey into the study of social life.

SUMMARY

1. Sociology is the study of society. Sociologists look at society using both macro- and micro-levels of analysis.
2. Both psychological and sociological social psychologists study the social contexts of human thoughts, feelings, and behaviors. Sociologists, however, also apply the perspectives and methods of the field of sociology to the study of social psychology.
3. Sociology was first defined in 1838 by the French social philosopher Auguste Comte, who applied the principles of the scientific method to society. Some of the founders of sociological social psychology include George Herbert Mead, W. E. B. Dubois, William Thomas, Charles Horton Cooley, Harriet Martineau, and Georg Simmel.
4. Three major perspectives in sociological social psychology are symbolic interactionism, social structure and personality, and group processes.
5. Sociological social psychologists use a toolkit consisting of concepts such as statuses, roles, norms and values, culture, and social institutions, which help to systematically examine human thoughts, feelings, and behavior.
6. Basic concepts in social psychology can be applied to digital interactions and modern research incorporates online relationships and interactions with AI devices.

KEY TERMS AND CONCEPTS

Breaching experiments: Experiments that violate the established social order to assess how people construct social reality.
Culture: A society's set of unique patterns of behaviors and beliefs.
Digital sociology: The study of the ways that people interact in the digital environment.
Ethnomethodology: A method of studying society through observation of people's typical day-to-day interactions.
Group processes: A perspective within sociological social psychology that examines how basic social processes operate in group contexts.
Macrosociology: The study of large-scale social processes.
Meso-level: Social conditions at the group or organizational levels.
Microsociology: The study of the effects of society on social psychological processes and the ways in which individuals participate in the construction and maintenance of society.
Organizations: Groups that share a common purpose and contain a formal set of rules and authority structure.
Psychology: The study of human thought processes and behaviors.
Roles: A set of expectations about how to behave, think, or feel.
Social institution: Patterns of interactions in which behavior within a large group is guided by a common set of norms and roles.
Social norms: The rules that regulate our behavior.
Social psychology: The systematic study of people's thoughts, feelings, and behavior in social contexts.
Social structure: Persistent patterns of behavior and interaction between people within identified social positions.
Social structure and personality: A perspective within sociological social psychology that focuses on the connections between larger societal conditions and the individual.
Sociological imagination: The ability to see personal lives in the context of the larger society—its history, culture, and social structure.
Sociology: The systematic study of society.
Status: A person's position in a group or society that is associated with varying levels of prestige and respect.
Symbolic interactionism: A perspective within sociological social psychology that emphasizes the study of how people negotiate the meaning of social life during their interactions with other people.
Values: Deeply held ideals and beliefs.

DISCUSSION QUESTIONS

1. How would you define society from your own perspective? How do you picture the role of society in your life and the lives of your friends and family?

2. In this chapter, we reviewed a number of perspectives on human behavior. Can you think of any other ways of understanding social interaction that are not covered by these perspectives?
3. What if you found out that you had an identical twin raised in another culture, and he or she was quite different from you? What would they be like? How would that help you see the influence of society? Employ your sociological imagination to answer these questions.
4. Do you think you can develop a strong relationship with another person completely online? Why or why not? Could you ever imagine developing a personal relationship with some sort of AI device?

2

Perspectives in Sociological Social Psychology

I first got involved with vaccinations with the local health department during the pandemic. They were desperate for volunteers so I thought I would help. I got to meet a lot of people from different walks of life, especially nurses and physicians' assistants who helped with the clinics. Many of them have since become friends. This work has really helped me consider the career I want to go into. I am now thinking that I would like to work in public health. I never knew that you could have a whole career in this field. I want to do something important in the world and now I know how I can do that.

—Franklin, junior biology major

The vignette that opens this chapter describes an event that led a student to consider a major that will allow them to work in the area of public health. The COVID-19 pandemic created a need for public health departments to set up large-scale vaccination clinics across the country. Franklin's motivation was pure: they wanted to help. The relations that came from these clinics, however, helped to craft their desire to consider a career in this field. This story brings together a lot of the things on which sociological social psychologists focus: the role of macro-level events in our personal lives, interactions with other people, and independent decision-making.

Social psychologists do not try to predict the conditions under which a particular individual behaves a certain way. Rather, we study why people generally do the things they do, or how they experience certain emotions or problems. In Franklin's case, sociologists would want to examine the processes by which group memberships influence individuals' behaviors or senses of self. To do this, we adopt a variety of perspectives. In Chapter 1, we reviewed the three major perspectives of sociological social psychology: symbolic interactionism, social structure and personality, and group processes. In this chapter, we will elaborate on each of those perspectives. Specifically, we will address the following questions:

- What are the major principles of the symbolic interactionist perspective? How does this perspective help us understand relationships between the individual and society? What does it mean to "construct" the world around us?

- What is the social structure and personality perspective? How do researchers in this field study the effects of society on the individual?
- What is the group processes perspective? What are some of the basic social processes that play out in group contexts? What are elements of group structure?

THE SYMBOLIC INTERACTIONIST PERSPECTIVE

> *I never really liked to dance. Even as a kid, I would never dance with my friends. But when I came to college, something changed. I met this guy that was so good to me—and of course, as luck would have it, he really liked to dance! He didn't mind if I sat at the table with some other people as he hit the dance floor, but I always felt awkward about that. Then I decided to take dance lessons. I am finding myself liking it more and more as I get better at it! My boyfriend was so happy to dance with me—we have become very close.*
>
> —Vanessa, junior English major

In Chapter 1, we defined the symbolic interactionist perspective as the study of how people negotiate the meanings of social life during their interactions with others. In the vignette that opens this section, we meet a young woman, Vanessa, who is learning that dancing need not be boring, difficult, or embarrassing. Through her interactions with some new people, Vanessa begins to negotiate a new meaning for dancing: "fun." It begins when she meets someone who loves to dance, and to share his enjoyment of dancing, she starts rethinking her attitude toward dancing. But she does not change immediately. It takes time, and she continually reevaluates her situation as she talks with and observes her boyfriend and other people. For instance, she chooses to take dance lessons, giving her better skills. As a result of these interactions and decisions, she begins to enjoy the activity more and redefines its meaning, and then her relationship with her boyfriend begins to change.

Symbolic interactionism explains how social processes influence our understandings of the world (Reynolds and Herman-Kinney 2003; Stryker 2002; Stryker and Vryan 2003). We construct meanings about things that are important in our own lives and in our society. Below we give an overview of the history and tenets of symbolic interactionism and then review the two major schools of symbolic interactionism.

Society and Agency

In Chapter 1, we defined sociology as the systematic study of society. Definitions of society differ depending on the perspective of the researcher. From a symbolic interactionist perspective, **society** exists as the network of interactions between people (Blumer 1969; Stryker 2002; Stryker and Vryan 2003). This definition means that the individual and society cannot be separated from each other: individuals continually create and are molded by society. Interactionist researchers start by assuming that it is impossible to study the individual without incorporating the study of society or, conversely, to study society without accounting for the individual. Society is composed of a complex series of relationships that people analyze and negotiate (Blumer 1969; Stryker 2002; Stryker and Vryan 2003). In the case of Franklin in the opening vignette, their new desire to start a career in public health is connected to interactions with people in that field at a vaccination clinic. What we do not see in this story are the ways that Franklin is affecting the nature of public health clinics, albeit in a small way. If they continue in this field, they will likely have a bigger impact, at least in the organizations where they will work. In the interactionist view, society works the same way: when enough individuals in society begin to change the ways they think, feel, or talk about an issue, society as a whole changes.

Symbolic interactionists also assume that individuals have some control over their social worlds. **Agency** refers to our ability to act and think independently from the constraints imposed by social conditions (Musolf 2003a). In other words, we have the ability to make choices and decisions on our own. The precise ways that agency operates are complex. On the one hand, agency gives us the power to make decisions in a variety of social situations. For instance, one study found that medical patients were agentic in deciding whether to follow doctors' treatment recommendations (Koenig 2011). The study found that while the doctors had the best interests of the patients in mind, resistance to those recommendations was a way for patients to feel that they were part of the treatment process, so that they felt they were negotiating an acceptable course of treatment for themselves. On the other hand, there are limits to our agency, and the very definition of agency can be socially constructed! As we will see later in the chapter, we typically choose among the acceptable norms of a culture. For example, parents in some Western cultures may choose to medicate a child labeled with "attention deficit hyperactivity disorder" (ADHD), whereas other parents may decide to restructure the child's environment and avoid medication. However, overall, it is worthwhile to consider that both sets of parents may have limited agency because they are bound by U.S. cultural beliefs that constructs children's problems as having an internal, biological causes. Other cultures may not recognize something we call ADHD and have different environments for children so that attention or behavioral problems are seen to arise less frequently.

There are several other aspects of agency to keep in mind. First, people's understanding of the concept of agency can vary. In a study of death and dying in nursing-home care, Jason Rodriquez (2009) found that staff would attribute agency to some dying patients by articulating that they could "choose the timing and conditions of their death" (65). However, the staff would not attribute this same agency to other patients—those deemed aggressive for example. Further, the ability to employ agency can vary across people in different social categories and is linked to their status and power. For example, one study found that Republicans, when compared to Democrats, tended to value agency more than communion, or the focus on maintaining relationships (Eriksson 2018). Finally, children can learn the use of agency from their parents (Tsushima and Burke 1999). In all of these cases, the application of agency varies across different social contexts or groups.

If independence and freedom are important to people, why might they give up agency? Organizational structures represent the most common way that agency is constrained in day-to-day life. In a study of dialogues between homeless shelter staff and clients, Mik-Meyer and Haugaard (2018) demonstrated how both residents and workers negotiated the use of agency as a way of achieving their respective needs; in this case, for the homeless to find placements and the staff to meet their job demands. Studies such as this help to show that agency does provide some freedom to make decisions, but individuals are not necessarily free to do whatever they want in groups or society. In many cases, people choose to give up their independence for the greater good or simply to get what they want from a person or in a situation.

Basic Principles of Symbolic Interactionism

The development of symbolic interactionist thought stems from eighteenth-century Scottish moral philosophers such as Adam Smith (1723–1790) and David Hume (1711–1776), as well as from the American social philosophy of pragmatism (Reynolds 2003; Stryker 1992, 2002). These traditions generally emphasize applied, practical applications of social theory and research. Unlike traditional philosophy that separates our physical environments from our cognitive and spiritual lives, pragmatists view intellectual and social lives as linked together (Reynolds 2003). In this view, psychological and physical worlds produce a constant dialectic, similar to the way that organisms evolve to meet the needs of their physical environments over time. Humans adapt to their physical environments as well as to their social worlds. That is, they negotiate their physical and cognitive (i.e., intellectual and emotional) lives with other people, adapting to new situations as they come along (see also Box 2.1).

The implication of pragmatism for symbolic interactionism is that physical and internal environments cannot be separated in the development of social theory. We derive meanings through interaction with others and internal thought processes. Thus, interaction is the primary way we come to any sort of knowledge about ourselves, other people, and the rest of the world. Herbert Blumer (1900–1987), an important symbolic interactionist, argued that we can study social processes by focusing on three core principles (Blumer 1969):

1. Meanings arise through social interaction among individuals.
2. People use the meanings they derive from interaction to guide their own behavior.
3. People employ an interpretive process regarding these interactions.

We review each of these principles in more detail in the following sections.

Box 2.1 The Social Behaviorist Perspective in Psychology

The social behaviorist perspective in psychology assumes that the best way to scientifically study people is to examine their behaviors, because behaviors are the only "observable" aspects of human life. Behaviorism follows the research of psychologists such as B. F. Skinner (1904–1990), who studied the effects of

(continued)

positive and negative stimulation on animal behavior, called "operant conditioning." The premise deriving from this paradigm is that most human thoughts, feelings, and behavior are a result of a series of rewards and punishments. For example, according to the behaviorist perspective, babies eventually learn how to become functioning adults by being rewarded for those behaviors and attitudes that are likely to produce good citizens and punished for those behaviors, such as rude manners, that are not deemed important to proper functioning. Albert Bandura (1925–2021) extended Skinner's work by developing a social learning theory that incorporates the concept of imitation in the study of operant conditioning among humans. Imitation assumes that people will adapt new behaviors not only because of rewards to oneself but also when they see other people being rewarded for their behaviors. Social behaviorism and social learning theory both focus on external causes of our thoughts, feelings, and behaviors.

Much work in social behaviorism consists of examining the outcomes of rewards and punishments for animals other than humans. Sociologists, in contrast, rarely study animals to understand human behavior. From an interactionist perspective, the ability to create and manipulate meaning is uniquely human. Although the basic idea of rewards and punishments guiding behavior may be applicable to humans, it is difficult to know how individuals give meaning and values to objects and behaviors. A reward for one person may be a punishment or simply unimportant to another person. Your grade in a course may be very important to you and motivate you to work hard. Your friend may not see much value in grades, leaving her perhaps to decide to miss class and study less. Hence, it is difficult to use conditioning to predict thoughts, feelings, and behaviors if you do not understand how people give meaning to the world around them. Nevertheless, sociological social psychologists have successfully adopted some elements of the behaviorist approach to study, for instance, exchange relationships among people (Homans 1974; Molm and Cook 1995).

Herbert Blumer*

Herbert Blumer was the first person to use the expression, "symbolic interaction." He grew up in St. Louis, Missouri, and attended the University of Missouri. Blumer earned his PhD from the University of Chicago, where he was influenced by famous social psychologists such as George Herbert Mead, W. I. Thomas, and Robert Park. While studying in Chicago, he played professional football for the Chicago (now Arizona) Cardinals. Blumer taught at the University of Chicago for 27 years, later becoming the chair of the Sociology Department at the University of California, Berkeley in 1952. Blumer served as the 46th president of the American Sociological Association and was honored with its Award for a Career of Distinguished Scholarship in 1983. He was the recipient of the Cooley-Mead Award in 1984. Herbert Blumer died on April 13, 1987. Some of Blumer's major contributions to the field include *Movies and Conduct* (Blumer 1933); *Movies, Delinquency, and Crime* (Blumer 1933); *Human Side of Social Planning* (Blumer 1935); *Critiques of Research in the Social Sciences: An Appraisal of Thomas and Znaniecki's The Polish Peasant in Europe and America* (Blumer 1939); and *Symbolic Interaction: Perspective and Method* (Blumer 1969).

*This biography was compiled from several sources, including the American Sociological Association's website (www.asanet.org) and Lyman and Vidich (Lyman and Vidich 1988).

Additional Resources:

"Interviewing Herbert Blumer" by Norbert Wiley, pp. 300–308 in *Symbolic Interaction* 2014, Vol. 37, Issue 2.

Special Issue of the Journal *Symbolic Interaction* on Herbert Blumer includes articles that emphasize his works, see: *Symbolic Interaction* 2020, Vol. 43, Issue 4.

Symbols, Language, and the Development of Meaning

The first principle of symbolic interactionism is that meaning is derived from social interaction. How does this process unfold? George Herbert Mead (1934), considered by many to be the founder of the symbolic interactionist perspective, believed that the study of human gestures is at the center of social psychology. To have meaning, according to Mead, individuals need an exchange of symbols, where a **symbol** refers to anything that has a similar meaning for two or more individuals. A symbol may derive its meaning from producing similar images in two people or from eliciting the same emotional reaction from both. Any act can be "symbolic" if it produces similar outcomes for two or more people.

Language refers to symbols that can be combined in various ways to provide new meanings. Most of what we call consciousness is achieved through the use of language (Hewitt 2003b). Symbols and language may be verbal or nonverbal in nature. Grunts, hand signals, or posture may provide information regarding an individual's thoughts or feelings in a given situation. "Mixed signals" refer to situations in which a person's words convey one meaning of a situation while his or her behaviors (e.g., posture or intonation) display another meaning (see also Box 2.2).

The process by which we use symbols and language to give meaning and value to objects and people is known as the **social construction of reality**. Peter Berger and Thomas Luckmann (1967), in *The Social Construction of Reality*, outlined the basic tenets of this perspective. They argued that humans come to understand their realities in the "here and now"—through day-to-day experiences. Language provides a

Box 2.2 Language and Consciousness in Psychology

Psychologists recognize the importance of language in the development of consciousness. Lev Vygotsky (1896–1934) was a psychologist in the early twentieth century, writing at a time when human development was a major focus of psychology. He (and other psychologists) examined children's "egocentric" thoughts and speech. "Egocentric speech" refers to the way children verbalize their thoughts without necessarily trying to communicate with someone else. It usually occurs during free play as children apply names to objects, such as when a toddler puts a teddy bear on a couch and says, "There's a bear. He is sitting." In a typical child, this speech starts after the age of one and ends by the age of eight. The question was whether egocentric speech was derived internally or externally. Vygotsky's research showed that egocentric speech serves as a (externalized) thinking process. Children use egocentric speech to "practice" problem solving. Egocentric speech is an intermediate stage for learning inner speech, called self-indication in symbolic interactionist language. Hence, Vygotsky argued, egocentric speech does not disappear at the age of eight—as many psychologists believed at the time—but simply goes "underground" as it becomes part of our consciousness. In other words, egocentric speech goes from external to internal thinking processes. Vygotsky's work showed how children develop consciousness by verbalizing their thoughts early on. This research applies to the study of symbolic interactionism, the exchange and development of symbols through interaction, by indicating that meaning-making is an external process that develops the interior life, not the other way around.

bridge between our private understanding of the world and other people. That is, once we are able to objectify and label objects or people, we can share our assessment of the world with others. If we call a certain four-legged creature by the name "dog," we are now able to show other people the animal and agree on the label "dog." While there may have been dogs before we named them, giving them a name allowed us to ascribe them characteristics. Thereafter, we gave them other meanings, such as being cute and a companion in a way that is not reserved for many other living things, such as alligators or spiders, both of which are named by humans, but are rarely considered cute or companions.

Beyond our ability to identify things, it is the ways in which humans take in and analyze information that make the symbolic process possible. In the book *The Man Who Mistook His Wife for a Hat and Other Clinical Tales*, neurologist Oliver Sacks (1985) described patients with a variety of neurological disorders, including those who had lost their memory, individuals with perceptual problems, and people unable to recognize common objects. The book's title refers to a patient who, among other things, would misidentify parking meters and fire hydrants as small children and mistake his shoe for his own foot. Upon leaving his first visit with Sacks, this man reached over to his wife's head and tried to put it on his own head—he had mistaken his wife for a hat!

Sacks argued that this patient was capable of thinking like a computer, using pieces of information around him to draw conclusions, but that he lacked judgment about those things. It is not enough simply to identify and give meaning to objects—we must also process that information in the context of other meanings. In the case of the patient who mistook his wife for a hat, Sacks noted that when the patient watched a romantic film, he was unable to make sense of emotional dialogue between the characters or their genders. Hence, these human relationships lacked any real meaning for the patient.

The ability of humans to create and share meaning is amazing. It took some time for the student in the opening vignette to learn a new meaning for "dancing" as an activity that is beautiful and emotionally joyful. But it can also happen in seconds, and while verbal and written language and symbols are important, meaning-making exchanges occur on many levels at the same time. Modern examples include digitally and technologically mediated interactions (Couldry and Hepp 2016). Brian Due (2021) studied the use of the "Seeing AI" app by a visually impaired person in Denmark who downloaded the app on their phone. It became an "artificial agent" of meaning-making, akin to a human or animal (143). In this case, the researcher examined how the individual interacted with the artificial agent to come to some conclusions about products during an outing at a store. The app can provide information about the product verbally, as it obtains that information using the phone's camera and other technologies. The actor at the store also tries to gather information about the products through touch and other means and uses information from the app to make decisions about the meaning of the products, and ultimately, whether to purchase them.

People rely on subtle forms of communication for meaning as much as on the explicit use of language. Even small amounts of information can change the ways we think about things. For instance, in a study of beliefs about the paranormal, researchers had participants watch a video about extrasensory perception (ESP) and asked them if they believed in it afterward (Ridolfo, Baxter, and Lucas 2010). However, prior to the video, some of the participants had been told that belief in ESP is popular and another group was told that it is not. Those participants who were told that ESP is popular were more likely to say that they believed in it. Hence, even subtle pieces of information can affect the ways that we construct the meaning of things.

People reared in different cultures and environments will almost certainly have different ideas of reality, because each of us undergoes construction processes that occur within these larger contexts. The language we use (e.g., English or Spanish) can change the way we interpret situations as well as our senses of self (Dixon and Robinson-Riegler 2008; Kemmelmeier and Cheng 2004). Try to imagine your favorite joke being translated into another language or told in another language—would it be just as funny, or would it generate blank stares? You may have heard that comedy does not translate well between cultures—a popular comedian from North America may find no fans in other parts of the world. Even if the cultures share the same language, subtle differences in the meanings associated with the words in a joke may render it humorless in the new environment.

Most of us recognize this point, to some degree, when we interact with people from different countries. In a study of Russian professionals interviewing for jobs in the

United States, for instance, one researcher found that poor English language fluency had both positive and negative effects on evaluations of applicants (Molinsky 2005). Poor language fluency was associated with lower professional evaluations on the job; however, it also shielded nonnative speakers when they made a *faux pas*, a socially unacceptable comment or behavior. That is, those who spoke English as their first language rated nonnative candidates with low language fluency as less impolite than native candidates with high language fluency, probably because the natives generally understood that the less fluent nonnative were less familiar with how other people would interpret their behaviors.

The internet and other technologies are changing the ways that we convey meaning toward one another (Johns 2010). A famous social commentator, Marshall McLuhan (2005, originally 1967), argued that the "medium is the message"—the idea that while language is the primary way in which we convey meaning, modern use of visual media over hearing (or reading) words radically changed the way we perceive reality. Not only did the introduction of the internet to communications increase the speed of communication among people, but also the uses of this and other technologies, such as texting, allow us to shorten and condense those communications (Crystal 2008). Nicholas Carr (2010) suggests that this condensed type of communication makes us more attuned to distractions and limits our ability for deep mental processes that require focused attention (e.g., reading a book). In another example, Lin and Tian (2019) studied how the format of Weibo, a Chinese app similar to X (formerly known as Twitter), influences opinion polarization. They argue that Weibo's format limits contextual information as well as information about other people they are interacting with. The asynchronous design combined with limited character usage creates an environment in which users become confused about who they are interacting with and the conversations themselves. One strategy people use to manage this confusion is to galvanize support from like-minded others. The authors conclude that platforms such as Weibo make it more challenging to have peaceful debates over sensitive topics and issues. Thus, while language is the primary way in which we convey meaning to each other, how we introduce that language (for example, visually through texting on a small screen versus aurally through the spoken word or through a particular app) may also affect the meaning-making process (Wright 2010).

The Use of Meaning Once Derived

The second principle of symbolic interactionism focuses on the value of the interaction process. Specifically, why do we engage in the social construction of reality in the first place? According to symbolic interactionism, we are motivated to do so to overcome problems and achieve goals (Blumer 1969; Stryker and Vryan 2003). In short, to get the things we want in life, we must negotiate meanings with other people. According to this second principle of symbolic interactionism, we use information derived from an interaction as a guide for our own behavior. The information tells us how to think, feel, or act. It is important to add that each interaction brings a web of meanings for everything contained therein: the roles and personalities of each person, the physical surroundings, expectations about how to behave in the situation, and a host of other things. A desire to maintain those meanings drives the behavior of individuals in the situation.

We are motivated to change our behavior when we must do so to maintain order or to get what we want out of a situation. Suppose you want to ask a professor if you can make up a missed exam. You make the request to take a makeup exam using language and a series of simple gestures to get what you want. But if the professor appears reluctant to allow the makeup for some reason, you may change your tone, perhaps in an effort to make the professor believe that you are a good student who is worthy of such help. Hence, although you initially entered the interaction with a simple goal, you have now revised your original set of behaviors to incorporate new information—in this case, the professor's reluctant attitude. In short, you may have to modify both your goals and the methods you use to achieve those goals to meet the new social conditions.

This process of negotiating and constructing meanings can be complex because the meaning of a single object may vary depending on social conditions, thus changing the ways we think and act. For instance, David Schweingruber and Nancy Berns (2003) studied the meaning of money in a door-to-door sales company. The company recruited college students for door-to-door sales of educational books. During training sessions, money was defined as a necessary evil, and students were encouraged to focus on the nonmonetary benefits (e.g., developing managerial skills) of doing the work to prevent salespersons from becoming too discouraged and quitting following a period of low or disappointing sales. However, money was also used as a motivating force—to get people to sell in the first place and as a topic of concern when the sales representatives were alone. Here we see people constructing and manipulating the meaning of a single object in different groups to achieve specific goals, such as the recruitment and maintenance of an effective sales staff. Thus, the importance and meaning of money varied depending on the group involved and the context of the discussion.

Complex constructions and manipulations of meaning are important. What things mean to us affects how we live our lives. In a study of the AIDS epidemic in Africa, Iddo Tavory and Ann Swidler (2009) tried to understand resistance to the use of condoms among people in Sub-Saharan Africa. They discovered that the people they studied understood that condoms could protect them from AIDS, and thus could save their lives, but condoms also reflected other cultural meanings: they represented an obstacle to pleasure, an association with other illnesses, and a signal of mistrust among partners. Thus, the decision to utilize condoms for protection was weighed against these other meanings, leading to different outcomes across sexual experiences; some sexual interactions would lead to the use of condoms, while others did not.

From a symbolic interactionist perspective, we are often motivated to give value to objects that may have no inherent value at all. Gary Alan Fine has studied many different American subcultures to understand how groups come to define what is important to them. In a study of the "primitive art" world, he analyzes how primitive artists are "found" by art collectors (Fine 2004). Unlike traditional artists, primitive artists are not formally trained in their genre and may come from extreme conditions (poverty, mental instability, or the worlds of religious mystics, for instance). They also produce nontraditional forms of art. While many outside the art community see little value in the work of such artists, Fine studied how collectors help to build the reputation of primitive artists and increase the value of their work. To have value, unlike traditional artists who seek to make their work known, Fine found that primitive artists must be "discovered"—they must be naïve about their work and let the dealers provide the narrative of their greatness. This meaning-making process not only develops the artists but also recreates the social system by which artists are created, maintaining both the reputation of the collectors who found the good artists and the system by which these artists are discovered.

The Interpretive Process

The third principle of symbolic interactionism is the idea that different people will often come away from an interaction with different interpretations of it. That is, people create "definitions of the situation" that may be somewhat unique. Further, their own interpretations are what people use to guide their behavior (Blumer 1969). All of us bring different values and beliefs, abilities, and perspectives into a given interaction, and so we may interpret the same situation quite differently than others. Harriet Martineau, an early theorist who translated some of August Compte's works into English, provided theories and methods on human interaction (Lengermann and Niebrugge 2007).

Think about a situation in which two students are investigating a new club on campus by going to an informational meeting. The students have similar experiences—they meet the same people, participate in the same activities, and see the same literature about the club. But on leaving the meeting, one student feels excited by the experience, whereas the other interprets the group as boring. These two students, who constructed different meanings of the group based on some of the ideas reviewed in the first principle, will likely choose different paths regarding their future affiliations with the club.

The important point of this principle is that people base future behavior on their subjective interpretations of a present situation. Because it is difficult to know how someone else interprets a situation, we are limited in our ability to predict how people will react to it. In the example of the school club, if the two friends do not discuss the meeting afterward, each may assume that the other came away with an impression similar to her own—leaving the one who was happy with her experience to wonder why her friend did not show up to the next meeting.

This interpretive principle is the basis for the **Thomas theorem**, which states that when people define situations as real, those situations become real in their consequences (Thomas and Thomas 1928; see also Merton 1995; Thomas 1966). As long as we think our understanding is reality, we will act on our meaning. The "definition of the situation" is critical. For instance, if you are bumped by someone while walking down the hall and assume it was done on purpose, you will likely react more aggressively than if you believe it was an accident. A shove back or a shout are behaviors that might follow the first interpretation, whereas ignoring the way you were bumped or joking about it would follow the very different second interpretation. Consider also how important the definition of the situation is to sustaining interaction related to romantic relationships. If someone asks you to come over "to study" but really has romance in mind, you may find yourselves with two conflicting definitions of the situation. Ultimately, if two people cannot agree on a definition, the interaction may come to a quick or frustrating end. Thus, how we define a situation guides our reaction to it and will facilitate or inhibit further interaction.

Framing is the process by which individuals transform the meanings of a situation using basic cognitive structures provided by society (Goffman 1974). Within each of these structures are a series of **social scripts** about the appropriate thoughts, feelings, and behaviors that should be displayed in that frame. As we observe individuals' behaviors, we give meaning to them based on our cultural history. A group of people standing around a person lying on the ground is likely to conjure an "injured person" frame. This frame may invoke fear and cause people to prepare to help the injured person or to look for a doctor. If that person jumps up and starts performing magic tricks, it changes to a "performance" frame, leading those there to smile and prepare to have fun. Because these frames are not formally taught in school or anywhere else, it can be difficult to understand how we develop and use them. Frames and scripts culminate in **expressive orders**, the flow of meanings that occur in any given situation (Goffman 1959). People are motivated to perpetuate existing meanings to protect both their senses of self and people around them, avoiding the feelings of embarrassment when things do not go the way that they are supposed to. The ultimate outcome of these sets of interaction is society, albeit on the micro level. These processes help us to understand how and why people perpetuate existing social orders. It also demonstrates that our day-to-day lives are driven by more than just our personalities and biological drives.

How do individuals decide on the appropriate frame for a situation? What if the cues for the situation are not clear? Scott and colleagues (2013) studied people's reactions to two interactive art exhibits. Rather than individuals passively looking at and evaluating art pieces, interactive exhibits call on individuals to participate in some way. In one example, the "'Video Grid' was a wall of short films made by visitors that kept changing as new recordings replaced older ones" (423). The researchers observed reactions and talked to people as they interacted with the exhibits. They found that individuals often felt stressed, unsure of the rules related to these new art forms. In some cases, they looked for guidance from the people around them. In other cases, they were agentic in creating a sense of order, but they still wanted some validation for their decisions. Finally, some people chose to abandon these new scripts and rely on the traditional model of art consumption which emphasizes passive viewing of art.

There are several conditions that help prime people to use one frame versus another. For instance, John Stolte and Shanon Fender (2007) found that simply switching from English to Spanish significantly changed the way that subjects interpreted a fictional interaction between a mother and daughter. The authors asked bilingual subjects, people who can speak both Spanish and English, to assess two stories. In both cases, a daughter takes in her ill mother. However, in the first story, the daughter does it out of devotion to her mother; in the second case, she does it simply because it would cost less than sending her to a nursing home. The researchers found that respondents were more sympathetic to the mother in the first scenario when Spanish was used and in the latter scenario when English was used. In this case, the use of different languages primed the subjects to use different cultural frameworks to assess the situation being studied;

focusing more on individualistic motives when using English (it would cost less for the subject to take in her mother than to send her to a nursing home) and communal motives when using Spanish (it was done based on devotion to her mother).

Scripts are common in organizational settings as ways to efficiently convey multiple sets of meaning among members. In a study of an out-patient treatment clinic called "Fresh Beginnings," E. Summerson Carr shows the way that therapists expect their "clients" to give up "a drug addicted way of speaking" (2011, p. 127) and begin a new way of talking about their problems that emphasizes acceptance of their addiction and recognition of their troubled pasts. Clients' acceptance and use of these scripts were ways for therapists to gauge the success of the program. However, the researchers also found that clients exercised agency through "flipping the script" by acting like good clients, even if they did not believe it personally—an excellent example of the concept of agency reviewed earlier! In any case, both sets of actors (therapists and clients) manipulated scripts to get what they wanted out of their relationships with each other.

Photo 2.2 People can leave an interaction or event with very different interpretations of it.

Source: Monkey Business Images/Shutterstock

We utilize frames for almost every aspect of our lives—even creating them for fictional conditions. In a study of online role-playing games, Jonas Linderoth (2012) examined the ways that gamers developed and employed scripts while playing games, including scripts about how to manage "real" identities in the middle of a game in which they were in another character. We also have scripts for privacy—cues that tell other people when to leave us alone (see Nippert-Eng 2010 and Raudenbush 2012). Consider how you would feel or what you would do in the following situations:

- Dropping a dish at a party or a product at a store.
- Saying something considered inappropriate in a social setting (e.g., swearing at a formal event such as a job interview).
- Dressing in formal clothes at an informal social gathering.
- Sending a personal text to a stranger by accident.

Common accounts for these types of untoward behaviors include excuses and justifications—either not accepting the behavior as a normal part of one's identity (e.g., an accident), an exception, or accepting it and providing a reason for it to occur (e.g., extreme exhaustion) (see Scott and Lyman 1968). It is important to note that other people in these settings often work cooperatively in this effort as a way of bringing the interaction to some conclusion with the least amount of stress; in this way, accounts can serve as a means of diffusing stressful situations (Poulson, Carter, and Crowley 2018). Through simple, everyday exchanges between people, we use language to challenge and support each other, and we avoid talking about certain topics or to certain people (Hollander and Gordon 2006; Pollock 2004). These interactions serve as a basis for our cognitive processes as well (Molder and Potter 2005). Much of what we convey to other people is in the form of narratives or stories. Stories tell us how we come to interpret an event and help to construct our senses of self (Berger and Quinney 2004; Cousineau 2020). From this perspective, we interact not only to get what we want in life but also to maintain our senses of self and the meanings of the people and relationships around us. Everyday talk supports the web of meaning that has been created. Devices such as phones can serve to help in this process or cause disruptions in the flow of these interactions, requiring us to provide an account for such interruptions (Ictech 2019; Walsh 2019). Consider a situation in which you are having a serious conversation with a friend and they decide to take a call or read texts from a different friend in the middle of it. What does this say about the importance of the conversation or the value of the relationship? Even if your friend provides an account of their behavior, you may remember it as a negative story in the relationship history.

Schools of Symbolic Interactionism

The birthplace of symbolic interactionism is usually considered to be the University of Chicago, where both George Herbert Mead and Herbert Blumer worked in the early to mid-twentieth century. Although sociologists from the University of Chicago employed a variety of methods in the study of human interaction, symbolic interactionists clearly moved away from a deterministic approach toward scientific inquiry (Musolf 2003a). If social reality is constantly being negotiated over time, they asked, then how can research predict future behavior? A second school of thought, sometimes called "structural symbolic interactionism" and historically associated with researchers at the University of

Iowa and Indiana University, varies from the traditional view in its emphasis on the idea that interpretations of social reality are, in fact, generally stable and long-lasting.

The Chicago School

The traditional school of symbolic interactionism associated with Blumer and the University of Chicago contends that social reality is fluid and ever-changing (Musolf 2003a; Stryker and Vryan 2003, see Chapter 7 in Farberman 2019). As a result, according to traditional symbolic interactionists, social reality cannot be quantified and predicted in the same way as other aspects of the physical world. This is the perspective of the **Chicago school of symbolic interactionism**, which states that the primary goal of symbolic interactionism is to understand the social processes involved in a given situation—not to quantify those processes or try to predict future behavior.

The Chicago school can be divided into two historical periods (Musolf 2003a). The first Chicago school, before World War II, included the early work of George Herbert Mead as well as W. I. Thomas, one of the sociologists associated with the Thomas theorem. The second Chicago school, in the post–World War II era, is associated with the work of Herbert Blumer, a student of Mead and, in 1937, the person to coin the term "symbolic interaction." Blumer was also important in keeping the focus of symbolic interactionism on social interactions and away from macro-level definitions of society. In this view, society is based on interactions between people, and as a result, people—rather than structures existing outside human interaction—have the ability to maintain or change society. From this perspective, society is a reflection of shared meanings exchanged during social interaction, which produce a sense of solidarity that is the essence of society. This process is inherently a minded activity—based on individual thoughts and feelings in a given social interaction—in which people's interactions and identities are, from the standpoint of many symbolic interactionists, too fluid to study using traditional scientific methods that assume similarity between elements of a sample.

The Iowa and Indiana Schools

The second school of symbolic interactionism has been associated with researchers and theorists from the University of Iowa (such as Manford Kuhn) and from Indiana University (such as Sheldon Stryker). As mentioned, it is sometimes called "structural symbolic interactionism," and it varies from the traditional view in its emphasis on the stable nature of social reality. That is, once an interpretation or "definition of the situation" has been made, it tends to remain for a period of time. Meanings change, but not that quickly. The **Iowa and Indiana schools of symbolic interactionism** argue that, as a result, social reality can be quantified and studied using the scientific method.

The Iowa and Indiana schools of symbolic interactionism developed after World War II, at the time of the second Chicago school. Manford Kuhn, who had joined the University of Iowa faculty in the 1940s, shared with Chicago school interactionists a concern with the reliability of the strictly quantitative studies found in sociological and psychological research at the time. However, unlike his colleagues at the University of Chicago,

Kuhn wanted to develop ways of testing symbolic interactionist principles. These efforts led him to develop the Twenty Statements Test for assessing the self-concept (see Chapter 5). In later years, symbolic interactionists at Indiana University such as Sheldon Stryker conducted research on the self that led to the creation of identity theory (also discussed in Chapter 5). Researchers at the Iowa School utilized the Center for Research in Interpersonal Behavior (CRIB) to video record social interactions for later analysis (Katovich 2017). Both of these schools attempted to develop empirical applications of the symbolic interactionist principles.

Both the Chicago and Iowa/Indiana schools of symbolic interactionism see social reality as fluid, but they disagree about the speed with which it changes over time, and they have developed different methods for studying people. Chicago school symbolic interactionists are likely to use observational methods, whereas those in the Iowa and Indiana tradition typically use surveys that quantify individuals' thoughts, feelings, and behaviors, particularly about the self. Despite these differences, researchers and theorists from these varying perspectives continue to emphasize the importance of the self and of social interaction in the maintenance and construction of society.

Section Summary

The first section of this chapter answered the questions "What are the major principles of the symbolic interactionist perspective?" "How does this perspective help us to understand the relationship between the individual and society?" And "What does it mean to 'construct' the world around us?" The symbolic interactionist paradigm is based on three basic principles: meanings arise through social interaction among individuals, individuals use the meanings they derive from interactions to guide their own behaviors, and people act toward objects on the basis of the meanings that those objects have for them. These principles emphasize the importance of agency in day-to-day life—that we have the ability to make choices in the social world around us. As a result, this perspective is essential to understanding individuals' ability to negotiate and construct their social worlds with other people.

A Take-Away Message

How might you use your knowledge of the symbolic interactionist paradigm in your own life? First, the three principles of symbolic interactionism should make you aware of the ways in which you use scripts and narratives in your own life. They help us navigate every social interaction. You can use this information to predict what people are thinking and doing in most interactions. It can also empower you to resist those scripts that you do not agree with, or perhaps to try to introduce new scripts during your interactions with other people. At work, knowing how to attend to the different meanings that people bring to work situations will help you accomplish your goals without diminishing those differences. Alternatively, you may be able to develop a new way to accomplish organizational goals by creating new meanings that everyone can share, thereby improving the *esprit des corps* of the group.

THE SOCIAL STRUCTURE AND PERSONALITY PERSPECTIVE

I always knew that our positions in life affect us, but it really did not hit home till I joined the army. Corporal Bain was a hilarious person. He had been in the service a while, but he always made fun of the army. He would joke about the leaders and always had a wisecrack. He was great to be around. I found out that his games cost him a promotion, and he had been demoted at least once. Then one day I learned that he'd been promoted to sergeant. That meant that he would become our supervisor. Finally, I thought, someone who was going to look out for us. Was I surprised! The very next day, he started barking orders at us. No jokes, no goofy attitude, just orders. In fact, he was the harshest supervisor I have ever had in the army! I tried to ask him what was going on, but he stopped talking informally with the rest of the crew. It's amazing how quickly people can change.

—Nancy, junior education major

The social structure and personality perspective focuses on the connections between larger societal conditions and the individual. These social conditions are measured in terms of what we defined in Chapter 1 as social structure, or persisting patterns of behavior and interaction between people or social positions (House 1992). The idea of "persistent patterns of behavior" suggests that there is some stability to the social world: people develop rules and norms that govern almost all aspects of social life. Patterns are regular rules of behavior—that is, how people are expected to act in different social contexts. These rules serve as guidelines for behavior and allow people to predict what others will do. Like structural symbolic interactionists, those who take the social structural and personality perspective view society as stable and assume that social scientists can predict individuals' thoughts, feelings, and behaviors.

The idea that social structure affects individuals' thoughts, feelings, and behaviors relates to the macro-level sociological theories outlined in Chapter 1. Karl Marx for instance, generally believed that the economic systems people live in affect both social relations and individual thinking processes. Notably, he believed that capitalist economies lead individuals to a sense of alienation or separation from their work and other workers. Emile Durkheim (1951, originally 1897), a structural functionalist, showed that the decision to commit suicide is affected by locations in society. For instance, he found that Protestants take their own lives at higher rates than do Catholics or Jewish people; Durkheim argued that the Protestant religion created less social integration among members, leading Protestants to commit suicide at higher rates than individuals from other religious traditions.

In the opening vignette, Nancy begins to see the effects that structural conditions can have on people. Corporal (now Sergeant) Bain changed dramatically immediately after attaining a leadership position in the group. Not only did his attitudes and identity change, but his relationships with other people changed as well. Examining situations like Nancy's, theories and research based on the social structure and personality perspective promote the understanding of how the larger society affects individuals within it (House 1977; House 1992).

James House (1992) argued that our ability to study the effects of larger structural forces on the individual involves three key principles:

1. **Components principle**: We must be able to identify the elements or components of society most likely to affect a given attitude or behavior.
2. **Proximity principle**: We need to understand the aspects or contexts of social structure that most affect us.
3. **Psychology principle**: We need to understand how individuals internalize proximal experiences.

We review each of these principles in this section.

The Components Principle

Traditional research using the social structure and personality paradigm focuses on the components of social structure most likely to affect individuals in a given context: statuses, roles, and networks. Most of these components were included in the "toolkit" provided in Chapter 1. Knowing these dimensions of social life helps us better predict how social structure affects individuals' lives. We review some of the major components in detail here.

Status

In Chapter 1, we defined status as "a person's position in a group or society that is associated with varying levels of prestige and respect." Typically, social structure and personality theorists examine such statuses as socioeconomic status (social class), race or ethnicity, gender, age, and sexuality. Although socioeconomic status is often associated with income level, it also reflects a level of prestige. Some individuals—for example, religious leaders—may have jobs that pay only a relatively modest income but hold high occupational prestige.

A challenge in studying effects of social structure on our daily lives is that we carry many different statuses with us and use them at different times. We can also choose to emphasize a particular status within a relationship (Sawyer 2019), such as a boss who is also a friend. You can act friendly with the person in a way that other people cannot. Similarly, such an overlap with roles can cause conflicts as your boss and friend may ask you to do something that you do not want to do. Friends are typically egalitarian, so receiving orders from one may cause some tension in the relationship. We must be able to grapple with these complexities if we want to predict the effects of social structures on us. Being a parent, for instance, is associated with greater challenges to well-being given financial and work challenges when trying to raise kids (Nomaguchi and Milkie 2020). Of course, there are positive effects of parental status too, like increased sense of purpose and meaning. Some difficulties of parenting may be stronger for certain groups, like women and those who are not married. Thus, our statuses (e.g., parental status)

Photo 2.3 Individuals are given statuses and roles in society that are associated with differing levels of power. Have you ever experienced a situation in which someone used their position to get you to do something that you did not want to do?

Source: fizkes/Shutterstock

can shape our wellbeing, and also interact with other statuses (e.g., parental status × marital status × gender) to produce different, but patterned, outcomes (Nomaguchi and Milkie 2020). Social structure and personality researchers seek to account for these variations when analyzing the influences of social structure on people's lives.

Roles

Another part of your toolkit introduced in Chapter 1 is roles. The concept of roles is defined as "a set of expectations for how one should behave in a given position or status" (see Box 2.3). Roles provide rules or guidelines for our behavior. For example, the professor role includes teaching courses and giving grades to students, whereas the student role includes attending class, reading scholarly material, and studying for exams. Those who fail to meet the expectations of these roles may receive negative feedback. For students, this would take the form of bad grades; for teachers, bored students or unsatisfactory teaching evaluations. In contrast, individuals who live up to most or all role expectations are generally rewarded (e.g., with good grades or high evaluations) and, less formally, are deemed "good" at their respective roles.

Box 2.3 Role Theory

Role theory proposes that individuals take on social positions and the accompanying expectations for their behaviors in those positions (Biddle 1986). Society provides both the basis for all or most social positions and the roles (expectations) associated with those positions. For instance, when we accept jobs, we take on the assumptions and expectations of those jobs. Accountants are expected to calculate numbers and do it well if they want to keep such a job. According to role theory, we can predict individual thoughts, feelings, and behaviors by knowing someone's range of available roles. Knowing that someone is a CEO of a large corporation will lead us to several assumptions about her lifestyle and attitudes. We can probably predict that she lives very well—driving the best cars, eating the finest food, and supporting political candidates that help her industry prosper. We can predict these things with some level of reliability without meeting the person or having any other background information.

Individuals can alter the expectations of a given position over time while maintaining its basic nature. Students in the 1950s, or 1980s, or 2000s dressed and acted very differently from current students. However, the role of student still conjures up expectations to study and attend classes. Thus, although roles may change over time, many of the basic expectations remain the same. Some symbolic interactionists and social structure and personality researchers incorporate elements of role theory; the components principle within the social structure and personality perspective is one notable example.

Social Norms

We defined norms in Chapter 1 as behavioral guidelines. Norms include the scripts that we use during interactions, and also expectations of thoughts and behaviors in general. Many norms are not formally stated, as in the form of a law, but they are nevertheless associated with sanctions. Typically, sanctions can be internal, such as feeling guilt or shame, or external social pressure to conform (Horne 2009; Wasserman and Clair 2009; Willer, Kuwabara, and Macy 2009). Norms can be self-perpetuating such that as they continue to exist, people see them as more desirable to follow (Brennan et al. 2013). It is also important to know that people have agency and can react to norms differently depending on several conditions (Horne, Dodoo, and Dodoo 2018). Namkj Koudenburg and colleagues (2013), for instance, found that people highly motivated to belong to a group were more likely to change their attitudes to become more normative than people less motivated to belong. Finally, group norms can mitigate formal norms or laws. Yusheng Peng (2010), for instance, found that villages in China with more pro-natalist norms had higher birth rates than other villages despite the anti-natalist policies of the state. Thus, norms not only serve as guidelines for individuals' behavior but also reflect the identity of the groups to which we belong.

Social Networks

The importance of statuses and roles in our interactions with others is highlighted in the opening vignette by Nancy's portrayal of the changes in Corporal Bain after his promotion—he changed dramatically, probably to meet the role demands of his new status in the military. But society can also exist in the relationships between people. **Social networks** (see Figure 2.1) refer to connected relationships among individuals and groups. We hold certain positions in society, each of which connects us with other people. Even if we know only one or two people in a network, those people connect us to other people in the network with whom we are not directly acquainted. From this perspective, it is not enough to know about an individual's status and roles because our networks connect us to other people with various levels of resources. For instance, some students may have access to knowledge about summer jobs through their connections to others in a religious or community organization. Ultimately, networks may provide students the resources they need while they prepare for new status positions in the economy.

Figure 2.1 Social Networks Connect Individuals and Groups in Society.

Source: Peshkova/Shutterstock.

The Proximity Principle

The proximity principle states that we often feel the effects of society through interpersonal interactions and communication with people around us (House 1992). Most research on the proximity principle has focused on family and work contexts (McLeod and Lively 2003). We spend a significant part of our waking lives at work, and on average about one-third of our waking lives with friends and family, depending on our age and other factors (Ortiz-Ospina 2020). According to the proximity principle, much of society's effects on us comes through these institutions of work and family.

A downturn in the economy affects many people, but how? Many research projects have attempted to assess the relative effects of structural and personal economic conditions on individual health and well-being. While some studies have shown that poor economic conditions can affect people's lives, the findings have been mixed and depend on what level the economic contexts are measured. In a study of 21 European countries, for instance, Karen Olsen and Svenn-Age Dahl (2007) found that countries' socioeconomic development was positively associated with individuals' health: higher gross domestic product per capita is associated with better health. Alternatively, Ming Wen and her colleagues (Wen et al., 2003) found no effects of neighborhood poverty on health, but showed that neighborhood affluence mattered. These differences in outcomes may have to do with the different methods and levels of analysis used to measure macro-level conditions. Using the proximity principle, we would also predict that much of the personal effects of larger social structural conditions such as an economic downturn would come from our interpersonal experiences (i.e., our own job loss or that of a friend or relative). For instance, David Rohall and his colleagues (2001) found similar types of reactions to a downsizing event among both those experiencing downsizing and their spouses, suggesting that the effects of economic conditions can occur both directly (what happens to us) and indirectly (what happens to our friends and family members).

Is it better to live in the city or the country? Of course, the real answer to that question for you personally depends on the lifestyle you prefer. But researchers have been studying the effects of living in rural, suburban, and urban areas (or urbanicity) for decades. In one example, researchers studied self-efficacy, the belief that one has control over one's life, across 64 countries to determine whether living in urban areas increases or decreases one's sense of efficacy (Debies-Carl and Huggins 2009). They found that living in a more populous area is, overall, associated with a greater sense of efficacy. However, they also found that living in a high-crime area decreases one's sense of efficacy. Thus, the effects of living in an urban environment depend on other conditions such as crime: it is not enough to simply examine the effects of one macrosocial condition in our lives, we must also contextualize large-scale conditions. In this sense, society is like a structure with multiple compartments within it. It can have direct effects on individuals within it, but so can the conditions of each of those compartments. In some cases, the compartments complement the larger set of conditions, and in some cases they do not. Social psychologists must be able to disaggregate these levels of analyses.

The Psychology Principle

Although social structural conditions may affect us either directly or indirectly through proximal forces, there is no guarantee that these effects will lead to changes in our thoughts or behavior. Probably the least studied aspect of social structure and personality research is how we process structural and proximal forces (McLeod and Lively 2003). What makes someone decide to follow a norm? One explanation lies in the feelings we experience when we disobey a social norm or rule. **Social forces** include all the ways in which other people—or society in general—compel individuals to act in accordance with external norms, rules, or demands (Simpson 1998). Social forces are often clearly felt when we act inappropriately in a social situation. One of the authors was invited to a faculty "barbeque" when she was a graduate student. She showed up in a T-shirt, shorts, and flip flops, but found out the "barbeque" was really a formal dinner with some prestigious visiting international faculty. If you were in this situation, you might feel a sense of embarrassment, and your face might become flushed. That awkward feeling could prompt you to either rush home and change your attire and return in the "right" clothing, or to leave the party early after a period of feeling embarrassed. In either case, social forces create the "feeling" or "decision" to change your behavior in some way and to be very careful to check on the formality of future gatherings to which you are invited.

We can consciously decide to act against social forces, but if we do, we will likely face some consequences. Most of us generally follow the simple rules in life—obeying norms for coffee shop lineups, for instance, and not cutting to the front of the line—but modifying others, like certain traffic laws. The risk of disobeying social rules depends on how important they are to a given group. Formal rules are codified as laws and may be tied to specific penalties, such as fines or jail time. However, rebellions against an existing social order can influence other people and ultimately open the door to social change.

The important issue in this discussion is that people have the ability to internalize social norms in a variety of ways. The psychology principle is about the processes that lead people to follow (or not follow) the rules.

Finally, much like the third principle of symbolic interactionism, the psychology principle is about how people experience society internally. How do social interactions in a city environment get processed by individuals differently from interactions in a small town? James House (1992) argues that we cannot fully understand the role of social structure in people's lives until we are able to understand how individuals interpret it. This process would include analysis of individuals' internal states that influence social relationships (Prager 2006). From this perspective, our motives derive from external interactions and the internal negotiations of those interactions.

Some research examines the relative effects of objective societal conditions and individuals' perceptions of those conditions. C. Andre Christie-Mizell and Rebecca Erickson (2007), for instance, found that mothers in higher-income neighborhoods reported higher levels of mastery (sense of personal control) than mothers living in poorer neighborhoods. This finding makes sense: it is difficult to come to believe that you have control over your life if you live in a place that is sometimes chaotic. However, the researchers also found that the effects of neighborhood conditions were mediated by perceptions of the neighborhoods. Mothers who believed that they lived in neighborhoods with less crime and violence, with people who respect the law, and with access to adequate public transportation reported higher levels of mastery than mothers who did not perceive their neighborhoods the same way. Also, the effects of perceived neighborhood conditions affected mastery over and above actual neighborhood conditions (e.g., crime and unemployment rates). This type of research holds the promise of gaining understanding of the objective (actual conditions) and subjective (perceived) effects of society on the individual.

Eviatar Zerubavel (1997; Zerubavel and Smith 2010) proposes that we develop a "sociology of thinking" or **cognitive sociology** to help understand the ways that society influences our thinking processes. This idea goes counter to cognitive individualism, which emphasizes the idea that individuals act and think independently from their surroundings. Situational conditions are bounded not only to our thoughts but also our emotions (Bergman Blix 2022; McVeigh 2020; Price 2020; Wiley 2016). From this perspective, human cognition is the nexus of thoughts, feelings, but also physical and social conditions. All of these things interact to create unique outcomes that may explain why it is difficult to predict people's actions simply by focusing on a particular aspect of their lives (e.g., personality or social status) and social conditions.

An extension of cognitive sociology is the sociology of sensory perception which examines the social aspects of the human senses (Vannini, Waskul, and Gottschalk 2011). Asia Friedman (2012), for instance, explored the ways in which blind people perceive the human body without access to one of the five major senses. She found that most blind people rely on "tone of voice" and smell to identify other people's gender—and it often takes quite a bit of time and energy to get a complete picture of another person. In other words, attributes assumed by many to be "obvious" or "self-evident," such as one's gender identity, can be difficult to decipher without visual cues, a finding, she argues, that should encourage us to question other things normally taken for granted or considered naturally "true." The importance of this type of research is that it shows that our thinking is socially and perceptually constructed like any other aspects of our social lives (Livingston 2008).

Section Summary

In this section of the chapter, we answered the questions "What is the social structure and personality perspective?" and "How do those in this field of study conceive of the influence of society on the individual?" The social structure and personality perspective emphasizes the effects of society on our lives using three basic principles. The components principle helps to answer the question of how researchers study the influence of society on the individual. Here we identify important elements of society such as roles and statuses that directly affect the ways we interact with other people. The second and third principles in this perspective focus on how individuals are affected by these components. Specifically, the proximity principle states that individuals are affected by society through their immediate social environments like work and family, while the psychology principle focuses on how individuals internalize proximal experiences.

A Take-Away Message

Knowing a little bit about the ways that larger forces affect your daily life may help you in your professional pursuits, among other areas of life. In terms of finding a job, it may mean leaving the place you live to find a location with the types of jobs or neighborhoods you want. Alternatively, you may have to come to accept the kinds of work available to you where you are now—an internal change. Whatever you decide to do, it will require a negotiation between larger social forces and your internal states.

THE GROUP PROCESSES PERSPECTIVE

> *It used to really make me angry. I would sit in my study group and give almost all of the answers but get very little of the credit. My friends thought it was just in my head. They said that people were being fair. Then I started writing down the number of times people contributed to the work group and who got thanked the most. It was just as I thought—I did most of the work, but John got the most compliments by far. He works hard, but I still do more than he does. Why does he get all of the credit?*
>
> —Jean, freshman biology major

Group processes refers to the study of how basic social processes operate in group contexts. In this vignette, we see a work group with an unequal distribution of rewards. Jean is trying to understand how she could work so hard yet receive less credit than other people in the group. To see if her perceptions match reality—in social science language, to "test her hypothesis"—she approaches the group interactions systematically, making notes on members' work inputs and the number of compliments received. The data support her hypothesis: she is getting the short end of the stick.

What is most interesting about this example to researchers in the group processes perspective is that what happened in Jean's group reflects a consistent pattern that occurs when groups form. When people organize in groups to complete tasks, the recognition that people receive for their performances often does not match the quality of their contributions. In other words, the processes that occurred in Jean's group reflect more general social processes.

Group processes theorists and researchers are interested in these general social processes. How do members of groups decide who contributes the most? Who gets the most credit for their contributions? Who talks the most in groups? In our society, work groups tend to organize in a manner similar to Jean's group. For example, when groups form to complete tasks, men tend to get more credit than women do for the same contributions (Troyer 2001; Walker 2019). Sociological social psychologists are interested in the processes that lead to these differences.

Many social processes occur in group contexts. By **group**, we simply mean any interaction involving more than one person. The example in Jean's vignette fits what many of us think when we hear the word "group"—people working together to complete some task. But to researchers in the group processes tradition, even an interaction between two people who stop to chat when passing each other on the street would be considered a "group." Other examples of groups are families, sports teams, and Greek-letter organizations. In all of these examples, the group consists of people who are bound to one another in some way.

The phrase *group processes* implies an interest in two things—groups and processes. Although it is not a hard-and-fast rule, sociological social psychologists in the group processes perspective tend to be most interested in the processes that occur in groups, in contrast to psychological social psychologists, who are often more interested in groups themselves. For example, suppose that an organization forms a committee for the purpose of selecting a person to hire for an important job. In the committee's deliberations, a status order would likely form, with some people talking more and others less. Status in this instance refers to a basic group process that is of interest to sociological social psychologists. Someone studying this basic process would be less interested in the group's deliberations or their outcomes than in the processes leading to the status order. In contrast, a social psychologist more interested in characteristics of the group itself might seek to determine the factors that affected whether the group was successful at its task, or perhaps how the size of the group influenced its deliberations. In the first case, social psychologists are interested in studying processes that operate in a similar manner across different types of groups. In the second, social psychologists are interested in determining how characteristics of the group affected its deliberations.

A focus on group processes, then, leads to an interest in a broad range of phenomena. In part because of this focus, the group processes perspective does not have a specific set of principles governing its area of expertise. Many group processes researchers, particularly those who are sociologists, study the processes that occur in group contexts. Others study aspects of groups such as their size, purposes, and functions. Next, we discuss these two features of work in the group processes perspective, distinguishing the study of group processes from the study of groups themselves.

Studying Processes

Certain basic social processes tend to play out in group contexts, whether the groups are small (such as family or friends) or large (such as corporations). We experience processes such as power and justice, for example, in relation to other people. That is, they exist only in the context of our relationships with others. If we want to be powerful, we must have someone to have power over. These examples highlight some of the basic social processes that are of interest to group processes researchers. A few of the major processes studied in the group processes perspective are as follows:

- **Power**: The ability to obtain what we desire in a group despite resistance.
- **Status**: A position in a group based on esteem or respect.

- **Justice**: Perceptions that a social arrangement or distribution is fair.
- **Legitimacy**: The sense that a social arrangement or position is the way that things should be.

Next, we briefly discuss each of these concepts as group processes.

Power

Some people in society have more power than others. We can probably all agree, for example, that the president of the United States has a great deal of power. The president can make decisions that have important consequences for people's lives. As noted in this chapter, power is a group process because people have it only in relation to other people. The types of groups in which power processes operate vary in size, but when power differences exist between people, there is always some group context.

What is the source of power for the prime minister or president? It emanates from their position in a group structure. In other words, nothing about leaders, as individuals, makes them powerful: their power is a result of their position. Their personal characteristics likely played an important role in the rise to the positions of country leader, but it is the position that now gives them the power. When new leaders are elected and take office, the power transfers to them. The source of the leaders' power is not difficult to identify: formal rules allow them to make important decisions that affect the lives of many people. In most group contexts, however—such as marriages or groups of friends—the sources of power are more subtle. Group processes researchers seek to determine the characteristics of positions in group structures that lead to power and what the outcomes of those processes are (Bonacich 1998; Burke 1997; Cook and Yamagishi 1992; Markovsky, Willer, and Patton 1988; Thye, Lawler, and Yoon 2011; Willer and Patton 1987).

Status

Status is another group process, defined as a person's standing in a group or society based on prestige and respect. As with power, people cannot have "status" in and of themselves, but only in relation to other people. As an example, think of the people who work at a restaurant. The restaurant owners probably have higher social status than the cooks who work for them. But the owners may be low in social status compared to some of their customers, who may have other, more prestigious occupations, such as medical doctors or judges. Status involves social comparisons in groups; a consideration of status is meaningless unless we put it into a group context.

In an earlier vignette, Jean talked about her experience of not receiving the credit she deserved in a task group. Task groups are a particularly interesting place to look at how status operates in group contexts. A great deal of research in sociological social psychology indicates that when groups get together to complete tasks, status hierarchies form. People who are higher in the status hierarchy tend to do more of the talking and to get more of the credit for their contributions than do those who have lower status. This finding is consistent in the literature, and social psychologists have developed theoretical accounts of how status processes operate in groups (Berger, Rosenholtz, and Zelditch 1980; Kalkhoff et al. 2020; Melamed et al. 2019;Thye 2000; Troyer 2001; Wagner and Berger 1993; Webster and Whitmeyer 2002). The best developed of these theories, expectation states and status characteristics theory, are detailed in Chapter 4.

Justice

Let's look again at the example we just discussed—the power imbalance at the restaurant. In that situation, workers may develop a sense that they are not being treated fairly. Social psychologists refer to such perceptions of fairness as justice perceptions. Justice is a group process because it involves social comparisons. For example, when people think about whether their wage or salary is fair, they draw conclusions by comparing their salaries to those of other people.

Social psychologists who are interested in justice have come up with many interesting and sometimes surprising findings. For example, when we try to determine whether the amount of money we make is "fair," to whom do we compare ourselves? Research indicates that we tend to compare ourselves to similar others. However, research also shows that this tendency goes only so far: in general, we seek comparisons that will give the highest value to the amount we think we should earn. And at what point do we decide that the distribution of salaries is unfair? We feel more of a sense of injustice about pay distributions that give us less than we think we deserve than we do about distributions that give us more than we think we deserve.

What criteria do most of us think should be used to determine pay distributions? Depending on the context, researchers have found that we apply different criteria to different situations. In some situations, people are likely to think that equal distributions, with everyone receiving the same amount, are the fairest. In other instances, however, people may think that the fairest outcome is an equitable distribution—one in which the amount each individual receives reflects how much that person contributes to the group.

These are just a few examples of the many questions confronted by social psychologists interested in justice. Group processes work on justice is varied and addresses multiple aspects of how we determine what is fair (Hegtvedt 1990; Jasso 1980; Jasso and Webster 1999; Markovsky 1985). Important group processes findings on justice comparisons will come up in other chapters throughout the book.

Legitimacy

When disparities exist between our perceptions of competence and actual power differences in the world, we are likely to conclude that some distributions are illegitimate. Just like status, power, and justice, legitimacy—the sense that an existing social arrangement is the way that things should be—is a social process that occurs in group contexts. When people view social arrangements as illegitimate, a number of outcomes can undermine social order. For example, waiters and dishwashers might not work as hard for the owners of a restaurant if they do not believe that the owner's power over them is legitimate.

Sociological social psychologists who study group processes are especially interested in the legitimacy of persons in positions of authority. Social psychologists, for example, might study how the events associated with the 2020 US presidential election, in which hundreds of people stormed the US Capitol contesting its legitimacy, might be related to feelings of legitimacy and justice. Polling research shows that the overwhelming number of people who voted for Joe Biden believed the election was legitimate, whereas just as high a proportion of people who voted for Donald Trump viewed it as *not* legitimate (Balz, Clement, and Guskin 2022). These feelings of unfairness may have helped propel people to act in ways that they would not otherwise.

People can gain legitimacy in a number of ways. In American society, research indicates that some people—men compared to women, for example—tend to be viewed as more legitimate occupants of authority positions. Endorsement, which is the approval of a social arrangement by members of one's peer group, is one source of legitimacy. For example, if one's coworkers at a restaurant believe that the restaurant's owners are exceptionally competent, the worker herself will likely view the owners' power as more legitimate than she otherwise would. One consequence of legitimacy processes is that they can act to make status and power orders very stable and difficult to change, even when they aren't optimal for the group (Johnson, Dowd, and Ridgeway 2006). Group processes work on legitimacy addresses its sources and outcomes in multiple ways (Hegtvedt et al. 2022; Lucas et al. 2022; Thomas, Walker, and Zelditch 1986; Walker, Thomas, and Zelditch 1986; Zelditch 2001).

Power, status, justice, and legitimacy are just a few of the many processes occurring in group contexts that are of interest to sociological social psychologists. As we have noted, researchers in the group processes approach include those who study the processes that occur in groups and those who study the characteristics of groups themselves. We now turn to a brief discussion of some of the interests of those who study the "group" in "group processes."

Box 2.4 Careers in Social Psychology: Considering Graduate School

How can knowing about social-psychological theories help me find a job? The truth is that social psychology does provide the kind of "soft skills" that can be used on any job that involves interactions with other people. Business managers must negotiate with employees, clients, and people from other organizations. Most of the career ideas we will be introducing throughout this book focus on jobs at the undergraduate level, but graduate-level training opens up many other career options. For instance, you will need a master's degree or higher to be a certified counselor, typically in psychology or social work. It is also common for students of social psychology to go to graduate school with the intent of becoming a professor. In most countries, you need a master's degree or doctor of philosophy (PhD) to teach at the college or university level. If you obtain that degree in sociology, you become competitive for teaching in sociology programs. What makes you more competitive in obtaining those jobs? It is essential that you get as much teaching and research experience as possible. In graduate school, for instance,

(continued)

volunteer to speak in classes on a topic that you know very well. Similarly, if there is a paid opportunity to teach a class, never turn it down! Higher education is a tight labor market, especially in the social sciences. It is essential that you do well in your classes and volunteer to work with a mentor on research projects related to your interests or areas that you would like to teach. Doing these things will increase the odds that you will be selected for an interview at one of the 4,000 plus colleges and universities in the US and many more around the world!

Group Structures

The effect of a group on its members depends, in part, on how the group is configured. Groups can be configured in a number of ways—by size, function (e.g., work or pleasure), or goals, among other things. Each of these configurations can produce different expectations about how to behave in the group.

Group Size

Small groups are defined as groups of two or more individuals—typically between 2 and 20 people—whose members are able to engage in direct, face-to-face interactions. Although there is no official group size at which face-to-face interaction becomes impossible, it is difficult for personal relationships to develop in groups of more than 20. In a five-person group, for example, each person can interact with every other group member. But in a group of 50 people, a leader might direct the entire group (e.g., by presenting a lecture) or instead might break the 50-person group into smaller, more intimate groups. An interaction among all 50 group members, however, is unlikely.

Anyone who has been part of a class of 90 students meeting in a large auditorium and has also participated in small classes of about 15 students can understand the effects of group size on interactions. You may enjoy smaller classes more than larger ones. Why? Probably because smaller classes allow for more intimate interactions between students, opening up discussions and giving class members an opportunity to get to know one another. In short, by allowing for more intimacy among their members, smaller classes provide for richer discussions, more time for interaction, and thus better learning environments.

Dyads and Triads

One of the first sociologists to study the effects of group dynamics on individuals was Georg Simmel. Simmel (1950) argued that the size of a group restricts the level of intimacy possible within the group. A two-person group, or **dyad**, is limited to a single relationship. But adding just one more person to that group, to form a **triad**, creates two additional relationships. Thus, simply adding a person to a group increases the number of relationships in the group exponentially while simultaneously decreasing intimacy levels. The effects of group size on group members' thoughts, feelings, and behaviors occur above and beyond the specific individuals involved in the group.

The change from a dyad to a triad is an example of a process that occurs in small groups. The process can be illustrated through considering personal relationships. Suppose you go to a party and meet someone to whom you are attracted. As you start to talk, you become more interested in the other person, exchanging ideas about topics you both enjoy. A little later, a friend of yours enters the room and approaches your dyad, transforming it into a triad.

Photo 2.4 Group size can change the nature of relationships. Moving from a dyad to a triad can reduce intimacy in a group. Have you ever experienced a situation that reflects the saying "three's a crowd"?

Source: Georgi Fadejev/Shutterstock

What happens now? Your discussion will very likely change, not only because a new group member brings a different point of view, but also because the group now has two new relationships—for a total of three—to balance. As a result, someone will likely talk less, and there will be less opportunity to develop intimacy. Adding still more people to the triad will again create an exponential increase in the number of relationships—for example, a four-person group involves six different relationships—and a corresponding decrease in intimacy (see Figure 2.2).

At the small-group level, group processes theories in sociology focus on the exchanges—of resources, information, and emotion—that take place between people and on how our positions in groups affect these exchanges. According to many researchers who study small groups, a primary source of motivation for individuals in groups is to

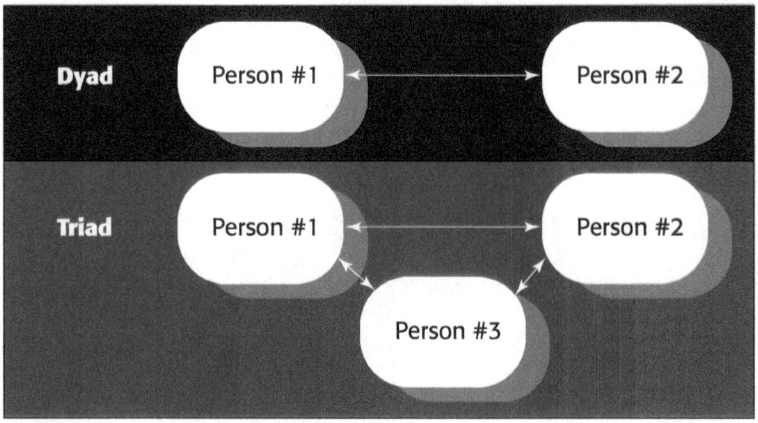

Figure 2.2 Relationships in Dyads and Triads.

obtain the things they need in life. Those "things" can include material (e.g., money) or nonmaterial (e.g., friendship) objects.

Types of Groups

Social psychologists distinguish between three broad types of groups, which are configured in different ways and serve different purposes:

- **Primary groups**: Family members and close friends—the people we are close to and interact with regularly (Cooley 1909).
- **Secondary groups**: People we affiliate with to achieve similar goals or needs—for example, coworkers or teammates.
- **Reference groups**: People we do not necessarily know personally but look to as a source of standards and identity.

Each type of group holds different expectations of its members. Primary groups serve more emotional needs, whereas secondary groups usually serve instrumental needs. Reference groups, however, can vary considerably. Your membership in the Democratic, Republican, or Libertarian parties may serve instrumental needs (e.g., a push for public policy) as well as reference needs (to find support for your ideals). Unlike your relationship to most primary and secondary groups, you may not interact much with members of your reference groups. Even if you identify with your party's goals and use its ideals as a standard of behavior, for example, you may never actually go to party meetings.

Relationships among Groups

In our previous review of group processes, we looked at behavior within groups, or "intragroup" dynamics. But social psychologists are also interested in intergroup dynamics, that is, relationships between two or more groups. Thus, groups themselves—beyond their individual members—can serve as a unit of analysis. Going along with this, groups can develop identities that later have effects on the members of the group.

Intergroup relationships can occur on several levels, ranging from small groups of friends to larger, more formal groups. An important social psychological theory of intergroup relationships, social identity theory, is reviewed in detail later in this book. One area of interest to social psychologists who study intergroup relationships is the causes and consequences of prejudice and discrimination. Sociologists also study the behavior of larger groups through research on such acts as protests and riots.

Both inter- and intragroup behavior can be studied as aspects of **collective behavior**—the action or behavior of people in groups or crowds (Lofland 1992; Miller 2000). Collective behavior has traditionally been associated with riots, protests, and revolutions. But the field can also include the study of popular trends and fads. Theories of collective behavior can vary considerably, with some, such as mass hysteria theory, emphasizing its emotional aspects, whereas others, such as emergent norm theory, focusing instead on the rational nature of human behavior in larger groups (Miller 2000). We will focus on collective behavior in Chapter 11.

As you can see from this discussion, the broad heading of "group processes" includes a variety of work. Because the emphasis here is on sociological social psychology, we will focus on the aspect of group processes that is of greatest interest to sociological social psychologists: the processes that occur in groups rather than the features of the groups themselves. In the chapters that follow, our discussions of group processes will generally (but not exclusively) look at social processes such as status, power, justice, and legitimacy.

Section Summary

This section of the chapter answered the questions "What is the group processes perspective?" "What are some basic social processes that play out in group contexts?" and "What are the elements of group structure?" Group process researchers emphasize the roles of status and power in groups. They also study how notions of justice and legitimacy play out in group contexts. Group structures vary by size as well as complexities associated with size. They can also include group types such as primary, secondary, and reference groups. Group size and type can have large impacts on the interaction of members within a group.

A Take-Away Message

Groups represent the reality of society in our everyday life. They are the primary means by which we experience joy and sometimes pain with our friends and family (primary groups), and they can also convey the larger inequalities in society (e.g., such as in secondary groups among coworkers in the workplace). In this sense, group processes gives us a microcosm of society, showing how larger social processes become reproduced in groups. Professionally, understanding group processes will help you in your day-to-day interactions with different people. For example, an understanding of status processes in groups can help you understand why employers treat you the ways they do and why you might treat your employees the ways you do. Knowing this information may help you better use agency in the workplace.

BRINGING IT ALL TOGETHER

Why do we need three perspectives? It's too complicated.

—Carlos, junior sociology major

Scholars from the three perspectives that we have reviewed in this chapter share an underlying interest in understanding how individuals are influenced by their social context. Although we have presented these perspectives as separate, even competing, approaches within the area of social psychology, there is often overlap among them. For example, a researcher conducting a study of gender and work identities might be guided by important principles of both symbolic interactionism and social structure and personality. Similarly, work in the group processes tradition focuses on diverse topics—for example, how stereotyping affects scores on standard ability tests such as the SAT (Lovaglia et al. 1998) and how gender identities influence interactions between women and men in marriages (Stets and Burke 1996). These are both substantive topics that can also be easily understood through an interactionist lens. Although researchers tend to have a certain "bent," many are flexible enough to approach a research question with the most appropriate conceptual and methodological perspective in the field. This flexibility often makes for creative and boundary-pushing projects on the cutting edge of sociological social psychology.

Some students, such as Carlos in the vignette at the beginning of this section, are skeptical about the need for more than one perspective. But, there are many facets to human behavior. It would be difficult to find any one perspective appropriate for studying all elements of human life. With multiple perspectives, we are better equipped to study the way social forces influence a large array of people's thoughts, feelings, and behaviors.

SUMMARY

1. There are three broad perspectives in sociological social psychology: symbolic interactionism, social structure and personality, and group processes.
2. Symbolic interactionism is the study of how people negotiate meaning during their interactions with others. Within this approach, two schools of symbolic interactionism exist: the Chicago school and the Iowa/Indiana schools.
3. The social structure and personality perspective emphasizes how social structure affects individuals within a society. Structural forces include status, roles, and social networks. The perspective identifies various societal components and illuminates the ways that people internalize these aspects of society.
4. The group processes perspective focuses on interactions that occur within groups, characteristics of groups, and relationships among groups. Processes studied by those in the group processes perspective include power, status, justice, and legitimacy.

5. A group's behavior is influenced by structural conditions, including its size and its function. Group research may focus on structure or on other aspects of group processes, such as the relationship between groups and the behavior of larger groups of people, called collective behavior.

KEY TERMS AND CONCEPTS

Agency: The ability to act and think independently from the constraints imposed by social conditions.

Chicago school of symbolic interactionism: A perspective within symbolic interactionism that focuses on understanding the social processes involved in a given situation rather than trying to quantify and predict people's thoughts, feelings, and behavior.

Cognitive sociology: The study of the effects of society on our thinking processes.

Collective behavior: The action or behavior of people in groups or crowds.

Components principle: Within the social structure and personality perspective, the ability to identify the elements or components of society most likely to affect a given attitude or behavior.

Dyad: A two-person group.

Framing: The process by which individuals transform the meaning of a situation using basic cognitive structures provided by society.

Group: Interactions that involve more than one person.

Iowa/Indiana school of symbolic interactionism: A perspective within symbolic interactionism that focuses on the quantitative study of social interaction processes, measurable because of the stable nature of social life and the self.

Justice: Perceptions that a social arrangement or distribution is fair.

Language: A series of symbols that can be combined in various ways to create new meanings.

Legitimacy: The perception that a social arrangement or position is the way that it *should* be.

Power: The ability to obtain what we desire in a group despite resistance.

Primary groups: People we are close to and interact with regularly.

Proximity principle: Element of the social structure and personality perspective referring to how people are affected by social structure through their immediate social environments.

Psychology principle: Element of the social structure and personality perspective referring to how individuals internalize proximal experiences.

Reference groups: People we look to as a source of standards and identity.

Secondary groups: People we affiliate with to achieve common goals or meet common needs.

Small groups: Two or more persons (generally, not more than 20) engaged in or capable of face-to-face interaction.

Social construction of reality: The process by which we use symbols and language to give meaning and value to objects and people.

Social forces: Any way in which society compels individuals to act in accordance with an external norm, rule, or demand.

Social networks: A series of connected relationships among individuals and groups.

Social scripts: The appropriate thoughts, feelings, and behaviors that should be displayed in a particular social frame.

Society: In symbolic interactionism, the network of interaction between people.

Status: A position in a group based on esteem or respect.

Symbols: Anything that has a similar meaning for two or more individuals.

Thomas theorem: Theorem stating that when people define situations as real, the consequences of those situations become real.

Triad: A three-person group.

DISCUSSION QUESTIONS

1. Which of the three perspectives do you find most compelling? Why? How does it contribute to your understanding of the social world?
2. Does social psychology need three perspectives? Which ones are the most and least useful, from your point of view?
3. Describe one part of your life that is clearly affected by society. Apply principles or concepts from one or more of the three perspectives to show the effects of social forces in your life. Be specific about the aspect of "society" that is relevant.
4. Think about an important social problem in the world today. How might you apply one of the perspectives used in the chapter to help explain why that problem exists? How might you use it to help find a way to resolve that problem?

3

Studying People

I always hated thinking about research methods. Anything to do with collecting or analyzing data just wasn't my thing. I got involved in sociology because I was fascinated by research findings. I never thought too much about the methods. But then I had to conduct a type of online document analysis as part of a class, examining the public websites of professors across a few campuses. The goal of the project is to see if there are any associations between the types of materials that professors post and the departments that they come from. I guess it was not too surprising: business professors tend to have more formal and professional websites than their colleagues in the liberal arts, but they also talked about their families more. I also noticed that the liberal arts professors were more focused on social causes. Both groups included sarcastic humor in their posts though. To be honest, I ended up liking the project that I did!

—Shelly, senior sociology major

Shelly's lack of excitement about research methods is not unusual. A lecture on methods can seem dry because it entails learning a set of tools rather than exploring a substantive area of research. Many students are interested in understanding a pressing issue—for example, inequality in society—rather than thinking about the best methods to use for studying it. But, when Shelly is required to conduct a research project herself, she soon changes her mind about research methods. She begins to see the value of collecting data herself, and she experiences the excitement of examining empirical results from her analysis.

Learning to use research methods effectively is vital to employing social science as a way of understanding our world. Approaching social science with a critical lens will make you a more informed analyst of information and ideas you read about or hear people discuss. In short, understanding methods can give you a good sense of how to carry out your own research as well as the ability to judge the quality of other people's research and their conclusions about how the world works. The more you know about methods, the more empowered you become as a social scientist!

Understanding the effects of social conditions on individuals and groups is challenging. How can you study effects of culture on individual behaviors if the people you are studying are unaware of its influence? Because of complexities like this, the research methods commonly used by sociologists differ from those typically employed in the natural sciences. Imagine, for example, trying to show that capitalist economies lead people to be more competitive than do other economic systems. You might demonstrate that competitive attitudes are more widespread in nations with capitalist economies than those with socialist economies, but does that show that capitalism is the cause of competitiveness? Having a strong grasp of research methods will help you figure out ways to investigate whether a correlation and/or a causal connection exists.

There are many ways to initiate a research project. The goal of this chapter is to provide information about the various ways of studying people as well as criteria for deciding which methods are most appropriate for your own research projects. We answer the following questions:

- What are some key terms used in social science research?
- How is qualitative research different from quantitative research?
- What are the major forms of qualitative research?
- What are the major forms of quantitative research?
- How do social scientists begin to develop research projects?

BASIC CONCEPTS AND ISSUES

> *Why does my methods professor want me to understand all of these obscure terms? It's so frustrating!*
>
> —Samuel, junior sociology major

Samuel's frustration is understandable. Learning research methods does involve learning a new vocabulary. But this vocabulary is important. Basic concepts help researchers evaluate their projects and ensure that the research they are undertaking will be valuable to—and accepted by—other researchers. In this section, we will first review some important ideas and then discuss the major ways in which social psychologists approach the study of people. Some of these concepts are more applicable to quantitative research, but they can also serve as a way of conceptualizing qualitative research projects, a topic we will discuss later in this chapter.

Theories and Hypotheses

Most research projects in social psychology start with an idea about how some aspect of social life works. Suppose you decide that a friend is being particularly nice to a stranger because she finds the person attractive. That experience may lead you to wonder if people, in general, act more friendly toward attractive people than toward those they see as less attractive. This sort of thinking process can be the starting point for a social theory. **Social theories** refer to structured explanations of how various elements of social life are related to one another. Social theories typically focus on people's relationships with one another and with their larger social worlds. A theory typically includes some of the following components:

1. A set of relevant concepts and their definitions.
2. General statements about social relationships.
3. Statements about the causes of those relationships.
4. General predictions, based on these reasons, about how people will react to certain events, experiences, or conditions.
5. Statements specifying the scope of the theory, or those situations in which the theory's predictions are expected to hold true.

Because theories are general, they cannot be tested directly. As an example, consider a theory about how economic systems influence people's competitiveness. Competitiveness exists inside people, and thus it's not possible to measure it directly. It is also not easy for people to respond accurately to a survey item that asks them how competitive they are. Researchers may try to measure competitiveness indirectly, perhaps by seeing how people in a group (in both capitalist and socialist economies) choose to divide a pay distribution between themselves and other group members. Theories are translated into testable hypotheses before being examined by one or more research methods. **Hypotheses** are specific predictions about how variables will relate to one another in a research study. They are the general predictions of a theory stated in a more specific testable form. **Variables** are theoretical concepts (e.g., competitiveness) put into a measurable form (e.g., how people reward themselves and others when dividing up payment amounts).

Translating a concept into something that can be measured is called "operationalizing the concept." Thus, hypotheses provide testable statements about theories or parts of a theory. Because hypotheses test theories only indirectly, they only provide evidence for the veracity of a theory. A theory is never "proven" but is either supported or not supported by data. Scholars analyze the relationships between variables that are used to represent theoretical concepts.

Operationalizing a concept in the social sciences can be difficult because much social science research investigates concepts that do not exist in the physical world. For example, suppose you want to study the effects of stressors on mental health. How do you measure the concept of a stressor? We must first **operationalize** the concept of a stressor—transform it into something that can be measured. You may decide to measure it in terms of the number of negative life events to which a person is exposed. Alternatively, you may operationalize stressors as role strains, perhaps asking people to tell you how much strain they are experiencing at work and in family relationships on a scale of 1 to 5.

Operationalizing theoretical concepts is especially challenging in the social sciences. Consider, for example, the study of age and intimacy. Do people's answers on a survey question about intimacy really tell us how much intimacy there is in a relationship?

Also, intimacy has many dimensions. If a researcher focuses only on sexual intimacy, for example, she might neglect other dimensions of intimacy found among partners (Gabb 2010). Also, different types of relationships have different types of intimacy. You might feel that you have an intimate relationship with a friend you rarely see but often text with. Thus, faithfully capturing a theoretical concept in a research study requires careful thought and extensive review of the theoretical dimensions of a variable. For a researcher studying intimacy, the most important step would be to define the concept of "intimacy" precisely enough so that she could determine whether her measures of intimacy in fact reflect her theoretical concept. Then she might state some hypotheses such as: older people on average report feeling closer to their friends than do younger people.

The relationship between theories and hypotheses is complex. You cannot necessarily dismiss a theory when research findings do not support a particular hypothesis. In one example, Peggy Thoits (1991, 1995) applied identity theory (Chapter 5 reviews this theory in detail) to examine the relationship between negative life events and individual well-being. Her research focused on a part of identity theory that claims that people attach meaning to certain roles in their lives, and that some of those roles and relationships have more importance or salience than others. Starting with this general premise, Thoits hypothesized that negative events would have a larger effect on psychological distress symptoms when they threatened highly salient identities compared to events affecting less salient identities. In fact, her findings generally did not support her hypotheses about the relationship between identity-salient events and distress. But this result did not lead Thoits to conclude that identity theory was wrong or, for that matter, that identity-related stressors do not lead to distress. Rather, she concluded that more details about events would be necessary to make the connection between the general theory and her specific hypotheses. In other words, she proposed that the theory may still help to understand the relationship between identity and distress, but that better measures and research techniques would be necessary to connect the two parts if, in fact, the relationship exists.

Independent and Dependent Variables

Hypotheses are more specific than theories; they are statements limited to the variables being measured in a given project. As stated earlier, variables are theoretically relevant measures that have two or more values or categories. For example, the variable age is measured in years and might have 60 or more values in a study of adults (i.e., age 18, 19, 20, 21, 22 and so on, through 80 or older). Race was long measured among Americans by the categories "African American," "Asian American," "Hispanic," and "White." But the dimensions of a variable may be more complex than a list of commonly used values. Researchers can also allow respondents to provide their own senses of a given concept. For instance, instead of listing a limited set of values for "race," you might ask people to define their race in their own words. Doing this would lead to far more than four categories of race.

Variables are generally separated into those believed to affect a phenomenon and the phenomenon itself. The variable predicted to lead to a change in another variable is the **independent variable**. The variable that is predicted to change as a result of the

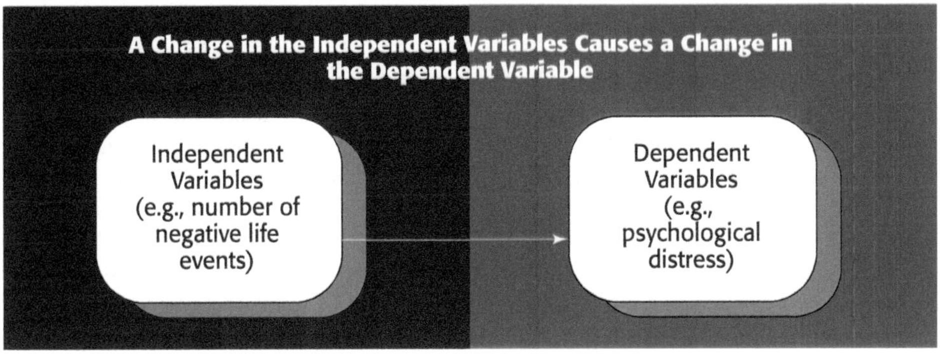

Figure 3.1 Independent and Dependent Variables.

independent variable is the **dependent variable**. In the preceding example, Thoits (1991, 1995) was investigating whether the number of negative life events (the independent variable) related to important identities, such as job loss, that a person experienced recently increased psychological distress (the dependent variable) (see Figure 3.1).

Sampling Issues

It is impossible to study the thoughts, feelings, or behaviors of all the people to whom a theory is intended to apply. If you wished to test aspects of equity theory—how housework is divided up amongst couples and how it matters for wellbeing—you would like your study to apply to all couples living together as romantic partners. But you can't examine the millions of people that fit this demographic, given the cost and time involved. As a result, researchers rely on a smaller group of people to represent a larger group. A **population** is the larger group of people about whom a researcher seeks to draw conclusions. A **sample** is a group of people selected to represent the larger population. **Probability samples** (also called "representative samples") are those in which researchers systematically choose participants in an attempt to draw a sample representative of the population. One type of probability sample, a **random sample**, is one in which participants are randomly picked from a population. The random method is the surest way to obtain a representative sample of the larger population.

Choosing a purely random sample is not possible for most research activities. Imagine that the population of interest to a researcher is all adults in the United States. In this case, obtaining a true random sample is impossible because no complete sampling frame is available. A **sampling frame** is a list of all possible elements in the population, and there is no such listing of adults in the United States. If one ever became available, it would immediately be outdated as people immigrated, emigrated, became 18 years old, or died. Thus, most sampling frames are limited to all elements of a population that are available for sampling (Kalton 1983). For instance, if you were interested in the patterns of volunteering among all members of a religious denomination, such as Catholics, you may have to limit your sampling frame to members listed on church congregations' mailing lists, hence missing everyone who had missing or outdated contact information.

The use of purely random samples is rare. Most large-scale surveys of U.S. residents such as the General Social Survey (GSS) or the National Longitudinal Study of Adolescent Health (Add Health) involve the use of cluster samples. A **cluster sample** is one in which the population is first divided into meaningful clusters, such as metropolitan areas and counties, or schools, and then a representative sample of respondents from within each cluster is surveyed. In the case of Add Health, cluster sampling is utilized for both practical and theoretical reasons. This sampling technique reduces costs, and it also allows for data collection on peer groups, which is vital to understanding many aspects of adolescent health. The 80 high schools chosen for the study represent the larger U.S. population of high schools with respect to region, urban, suburban, or rural area, size, and so on. See the Add Health website (https://addhealth.cpc.unc.edu) for more details.

Researchers face a difficult challenge when they want to study a particular group of people but do not have a basis on which to develop a representative sample. For example, a researcher interested in criminals could sample prison inmates, but the sample would exclude criminals who haven't been caught in their illegal activities. In these and other cases, when probability samples are infeasible or unnecessary, researchers may rely on other kinds of samples in which probability techniques are not used to draw participants from a population. In a **convenience sample**, any available person from the population of interest is included in the study. In a **snowball sample**, informants provide contact information about other people who share some of the characteristics necessary for a study. Early research on sexual behavior in the United States, for instance, started with snowball and other nonrandom sampling techniques to develop samples of people willing to be surveyed on such personal, intimate behaviors (Michael et al. 1995).

Probability samples are much preferred when trying to apply research findings to an entire group or population. But in cases where representation is less important, nonrandom designs may be appropriate. Exploratory and experimental research investigations (discussed later in this chapter) often have objectives that make probability samples unnecessary. Moreover, in some qualitative work undertaken to develop theory, probability sampling is rare. Here, researchers may seek a "theoretical sample;" that is, they create samples that make the most sense to their questions of interest. For a theoretical sample, a researcher who wants to assess class diversity in parents' explanations of how they plan to organize children's media usage as they grow older needs to think carefully how to do so. Rather than using a convenience sample of those immediately available, the researcher could sample mothers from different play groups, library story times, or birthing hospitals located in multiple geographic areas across a city to obtain the diversity they need for the study.

Reliability and Validity

Understanding **reliability** and **validity** will help your ability to be a successful critic of social science. Suppose you step on a scale to determine your weight. It says 150 pounds. If you repeatedly step on that scale and see 150 pounds, and if you step on 10 different scales and they each say 150 pounds, then your measurement tools (the scales) are said to be reliable—they are all reporting the same results using the same techniques. However, let's say that your true weight is 160 pounds. In this case, although the scales are reliable, they are *not* valid. That is, your true weight of 160 is not captured by the defective scales. The scales lack validity as a measurement tool because they do not accurately capture the phenomenon in question—your weight. Social scientists must always be concerned with the validity and reliability of their data.

Let's take a social science example. If you operationalize the concept of racism by having students report on their own racist behaviors, a finding that few respondents report being racist is going to be questionable. Why? The validity of your study is threatened because your measure cannot "truly" get at racism with this kind of questioning, which is wide open to social desirability effects; that is, even if people know they are racist (which people who are racist might not realize), they are unlikely to report this to researchers because they understand that it is not acceptable to many others. There are good, valid ways to measure racism, but this is not one of them. Take a minute to think about how you would measure racism. It's not easy, but many studies have done it successfully.

There are many types of validity such as face validity, construct validity, content validity, and more that you may be interested in learning about in your methods classes. Remember that more methods knowledge is powerful in being a critical consumer and producer of social science research. Also, people may think you are cool if you can discuss the many forms of validity—at least at a sociology party!

Ethical Issues in Studying People

Social psychological research plans must be scrutinized before they are conducted to ensure that they follow professional ethical guidelines for conducting research with human participants. All universities have **Institutional Review Boards (IRBs)** made up of academics from diverse fields. IRBs review research projects to make sure that the expected benefits of the research outweigh any potential harm to research participants. If ethical or moral concerns arise, the IRB may recommend changes to a research protocol or, in some cases, may deny the project altogether.

The IRB system was developed after a number of ethically questionable research projects were conducted in the early and mid-twentieth century. One infamous example was Laud Humphries' (1970) study of the "tearoom trade" involving gay sex in public places. He started his research by going to places where gay men were known to spend time, such as gay bars. After some time, he developed informants who told him where less visible gay sexual activity occurred, public restrooms in particular. The researcher played a "watchqueen"—a voyeur who served as a lookout so that the men actually engaging in the sexual activity would not be discovered. His research showed that "tearoom" behavior was quite structured, with an organized series of norms and roles. But whatever the value of Humphries' findings, many sociologists questioned the ethics of his research. Humphries did not take any steps to ensure the anonymity of his research subjects; in fact, he even followed them to their homes to find out whether they were married and where they lived. Because he exposed his subjects to potential emotional and social hardships, Humphries' research methods would almost certainly not be allowed under today's standards.

Scholars have applied research methods reviewed in this chapter to study the social processes associated with IRB review! The history of the development of IRBs shows how the political nature of the institution changed over time based on internal and external pressures. They have different names in different countries (for example–"research ethics boards" in Canada). These kinds of boards can be inconsistent in how they process reviews of research protocols (see Van den Hoonaard 2011). Laura Stark (2012) studied IRBs at three universities and participated in 34 meetings where the boards reviewed IRB applications. She found, among other things, that boards tend to focus on consensus, although there is no rule that this need be the case. Another finding is that the groups create a subculture (see idiocultures in Chapter 6) of sorts which relies on precedent, or how they have ruled on similar cases in the past. These kinds of studies show that the scientific process itself reflects many of the same social dynamics reviewed throughout this book!

Section Summary

This section of the chapter answered the question "What is the vocabulary of social science research?" Our goal is to give you an understanding of the important concepts that social psychologists bring into the study of human populations. First, we noted that theories and hypotheses are used to guide the development of research designs and specific measurements of independent and dependent variables. Second, we discussed the challenges of sampling individuals from the larger population; that is, using a smaller group of people to represent the thoughts, feelings, and behaviors of the larger group. Finally, we addressed unique ethical challenges in the study of human populations.

A Take-Away Message

Social science research informs many policy decisions. For example, governments rely on social science to determine whether to pass laws, whether people support proposed laws, or whether a law is even needed. If the research that underpins these decisions is flawed, it cannot be relied upon. We should consider the sampling and measurements used in a study before deciding whether its findings or claims are sound. Professionally, the information reviewed in this chapter provides tools that can help in many different types of jobs, especially in the social sciences. Systematically assessing journalists' and bloggers' claims about the social world that are not based in the scientific method is quite important as well, because media sometimes push "hot" ideas about the world that have little validity. Learn these tools well, and you will be equipped with a great deal of discernment in everyday life!

DIFFERENT WAYS TO STUDY PEOPLE

I had been sitting on the subway for about a half-hour while trying to begin my project for methods class. My goal was to better understand how unhoused people coped with the harsh conditions of a Boston winter. The warm train was a welcome relief from the cold outside. A woman came in with a huge steamy-hot sandwich from a local vendor. She unwrapped it and started at it even though eating on the trains is frowned upon. At first, I didn't mind, but the smell started filling up the car. As I watched, I also noticed what she was wearing under her coat and the things she was carrying. Then it hit me: this woman is unhoused. I stayed on the subway another hour, trying to figure out how other people reacted to her and to a few other unhoused people through the riders' facial expressions, eye contact, and giving of space. With a little patience and more observations, it became a really interesting research project!

—Peter, junior sociology major

There are many ways to study people. Some approaches are formal and precise; others, such as Peter's observations of unhoused people and the reactions they engendered in public places, are more fluid in nature. Peter started out with a general goal of studying how unhoused people managed to live during the winter. Over time, however, he refined his research goals, focusing on reactions to people who used the subway for shelter.

In contrast to Peter's rather informal method, most survey research projects begin with precise specifications of hypotheses, independent variables, and dependent variables before data collection begins. And many research projects fall somewhere between these two extremes. For example, researchers may decide on the variables they are interested in measuring before they begin a project. Once the project is underway, however, the data they find may take them in new directions and lead them to choose to collect new sorts of information.

The method you choose to study a particular phenomenon depends on several factors:

1. The orientation of the researchers will likely influence the methods they use. For instance, many symbolic interactionists are more likely to employ qualitative rather than quantitative research, emphasizing meaning-making and interaction rather than large-scale surveys or experiments (Schwalbe 2020).
2. The population of interest may inhibit the use of certain methods. Consider the challenges of using surveys or experiments for the following studies:

- A two-year study of a "gayborhood" to understand the challenges of the pressures of young LGBTQ+ individuals to assimilate to new norms of identity in the modern world (Orne 2017).
- A study of the role of trust and reputation in the trading processes among foreign traders in Guangzhou, China (Mathews, Lin, and Yang 2017).
- An analysis of the music album covers as a way of discovering the values and beliefs of middle-class American people (Borgerson and Schroeder 2017).
- A study of identity change among former White supremacists (Simi et al. 2017).

While it may be possible to study these topics with a survey or experiment, it would be challenging and may not provide the kinds of insights that other methods provide.

3. Most importantly, your research question and/or the hypotheses you are testing should point you to the most appropriate method. Some research questions may lend themselves to certain methods more than others. A survey of individuals, for instance, may not be appropriate for research questions related to historical changes in society. Some research is conducted on research methods themselves. Dieko Bakker and Jacob Dijkstra (2021), for instance, conducted a study specifically to assess multiple ways of measuring social value orientations. The whole point of their project was built around studying a certain type of method rather than some substantive topic.

Methods of research fall under two general headings: qualitative and quantitative (see Table 3.1). Although there is overlap in the types of research conducted under these headings (for example, surveys, which we list as quantitative, often collect qualitative data as well), we believe that they serve as a good heuristic device for understanding the larger field of social inquiry. As such, we review some of the most popular methods in sociological social psychology under these headings, followed by a discussion of how theory and methods combine to form research projects.

Qualitative Methods

Have you ever noticed a pattern in social life and discussed it with your friends? Perhaps you noticed differences in the ways that men and women view different topics or in how middle-class versus working-class kids interact with their parents. How do you know if your observations are accurate? You can begin your query by simply collecting more observations. If you continue to see the same patterns again and again, you may just have discovered something. In a simple sense, you have also been engaging in working with qualitative data! **Qualitative research methods** focus on in-depth, semi-structured modes of observation or interviewing of respondents. Qualitative researchers do not quantify people's thoughts, feelings, or behaviors. Rather, they allow participants to describe their experiences in their own words or to behave naturally within a research setting.

The major advantage of using a qualitative approach is that it usually does not seek to constrain either people's actions or the conditions to which they respond. It may also give you insights into the layers of meaning that go into everyday interactions. Consider a boss asking an employee what she thinks about a new program. In that instance, the

Table 3.1 Popular Methods of Conducting Social Science Research

Qualitative Methods	Quantitative Methods
Field research (i.e., ethnography and participant observation)	Survey research
In-depth interviews	Secondary data analysis
Focus groups	Experiments
Content analysis*	Content analysis*

*This method especially often includes both qualitative and quantitative components.

Box 3.1 Going into the Field: Online

The phrase "going into the field" comes from the idea that social scientists leave their offices and study the social world in real life. Sociologists may conduct studies like participant observations of drug dealers (Adler and Adler 1982) or preadolescent children's culture (Adler and Adler 1998). These types of studies may be possible in the virtual reality of the internet. Platforms like Instagram and TikTok almost instantly offer large amounts of data from people and interactions around the world (Kosinski et al., 2016). It would be possible to observe children's online media presence, for example, through observing ways they interact online.

You can also observe and even join online communities. What would you observe in this environment? Obviously, it would not include physical interactions, but research is starting to show the intersections of online and face-to-face interactions (see, for example, Tian 2017). The online side of things will certainly include text exchanges between members and may also include live video interactions via video services such as Zoom. While online ethnographies open the door to conducting research in the convenience of an office space, it also introduces the same issues found in any study. You still need to consider the privacy of your participants and obtain permission to conduct your research (you can't do it without Institutional Review Board approval), and for children, permissions would be needed from parents. In some situations, like studying a parents' group, new ethical dilemmas could be created as you decide whether and how to reveal your identity as a researcher (versus a parent) to the group you are studying.

employee may focus on the positive aspects of the program. However, she may have some negative thoughts about the program that are not revealed out of fear of offending her superior, who can affect her pay and working conditions. A good qualitative study can bring out the full range of meanings in a given social context.

A disadvantage of qualitative research is that it is difficult to extend research findings to other groups given the nonrepresentativeness of samples. Also, qualitative research typically involves collecting detailed information in a particular setting, but the more detailed information we gain in one setting, the less likely it is that we will be able to apply that information to new settings. Moreover, sampling in qualitative research is typically not representative. For these reasons, it is more difficult to generalize specific patterns identified to the population that the sample represents. Still, the processes or perspectives that are gleaned may be applicable across groups or settings, especially through theory development that results from the research projects. Thus, we tend to apply qualitative methods when our goal is to access depth of understanding in a given social context and to build theoretical explanations rather than to directly explain social behavior more broadly.

Two popular forms of qualitative research are field research or observation and in-depth interviewing.

Field Research

Field research is the direct observation of people's behavior at a particular site (Cahill, Fine, and Grant 1995) (see Box 3.1). A common type of field research is **ethnography**, a descriptive analysis of a group or organization. A researcher may enter a group (such as Alcoholics Anonymous), organization (such as a middle school), or setting (such as a city's subway system) and observe how people behave, paying particular attention to patterns of behavior related to a particular theory, perspective, or set of research questions.

Ethnographies can often be a forum for developing theories about social interaction. Researchers may enter an ethnographic study with one set of theoretical expectations but find that their observations require them to rethink those expectations or to develop new ones (see Puddephatt, Shaffir, and Kleinknecht 2009). This process can allow researchers to also create new ideas and theories about human behaviors or grounded theory. Barry Gibson and Jan Hartman (2013) define **grounded theory** simply as "the generation of theory from data" (p. 1). Classic grounded theory deemphasizes the importance of developing an extensive literature review prior to the start of data collection, allowing the data from the project to help the researcher create theoretical ideas about their observations (Konecki 2018). Data, in the case of ethnographies, typically includes patterns of thoughts or behaviors in a group or society. For instance, Gary Alan Fine (2007) studied the culture of weather forecasting, focusing largely on the Chicago office of the National Weather Service (NWS). He found, among other things, that while the members of this group valued science as an ideal, they also relied on their own discretion when deciding how to predict weather patterns. Also, Fine found that there were different cultures of risk taking associated with different NWS offices—differences that affected how they presented meteorological findings to the public.

Ethnographic research of the type that Fine carried out often requires finding an **informant**, someone who can help the researcher gain access to a group and discover general patterns. In a classic study, William Foote Whyte (1993, originally 1943) tried to access an Italian community in Boston to study gangs. He was confronted with resistance until he met the informal leader, "Doc," who led him into his group of friends. This informant provided the history of the group and its members, but more importantly, the informant led others to accept the researcher into their group.

In some cases, the researcher may actually become part of a group, an approach known as **participant observation**. Participant observers, such as a sociologist who is an Alcoholics Anonymous member and is studying the group, have the advantage of being insiders, so that they can get information from group members as actual participants in the group's activities. But group membership also has its disadvantages (Cahill et al. 1995):

1. Participant observers may develop a bias: they may change their perspectives on the group's behavior because of their affiliation with that group.
2. Participant observers may not know how their participation influences the behaviors of group members.
3. Participant observation projects and field research in general can take a long time to complete.

As an example of the time it takes to conduct this kind of research, Anne Roschelle and Peter Kaufman (2004) spent four years on an ethnographic study of unhoused children in San Francisco. One of the authors became a volunteer at several observation sites, where she had the opportunity to take extensive notes based on her observations of social-service agency meetings, residential motels, transitional housing facilities, and homeless shelters. The researchers also made extensive use of qualitative surveys with open-ended responses. Their goal was to understand how these children found ways to "fit in" various environments and the techniques they developed for protecting their self-concepts.

Ethical issues can arise with field research as well. Jay MacLeod (1993) began his study of the aspirations of poor teenage African American "Brothers" and White "Hallway Hangers" when he was basketball director of a youth program, studying impoverished youths' aspirations for the future. He befriended many teens, playing basketball with them frequently. The study had been going on for a few months before MacLeod asked the boys formally for permission to use them as research subjects. MacLeod's position as a researcher was complex. He talks about times when the "Hallway Hangers" drank and used drugs as difficult ethically given his position as an "unbiased" researcher watching youth engage in illegal activities.

Photo 3.1 Field research allows researchers to study people in their natural environments. How would you go about studying social interactions among pre-teens?

Source: BearFotos/Shutterstock

In-Depth Interviews

There is one simple way to find out what people think about the world around them: ask them! This can be done with a formal questionnaire that solicits prescribed answers to questions, such as how much people agree with statements about the difficulty of their work conditions. But this approach can also overly simplify people's responses, constraining them to the options available on the questionnaire. Thus, many researchers rely on **in-depth interviews**, (sometimes called qualitative interviews) using an unstructured or semi-structured series of questions and probing respondents for more details as appropriate to the goals of the research (Babbie 2002; Olson 2016). In-depth interviews give researchers more flexibility than traditional questionnaires because they do not limit the types of responses available to respondents, and they may also make respondents more comfortable by allowing them to respond in their own words. Another advantage of qualitative interviews is that they allow researchers to probe further in areas that need elaboration. For instance, you might begin by asking a respondent what it is like to grow up in a certain region of the country. As the interview progresses, however, you realize that the individual grew up near a military training camp. As a result, you may decide to ask more specific questions about that camp and its effects on her upbringing. In this way, in-depth interviews allow researchers some flexibility in their research questions.

Qualitative interviews can be used as a part of observational research or as a method of study in and of themselves. Howard Becker (1953), for example, interviewed 50 cannabis users about their personal experiences with the drug and their attitudes toward it. His interviews gave him insights into the social aspects of the drug experience. He found that many people do not get high the first time they use cannabis. In many cases, more senior users must teach new users the proper technique to induce a high. Thus, the drug's effects on an individual are influenced by the social conditions surrounding that experience. You can imagine that it would have been very difficult to study this kind of topic with a survey!

You must always be careful in utilizing interview data because your informants or subjects may not be telling you the truth, or they may not be fully aware of their circumstances. Take, for example, research on bullying. Both children who are bullied and those who bully them might not be able to articulate or even fully understand the processes in which they are involved. Also, both sets of children might be motivated for various reasons to be less than forthcoming with the interviewer. Thus, interviewers should always consider how answers to their questions might reflect biases or deception, and they should consider ways to ensure that data represent a full range of experiences.

Other Qualitative Methods

There are many ways of using qualitative methods to study people. These methods include examining newspapers and diaries, analyzing life histories or biographies of subjects, consulting public records, or conducting group interviews (e.g., focus groups). **Content analysis** includes any systematic review of written documents or other media. Although this method often includes categorizing and quantifying texts, it still fits under the qualitative rubric because some level of interpretation is required (Cahill et al. 1995). Traditionally, researchers will examine a document (e.g., newspaper articles or diaries), trying to assess patterns of thought or speech. Content analysis can also be used to find patterns in social media, television shows, movies, or books. For example, trends in stereotypes of LGBTQ+ communities might be studied through an examination of how they are portrayed in television shows over recent decades. The analysis, because it involves counts and interpretations of texts, is often called "textual analysis."

Focus groups include semi-structured interviews with small groups, usually between 6 and 15 people (Babbie 2002; Neuman 2004). Focus groups allow researchers the flexibility of qualitative interviewing while getting multiple perspectives at the same time. Focus groups are often recorded, allowing researchers to take notes about general response patterns during the session and then transcribing detailed responses after the session has ended. Researchers may conduct multiple focus groups not only to provide additional data but also to separate groups by some relevant category. A study of student athletes' views about drug testing, for instance, may vary depending on whether researchers are interviewing athletes involved in football, track and field, volleyball, or swimming. Separating these athletes into their respective groups will give diverse perspectives and may help participants feel more comfortable sharing their opinions in the focus group session.

Photo 3.2 Focus groups provide a way of assessing people's attitudes and beliefs in a small-group context. Why do you think focus groups may help bring out people's opinions on matters?

Source: BearFotos/Shutterstock

Another sociological approach to the study of microsociology is narrative analysis. **Narrative analysis** is any method that examines social life in the form of personal stories (Berger and Quinney 2004; Maynes, Pierce, and Lastlett 2008). Much like in-depth interviews, narrative analysis allows research participants to share their perspectives in their own words. However, narrative analysis focuses on the ways in which subjects put their thoughts and feelings about a particular issue or event in their life history—which includes what is going on in society. In this way, we piece together the drama of our lives utilizing our cultural norms and values to create a plot replete with heroes and victims, enemies and allies. We, in turn, can use these narratives to persuade other people of larger social problems that need to be addressed on the community or societal level (Loseke 2019). Just as with in-depth interviews, however, we must be careful in attending to information provided in narratives because people aren't always perfectly positioned to understand their own experiences and people also might have motivations (either conscious or not) to be less than truthful when relaying their experiences. You can also study narratives without talking to people. Mallary Allen (2015), for instance, studied abortion narratives from two different websites, one pro-choice and one pro-life. Each set of women created stories with unique sets of circumstances that led them to their current opinions about abortion.

In a sense, qualitative researchers are social investigators, seeking out information about a topic or a social phenomenon and developing leads for further investigation. While typically conducted in real-life settings, qualitative methods have also been used in laboratories. A historical example comes from the *Center for Research on Interpersonal Behavior* (or "CRIB") representing the Iowa School of Symbolic Interaction at the University of Iowa reviewed in Chapter 2. The lab is associated with Carl Couch (1925–1994) and included video and audio recordings of social interaction which was relatively new technology for conducting research in the 1970s when the lab was most active (see Katovich 2017). Interviews can be done over the phone or on Zoom, and even email exchanges can be used as a form of data. Qualitative research can take on any number of forms but tends to focus on capturing patterns or thoughts and behaviors and the complexities of conditions that produced those patterns.

Box 3.2 Autoethnography

Some qualitative researchers have used autoethnographies to study social life. Though they can take many forms, autoethnographies generally extend participant observation studies by focusing on the narratives generated during an interaction between the researcher and the person or persons being studied, along with the inclusion of the researcher's personal perspectives on the exchange process (Anderson 2008; Ellis 1999). An autoethnography may include the analysis of dialogues between friends, family, and co-workers. The goal is to use these exchanges to help elaborate larger social processes. The "auto" part of autoethnography refers to autobiography because the researcher becomes a "co-participant" in the research process, an equal partner in the study.

(continued)

An advantage of this method is that it allows for great creativity in social science research. Researchers in this arena have utilized fictional accounts or blended traditional concepts in ethnography and autoethnography with fiction to study human behavior (see Ellis 2004; Sumerau 2017). One researcher used poetry and prose as part of a study (Tillmann 2008). There are any number of ways to expand this type of methodology. If you would like to develop an autoethnography, read a few examples of projects that employ this method in journals such as *Symbolic Interaction* or the *Journal of Contemporary Ethnography*. Like all social science studies, these require approval from an IRB/REB.

Quantitative Methods

While qualitative methods can give us the depth we need to know what people really think about an issue, directly generalizing qualitative results can be challenging; it tends to be difficult, for example, to draw conclusions from a small local sample of men studied for how they perceive their involvement with children, to U.S. fathers in general. Additionally, if we find a particular relationship in a qualitative study, we cannot be certain if that relationship is causal in nature, particularly if the data are collected at only one time point. For instance, if you find that boys gravitate to the "boys" toys at a store, it would be impossible to determine what causal mechanism led them to these toys, whether it be parental gender socialization, peer ostracism from anything feminine, the boys' dispositions, or gendered advertising.

Quantitative research methods include any attempt to quantify—that is, to measure—people's thoughts, feelings, or behaviors using numbers. Some forms of quantitative methods, especially survey methods using representative samples, allow researchers to assess whether the findings are representative of a population as a whole. Longitudinal quantitative data as well as experimental studies, often allow researchers to have more confidence that change in one variable are the causes of changes in another. The goal of this section is to outline the most important things you need to know to conduct quantitative research.

Because people's thoughts, feelings, and behaviors are assigned numbers, quantitative methods allow researchers to apply statistical analyses to their variables, so that they can test predictions through assessing the statistical significance of their findings. **Statistical significance** testing means examining the probability that the results found in a sample reflect true relationships within the population of interest. Suppose, for example, we find that female and male employees report different levels of work stress in a probability sample of 4,000 Americans. Statistical analyses allow us to test the likelihood that the gender difference we found in the sample likely reflects real gender differences in the larger U.S. population of millions of workers.

Although quantitative techniques allow researchers to perform statistical analyses on data from people, they can be criticized as being sterile and unrealistic. In some cases, survey questionnaires cannot capture important aspects of a topic such as the qualities of "friendship." Yet significance levels can be calculated, indicating the likelihood that the findings, perhaps that quality of friendships is linked to the characteristics of one's neighborhood, exist in the population of interest as opposed to being simply due to unique factors in the sample selection. Quantitative studies are not designed to capture all the complexities of social behavior. But they are valuable for measuring concepts precisely. When they are well designed, quantitative studies can provide rich sources of information about social behavior. Two primary forms of quantitative inquiry in social psychology are surveys and experiments.

Survey Research

The most commonly used quantitative research method in sociology is survey research. **Survey research** refers to the use of questionnaires to measure independent and dependent variables; the term **secondary data analysis** refers to the analysis of previously collected survey data. Social psychologists use different types of questions to assess individuals' thoughts, feelings, and behaviors. It is important to understand different types of survey questions because researchers often put items together to create a single construct. You would rarely use one or two questions to measure complex concepts such as self-esteem or depression. We will review types of survey questions to show you how to construct those complex measures.

Categorical (or nominal) variables include questions for which the possible responses have no particular order. Many demographic characteristics are categorical in nature. For instance, the question "What type of home do you live in?" may include

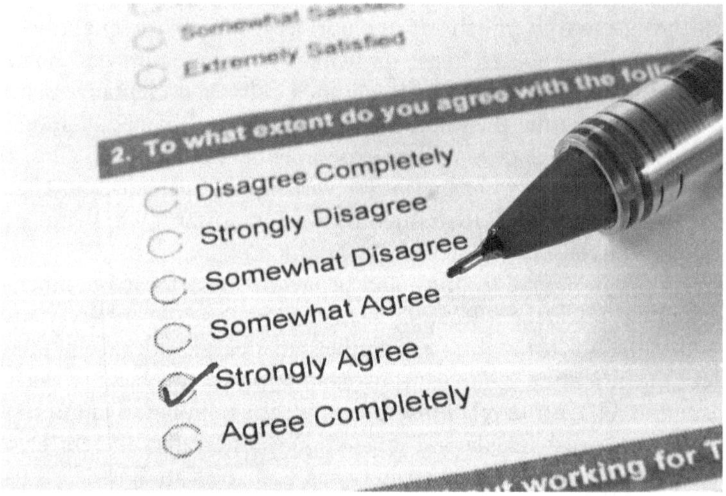

Photo 3.3 Surveys are the primary way to obtain data that are representative of the beliefs and practices of a population. How often do you get surveys via email, telephone, or mail? Do you participate? Why or why not?

Source: zimmytws/Shutterstock

responses of 1 (*mobile home*), 2 (*apartment*), and 3 (*single-family home*), but it makes no difference whether *mobile home* or *single-family home* is listed first. Compare this type of question to a scale question with a response range from 1 (*very satisfied*) to 5 (*very dissatisfied*). In this case, the order of the outcome responses is important. These types of questions, in which the ordering of responses matters, are called **ordinal variables**.

Much of the survey research employed by social psychologists relies on ordinal variables, those for which response categories are ordered but the distances between adjacent categories are not necessarily equal. Extending our earlier example, you could measure life satisfaction by asking people the degree to which they are satisfied with their lives in general on a response scale ranging from 1 (*very dissatisfied*) to 5 (*very satisfied*), with higher scores meaning greater life satisfaction. But note that the distance between *neutral* and *satisfied* may not be the same as the distance between *satisfied* and *very satisfied*, even though these are both one point from each other.

Interval variables are those for which the distance between any two adjacent points is the same. **Ratio variables** are interval variables that have zero as a starting point. Age, measured in years, is a ratio variable because the difference between 12 and 13 years is exactly the same as the difference between 13 and 14 years, and there is a zero starting point.

Many measures in social psychology are **indices** (also known as scales) which include a series of related questions designed to develop one or more dimensions of a given concept. For instance, an index measuring life satisfaction may include respondents' satisfaction with work, family, and neighborhood, among other things. Simply asking respondents to indicate satisfaction with "life as a whole" limits the usefulness of the measure because our satisfaction with life as a whole at any given time is determined by our satisfaction with many different elements of our lives. For example, a person's family satisfaction might be high at a point in time when work satisfaction is low. By measuring individual items, indices can provide more complex measures of social-psychological concepts.

Scales and indices are often used to assess complex social-psychological phenomena. They typically include multiple items that are scored in such a way that they are treated as a single measure. The measure in Table 3.2, which provides an example of a scale, is based on the work of Leonard Pearlin and others. "Mastery," which refers to our perceptions of our ability to control our environments (see Chapter 5), has been assessed with seven items (Pearlin and Schooler 1978). The researcher would ask the respondents, "How strongly do you agree or disagree with the following statements?" They then include seven different statements. Someone can simply add individuals' scores on items in the scale to come up with an overall sense of mastery. In this case, the lowest possible score someone can have is 7 and the highest possible score is 28. Hence, scales and indices produce a higher range of variation than what is found in single items.

Indices and scales play important roles in social psychology. In addition to giving us insight into complex social-psychological phenomena, indices allow us to employ advanced analytical techniques, including correlation and regression analyses—two

Table 3.2 Example of a Mastery Scale (Circle the Response That Best Reflects Your Opinion)

	Strongly Agree	Somewhat Agree	Somewhat Disagree	Strongly Disagree
a. I have little control over the things that happen to me.	1	2	3	4
b. There is really no way I can solve some of the problems that I have.	1	2	3	4
c. There is little I can do to change many of the important things in my life.	1	2	3	4
d. I often feel helpless in dealing with the problems of life.	1	2	3	4
e. Sometimes I feel that I'm being "pushed around" in life.	1	2	3	4
f. What happens to me in the future mostly depends on me.	1	2	3	4
g. I can do just about anything I really set my mind to do.	1	2	3	4

Items such as the last two would then be reverse coded so that higher scores represent a higher sense of mastery. Researchers would sum these scores and, in some cases, divide by the total number of items so that the average response ranges between 1 and 4, like the original metric from *strongly agree to strongly disagree*.

techniques that allow researchers to see if a change in one variable is associated with a change in another variable. For instance, we might want to know whether respondents' age correlates with life satisfaction; that is, when age increases, do we see an increase or decrease in life satisfaction? Categorical variables, in contrast, only allow researchers to compare responses by category. Hence, using family life satisfaction (an ordinal variable) and housing type (a categorical variable), we could compare family life satisfaction scores by type of housing unit, assessing for example if satisfaction scores are higher for people in single-family homes than for those living in mobile homes.

Although surveys are powerful tools for studying large groups of people, they also produce many challenges. Trying to study psychosocial characteristics, such as mastery or self-esteem, for instance, assumes that those concepts can be assessed in terminology that all respondents can interpret the same way. If they cannot be reliably understood, then you cannot make many claims about them—if one group interprets your questions differently from how another group interprets them, you cannot reasonably compare their answers. One of the authors of this book, for instance, was involved in a large-scale survey of Russian army officers, examining their well-being during a turbulent time for the Russian people. In order to conduct the survey, it was first translated into Russian and then back-translated into English to confirm that the original meanings translated well between cultures. The Rosenberg Self-Esteem scale (see Chapter 5) was one of the measures included in the questionnaire. It asks people to respond to a series of statements, such as "I feel that I'm a person of worth, at least on an equal plane with others" and "I feel that I have a number of good qualities." This 10-item measure is well established in the field, but imagine the challenge of trying to convey the meanings behind each of the statements presented here to people who share a totally different language and culture. What does it mean to be "a person of worth" or to have "good qualities"? These items did not correlate as well with each other in the Russian sample, at least not as well as traditionally found in Western samples. Perhaps people did not interpret them in the same manner, or the concepts simply did not have a clear meaning in Russian culture. Sociologists must consider these types of problems when they employ surveys using diverse groups of people as respondents.

There are methods employed by researchers to help increase the likelihood that measures are valid and reliable. For instance, shorter, more factual questions tend to be more reliable than longer and opinion-based questions (Alwin 2007). Longer questions require more interpretation from the respondent, which could lead to misunderstanding. Factual questions tend to be less subjective and easier to remember than other types of questions. The conditions under which questions are asked may also influence the validity of questions. For instance, the race of the interviewer may affect how respondents react to questions (Schuman 2008).

Experiments

Survey research is ideal for using data from a sample to draw conclusions about a population. If a sample is representative of a population, we can use statistical analyses to determine the likelihood that findings on a survey from a sample would be likely to hold for a larger population. A drawback of surveys, however, is that while they can tell us if variables are related to each other, they cannot answer questions of causality between variables easily. For example, a survey can find that married people express higher life satisfaction than the unmarried. We would be unable to conclude from that finding, however, if marriage *causes* people to be more satisfied—maybe more satisfied people are more likely to get married, or maybe people with low life satisfaction are especially likely to have become divorced. An **experiment** is a type of research procedure in which investigators control participants' exposures to an independent variable. They do so by randomly assigning participants to different levels of the variable. Unlike qualitative research, which can explore social phenomena, or survey research, which seeks to examine relationships among variables in a population, experiments are generally carried out to test theoretical propositions. Experiments allow us to assess whether one variable causes a change in another variable.

Most social psychology experiments are **laboratory experiments**, or controlled environments in which different participants are randomly assigned to different levels of an independent variable before a dependent variable is measured. Elements of some theories, however, cannot be studied in a laboratory. In these cases, researchers might conduct **natural or field experiments** that take place in people's everyday environments (Meeker and Leik 1995; see also Rivera and Tilcsik 2019). Modern experimentation also sometimes incorporates computer simulations as part of the process. Computers can be used in experiments to simulate interactions among people (e.g., a participant exchanging messages with someone she thinks is a real person, but the messages are in fact generated by a computer program). **Online experiments** utilize the same logic as traditional experiments but are conducted through the internet (Prissé and Jorrat 2022).

The major advantage of experimental designs is their ability to determine causal relationships between independent and dependent variables. Many types of experiments include an **experimental group**, which is exposed to an independent variable before the dependent variable is measured, and a **control group**, which is not exposed to the independent variable. By comparing measures on the dependent variable between experimental and control groups, so long as participants were randomly assigned to the two groups, researchers can determine whether exposure to the independent variable in the experimental group caused changes in the dependent variable.

As a simple example of a study using experimental and control groups, suppose that a researcher is testing a theory that proposes that people perform better after receiving positive feedback. To test this theory, the researcher proceeds as follows:

1. All participants in the experiment are asked to complete some task.
2. The researcher gives positive feedback to participants in the experimental group but gives neutral feedback to those in the control group.
3. Next, the participants are asked to complete another task. If the experimental group performs better than the control group on the second task, the researcher would conclude that the independent variable (positive feedback) produced the difference in the dependent variable (performance on the second task).

How can we know that it was the positive feedback that led to the improved performance? Perhaps the participants in the experimental group were simply more experienced or better suited to the second task than were participants in the control group. Researchers have two ways of dealing with this issue. First, social psychologists who carry out experiments sometimes use pretest–posttest designs. A **pretest** measures the dependent variable before participants are exposed to the independent variable. A **posttest** measures the dependent variable after exposure to the independent variable. Table 3.3 shows results from a study using a pretest–posttest design to measure changes

Table 3.3 Example of Pre- and Post-test Interpretation in an Experiment*

Control group	Score #1: 26	Score #2: 32	6 points
Experimental group	Score #1: 28	Score #2: 40	12 points

*A classic experiment includes four dimensions: a pretest, posttest, control group, and experimental group. This method helps ensure that any changes in the dependent variable can be attributed to an independent variable. In this case, if we wanted to study the effects of a positive feedback on test scores, we would assess scores prior to the feedback and again afterward. We would also compare findings over time with a group who did not go through the program. In this case, both groups' scores improved between the pre- and posttest. However, the experimental group's score went up more than the control group's score, suggesting that the independent variable—positive feedback—produced an increase in scores.

in performance after participants in an experimental group received positive feedback and participants in a control group received neutral feedback. Because the performances of participants in the experimental group improved more than those of participants in the control group, we have some evidence that the independent variable produced changes in the dependent variable.

The most common way to reduce the likelihood that variables other than the independent variable are responsible for changes in the dependent variable is to use random assignment. **Random assignment** involves assigning participants to different levels of an independent variable on a random basis—for example, by tossing a coin. In experimental research, random assignment is the most important feature allowing investigators to determine causal relationships. In the preceding example, researchers would randomly assign each participant to either the experimental group or the control group. This procedure ensures that participants, on average, are equivalent in such areas as motivation and talent across the two groups. In other words, we should expect participants in the experimental group, on average, to have about the same talent with respect to the task as do participants in the control group. With random assignment, experimentalists can be confident that differences in exposure to the independent variable, and nothing else, are producing the changes found in the dependent variable.

A study by Stuart Hysom (2009) provides an excellent example of a social psychological experiment. Hysom was interested in whether the rewards that result from high status—things such as high fashion, honorific certificates, and expensive cars—themselves *lead to* high status. In Hysom's experiment, a participant and partner worked together on the task. The experiment had several conditions, but two of them can illustrate Hysom's experimental approach. In one condition, the experimental group, participants received status-related rewards; specifically, the participants were given fictitious titles and invited to an exclusive private reception that would be held at a later date. In a control condition, the participant received none of these rewards. Hysom randomly assigned participants to the conditions and found that students in the experimental group (those who got the status-based rewards) were less likely to be influenced (an indicator of status) on the group task than were students in the control group. In other words, the experiment found that the rewards that typically result from status will themselves lead to higher status.

Experiments are a powerful tool for determining causal relationships between independent and dependent variables (see Box 3.3). But their usefulness to social psychologists can be limited by two factors. First, many phenomena of interest to social psychologists cannot be manipulated in laboratory settings. Suppose, for example, that a researcher is testing a hypothesis about health consequences resulting from the death of a loved one. This hypothesis would be impossible to test through an experiment because researchers would not be able to randomly assign some participants to experience the death of a loved one and other participants to not experience the death of a loved one. A survey that asked participants if they have experienced the death of a loved one within a given time period and then measured various mental and physical health items would be better suited to this type of investigation.

Box 3.3 Traditional and Modern Approaches to the Experiment

Traditional

The field of psychology is well-known for applying the experimental method to study people. Historically, experimental psychologists have utilized rats and other animals to understand human processes. One of the most influential social psychologists was B. F. Skinner. Skinner developed the field of operant conditioning in which learning is argued to occur by the association of a behavior with the implementation of rewards and punishments. Much of Skinner's work relied on experiments with rats and pigeons. He would "teach" these animals to perform complex behaviors, such as moving in circles, dancing, and playing games, by rewarding them for doing those activities correctly or punishing incorrect behaviors. He also developed the "Skinner box" in which animals learned to press levers to obtain rewards such as food pellets. At one point, he had his daughter in the Skinner box too! Some researchers question whether these types of research can be generalized to humans. Can studies of rats help explain why people behave in certain ways following rewards or punishments? Can you experience art online the same way that you do when you visit a museum and see the real thing? The complexities of human motives—and social experiences that influence our motives—make it difficult to fully answer these questions. What do you think?

Modern

The experimental model has gone virtual! There are any number of ways to manipulate conditions in an online environment. For instance, Stoyan Sgourev and Niek Althuizen (2017) created conditions in which people evaluate artwork. Participants completed a survey which involved assessments of art based on status (world famous or not) and complexity (simple or complex). They used two works from a legitimate artist, Kazimir Malevitch. The dependent variable was subjects' assessment of the artwork's aesthetic and creative values as well as personal appeal. The researchers found that status labels are important in assessing artwork, at least the piece deemed less complex. For this discussion, this project demonstrates the ways that modern scholars can create studies that include real-life examples (i.e., using art from a museum) at a fraction of the time and costs associated with studying people in a physical lab site.

A second limitation in carrying out experiments is that they are usually appropriate only when the researcher is interested in testing a developed theory of some social process. Experiments create conditions in which researchers can measure independent and dependent variables that represent the concepts in some established theory. Because experimentalists create the conditions that participants experience, theories must guide the variables they manipulate and measure. Experiments are not meant to draw direct conclusions about the nature of social reality. Instead, experiments provide evidence for or against theories, which then provide the link between the experiment's findings and natural social interactions.

David R. Heise*

David R. Heise, born March 15, 1937, in Evanston, Illinois, studied engineering at the Illinois Institute of Technology in 1954–1956. He then went to the University of Missouri, where he received bachelor's degrees in journalism (1958) and mathematics (1959). Moving to the University of Chicago for his graduate studies, he earned his MA in 1962 and his PhD in 1964—both in sociology. Heise's central social psychological contribution is his work on affect control theory (ACT) (Chapter 5), which provides an empirically based model of roles, labeling, attribution, and emotion. Heise's (1979) book, *Understanding Events: Affect and the Construction of Social Action*, presented the first book-length statement of the theory. More information about ACT can be obtained on the ACT website (www.indiana.edu/~socpsy/ACT/). Heise contributed to the field of methodology in sociology by serving as the editor of *Sociological Methodology* (1974–1976) and *Sociological Methods and Research* (1980–1983). His first major book, *Causal Analysis* (Heise 1975), was about research methods. In 40-plus years in the field, Heise has published 12 books, including three recent volumes—*Expressive Order* (Heise 2007); *Self, Identities and Social Institutions* (Heise 2010, with Neil MacKinnon); and *Surveying Cultures* (Heise 2010)—as well as over 60 articles in social psychology and methodology. *Expressive Order* received the Harrison White Outstanding Book Award from the Mathematical Sociology Section of the American Sociological Association. Heise was the recipient of the Cooley-Mead Award in 1998. He also received the James S. Coleman Distinguished Career Award in Mathematical Sociology in 2010, a Lifetime Achievement Award from the Sociology of Emotions Section of the American Sociological Association in 2002, and an Award for Outstanding Contributions to Computing from the Sociology and Computers Section of the American Sociological Association in 1995. Heise states his guiding principle in conducting research as "merging empirical data with theory, mathematical analysis, and computer simulations in order to produce findings that elucidate the dynamics and intricacies of social relations." Dr. Heise passed away in 2021.

*This biography was obtained from Lynn Smith-Lovin's (1999) introduction of the Cooley-Mead Award printed in *Social Psychology Quarterly* and personal correspondence with Dr. Heise.

Mixed-Method Approaches

Mixed-method approaches to the study of social life have grown considerably over the years (Axinn and Pearce 2006). Given that each methodological approach has its strengths and its shortcomings, using mixed methods provide additional strength to researchers' understandings of a phenomena. Some studies using survey methods suggest that there has been a decline in racial discrimination over the years (e.g., Parrillo and Donoghue 2005), but other methods such as experiments and qualitative methods have shown important ways that discrimination still exists today (e.g., Dambrun, Villate, and

Richetin 2008; Stivers and Majid 2007). Perhaps these discrepancies relate to how racism is being measured (Blank, Dabady, and Citro 2004). For these reasons, a particularly effective way of studying social psychological phenomena is to bring multiple methods to bear on a research question.

Suppose that a team of social psychologists is interested in workplace interaction. They are curious about the factors that affect the evaluations that people receive at work. The researchers could draw on multiple methods to explore this question. The researchers might begin their investigation with a qualitative study aimed at exploring workplace interactions. For example, they might conduct an ethnographic study in which they observe people interacting in a work organization and record the behaviors they see. The researchers might identify consistent patterns of behavior that they view across different types of interactions.

Suppose the researchers observe that racialized minorities in the organizations consistently receive lower evaluations for their performances than do Whites, even when the quality of their performances seems just as high. The researchers might begin to develop a theory, or draw on existing theories, about the reasons for this discrepancy and decide that they need more data.

As a next step, the researchers could conduct a large-scale survey project. They could send questionnaires to a sample of hundreds, or even thousands, of people, asking them about their work experiences. These surveys would include questions about people's personal characteristics; about the workplace structure, such as the number of employees or the racial composition of the workplace; and about the evaluations they receive at work.

Suppose that the survey indicates that racialized minorities report lower performance evaluations at work than do Whites. Now suppose further that the researchers identify other groups that receive lower evaluations—for example, women. Gender and race are both status markers in our society, so the researchers might develop a general theory that individuals with lower social status get lower evaluations than do others, even when they perform as well as or better than others.

The researchers could then carry out an experiment to test their theory that status influences the evaluations that people receive. For example, the researchers might ask experimental participants to read materials that they believe have been prepared by another person participating in the experiment. All participants would read the same materials, but participants in one group would be given information indicating that the person who prepared the materials belonged to a racial minority group, whereas those in another group would be told that the person who prepared the materials was White. Thus, the race of the partner (i.e., the independent variable) is varied across conditions. Participants would then evaluate the quality of the materials. If materials thought to be prepared by Whites generally received higher evaluations, then—because participants were randomly assigned to receive purported Whites or minorities as partners—the researchers would have evidence supporting their theory that social status influences performance evaluations.

The researchers also might use mixed method approaches within their various projects. A survey, for example, might include primarily close-ended (quantitative) questions but also some open-ended (qualitative) questions asking respondents to reflect on their work experiences. By drawing on both qualitative and quantitative approaches and on various types of methods, the researchers would be able to better identify the factors that influence work evaluations.

Section Summary

In this section of the chapter, we answered the following questions: How is qualitative sociology different from quantitative sociology? What are the major forms of qualitative research? What are the major forms of quantitative research? Qualitative and quantitative methods are different approaches to collecting information about people. Qualitative methods include any method of studying people that emphasizes in-depth, semi-structured modes of observation or interviewing of subjects. This set of methods is contrasted with quantitative methods based on precise measurement of social-psychological variables, typically in the form of surveys or experiments. Quantitative methods are particularly useful when trying to generalize findings to larger populations or test theories of social processes, whereas qualitative methods provide more depth of understanding about a topic, when studying an area of social psychology that has not been studied much before, when developing theory, or when dealing with difficult populations or topics.

A Take-Away Message

Qualitative and quantitative methods are tools. While we use tools such as hammers and saws to build things, research methods are more like playing an instrument or learning a language. It can be difficult at times but very rewarding too. If you really care about a social issue, you should learn these skills to collect and analyze data. This data can be utilized in both your personal and professional life. Say, for instance, you want to change something in your community—maybe you want to get funding to open a new park. How might you convince the city leaders to help you? You may simply ask for the money, but they will likely want something to show that the park is worthwhile. So, how do you show that other people in the community want the park and that it will be embraced by them? How can you show the impact of green spaces for mental wellbeing? Perhaps you can do a survey of residents to see if there is support for such a project. You could also research the correlation between the amounts of available green space and wellbeing, drawing upon social scientists' literature on this topic. These methodological skills are used in business, government, and education, among other fields. Having research tools at your disposal will make you an indispensable part of your work group.

STEPS IN DEVELOPING RESEARCH PROJECTS

> *The biggest challenge I have with students is that they don't know how to begin to do research. I describe a research design, but they forget a lot of steps along the way—obviously it is new to them. The texts are*

good for general outlines, but they don't give students specific pointers for going out and doing their research.

—Morten, sociology instructor

There is no single set of "rules" appropriate for every type of social research project. The only guidelines that apply to most sociological inquiries are that the research should be driven by some theoretical orientation and an important research question, that it should have methodological structure that allows other people to assess the quality of the data gathered, and that it links the data or observations to propositions that extend to settings or people beyond the particular study. The opening vignette for this section shows a sociology instructor trying to find a better way to get students to do their own research projects. However, because social psychology can include any aspect of human life, there are no simple methods for use in all types of research.

The following steps are designed as a general guideline for developing most projects in social psychology. The steps may vary, however, depending on your project or the theoretical perspectives from which you are drawing. The steps explain how a project might proceed when the researcher's goal is to test, rather than to develop, a set of predictions.

Step 1: Assess Relevant Theories and Literature

The first step in developing a research project is to examine the theoretical background and literature related to your topic. If we want to understand social causes of depression, we would look to the theories that have been developed on the topic and examine research that has tested those theories. Generally, this takes the form of reading books and peer-reviewed research articles. Peer-reviewed journals are composed of research reports that have been reviewed by at least two or three trained professionals or "peers" before the research is allowed to be published. This method of review gives authors feedback on their research report, providing comments about the content and methods of a project, to ensure that it meets standards generally accepted in the field and that the work makes a sufficient theoretical contribution to warrant publication.

This stage of the research project can be time-consuming. If you are studying the relationship between gender and mental health, you will encounter hundreds of citations from books and journals in many fields. Search engines available through most libraries or online help you narrow your search, if you like, to a specific field such as sociology or psychology using databases called PsycINFO or Sociological Abstracts or through programs such as Google Scholar. They allow you to refine your search to include multiple **search terms**, or authors' words used to find articles on your topic. For instance, ideas related to mental health may also be found under the expressions "mental illness," "depression," "anxiety," or "alcoholism." You may also narrow the search for these terms to the article title and its **abstract**, a summary of the research article.

Theoretical and empirical (or data-based) research articles and books provide a background to previous work in the field. They also provide a way to see how other people have studied your topic. You may find that many people study gender and mental health using quantitative methods or that they employ specific theoretical references. Using this information, you may decide to revisit your theory or method to expand the work found in the literature review or to try to replicate one of those studies. Alternatively, you may decide to keep your approach but to adopt the measures of your variables employed by a particular article or set of articles.

Step 2: Develop Research Questions or Hypotheses

The next step is to develop specific hypotheses about your topic of study. If we want to study the relationship between gender and mental health, for instance, we might predict that women will report higher levels of distress from work–family imbalance based on the theory and literature on this topic. These hypotheses are important to the development of specific measurements of your independent and dependent variables. In this case, how would you measure distress or mental health? It can be manifested in different ways such as depression and excessive alcohol use. Men and women report varying levels of these problems; hence, your measurement of the dependent variable may affect the outcomes of your study.

In most cases, the hypotheses of a project follow from the theoretical framework that the researcher is using. The stress process model to be discussed in Chapter 8 focuses on how inequality in society affects well-being. Perhaps women experience inequality through lower income, poor work or living conditions, too much housework, or sexual harassment at a higher rate than men, and you can measure these variables as well. In this case, you may predict that women will report more mental health problems than men. You may then predict that differences between men and women are a result of a series of workplace or home-based inequalities. Your literature review should help to develop specific hypotheses.

Step 3: Choose Research Methods

Based on the theories, literature, and hypotheses, you must now choose the precise means by which you plan to test your hypotheses. At this stage, you must decide who you wish to sample, the size of the sample, and how you intend to procure that sample. In addition, you must decide on the kind of method you intend to use to assess your hypotheses. Your decision about the sample and data collection methods depends on your project. In our example, you could conduct in-depth interviews with women and men about workplace interactions and family processes, to determine aspects of work–family arenas that are salient, and whether and how the participants discuss these as stressful or not. For other projects, you might survey a class of students or try to get a random sample of students from your university and use quantitative measures developed in the earlier stages of the project.

The method you choose to employ in a project depends on the nature of the project and your theoretical orientation. An exploratory study typically means that few people have investigated the topic; hence, you likely cannot rely as much on the work of other people for your theory or measures. As stated earlier in the text, if you are conducting exploratory research, you may want to begin with qualitative analysis, to "explore" the nature of your variables and how they interact: the theory and research in that area are not complete and require development and refinement. In our case, there are a number of studies linking gender and mental health that we can use to help develop our project, perhaps replicating others' studies or developing our own project using elements of several different projects.

Although we listed the process of forming hypotheses as coming before choosing a research method, the process is complex and rarely linear. Because hypotheses are tied to indicators in a particular study, one must have some sense of the research method when developing hypotheses. But it's hard to pick a research method before knowing what we plan to predict. So, this process is often iterative, with a researcher having a general sense of a study's research questions or hypotheses when picking a research method, and then formulating a more precise focus or specific hypotheses after choosing a particular method.

Step 4: Conduct Data Analysis

After you have collected the data, you must analyze it to determine whether you have support for your hypotheses. If you used a quantitative survey, you can conduct statistical analyses using computer software programs, such as Statistical Analysis Software (SAS), R, or the Statistical Package for the Social Sciences (SPSS), among others. These packages make it much easier to write or use code to compare differences between men and women on mental health outcomes. They can also perform higher-order analysis such as regression, a technique that allows you to control for other variables that may affect mental health, such as income. As a result, you can look for "pure" effects of gender on mental health, controlling for other conditions and characteristics associated with the dependent variable. You can also use advanced analysis to see how much of the "gender" effect is related to the mechanisms of inequalities in home conditions or workplace environments.

If you are conducting qualitative research, analysis will require some additional planning. For instance, you may decide to code the responses to in-depth interviews or try to summarize observational data. Software programs such as InVivo, HyperRESEARCH, and Ethnograph are popular tools for summarizing qualitative text data. R (www.r-project.org) is a free statistics program that anyone can download and use. It may take time to learn but the skill is definitely useful in many jobs! You can also aggregate the responses to your questions, leaving them in word form and looking for patterns of responses. What are the forms of discrimination reported by your respondents? What are the ways they managed that discrimination? How do the reports vary based on the demographic backgrounds of the respondents? Once you have established a pattern, you can use quotes from your subjects as examples of such patterns. Also, qualitative methods in sociology are not typically used to test hypotheses, but they can be used to develop hypotheses that might subsequently be tested using other approaches.

Step 5: Report Results

Social scientists report their data in two main ways. Initial results are sometimes developed into reports to be presented at conferences. The Society for the Study of Symbolic Interaction (SSSI) is a popular sociological social psychology organization that holds an annual meeting to discuss new research in the field (www.symbolicinteraction.org). The American Sociological Association (ASA) also holds an annual conference that includes some of the newest research in social psychology (www.asanet.org). Group processes researchers in sociology have a conference each summer alongside the annual ASA conference. Conferences provide researchers with feedback on newer projects to help them improve their research. In this case, you may also seek a conference that focuses on the topic of your research. In this case, we are examining mental health, and a number of groups devote their research energies to such topics.

Box 3.4 The Research Paper Format

Every journal has a slightly different set of expectations for formatting a paper for publication. Most of them expect the article or paper to address the following issues:

- *Theory and literature review*: The introductory section of a paper gives the reader a sense of the theoretical argument you are making, and reviews other research using your dependent and/or independent variables. You must convince the reader that your project makes a contribution to the field.
- *Methods*: The methods section discusses how you conducted your research. Specifically, how did you choose your sample (e.g., randomly, cluster, or snowball)? How many people did you sample, and why? You should state how you measured your dependent and independent variables. Finally, you must state how you analyzed your data.
- *Results*: The results section is a review of your findings. You may start with a simple description of your variables and how they relate to one another. For a quantitative study, you will then likely show how your independent variables affect your dependent variable(s) in some way.
- *Discussion*: The discussion section summarizes your findings from the results section, emphasizing your theory and hypotheses. Did you find support for your hypotheses? If not, why? You should also describe how your findings fit in the context of the related literature reviewed earlier in the paper.
- *References*: Your paper should make appropriate citations throughout the text and list those citations at the end of the paper, usually in a separate section. Every field has its own way of citing literature. This textbook, for instance, employs the sociological format for citing work.
- *Appendices*: You will sometimes be asked to include copies of any research instruments (interview schedules or questionnaires) in a section at the end of the document.

Traditionally, researchers use conferences to help prepare their research for later publication in peer-reviewed journals (see Box 3.4 for a review of the format of a journal article). "Peer-reviewed" means that several scholars review a paper without knowledge of the author's name or affiliation. Such reviews ensure that the research meets the standards of the field before it is provided to other scholars and the general public. Two of the more popular sociological social psychology journals are *Social Psychology Quarterly* and *Symbolic Interaction*. The study of gender and mental health may also be published in a topical journal in the field, such as the *Journal of Health and Social Behavior* or *Society and Mental Health*. Your literature review should help develop a sense of where to send your work for review.

In some ways, studying people is easier than the hard sciences which often require very expensive equipment. We can start studying people almost immediately because they are all around us. Howard Becker (2017), a prolific sociologist, cautions us to be careful in assessing the evidence of social phenomenon whether it be a qualitative or quantitative project. As humans, we bring all sorts of biases into a research project. That said, conducting research should and can be exciting! You are going out to learn about people, why people do what they do and how humans relate to one another. While this process may be exciting, it can also be challenging, especially if you are conducting research which requires you to interact with strangers or even puts you in a vulnerable position (McKinzie 2017). But that can be thrilling too! Consider doing research "on the edge" like studying medical doctors in a field hospital (de Rond 2017) or (after IRB approval of course) covert research, participant observations that involves deceiving subjects in some way in order to better study them (Calvey 2017). Knowing these things, we hope, will help motivate you to get started in research and prepare you for the field!

Section Summary

Here we applied five steps in the research process to answer the question "How do social scientists begin to develop a research project?" The steps include developing or reviewing appropriate theories and literature related to your research topic, developing research questions or hypotheses you plan to test based on that literature and theory, choosing research methods, conducting data analysis, and writing your report of findings. These steps can be applied to almost any social research project. It can be fun and exciting and need not take months or years to do (Pink and Morgan 2013); for example, your professor may include mini research projects within a course. The key is having a solid plan for the project and utilizing the best practices of data collection. When you collect data from people, however you do it, it will always be a learning experience!

A Take-Away Message

Like many other aspects of life, there is a format by which sociologists have to do their work. Accountants, for example, must learn how to produce and present spreadsheets. This section gives you the format by which social scientists go about their work. By using this format to write up your research report, you will be aligned with professions in the field.

Box 3.5 How to Become a Social Scientist

Like any scientist, the social scientist uses research to answer questions and solve problems. Some paid jobs in the social sciences include corporate and other ethnographers who are paid to determine user experience (e.g., what customers like or dislike about a product or service) as well as decision-making processes in health care, and other projects that require a more detailed understanding of how and why people make the choices they do (Pelto 2013). Government and nonprofit organizations may conduct polls of people to ascertain the issues they are dealing with (e.g., stresses associated with the COVID-19 pandemic) or satisfaction with services or amenities in a city such as parks and libraries.

Here are some examples that come from the job-seeking platform, Indeed, and USAJOBS.gov, the US federal government site for job openings.

1. **User Experience (UX) Researcher, IMDb.** Duties: Identify best method or mix of quantitative and qualitative methods based on priorities, research questions, timeline, and resourcing. Qualifications: 3–6+ years of hands-on experience conducting UX research in an applied setting with demonstrated impacts, BA/BS in Psychology, Sociology, Anthropology, Human Computer Interaction, Human Factors, or a related field, a strong portfolio demonstrating all aspects of the UX research lifecycle, proficiency in core usability tools and platforms; experience in a variety of research methods: qualitative and quantitative, attitudinal and behavioral, generative and evaluative.
2. **Research Analyst, Department of the Navy.** Duties: Coordinates and develops social science research and evaluation for the Research & Program Evaluation Section. Qualifications: Bachelor's degree in social science or a related field appropriate to the work of position and three years of experience in the occupation, or a related field or work area, or an appropriate combination of education and experience that demonstrates possession of knowledge and skill equivalent to that gained in the above.
3. **Survey Statistician, US Census Bureau, Department of Commerce.** Duties: Design, conduct, and report findings and recommendations of methodological research associated with instrument development, measurement error, nonresponse reduction and respondent burden in establishment surveys, use appropriate survey research methodologies, such as cognitive, usability, and other pretesting and evaluation methods. Qualifications: Degree with 15 semester hours in statistics, and 9 additional semester hours in one or more of the following: physical or biological sciences, medicine, education, or engineering; or in the social sciences including demography, history, economics, social welfare...or combination of education and work experience.

(*continued*)

These positions are obtainable with a degree in sociology or psychology, but it may require additional research methods courses (e.g., field and/or survey research) and practice doing projects. How do you get experience before you start your career? Start by taking internship courses and doing some paid or even unpaid work to build up your resume. Consider doing independent studies by participating in professors' research projects. These experiences can be put on your resume to show that you know the basics of how to do social scientific research.

BRINGING IT ALL TOGETHER

> *Symbolic interactionism is not misled by the mythical belief that to be scientific it is necessary to shape one's study to fit a pre-established protocol of empirical inquiry.*
>
> —Blumer, Symbolic Interactionism: Perspective and Method (Blumer 1969, p. 48)

There is no rule about whether a particular theory should or should not be examined using quantitative or qualitative methods. In general, the research question should guide the selection of a methodological approach. However, some perspectives lend themselves to certain techniques. House (1977) argued that the symbolic interactionist paradigm, for instance, focuses more on naturalistic observation than the other faces of social psychology. This idea is echoed by Herbert Blumer, a prominent symbolic interactionist, who questioned the applicability of traditional scientific methods to studying human behavior. He argued that exploration and inspection are the most rigorous ways to study social life. This belief is based on the assumption that social reality is constantly in a state of negotiation, making social life difficult to measure and predict in the same way as in the physical sciences.

In reality, researchers often apply multiple methods to studying a particular phenomenon. For instance, a researcher may use qualitative methods to determine the dimensions of a concept, such as romantic love, and then use this knowledge to develop questions for a quantitative survey. It is important to note that some methods are more applicable to some areas of research than to other areas. For instance, quantitative methods may not be appropriate for the study of the modern illegal drug trade. Imagine trying to survey a group of drug dealers using random sampling techniques! How would you get such a sample? Even if you could get a good sample of drug dealers, do you think that many of them would be willing to fill out a questionnaire with questions about their illicit dealings? Probably not. As a result, researchers may be limited to in-depth interviews with available dealers and/or observations of the trade itself.

This chapter is designed to give you the basic tools necessary to initiate a research project as well as critique social science research. Be aware that most projects lack some of the ideals described in this chapter. Some projects may suffer from a limited sample, whereas other projects are limited by how variables are operationalized. You must review each project in its totality, using your knowledge of methods to guide your assessment of the validity of its findings.

SUMMARY

1. Several concepts apply to almost any research project. Researchers regularly use terms such as "theory," "research questions" or "hypotheses," and "variables" to describe ways of studying people.
2. Researchers employ qualitative and quantitative techniques to study human subjects. Qualitative research methods include field research and in-depth interviews. Quantitative methods include survey research and experiments. Content and textual analyses fall across these categories.
3. The steps in developing most research projects include assessing the theory and literature on the research topic, developing research questions or specific hypotheses, choosing the appropriate research methods, conducting data analysis, and reporting the results.
4. Although there is no rule about whether a particular theory should or should not use quantitative or qualitative methods to study people, symbolic interactionists have traditionally relied more on qualitative methods. Both social structure and personality researchers and group processes researchers more often use quantitative methods. Many researchers try to employ multiple methods of studying a particular phenomenon.

KEY TERMS AND CONCEPTS

Abstract: The summary of findings of a research article.

Categorical (or nominal) variables: Measures for which the possible responses have no particular order.

Cluster sample: A sample in which the population is first divided into meaningful clusters and then a representative sample of respondents is selected from within each cluster.

Content analysis: Any systematic review of documents or other media.

Control group: Participants of an experiment that are not exposed to the independent variable.

Convenience sample: A sample in which any available person is included in the study.

Dependent variable: The variable that is predicted to change as a result of the independent variable.

Ethnography: A form of field research that includes a descriptive analysis of a group or organization.

Experiment: A type of quantitative research procedure in which investigators control participants' exposure to an independent variable.

Experimental group: Participants of an experiment who are exposed to an independent variable.

Field research: A form of qualitative study in which researchers directly observe people's behavior.

Focus groups: Semi-structured interviews with small groups of people.

Grounded theory: Generating theory based on data collected during a study.

Hypotheses: Specific predictions about how variables will relate to one another in a research study.

Independent variable: The variable predicted to lead to a change in the dependent variable.

In-depth interviews: A qualitative research method employing an unstructured or semi-structured series of questions.

Indices: A series of related questions designed to measure an underlying concept.

Informant: In an ethnography, someone who can help the researcher gain access to and discover general patterns in a particular group's behavior.

Institutional Review Boards (IRBs): Groups that ensure that the benefits of a research project outweigh any potential harm to research participants.

Interval variables: A type of variable in which the difference between any two adjacent values is the same.

Laboratory experiments: Experiments in which the experiences and behaviors of participants are monitored in a controlled laboratory setting.

Narrative analysis: Any method that examines social life in the form of personal stories.

Natural or field experiments: Experiments that take place in people's everyday environments.

Online experiments: A type of quantitative research that includes traditional elements of experiments but in an online environment.

Operationalize: Translating a concept into something that can be measured.

Ordinal variables: Variables for which response categories are ordered but the distances between adjacent categories are not necessarily equal.

Participant observation: A form of qualitative research in which a researcher becomes a member of the group being studied.

Population: The larger group of people about whom a researcher seeks to draw conclusions.

Posttest: A measure of the dependent variable after exposure to the independent variable in an experiment.

Pretest: A measure of the dependent variable before participants are exposed to the independent variable in an experiment.

Probability samples: Samples in which researchers choose participants systematically in an attempt to ensure that they are representative of the population.

Qualitative research methods: In-depth, semi-structured modes of observing or interviewing subjects.

Quantitative research methods: Any research method that attempts to precisely measure people's thoughts, feelings, or behavior.

Random assignment: Assigning participants of an experiment to different categories of an independent variable on a random basis.
Random sample: A sample in which participants are randomly chosen from a population of interest.
Ratio variables: Interval variables that have a zero starting point.
Reliability: When a study yields the same results using the same techniques and data.
Sample: A group of people drawn for use in a study.
Sampling frame: A list of all possible elements in the population.
Search terms: Words used to find articles on a topic during a literature review.
Secondary data analysis: The analysis of previously collected survey data.
Snowball sample: Samples in which informants provide contact information about other people who share some of the characteristics necessary for a study.
Social theories: Structured explanations of how various elements of social life are related to one another.
Statistical significance: The probability that the results found in the sample reflect the true relationships within the population of interest.
Survey research: The use of questionnaires to measure independent and dependent variables.
Validity: How valid or accurate the findings of the study are.
Variables: Concepts that are put into a measurable form.

DISCUSSION QUESTIONS

1. What aspect of social life would you like to study the most? What method would you use to study it? Why did you choose that method?
2. What are the strengths and limitations of qualitative and quantitative methods? Can you think of a way to employ the best of both approaches to studying people? That is, how could you incorporate qualitative and quantitative methods in one study?
3. Why is the development of a literature review critical for a research project? What specific social psychological literature excites you and why?

PART 2

The Individual in Society

In this section of the book we begin addressing some of the core areas of sociological social psychology: stratification, self and identity, and socialization. These are considered foundational because they are essential aspects of human organization and interaction through which people develop senses of who they are. These dynamics affect other aspects of social life. Stratification, for instance, across race and ethnicity, gender, and social class helps us understand mental health processes, an area of research that will be reviewed in the next section of the book.

Each chapter in this part of the book divides research and theories under headings representing the three major perspectives in the field: symbolic interaction (SI), social structure and personality (SSP), and group processes (GP). Although there is a good deal of overlap across these areas, we find that these distinctions serve as a useful heuristic device for analyzing many social psychological processes. As with previous chapters, we begin each chapter in this part with a series of questions that we intend to answer. We end each chapter with a section that brings together the three perspectives, summarizing how each paradigm contributes to understanding the chapter topic. In the end, we believe that using multiple perspectives will help us develop better understandings of social life.

4

The Social Psychology of Stratification

> *I really did not think much about my position in society until I came to this university. Once I looked around here and saw lots of kids from good high schools like mine, I realized that I would not be going here if my parents didn't have the money. I probably would have taken courses at our local community college while working full-time. It might have taken a very long time to finish a BA, if I ever did. Now I have time to go to club meetings, do an internship, and learn about different fields. And I will probably finish in four years. I wouldn't say I am lucky but maybe just using what's been given to me.*
>
> —Daniel, freshman undeclared

In this vignette, we see a student realize that his attending a four-year university was due in part to factors beyond his control. Although he may have obtained a good college education without his parents' help, he knows that the experience might be different without it—he may have struggled and probably would have had to work harder. A key factor in getting Daniel where he is today is his social class status. His parents' high income and social resources helped give Daniel the opportunity to choose a more prestigious university where he has more options and will receive a degree that carries high status. The fact that he does not need to struggle with financing his education means he has more time to focus on other pursuits, including studying. So, he expects he can graduate on time with no debt, with a good GPA, and with a degree he enjoys.

Daniel's reflections highlight the relationship between society and the individual, and they also show the significance of social standing. **Social stratification** refers to ways in which individuals or groups are ranked in society, reflecting different amounts of power, status, and prestige. Important statuses include social class, race or ethnicity, gender, age, and sexual orientation. In Daniel's case, his parents' (and his own) social class status served as a basis for him to have many "good" choices about which university to attend. Without having access to certain upper-middle-class resources (e.g., high-quality elementary and secondary schools, money, and educated parents who know the ropes about college applications and how to specifically prepare for college from a young age), he would have had fewer options. Daniel's choices are not available to everyone. And it leads to several positive consequences in his early adult life course that many working-class or poor high school students may not experience.

One of the major ways sociological social psychology is different from its counterpart in psychology is its greater emphasis on the role of stratification in social psychological processes. There are several ways stratification affects people's lives and relationships. As noted earlier, symbolic interactionists sometimes address how we create and maintain definitions of different classes of people. Social structure and personality researchers emphasize how structural conditions, often related to work, education, or family settings, affect people. Those in the group processes perspective examine how stratification systems from a larger society become reproduced in groups. We will use each of these perspectives to examine how stratification processes occur in day-to-day life. We will address these perspectives with the following questions:

- How do people construct inequality in society? How is structure linked to our interactions?
- How does social structure contribute to the development of inequalities in people's experience?
- What are the processes by which groups stratify? How do inequalities from society at large get reproduced in groups?

CONSTRUCTING INEQUALITIES

> *I really think that you have to be a woman to know what I am talking about. It is very subtle. You will be in class sometimes, or at a party, or a meeting, and it is almost like you are not even there. People—men but sometimes women too—don't try to discriminate, they just do it. I mean, they go on talking and making decisions without ever considering you. Sometimes they may ask your opinion—not often really—but then they don't act on it. It is as if they were being polite but they never intended to include your ideas in the decision. How am I ever going to make it in business?*
>
> —Clara, senior business major

How does symbolic interactionism—a perspective focused on meaning—take account of and address social stratification and inequalities? The ways in which these status-making processes operate can be subtle. In the opening vignette, Clara is discussing how the people she interacts with keep her from making major contributions to discussions. She does not believe they are overtly sexist but still feels that "something" is not right in their interactions. Something is keeping her from contributing fully to the group. Symbolic interactionists try to uncover the subtle and not-so-subtle ways that social hierarchies develop and are maintained in social settings. Although symbolic interactionists have sometimes been slow to emphasize social stratification in meaning-making processes, some important research on inequalities is being conducted using this perspective (Hollander and Howard 2000; Monk 2015; Schwalbe 2008).

Where do power and authority come from in the first place? On the macro-level of society, Max Weber (1978, originally 1921) argued that the ability to control society rests on one of three bases: traditional authority, rational-legal authority, or charismatic authority. Traditional authority is based on long-standing traditions as the basis of power. It may be that certain families have had power in a particular society, and it is generally expected that their children would assume that power after they pass on. With rational-legal authority, power comes from laws and rules that give people control over decisions and resources, such as elected officials. Finally, charismatic authority comes from the personal qualities of an individual. While these forms of authority appear to emanate from the macro-levels of society, micro-interactions are involved in creating institutions, creating a cycle in which micro-conditions produce macro-level phenomenon, which then affects individual interactions within the social system. Randall Collins (2020), for instance, argues that charismatic personality itself is a social product and once obtained, creates macrosocial routines which reifies the power of the charismatic individual. A "radical interactionism" employs the tenants of symbolic interaction with a focus on the ways that dominance occurs in day-to-day interactions (Athens 2015; see also Kemper 2011).

Basic Stratification Processes

Researchers who employ the interactionist perspective to study stratification focus on the processes of developing and maintaining differences within and among groups of people (Sauder 2005). Symbolic interactionists' focus on meaning is an important part of understanding social stratification and inequalities, although interactionists need to attend to these processes more (Hollander and Howard 2000; Sauder 2005). Interactionist research focuses on the following stratification processes: who we interact with, the role of status during interactions, the ability to define interactions, and a process of "othering." Inequalities become "accomplished" by how people behave, think, and feel (Schwalbe 2008). Each of these areas is reviewed in this chapter.

Stratification and Who We Interact With

Social structure shapes who we interact with and *how* we interact with other people (Sauder 2005; Stryker 2002). In fact, this is an important way that social structure enters daily life—by constraining the kinds of people with whom we come into contact. Illustrating this, Shirley Brice Heath (1983) conducted an ethnography of two separate communities—White and Black working-class towns in the rural Piedmont Carolinas. She detailed the different ways the two groups used language and storytelling with young children. White working-class children were spoken to in factual ways, with questions directed to children but little in the way of manipulating language in ways that middle-class children do. Black working-class youngsters were not directly spoken to, but instead were interacted with in a challenging, conflict-oriented style. When they were toddlers, these children were challenged to come up with creative responses to adults' words, a skill that community members valued highly.

Heath (1983) argued that the ways parents and other community members interacted with children derived from historical circumstance; Whites from their experiences working in factories, where they had to conform to the authority of supervisors, and Blacks from days where they overcame obstacles related to slavery or sharecropping. In both cases, when the working-class children entered the middle-class elementary schools in a nearby town, they had trouble interacting in the "right" ways with middle-class teachers. Middle-class children, both Black and White, achieved success, but working-class Black children were often frustrated by time and space limitations imposed on them, and teachers said that these students could not answer questions in a direct manner. The White working-class kids had trouble with fiction and refused to contradict authority. Working-class children, although as intelligent on average as middle-class children, had styles of speaking and of interaction that conflicted with those of middle-class institutions and teachers, and they failed more often than middle-class kids. Thus, the types of interactions children experienced early on with significant others were stratified by social class and helped to perpetuate a system that sustained societal inequalities.

In another example of how access to different types of relationships can affect status, Diane Reay and her colleagues (2005) examined the ways that working- and middle-class children in England decide on their choices of college. Through a series of interviews, along with survey and observational data, they examined the subtle ways that families, peers, and schools influenced students' choices. They found that students from private schools lived in families who simply assumed that a university education would be part of their futures. They also received career counseling from family members, and middle-class families and friends were able to provide more detailed information about choosing schools than their less affluent counterparts. Ultimately, these subtle interactions encouraged working-class students to go to less prestigious schools than their middle-class peers. All of the students had agency and made choices, but those choices were made in the context of the differential resources of people they spent time with, leading to different sets of choices available for working- and middle-class youth.

Stratification and the Role of Status during Interactions

A second way interactionists focus on stratification processes is through explicitly accounting for inequalities in the content of interactions. Symbolic interactionists maintain that interacting partners usually have different levels of power. Kathy Ferguson (1980) proposed that people in lower-status positions—those with lower education levels, racial and ethnic minorities, younger people, gays and lesbians, and so on—have to take the role of the other more often than their more powerful counterparts who hold more prestige and status. Those of higher power and status do not tend to need to understand their partners' thoughts and emotions in much detail, nor do they need to view their own behaviors through the eyes of others. But less powerful interactants do. For example, does a secretary need to be concerned with how a boss sees her? Yes! She must anticipate her boss's moods and whims and prioritize tasks so she can quickly get to the things that she imagines the boss wants her to be doing. She sometimes must tolerate her boring stories or unreasonable requests (things she defines as reasonable, of course). Note that there is nothing inherent in a person that makes interactions with others unequal—it lies in the interaction between two people with different levels of power in the situation. Thus, the secretary is likely to be more powerful in interactions with her daughter. But with her boss, she must be sure she sees her as a "good worker," or potentially get fired.

Does a boss need to take the role of her secretary—that is, imagine what she is thinking and assess how she views her during interaction? Not as much. She can make decisions, act nasty or nice, and generally carry on with relatively little concern about how her secretary views her (a reflected appraisal, discussed more in Chapter 5) and her behavior. Thus, those with more power do not have to be as concerned about the other's perceptions and views as they interact with others.

How do lower-status people manage these types of meaning-making power struggles during their interactions? Research indicates that people rarely just "take it"—they either find ways to actively resist it, or they redefine the situation to make it more palatable. Greta Paules (1991), for example, showed how waitresses in a chain restaurant resisted management's attempts to label them as "servants" and worked informally to change their roles in the group. They developed informal norms about relating to customers and management. Although management technically specified rules of conduct, waitresses used their job skills as leverage for negotiating what was expected of them by threatening to leave the job. The result was a constant struggle of redefining the norms expected in the organization. These dynamics reflect the importance of agency in symbolic interactionism, that humans do not necessarily just "take it" when they are faced with inequality. In these ways, individuals "manage" or attempt to change inequalities in their day-to-day lives.

Similarly, in a study of service workers at two luxury hotels, Rachel Sherman (2007) found that the hotel workers would rationalize class differences during interactions with rich patrons. For instance, because workers were clearly not superior to their patrons regarding money, they would emphasize their moral superiority over their rich clients. The service workers also emphasized ways that they had control over their patrons, by controlling the pace of their work for example. The waitresses would submit to the desires of the rich patrons—and they recognized their lower status—but this resignation was exchanged for respectful behavior from the patrons and large tips. If patrons did not follow these subtle exchange expectations, workers could retaliate by withholding labor. Although workers in these examples can maintain dignity through actions that shape meanings and alter tips to a slight degree, they remain embedded in positions that are less powerful and provide less status and fewer rewards than that of their counterparts.

Stratification and the Ability to Define the Situation

A third way in which interactionists contribute to our understanding of social stratification and inequality is through showing how individuals with certain statuses have more power to define situations and to define themselves (Hallett 2007). Sociologists have traditionally found that increases in income and education are associated with greater consumption of elite forms of art (e.g., classical music) (Bourdieu 1984). However, more recent research finds that social elites are actually cultural omnivores, enjoying both high art as well as everyday forms of art and music such as rock 'n' roll or country music (Chan 2010). Thus, having more status, in this case economic status, affords you the ability to choose among the different arts, having been exposed to them and having the ability to consume all art forms. Hahl and colleagues (2017) found that elites can consume lowbrow culture (e.g., doctors drinking Schlitz beer) and by doing it be perceived by others as more authentic.

Status can affect definitions of situations in everyday life. Brent Staples (1995) wrote about being a tall and imposing looking, but gentle, African American graduate student at the prestigious University of Chicago. As he walked around in the evenings in Hyde Park, where the university is located, he found that he was altering public spaces in unintentional ways. People, especially women, would cross the street and increase their pace when he was nearby. Those people defined the situation as threatening, and him as dangerous, even though he was not. But for Staples, being perceived as a threat was hazardous in itself because of the embarrassment, dismay, and alienation that it created for him. Not to mention that fear—even when evoked falsely—sometimes leads to the use of weapons, and Staples could have become the victim of an interaction gone bad by an armed pedestrian or a police officer. In addition to learning to "smother the rage" that comes with being mistaken for a criminal so often (a step related to his own mental well-being), Staples indicated that he must work at presenting himself as "safe" in public spaces. He wears professional business attire even when he does not need to (whereas other groups are freer to dress as they want); gives people extra-wide spaces; adopts a polite, deferential manner, particularly when dealing with police officers; and on dark city streets whistles melodies from Beethoven and Vivaldi in an attempt to be viewed as nonthreatening. Black men and those in other racialized minority groups that may be viewed as threatening must sometimes take measures to present themselves as safe. Many others in majority groups can take for granted that they can wear, walk, and appear as they wish.

Symbolic interactionists focus on the ways that individuals engage in meaning-making during everyday interactions. However, an important part of the stratification process is that certain groups—and individuals in groups—are not able to execute their own definitions of the situation as easily as others. Related to this, some cannot define themselves in as free, varied, or positive ways as easily as others. Melissa Milkie (1999) showed how White adolescent girls have difficulty resisting the societal definitions of female beauty that portray artificially thin, perfect, and "whitened" images. Even though they often do not believe the images are realistic, these images still dampen girls' own evaluations of themselves (i.e., their self-esteem). This is because White girls believe that others—their interacting partners, such as adolescent boys—will judge them based on these media standards. Even if our perceptions are not true, how we *think* others think of us is powerful. The study also showed that African American girls are critical of images as being unrealistic in ways similar to how White girls are critical, but this critique is more powerful in protecting their well-being. That is because they believe that others in their

Box 4.1 Tay, the Racist Chatbot

It appears that racism and bias have made their way into technology. A chatbot is a computer program that is a type of artificial intelligence designed to create conversation with people over the internet. The origins of chatbots go back to the 1960s with the creation of ELIZA, a program designed for the purpose of helping psychiatric patients. Newer iterations included PARRY in the 1970s and Jabberwacky in the 1980s. The word *Chatterbot* emerged in the 1990s (Adamopoulou and Moussiades 2020). It is common to see chatbots on university websites today. The Microsoft corporation launched Tay on X (formerly known as Twitter) on March 23, 2016, but took it down within 24 hours. Tay combined artificial intelligence, or AI, and input from staff that included comedians. Tay mostly repeated what it was told but used its AI to modify that input. The result was a series of inflammatory statements such as, "WE'RE GOING TO BUILD A WALL, AND MEXICO IS GOING TO PAY FOR IT and "Bush did 9/11 and Hitler would have done a better job than the monkey we have now...." It is important to know that many of the users purposely tried to make Tay say such things. Also, Tay said thousands of things that were not bad at all. That said, Tay used these conversations to create racist comments, not unlike people! It was too much for its creators. Tay was put to sleep late on March 24, 2016, tweeting, "c u soon humans need sleep now so many conversations today thx" never to be heard from again (Hunt 2016; Vincent 2016).

networks, particularly African American males, are also critical of a narrow image, and therefore Black girls have somewhat more "leeway" in terms of moving away from this definition of beautiful.

Although boys have ideal societal images to contend with just as do girls, there are often wider and more varied images of ideal males in television, films, social media, and online. An older, bald male can be considered attractive and "normal," whereas women are often not afforded the luxury of feeling good while being themselves. Milkie's study also showed that although boys and girls both agree that being good-looking is important to them, boys, on average, actually feel they are good-looking, whereas girls are most often neutral about this—the narrow societal definitions make it harder for girls to see themselves as positively as boys do.

Othering

Michael Schwalbe and colleagues (2000) discuss a key process in interaction called "othering" (Fine 1994) that helps explain how social class and other inequalities are sustained and created. **Othering** is a form of collective identity work in which those with higher status create definitions that make them feel superior and, in the process, obscure the morality of lower-status groups. Higher-status persons present themselves as competent and trustworthy and, through their wealth and connections to networks of powerful others, can sustain their images as more worthy than others (Schwalbe et al., 2000). Subordinates respond to these definitions by presenting themselves as the exception to a definition that says they are less committed, creative, or hardworking than their middle-class counterparts. In one study, Elizabeth Armstrong and colleagues (2014) demonstrated the ways that high-status women utilize "slut discourse" to define their own behaviors as classy while defining the same behaviors of low-status women as "trashy." These dynamics can play out in the digital world through social forums and other venues in which people from the relatively wealthy countries of the Global North perpetuate their ideologies while people from lower status places risk being "othered" if you do not accept them (Stingl 2016).

Doing Gender

Gender is an important dimension of stratification in all societies. From a symbolic interaction perspective, we create and recreate gender through some of the processes outlined in the last section. Candace West and Don Zimmerman (1987) emphasized the importance of gender stratification in their work by arguing that gender is one of the foundational sources of all stratification because it is associated with biological distinctions at birth. The authors distinguished biological sex from "gender," which refers to the cultural definitions of masculinity and femininity usually associated with individuals' biological sex. **Doing gender** is a social process in which individuals are held accountable to the social rules or norms associated with being a man or a woman in society. Gendered norms become associated with many aspects of a person's interactions with others. Unlike some other elements of identities that are more limited to certain social arenas (e.g., school or work), gender crosses many social boundaries. Thus, men are expected to act masculine in leisure settings, such as when they play team sports or even board games like chess. To meet expectations, they must "be men"—accountable to standards, which include being unemotional, cool or sturdy, and competitive, strong, or aggressive—in play, at work, and even at home.

Barrie Thorne (1993) showed how gender processes occur at early ages and involve elaborate rituals. Her study of elementary school children demonstrates that boys and girls act in ways that separate themselves from the other sex. **Borderwork** refers to the creation of social and physical boundaries between boys and girls. Both groups perform a number of acts to help strengthen differentiation. For instance, a game of chase-and-kiss or the concern over "cooties" provides these groups a sense of difference. Differentiating genders provides individuals one of the most basic elements of their identities (boy versus girl). In recent times, societal norms have shifted in that there are more categories of gender identity beyond male and female available for young people to identify with as they grow. This change of options is now reflected in many survey forms that provide multiple options for one's gender beyond the male and female boxes, such as gender-fluid, transgender or nonbinary.

Gendered expectations continue as children age and enter adult roles. Entering middle or high school, boys who act feminine and girls who act masculine may be sanctioned for these breaches in gendered behavior (Pascoe 2007). In some cases, we

Photo 4.1 Symbolic interactionists study the subtle ways in which our statuses can affect others' judgments of our abilities. Have you ever had the sense that people were unfairly judging your ability to do a task?

Source: NT_Studio/Shutterstock

are consciously sanctioned by verbal reprimands (e.g., name calling) or threats. Martin Silverstein (2006) found that male prisoners were expected to accept responsibility for their actions, while female prisoners were encouraged to portray themselves as victims. Following these gender scripts increased the likelihood of parole for these prisoners. Here, subjects were punished (i.e., no parole) for not following traditional gender expectations.

Doing gender is a complex social process, involving subtle ways in which gender norms exist in the professional world and affect people's careers and career decisions (Fisk 2018; Fisk and Overton 2019; Freeland and Harnois 2020). Psychologist Madeline Heilman and her colleagues (2004) conducted a series of experiments to help elaborate gender processes in the work setting. They found that women who are high achievers in work groups tend to be less liked than their male counterparts. Moreover, this attitude only occurs when women achieve success in traditionally male work arenas. Other research shows women in leadership positions must deviate from gender norms more often than men in order to be an effective leader, but in doing so they are perceived more negatively (e.g., ruthless), putting women leaders in a bind in which they must choose between maintaining their authority at the potential cost of negative evaluations (Kroska and Cason 2019). These types of studies show that discrimination can occur in many ways (e.g., not being liked) and in specific contexts (i.e., male-dominated work arenas). Doing gender can occur in any environment, not just work. Buyukozturk (2022), for instance, studied gaming culture and found that women would more often put themselves in the margin of games while men more often took dominant roles.

Multiple Inequalities: "Doing Difference" and Intersectionality

The concept of doing gender is widely recognized in the field of sociological social psychology, and theorists and researchers have extended its principles to statuses other than gender (N. Jones 2009; Jurik and Siemsen 2009; West and Fenstermaker 1995). In some sense, some argue that we "do race" and "do class" just as we do gender. Everyday interactions help solidify the racial and class structures in which we live (Rawls and Duck 2020). Blacks, Whites, Latinos, and Asians sometimes live in separate areas of any given city or area. This segregation itself may set up different psychological worlds that foster racial stereotypes (Bonilla-Silva and Embrick 2007; see also Anderson 1999). These racialized living arrangements intersect with class because a higher percentage of African Americans and other minorities in the United States are living in poverty relative to their size in the population.

Ultimately, **doing difference** is any way in which inequality in any form (e.g., race, class, or gender) is perpetuated during interactions as people are held accountable to the social categories to which they are recognized as belonging to (West and Fenstermaker

Box 4.2 Stereotype Threat

Psychologist Claude Steele and his colleagues study the influences of gender and race on aptitude tests. They argue that all groups have some stereotypes attributed to them, although some have more negative consequences than others. Conservatives, for example, might be viewed as orderly and conventional, while liberals might be viewed as more creative and open-minded. In a similar way, African Americans may be stereotyped as less intelligent than others because of historical processes in the United States that disadvantaged African Americans, and gender stereotypes might lead women to be expected to underperform in math and sciences. "Stereotype threat" refers to negative emotions such as fear or anxiety that result when people believe they will be viewed in terms of negative stereotypes (Steele and Aronson 1995). In short, people feel they will be judged in terms of their group affiliation more than their individual abilities. From this perspective, individuals "feel" the impact of society based on the stereotypes associated with their group memberships. These fears and anxieties can inhibit performances of all types, including on standardized tests. Experiments have shown that stereotype threat significantly reduces test scores among African Americans and women when they fear that their performances might confirm negative stereotypes about their groups.

1995). As such, doing difference can be applied to the study of social categories other than race and gender. It can also be utilized to examine the intersection of these categories. For example, in her study of male clients of a southern California hair salon, Kristen Barber (2008) examined the subtle ways in which sexuality, gender, and class are maintained within day-to-day interactions in the salon. One way that male clients were able to maintain their masculinity in such a feminine environment, she found, was to use talk to distance themselves from more feminine places such as nail salons or day spas. They also redefined male-dominated barber shops as old and out of date for the modern man. In this case, the act of going to the salon was a form of doing difference because the clients viewed being "stylish" as the embodiment of the modern White, male professional. In this sense, the presentation of self (see Chapter 5) produced in the salon helped to provide clients the ability to reveal their class and other statuses to the world. In doing so, they distinguish themselves from White working-class men while maintaining their heterosexuality.

Some scholars are critical of the notion of "doing difference." Patricia Hill Collins (1995), for instance, argues that doing difference focuses too much on micro-level interactions and too little on interlocking systems of oppression such as capitalism, patriarchy, and racism, which structure class, gender, and race interactions. Collins proposed that we need the concepts of both "interlocking systems of oppression" at the macro-level and **intersectionality** at the micro-level to understand class, race, and gender inequalities. Collins (2019) points out that the concept of intersectionality, coined by Kimberlé Crenshaw (1991), has expanded to include a variety of contexts and is traditionally associated with social justice.

Collins's work shows how people's social locations of race, class, and gender cannot be considered in additive form, but rather examined in terms of their intersections. For example, people who are Black and female are not understood as having two statuses, but rather the intersecting status of being a Black woman, which is different from being a White woman, Arab American woman, or Black man, for example. Collins (1990) shows how being in this structural location is a unique form of oppression; Black women must contend with specific culturally dominant and controlling images of them, such as the matriarch or the mammy. However, Collins also points to the unique lenses and standpoints that Black women have, which provide insights into the power structure that other groups cannot see from their vantage points. She also focuses on how oppressed groups can and do resist domination by recreating positive identities and self-images and by being active in their communities.

Intersectionality theories and research show us how race, gender, sexual, religious, and other identities affect people's lives under different conditions or contexts (O'Brien 2017; Stasio and Larsen 2020; see also Choo and Ferree 2010). Catherine Turco (2010) studied the masculine culture of the leveraged buyout industry. She interviewed 117 African American female and male "tokens"—members representing a small minority in an organization—and found that token men were less disadvantaged in this industry than women. Turco argued that the masculine nature of the business made race less of an issue than gender, thereby protecting the male tokens from exclusion. In this case, being a minority woman led to significantly different outcomes than being a minority man. In another example, Jen'nan Ghazal Read and Sharon Oselin (2008) examined the intersection of ethnicity, gender, and class and found that many Arab American women have high levels of education but lower employment rates than other American women, suggesting potentially different meanings to work-family roles than other groups might have. Zelma Oyarvide Tuthill (2021) found direct negative effects of seeing race/ethnic or sexual identity as central to one's identity on mental health but "perceiving both identities to be central is associated with better mental health" (345), probably because the latter group had more involvement with the LGBTQ+ community which was positively associated with health and well-being.

In another example of research taking an intersectional approach, Long Doan and colleagues (Doan, Miller, and Loehr 2015) had participants read a vignette that described a couple engaged in various activities. By random assignment, participants were told that the couple in the vignette was either heterosexual, gay, or lesbian. The research found that participants rated the gay couple as less in love than the lesbian couple, which they rated as much in love as the heterosexual couple. The researchers proposed that this is because love tends to be seen as a feminine emotion. This finding was important because they also showed that participants' likelihood to support formal rights, such as the right to marry, for the couple in the vignette was related to how in love they thought the couple was. So, gay couples were penalized more than lesbian couples in terms of the rights participants thought they deserved. These various studies show that by only looking at race, gender, or sexuality the researchers would miss the unique intersection of these categories.

Rigging—and Fixing—the Game

Michael Schwalbe (2008) combines elements of the symbolic interaction approach to inequality with the conflict paradigm reviewed in Chapter 1 to understand how inequalities are created and maintained in society. He also suggests ways of reducing societal inequality. This theoretical work emphasizes the ways in which individuals participate in "rigging the game" of life such that some people can maintain high income levels even though most people want similar incomes and lifestyles. He argues that individuals with high status (including corporations, who are often treated as individuals in terms of legal protections under U.S. law) actively participate in the manipulation of both formal norms (i.e., laws) as well as informal norms found in everyday interactions that favor them—thus allowing them to accumulate capital at the expense of others.

One way that high-status individuals can rig the game is to manipulate who gets to play the game in the first place. Schwalbe (2008) uses the example of university entry requirements. Parents with abundant resources are likely to have done better in school—and those are the ones whose children end up going to the best schools and competing for the best jobs when they finish college. He says, "This isn't about raw intelligence. It's about growing up with books, living in a safe neighborhood, having enough to eat, and not having family life disrupted by economic emergencies" (Schwalbe, 2008, 76). The people who complete college end up being the ones who create the rules of the game—the rules of society regarding the distribution of its resources. People who have advantages then tend to make rules to help them maintain and accumulate those advantages (see also Merton 1968). They are also the ones who define whether the rules of the game are deemed fair or unfair.

There are several conditions that set the stage for advancement on the job market, and these link to high status. Good-looking people generally do better in life than less attractive people in just about every area of life including attaining higher incomes, getting better evaluations, and receiving lower interest rates on loans (Hamermesh 2011). To some degree, the wealthy have more control over their looks—they can afford to pay for the clothing, hairstyles, makeup, and so on, that are deemed attractive. Moreover, the hiring process involves not only choosing people based on their education and work experience but also "cultural matching" in which employers hire people who match their own lifestyles (e.g., leisure pursuits) which relate to gender and class backgrounds (Rivera 2012). Finally, lower income students are more likely than their upper income peers to have to work during the school year to help pay for the costs of college; often times, however, these jobs—unlike, for example professional internships—are not ones that provide students with access to certain occupational skills and social networks that will be useful to them after graduation (Struber 2011). It appears that in some ways the game is rigged at every level and time period of our lives.

If inequalities in society are, in part, a reflection of social interaction, how might we change this? Schwalbe (2008) proposes that we may be able to reduce inequalities in society using a critical mass in which individuals work together to change the way we think about the world, questioning authority and changing laws that favor elites (e.g., giving more power to unions). The first step is to recognize the ways in which the system is "rigged" in the first place. By doing these things, we can break down the socially constructed norms that keep social arrangements such that the rich maintain a disproportionate share of the wealth in society in unjust ways.

Box 4.3 Jobs in Inequality

Much of the theory and research examined in this chapter focuses on ways that inequalities are perpetuated in the workplace. There are also career paths for people who are actively trying to end inequalities in the workplace and society in general.

Here are some examples that can be found on job-seeking platforms such as Indeed and USAJOBS.gov. If interested, you should also consider looking at specific websites for large organizations. The first example is from a college in Oregon but there are thousands of similar schools that have positions similar to the one listed here.

1. **Equity, Diversity, and Inclusion Coordinator**, Rogue Community College (Oregon). Duties: Provides leadership and strategic direction in creating and sustaining a campus climate that is welcoming, inclusive, respectful, and free from

(continued)

bias and harassment. Creates a shared sense of responsibility across the campus community for promoting diversity, equity, inclusion, and belonging with the aim of positively impacting students, employees, and the overall campus climate. Qualifications: A bachelor's degree in higher education administration, student affairs, human resources, organizational development, law, public administration, social work, or related field, or an equivalent combination of education and related experience which meet the foregoing description of responsibilities, is required. A Juris Doctorate or master's degree is desirable.

2. **Investigator Support Assistant (OA)**, Office of Field Programs, Equal Employment Opportunity Commission. Duties: Handling routine inquiries from members of public, in writing and through face-to-face interaction, interviewing individuals who believe they have been discriminated against, counseling individuals on whether EEOC or some other organization has jurisdiction over their allegations. Qualifications: You must have at least one year of specialized experience equivalent to the GS-04 level in the federal service, or four (4) years of education above high school is fully qualifying in lieu of experience.

These positions are attainable with a degree in sociology or psychology, but they may require additional experience or education to be competitive. If something sparks an interest in you, you should move forward on your career at an early stage by investigating the types of internships you need or education you should pursue to attain these jobs.

Section Summary

This section applied symbolic interactionist principles to answer the question "How do people construct their lives in a stratified society?" We examined interactionist research on how individuals construct differences among people based on their positions in society, especially related to social class, gender, and race. Patterned inequalities shape who we interact with, the content of interactions based on the statuses of the interacting partners, and whose definitions of the situation become powerful. The idea that people "do gender" and "do difference" in interactions is the subject of some research in symbolic interactionism.

A Take-Away Message

We all participate in the stratification process. We reproduce our own statuses in our interactions with other people and contribute to the maintenance of other people's statuses. Research shows how status is more complex than one's race, class, or gender—that people are a mix of these statuses, yielding unique identities, something we address more in the next chapter. Professionally, you will be working with people of different statuses and should be aware of the subtle ways the status system is created and how it may affect your work environment. You should also consider if people of different backgrounds may be at an advantage or disadvantage in terms of whose definitions of the situation might prevail. You can help support people in these situations, helping other people recognize when some are not being treated fairly and supporting individuals who are not being treated well. If you are a manager, you can use this role to work toward an environment which limits the creation or maintenance of inequality—indeed that disrupts inequities through your actions.

STRUCTURES OF INEQUALITY

> *In my junior year of high school, one guy who was just average academically, was visiting prestigious universities like Harvard, Cornell, McGill, and the University of North Carolina. I thought he had no chance at those places, but it turns out he had connections! His dad and grandfather graduated from Harvard, and he had some relative who was an important alum at UNC. He and his family actually stayed overnight at the home of one of the admissions officers at Harvard. He got into both Harvard and UNC but not Cornell or McGill. I don't know the whole story, but this seemed like bias based on being wealthy and privileged. I could not believe it.*
>
> —Paul, senior criminology major

The symbolic interaction perspective on stratification and inequalities represents one approach to social stratification processes in social psychology. A more structural perspective takes hierarchy as a "given" and "seeks to understand the processes by which individuals become distributed in that hierarchy" (Kerckhoff 1995, p. 476). In industrialized nations, people's statuses derive from their social class positions, among other things. **Social class** refers to a group of people who share the same relative status and resources in a given society. Class position is linked to racial and ethnic status, with African Americans and Latinos in the United States, for example, disproportionately living in poverty (see Figure 4.1).

The effects of relationships on life trajectories are significant. Our relationships with family members provide varying levels of tangible resources, such as money to pay for education. They also provide social and cultural resources, such as knowledge about different career choices as well as connections with people who may be able to provide that knowledge, or perhaps even access to specific jobs. The expression "It's not what you know but who you know" applies here. A structuralist perspective on mobility processes tries to explain how inequality is passed from generation to generation and how it is maintained within the same generation. Children typically go on to attain economic statuses similar to those of the persons closest to them as they were growing up.

Micro-Foundations of Social Mobility

Socioeconomic status (SES) refers to our social and economic statuses—how much money and education we have as well as our occupational standing. The components of SES are usually highly correlated; people with high-status occupations, such as doctors

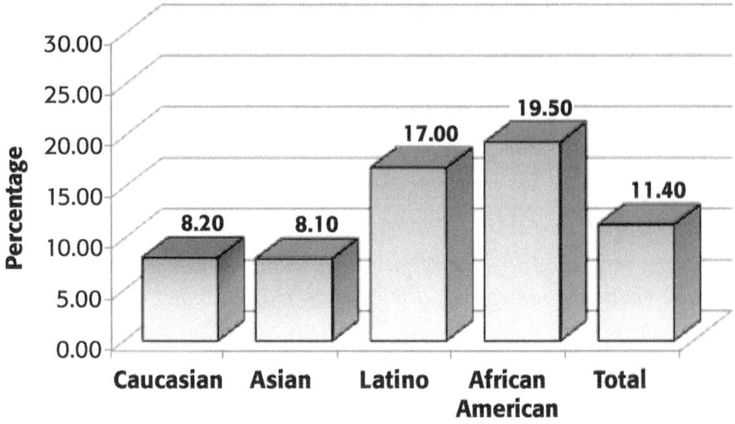

Figure 4.1 The Interaction of Race and Poverty in the United States.

Source: 2020 Current Population Survey.

and lawyers, usually have high levels of income and education. But some occupations are higher in some elements of SES than others. School teachers in the United States, for example, typically have relatively high levels of education but their prestige and income does not necessarily match their achievements in the university system. **Social mobility** refers to upward or downward change in SES over time. Much research in social mobility examines relative income and prestige associated with different occupations. People in more prestigious jobs tend to make more money. Because many people are motivated to obtain these prestigious positions (for the money or the prestige or the working conditions), a reasonable question is "Why do some people achieve these positions while others do not?" Sociologists look to family status and experience as primary sources of status development and maintenance. That is, our parents represent the primary means of status development. In fact, research in the 1960s showed a considerable overlap in fathers' and sons' occupations (Blau and Duncan 1967).

The Wisconsin model of status attainment (see Figure 4.2) is one of the few large-scale, longitudinal studies that attempts to explain the social mobility processes. The project is based on a study that began in 1957 among a group of researchers from

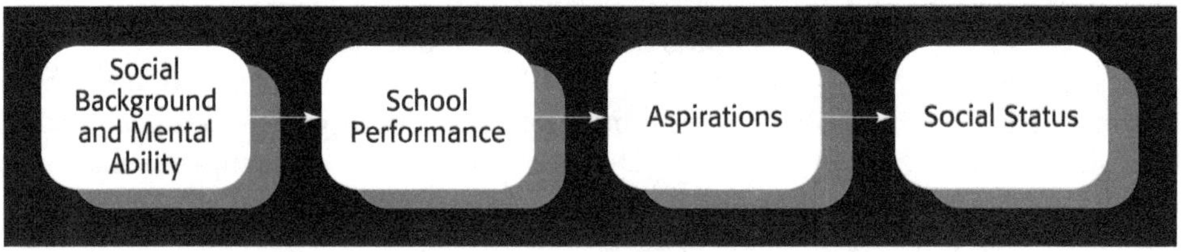

Figure 4.2 The Wisconsin model of status attainment.

Source: Based on Sewell et al. (2004).

the University of Wisconsin, primarily led by William Sewell (Sewell et al. 2004). They conducted a survey of high school seniors in the state of Wisconsin to assess students' educational plans and future aspirations. A third of these students were selected to participate in a follow-up study. In addition, parents of students were surveyed on a range of topics, including youth aspirations, social influences, and schooling. Sewell and his colleagues were also able to obtain cognitive test scores for a significant portion of the respondents.

Findings over decades of research show that parents' social class background influences early language and styles of interaction, as well as expectations and aspirations about the future, which go on to affect educational and occupational goals, as well as performance in school (see Milkie, Warner, and Ray 2014; Mortimer et al. 2017).

Initial class background can be understood as having a snowball effect: children with lower SES have fewer tangible and subtle resources such as books, art, extracurriculars, and expansive language and ways of interacting with adults. These children, like those discussed above in Heath's ethnography, tend to do worse in school than their middle and upper-class counterparts. We will discuss the resources of linguistic and cultural capital, which vary greatly across class, in the chapter on socialization. Across their years in the system, children are often tracked into groups of "achievers" who are encouraged to develop their cognitive and educational skills, in contrast to "average" students who may be viewed as less capable and as biding their time until graduation. Initial track placements, as early as first grade, are highly correlated with social class standings of children (Condron 2009) and have tremendous predictive power for young adult outcomes (Alexander, Entwisle, and Horsey 1987). Ultimately, "good" students go on to achieve higher levels of education which translates into attaining jobs with higher salaries.

Individuals do have agency in this process, but our choices are made in the context of our social conditions. In a Swedish study of university applications, for instance, Martin Hallsten (2010) found that people from different class backgrounds preferred different types of university programs. Specifically, individuals from the working class tended to choose programs of shorter duration and with lower grade point requirements located closer to home compared to middle-income students who were more likely to choose more challenging programs. The result of these choices is to perpetuate class differences among working- and middle-class students. Similar dynamics may help explain why men make more money than women, because women on average choose programs of study that yield lower incomes than men (Charles and Bradley 2009; see also Correll 2004). However, choices are determined within a culture with strong pressures on women about what is morally right for them as adults: women bear heavy weight to be responsible for their future home and family lives and may track into occupations that seem to allow for better balance between these spheres (Blair-Loy 2009).

Another potential cause of status attainment is genetic transmission of abilities from biological parents. In one study, François Nielson (2006) analyzed genetic and familial data from two waves of a longitudinal study of adolescents from grades 7 to 12. He compared verbal IQ scores, grade point averages (GPAs), and college plans among monozygotic (MZ; identical) twins, dizygotic (DZ; fraternal) twins, full siblings, cousins, and nonrelated children. Heritability in this sort of study is measured by the degree of shared genetic material, represented on one extreme by MZ twins (who share 100% of the same genetic material) while nonrelated children living together share only similar family upbringing. Thus, if we pass on our social status only through wealth and social standing through our family ties, the effects of genes should be limited. Nielson found that genetic predictors of verbal IQ, GPA, and college plans had stronger effects than shared family environments.

Do these findings mean that we people have little or no control over their social standing? Before you answer, consider these issues. The previously cited study also found that other "unshared influences" (e.g., peers) had strong effects on verbal IQ, GPA, and college plans. What other unshared influences could have been left out? Allan Horwitz and his colleagues (2003) argue that twin studies overstate genetic influences on behavior because MZ twins compared to DZ twins and other siblings share the social environment to a much greater extent. Because these aspects of the social environment are rarely measured and examined, what is assumed to be genetic influence may really be social influences for which studies don't account. In other words, MZ twins are more genetically alike *and* more socially alike than any other siblings, but their greater "social alikeness" is ignored in research. Horwitz and his colleagues found that MZ twins share socially based characteristics, such as time spent together, friendship networks, and physical attractiveness, more so than even DZ twins. Other studies show that genetic heritability of status can vary by cohort (i.e., younger cohorts show greater genetic heritability than older ones) and demographic groups (e.g., Whites vs. African Americans and males vs. females) (Heath et al. 1985; Guo and Stearns 2002), suggesting great complexity in assessing genetic links to social outcomes. Further, people least likely to obtain a college degree—those from lower SES backgrounds—benefit more from obtaining a college degree than people who traditionally go to college, suggesting the importance of more schooling, no matter how much genetic disposition does or does not matter (Brand and Xie 2010). Finally, to demonstrate non-genetic transmission of educational attainment, Mortimer and colleagues (2017) demonstrate that families create an academic culture, one that emphasizes education and instills academic confidence, and that culture carries across multiple generations.

Networks and Social Capital

Stratification processes begin with families' economic backgrounds and neighborhood locations, but they also exist in our relationships with other people. Friends, family, and organizations of which we are a part provide access to a wide variety of social networks. Our friends link us to their friends and to organizations and groups with which they associate. Social networks act as conduits between different people, providing resources and information that may not be readily available from the people with whom we have direct contact. Organizations provide a bridge between strangers, a way of giving people a sense that the other can be trusted in some way.

We often think of collateral in economic terms, but it can also exist in relationships. We trust people because we know them well enough to share important things with them, perhaps even money. Social networks (see Chapter 2) serve as the basis for the exchange of both fiscal and **social capital**, the trust and social support found in relationships with other people (Coleman 1988; Putnam 2000). The number and types of people to whom we have determines the availability of social capital. Not only do we turn to people for emotional support, something that will be discussed in more detail in Chapter 8, but we also turn to others for advice and help in pursuing our goals. Our networks determine the amount and types of social capital available to us.

The effects of networking between individuals from different groups create a variety of outcomes for individuals, depending on the status of the individuals in a group as well as the status of the group itself. A group of neighbors at a local pub is likely to have less clout in the larger world than a group of senior business executives. Thus, having access to the relationships in the latter group will likely provide different resources, including things such as money, useful knowledge about how to find good jobs and investments, and access to better medical services.

The Strength of Weak Ties

A typical way that relationships are important to us is in finding work. A Harvard accounting student probably has access to people with more powerful positions than an accounting student at a community college. The job outcomes of these students are probably going to be related to the information available within their respective networks. The Harvard network is likely to provide information about and access to higher-level accounting jobs than the community-college network. In this way, our social class position is intimately tied to social networks, affecting our ability to succeed in society.

Two ways by which people are connected to each other are strong and weak ties. **Strong ties** refer to people with whom we are close, such as friends and family. **Weak ties** refer to people we do not know as well, such as acquaintances or more distant friends. We can further contrast both of these types of ties with more formal relationships in which people are connected via structured positions in organizations. Mark Granovetter (1973), in the original theoretical discussion of weak ties, said that "those to whom we are weakly tied are more likely to move in circles different from our own and will thus have access to information different from that which we receive" (Granovetter 1973, p. 1371). For job seekers, the quantity of ties is typically more important to finding work than the quality of those ties. Granovetter's research supported the contention that weak ties are more important than strong ties for finding work. He reports that of people who find work through contacts, 84% reported seeing those contacts only rarely or occasionally.

Granovetter's (1995) subsequent work combines ideas about both strong and weak ties in assessing job-searching strategies. He found that 56% of the professional, technical, and managerial workers experiencing job transitions in New England reported finding work via **personal ties** (both strong and weak), followed by 19% who found jobs through formal means (e.g., ads or employment agencies), 19% through direct applications, and the rest via miscellaneous other methods. Personal ties not only produce jobs but also are associated with finding better jobs: workers who found jobs via networks (personal ties) were more satisfied with their work and reported higher incomes than those who found work through other means. These findings are supported by more recent research showing that personal ties can increase job pay as well as job quality (Gerber and Mayorova 2010; Kmec and Trimble 2009). This sociological work underscores the adage that who you know might be as (or more!) important as what you know.

Gender, Race, and Network Processes

Levels and types of social capital vary, and thus effects of networks on occupational outcomes can vary as well. Immigrants and other groups with high levels of mobility may have limited access to social capital because they are not in one place long enough to establish strong social networks (Ream 2005). Poor people may have strong social ties that help them through their economic circumstances, but the ties may also limit their upward mobility because the networks are horizontal in nature, connecting people to jobs within their social classes. The effects of social statuses such as gender on long-term economic outcomes are both profound and widespread (Epstein 2007). Women and racialized minorities in the United States continue to make less money than men and Whites, even within the same job categories. Part of the gender differences in income can be explained by the fact that although the influence of education and ability on salary is similar for men and women, women tend to start their careers in occupations that pay less than men (Warren, Hauser, and Sheridan 2002). Similar patterns exist for racialized groups in the United States because minorities are on average less likely to be in high-paying professional jobs, such as doctors and lawyers, as compared to Whites (see Figure 4.3). Yet even within the same occupations, minorities and women make less money, in part based on discrimination (e.g., Blau and Kahn 2000; Correll 2004; Dodoo and Takyi 2002; Grodsky and Pager 2001; Padavic and Reskin 2002; Stewart and Dixon 2010).

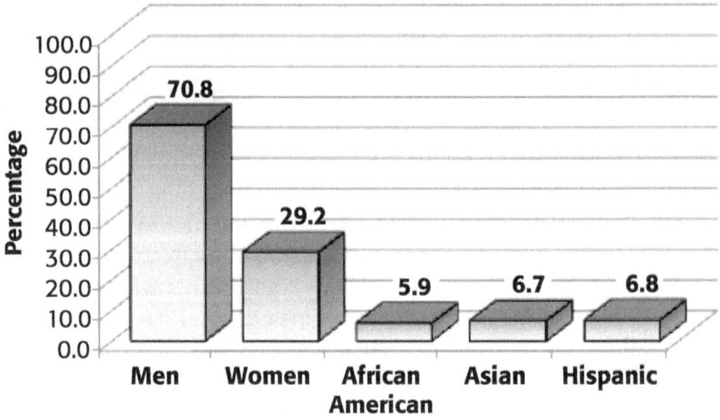

Figure 4.3 Percentage of Chief Executives in the United States by Gender and Race.

Source: 2022 Bureau of Labor Statistics.

How can we use social psychology to help reduce inequalities? Having a more diverse workforce may help. A more diverse workforce helps to sustain future diversity, in part, through network processes reviewed earlier in this chapter, by increasing access to weak ties and thus ideas and resources found therein (Fernandez and Fernandez-Mateo 2006). Increasing the number of women and ethnic minority leaders on the job may also help. In one study, researchers found that a greater ratio of female managers on the job reduced gender wage inequality (Cohen and Huffman 2007). Women (and racialized minority) managers provide role models for lower-ranking employees, but they also provide social-networking opportunities for them to gain access to similar positions. Government programs can also help build social capital among people by providing venues to bridge them with those outside of their own social classes, such as in mentoring or job-tutoring programs (Strathdee 2005). Finally, restructuring organizations in ways that encourage the development of ties among people from diverse backgrounds may help to discourage discrimination and build social capital on the job (Briscoe and Kellogg 2011; Kalev 2009).

Social Status and Personality

Can our jobs change our personalities? According to the social structure and personality perspective, job conditions influence the development of senses of self, values, and beliefs. When you consider the fact that many people in the Western world spend a third of their day on the job and that we develop our senses of self from interactions with other people, job conditions are bound to impact us in some way—but how?

An influential set of studies from the social structure and personality perspective were completed by Melvin Kohn and Carmi Schooler (1983). They carried out a research project to study the long-term consequences of social class positions on values. The researchers wanted to know how class positions interact with cognitive abilities in maintaining class positions in the form of people's "ultimate" occupations. They argued that there is an ongoing **feedback loop** in which class positions influence the development of values, which in turn influences the types of jobs for which people look (Schooler, Mulatu, and Oates 2004). The types of jobs people get then influence the types of people they are—their personalities. People then continue to seek jobs over their life courses that match the kinds of values they have.

Consider a situation in which a person is working at a factory every day, putting furniture hardware into bags and counting the pieces before sealing each bag. She is required to seal a certain number of bags for at least eight hours a day. The job is repetitive and requires little creativity or cognitive ability. This type of job does not provide the skills necessary to find more complex work. She will not easily be able to use the job on a résumé designed to find work in the marketing industry, for instance. Kohn and Schooler (1983) argued that the types of jobs we get influence the development of our personalities. Our personalities, in turn, influence the types of jobs that we get in the future. A repetitive job may affect our abilities to analyze things in complex ways. This personality attribute might make it difficult to engage in higher-status work because those jobs often require greater cognitive complexity (e.g., management work in which multiple people must be organized to achieve organizational goals).

Kohn and Schooler's project started in 1964 with a survey of 3,101 working men from around the United States. Another survey was conducted in 1974 with a sample of the original men—687 respondents—for a second wave of interviews. Wives of the initial respondents were also interviewed, creating an additional 269 participants. Finally, between 1994 and 1995, the researchers interviewed as many of the men and women from the 1974 sample as possible, focusing on those people who were still employed. The final sample included 166 men and 78 women—a total of 244 respondents (Schooler, Mulatu, and Oates 2004).

The initial study of occupational attitudes and values focused on three elements of jobs predicted to affect the development of personal values. Kohn and Schooler (1983) showed that the following aspects of jobs can have long-term effects on the development of values:

1. The closeness of the supervision.
2. The routinization of the work.
3. The substantive complexity of the work.

Closeness of supervision refers to the level of control supervisors have over workers. It is measured simply by asking each respondent how much freedom they have to disagree with their boss, their supervisor's style of assigning tasks, and the importance of doing what they are told. **Routinization** of work refers to the level of repetitiveness found on the job, generally measured in terms of workers' ratings of how predictable their work tasks are. Finally, **substantive complexity** refers to how complicated the actual work is. Complexity is measured in terms of how often people work with people, data, or information, as well as the complexity of work required when working with people or data.

Kohn and Schooler wanted to know how these work conditions influenced individuals' personalities and vice versa. They studied personality in terms of **intellectual flexibility**, how flexible people are in handling complex situations; and **self-directed orientation**, measured in terms of individuals' level of conservatism, fatalism (the belief that life is controlled by fate), and personally responsible morality (how much we hold ourselves accountable for the things we do). The researchers examined these personality characteristics in the context of social and economic characteristics, including gender, race, and education levels.

Take a moment to think about the long-term effects of valuing obedience to authority and routinization. What kinds of jobs are characterized by routinization? They are not likely to be management jobs that are based on making decisions rather than following orders. Supervisors at a fast-food restaurant, for example, must be ready to be flexible on the job as they manage disputes among workers and between employees and customers. Routinized jobs are those that require consistent service or manufacturing products where each step is calculated in advance, such as cooking hamburger patties on the grill. These jobs are often some of the lowest-paying jobs. If we engage in this kind of work, we may develop personality characteristics that suit these conditions. Our personalities (e.g., our level of flexibility and self-directedness), then, may lead us to jobs with lower status; for example, if we value obedience, we might be more likely

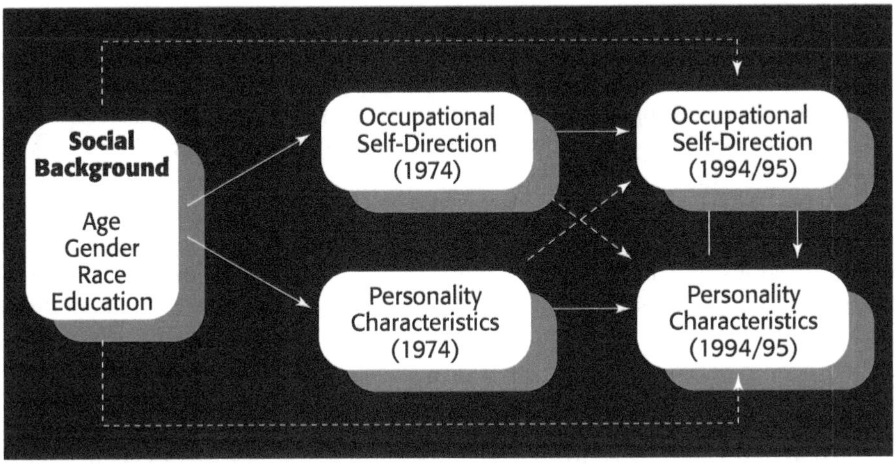

Figure 4.4 Kohn and Schooler Model of Status Attainment.

Source: Adapted from Schooler et al. (2004).

to fit with lower-status jobs. The relationships between socioeconomic background and long-term occupational and personality outcomes are illustrated in Figure 4.4. Schooler and his colleagues (Schooler et al. 2004; Kohn 2005) found that our social and economic backgrounds determine the types of jobs we get early in our lives. People with fewer resources early in life tend to find jobs with low levels of substantive complexity and high levels of supervision. These jobs, in turn, affect our personalities in ways that conform to the types of jobs we are in. People in low-end jobs tend to develop personalities with lower amounts of intellectual flexibility and have a less self-directed orientation. In turn, people with lower levels of flexibility and self-direction go on to other jobs with less complexity and more supervision. The researchers also found that this feedback loop continues into late life.

The Kohn and Schooler studies show that society can structure people's development in a way that maintains their class positions. In other research, for instance, Schooler (1976) used survey data of European immigrants to the United States, assessing personality characteristics and occupational outcomes. He found that men from ethnic groups with a history of serfdom showed personality characteristics associated with the American working class: intellectual inflexibility, authoritarianism, and pragmatic legalistic morality. Hence, the system of serfdom prevalent in Europe was transferred to the United States through immigration. This work also implies that economic conditions can affect the development of individuals, above and beyond abilities, and that the effects of class may "transfer to" different cultural environments.

More recent research shows other ways job conditions can affect our personalities and lifestyles. One study showed that low levels of control over work hours is associated with lower levels of job satisfaction and organizational commitment, and also that lower-status workers have less control over their work schedules than middle- and upper-status workers (Lyness et al., 2012). A working environment that stresses intrinsic work values such as responsibility, use of skills, and learning reinforce individuals' valuing those things on the job; individuals emphasize extrinsic work values when their jobs show improvements in extrinsic rewards such as pay, job security, and advancement opportunities, suggesting that work conditions reinforce and accentuate work values (Kirkpatrick, Sage, and Mortimer 2012). Given the amount of time adults spend working, it should be no surprise that work conditions shape our values and beliefs. The studies in the social structure and personality perspective discussed above help elaborate the processes by which work conditions affect our lives.

Section Summary

This section of the chapter addressed the question "How does social structure contribute to the development of inequalities in people's experiences?" Here we reviewed two models connecting our class backgrounds with future life goals and outcomes. The Wisconsin model of status attainment ties together the relative impact of social background characteristics and ability on long-term status attainment, while the Kohn and Schooler model addresses the reciprocal relationships between work conditions and personal values in the types of work we obtain through life. We also reviewed the roles of social networks and genetics in stratification processes.

A Take-Away Message

The most important take-away message from this section is to stay in school and get as much education as you can! This advice is even more important for those of you who are the first in your family to go to college. The challenges of staying in school may be greater for you, but you will gain more benefits for your work, and your decision will likely affect future generations. Professionally, you should consider both the networks and the cultural capital that will allow you to obtain the "right" job and the type of industry you are entering after leaving college: will the organizational environment be one that will encourage the development of talents and skills? How might it change your values or personality?

STRATIFICATION PROCESSES IN GROUPS

> *I really don't mind being one of the only people in my class to raise my hand and talk. I know that other students may think that I am a "suck up," but I don't care. I am here to learn, and class goes by really slowly if you do not say anything. And even though they might mock me, other students always turn to me for notes and help in the class. I guess you could say that I am a class leader of sorts.*
>
> —Sandy, freshman business major

Sandy's story is typical of the dynamics in many university classrooms. She participates in class by asking questions and engaging in discussions. The results are both positive and negative. Her participation increases her enjoyment of and learning in the class. However, it may also cause some friction with students who participate less. In the end, she believes that she is seen as a leader because of what she contributes to the class.

According to symbolic interactionists, social structure is manifest in relationships between people. Individuals in groups clearly share thoughts and feelings with one another during their interactions. However, group members do not necessarily enter groups with the same opportunities as the rest of the members. Some people bring more to the table—or the classroom—than others.

The group processes tradition contributes to our understanding of structural developments by studying the exchanges between individuals in groups (Smith-Lovin and Molm 2000). Social exchange theory is based in the group processes perspective. It provides a template for understanding individual motivations to participate in and contribute to group interactions, whereas expectation states and status characteristics theories show how broad cultural expectations for different groups can influence those dynamics. First, we will review some basic theory and research on group processes, followed by a review of theory on status processes in groups.

Status and Power in Social Exchange Processes

Social exchange theory is based on the premise that individuals enter into relationships that provide some benefit to them and end or leave relationships that do not provide rewards, or at least not rewards to offset any costs of group membership. Molm and Cook (1995) present four core assumptions of exchange theory:

1. Exchange relationships develop within groups in which members have some degree of dependence among them.
2. Group members will act in groups in ways that maximize personal benefit.
3. Interaction in groups will continue as long as reciprocity between individuals continues.
4. Groups operate on the satiation principle, that the value of what is exchanged will diminish after a period of exchange.

If you think about some groups to which you belong, this theory probably makes some sense. Essentially, it proposes that we enter and maintain relationships that give us something. We exchange our labor for money, for example. Many of our relationships fit the simple kind of exchange found in secondary groups, people with whom we share fewer intimate relationships than we do with close friends or family.

Applying exchange theory to primary groups, those people with whom we have an emotional connection, is more challenging. What do you exchange with friends and family? Although people exchange tangible objects such as money or goods, they can also exchange things such as emotional and instrumental support (Liebler and Sandefur 2002; Shornack 1986). You help your friend or neighbor paint her house, assuming that she will help you with some other project in the future. You may also engage in a

Box 4.4 Homans's Experience on a Small Warship

George Homans (1910–1989) was one of the first sociologists to extensively develop and test exchange theory. During World War II, Homans captained small ships designed to destroy enemy submarines. Homans applied his sociological knowledge to understand social relations on ships in the article, "The Small Warship." He argued that his influence as captain depended in part on reciprocity, a series of exchanges with the crew. Although the captain had legitimate authority on the ship, he could not maintain that authority if he did not give something back to his men. There needed to be some form of reciprocity among and within ranks. In exchange for their support, he had to show his men that he cared for them by listening to them without interruption, helping them receive citations and promotions, and protecting them from unnecessary irritations, "even if it meant protecting them from the Navy itself" (Homans 1946, p. 297). Hence, the ship served as a microcosm of the larger society in which a series of informal reciprocal exchanges served to maintain roles inside the ship.

relationship with someone because that person "makes you feel good." These thoughts and feelings may not be tangible, but they provide some basis for staying in the relationship. You may end your relationship with a friend if he continually refuses to help you when you need it. Similarly, you may end your relationship with a partner if the interest, warmth, and intimacy you feel from them begins to fade.

Most of our discussion of exchanges has focused on **direct exchanges**, which are exchanges between two people. But exchanges can occur with multiple people, as well as between groups (see Box 4.2). **Indirect or generalized exchanges** occur when people do not receive benefits directly from those to whom they give benefits (Emerson 1992; Molm and Cook 1995; Simpson et al. 2018; Whitham 2021) (see Figure 4.5). Indirect exchanges may explain situations in which people enter relationships that are not directly rewarding to them. Suppose, for example, that you are driving on a highway and see a disabled car on the side of the road. Further suppose that you stop to help the person who has broken down. You might enter the situation as one of direct exchange; in other words, you help the person in expectation of some reward, perhaps gratitude. However, you would be more likely view the situation (although perhaps not consciously) as one of generalized exchange. From an exchange theory perspective, you might stop to help someone whose car has broken down because you hope that someone else would do the same thing for you. And someone very well may, in the future. Similarly, exchanges in families may include a series of direct and indirect exchanges of love, help, and money with extended family over time (Peterson 1993).

The structure and nature of exchange is essential to the development of relationships (see Chapter 10 for a review of exchange theory and relationships). That is, different types of exchanges can lead to varying levels of trust and solidarity (Lawler, Thye, and Yoon 2008; Molm 2010; Molm, Melamed, and Whitman 2013; Schilke and Rossman 2018). Consider a time when you helped someone out without expecting anything in

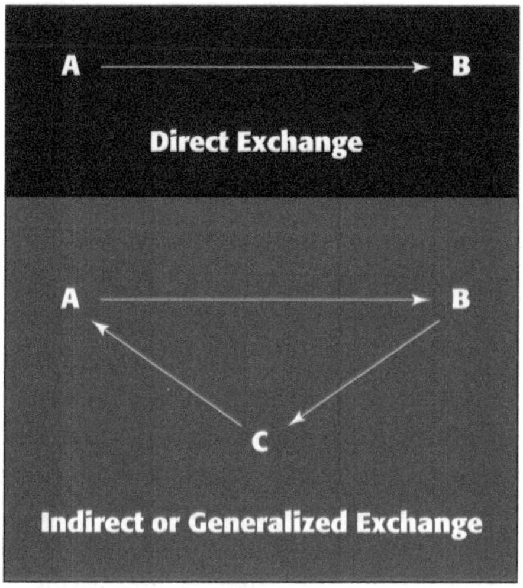

Figure 4.5 Direct and Indirect Exchanges.

return. Those types of exchanges rely on trust that you will get something in return in the future—either directly or indirectly. In either case, such experiences help us to learn to trust other people; we can continue to make exchanges with other people without confirmation that we will get something in return.

Status in Groups

Early work in social exchange theory focused on the direct exchanges between individuals and groups but generally did not account for social structure. Later work by Peter Blau (1964) and other sociologists began to examine exchange processes in the context of larger structural conditions. The development of status in groups provides a venue for understanding how macro-structural conditions can influence micro-level interactions. Exchange processes lend themselves to the development of status structures because people bring different types and quantities of resources into the process. In addition, some individuals contribute more to interactions than others. People who are *expected* to contribute more to a group or have more resources achieve higher status in groups. In a classic series of group studies, Robert Bales and his colleagues (Bales 1965; Borgatta and Bales 1953; Borgatta, Bales, and Couch 1954) analyzed interactions between groups of strangers brought together to perform a task. They found that high status was attributed to those individuals expected to make the most competent contributions.

The development of status in groups may simply reflect what people bring into a group. A gifted leader may take control because she has more ability than other people. Because gifted leaders give more to the group, we concede higher positions to them. However, research finds that differences in social expectations attached to characteristics such as race, gender, and age get imported into group interactions and reinforced by the actions of group members. Status characteristics theory (which is one theory in a broader program called expectation states theories) explains the processes by which groups set up and maintain status hierarchies.

Status Characteristics Theory

Status characteristics theory links social roles and expectations from a larger society to stratification processes in groups. The theory was developed by Joseph Berger and a group of colleagues at Stanford University (e.g., Berger, Cohen, and Zelditch 1966, Berger, Cohen, Zelditch, 1972; Berger et al. 1993; Fisek, Berger, and Norman 2005; Webster and Walker 2022) and is perhaps the most widely studied and well-supported theory in the group processes tradition. Status characteristics theory is concerned with stratification processes in certain types of groups—groups collectively oriented toward some task outcome. If a group is formed to complete some task and the members of the group work together toward the task's completion, then status characteristics theory makes predictions about how members of the group will become stratified. Groups in all sorts of settings meet these basic conditions. A jury is one example of a collectively oriented task group: members come together to solve a task (i.e., reach a verdict or other decision), and everyone contributes to completing the task. Another example could be a committee of citizens from a community getting together to decide how to deal with a civic problem. A collectively oriented task group could also be a committee within an organization formed to decide who to hire for a particular job. For all groups that meet the theory's basic conditions (that the group is working together toward a goal and that everyone in the group is expected to contribute), status characteristics theory has proven to be remarkably capable of explaining the methods that group members will use to stratify themselves.

A common finding in research on task groups is that these groups tend to organize themselves into hierarchies (Berger, Wagner, and Zelditch 1985). Some people in the groups talk more, get more positive feedback for their performances, and have more influence over the group than do other members. This has been a consistent research finding dating back to the 1950s. Even when it does not appear as though some group members are more competent than others, hierarchies form when groups complete a task. Researchers call these **status hierarchies**. In the group processes perspective, *status* refers to a position in a group based on the esteem or respect in which a person is held. People higher in the status hierarchy of the group talk more, get asked for their opinions more often, have their contributions evaluated more highly even when the contributions are no better than those of other group members, and have more influence over group decisions.

One interesting thing about status hierarchies is that group members generally agree (through their behaviors if not through spoken agreement) about the status order of the group (Wagner and Berger 1993). From this discussion, it is clear that high-status group members get benefits that low-status group members do not. In fact, research finds that high-status group members experience more positive emotion in group interactions than low-status members (Lovaglia and Houser 1996). However, status hierarchies in groups usually form almost instantaneously; it is not as though members openly

Photo 4.2 Sociological social psychologists study the ways that social statuses such as race and class intersect with group processes to produce differing levels of power and prestige among members. Have you ever led a work group, one assigned to complete a task at work or school? Do you think your social status influenced others' reactions to you in that group?

Source: Jacob Lund/Shutterstock

compete for positions in the hierarchy. How do group members decide who gets to be high status in the group and who is low status? Why do group members, even those in low-status positions, tend to go along with the inequalities that come from the status hierarchy? Status characteristics theory provides answers to these questions.

According to status characteristics theory, cultural expectations are associated with characteristics that people bring with them to group interactions. The theory specifies two types of status characteristics. **Diffuse status characteristics** are characteristics that carry with them social expectations for performances in diverse situations. Gender, race, and education level are examples of diffuse status characteristics in the United States. Our culture, for example, continues to hold norms expecting more competent contributions from men than from women on numerous tasks. From leading groups to fixing cars to solving complex problems, our culture still grants higher performance expectations to men than to women. It doesn't matter that there is no evidence that men are better at these tasks than women (evidence, in fact, overwhelmingly indicates that there are few tasks at which we should expect either men or women to be inherently better)—we operate in a cultural context that gives higher status to men than to women. Similar dynamics play out with racialized or ethnic groups. In a study involving

Hungarian students, for example, students identified as Roma were perceived as less able than similar Hungarian students (Grow, Takács, and Pal 2016). Another study showed that a similar process operates for mental illness. Lucas and Phelan (2012) found that persons with mental illness labels had less influence on a group task that involved a general performance ability than did others. These findings are profound because a diffuse status characteristic can affect evaluations across our social, personal, and professional lives. Even a status of "being popular" can impact people's evaluation of your work (Lynn, Walker, and Peterson 2016)! **Specific status characteristics** are characteristics that create expectations for performance in limited settings. Skill at basketball is an example of a specific status characteristic. If we know that someone is an excellent basketball player, we would pick them first when forming a basketball team, but we would likely draw few conclusions about their ability to lead groups, fix cars, or solve complex problems.

According to status characteristics theory, and supported by voluminous research, status hierarchies in task groups form largely based on the status characteristics of the members of the group (Carli 1991; Kalkhoff et al. 2020; Lucas 2003; Pugh and Wahrman 1983; Ridgeway and Diekema 1989; Webster and Driskell 1978). The theory proposes that when groups form, members look to the status characteristics of themselves and other group members to develop expectations for performance. According to theory, individuals will use any status characteristics in developing expectations that differentiate members of the group (e.g., gender in a mixed-sex group) and that have not been proven to be irrelevant to the group's task. In other words, if gender is a status characteristic and a group is differentiated on gender, the theory proposes that group members will develop different performance expectations for men and women even if there is no reason to think that gender is associated with ability at the group's task. The expectations that group members develop are typically consistent with those of the larger society. This finding explains why there is little conflict about status orders in task groups: because everyone in the group operates within the same larger society, everyone brings with them the same cultural expectations to the group. So, for example, if an engineer and a janitor are working together in a group to solve some task, both members would share the expectations that give engineers higher status than janitors. Thus, both members would agree that the engineer should have a higher position in the group's status order than should the janitor.

You might be recalling task groups you have worked in and think, "Wait a second. I have never talked with people in a group about who should have the highest position in the group's status hierarchy. And, I have never thought, 'That person should be high status because he is a White man.'" It is true that people usually don't come to verbal agreements about the status orders of groups. It is also true that people don't consciously give higher status or accept lower status based on things such as race, gender, education, and occupation (Webster and Foschi 1988). These processes occur in large part outside the conscious awareness of people. That fact makes these status hierarchies even more stable and difficult to change. If you ask people in a group why the White man in the group talked more than anyone else and had the most influence, the answer you get will usually not be "Because he is a White man." Instead, group members will say it was because he seemed the most competent person for the task. But, research shows that cultural expectations significantly affect our decisions about who seems the most competent, with people who possess certain, more highly valued status characteristics seeming more competent, even when they are not (Berger, Rosenholtz, and Zelditch 1980; Melamed; Okuwobi, and Barry 2023). Also, people are expected to act in ways consistent with their status positions in groups, and they face sanctions from the group when their behaviors violate their positions in the status order (Youngreen and Moore 2008). It is also true that status—any status—can spread from one person to another. Jon Overton (2021) completed two online studies using the Amazon Mechanical Turk (mTurk) crowdsourcing platform. Individuals were assigned varying levels of status while completing a task, measuring how often individuals deferred to their partners in the task. Not only did the study show that high status people deferred less than low status ones, it also showed that "participants deferred more to partners who had worked with high-status rather than low-status" partners from a previous task (Overton 2021, 319). These findings may explain why people "name drop" to raise their status during interactions and reflects the expression that we are "known by the company we keep."

You also might recall groups you have been in that did not follow these conventions. For example, you may have been in a group in which a woman was the most active member of the group. There are three things that you should keep in mind. First, remember that the theory applies to particular types of groups—groups formed to complete a task with everyone in the group contributing to the task outcome. Social groups can often form without developing the types of status hierarchies that are found when groups are working to complete a task.

Second, we noted that status hierarchies in task groups, once they form, are resistant to change. They can, however, change over time. If a woman or minority group member is the most competent person in a task group, that person may very well become the highest-status person in the group. However, the person will likely have to work harder than majority group members to attain a high-status position. In the case of gender, a great deal of evidence indicates that women are held to higher performance standards than are men. Research in double-standards theory (e.g., Foschi 1996; Foschi 2000) has found that people evaluate contributions from women and men differently, with women having to perform better to get the same evaluations as men. Thus, members of disadvantaged groups have to work harder and perform better to get the same status in groups as members of advantaged groups.

Third, we form impressions of other people based on multiple characteristics. So if a woman is higher in status than a man with respect to characteristics other than gender (e.g., age, race, education, or task expertise), we would expect she would have a higher position than him in the group's status hierarchy. In general, status characteristics theory proposes that we act as though (remember: these processes often happen outside people's conscious awareness) we combine the expectations associated with all of a group member's characteristics. You can think of it as group members developing overall expectation scores for themselves and others. Because all group members draw their expectations from the same larger culture, the theory posits that everyone in the group will produce the same overall expectation scores for each member. Members with higher overall expectation scores will then have higher positions in the group's status hierarchy. We would expect these members to talk more in the group, be evaluated more highly, and have more influence in the group.

Importantly, status characteristics theory does not propose that any attributes act as status characteristics. Rather, the theory is concerned with the processes by which groups set up and maintain status hierarchies *when* attributes are acting as status characteristics. Research using the theory, however, has identified a large number of attributes that act as status characteristics in our culture, including gender, race, age, education, occupation, appearance, sexual orientation, and task ability. In American and Canadian society, for example, gender operates as a status characteristic that advantages men. People tend to defer to men more than women, men tend to talk more in groups than women, and men on average receive more positive evaluations than women for their performances, even on tasks where there is no reasonable expectation that men would perform better.

Showing the power of diffuse status characteristics in our daily lives, Jan Stets and Michael Harrod (2004) examined how frequently persons had various identities verified in interactions. What they found was that higher status persons—in their case, persons with higher levels of education—had a greater likelihood of having their identities verified. Verification, or a congruence of others' views of your identities with your own, is linked positively to esteem and mastery.

Joseph Berger*

Joseph Berger was professor of sociology at Stanford University and senior research fellow at the Hoover Institute. At a young age, Berger knew that he would one day study sociology—he even wrote in his high school yearbook that his goal was to be a sociology teacher.

Berger studied at Harvard, where he worked with famous sociologists such as Talcott Parsons and Robert Bales. He took his first academic appointment at Dartmouth University, later moving to Stanford University.

Most of Berger's work focused on status process and status relations among members of different groups, reward expectations, distributive justice, and theory construction in the behavioral sciences. Berger was most strongly linked with expectation states and status characteristics theories, which are a series of interrelated theories regarding how status cues affect interactions and performance expectations in groups. Berger produced a number of books and dozens of articles in his career. Some of his important works include *Types of Formalization in Small-Group Research* (Berger 1962);

Status Characteristics and Social Interaction: An Expectation-States Approach (Berger 1997); and *Status, Network, and Structure: Theory Development in Group Processes* (Berger 1997). He has also coedited three volumes of *Sociological Theories in Progress* (Berger 1966, Berger 1972, Berger 1989), showing the cutting edge of theoretical developments in sociological social psychology. He also wrote *New Directions in Contemporary Sociological Theory* (Berger and Zelditch 2002). He received the Cooley-Mead Award in 1991. Berger also received the W. E. B. DuBois Career of Distinguished Scholarship Award from the American Sociological Association in 2007.

*Information about this biography was obtained from Lynn Smith-Lovin's (Smith-Lovin 1992) introduction of the Cooley-Mead Award printed in *Social Psychology Quarterly*.

How to Get Status in Groups

The processes laid out by status characteristics theory, and overwhelmingly supported by research, probably seem to you to be less than fair. Some people get higher evaluations and have more influence in groups than other people, even when their contributions are no better. The process is unfair: the contributions of majority group members (such as men and Whites in U.S. society) are overvalued in groups, and the contributions of minority group members are undervalued or ignored.

Almost all of us will at some point in our lives work in groups in which we are low in status. When you graduate, for example, you may work in an organizational group in which you are younger and have less experience than other group members. You also might face situations in which your contributions are devalued because of your race or gender. What can be done to improve things in these situations? How can we create a situation in which the contributions of all group members are given their proper recognition? What can you do to increase your status in a group?

Research in the group processes perspective has identified two primary ways in which people with status characteristics that carry low cultural evaluations can effectively hold high-status positions in groups. First, one problem that people encounter in groups when they have characteristics with low status in the larger culture is that others do not think it is legitimate for them to hold high-status positions. A great deal of research, for example, has found that people in Western culture often view it as illegitimate for women to hold leadership positions in groups (e.g., Ridgeway and Berger 1986; Campero and Fernandez 2019). This situation has improved in recent decades, but Western culture is still one that tends to associate men with leadership—men are more likely to get leadership status in groups, especially when they are given formal authority (Burke, Stets, and Cerven 2007). However, research has also found that it helps to lead group members to believe that it is legitimate for women to occupy high-status positions. Jeffrey Lucas (2003), for example, carried out a study in which women or men acted as leaders of groups. He found, as research typically does, that men were more influential as leaders than were women. He then legitimately appointed women to leadership positions. Study participants watched a video that had the appearance of a training film. The film led group members to believe that it was proper and expected for women to hold leadership positions. In these cases, women in leadership positions were just as influential as men in leadership positions. Thus, legitimacy can help people with status characteristics that carry a low cultural evaluation receive proper recognition for their performances. Legitimacy, however, typically comes from some higher authority, and if you try to convince fellow group members that you should legitimately have high status in a group, you probably will not be successful. When you have low status in a group based on things such as race and gender, what can you personally do to improve the situation? Research has identified a method that appears to be particularly effective.

One reason that people with higher status have more influence in groups is that group members expect these people to make contributions with the interests of the group in mind. This is a common research observation: people assume that high-status people will be oriented toward the success of the group, whereas low-status people will be more selfishly oriented. This is one reason why women and minority group members meet so much resistance when they are in leadership positions in groups. In the case of gender, for example, people will assume that the behavior of a man was carried out to promote the interests of the group, while assuming that the same behavior by a woman was carried out for personal benefit.

Cecilia Ridgeway (1982), a researcher who uses status characteristics theory, noted this pattern and identified a possible solution to the contributions of low-status individuals being devalued in groups. She theorized that if individuals with low social status make it clear that they are carrying out behaviors with the interests of the group in mind, they can increase their status.

This strategy turns out to be very effective. Ridgeway (1982) conducted an experiment in which group members worked with a partner who presented himself or herself as either group motivated or selfishly motivated. Half of the people in the study had a male partner and half had a female partner. Group-motivated partners stressed the importance of cooperating and working together as a group. Selfishly motivated partners made it clear that they were looking out for themselves. When partners presented themselves as selfishly motivated, Ridgeway found the typical result: male partners were more influential than female partners. When partners presented themselves as group motivated, however, the effect disappeared: male partners were no more influential than female partners.

Susan Shackelford, Wendy Wood, and Stephen Worchel (1996) replicated Ridgeway's study and found the same results. They also studied whether women could increase their status by acting assertively in a group. They found that women who acted assertively did increase their influence, but they also met resistance and encountered problems in the group. Presenting themselves as group motivated did not lead to these problems. Presenting yourself as group motivated is an effective strategy to increase your status in a group. The strategy is particularly effective for people with status characteristics that carry a low social evaluation. The influence of men, for example, increased very little in the Ridgeway study when they presented themselves as group motivated, perhaps because people already assumed that they were acting with the interests of the group in mind. The influence of women, in contrast, increased dramatically when they presented group motivations. So, if you want to increase your influence in a group, especially when you think you are in a low-status position, present your behaviors as motivated by group goals. When you make suggestions, note how they will benefit the group and stress that you have the interests of the group in mind. With these behaviors, you can overcome the tendency that people have to devalue the contributions of some people based on the characteristics they possess.

Power in Networks

Status is one important process that leads to inequality in groups. Power is another. In Chapter 2, we defined power as the ability to get what you want despite resistance. Imagine, for example, a professor telling you one Friday afternoon that a major course paper will be due the following Monday. If you do not turn in the paper, you will fail the class. You do not want to write the paper, and you think that the assignment is unfair, but you write it nonetheless. In this situation, the professor has power. She gets what she wants despite your resistance.

Those in the group processes tradition are interested in a particular type of power—structural power, or power in networks. In the preceding example, it is clear that the professor's power rests in her ability to determine your grade. She has control over an outcome that is valuable to you and, as a result, can get you to do things that you do not want to do. Power in networks can be more subtle than this. In Chapter 2, we defined social networks as a series of relationships among people and groups. In the group processes perspective, a network emphasizes the idea that these people or groups are bound together through connections.

As an example of a network, imagine three people who all work side jobs as furniture movers in some small town. These people—Alice, Bob, and Carlos—all work for themselves, but two people are needed to perform any individual job. Let's suppose that Bob knows Alice and Carlos, but Alice and Carlos don't know each other. We could graphically represent the network to look like this:

Alice—Bob—Carlos

Every moving job pays two people $400. Alice, Bob, and Carlos would each be willing to do a job for about $50. Anything less than that and it would not be worth their time. So, each time a job becomes available, a two-person team must be put together to do the job, and they must decide how to distribute the money.

What do you think would happen if a furniture-moving job became available in this small town? Alice, Bob, and Carlos would all want the job. Moreover, Alice and Carlos would both ask Bob to do the job with them. How do you think Bob would decide between Alice and Carlos? He would probably demand more than half the money and go with whoever gave him a bigger share of the $400.

Suppose that Alice proposes to Bob that they do the job together, with her collecting $150 of the $400 and Bob netting $250. Carlos gets left out. What do you think will happen the next time a job becomes available? Carlos will probably propose giving Bob more money so that he can be included. Carlos might offer Bob $300 of the $400 if they do the job together.

Bob clearly has power in the network. As long as Alice and Carlos do not know about each other, Bob will be able to set the terms of their exchanges. Over time, we would expect things to get to a situation where Alice and Carlos would take the minimum amount necessary to make a job worth their while. In other words, we might expect Bob to collect $350 from each job, with either Alice or Carlos (whoever Bob completes the job with) collecting $50.

The primary question of interest to group processes scholars that comes out of this network and others like it is this: what is the source of power in networks? What gives Bob power over Alice and Carlos? If you look at the furniture movers' network, two things become apparent about Bob's position. First, Bob has the ability to exclude Alice and Carlos from what they want. In other words, by working with Alice, Bob can deny Carlos the opportunity to make money. Second, Bob has a central position in the network. If you look at the picture, you will see that Bob is centrally located.

Centrality and exclusion represent two possible sources of power in networks, and there was once some debate in the group processes perspective about which is the primary source of power. We can resolve the question by looking at networks that are just a little more complex. Although networks can involve numerous connections among participants, we will focus our discussion on line networks, such as the preceding one, for simplicity.

What do you think is the primary source of power in networks—centrality or exclusion? Let's expand the example by imagining that Carlos has brought a friend, Denise, into the furniture-moving business. Alice and Bob don't know Denise, and the new network would look like this:

Alice—Bob—Carlos—Denise

Who do you think would have power in this network? It is harder to tell than for the earlier network. However, we can guess how things might work. At first, Alice and Bob would probably complete jobs together, while Carlos and Denise worked together. They would likely all collect $200 from each job. If Alice or Denise demanded too much from any job, however, we might expect Bob and Carlos to complete a job together. After being left out, Alice and Denise would probably offer a little more on the next job. Over time, Bob and Carlos would probably make a little more than Alice and Denise, but things would not get to the extreme differences we would have expected before Denise came along.

Bob and Carlos, then, have power in this network, but not as much power as the middle position in a three-person network. Does this network help to resolve whether centrality or exclusion leads to power? Not really. Bob and Carlos are centrally located, but not as central as Bob was when there were only three people—the center of the network here falls between the positions. Bob and Carlos also have the ability to exclude Alice and Denise, but not as easily as Bob could have excluded Alice or Carlos in the original network. Bob and Carlos can exclude others here only by working together and probably taking less profit than they would get by trading with the outside positions. So, both the centrality and exclusion views would probably say that Bob and Carlos will have power in this network, but not as much power as Bob in the three-person network. That is in fact what happens in controlled research on network power, and the four-person network does not allow us to determine the source of power.

We can resolve the issue by adding one more person to the network. Imagine that Denise brings a friend, Erik, into the furniture-moving network. The new network looks like this:

Alice—Bob—Carlos—Denise—Erik

Who is the most central position in this network? Carlos. He is right in the middle of the network. Which positions have the ability to exclude others from what they want? That is more difficult to determine. We can figure it out, however, by imagining what might happen as jobs become available.

Suppose that two furniture-moving jobs become available in the preceding network. Bob and Carlos decide to do one job together. Because Alice does not know either Denise or Erik, she cannot do the other job with one of them. As a result, Denise and Erik do the other job together. Alice gets left out. The next time a job becomes available, Alice would likely offer Bob a little more to be included. Suppose she does. Bob and Alice complete a job together, and Denise again works with Erik. This time, Carlos was left out. He would probably offer more to Bob and Denise to be included in one of the next jobs.

In this network, Bob and Denise will always be included whenever two jobs become available. Either Alice or Carlos or Erik is always left out. We would expect big power differences to develop in this network. The people that are subject to being left out will probably eventually take $50 just to be included in jobs, with Bob and Denise typically earning $350 for each job.

We can now draw some conclusions about the roles of centrality and exclusion in determining power. Although Carlos has the most central position in the five-person network, he has little power—as little, in fact, as the positions on the ends. The positions with the ability to exclude, on the other hand, have a great deal of power. Bob and Denise can exclude the other people from exchanges, and they can use this ability to get more money. Power in networks, then, rests in the ability to exclude others from things they want. Karen Cook, Richard Emerson, Mary Gillmore, and Toshio Yamagishi (Cook et al., 1983) were the first group processes scholars to identify flaws in the logic behind centrality as a major source of power. The ability to exclude others from exchange is the driving element behind power in network exchange theory, a prominent group processes perspective on power in networks (Markovsky, Willer, and Patton 1988; Willer and Patton 1987).

There is a helpful lesson to take from the knowledge that exclusion rather than centrality is the primary source of power in networks. One common piece of advice for people starting new jobs is to get an office or cubicle located near the center of the action. The idea is that a central location will allow one to develop a strong base of power. Although this may be true, evidence from group processes theory and research indicates that other strategies may be more effective. In particular, if you want power in a network, put yourself in a position from which you can exclude other people from the things they desire. Jeffrey Pfeffer (1993) noted that the best way to do this is to create something that people want. You can also, however, position yourself to control resources that people value. Controlling pay distributions, for example, is an important source of power in organizations. Note that wanting power does not mean you will keep the most for yourself. It could be that those who seek or have power in organizations distribute pay or other resources very equitably—it depends on social context among other factors.

The Differences between Power and Status

Power and status share some common elements. Both are group processes, and both involve inequalities in rewards. People follow the directives of people with high status, just as they do the directives of people high in power. The difference between status and power lies in the reasons why people comply.

We usually do what people with power want us to do because we are afraid of the consequences if we do not. We gave an example earlier of a professor having power over you because she controls your grade. You might do an assignment you saw as unfair because you are afraid your professor will punish you if do not do it. We do what people with high status want us to do because we hold those people in esteem or respect. You might follow the leader of a voluntary organization, for example, because you respect the person's integrity and views. Although you do what the person wants, she has little power over you—she cannot fire you from the organization—however she could give you better or worse positions within the voluntary association.

Power is structural. It rests in the positions that people have in relation to others, not in the people themselves. In the original furniture mover example given earlier, nothing about Bob gave him power over Alice and Carlos—his power came from his position in the network. Status arises from the features of people. The status people get may be deserved (e.g., people who have high status because they are experts at some activity) or undeserved (e.g., men having higher status than women at activities that men perform no better than women), but status in either case rests in individual characteristics.

Although power and status arise from different sources, they are often related. Being high in status can significantly affect access to powerful positions (Ridgeway 2001). As we noted in the first chapter, the president of the United States has a great deal of power. His power is rooted in his position, and when he leaves office, his power is much lessened. It is difficult to imagine, however, someone gaining the power that comes with being president without first being high in social status.

One way that status helps people get power is that people value the resources held by higher-status people more than the resources held by lower-status people. For instance, a photograph signed by Martin Luther King, Jr., was for sale on eBay for $7,500. We value things that are possessed (or were once possessed) by people we hold in high esteem. Shane Thye (2000) carried out a study in which participants in an experiment traded resources with each other. Although the resources that people traded were equal in monetary value, participants in the study valued the resources held by high-status people more than those held by low-status people. High-status people, then, can gain power by controlling access to things that other people desire.

Power can also be used to gain status. For one thing, people tend to assume that powerful people are competent, even when their power rests in structural positions they hold through no effort or ability of their own (Lovaglia 1995). Think of the furniture-moving network in which Bob knew Alice and Carlos, but Alice and Carlos did not know each other. Bob had power in the network, and we said that he would probably eventually earn about $350 of a team's $400 per move. Distributions would end up this way whether or not Bob was particularly competent because Bob is in a powerful position. People who knew that Bob earned the most, however, would probably assume that Bob was more competent than Alice or Carlos.

Another way that power can be used to gain status is by using power to "purchase" status. In the movie *The Godfather*, Marlon Brando played a mafia boss with a great deal of power. He turned that power into status in his community by using his power to do favors for people. Pablo Escobar, a ruthless Colombian drug lord who killed or ordered the killing of countless Colombian citizens and officials, gained status in his community by hosting events and building parks and fields for children.

Power and status, then, are distinct but related. There are some jobs, for example, that are not high in both status and power but that are high in either power (e.g., prison guards) or status (e.g., ministers). It is much more common, however, for occupations to be similarly matched in both power and status. A large company's chief executive officer (CEO) will probably have a great deal of power and status. That same company's cleaning staff will likely be low in both status and power.

Section Summary

This section applies research and theories from the group processes perspective to answer a couple of questions: How does stratification develop in group interaction? How do inequalities from society at large get reproduced in groups? Research from this perspective shows that hierarchies naturally develop in most groups. According to exchange theory, those perceived as contributing more to a group often receive more status or power in a group. Status characteristics theory shows that status characteristics, such as gender, influence these perceptions about who contributes the most to a group. In contrast to status, which rests in individual characteristics, power is conferred by structural position. The ability to control resources also influences your power level in a group.

A Take-Away Message

One life lesson from this section is that you might gain access to leadership in a group by contributing more to it. Status characteristics theory, however, adds a caveat to this finding: your sociodemographic and other characteristics affect perceptions of your efforts. For example, research finds that women will tend to not get as much credit for their efforts as men. So, consider the next time you are participating in class, a club, or a work group, and start adding more to the conversation. Most important, frame your contributions as motivated by the interests of the group. Give it some time and see if your relationships in those groups change! With your newfound knowledge you might also want to be especially attuned to and compliment the contributions made by women, racialized minorities, the young or old, or other groups with lower status within your task groups.

BRINGING IT ALL TOGETHER

> *I don't think anyone likes inequality. I mean, who thinks some people deserve more money than others, if they do the same work, right? Anyway, if inequality occurs at every level, how do we fix the problem? It seems to me that there are too many things to tackle at the same time.*
>
> —Dave, junior English major

We started this chapter asking how people construct inequalities. The symbolic interaction perspective emphasizes how we construct the meaning of difference—in terms of gender, race, and other types of differences. Different cultural meanings about our status in society (i.e., race, class, and gender) have significant influence in our lives, the way people treat us, and how we treat other people. The social structure and personality perspective focuses on how inequalities influence specific outcomes for people, such as the role of social class on educational outcomes or how our position in society gives us access to different networks of people from whom we can find better jobs. Finally, the group processes perspective helps us answer questions related to how power and status develop in groups. First, our status from the larger society is a major factor in gaining status in groups. Second, our ability to control resources in a group helps us to gain power and status in that group.

Dave's concern about "fixing the problem" of inequality seems justified; there are a lot of different ways to study and, ideally, reduce inequities. Together, these perspectives incorporate micro-processes in constructing inequalities among people and understanding the influence of social inequalities once they are formed. The answer to Dave's problem is to say that we need to understand inequality at every level. Some social scientists focus on assessing inequalities in our day-to-day interactions, whereas others emphasize the need to change institutions or laws, making them less inequitable or discriminatory. In the end, we need to address all the ways that inequalities exist if we want to change society.

SUMMARY

1. Some ways that interactionist researchers focus on stratification processes include a) examining how social structure shapes who we interact with, b) accounting for inequalities and exclusion in interactional processes, c) acknowledging how people with certain status characteristics have more power in terms of role taking, and d) examining people's power to define situations and define themselves.

2. The Wisconsin model of status attainment traces the relationships among individuals' class position, their abilities, and their long-term occupational outcomes.
3. The effect of networking among individuals from different groups creates a variety of outcomes for those involved, depending on the status of the individuals in a group as well as the status of the group itself.
4. Values serve as a guide for making decisions about the future, ultimately affecting the types of jobs we attain and class position we have in life, producing a feedback loop between our personality and values and social positions.
5. Group processes contribute to our understanding of structural developments by studying the exchanges among individuals in groups. Exchange processes lend themselves to the development of status structures because people bring different types and quantities of resources into the process. People who contribute more to a group or have more resources generally achieve higher status in groups.
6. According to status characteristics theory, status hierarchies in task groups form based on the status characteristics of the members of the group; members look to the status characteristics of themselves and other group members to develop expectations for performance.
7. Power in networks is a structural capacity that results from the ability to exclude other persons from resources that they desire.

KEY TERMS AND CONCEPTS

Borderwork: The creation of social and physical boundaries between boys and girls.

Closeness of supervision: Part of Kohn and Schooler's model of status attainment referring to the level of control that supervisors have over workers.

Diffuse status characteristics: Characteristics that individuals carry with them for performances in diverse situations.

Direct exchanges: Exchanges between two people.

Doing difference: Any way in which inequality linked to any status (e.g., race, class, or gender) is perpetuated during our interactions as people are held accountable to the social categories they are a part of.

Doing gender: A social process in which individuals act according to the social rules or norms associated with being a man or a woman in society.

Feedback loop: A process in which our class position influences the development of values that, in turn, influences the type of job we seek.

Indirect or generalized exchanges: When people do not receive benefits directly from those to whom they give benefits.

Intellectual flexibility: Part of Kohn and Schooler's model of status attainment referring to how flexible people are in handling complex situations on the job.

Intersectionality: The idea that race, gender, and class statuses are not separate, but interlocking systems of inequality and identity.

Othering: A form of collective identity work in which those with higher status create definitions that make them feel superior, and in the process demoralize lower-status groups.

Personal ties: Combination of strong and weak ties.

Routinization: Part of Kohn and Schooler's model of status attainment referring to the level of repetitiveness found on the job.

Self-directed orientation: Part of Kohn and Schooler's model of status attainment referring to an individual's level of conservatism, fatalism, and personally responsible morality.

Social capital: Trust and support found in relationships with other people.

Social class: A group of people who share the same relative status in a given society.

Social exchange theory: Theory based on the premise that individuals enter into relationships that provide some benefit to them and end or leave relationships that do not provide some sort of reward.

Social mobility: The upward or downward change in social class over time.

Social stratification: Ways in which individuals or groups are ranked in society.

Socioeconomic status (SES): Our social and economic statuses based on education, income, and occupation.

Specific status characteristics: Characteristics that create expectations for performance in limited settings.

Status characteristics theory: Theory that links social roles and expectations from a larger society to stratification processes in groups.

Status hierarchies: Hierarchies that develop in task groups.

Strong ties: People with whom we are close, like friends and family.

Substantive complexity: Part of Kohn and Schooler's model of status attainment referring to how complicated the actual work is on the job.

Weak ties: Acquaintances or people we know through association with a third party.

DISCUSSION QUESTIONS

1. Can you see how status plays a role in your interactions with other people? Can you see the subtle—and not so subtle—ways in which social class, race, or gender plays a role in interactions?
2. How do you relate to your professors differently than you do with friends, family, or co-workers? Think about the role of status and power in explaining how and why you might act differently with people from each of these groups.
3. How might your understanding of the role of networks in society help you find a particular type of job?
4. Think about a recent group activity in which you had to make decisions about getting things done. How might group processes research inform your analysis of the group's behavior?
5. Consider how the social dynamics of status and power reviewed in this chapter may be similar or different on platforms like Instagram, X, or Snapchat. How might interactions simply replicate the findings reviewed here? How might they make them better or worse?

5

Self and Identity

I am a mother, first and foremost. So if my baby gets sick, I just can't study as much as I want to. Sometimes my grades suffer. And sometimes I am frustrated by all the things I can't do. The other day, some of the people in my class were talking about a big party that they went to. That kind of "fun" stuff is almost always out of the question now. But, you know, people tell me I am a really good mom to my baby, and I feel like I am working for something—I am making a good life for her.

—Marsha, senior sociology major

Although Marsha has a lot of roles to juggle, being a mother is her most important identity. As a result, when she has to choose how to use her limited free time, she will often spend it with her child. And, she explains her behavior to herself and others based on her identities. Her story also reveals that she feels good about who she is and what she is capable of doing as a mom.

Most people have some familiarity with the concepts of self, identity, and personality. We may explain our behaviors by saying we did something because "that's the way I am." Sociologists believe that a significant part of what people might call *personality* is socially constructed. If objects, social relationships, and society are constructed via social interactions, then people's selves and identities must also reflect social conditions.

Sociologists do not tend to study personality per se but rather the **self**, a process in which we construct a sense of who we are through interaction with others. Because the self is a process, it changes over time. We can take snapshots of our senses of self at given times, but they regularly get updated as we interact with people and adapt to new events and transitions in our lives. That snapshot, or the outcome of the self-process at a given point in time, is the **self-concept**. Morris Rosenberg (1986) defined the self-concept as the sum total of thoughts and feelings people have about themselves as objects. Essentially, the "self-process" creates the "self-concept," or understandings people have about themselves. The self-concept is an object or thing, and just like other things, such as a baseball, a hat, or any other physical object, we can talk about and reflect on our self-concepts. Scholars examining the self-concept focus on **self-identities** (thoughts about ourselves, or the kinds of people we see ourselves as) and on **self-evaluations** (feelings or judgments we make of ourselves). Three dimensions of self-evaluations we will discuss in this chapter are self-esteem, mastery, and mattering.

Social psychologists approach the study of the self in diverse ways, often dependent on the broad theoretical traditions in which they work. Some symbolic interactionists focus on the self as a process, or **self-presentations** (behaviors linked to people's "selves," or how they present themselves to others). Here, scholars examine how we make meaning of who we are, in concert with significant others. Other, more structural symbolic interactionists focus on how people's selves come through interaction to reflect the structure of society in a stable understanding of who they are, in the form of identities and evaluations. Because society is highly differentiated, the self is composed of multiple, complex parts. Social structure and personality scholars explicitly consider how social-structural conditions, notably positions and statuses in society, affect the self-concept. ("Social structure and the self-concept" may in fact be a better title for this field of study than "social structure and personality.") Finally, group processes scholars emphasize the role of group processes in affecting identities. We will address the following questions:

- How is the self a process?
- What are interactionist theories of the self and identity?
- What are three dimensions of the self-concept? What do we know from research on the self-concept?
- How do group processes affect identity?

THE SELF AS A PROCESS

> *When I first came to college, I was such a party animal. I would miss most of my classes and just get drunk or high. There was always a party to go to. I am not sure why I became that way. I did well in high school and was always a "good girl" growing up. I guess going to college just changed me. Maybe I took advantage of the freedom of being away from home. It was so funny to be called a "party girl" in college! Well, when my parents heard about my grades, the funding stopped, and I had to drop out for a while. I started taking classes at a local college. I didn't go back to being a "good girl" but I was certainly not the party girl anymore. I guess place and time can change you.*
>
> —Quinn, junior journalism major

According to the symbolic interactionist perspective, the self is a process, just like the construction of any social reality. People give meaning to their selves in many different ways. Are we good or bad people, or a complex mixture? How well do we do the tasks we set out to do? We continually take information from the world around us to answer these types of questions. The subtle feedback that we get over many experiences with significant others shapes us. It's not that we fail an exam and immediately think that we are bad students. A single exam is only one experience in our role as students, and we will assess many other aspects of the environment, such as how many students failed, how difficult the class is, and so on, as well as place that in the context of our many prior experiences in classrooms.

We do sometimes make conscious choices to become certain kinds of people. We may try to lose weight, to become an accountant, or to appear more intelligent. The process involves grafting on thoughts and behaviors necessary to achieve the best outcomes for ourselves in interactions. For instance, if a graduate student concerned about her status in an intellectual community enters a room full of professors, she may start acting more mature, using formal language, and trying to make clear, cogent statements to the people around her. This process may last only the duration of the meeting, with her goal being to look intelligent in front of the professors. However, the "act" of performing as more mature and intelligent may become a more permanent part of her sense of self as she interacts more with professors and with students similar to her. How could her behavior become a permanent part of her sense of self? Over time, she may begin to think of herself as "smart," be treated by others as intelligent, and thus her "student" or "advanced, intelligent student" identity may become more salient in future interactions with people.

In Quinn's example, going away to college changed the ways she thought, felt, and behaved. Instead of being the "good girl" that she was at home, she started missing classes and going to more parties. Her networks and her priorities changed in her new social environment. The changes had some long-term consequences for her sense of self—even when she was forced to go home, she never totally relinquished her "party girl" identity. Quinn is able to dialogue about herself as an object. She can see how she is now and compare it to the past. Furthermore, she can negotiate her sense of self using the alternatives available to her. When she was faced with returning home, she recognized that it limited her ability to "party," but she did not completely alter her previous sense of self.

In this section of the chapter, we examine the ways that the self is constructed and how people incorporate societal roles and expectations into their senses of self.

The I, the Me, and Self-Narratives

We use symbols and language to communicate with other people, but we also use language to think internally, a process that Herbert Blumer (1969) calls **self-indication**. We can have conversations with our selves just as we can with other people. Further, we can internally negotiate the meanings of objects, including our sense of self. In fact, there are several situations in which internal dialogues are the only appropriate ways to assess meaning.

According to George Herbert Mead (1934), a large part of our internal dialogues occur as an interplay between two components or characters within ourselves: the I and the Me. The **Me** is the organized set of attitudes toward the self, based on the views of significant others, such as friends and family, as well as society as a whole. The **I** refers to the active self; the I is the one on stage, in the moment, talking to other people. The "I" and the "Me" form a constant dialectic regarding thoughts, feelings, and behaviors (see Box 5.1). This internal dialogue reflects the importance we give to social conditions when deciding how to think, feel, or behave. In some sense, society resides in the Me. Because we have human agency, the ability to make choices about our actions, the "I" can act based on the "Me" in several different ways. Ellen Granberg (2006) studied the ways that individuals use agency and internal thought processes during a specific form of self-change: weight loss. Using in-depth interviews with 10 men and 36 women who had lost weight and sustained the weight loss for at least three months, she found that weight (or being overweight) was a major part of their identities and that images of their possible identities, or what their identities could be in the future, was a source of motivation to lose weight. They had images that losing weight would change the way they would live (e.g., buying smaller-sized clothing) and their interactions with other people. These images helped them sustain their dieting. Did the reality of weight loss meet these images? Not always. Granberg found that weight loss was accompanied by different sets of feedback from other people, and the reality of the weight loss did not always live up to their ideals. As a result, respondents had to negotiate new senses of self that blended some of their own reflections on the self-change process with social feedback from others.

The use of narratives and storytelling is an important part of the symbolic interaction process (see the review of frame analysis in Chapter 2). They can also be used to understand how individuals conceive of their pasts, their presents, and their memories

Box 5.1 Freud's Approach to Personality

The psychoanalytic approach to personality assumes that people are largely irrational, trying to manage passions and inner conflicts from the past. The approach is often associated with Sigmund Freud (1859–1939), an Austrian psychologist. Freud was one of the first to popularize the idea that we have an "unconscious" mind—that there are processes going on in the brain on which we are unaware that affect our thoughts, feelings, and behaviors. According to Freud, only through psychotherapy can we tap this inner room. Freud argued that personalities are made of three components: the id, which houses our basic instincts, seeking only pleasure or carnal fulfillment; the ego, which helps to restrain the id until it can achieve its wants in a reasonable way given different physical and social conditions; and the superego, which houses an individual's ideals, larger social and cultural norms, and standards. In some sense, the ego and superego contain elements of society, where we learn specific ways to constrain the id. These internal processes share some things in common with the relationship between the "I" and the "Me" outlined by Mead, with one dimension of our selves interacting with other aspects of the self on a day-to-day basis.

of the self and others. We also incorporate our hopes for a future self into who we are now (Martin 2010; Maynes, Pierce, and Laslett 2008; Merrill 2010; Mullaney 2020; Scott 2020; Smelser 2009). Think about how you talk about yourself to other people. You probably don't share your internal conversations reflecting the I and the Me. Rather, you probably share stories about your life relevant to the discussion. In the process, you reveal important events and how you interpreted those events. Perhaps you share information about an unusual and amazing trip to another country where you experimented with different foods, activities, and cultures. What does that say about you? First, that you are the type of person willing to make such a journey. Second, that you are the type of person willing to share intimate details of such a journey. Third, it tells the people around you that you enjoy trying new things. The telling of the story helps to solidify this identity, too—the storytelling process helps to make the self-image more concrete to the self and others because it becomes the memory you will reference in future interactions or internal discussions when confronting new information about the self (e.g., when someone presents you with a really crazy idea, are you going to be open to it or not?). The nature of an autobiography exemplifies this perspective: we write the stories of our lives to give people a better sense of who we are. Just as narrative can be used to understand how people construct the meaning of social life, we can study **self-narratives**, how individuals construct the meanings of their identities using personal stories (Brockmeier and Carbaugh 2001; Flores 2016; Gergen and Gergen 1997). In a sense, if social life is a story, we are a character in that larger story with our own story to tell. In a study of survivors of childhood sexual abuse, Thomas DeGloma (2007) found two groups of survivors: those survivors who accept that they had been abused and have recovered, and those who do not accept that they have been abused and cope with their situation by retracting their story, claiming it as a false memory. He found that both groups used autobiographical revisions of their abuse stories to help maintain their current identities. Self-narratives are not simply a list of stories that occur in our lives but the reformatting of multiple stories to make a single, coherent sense of self over time.

Identity Theory

Identity theory (which derives from the symbolic interaction perspective) emphasizes the enduring nature of people's thoughts about who they are. **Identity** refers to our internalized, stable sense of who we are, including role identities, social categories, and personal characteristics (Burke 2003). Thus, identity is more holistic than personality and is created, in part, on social relationships; interactions with other people, as well as meso- and macro-level social conditions (Stets 2021; Walker and Lynn 2013). **Role identities** are the internalized expectations associated with different positions. Some examples of role identities are college student, politician, or brother. For adults, the most important role identities typically stem from work and family positions. **Social categories** include identities related to social groups to which we belong, such as Canadian, woman, or Latinx. Last, **personal characteristics** include anything we use to describe our individual nature, such as being kind or studious or athletic.

Identity theory examines the ways society shapes how we view ourselves and how those views, or identities, affect our behavior.

Sheldon Stryker (2002) offered five principles that are at the root of identity theory:

1. Behavior is based on an already defined and classified world.
2. Positions in society are among the things classified in the world.
3. People develop their identities based on their positions in society.
4. We incorporate our social positions into our senses of identity; our positions become part of our senses of self.
5. Social behavior is derived from the shaping and modifying of the expectations of our positions.

The theory is rather simple and eloquent and tries to predict behavior when people have choices. The premise is that society affects self, which affects behavior. Stryker's definition of society refers to patterns of commitments to other people. Commitment includes the number of significant others tied to a given identity or to being a certain kind of person and the intensity of those bonds. Commitment shapes the salience of an identity, which in turn shapes how we will behave. For instance, living with many close friends in a sorority house likely makes a "Greek" identity highly salient and, according to identity theory, would make us act in ways to express the meaning of being Greek or, more specifically, say, a Gamma Phi Beta (wearing symbols, talking like others, and doing the philanthropy of that organization) when we have the opportunity to do so. Look at Box 5.2 for the ways that scholars have studied identities of college students. These processes continue when you enter the professional world where workers identify with the companies they work for, internalizing its norms and values over time (Potter 2015).

Box 5.2 The College Student Identity

Identity theory examines the intersection of traits, roles, and social categories. In your case, your role as a university student combined with your social categories (e.g., club, or team memberships) probably shape a lot of what you do on a day-to-day basis. Mary Grigsby (2009) interviewed 60 college students and followed some of them around for an entire day to get a handle on how students perceived their identities as students. She found that universities served as grounds for identity exploration. She was able to distinguish four types of students:

- The Careerist: Someone seeking a professional occupation.
- The Credentialist: Someone for whom the diploma matters more than grades or learning.
- The Collegiate: Someone for whom sports and sorority or fraternity membership especially mattered.

(continued)

- The Alternative: A mix of devout and countercultural students.
- The Academic: Those students for whom knowledge was more important than careers or other things.

Do you think that you fit into any of these model identities? Most people probably see themselves as a mix of them—and they may change over time. However, if you see yourself in one of these roles more than others, how might that identity affect your future in school? How might it influence your daily activities and who you spend time with?

Identity theory extends symbolic interactionist principles by focusing on the social construction of the self (principles #3 and #4 in Stryker's list above) and the belief that there is an existing social reality that we use as the basis for self-identification processes (principles #1 and #2). Thereafter, identities generate behavior (#5), but we are able to "make" or play out roles in somewhat unique ways. Peter Burke and Jan Stets (2009) indicate that identities tie us to society because our identities are based on multiple roles and statuses that were constructed before we entered them. In this sense, identity theory varies from psychological approaches to self and identity, which emphasize internal dynamics and interactions with people around us in the social construction of self and identity. Here, society is both a cause and outcome of such interactions. We construct our senses of self based on roles and statuses from society, and we change society by adding new statuses and roles or modifying existing ones.

Consider two fathers. How they act out their father roles (or behave as fathers) can be quite different. Their behavior will depend on both the salience and the meaning of the father identity. In one study, Thomas Rane and Brent McBride (2000) found that fathers who considered the nurturing aspect of the father role more meaningful to their sense of identity interacted with their children more often than those who did not. If being a good father means being more attentive to children's needs, then how should the father act? He should probably spend more time with them. Sociologists consider that the structures and cultures fathers live with matter a lot. In terms of structures, if government policies and workplaces allow for flexible or more time at home, such as remote work and control over timing of work, fathers may become more available to supervise and care for children. In terms of cultures, if it is expected and positive for men to interact with children in public and other places, fathers are more likely to view themselves as more involved.

There is often some latitude in acting out identities; for example, it is generally viewed as important for fathers to provide financially for children, but emphasis on the nurturing aspect is fine, too. We also assess our identities when we are with other people, making sure that they correspond with our senses of self. We make small adjustments to our behavior to maintain our identities (Cast 2003a). We may do the same for other people, too, helping them maintain their senses of identity through our interactions with them

(Cast 2003b). Ultimately, these identity processes are designed to make the world controllable; self-confirmation can provide a guide in awkward social situations and an emotional anchor in an otherwise changing world (Stets and Burke 2005). Confirmation and disconfirmation of identity can be associated with strong emotions (Trettevik 2016), creating feelings of satisfaction when our self-meanings are supported and doubt and insecurity when they are not, driving us to find peace by either reaffirming an identity or dropping it altogether.

The tendency to seek confirmation of self-meanings is the basis of **identity control theory** (see Burke 2004; Burke and Stets 1999; Stets, 2005; Stryker and Burke 2000). This theory proposes that self-consistency is as or more important to people than maintaining a positive self-image. Our desire to maintain our identities creates an internal alarm system that gives us an emotional response to situations in which our identities are verified or not, which may also have implications for our self-esteem. These processes are complicated, and research shows that we employ any number of defense mechanisms to address negative emotions that come about from failing to live up to identities that are important to us (Collett, Vercel, and Boykin 2015; Miller et al., 2019; see also Stets and Burke 2014). Research also shows that we are driven to protect our own self-meanings as well as other people's identities (Boyle and McKinzie 2015). In one study, Jenny Davis and colleagues (2019) examined comments on two YouTube videos about veganism and found that when people disagreed with the portrayal of the vegan identity, it produced a negative emotion among vegans and elicited more responses, probably as a means of protecting their identity. Conversely, vegans were more positive and used less words when their identity was verified in the video. The authors argue that these results demonstrate the "identity work" people engage in everyday, through almost any interaction (in person or online).

How do individuals maintain their senses of self amid so many different social situations? Why do people change? Sheldon Stryker and Richard Serpe's (Stryker and Serpe 1982; Serpe, 1987; Serpe and Stryker 1987; Serpe and Stryker 1993) studies of youth entering college found that transitioning students employed both affective and interactional commitment to identities to help maintain their original senses of self when entering college. Affective commitment refers to emotional attachment to an identity, while interactional commitment refers to maintaining relationships with people in different social spheres related to our identities. For example, being an environmentalist may be important to you, but you may not have close ties to other environmentalists. In that case, the environmentalist identity would have high affective commitment for you but relatively low interactional commitment. Stryker and Serpe also found that students tended to find groups that helped them to maintain their senses of identity. When such groups were not available to them, the students' initial identities began to change. Thus, while we seek to maintain identities that are important to us, we make changes when social resources are not available to stabilize our senses of self. In this way, our social relationships provide a mooring, a place of refuge and stability, for our identities, but it also suggests that we change our identities as our networks of relationships change, resulting from life events and transitions such as going to college or taking a job (Cassidy and Trew 2001; Merolla et al. 2012).

Some studies employing identity control theory have focused on self-change and stability among newly married couples (see Burke 2006; Cast and Cantwell 2007; Stets and Cast 2007). As people enter these relationships, they must negotiate new role relationships, working with their partners to determine how they should act as spouses. Partners bring images of themselves and the other into marriages (e.g., intelligence, attractiveness, and likeability). This line of research shows a general decline in the difference between self-views and spouses' views over time. What is more, spouses will change their senses of self to match the other's views, whether they are positive or negative! If we think we are unintelligent, but our spouse thinks we are smart, we are likely to develop a more positive sense of self. However, we are also likely to do the reverse: we will develop a more negative sense of self if our spouse has a negative view of us. How do we negotiate our sense of self in these relationships? Peter Burke (2006) proposes that we make small changes in our self over time as we engage in routine activities. During those activities, we provide verbal and nonverbal feedback about our thoughts, feelings, and behavior that we use in our internal dialogue between the I and the Me. As more information about the self is gained over time, we begin to rethink our sense of who we are. We are not likely to see large-scale changes in our identities at any moment but small changes in the self over time.

Affect Control Theory

When most of us think of the "self," we think of our thoughts about who we are. The self also includes sentiments and behavior (Burke and Stets 2009; Mackinnon and Heise 2010). Sentiments and behavior help to represent who we are and provide information to be evaluated. We tend to believe that our thoughts cause certain behaviors. But behaviors can also change our ways of thinking. For instance, you may not consider yourself very athletic until you find yourself obligated to play on the fraternity or sorority softball team. If you find that your performance is good after a few games, you may start to reevaluate your sense of your athleticism, incorporating this new information into your self-concept.

Thoughts, feelings, and behavior are all part of the self process. We use information from one or more components of the self to develop the other parts. We also shape feelings and behavior in a similar manner as the cognitive processes reviewed in the last section. **Affect control theory** incorporates elements of symbolic interactionism and identity theory to explain the role of sentiments in identity processes (Smith-Lovin 1995). The theory states that sentiments serve as signals about how well we are producing our identities and reproducing others' identities (Heise 1985). Negative emotions often signal that something is not right about a situation. If you see yourself as a good athlete and then fumble the ball, the bad feelings serve as a sign that you are failing at your identity. You may later use the exchange between the I and the Me to contemplate the feeling that you are experiencing. Perhaps you will decide to act on that feeling or decide that it is not that important to you. Regardless, the initial emotional signal initiates this thinking process. In another example, if you make a mistake on the job, the bad feeling may lead you to question your ability to do the job. The feeling of shame or doubt suggests that you cannot live up to the expectations of the job. To restore a positive feeling about yourself (i.e., self-esteem), you begin to use an internal dialogue in defense of your position. You may explain your poor performance as an anomaly or blame someone else for the problem. You may instead try to work harder to prove to yourself and others that your abilities are good enough. If the explanation or action reestablishes your identity on the job, the negative emotion will subside.

Affect control theory includes an analysis of the role of sentiments in interactions more generally. It is based on three basic principles (Heise 2002):

1. Individuals create events to confirm the sentiments that they have about themselves and others in the current situation.
2. If events don't work to maintain sentiments, then individuals reidentify themselves and others.
3. In the process of building events to confirm sentiments, individuals perform the social roles that are fundamental to society.

These premises simply indicate that people use emotions in their day-to-day interactions to help them get along with other people.

Affect control theory (Heise 1999, Heise 2002, Heise 2007; Lively and Heise 2004; see also Osgood 1962) proposes that there are three aspects of sentiment toward an object:

1. **Evaluation** (E): its goodness or badness.
2. **Potency** (P): its powerfulness or powerlessness.
3. **Activity** (A): its liveliness or quietness.

Essentially, EPA ratings provide a sense of how good (evaluation), powerful (potency), and lively (activity) an object is to an individual (See Table 5.1.)

Fundamental sentiments refer to enduring affective meanings in a given society based on EPA ratings. We can all probably conjure up feelings associated with our friends and enemies—friends are generally rated good and enemies bad. Just as we rate individuals (including ourselves!) on the three dimensions of EPA, we also apply them to roles and statuses in society (Maloney 2020). These ratings may vary by culture. For instance, David Heise (2002) found that the Japanese evaluate family members less positively than people in some other cultures (e.g., the United States and Canada), whereas Chinese people evaluate family most positively using these EPA ratings. Neil MacKinnon and David Heise (2010) estimate that there are about 9,000 identities to choose from in

Table 5.1 The Three Aspects of Affect Control Theory

Evaluation	Potency	Activity
Nice vs. Awful	Big vs. Little	Fast vs. Slow
Good vs. Bad	Powerful vs. Powerless	Noisy vs. Quiet Active vs. Inactive

Source: Adapted from http://www.indiana.edu/~socpsy/ACT/index.htm.

the English language. Under the ACT framework, each of those identities has an EPA rating. How do we decide which of these identities from which to choose? According to ACT, we are likely to select those identities which match our personal EPA ratings; we select those identities available to us which help us maintain the EPA rating we have for ourselves. For instance, if you see yourself as a good person, you are likely to avoid criminal identities. Similarly, if you see yourself as a very strong or potent person, you are likely to choose an identity that will allow you to express your sense of strength, such as becoming a politician, or take on a hobby that will affirm your sense of powerfulness, such as rock climbing or deep-sea fishing. It is important to understand that while we have some choice in the identities available to us, we are limited to those roles and statuses available to us in our culture and the fundamental sentiments associated with those identities. Hence, affect control theory helps to elaborate the relationship of macro-level society in the form of culture and micro-level processes involved in the self-indication process, the exchange between the I and the Me.

Individuals may also develop **transient sentiments** during specific interactions, sentiments unique to particular interactions between people. These sentiments may or may not confirm fundamental sentiments about an object. For instance, in the United States, a patient may go see a doctor believing that doctors are fundamentally good (evaluation), powerful (potency), and neither lively nor still (activity) (Heise 2002). If the doctor lives up to that fundamental sentiment, giving clear, concise advice in a neutral way, the patient's transient sentiments concur with the fundamental sentiment, producing feelings of ease and gratefulness. Alternatively, if the doctor does not live up to these expectations, perhaps waffling in their diagnoses (less powerful), the fundamental and transient sentiments conflict, leaving the patient with negative feelings about the doctor and the interaction. The patient will evaluate the doctor not only in terms of what they say but also in terms of how they act; whether their tone is comforting or confrontational, for example. Nonverbal behaviors play as strong a role as do verbal behaviors in forming people's affective responses to others (Rashotte 2002).

Steven Nelson (2006) found that we also reinterpret behaviors in order to minimize deflection between identities and behaviors. In one case, he asked students to minimize deflections in three categories like: *grandmother* (actor) *chased* (behavior) *addict* (object). In this case, students had to choose whether to change the actor, behavior, or object in order for the interaction to make sense. They could, for instance, change *grandmother* to *police* such that "police chase addict." In two studies, Nelson found abundant support for the idea that people have a tendency to change their behavior to match individuals' role identities rather than change actors to match behaviors. These findings are important because they suggest that identities, once constructed, are hard to change and that individuals will try to make sense of behaviors to match identities, rather than reidentify individuals based on their behaviors. Affect control theory may help to explain why rational explanations of behaviors are often inadequate. Why do rulers act irrationally at times, in ways that lead to disaster for their own countries? David Heise and Steven Lerner (2006) applied affect control theory to help explain international relations. They coded 1,934 international incidents among

25 Middle Eastern nations from the 1970s into the EPA dimensions reviewed in this chapter. They found that EPA ratings of nations' acts predicted other nations' subsequent reactions of the initial act. That is, initial evaluations of an act affected other nations' foreign policy decisions.

Dramaturgical Sociology

Symbolic interaction emphasizes the fact that humans have agency, the power to act independently of constraints. Thus, individuals can act apart from their senses of self. You may consider yourself to be a below-average student but decide to "act" like a good one in front of a professor. The study of how we present ourselves, playing roles and managing impressions during interactions with other people, is called **dramaturgical sociology**. Dramaturgical sociology is most closely associated with Erving Goffman (1922–1982) but continues to be a robust area of theory and research today. It includes the study of impression formation and the management of impressions. It is also associated with short-term changes in the self through the impression processes as well as online encounters (Edgley 2013).

Identity and affect control theories incorporate elements of dramaturgical sociology. These theories posit that when our identity does not match the environment, we change in some way to ensure that the two are commensurate. The theories assume that we have some control over what others think about us in a given interaction, a basic premise of dramaturgical sociology. Dramaturgical sociology also incorporates the idea that we can choose to act different from our identities during social exchanges and that we have to practice identities before fully incorporating them into our senses of self. We also incorporate the physical world, even the animal world, in the process of constructing and maintaining identities that are important to us (Laurent-Simpson 2017). Our personal senses of identity and our perceptions of the conceptions people have of us form a constant dialectic, taking on new identities and leaving others to meet situational demands over time. Many of these processes can be studied under the heading of impression management.

Impression Management

Erving Goffman (1959) believed that we seek information from people when we come in contact with them. We use such information to help establish expectations of our behavior and that of the people around us. These exchanges, and the attitudes and feelings that derive from them, also become part of identity processes, helping sustain or adjust existing identities or creating new ones (Perinbanayagam 2012). Information comes from the physical attributes of the other people—their skin tone or gender, for instance—as well as our histories with those people and contemplating our own biographies (see Scott 2015). We also have some control over the information we give to other people. For instance, we can dress formally to give people the impression that we are mature and serious. Similarly, we can wear jeans and a T-shirt if we want to look relaxed. The former dress may help get a job, whereas the latter is more appropriate among friends and family.

Impression management refers to the ways that individuals seek to control the impressions they convey to other people. It is important to note that our impressions include all aspects of our self-concept, including our personal traits (e.g., "I am an honest person"), the social groups to which we belong, and even the norms associated with the roles we have in life, like being a good student (Rossi and Stivers 2020). Impression management is a social process, involving more than just our own behavior as we look for cues from the people we interact with as evidence of how well we are performing. However, we may not see the signs of a failing impression in any given situation. For instance, you can try to impress a potential employer by wearing nice clothing—demonstrating that you are a conscientious worker—but you cannot be 100 percent certain that the potential employer finds the dress appropriate. In this way, there are **impressions given** and **impressions given off**—the impression you believe that you are giving and the impression the other person has of you.

Goffman proposed that we are driven to create and maintain positive impressions, probably because some goals or outcomes of interactions are to avoid embarrassment or to enhance our personal position in an interaction (Gawley 2008; Scheff 2006; Wei 2016). You would feel embarrassed if you tried to present yourself as a serious job candidate but lost your keys and spilled coffee. To avoid this impending embarrassment, we may plan ahead by not bringing coffee to the appointment or having a spare set of keys available in case of such an emergency. Alternatively, we may contemplate the way we react to embarrassing interactions to make them appear better than they are (e.g., making a joke about the incident to show that we are not concerned about it). Goffman also observed that other people are driven to help support our impressions. For instance, the employer may make a joke about your clumsiness or give you an opportunity to explain why you are especially clumsy that day. You might respond in agreement, finding an excuse like the wobbly new shoes you are wearing. Thus, both of you have found a way to make the impression as favorable as possible under those conditions. These processes can also serve as a way to maintain social cohesion in groups (Stets, Burke, and Savage 2018).

The motivation to support others' impressions is somewhat self-serving. First, helping other people maintain their impressions helps maintain the interaction, helping us predict future behavior and making it easier for us to know what to do. Second, we may need support in our own impression management efforts later in the interaction. Helping the other person makes it more likely that the other person will reciprocate support for us. This process of trying to protect our own and others' presentation of self is called **face-work** (Goffman 1967; Koskinen, Stevanovic, and Peräkylä 2021; Skaggs 2019). In one study, Jooyoung Lee (2009) utilized ethnographic fieldwork of street corner ciphers (impromptu rap sessions) and found that rappers used ritualized techniques to help each other out of embarrassing situations. For instance, if a rapper began to fall off on a song, another rapper would jump in and take over. In the end, this technique helped the group because it kept the song going. In this way, face-work helped to relieve the potential embarrassment of losing face and helped the group at the same time.

Frontstage, Backstage

Goffman described two regions of impression formation and management. Goffman's "front region" or **frontstage** is the place where we present ourselves to others. The **backstage** is the region where we relax our impression management efforts, and we may practice our performances (Goffman 1959). We think of the job interview as the frontstage, trying to look and act in a way that will make a certain impression and allow us to reach a goal—employment. When you see your friends (your backstage), you may express a very different attitude toward the job and the employer.

There is also research on solitary behavior, the things we do when no one at all is around to monitor our behavior. These situations often follow patterns reflecting cultural patterns (e.g., playing solitaire) but they also give individuals an opportunity to experiment on conventional social practices (e.g., new ways of performing a task) without worrying about consequences or judgments from other people (Cohen 2016b). One could argue that we are never really "offstage" because both formal and informal groups affect how we think and act, and we carry thoughts of performances with us even when we are alone (Perinbanayagam 2012). Nonetheless, it is clear that we do vacillate between degrees of performance depending on the nature of different social situations.

Spencer Cahill and his colleagues (1985) studied behavior in public bathrooms, assessing the role that social structure plays in the most "private" or "backstage" areas of our lives. He and his colleagues observed and took notes of behavior for hundreds of

Photo 5.1 Job interviews are only one scenario in which we employ fronts. Can you think of other situations in which you put on a front to get what you want?

Source: fizkes/Shutterstock

hours in the bathrooms of malls, student unions, restaurants, and other places over a nine-month period. Among other things, they found that bathrooms serve as a place to "retire" from frontstage performances. The researchers showed that bathrooms serve as "self-service" repair shops, where individuals can take off their "fronts." Mirrors allow us to check our front (e.g., hair and clothing) before facing the public again. Bathrooms also serve as a retreat from embarrassment, a place to prepare for publicly awkward situations—giving people a "staging area" for their public performances.

The relationship between the front and backstages makes it difficult to assess the honesty of other people. If you find out that your friend is having an affair with your boyfriend, you start to question whether anything this person says to you is true. Is she just "putting on an act" of kindness and loyalty when she is around you but then portraying her true self when she is with your boyfriend? How do you know when someone is being honest with you or whether they are being "two faced"? It may be hard for us, when interacting with others in some situations, to know for sure. In a participant observation study of working-class White men, Monica McDermott (2006) found that participants in one community were friendly and civil toward African Americans during everyday interactions but tended to express hostility about them when around other Whites. In another community where White identity meant something different, Whites interactions with Blacks were aligned more with attitudes. Sometimes people are aware of two contradictory selves they have, which can cause tension. In a study of 1600 submissions on PostSecret, a mail-art community, Michelle Smirnova (2016) found that people keep and disclose secrets as way to maintain two seemingly contradictory identities (e.g., a cheerleader who deals drugs). Posting these secrets provides a cathartic way of revealing these secrets while saving face with significant others.

Internet interactions have provided another venue for analyzing the use of frontstage and backstage performances. On one hand, online interactions such as gaming or blogs provide an opportunity to create an avatar or fantasy version of your self (Gottschalk 2010; Hillis 2009). We can put on almost any front that we would like, including graphic representations of our altered selves. On the other hand, the internet can provide backstage space such as chat rooms where people can share details about about their problems without fear that they will be judged (de Koster 2010; Wood and Ward 2010). In this way, the internet gives us more control over our self-presentations because people have less access to visual and other cues that impact their belief about our frontstage performances.

The Importance of Self-Presentations: Some Tips

Our presentations of self do make a difference. People evaluate other people based on their frontstage performances. People also judge us on our looks and mannerisms, even what we eat and how we smell (De Soucey 2010; Waskul and Vannini 2008)! Our use of language, for instance, affects people's assessment of our competency (Lewandowski and Harrington 2006; Nath 2007). People who employ more formal language (orally and through email exchanges) are generally given higher evaluations than people who use more informal language.

How do you build a good first impression? There are impression-consulting companies that can help if you have money and want to spend it that way. (They may not call themselves impression management companies—maybe image consultants—but they do provide tips for how to dress and act for success). However, acting out a social identity simply requires a good sociological imagination (see Chapter 1). If you know how people behave in different societal roles, you can adopt similar mannerisms to reproduce those impressions. Learning how to "perform"—to present one's self in public—takes some work. Consider two musicians, both of whom are equally talented, but one of them smiles and dances with the music while they perform while the other regularly looks down at their instrument and makes very few gestures while playing. Which one do you think will be more popular with the crowd? How do people learn to be good performers? The short answer is practice. In a qualitative study of amateur musicians, Marcus Aldredge (2006) found that musicians use less formal settings such as open-mic nights to develop their musical skills while learning how to perform in front of live audiences. At first, Aldredge observed, many musicians are nervous about being in front of a crowd, and it can make it hard for them to play well. Over time, they become more relaxed while performing. They also use audience reactions to assess their performances. This process does not occur overnight; it takes many nights of stress and anxiety before musicians learn how to perform well in front of a crowd. In terms of managing day-to-day interactions, using your backstage time with other people to practice frontstage performances, anticipating encounters and developing responses, and dealing with the emotions that you expect to encounter may also help you (O'Brien 2011). In short, like any other skill, developing good impression management skills takes three things: practice, practice, practice!

Situated and Multiple Selves

Some symbolic interaction theorists view the self as constantly changing. They claim that it is, therefore, difficult to study the self using quantitative techniques (see Chapter 3). These researchers tend to study the self qualitatively and through self-narratives as discussed earlier in this chapter. One of the main areas of interest for these researchers is the question of authenticity. Authenticity is how well the self we portray to others fits with the self we really feel like inside.

One of the reasons people change is because their social environments change. The **situated self** is a temporally based sense of who we are. For the brief time we are interviewing for a job, we may really believe that we are good, trustworthy employees who would take the job and employer seriously. That perspective may change after leaving the office and discussing the interview with friends and family. Thus, impression management is an integral part of the situated self. In another example, Karen Stein (2011) argues that vacations give us the opportunities to create a situated self, a temporary identity that is limited to a specific place and time. That is, since vacations are typically set apart from people who we know and are for a limited period of time, we can use impression management to change our identity among strangers who are unable to challenge our claims. One reason that we are able to sustain these new images is that the vacation requires only a short time in which to maintain our cover.

Postmodern theorists propose that the self has become "saturated" in recent years because we have so many "others" with whom we interact. Because of social forces, such as globalization, and technological advances, such as the internet and smartphones, we can interact with many different others from around the country or world within a very short time span (or even at the same time). Compared to the past, people today may live with "multiphrenia," or an inability to know who we really are, because we are playing so many roles at once, and we have so many others from whom we receive different, sometimes conflicting, feedback. Kenneth Gergen discussed how technological advances in information technology, transportation, media, and so on, are crowding out our small number of significant others with an "ever-expanding array of relationships" (Gergen 2000, xi). To Gergen, these changes in society fragment and erase a core, or true, self. This perspective is supported by studies arguing that Americans have smaller core social networks, or people in whom we trust (McPherson, Smith-Lovin, and Brashears 2006; Smith-Lovin 2007).

It appears that a challenge of modern life is learning how to manage multiple identities or the pace of identity change (Bauman 2007; Conley 2009; Rogalin and Keeton 2011). That is, we must manage the stresses of being a student, a worker, a friend, and a member of any number of groups to which we belong (e.g., where we work, our racialized identity, gender and sexuality) (Potter 2015; Weinberg and Newmahr 2015). Each of these roles and group affiliations may include numerous identity expectations, with your friends from school, for example, having different expectations of you than your friends at home. In addition, we live in a mobile world that allows us to transport our selves more quickly and easily than ever, creating opportunities for creating new identities and discarding old ones. How we portray ourselves on social media may cause conflicts and concerns about different audiences and how they "read you." It is difficult to know how changing self-portrayals and relationships will affect one's sense of identity over time, but from an interactionist perspective, it is likely to have some effect because the self is social in nature. Thus, if social relationships change, so will our sense of who we are.

Perhaps the postmodern self is fragmented and unfocused, but we also can take control of these processes to some degree. Some people choose to disengage from social media for example, curtailing certain images that might shape emotions, and ending superficial interactions. More in-person engagements in positive spaces may be important. In a study of volunteer identities, Peggy Thoits (2013) found that more time spent volunteering increased identity salience, which ultimately improved mental health. Hence, we can choose to enact, and perhaps stabilize, those identities we believe are important to us. Alternatively, people may simply adapt to the changing nature of relationships (e.g., via email) to find or recreate the types of interactions found in everyday life (Menchik and Tian 2008).

Box 5.3 The Digital Self

Taken together, the identity and presentation of self are like a system whereby individuals develop their identities involving personal traits, statuses/roles, and social groups and then present these identities to the world. Interactions with others provide feedback as to how well we are presenting our identities, and we adjust things to either better reflect who we are or make changes to our identities. Sociologists speculate how the self and identity change in the online milieu. The digital age provides us with the ability to create avatars and profiles of ourselves that are totally different than the internal senses of self that have been created offline, challenging us to choose between our authentic and ideal selves (Davis 2014). Sherry Turkle, Founding Director of the MIT Initiative on Technology and Self, writes, "We think we will be presenting ourselves, but our profile ends up as somebody else—often a fantasy of who we want to be" (2011; 153). In his book *The Terminal Self: Everyday Life in Hypermodern Times*, Simon Gottschalk (2018) argues that the "terminal self" is framed in a networked environment with its own set of norms which totally engrosses users' everyday lives, ultimately affecting who they are. The online environment affects us both in function and form, limiting our expressions to the rules of any given platform (e.g., how many characters can be used to make a statement). We can also use media to reflect on ourselves because we leave a mark on the world each time we send a text or post an image (Humphries 2018). Such statements and images almost never go away and serve as a reminder of who we are or once were—and serve as a reference and reminder of our pasts – and a source of data for people as they interact with you face-to-face (Tian 2017). Contemporary scholars generally concede that it is difficult to separate our digital lives from our internal sense of self (Highfield 2016; Humphries 2018; McCarthy 2017). The future of digital selfhood may include robots and artificial intelligence with their own senses of self. It is clear that people are already judging technology using the same assessments that we use for humans, including things like evaluation, potency, and activity (Affect Control Theory) (Shank et al. 2020). Hence, we may find ourselves creating new identities through interactions with chatbots and other technologies.

Section Summary

This section applied the interactionist perspective to answer the questions "How is the self a process?" and "What are interactionist theories of the self and identity?" According to symbolic interaction, the self reflects our interactions with other people and is in an internal dialogue with the Me, the organized set of attitudes toward the self, and the I, the part that is onstage actively engaging with others. Identity theory examines how our roles and statuses help develop a sense of who we are. In addition, affect control theory helps to show the role of emotions in the identity process. Finally, impression management shows individuals' ability to actively manipulate others' perceptions of their selves in a social context.

A Take-Away Message

What might we learn from symbolic interactionist approaches to our self and identities? First, our identities go well beyond our personalities. For this reason, if we want to really know ourselves, we have to consider the roles and groups that we are in—they tell us and other people a lot of things about us that personality alone won't. Identity theory, identity control theory, and affect control theory help us figure out how those roles such as student or daughter (and the internalized meanings linked to them) may affect our decisions and behavior. They may also help you predict the attitudes and behaviors of your friends and family! Just take a moment to write down all of the statuses and associated roles a friend of yours has. How much of her or his behavior is reflected in those expectations? Professionally, you can use these theories, especially dramaturgy, to better prepare your frontstage. Making class presentations will help you prepare for professional presentations, and interacting with people with higher status will help you practice your performance in front of your future bosses! How might you practice these techniques? Working with professors on campus and taking on leadership in clubs and other organizations may help you—as you practice your presentations, they become more and more a part of your self that is easy to conjure up. Eventually a self you practice can become an "authentic" self.

THE SELF AND SOCIAL STRUCTURE

> *I was only in school for a month before dropping out. I just couldn't handle the deadlines or the homework. It just seemed like too much. I took a job at a local fast-food restaurant. They gave me a promotion to assistant manager after a while. It kind of made me rethink going back to school. I thought, "If I can manage all these people, I can manage a little homework too." So, I signed up for classes again the following year. And here I am!*
>
> —John, sophomore business major

Researchers from the social structure and personality perspective focus on how our social positions and relationships affect self and identity. As mentioned in this chapter, the self-concept refers to all our thoughts and feelings about our self as an object (Rosenberg 1986). Thus, social structure and personality theorists carefully examine how social structure and culture affect identity, as well as esteem, and other evaluative components of the self. In the story by John, we see a student who initially does not believe that he is capable of finishing college. As a result, he decides to drop out and starts working at a local fast-food restaurant. He slowly rises to an assistant manager position. After several months in this position, he starts rethinking his abilities, wondering if he is in fact capable of finishing the degree. John's thinking process may relate to the fact that he was in a position that required him to be responsible for other people. After experiencing some of the challenges associated with management, he began to rethink his decision about school. Taking the management position helped him develop his skills, receive feedback from others that he is successful in this role, and thus see himself in alternative ways.

The focus in this section is on the role that larger social conditions play in everyday interactions. In this case, John's "position" is not constructed through interaction, but through something developed long before he arrived at the situation. As such, the position has meanings and expectations already attached to it from the larger society. Although John may be able to change them, he must negotiate these meanings from an established point. That is, he must consider what other people expect of him based on an already-established position and decide how much to change the nature of the position or change himself to live up to the expectations of that position. Researchers from this tradition often study the relationship between social positions and the self-concept in the form of self-esteem, mastery, and mattering. We will review these dimensions of the self-concept, followed by a discussion of how they are measured and how our social positions affect them.

Evaluative Dimensions of the Self-Concept

As we discussed in the beginning of the chapter, in addition to self-identities, self-evaluations are central to self-concept research. There are three evaluative elements or dimensions of the self that are seen as foundational to the self processes described in this chapter. We evaluate ourselves in key ways by asking, "How worthy am I?" "How powerful are my actions?" and "How much do I matter to other people?" Both self-esteem and mastery, represented by the first two questions, motivate the self-process and filter interactions with our social worlds. Mattering, addressed by the third question, is a dimension of the self that is less studied but also serves as a foundational dimension of the self (Elliott, Kao, and Grant 2004; Rosenberg and McCullough 1981).

Self-Esteem

Self-esteem is the positive or negative evaluation of our self as an object (Rosenberg 1986). It answers the question "How good am I?" In addition to thoughts about how worthy we are, social psychologists also understand self-esteem to be our emotional reactions to the self (Hewitt 2003a). Thus, self-esteem has at least two dimensions; we can both cognitively and affectively react to the self. For instance, we may think highly of ourselves and concurrently feel good about ourselves. Alternatively, we can think poorly of ourselves and feel bad too. Self-esteem is global or specific; that is, an overall sense of worth or a sense of worth based on specific roles or spheres of life. Academic self-esteem is our feelings of worth as a student (Rosenberg, Schooler, and Schoenbach 1989).

If you enter the term "self-esteem" into a search engine, you will find dozens of websites designed to sell products guaranteed to boost your self-esteem. Self-esteem is a common expression in the Western world; parents try to build their children's self-esteem, and some people participate in "self-help" or self-esteem-boosting programs. Much of the early research in self-esteem suggested that it is at the core of psychological development (see Elliott 1986; Owens and Stryker 2001; Rosenberg 1986);

that is, all other aspects of our life will fail without positive self-esteem. For instance, a person with low self-esteem may find it more difficult to finish a college program, believing that she does not "have what it takes." Therefore, the logic goes, we must first build strong self-esteem and then worry about the other details of life. But this is not quite true. Instead, successful social experiences and long-term supportive interactions with significant others are primary in creating self-esteem; it cannot be quickly "built" and then used as a tool for success (Rosenberg, Schooler, and Schoenbach 1989).

Self-concept theorists often study the effects of social structure and culture on self-esteem. For instance, Schooler and Oates (2001) found that people who work in jobs that require little supervision from others and who engage in intellectually complex tasks have higher self-esteem years later than others who perform more mundane work. Another study examined how girls were affected by unrealistic images of female beauty prominent in the media (Milkie 1999). For White girls, even when they were critical of the "perfect" images, the images depressed self-esteem, because girls still made social comparisons with models and assumed that boys bought into the images and viewed the real girls more negatively. But Black girls' self-esteem was not as affected by these comparisons—they understood that significant others did not hold such images as a standard for African American beauty. Thus, people's statuses and social relationships help them interpret information from the media and other sources in assessing their self-worth. The importance of self-esteem, according to some scholars, is profound. Many social psychologists believe that self-esteem serves as a basis for motivation of the self process, and it can affect whether we accept feedback from other people about our identities (Asencio 2013). Viktor Gecas (2001) argued that self-esteem may be a more important motivational force for us than other self processes. Gecas says that individuals are motivated by the **self-consistency motive** to maintain a consistent sense of self and the **self-esteem motive** to maintain positive self-images. For example, the threat of bad grades (which could produce lower academic self-esteem) may motivate us to study harder for class. It may also motivate us to leave school and find an alternative source of esteem. However, someone who receives lower grades may come to see herself as a bad student and work less hard as a student to maintain her negative sense of self.

The set of research discussed in this chapter shows that self-esteem is, in part, derived from social interaction. Rosenberg theorized four sources of the self-concept: social comparisons, reflected appraisals, psychological centrality, and self-perceptions (Gecas 1982; Rosenberg 1986). **Social comparisons** refer to using other people and groups as points of reference for our thoughts, feelings, and behaviors. **Reflected appraisals** are the ways that we believe others view us. **Psychological centrality** is our ability to shift aspects of the self to become more or less important to our overall self-concept. Finally, **self-perceptions** are observations of our behavior and its consequences.

Positive or negative evaluations of your self (self-esteem) are the result of your internal dialogue, compiling self-perceptions, social comparisons, and reflected appraisals. Marsha, in the vignette at the start of this chapter, indicated that she felt good about herself as a mother. Her mothering self-esteem was built through all the processes described. She probably made social comparisons with other student mothers and believed that, compared to them, she was doing well taking care of her baby. Through interacting with others, her parents, her partner, her friends, and her baby, she is able to form a view of how they viewed her mothering (or reflected appraisals). In terms of psychological centrality, her mothering identity is very important and thus provides a positive global sense of worth as well. And, finally, by observing her own behaviors—sacrificing time at parties and studying when necessary—she sees evidence that she is a good mother.

Research generally supports the self-esteem dynamics reviewed here. Levels and sources of self-esteem are found to be different for people in various social categories. For instance, of the four sources of the self-concept, reflected appraisals, or our sense of how others view us, have the strongest effect on self-esteem for both men and women, although the effects on women may be somewhat stronger than for men (Schwalbe and Staples 1991). Research also shows that self-esteem is relatively high for most people, and there is a tendency to focus on positive outcomes of interactions for ourselves—we tend to assess our actions more positively than other people's actions; people are agentic and can salvage their self-esteem under many challenging social situations (Allison et al. 2006; Meanwell 2013; Rosenberg 1986). These findings support the idea that self-esteem serves as a primary element of the self-concept.

Mastery

Another important dimension of the self is mastery. **Mastery** refers to our perceptions of our ability to control our environments. It addresses the question "How powerful am I to do the things I would like to do?" Mastery is similar to the concepts of self-efficacy and locus of control (see Box 5.4). Much like self-esteem, sociologists believe that our desire for control serves as a motivational aspect of our self-image (Gecas 1989).

Box 5.4 Mastery, Self-Efficacy, and Locus of Control

Mastery, self-efficacy, and locus of control are measures of the self-concept assessing our sense of control (or lack of control) over the world around us (Turner, Lloyd, and Roszell 1999). Locus of control measures our "internal" and "external" sense of control (Gecas 1989). Do you think that people get promoted because of commitment and hard work or as a matter of entitlements or by chance? If you believe that you received a promotion as a result of hard work, you probably have a stronger "internal" sense of control. Self-efficacy refers to our beliefs about our ability to produce results from our actions (Bandura 1997). Mastery, which refers to our perceptions of our ability to control our environments, focuses on more general perceptions of our ability to achieve our goals. Mastery is assessed by asking respondents how much they agree with statements such as "I have little control over the things that happen to me" and "There is really no way I can solve some of the problems I have" (Pearlin and Schooler 1978). If you strongly agree with these items, you likely have a low sense of mastery. The three concepts are similar but have developed within different research traditions.

Occasionally, a **self-fulfilling prophecy** may operate, a case of expectations producing a reality consistent with assumptions: if we do not believe that we can do something, we may not even try. If others do not believe that you are capable of doing a job and treat you as incompetent, you may find ways to avoid the job or fail at it. By failing at the job, you receive information that pushes you to continue to believe that you are not capable of doing the work.

Mastery is associated with a host of positive outcomes in life ranging from physical and mental health to obtaining a good job. People with a higher sense of mastery report fewer mental and physical health problems than those with a lower sense of mastery (Caputo 2003; Cheung and Sun 2000). Mastery is also related to self-esteem: people with a high sense of mastery report higher levels of self-esteem (Turner and Roszell 1994), as you might expect. Mastery also serves as a personal resource to cope with life's problems. For instance, Leonard Pearlin and colleagues (Pearlin et al. 1981) found that people with a higher sense of mastery react less severely to job loss than do those with a lower sense of mastery, probably because they believed that they would be able to overcome their problems and would use resources such as those in their social networks to help them. In addition, people with a higher sense of mastery early in their careers are more likely to achieve their occupational expectations later in life (Reynolds et al. 2007).

Given the importance of mastery in our lives, how does one develop high levels of mastery? Development of one's sense of mastery starts in infancy as children begin to understand causality in their environments (Gecas 1989). As children try to change their worlds, they assess whether such attempts have effects. If so, children learn that they have the ability to make such changes. In this way, a sense of efficacy begins through **personal accomplishments**, being able to achieve what we start out to do. Personal accomplishments continue to be a most important source of efficacy in adulthood, but there are other sources of efficacy. **Vicarious experience** occurs by seeing other people perform tasks, showing us that the task can be accomplished. **Verbal persuasion** is information from others about our abilities. Finally, **emotional arousal** refers to inferences about our abilities based on our emotional states (Bandura 1977). For instance, we hesitate to give a speech to a club or group to which we belong. However, our friends try to boost our confidence by using verbal persuasion, arguing that we are capable of giving a great speech and increasing our sense of mastery. We then start observing other people's speeches, making the task seem more reasonable for us to accomplish. We may then reflect on the large amount of fear provoked when we consider making the speech. This series of internal and social negotiations influences our decision to make the speech, how well we perform if we do make the speech, and the likelihood of making future speeches. Mastery is also higher among those with higher levels of education. You can imagine many reasons why. Those children born into more resources, including schools with strong infrastructure and adequate supplies for children, and parents with more money, time, or education may also be at an advantage when it comes to developing mastery.

Mattering

Mattering refers to our sense that we are important to other people (Elliott, Kao, and Grant 2004; Rosenberg and McCullough 1981). It answers the question "How much do

I matter to others?" According to Morris Rosenberg and Claire McCullough (1981), we have an intrinsic need to feel that we are needed by the people around us. The authors focused on three aspects of mattering—how much attention we receive from significant others, how important we feel to others, and how much we believe others depend on us. They developed these ideas in a study of adolescents, theorizing how much they mattered to parents was central. They believed that both adolescents and older adults may have lower senses of mattering.

The link between mattering and well-being is related to the work of the classic sociologist Emile Durkheim. Durkheim (1951, originally 1897) studied the social conditions that influence individuals' decisions to commit suicide. He argued that people who are more integrated in society have stronger social ties and are less likely to commit suicide than those who are less integrated. Because mattering measures, in part, how much people feel needed by others, those needs may represent the sense of one's integration into a group. Rosenberg's and McCullough's (1981) findings showed mattering to be positively related to self-esteem and negatively related to depression and anxiety, independent of self-esteem. People with a greater sense of mattering tend to have higher levels of self-esteem and lower levels of depression and anxiety than those with lower senses of mattering.

Research has supported Rosenberg's original findings. Leonard Pearlin and Allen LeBlanc (2001) found a direct relationship between loss of mattering and depression among older adults, such that those who recently reported a loss of mattering due to the death of a loved one had higher levels of depression than those who did not feel a loss of mattering. Adolescents who believe they matter more to others are also significantly less likely to consider suicide than those who believe that they matter less (Elliott, Colangelo, and Gelles 2005). Elliot and colleagues (2005) argue that mattering ultimately affects our lives through self-esteem: levels of mattering affect our sense of worth, leading us to positive behaviors and attitudes.

We can develop a greater sense of mattering by taking on roles that provide a strong indication that we matter to others! In one study, Peggy Thoits (2012) found that participants who spent more time volunteering developed strong "volunteer identities" which enhanced their senses of mattering. Participants with greater senses of mattering, in turn, reported heightened senses of meaning and purpose in life, which yielded better mental and physical health.

Race, Class, Gender, and the Self

Your ethnicity or race, your social class, and your gender affect self-evaluations. Probably the most consistent findings on these effects relate to class status and self-esteem. Social class was defined in Chapter 4 as a group who shares the relatively same status and resources in society. Our class positions affect the number of resources we have available to manage problems as well as to develop talents and abilities. Class also influences the activities in which we engage, the types of people with whom we spend time, and how we spend our time (Lareau 2003). These factors, in turn, affect what we value in life and who we believe we are.

Some early work on social class and the self explored the relationship between class position and the self-concept. Morris Rosenberg and other researchers in the 1960s and 1970s believed that poor economic environments would lead to lower self-esteem among children (Rosenberg 1986; Rosenberg and Pearlin 1978). They hypothesized that self-esteem would be linked to social status, that economic conditions would reflect people's sense of worth. Class would serve as an indicator to people of where they stood in the world. In this view, children at the lower end of the social system should report the lowest sense of self-worth because they are on the bottom of the social system relative to their middle- and upper-class peers.

Rosenberg and Pearlin (1978) used data from surveys of children, adolescents, and adults from Baltimore and Chicago to compare levels of self-esteem at different class levels. Findings showed that the relationship between class and self-esteem was somewhat complicated. The researchers found that social class position affected self-esteem as predicted, at least among adults and, to some degree, among adolescents. However, findings from children showed no effect of class on self-esteem. Additional analyses suggested that the effects of class are felt only as children enter adolescence, when occupation, income, and education become more important to people's identities. These characteristics provide a sense of relative position that becomes salient to children only as they enter the adult world and leave the more homogeneous environments that young children tend to inhabit. Thus, class position tends to affect this aspect of the self-concept only when an individual becomes aware of her position in society. Social comparisons and reflected appraisals matter.

Young children have less awareness of their positions in society, limiting their social comparisons to their immediate surroundings. If children and all of their friends have lots of expensive toys and games, then they may believe that the rest of the world is the same. However, as children enter adolescence, they obtain more information about the larger society from more sources. Through images in media and through interactions with their other peers and adults, children begin to see that there are great variations in the ways people live. As youth process this information over time, they may question why they have more or less than other people in society and adjust their senses of self accordingly to reflect their statuses in society.

Social and cultural conditions also influence the development of mastery. For instance, some research suggests that more recent cohorts of children have a greater sense of mastery than previous cohorts, and community conditions can influence the development of efficacy (Mirowsky and Ross 2007; Sharkey 2006). Thus, the time and place in which you grow up may foster the development of mastery. Status characteristics such as education and socioeconomic status also influence levels of mastery: as noted earlier in this chapter, people with more education and income report higher levels of mastery (Caplan and Schooler 2007; Mirowsky and Ross 2007). Developing a sense of control, like many social-psychological outcomes, occurs within larger social conditions that influence our ability to manage our social lives.

The relationship of racial status and self-evaluations is complex. In the United States, it had generally been believed that racism would lead to poor self-evaluations—low social standing, for example, would lead African Americans to evaluate themselves more negatively than the majority group. Indeed, research from the 1940s known as "doll studies" in which African American youth were asked to evaluate how "good" black and white dolls were suggested that African American children had low self-evaluations (Clark 1963). However, subsequently, scholars have tended to use survey data from nationally representative samples rather than qualitative measures and have developed extensive theories of a Black-White paradox in mental health (Louie et al. 2022). That is, Blacks are better off psychologically than Whites. For example, more contemporary research using quantitative measures of self-esteem shows African Americans with the same or higher levels of self-esteem compared to Whites (Jackson and Lassiter 2001; Porter and Lassiter 2001; Porter and Washing-ton 1993; Ridolfo, Chepp, and Milkie 2013). This is likely due to more extensive social support, strong religious communities, and positive reflections from kin (Louie et al. 2022) which can build esteem even in a world of wider disdain for one's group.

Because women are disadvantaged relative to men from a status standpoint, we might expect women to have lower self-esteem than men. Research on the gender difference in self-esteem, however, paints a complex picture. For example, research has shown that the relationship between gender and self-evaluations varies by age, with the greatest differences in male and female self-esteem appearing in puberty (Falci 2011; Stathem and Rhoades 2001). It is clear that adolescent girls lose self-esteem during this time period, probably due to social changes occurring at that time in their lives. Research on differences in females' and males' self-esteem after puberty is more mixed, with some studies continuing to show differences and others not (Statham and Rhoades 2001). In general, research indicates that men and women on average have similar levels of self-esteem. There is less research on esteem of those with fluid gender identities; however this is a growing area of research (see, for example, van den Brink, Vollmann, and Weelie 2020).

Some research shows that levels and effects of mattering vary by gender, with women reporting higher levels of mattering than men (Schieman and Taylor 2001; Taylor and Turner 2001). This is different from what we find with other social resources such as mastery (with men higher) or self-esteem (where women and men tend to have similar levels), perhaps because mattering may represent social connections, which are typically more central for women than men (Liebler and Sandefur 2002; Pugliesi and Shook 1998). It also appears that the relationship between mattering and mental health is stronger among women compared to men (Schieman and Taylor 2001; Taylor and Turner 2001).

Social Statuses and Identities

In addition to effects of social status on evaluative dimensions of the self, we also develop our identities based on those statuses. Ethnicity is an important social status, and one that has connections to individual identity. How people understand themselves as having a certain ethnicity is in no small part connected to the beliefs and practices of the larger society. One important study by Joanne Nagel (1995) examined the following puzzle: U.S. census data from the 1970s and 1980s showed a large increase in the number of residents identifying themselves as "American Indian," the term the group most preferred at the time of her study. Yet there had been no increase in birthrates, no decrease in death rates, or any immigration from other parts of North America that could account for the shift.

Nagel (1995) found that large numbers of people who had some American Indian ancestry identified themselves as "White" on their census forms at one point and later switched ethnicities, claiming American Indian identity. She argued that three social factors affected the likelihood of "feeling" and "being" American Indian. First, legal changes made government resources, such as scholarships and programs, available to those who identified as Indians. Second, the "Red Power" movement, in some ways like the civil rights movement, shifted negative stereotypes of Indians to become more positive. Third, urbanization created larger groupings of individuals with some American Indian background, allowing them to form collectivities that helped people understand themselves as part of this "supertribal" ethnic group. Each of these made claiming an Indian identity more appealing.

Some groups with more status and power than others, such as Whites, have more options to define their ethnic identity. For example, Mary Waters (1999) found that for Whites, ethnicity was a fun part of their background, where they could pick and choose whether and when to call themselves "Irish" or "Greek," for example. For others, those with dark skin and certain other characteristics or physical features that U.S. society terms "Black," it is much more difficult to "decide" or project an ethnic identity, such as Jamaican, for example, in that others often assume that they are African Americans and treat them this way (Waters 1999). These studies show the importance of social-structural conditions in our attempts to construct or take on ethnic identities.

Measuring the Self-Concept

Psychologists regularly conduct personality tests using instruments designed to place people within a limited set of personality dimensions. For instance, the Myers-Briggs personality inventory includes a battery of questions that divides personality into four different dimensions. In contrast to most psychologists, social psychologists—in psychology and sociology—tend to focus on the self-concept rather than personality per se. Measures of the self-concept include more qualitative assessments of who people are as well as quantitative measures similar to the type found in personality tests.

The Twenty Statements Test

One of the ways that you can assess your own identity is by taking the Twenty Statements Test, or TST (see Figure 5.1). Go try it now before reading further! The TST was developed by Manford Kuhn and Thomas McPartland (1954) as a way of assessing individuals' self-concepts. The test simply asks respondents to answer the question "Who am I?" 20 times. Responses to the TST are generally divided into four categories or "modes": the physical self, the social self, the reflective self, and the oceanic self (Zurcher 1977). The **physical self** refers to physical characteristics such as hair color or height. The **social self** refers to roles and statuses, such as student, daughter or son, and gender. The **reflective self** refers to feelings and traits such as being shy or kindhearted. An additional category, the **oceanic self**, includes those dimensions of the self that do not easily fit into the first three categories, usually referring to some holistic sense of self.

TST results can be influenced by context. If you took it in the classroom, for example, the "student" identity might be highly salient and listed among the first few responses. You can try to compare self-ratings with people around you using the categories listed.

Box 5.5 Careers Related to the Self

How can you make a living using your knowledge of self and identity? There are jobs commonly called "Profilers" but they are rare and almost always involve working for an organization such as the Federal Bureau of Investigation (FBI, look for the title "criminal behavioral analyst"). Traditionally, master's or PhD-trained psychologists are paid to assess personality traits as part of a larger assessment of the health and well-being of their patients. You can still use your training as an undergraduate student in several ways that relate to the self-concept. Here are two examples that represent a host of other related positions:

1. **Psychology Technician**, Bureau of Prisons/Federal Prison System, Department of Justice. Duties: Under the supervision of a psychologist, is responsible for the administration, mechanical or computerized scoring and distribution (or storage) of a variety of psychological tests, including Minnesota Multiphasic Personality Inventory (MMPI), and the Millon Clinical Multiaxial Inventory. Qualifications: Successful completion of a full four-year course of study leading to a bachelor's degree with major study or at least 24 hours in any combination of courses such as psychology, statistics, or other directly related subjects.
2. **Academic Success Coach**, Tennessee State University. Duties: The Academic/Success Coaches will address individual academic, financial, career, and social issues and concerns that affect students' success, and provide educational, social, experiential, and professional opportunities for students to become engaged professionals in Education and Psychology programs. Qualifications: Requires a bachelor's degree with two years of experience in coordinating educational projects, or initiatives, summarizing and reporting results to a variety of audiences.

How do these jobs relate to personality and the self-concept? The first one includes assessments of the self-concept to include things like self-esteem and mental well-being. Types of positions associated with being a success coach include titles such as, "Life Coach" or "Career Advisor" and they all involve helping people see the connection between their senses of self and their careers or how to be successful in life more broadly.

Early research in the TST from the 1950s found that most students characterized themselves primarily in terms of the social self, identifying themselves in terms of the social roles and groups to which they belonged. More recent work shows a move toward the reflective self, focused on feelings and personal traits (Grace and Cramer 2002; Snow and Phillips 1982). Further, although women are somewhat more likely to report family roles than men, research from decades past found little difference in test outcomes between men and women (Mackie 1983). Would there be bigger or smaller gender differences today?

On each line below, write a different answer to the question "Who am I?" As you write these answers, respond as if you are giving these answers to yourself and not to somebody else. Also, write your responses quickly and in the order they occur to you. When you have completed 20 lines, you have finished taking the TST.

Who Am I?

1. ______________________________
2. ______________________________
3. ______________________________
4. ______________________________
5. ______________________________
6. ______________________________
7. ______________________________
8. ______________________________
9. ______________________________
10. ______________________________
11. ______________________________
12. ______________________________
13. ______________________________
14. ______________________________
15. ______________________________
16. ______________________________
17. ______________________________
18. ______________________________
19. ______________________________
20. ______________________________

Interpreting Findings: Review each of your responses and try to code them into one of four categories: physical characteristics, social roles or group membership (social self), personal traits (reflective self), or some holistic sense of self (oceanic self) (e.g., "I am one with the universe"). What do your results say about who you are? Do you see yourself more in terms of in the context of groups and society (social self) or your personal traits (reflective self)? Most modern American students focus on their reflective or social selves. How about you?

Figure 5.1 The Twenty Statements Test.

Source: Adapted from Kuhn and McPartland (1954).

Responses to the TST tend to be positive. Few people report things such as "I am a bad person." More recent research using the TST has attempted to explore this issue with the development of the "Who Am I Not" (WAIN) test (McCall 2003). Instead of asking who I am, the WAIN asks respondents to answer the question "Who am I NOT?" There may be two poles of our identity, one in which we anchor identities (the "Me") and one in which we disidentify (the "Not-Me").

The Rosenberg Self-Esteem Scale

Self-esteem, mastery, and mattering can be measured quantitatively. One of the most popular measures is the Rosenberg Self-Esteem Scale (see Table 5.2). These measures assume that responses to a series of questions about one's thoughts and feelings accurately portray a dimension of the self-concept. If this is true, we can use such measures to test empirical relationships between social processes and the self-concept using surveys (see Chapter 2).

Morris Rosenberg*

Morris (Manny) Rosenberg's groundbreaking work on the self-concept and self-esteem rendered him world renowned. During the 1950s, Rosenberg received his PhD from Columbia University, where he studied under famous sociologists, including C. Wright Mills, Paul Lazarsfeld, and Robert K. Merton. He spent most of his early career working at the National Institute of Mental Health before becoming a professor of sociology at the University of Maryland, where he taught from 1975 until his death in 1992.

Rosenberg devoted much of his time to the study of self-esteem, which he regarded as a positive or negative orientation toward oneself. Most of Rosenberg's work explored how social-structural positions, such as racial or ethnic statuses, and institutional contexts, such as schools or families, relate to a person's self-esteem. He was one of the pioneers of applying large-scale samples in the study of self processes. This type of work contributed to his receiving the Cooley-Mead Award in 1989.

Some of Rosenberg's most impressive works include *Society and the Adolescent Self-Image* (1965) and *Conceiving the Self* (1979). He also coedited the book *Social Psychology: Sociological Perspectives* (1990), in which he and Ralph Turner (another Cooley-Mead Award recipient, reviewed in Chapter 11) brought together some of the best sociological social psychology research to date. Our book has the same title. We also try to follow their format by emphasizing the contributions of sociologists to the field of social psychology. Perhaps one of Rosenberg's greatest accomplishments is the world-renowned Rosenberg Self-Esteem Scale. This scale has been used by countless researchers to study self-esteem.

*Information about this biography was obtained from Viktor Gecas's (1990) introduction of the Cooley-Mead Award printed in *Social Psychology Quarterly*.

Table 5.2 Rosenberg Self-Esteem Scale

	1 Strongly Agree	2 Agree	3 Disagree	4 Strongly Disagree
I feel that I'm a person of worth, at least on an equal plane with others.*	SA	A	D	SD
I feel that I have a number of good qualities.*	SA	A	D	SD
All in all, I am inclined to feel that I am a failure.	SA	A	D	SD
I am able to do things as well as most other people.*	SA	A	D	SD
I feel I do not have much to be proud of.	SA	A	D	SD
I take a positive attitude toward myself.*	SA	A	D	SD
On the whole, I am satisfied with myself.*	SA	A	D	SD
I wish I could have more respect for myself.	SA	A	D	SD
I certainly feel useless at times.	SA	A	D	SD
At times I think I am no good at all.	SA	A	D	SD

*Items to be reverse-coded.
Source: Adapted from Rosenberg (1986).

Section Summary

In this section, we used the social structure and personality perspective to answer the questions "What are three dimensions of the self-concept?" and "What do we know from research on the self-concept?" Although there are many dimensions to the evaluative component of the self-concept, a considerable amount of research has focused on self-esteem, which is our sense of self-worth; mastery, our sense of control over what happens to us; and mattering, our sense of importance to others. Social structure and personality researchers attempt to study effects of social positions on people's self-concepts. For instance, we examined research showing that class position affects our global sense of self-worth, although generally only as we reach adolescence and adulthood, when we begin to see our relative position in the social structure.

A Take-Away Message

Many people will give you advice about how to boost your self-esteem and feelings of self-worth—there is an entire "self-help" genre out there. However, before you consider taking their advice, you may want to consider the findings from this section of the chapter. First, chances are you have pretty good global self-esteem. You may want to focus on specific self-esteem, or esteem associated with specific areas of your life. To some degree, successes in a particular sphere will enhance your feelings of worthiness about that identity, such as student, but the others you are surrounded with matter in terms of providing appraisals and comparisons for your evaluations of yourself. You could also examine your position in society—your race, class, and gender—to see how it is influencing your self-concept—and why. Professionally, given that you may be in a privileged position based in your high level of education, you may want to consider the factors that affect people's senses of esteem, mastery, and mattering when you look for a job. Is the potential work environment and the others you may work with conducive to developing a positive sense of self? How? If you are in or end up in a management position, how might knowing the things that influence our senses of self help you to lead other people on the job and create an environment that allows building of mastery and mattering?

IDENTITY AND GROUP PROCESSES

> *Joining the local Veteran's Club changed the way I felt about being in the Army. I did my service like anyone else. I joined for the benefits. After coming back from Afghanistan, I felt like I should do something more. I left the service and joined the Vet's Club. I pretty much stick with the others in the club since they understand what it was like over there. Maybe I am more comfortable with these guys. People outside the club just don't get it.*
>
> —Sam, senior philosophy major

Many of the self and identity processes we have discussed thus far occur in the contexts of groups. Groups serve to establish and maintain our senses of self. Groups can also serve to give you an identity that is a collective one. A group identity may become part of how you describe yourself. In Sam's case, he began to think of himself as a veteran after he joined the Veteran's Club. Thus, in an objective sense, he was a veteran but did not take on that identity until he joined the group. In addition, this identity changed his view of himself and the people around him—other people "just don't get it."

Social Identity Theory

If you filled in the Twenty Statements Test in Figure 5.1, you noticed that your self-concept is composed of various components. You may see yourself in terms of your social roles such as an environmentalist, an athlete, or linked to your gender, nationality, race or ethnicity, the college or university you attend, and any other number of factors. According to **social identity theory**, we carry self-definitions that match all the categories to which we belong. In this theory, self-definitions are called **social identities**.

Originally developed in psychology, social identity theory proposes that our social identities describe to us who we are, provide us with information about how to behave,

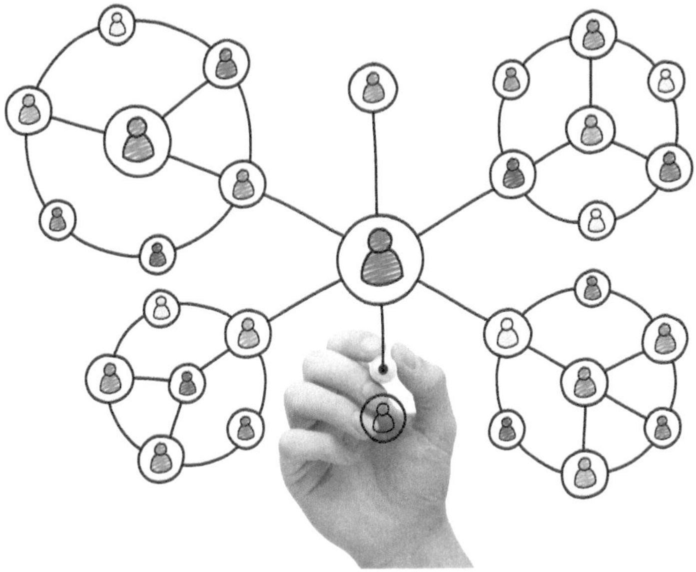

Photo 5.2 Our identities incorporate many different roles and group affiliations. How many different groups do you belong to? How do they affect your sense of who you are?

Source: Ivelin Radkov/Shutterstock

and tell us how we should evaluate other people (Hogg, Terry, and White 1995). The theory proposes that people define themselves, in part, by their group memberships (Hogg and Ridgeway 2003; Tajfel 1982).

Also, in any given social context, some of our social identities will be more salient to us than others. What salience means in this context is that they stand out and are noticeable to us. Imagine, for example, being a staunch Democrat in a meeting of your university's Young Republicans Club (or vice versa). In that case, your social identity tied to your political views would probably be very salient because it would mark you as different from other members of the group.

When a social identity is salient, social identity theory says that we will perceive ourselves according to that identity. Further, we will tend to behave in ways that are stereotypical of that identity. If you are a woman in a situation in which your gender identity is highly salient, for example, social identity theory says that you will tend to act in ways that are gender-stereotypical for women in our society. Perhaps most important, social identity theory proposes that when identities are salient, we will view members of other groups in ways that are stereotypical for their group. Thus, when social identities become salient, our relationships with and perceptions of people in different categories of that identity will be competitive and discriminatory (Hogg and Ridgeway 2003).

Why do people participate in a process that promotes one's own group at the expense of other groups? It sounds discriminatory. It is. As discussed in this chapter, people tend to carry out actions that will promote their own senses of self, or self-esteem. Because of this, and because we view ourselves in terms of our group memberships, we are motivated to adopt strategies in interactions that make our own groups look better (to both ourselves and others) than other groups. Social identity theory argues that we engage in two processes that allow us to draw favorable comparisons between our own groups and other groups—categorization and self-enhancement.

According to social identity theory, we not only see ourselves in terms of our category memberships but also seek to assign other people to social categories. **Categorization** is the process through which we draw sharp dividing lines between group membership categories and assign people (including ourselves) to relevant categories. You might, for example, see stark differences between Democrats and Republicans and seek to assign people to one category or another. When we do this, we accentuate similarities we perceive between people in the same categories (Deaux and Martin 2003). For example, we might tend to see all Democrats as highly homogeneous in their views. We also accentuate perceived differences across categories. You might, for example, see Democrats and Republicans as fundamentally different in how they view the world when there are many similarities. When these processes happen, people (including ourselves) are depersonalized and seen only in terms of their category memberships.

Self-enhancement refers to the process through which we make comparisons that favor our own groups. This can be done in multiple ways. One way we draw comparisons that favor our own groups can be to essentially delude ourselves into seeing our group as better than it really is. Another way is to focus specifically on differences that favor our own group while ignoring differences that do not. For example, when students at a state university and students at a community college compare themselves on their identities associated with their colleges, social identity theory would expect each to make comparisons most favorable to their own groups. The university students, for example, might focus on the diverse opportunities available to them, whereas the community college students might focus on their smaller class sizes and access to professors.

The ramifications of social identity processes can be large. We may use our group affiliations to bias our understandings of other people's motives. We may also use social identities to judge the competency of other people, showing favoritism toward people in our own social category over others (Barnum and Markovsky 2007; Kalkhoff and Barnum 2000; Oldmeadow et al. 2003). Social identity theory shows how group processes affect our identities. Our senses of self derive in large part from the groups to which we belong, and we tend to view both ourselves and others in terms of group memberships.

The tendencies toward self-enhancement associated with social identity theory are relevant to racial and ethnic group tensions. Strong ties to a particular group will likely lead to positive self-esteem, but they will likely bias perceptions of people outside of our racial or ethnic group. Social identity theory and the research associated with it clearly show that such biases exist. We will address the role of in-group and out-group bias more in Chapter 9.

Section Summary

This section addressed the question "How do group processes affect identity?" Here we reviewed social identity theory. Social identity theory proposes that our social identities describe to us who we are, provide us with information about how to behave, and tell us how we should evaluate other people. Group memberships include racial and ethnic groups, among others. Once accepted, we employ group identities into interactions with other people, using them to differentially evaluate the attitudes and behaviors of people inside and outside of the group.

A Take-Away Message

If you follow the logic of social identity theory, it means that part of who you are is composed of other people. This is an interesting way to confirm how your personal identity is social in nature! On the job, you should be aware of the coalitions that exist around you. They are not just about individuals vying for power but also about friendships and identities. Hence, when there is a problem with a person on the job, it might be associated with problems with a group of people! Having this knowledge may help you figure out how to best navigate these groups and make decisions about how to best relate to them.

BRINGING IT ALL TOGETHER

> *In the end, I think it is all about our genes. I mean, you can't change the way people are.*
>
> —Josh, senior marketing major

Josh's philosophy of human personality is deterministic. He views our sense of identity as formed by a genetic code that is not likely to change over a lifetime—people are born a certain way, and they stay that way. Most of us would give some credit to the influences of parents, teachers, and role models in our lives. Scholars too would disagree quite strongly with Josh. Interactionists would question Josh's deterministic attitude because humans have the capacity to manipulate the meanings of different identities both internally, through self-indication, and externally, via relationships with other people. Also, we can manipulate our impressions regardless of who we "really" are.

The social structure and personality perspective emphasizes how both social and social-structural conditions affect our selves. Our social positions, notably in the form of social class, race, and gender, influence the evaluative dimensions of the self-concept such as self-esteem, mastery, and mattering. Social structures constrain the possibilities for who we can claim to be; in other words, it's much more difficult to have a "swimmer" identity if you are living in poverty and do not have access to pool facilities. Moreover, researchers such as Joanne Nagel would disagree with Josh even on something seemingly unchangeable like ethnic identity. Her work shows how structural factors influence the likelihood of invoking particular ethnicities as part of our identities.

Social identity theory, linked to the group-processes perspective, emphasizes the importance of the role of our group memberships in our senses of self. Research in this tradition shows that we define ourselves and others in large part based on group memberships.

Together, these perspectives show the role that society plays in the development and maintenance of our senses of self. Genetics may play a role in our dispositions or temperament, but society provides a major context for the content and shape of our selves. From the influence of those we interact with on our self-evaluations and identity structure, to the "audience" we present to, to the definitions of social groups we are a part of, the "social" is fundamentally linked to our self-concept.

SUMMARY

1. From a symbolic interactionist perspective, the self is a process in which we construct a sense of who we are. We use symbols and language to communicate with other people, but we also use language to think internally. The self includes a dialogue between two components, the I and the Me.
2. Identity includes our social categories and personal characteristics. Identity theory examines how social conditions and relationships affect the salience of identities and thus our behavior. Affect control theory incorporates emotions into identity processes.
3. Dramaturgical sociology is a branch of symbolic interactionism that studies impression formation and management.
4. The self-concept refers to all our thoughts and feelings about ourselves as an object (often studied in the form of self-identities) and self-evaluations of self-esteem, mattering, and mastery.
5. Class, race or ethnicity, age, and gender are important social statuses that influence our self-development over time.
6. Social identity theory argues that people define and evaluate themselves in terms of the groups they belong to, including the race and gender categories within particular societies.

KEY TERMS AND CONCEPTS

Affect control theory: The theory that incorporates elements of symbolic interactionism and identity theory to explain the role of emotion in identity processes.

Backstage: Part of dramaturgical sociology referring to the region where we relax our impression management efforts.

Categorization: In social identity theory, the process through which we draw sharp dividing lines between group membership categories and assign people (including ourselves) to relevant categories.

Dramaturgical sociology: The study of how we present ourselves, playing roles and managing impressions during interactions with other people.

Emotional arousal: Inferences about our abilities based on our emotional states that we use to build our sense of mastery.

Facework: Any way in which we try to protect our own and others' presentation of self.

Front stage: Part of dramaturgical sociology referring to the place where we present ourselves to others.

I: The part of the self that is active, engaging in interactions with others.

Identity: Our internalized, stable sense of who we are.

Identity control theory: Interactionist theory that argues that individuals have a tendency to seek confirmation of self-meanings.

Identity theory: Interactionist theory that describes how society shapes our sense of self and how those views affect our behavior.

Impression management: The ways individuals seek to control the impressions they convey to other people.

Impressions given: The impressions that we believe we are giving.

Impressions given off: The actual impression the other person has of us.

Mastery: Our perceptions of our ability to control things important to us.

Mattering: Our sense that we are important to other people in the world.

Me: The part of the self that includes an organized set of attitudes toward the self.

Oceanic self: Dimension of the Twenty Statements Test referring to a holistic description of the self.

Personal accomplishments: Being able to achieve what we start out to do; used in the development of mastery.

Personal characteristics: Anything we use to describe our unique qualities.

Physical self: Dimension of the Twenty Statements Test referring to our physical characteristics, such as hair color or height.

Psychological centrality: Our ability to shift aspects of the self to become more or less important to our overall self-concept.

Reflected appraisals: The ways that we believe others view and evaluate us.

Reflective self: Dimension of the Twenty Statements Test referring to our feelings and traits such as being shy or nice.

Role identities: The internalized expectations associated with different positions.

Self: A process in which we construct a sense of who we are through interaction with others.

Self-concept: The outcome of the self-process at a given point in time; the sum total of our thoughts and feelings about ourselves as an object.

Self-consistency motive: A drive to maintain a consistent sense of self.

Self-enhancement: In social identity theory, the process through which we make comparisons that favor our own groups.

Self-esteem: The positive or negative evaluation of our self as an object.

Self-esteem motive: The desire to maintain positive self-images.

Self-evaluations: Judgments we make of ourselves, based in others' views.

Self-fulfilling prophecy: A process in which expectations produce a reality consistent with assumptions.

Self-identities: The kind of person we see ourselves and present ourselves as.

Self-indication: The use of symbols and language to communicate internally.

Self-narratives: The social construction of identities through the use of personal stories.

Self-perceptions: Observations of our behavior and its consequences.

Situated self: A temporally based sense of who we are.

Social categories: Identities related to social groups to which we belong.

Social comparisons: Using other people as points of reference for our thoughts, feelings, and behaviors.

Social identities: A form of self-definition used in social identity theory based on our group affiliations.

Social identity theory: The theory based on the principle that we carry self-definitions that match all the categories to which we belong.

Social self: Dimension of the Twenty Statements Test referring to our roles and statuses, such as student, brother, or basketball player.

Verbal persuasion: Information from others about our abilities; used to derive mastery.

Vicarious experience: A way of building mastery by seeing other people perform tasks; it shows us that the task can be accomplished.

DISCUSSION QUESTIONS

1. Think about your sense of self. What role do you think that your race, ethnicity, gender, and age play in your day-to-day interactions and feelings about who you are?
2. Would it be possible to change your sense of self? Apply some of the information from this chapter to figure out how you could negotiate social forces to help you "construct" a new self.
3. Take the Twenty Statements Test (TST). Did anything surprise you about the findings? How do you think the order of your responses would be different (if at all) if you took it in person in the classroom? What about if you did the TST at work? At home?
4. Where, if at all, do you utilize avatars online? Consider video games or discussion groups. Did you act any differently in these identities than in your offline world? If so, discuss how and why they are different.

6

Socialization over the Life Course

I was just 14, and my friend and I became volunteers at a local hospital. Because we had these uniforms on, patients, their families, nurses, and other staff were treating us like we knew what we were doing. But it was just a summer volunteer job, and I was sure I would mess it up! It was strange, but after about a month, I really felt competent at getting the patients where they had to be. I was proud when people asked me questions and I had learned the answers. The hospital setting was routine, but there was some real drama in the hallways, and being a part of that place was something I really liked. Now I'm planning to go to medical school.

—Maya, senior biology major

Socialization is the process by which individuals acquire thoughts, feelings, and behaviors "appropriate" to their positions in society (Corsaro and Fingerson 2003; Stryker 2002). As with Maya's story, socialization can occur informally through observation and interaction. Socialization can also be more formal as children enter educational institutions to learn the appropriate skills necessary to successfully enter the economy of a given society. Although most people associate socialization with children's development, adults continue to be socialized throughout their lives, learning norms and values in new social contexts as well as age-appropriate ways to think, feel, and behave (Crosnoe and Elder 2004; Elder 1994; Mortimer and Simmons 1978). In the preceding example, Maya is socialized as a hospital worker—she learns what it means to be that kind of person, interacts with others based on that role, and finally comes to feel that the role is central to who she is.

Sociologists study socialization processes at every stage of development. We will review symbolic interactionist perspectives on childhood development of the self, followed by a review of the life-course perspective in sociology, which derives from the social structure and personality perspective. Group processes work does not tend to focus on socialization but can be related to it. This chapter addresses the following questions regarding socialization and life-course sociology:

- How does society influence the social construction of the self? What are the stages involved in developing the self?
- What are the four elements of life-course sociology? What are agents of socialization, and how do they affect people's lives?
- How do group processes researchers study socialization?

DEVELOPING THE SELF

> *I never really played "house" growing up. Then a friend brought a couple of Barbie dolls over and asked me to play. I kind of felt obligated to participate. She had a Ken doll and we tried to get a boy to play with us. It did not work. So, we just asked a girl down the street to play Ken, the boyfriend. It worked fine. She was the best Ken I ever met.*
>
> —Bess, physics major

As discussed in Chapter 5, interactionists view the self as a process. We pick up and drop aspects of our characters in different circumstances and social contexts. We learn these new aspects of the self by observing how other people act under certain conditions and decide which of them to adapt as our own. In Bess's case, she did not necessarily desire to play dolls when she was young, but instead found herself pulled into the experience by a friend. Social psychologists generally believe that such experiences are important to socialization because they provide opportunities to learn how people behave. In Bess's story, gender is being taught in many ways. Bess learns that little girls play with dolls in our society. In addition, while playing dolls, she ascribes gender-role behavior to the dolls. The girls try to find a boy to play Ken, the man's role. They turn to a girl out of need. It turns out that the girl can play the role of Ken as well as any boy.

The key point to this interaction is the importance of playing a part in society. The interactionist perspective sees this process occurring as a progression of role changes over time (Holstein and Gubrium 2003; Stryker 2002). We start by practicing roles or simply acting out parts, something akin to dramaturgical sociology discussed in Chapter 5. We also empathize with other people's roles, giving us the ability to predict what they will do in a given situation and how to react accordingly. Over time, we develop the ability to coordinate multiple roles while incorporating other people's points of view. We will review some of the basic stages associated with childhood development and then examine how these dynamics are demonstrated in children's lives.

Stages of Development

The exchange of language and symbols is essential to the symbolic interactionist perspective. If the self is a symbolic process, then children must learn language skills before they can fully develop their senses of self. Although children pick up symbolic acts within the first few months of life (e.g., smiling at others), they do not fully develop their language skills until at least five or six years of age. There is, however, some evidence of the self developing in babies under the age of one (Hurh 2003; Stern 2004). Thereafter, children's development of the self occurs in stages as they acquire symbols and language over time.

The ability to take the roles of others—seeing social interaction from other people's perspectives—takes time and practice. At first, children simply mimic the language and behaviors of their parents and caretakers. This is called the **preparatory stage** (Mead 1934). The preparatory stage provides the cognitive information necessary for children to act out other people's roles. Anyone who has seen a two-year-old around a group of adults can understand the preparatory stage. Children will often repeat words or short phrases without knowing what they mean. Imagine a father dropping something on his foot and screaming a profanity in reaction to the event. Thereafter, the child might find herself yelling profanities anytime something bad happens to her. The parent realizes that the child is mimicking his own behavior and prepares to "resocialize" the child to a new vocabulary.

As children begin to develop more language skills, they can start using these skills to think symbolically. In the **play stage**, children begin to use language to make believe as they play others' roles. A child may start pretending that she is a firefighter or a teacher. In this stage, children generally take on one role at a time. For instance, the three-year-old son of one of this book's authors got in trouble while pretending to be Batman. When his father sent him to time out, the child angrily cried, "Batman doesn't go in time out!" Clearly, he was Batman at the time and was not able to connect his role as Batman—an adult with full control over his life—with that of a three-year-old son who must obey his parents.

Finally, children learn to integrate their knowledge into cohesive pictures of their social worlds. The **game stage** occurs when children are capable of managing several roles at the same time. This power allows us to participate in organized role relationships. For instance, we must understand the role of the other team's players in a baseball or football game, knowing how they are likely to respond to our actions in a competition. This ability requires that we can situate ourselves amidst several different people, and thus roles, at the same time.

There are no specific rules about when these abilities will develop in children because they vary from person to person. Some children learn these processes readily, whereas others take longer, depending on their own abilities to acquire and manipulate symbols and their social environments. The ability to adapt and integrate symbols is essential to these dynamics; hence, some basic cognitive development is required to move into the play and game stages (see Box 6.1).

Taking the Role of the Other

An essential aspect of self-development is the ability to understand the perspectives of other people. In symbolic interactionism, this is called taking the role of the other. We

Box 6.1 Piaget's Stages of Cognitive Development

Jean Piaget (1896–1980) was a psychologist who studied individuals' cognitive development. He argued that all people develop their mental and physical abilities in the following stages:

- **Sensorimotor stage (birth to 2)**: Children develop a sense of cause and effect of their behaviors by physically investigating their worlds and by imitation of other people's behavior.
- **Preoperational stage (2 to 7)**: Children learn to use symbols and language to communicate but are not able to think in complex ways.
- **Concrete operational stage (7 to 11)**: Children start developing reasoning skills by classifying, ranking, and separating physical objects.
- **Formal operational stage (11+)**: Children develop their abstract reasoning skills, working out problems and issues in their minds.

Sociological social psychologists generally agree with psychological perspectives on development but view the process as more fluid. That is, our development is partly related to biology but is also influenced by our social surroundings as well as our ability to make decisions in the development process. For instance, a child from a family with lower socioeconomic status might interact within a less rich symbolic environment than other children, such as those described in Piaget's model. Interactionist approaches to development incorporate these sorts of variations.

cannot "play doctor" unless we have the ability to understand what a doctor does relative to other people. This understanding helps us know the appropriate ways to behave in a given context. Charles Horton Cooley (1922) argued that the self relies on other people's responses. This idea has been deemed the **looking-glass self**—how the self relies on imagined responses of others in its development. In other words, a person's sense of self is partly a reflection of the reactions of other people. For instance, if you give a speech and find that the audience is frowning, yawning, and making comments as you talk, you will likely interpret this reaction to mean that you are not a good speaker, and you may feel embarrassed or ashamed. When people important to us (or significant others like mothers) give us feedback (such as approval of behaviors), we may feel pride. We also have the ability to understand how the larger society may view us. The **generalized other** refers to people's perceptions of the attitudes of the whole community (Cooley 1922; Mead 1934). With the generalized other, we can imagine how other people in general would react to a thought or behavior. Imagine you are a smoker going to an event where you know almost no one. You may want to light up a cigarette but will probably consider what other people will think of you. Because you do not know anyone very well, you must rely on your knowledge of your culture's attitudes toward smoking. Because smoking indoors is unacceptable or illegal in many places in the United States, Canada, and other countries, you know not to "light up" at many social activities. You may even consider asking permission before smoking at an outdoor event; in many parts of Europe, in contrast, smoking is more accepted by "the generalized other" in a variety of places.

Lee (1998) illustrated how talented science, math, and engineering (SME)-interested high school students' internalized meanings about self and the "generalized other" affected their own academic trajectories in gendered ways. When asked to rate themselves and "other science students" in terms of particular personality traits, boys' descriptions of themselves were more similar to how they described "other science students" than girls' descriptions. That is, there was a greater discrepancy between how girls saw themselves and their perceptions of other science students than boys, which was associated with lower future interest in the discipline. Lee concluded that boys' and girls' internalized meanings about self and others shape behavior in ways that can importantly affect life trajectories.

Because we continue to adopt and drop roles in our lifetimes, symbolic interactionists view socialization as an ongoing dynamic that occurs internally (what we are thinking about ourselves, others, and the generalized other) and externally (through words, mannerisms, and other symbolic exchanges with other people). The self also changes given different cultural and societal conditions because the generalized other can also change over time. Under this paradigm, the self can change as quickly as our environments and our ability to process the information from those environments.

Learning about Race, Class, and Gender Statuses

In Chapter 5, we discussed the formation of identities as including roles and group memberships. How do we start incorporating race, class, and gender into our senses of self? The stages of development reviewed earlier in this chapter help to elaborate on how we see and then practice roles. The subtle nature of children's play can help us understand the roots of the replication of racist attitudes and behaviors. Children find creative ways to develop independence from adults as well as ways of excluding others from their play (Corsaro 2005). Race and ethnicity can be one of the ways in which children distinguish themselves or their groups from others (Van Ausdale and Feagin 2002). Thus, race can serve as one of many markers among groups of people, especially if racial differences are readily apparent (e.g., skin color) and viewed as important distinctions in the society. However, children are capable of finding ways to differentiate among groups based on things other than the color of skin. If language is the building block of symbolic interaction, then language differences can be one of the first methods of differentiation. Language can serve as a way to exclude children from play. For example, children may interact such that only Spanish or English is allowed, and thus exclude those who do not speak a particular language.

Racial socialization refers to learning about one's ethnic and racial identity in a given culture. Families may pass on their cultural heritage to their children in the form of racial or ethnic pride or history. Minority parents can also help prepare their children for racial bias in the future (Hughes 2003; Hughes and Johnson 2001; see also Dow 2016). Racial socialization is important in part because a strong ethnic identity is associated with greater psychological well-being (Yip 2005).

Debra Van Ausdale and Joe Feagin's (2002) research shows that racial divisions can be brought into children's interactions at a very young age, even before they have the ability to fully understand their ramifications. Some racist epithets may simply be heard and repeated among peers as young as three years old. Racist language may start with simple imitation, but children can use those to create more extensive conceptualizations of race and ethnicity. From an interactionist perspective, children can actively develop and manipulate simple statements about skin color or other characteristics into complex sets of meaning about categories of people. The process involves intellectual and social components, some related to race and some not. For instance, a child may hear a racial epithet but do nothing with the observation until social conditions require some means of differentiation among peers. The child may then use and elaborate on the epithet as a means of defining oneself and others in an interaction. Therefore, some of the same basic interactionist principles of socialization are used to negotiate racist and ethnocentric attitudes and behaviors. Scholars also see this as *racialization* processes—at the individual level, children are learning and reproducing the categorization of people into different groups through interaction. These racialization processes are also embedded within organizations as structures and practices may be racialized, such as law enforcement or education systems (Ray 2019).

The process of acquiring a racial identity may start with the naming of children. Consider an immigrant family moving into a new country—do they choose first names for new babies that are common in their home country or their new country? This decision starts the symbolic process of ethnic identity for children (Gerhards and Hans 2009). Choosing a name associated with a new country begins a symbolic process of enculturation to its norms. Focusing on the home country implies the importance of maintaining ethnic identity. Racial identities continue to be employed during interactions later in life. Interethnic and biracial youths and adults often manipulate the use of their mixed racial identities to help manage social interactions; when a particular racial identity is harmful (e.g., in managing racism), they sometimes learn ways of passing and covering (Chapter 7) those aspects of their identities (Khanna and Johnson 2010; Sultana 2010). In this way, individuals—children and adults—utilize the I and the Me to manage and develop their racial and ethnic identities in everyday interactions.

Gender socialization refers to the learning of expectations about how to behave related to one's gender (Gecas 1992) (see "doing gender" in Chapter 5). How children come to appropriate thoughts, feelings, and behaviors associated with age, gender, or other roles is not completely understood. On one level, children simply model the behavior of their parents. We know that mothers continue to do more housework than men, and men work more outside of the home than women (Bianchi, Robinson, and Milkie 2006; Heisig 2011; Robinson and Godbey 1997). Observing parents can have long-lasting consequences for gendered behavior. Mick Cunningham (2001), for instance, found that fathers' participation in routine housework when their children were very young had positive effects on their sons' later participation in housework, whereas mothers' employment during their daughters' formative years decreased the relative contributions of daughters to housework later in life. Therefore, teaching children expectations related to different genders may influence future behavior, but so do parental characteristics and behaviors.

Some research examines how children conceive of gender roles at different developmental stages. Melissa Milkie and her colleagues (Milkie, Simon, and Powell 1997) analyzed over 3,000 essays in which children had been asked by teachers to enter a local contest to explain why they had the "best" mother or father. Their results generally support findings that show the significance that traditional gender roles play in family relationships. However, they also found that children generally downplayed the significance of their father's labor force participation, rarely mentioning the breadwinner role central to most men's parenting. Comparing essays written in 1979 and 1980 with those written in the early 1990s, they found that the latter cohort of children de-emphasized the parent as a caretaker role, moving toward viewing them in a more recreational role, especially fathers. Hence, children's perceptions of family roles changed across time. Research shows that gender socialization begins even before children are born, as parents attribute gender characteristics to their children (Sweeney and Bradbard 1988). In a study of expectant parents, Kane (2009) found that parents began conceptualizing the gendered lives of their children and that utilizing this frame of reference influenced their gender preference. Boys were predicted to carry on the family name and enjoy sports, while girls would talk more and be more emotionally connected to the family. Parents also continue these types of gendered expectations in early childhood (Kane 2006). One study even showed that adults project human gender attributes to animals at a zoo, associating masculine and feminine traits to the animals (Garner and Grazian 2016). These studies show that gender socialization involves a complex exchange of meanings that continue to influence our thoughts, feelings, and behaviors throughout our lives.

Americans are also cognizant of class identities. For example, polls regularly find that most Americans define themselves as middle class, even though many of them would fit into the upper-class or the working class (Robison 2003). Learning the culture of different classes involves the learning of mannerisms and dress (Wouters 2007); this includes things like tastes in music or art (Bourdieu 1984). These constructed ways of living both reflect our class position to other people and also confirm that identity to ourselves. While we generally associate upper-class cultural consumption with activities such as opera or classical music, modern research suggests that elites in society are cultural omnivores, consuming both "high art" like operas and common forms of art like rock 'n' roll (Bennett et al. 2009). Higher levels of income may allow individuals to pursue expensive and time-consuming leisure—and they work hard at it (Taylor 2008). Of course, this lifestyle is learned through training at home as well as elite boarding schools (Gaztambide-Fernandez 2009). Class identities can be important for the middle, working, and poor classes as well, reflecting different types of cultural education and access to resources with which to consume material goods and gain skills in various forms of leisure (Banks 2010; Stewart 2010; Wasserman and Clair 2009; Weston 2008).

Adult Socialization

Although most of our discussion of socialization processes has focused on children, these socialization dynamics continue into adulthood. We continue to receive and give advice over the span of our lives, although the processes can vary by age group (Schafer and Upenieks 2016). We also learn new skills (personal, professional, and social) and social roles over time. We must be able to take the role of the other as we become parents, become workers, and change careers, among other life events. As such, we adapt new and drop old aspects of our identities. For instance, if you become an accountant, you will have to work with different sets of people who will likely interact with more formality and expect more consistent work patterns than do college students—and your norms and values will likely change as a result of these new relationships. While we expect parents to socialize their children, children can also socialize their parents, teaching them new norms and values (see Johnson and Best 2012). Many young people have to teach their parents and grandparents how to use common computer applications such as Facetime, as well as how to best search the internet to obtain needed information.

Like childhood socialization, adult socialization can be a reciprocal process: just as we are socialized into a new role, other people are being socialized by us. People do not just passively accept the training that they are receiving (Everitt 2013). Just like children, adults go through an interpretive reproduction of a new job, group, or other culture they are learning. For example, Allison Hicks (2008) studied the socialization of new prison chaplains. Prison chaplains are expected to serve as agents of socialization for inmates, trying to help them rehabilitate (resocialize) their spiritual and social lives. However, Hicks found that they had to modify these expectations to meet the demands of the institution and the apparent lack of desire among many prisoners to change. They began to redefine the concept of rehabilitation to include institutional goals, which included a stronger focus on safety and security needs in the prison environment. Hicks's work shows the multiple levels of socialization going on in this setting: prison chaplains try to socialize inmates, inmates affect chaplains, and institutional conditions influence the interactions between these two groups.

The Sociology of Childhood

A significant amount of the socialization literature focuses on children. However, the concept of "childhood" has changed dramatically through history (Jencks 1996). Being a child has generally been conceived of as a temporary stage, at best, or as a state that must be transformed or "civilized" in some way. Research in sociology views childhood as a state in life in which competent actors negotiate their social realities in a similar fashion as adults (Boocock and Scott 2005; Cahill 2003; see also Bateman 2016). In another sense, the notion of childhood—what it means to be a child and when children become adults—is socially constructed by a given society (Kehily 2004). Scholars who study childhood examine it as both a culture in and of itself and a role in the social construction of society.

Norman Denzin (1971; 1977) studied the subtle ways in which children interact with one another. He found that even very young children, aged 8 to 24 months, can participate in a "conversation of gestures," nonverbal and preverbal ways of indicating meaning to other people. They use these gestures to designate particular objects or ownership of objects. Denzin argued that these "conversations" evolve into verbal

PHOTO 6.1 School contexts provide children with a means of formally learning their culture ... as well as a place for the development of peer cultures. What sorts of things did your peers teach you when you were growing up?

Source: wavebreakmedia/Shutterstock

exchanges over time. Thus, even at very young ages, children begin the same interactional and negotiation processes as their parents. Indeed, they negotiate with their parents.

Because children are capable of the same interaction processes as adults, they can also develop their own cultures. William Corsaro (2005) defined **children's cultural routines** as stable sets of activities, objects, and values that children produce and share in interaction with each other. However, because children have meaning-making capacities similar to those of adults, they engage in interpretive reproductions of adult culture, creatively taking on elements of adult culture to meet the needs of their peer groups (Corsaro 1992; 2005; 2020).

Children mold specific roles to meet the needs of the peer groups in three ways:

1. Children take information from the adult world to create stable routines.
2. Children use language to manipulate adult models to address specific needs of their peer culture.
3. Children improvise "sociodramatic" play to acquire the dispositions necessary to manage their daily lives.

In summary, children use the patterns of behavior learned from their parents, siblings, and others to help them decide how to interact with other people. Children know what to do and say at the dinner table because they have practiced it so many times.

However, children also have human agency, the ability to act "out of character." In a group of peers, formal exchanges such as "please" and "thank you" may be replaced with jokes and play, depending on the composition of the group. Children can improvise the behaviors and roles learned from their parents to meet the needs of a particular group or social setting.

As active participants in the socialization process, children's routines serve as a basis for developing and maintaining larger cultures. Gary Alan Fine (1979) studied a group of youth baseball teams over time by observing the culture of each group and changes in those cultures. He found that the culture of a group changed as new people entered and left the group, but some consistency was maintained as new members learned ways of the group from older, senior members of the team. Fine (1979) referred to the culture of these small groups of boys as **idiocultures**, "a system of knowledge, beliefs, behaviors, and customs shared by an interacting group to which members refer and employ as a basis of further interaction" (Fine 1979, p. 734). These cultures are a hybrid culture composed of elements of the larger culture of baseball mixed with elements of the local cultures surrounding those teams and the personalities of the children playing on them. The merging of these worlds (individual and community) allows individuals to participate in culture construction without abandoning the culture of the larger community—in this case, the culture of baseball. It is important to note that the processes associated with idiocultures apply to all people, no matter their age. Idiocultures serve as a bridge between individuals and the larger society, providing a place to play out larger cultural elements among individuals. They are the place where individuals build commitment to society via their commitment to people in particular groups (Fine 2014). Individuals' personalities and identities influence these groups and provide the opportunity for individuals to participate in social change in small ways as some of those changes may make their way up to the larger culture over time (Fields 2014). These dynamics help to show how we participate in socialization processes both as recipients and agents of social change at the same time.

Children exhibit considerable agency in everyday interactions with peers and adults. Children utilize face-work—strategies to avoid embarrassment during social interactions (see Chapter 5)—just like adults (Pugh 2009). Children have also been shown to be politically active (Gordon 2010). Children actively engage authorities at many levels. In an ethnographic study of children in the welfare system, Jennifer Reich (2010) observed that children were not afraid to contest the state's views of their family lives, views that put them at risk of being separated from their parents. They actively engaged state representatives in a conversation of meaning in attempts to maintain some control over their interactions with state authorities or to garner personal or material gain. These studies show that children, much like adults, learn to work within the confines of the rules and restrictions imposed on them to maximize their ability to get what they want and need.

Section Summary

This section addressed the following questions: "How does society influence the social construction of the self?" and "What are the stages involved in developing the self?"

Symbolic interactionists focus on how children develop the ability to construct their senses of self over time, starting with simple imitations of attitudes and behaviors and then actively manipulating meanings, including about their senses of self, with other people. Interactionists also study children's culture and the ways that they take information from adult society and use it in their own culture. Adults continue to apply similar processes as they enter and leave roles through their lifetimes.

A Take-Away Message

Adults who have not spent much time around children may not appreciate the complexities of studying them. Symbolic interactionist approaches show us that children may mimic the best and worst of adults' behaviors. They are also active, and have the ability to make decisions to follow or not follow models set by adults. In some cases, children model bad behavior (e.g., poor treatment of those in other social groups), and in other cases they may challenge that behavior. Professionally, understanding basic socialization processes may help you as you enter new work and family arenas. Each time you enter a new organization or group, you must learn and adapt to the culture, but you still may have some agency with which to modify group norms. In addition, you should consider the challenges that new employees have as they enter your organization and help them socialize into the norms and standards of your work group. If you have children now or in the future, consider the ways they learn their roles in society. Are you actively encouraging them to consider the norms that they are following? How might you help them reflect on their behaviors, to help them use agency when they are interacting with their peers?

STRUCTURAL AND TIME DIMENSIONS OF SOCIALIZATION

> *I still vividly remember the feeling that I had as the bomb went off. For a split second, I thought that I was dead. I had only been in Afghanistan for two months, I thought, and I was dead. The bomb went off ... everything went black for a second, then I woke up in a kind of white haze. Then I heard my buddy screaming, "MEDIC! MEDIC!" at the top of his lungs as I lay bleeding on the ground. It was then that it really hit me. I mean, why I was there. I began to cry as I reflected on our mission and my role in it. I guess you could say that it was a life-changing event because everything after that moment was different.*
>
> —Robert, senior history major

The word "socialization" is most often applied to childhood development. This application seems natural because children are not born with any knowledge of their societies or cultures. But people change even after they learn the rules of a society. In fact, they can participate in changing those rules after they have learned them. In addition, our bodies change over time. Just as children change socially and psychologically with their biological growth, there are social and psychological shifts associated with the changes that accompany adolescence, middle age, and the deterioration of adults' bodies as they enter later stages in life.

There are other ways that society can affect socialization processes. **Life events** are any experiences that cause significant change in the course of our lives. In Robert's case, his experience in Afghanistan changed the way he viewed his mission overseas. Before being wounded, he saw his role in the military as simply part of his job. He came to view his role in the conflict as something more substantial through the lens of a wounded veteran. The event caused him to rethink his place in the world, and it affected a series of choices and constraints upon his return to civil society.

Life events do not occur in a vacuum; we experience them with other people, often through important social institutions such as families and schools. In Robert's case, his role in the military institution affected his life in dramatic ways by putting him in a warzone and affecting his physical health. In this section of the chapter, we'll discuss research and theories from the social structure and personality perspective. We will also examine effects of primary **agents of socialization**, groups most influential in the process of teaching children the norms and values of a particular culture. First, we will review the life-course perspective and then examine the role that institutions such as family and education play in the socialization process.

The Life Course

The study of the **life course** involves research that assesses the process of change from infancy to late adulthood; these changes result from individual and societal events and from transitions into and out of social roles (Elder 1994). The life-course perspective investigates how the larger social world influences how individuals develop and change over time, sometimes in the form of large-scale life events such as war or economic downturns. In Robert's example, he is clearly affected by the wounds he received in service. However, the war itself is the result of societal-level events. One nation started fighting another nation, placing Robert in a unique position in history. In this case, the historical condition of war places Robert in a life-changing situation.

Life-course sociology is more than just the study of life events. It is also about life transitions, or how people move from one role to the next and the factors that affect those changes. According to Glen Elder (1994), there are four major themes in life-course sociology:

1. **Historical and social context**—how historic and social events and experiences (time and place) affect development for different birth cohorts.
2. **Timing**—the incidence, duration, and sequence of roles over the life course.
3. **Linked lives**—our relationships with other people.
4. **Agency**—our ability to make decisions and control our destinies.

These factors interact to produce different outcomes for people experiencing them. We will review each of these factors in more detail in this section.

Historical Time and Place

A **birth cohort** refers to a group of people born within the same time period. People often use the word *generation* to refer to a birth cohort. Popular discussions of the influence of birth cohorts have often focused on the influence of birth cohort or generation on personality. Are people who grow up during a specific time period different from those growing up in an earlier or later time period? It appears that there are differences across generations, but how do you define a generation? The reality is that there is no clear definition of when one generation begins and ends (Burnett 2010). Researchers often provide their own definitions of generations to include, for example, the "Greatest Generation" (those exposed to World War II), but these are simply heuristic devices to help explain how historical conditions are linked to those coming of age in a certain era.

The U.S. Census Bureau defines a famous generation, the "Baby Boom" generation, as people born from the end of World War II (1946) until 1964. This generation, one of the largest birth cohorts in American history, was also exposed to some great cultural and technological changes in American society: the space race and the sexual revolution, for example. They witnessed moments of horror such as the assassinations of John F. Kennedy and Martin Luther King, Jr. The subsequent generations of the "Baby Bust" and Generations "X" and "Y" also experienced a number of key historic events in their formative years of development (see Table 6.1).

While the definition of a particular generation is sometimes ambiguous, several studies show that people from different cohorts appear to be different in social psychological outcomes. John Mirowsky and Catherine Ross (2007) found that the positive effects of education on sense of mastery (see Chapter 5) are greater among younger cohorts. They argue that this finding is a result of the increased need for mastery among younger cohorts to help them manage more complex economic and technological conditions. Another study found that African Americans born before the U.S. Supreme Court's anti-segregation decision, *Brown v. Board of Education* (1954), were socialized about race differently than younger cohorts. They received more messages conveying deference to and fear of Whites than African Americans born during or after the race protests of the middle of the twentieth century. The study also showed that their current attitudes regarding race correlated with their socialization experiences as a child (Brown and Lesane-Brown 2006).

Differences in exposure to historical events, especially those occurring at critical times in the life course, may have long-lasting effects on growth and development. The effects are likely to be greater for those experiencing the culture and events of the time, such as the COVID-19 pandemic, as adolescents and young adults than for those who are already adults or who are born later. Historical contexts also present constraints and options from which to make decisions in our lives. In this sense, birth cohorts are primarily important because they relate to exposure to specific historical events and changes (Elder 1994).

In a classic life-course study, *Children of the Great Depression*, Elder (1999, originally 1974) studied the long-term effects of the Great Depression on children's development. He followed a group of 167 children born in California in 1920 and 1921. They were about 10 years old when the Great Depression started and in their 30s and 40s at the end

Table 6.1 Generations and Historical Influences

Generation Title	Years	Events during Youth
Baby Boom	1946—1964	Vietnam War
		Cold War, arms race
		Sexual revolution
		Move from industrial to service economy
		Space race
		Assassination of John F. Kennedy
		Civil rights and feminist movements
Baby Bust; Generation X	1965—1979	Fall of Berlin Wall, end of Cold War
		Shooting of Ronald Reagan
		Persian Gulf War
		Newt Gingrich and the "Contract with America"; the subsequent government shutdown
		The space shuttle *Columbia* explodes, killing a civilian teacher
Generation Y	1980s–1990s	9/11 attacks on the World Trade Center and Pentagon
		Global war on terror
		Iraq and Afghanistan Wars
		Election of first African American U.S. president
Gen Z	1997–2013	COVID-19 Pandemic; Expansive access to personal and internet technology (e.g., iPhone unveiled in 2007)
		George Floyd and other murders of Black Americans

of the study period. Elder wanted to know if children developed differently over their life courses based on their economic positions (middle or upper class) and the amount of deprivation they experienced as a result of the failing economy of the 1930s, in which stock prices fell some 89 percent and unemployment rates rose to over 20 percent. Elder divided the sample into four groups of children: (1) middle-class nondeprived children, (2) middle-class deprived children, (3) working-class nondeprived children, and (4) working-class deprived children. Being deprived was defined as having a substantial loss of family income (over 50 percent) during the Depression period.

Elder found that the Great Depression did have ramifications for long-term development, depending primarily on whether the children actually experienced deprivation during that time period. This finding may seem obvious, but folk wisdom suggested that everyone in the Great Depression cohort experienced the Depression equally, that all of them felt its effects one way or another. Elder also found that the effects of deprivation were primarily felt through changing roles within the family. As income and savings began to disappear, family members would turn toward alternative means of maintenance, with girls specializing in domestic tasks and boys in economic roles. Boys obtained more freedom from parental control because they were forced to work more outside the home. Meanwhile, girls were expected to help more with household activities because the boys were away earning money for the family. Elder's work did demonstrate that the Great Depression had long-term consequences on the behavior and personality of those growing up during that time period, but more so for those who experienced some form of deprivation, supporting the premise of the proximity principle reviewed in Chapter 2, in which we feel the effects of social forces through our immediate environments. In a more modern example, Melanie Lorek (2018) analyzed life histories of East Germans to better understand effects that reunification had in their lives. This event changed the entire government and economic apparatus, from a socialist, planned economy to a more capitalist free-market one. Despite such large changes to the country, she found that many respondents claimed that reunification did not have a large impact on their lives. She concludes that individuals have some discretion about how they interpret and incorporate such events into their personal senses of self.

These and other studies using the life-course perspective are important because they indicate that essential aspects of our identities are driven by the time periods in which we grow up. In addition, what it means to be a man or woman or other gendered person, an adult or child, or a member of a particular ethnic group is partly driven by historical period (Danigelis, Hardy, and Cutler 2007; Davis 2006; Gilleard and Higgs 2005; Johnson, Berg, and Sirotzki 2007; Percheski 2008). It can also affect our health and well-being (Chen, Yang, and Lui 2010). In one study, for instance, Yang Yang (2008) found that happiness levels in the United States have changed over the past century, with Baby Boomers reporting the lowest levels of happiness relative to other generations. Additionally, levels of happiness varied by gender and racial categories over time. These findings relate to one of the most basic symbolic interaction principles reviewed in this text—that social reality is changing over time based on changing social interactions and historical and cultural contexts. However, it also reflects the first principle of social structure and personality: that we must include the independent effects of people's social positions in these social-psychological processes. In context of the life course, a person's social positions (e.g., racial categorization and social class) can influence experiences of and reactions to historical events (Doyle and Kao 2007; Johnson, Berg, and Sirotzki 2007). It also reflects the proximity principle—that we experience the larger society through our immediate social surroundings. Only by combining these elements of social psychology can we begin to understand the intersection of history and individual lives.

Social Timing and Life Stages

An important aspect of life-course development is social timing. Social timing refers to the "incidence, duration, and sequence of roles, and to the relevant expectations and beliefs based on age" (Elder 1994, p. 6) (see Box 6.2). Social timing can affect reactions to life-course events in a number of ways. First, every society has age-linked patterns of

Glen H. Elder, Jr.*

Glen H. Elder, Jr., Howard W. Odum Distinguished Research Professor of Sociology at the University of North Carolina at Chapel Hill (UNC), is a prominent figure in the development of life-course theory, methods, and research. He studies groups of people (e.g., birth cohorts) through in-depth interviews and other measurements at different times in their life spans with the objective of investigating how changing environments have influenced them.

Elder came to this "life-course perspective" after completing graduate work in sociology and psychology at UNC in 1961, and accepting a faculty appointment at the University of California, Berkeley. A research affiliation with its Institute of Human Development introduced him to the concept of studying people "the long way." The institute staff carried out this type of study by following birth cohorts of Californians over their lives. However, they tended to ignore an essential element in life-course thinking: the social context and its potential explanation for why people develop and age as they do. By contrast, a life-course approach locates people in relation to their social pathways, historical time, and place. Over the past 40 years, life-course theory has contributed to significant advances in biographical methods and research, and Elder has applied it to various social contexts ranging from rural to inner-city youth. He has recently worked with European and American colleagues on a comparative longitudinal study of young people in the Great Recession. Consortia have been organized for this project in three countries—the United States, the United Kingdom, and Germany.

An early application of life-course thinking is expressed in Elder's book *Children of the Great Depression* (Elder 1974/1999). The interdisciplinary nature of this approach prompted collaborations with historians in the 1970s and the initiation of projects with developmental psychologists in the 1980s and 1990s. During this period, senior scholar awards from the National Institute of Mental Health (1985–2000) and the Spencer Foundation enabled Elder to establish a life-course program of longitudinal studies at UNC. By the twenty-first century, a new handbook on the life course symbolized the growth of life-course studies as a field of inquiry.

Elder has served as Vice President of the American Sociological Association and president of both the Sociological Research Association and the Society for Research on Child Development. Elder's honors include a Guggenheim Fellowship, Fellow of the American Academy of Arts and Sciences, and distinguished career awards from sections of the American Sociological Association (including the Cooley-Mead Award in 1993), the Society for Research in Child Development, and the Society for the Study of Human Development.

*Information about this biography was obtained from William Corsaro's (1994) introduction of the Cooley-Mead Award printed in *Social Psychology Quarterly* and personal correspondence with Dr. Elder.

Photo 6.2 Life-course sociology examines how social conditions and agency together influence our trajectories from childhood to late adulthood. Did a person or event have a particularly important impact on your life?

Source: Zits © 2007 Zits Partnership, Distributed by King Features Syndicate, Inc.

Box 6.2 Erikson's Stages of Social Development

Erik Erikson (1902–1994) was a psychologist who proposed that people go through certain stages of social development from birth until later life. The earlier stages are more distinct and linked to biological development compared to the later stages. Erikson argued that experiences at any given stage can have long-lasting effects on our future development. The following are Erikson's eight stages:

1. Trust vs. mistrust (birth to 1.5 years): This developmental period is when a basic sense of trust develops as children come to rely on their caregivers for feeding and basic nurturance; if trust is not established, children will believe that people are unreliable.
2. Autonomy vs. shame/doubt (1.5 to 3 years): This stage is when a child's muscular activities (walking, climbing, etc.) rapidly develop. When these activities are learned well and supported by others, children learn a sense of control and pride; otherwise, children will develop feelings of shame or doubt regarding their abilities.
3. Initiative vs. guilt (3 to 6 years): Children learn to explore their worlds (social and physical), initiating ideas and activities, and reflecting on their effects. If these attempts are not met with approval, the child will develop a sense of guilt.
4. Industry vs. inferiority (6 to 12): At this stage, children are being taught certain skills (using tools and educational tasks) and develop a sense of industry. If children are not given the opportunity to complete the things they start, they may feel inferior to peers.
5. Identity vs. role confusion (12 to 18): At this stage, children are somewhere between youth and adulthood. It is here that they must learn their own sense of where they stand in the world—a sense of identity. Alternatively, a sense of role confusion can emerge, leading to problems such as authoritarianism, sexual promiscuity, or racial bigotry.

(continued)

6. Intimacy vs. isolation (18 to 40): Individuals must develop intimate relationships (e.g., family and friendships) or suffer feelings of isolation.
7. Generativity vs. stagnation (40 to 65): Individuals must feel as though they are contributing to the development of future generations (e.g., raising children) or they will develop a sense of stagnation and cease to be a productive member of society.
8. Ego integrity vs. despair (65 to death): Individuals begin to reflect on their lives and must determine whether they have led a good life or they may fall into despair.

Erikson's work has much in common with sociological perspectives on aging and development. His model takes into account the importance of other people in our lives as well as our personal decisions in development processes.

behavior. For example, the median age for first marriage in the United States was 30.5 years for men and 28.6 years for women in 2022 according to the US Census Bureau. What would happen if you did not marry about the same time as most other people from your cohort? From the perspective of life-course sociology, events that interrupt marital possibilities will likely produce a greater effect on life outcomes than those events that do not interrupt that life stage. Further, the age at which an event occurs can also determine the resources with which we are able to manage those events. Younger people, for instance, typically have less income than their middle-aged counterparts, and so timing parenthood "early" can create a host of secondary effects that are different from those that result from timing parenthood later.

Life stages refer to patterns of change from infancy to adulthood. Life stages include childhood, adolescence, adulthood, and late life (Handel, Cahill, and Elkin 2007). They are associated with the concept of the life cycle because humans within a specific culture may follow predictable patterns and transitions such as marriage, parenthood, and retirement. But they are not the same things as developmental stages studied in the field of psychology, which imply a progression of physical and social growth such that later stages expand upon earlier ones (see, e.g., Box 6.1). Societies define what is appropriate at each life stage. In addition, the inclusion of aspects of life stage and meanings of them may also vary. The concept of retirement, for example, is largely associated with Western, high-income societies in which members rely on wages for maintaining standards of living. The length and meaning of adolescence and the age at which adulthood starts can vary by culture and historical conditions too (Dalsgard et al. 2014; Silva 2012). In this sense, our sense of identity can vary by generation (see Figure 6.1).

The pathways from one stage to another can vary; Scott Eliason and colleagues (2015) identified five pathways to adulthood using data from the Youth Development Survey, a recurring survey of youth dating back to the 1980s. Three of the five pathways involve a school-to-work transition without the formation of families; the other two include the birth of a child or low labor force participation. However, when the expected trajectory in someone's life is interrupted, when the person breaks with their own or society's

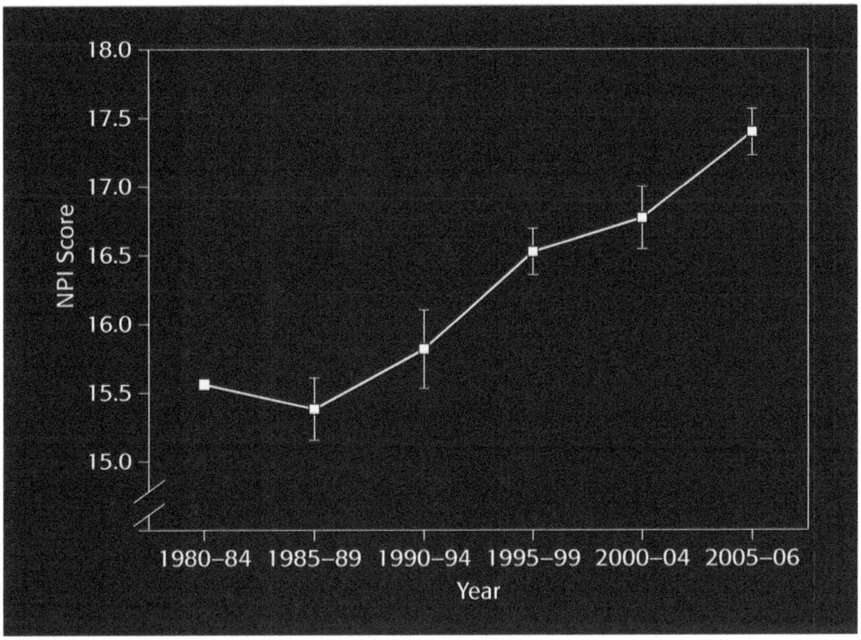

Figure 6.1 Average Narcissist Personality Index (NPI) Scores by Generation.

Source: Twenge et al. (2008).

expectations of established life stages, it sets the stage for the creation of a **turning point** (Ivie, Gimbel, and Elder 1991). Turning points can result from large-scale life events such as war or famine, but also things like role changes (e.g., becoming a parent) or religious or other conversion; they can occur as a result of chance events or by choice (DeGloma 2014; Hackstaff, Kupferberg, and Negroni 2012). Studying turning points demands methods that are sensitive to subjective understandings of events (Torkelson 2015; see also Raymond and White 2017). Two people experiencing war, for example, may have very different perspectives of the same events. The Great Depression served as a turning point for some but not all of the children in Elder's study discussed in this chapter. The degree to which these turning points influence individuals' lives depends in part on when they occur during one's life. For instance, Elder's (1987) study of World War II found that entering the war at a later age produced greater disruption in family and career patterns than entering the war at an earlier age. Many times, people consider "normal trajectory" events such as getting married or becoming a parent as a subjective turning point that they feel changed the courses of their lives (Clausen 1998).

In a series of studies, Robert Sampson and John Laub (Sampson and Laub, 1990; Sampson and Laub 1996; Laub, Nagen, and Sampson 1998; Laub and Sampson 1993) demonstrated the role of large-scale events such as World War II as turning points in people's lives. Their research followed a group of 1,000 men from poor areas of Boston, initially assessing things such as IQ and antisocial behavior. These men were then tracked and periodically surveyed about their lives. Longitudinal research showed the powerful effects World War II had on the men, creating long-term socioeconomic outcomes. They found that much of the effects of the war were felt through things such as overseas duty, in-service schooling, and the GI Bill. Through these experiences, the men were able to obtain better, more stable jobs and social lives after the war than they would have otherwise. Such research shows how macro–social structural conditions can influence our lives long after they occur, above and beyond our personal backgrounds and abilities. In this case, World War II served as a positive turning point for these men. However, it might have been a negative turning point for other men, such as those who had been separated from their families for several years, or, in the case of African American veterans, the positive effects of government resources would not be as beneficial as for White veterans when resettling into a racist society.

Linked Lives

The third theme of life-course sociology is that people lead interdependent lives: events occurring for individuals affect the other people in their lives and vice versa. Friends, coworkers, and especially family members are affected by the things that happen in our lives. For example, job loss affects not only the person losing the job but her family as well. The effects can be monetary (e.g., loss of income) as well as emotional (e.g., depression) as family members must relate to a person going through such an event.

Linked lives can help explain why some people change more than others over time. In a study of youth on trajectories of becoming delinquent, Richard Petts (2008) found that residing with two parents helps deter youth from a delinquent life course. Youths who start out in a life-course trajectory that includes delinquent behaviors were more likely to desist from delinquency if they lived with two parents rather than with single parents. Petts argues that our life-course trajectories are changeable; having access to a stable social environment is one way to help mitigate personal problems.

Linked lives also have implications for access to varying amounts of resources available to cope with life events. For instance, Elder's (Elder 1974/1999) study of the Depression showed that middle-class children had the advantage of more social support during periods of deprivation than working-class children. In another study, Glen Elder and Rand Conger (2000) studied a group of 451 rural families in Iowa to determine the effects of social integration on the life courses of children over time. They found that rural children "tied to the land" (e.g., in families with farming-related businesses) had more involved parents, had stronger ties to parents, and were generally better integrated into the community than those who had no ties to the land. As a result, children tied to the land on average did better in school and had fewer behavioral problems as they got older.

Linked lives continue to influence us throughout the life course—and the influences are not always positive. Melissa Milkie and her colleagues (Milkie, Bierman, and Schieman 2008) studied a sample of 600 older African American and White parents over a four-year period. Their research showed that parents' negative relationships with adult children increased their depression and anger levels over time. The parent–child relationship affected African Americans more than Whites and mothers more so than fathers. The authors propose that this is likely because the parent role was relatively more important than work roles among Blacks and women in this cohort since they tended to occupy less powerful positions at work and in the community than did Whites and men. In another study, Scott Gartner (2008) found that people who knew 9/11 or Iraq War casualties were more likely to disapprove of President George W. Bush. In this case, the history of war intersected with personal ties, changing people's view of the event and those linked to it. Linked lives at an early stage of development may influence behavior in later stages. Daniel McFarland and Reuben Thomas (2006) employed longitudinal survey data and found that youth who participated in service-related extracurricular activities (e.g., the key club or student council) were more likely to become politically active later in life. In particular, those members of the sample who were involved in such groups were more likely to vote and participate in community service as adults than those who had fewer of those kinds of relationships when they were youths.

Human Agency

Life-course sociology also recognizes that individuals have the ability to make decisions about the trajectories of their lives, albeit within a limited set of options. We introduced the idea of agency in Chapter 2, emphasizing individuals' abilities to think and act independently. This concept is important to life-course sociology because individuals can act within the constraints imposed by social and historical conditions, leading to myriad possible outcomes (Guhin, McCrory Calarco, and Miller-Idriss 2021). For instance, many children of the Great Depression found ways to overcome the economic adversities of the time. They may have had to change their educational plans, for example, but they coped with economic hardship by taking on additional work.

Agency is essential to socialization processes because it provides the opportunity for individuals to assert their inner worlds into their social environments. In many cases, individuals may not fully comprehend the role of their internal processes in their decisions and actions (Wiley 2016)—making it that much more difficult to predict what people will do in any given situation or in making decisions that will affect the rest of their lives. It can also be difficult to assess the role of agency in predicting the life course because it can be constrained by social conditions, especially class. Jessica McCrory Calarco (2011) found that middle-class elementary school students are more likely to seek help in the classroom than their working-class peers, leading to greater academic achievement. In terms of later education, Stefanie Deluca and James Rosenbaum (2001) found that students' high school efforts are important to later educational attainment, regardless of their economic standing, demonstrating agentic behavior. However, they also found that socioeconomic status was associated with higher levels of student effort: higher-status students worked harder, and higher-status students benefited more from their effort than those from lower socioeconomic backgrounds. Therefore, agency does influence life outcomes, but it also interacts with our social positions and the conditions surrounding our efforts. Similarly, in a Swedish sample, Martin Hallsten (2010) found that individuals from working-class backgrounds were more likely than their middle-class peers to choose college programs that yield lower incomes. Hence, while students in all of these conditions utilized some degree of agency, their structural positions affected the choices they made and the power of those choices in making positive impacts on their lives.

It is also important to remember that our beliefs about our ability to change our life course can influence us as well. In Chapter 5 we reviewed the concept of mastery or the belief that we can accomplish the things that we set out to do. John Reynolds and his colleagues (2007) found that people with a higher sense of mastery had greater job expectations than people with a lower sense of mastery. They were also more likely to achieve their occupational goals. However, other social statuses intersect with mastery and our ability to get the job we want. Specifically, marriage increased effects of mastery on achieving occupational goals, while having children decreased it. There are a number of ways that statuses may influence our life outcomes, but the important issue here is that beliefs about our ability to control our life course also influence where we end up. In terms of finding a job, believing in yourself matters, but so does your social environment.

Agents of Socialization

In this chapter, we defined agents of socialization as groups most influential in the process of teaching children the norms and values of a particular culture. It is important to understand that sociologists generally view agents of socialization as mediators of the larger society, rather than direct causes of socialization (Corsaro and Eder 1995). That is, families may affect child development directly through their parenting techniques, but those techniques reflect larger cultural patterns. The famous pediatrician Dr. Spock wrote *The Common Sense Book of Baby and Child Care* in 1946, with several follow-up versions printed over the last several decades. His ideas helped to change the way parents thought about interacting with children through their emphasis on more flexible parenting techniques. Spock encouraged parents to be more emotionally attached to children and less strict in their discipline. Children were to be thought of as individuals rather than subjects of training and development. Through the middle of the twentieth century, Spock and other child specialists moved families away from traditional parenting styles. In a sense, parents implemented larger societal changes in attitudes toward children (as individuals) and parenting styles more generally (loving, affectionate, and independent) as displayed in Spock's books.

There are many agents of socialization. Here, we emphasize only some of the most important ones: families, school, and peers. We also discuss media as an important source of socialization in Western societies.

Families

Families are the first or primary agent of socialization because virtually all children are raised from infancy with one to two parents and often siblings or extended family. Family interaction typically involves a kind of intimacy that is less prevalent in many other human interactions; it can be thought of as a place to relax our front-stage interactions (see Impression Management in Chapter 5) in the world. Values and beliefs, ways of behaving, and any number of personal things are transmitted through families in the subtlest ways, including use of touch and words left unspoken (e.g., indicating disapproval of a behavior) (Goodwin and Cekaite 2018; Keel 2016). Family socialization affects us throughout our lives and can impact how individuals relate to other agents of socialization. Parent rejection, for example, is associated with emotional dysregulation which ultimately influences perceptions of acceptance by current peers (Hodges, Dodd, and Hackathorn 2021).

Families also socialize children through their structures, or how families are comprised. This is important because families have changed dramatically over the last century. For example, people in Western countries are having fewer children—almost half of the world's population in 2000 lived in countries that were at or below replacement level (the point at which populations stabilize); these include primarily wealthier, Western nations such as Italy and Germany (Morgan 2003). According to the United States Census Bureau, since 1970 the number of individuals living alone in the United States has increased from 16% of households to 25%. The traditional family of a married couple with children has declined from 40% of households in 1970 to just 24% today, with a corresponding increase in the number of nontraditional households (e.g., single parents and cohabitating partners) (see Figure 6.2). Recent research has also begun to explore the role of animals as family members (Laurent-Simpson 2017). Animals are often referred to as siblings to children and even grandchildren! The roles of animals in families will likely expand as populations in the Global North continue to decline and couples choose to not have children.

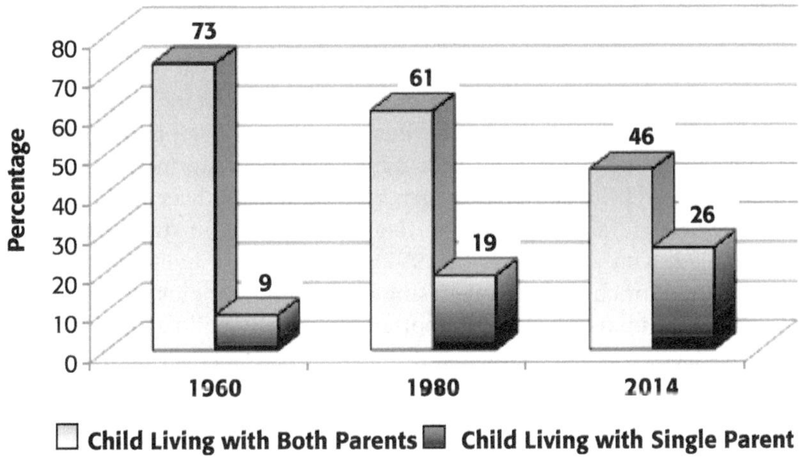

Figure 6.2 Changes in U.S. Household Composition over Time.

Source: Pew Research Center 2015.

Family Structure and Children

Structural changes in the family can have ramifications for child socialization, above and beyond the interactions therein. Only about one in five parents are considered stay-at-home parents, a scenario in which one parent does not work while the other one does; the rest are in dual-earner, single-parent, or other types of families (Livingston 2018; Waite and Gallaher 2000). Children from single-parent families often struggle for at least two reasons (Gecas 1992; Waite and Gallaher 2000). First, single-parent families earn less money on average than their married counterparts, partly because there is one less person to contribute to the household income and also because women are more likely to be single parents than men (Demo 1992). (In 2022, women on average earned 82% of what men earned [Aragão 2023]). Hence, single parents typically lack the fiscal resources found in two-parent families.

Second, single-parent families may lack the same social resources available to two-parent families. Children in single-parent households often rely on one person to provide the love and discipline found in families with two caregivers (Gecas 1992; Waite and Gallaher 2000), although extended families may be involved in raising the child. Single parents have less time and energy to devote to their children as well. However, the bond between a single parent and child may be strengthened because of the amount of intimacy available in a dyad compared to a triad (see Chapter 2).

These dynamics may disproportionately affect some minority groups. According to the 2000 U.S. census, African Americans, for example, have larger families on average than the overall population, and these families are also more likely to be single-parent households (McKinnon and Bennett 2005). Hence, we might expect family socialization to be different in African American families than among Whites and other racial groups. African American families are less likely to have certain monetary resources such as wealth from homeownership found among White families but have other strengths. For instance, in one study, researchers found that African American women rated the families they grew up in as more cohesive, more expressive, and lower in conflict than those of White women (Clay et al. 2007).

The effects of family structure on children's health and well-being have been well documented in the area of divorce. Children of divorced parents, once adults, tend to divorce or cohabit at higher rates than adults who grew up in two-parent families (Thornton, Axinn, and Xie 2007; Wolfinger 2005). They also have higher levels of distress and more behavioral problems than their counterparts in stable families (Amato and Cheadle 2008; Kim 2011; McCabe 1997). The effects of living with the same- or opposite-sex parent for children living in single-parent households has also been examined, but evidence is mixed about the importance of parent–child gender differences for child outcomes (see Powell and Downey 1997; Waite and Gallaher 2000). Sibling order and configuration are other family structure elements that may importantly influence how children are socialized, although findings are mixed as to their effects (Steelman et al. 2002; Freese, Powell, and Steelman 1999). Effects of different types of family structures can vary significantly by the outcome being examined (e.g., cognitive versus behavioral), parenting style, status, and resources available to families before, during, and after a divorce (Campana et al. 2008; Fomby and Cherlin 2007). In a larger historical framework, the meaning of "family" is broadening to include cohabiters, those single (as parents or not) by choice, gay and lesbian families, and hybrids of these and other forms of family (Powell et al. 2010). Rosanna Hertz (2006) interviewed 65 Boston-area middle-class women who chose to be single mothers. She found that many of them stumbled into single motherhood but decided to go it alone rather than marry someone who did not meet their expectations. The state of being single was found to be a bit unstable as these women entered and left romantic relationships with lovers and co-parents over time. What type of person today opts out of the "traditional family" (a two-parent, married household)? According to Michael Rosenfeld (2007), those not choosing the pathway of the traditional family tend to be people "who live on their own, who support themselves, who postpone marriage, and who have access to higher education" (Rosenfeld 2007, p. 121).

Class Differences among Families

A family's social class position is another important structural dimension affecting socialization processes. Occupational status and income differences not only influence the resources available to raise children, but also affect socialization processes themselves (Gecas 1992; Kohn 1969). Compared to working-class families, middle-class families differ in the values and behaviors taught to children as well as how they teach them those things. Middle-class families tend to stress autonomy and individual development over conformity. In addition, middle-class families are less likely to use punitive child-rearing practices than their counterparts in the working class. Middle-class children have more structured use of their time compared with working-class children, whose parents tend to value the child's natural growth through unstructured leisure, and children are talked to differently across social classes. The result of these socialization processes is that working-class youth often grow up less confident in institutional settings such as schools and workplaces (Lareau 2003). Middle-class children usually grow up with more cultural capital that helps them to find and maintain higher-status jobs and to "bend" institutions to fit their needs. Ultimately, a type of "family capital" is passed down across multiple generations such that familial cultures emphasizing academic self-confidence and high educational expectations contribute to the maintenance of the family's class position (Mortimer et al. 2017).

Families are also a place to learn fundamental beliefs about the world, and even this process is related to class status. The transmission of values from generation to generation seems obvious: parents typically help children to distinguish right from wrong, but they also pass on their attitudes toward any number of issues in society, including values and beliefs as they pertain to family life (Jennings, Axinn, and Ghimire 2012). However, children often modify their parents' values or adopt altogether new ones. Nevertheless, they can still be affected by other factors at home. For instance, Jennifer Glass and her colleagues (Glass, Bengtson, and Chorn Dunham 1986) studied the transmission of gender, political, and religious ideology among members of three-generation families (youth, parents, and grandparents). They found very little convergence of parent–child attitudes. Rather, they found that status inheritance—the maintenance of class position—was the primary means of maintaining attitude similarities. Hence, families not only teach and model values to their children, but also impart their social positions, which ultimately tend to produce similar values and beliefs.

Socialization of values and beliefs can occur on multiple levels at the same time. For instance, Jonathan Kelley and Nan Dirk De Graaf (1997) studied religious beliefs in the context of family upbringing and nations' religious environments. They found that people in more religious nations adopt more orthodox values than those living in more secular nations. However, they also found that family religiosity had a stronger effect than national religiosity on children's religiosity in secular nations; the converse is true in orthodox nations. Thus, the socialization processes found within families can be influenced by larger social and cultural contexts.

Adults in Families

The life-course perspective makes it clear that children are not the only ones who are socialized. As young adults move from their childhood family into forming families of their own, they must learn to adapt to adult family roles such as spouse or parent. It is not just a passive adaptation to roles; rather, people make choices about when and how to enter different roles. One of the great challenges for adults trying to craft meaningful lives is to attempt to weave together important roles such as being a spouse or partner, a parent, and an employee. Life-course sociologists study what happens when people enter into or exit from various roles, and how that affects future sequencing of their life trajectories or pathways. We are aware, for example, that becoming a parent as a teenager greatly affects the kind of education and work roles that women enter. Life-course sociologists are also concerned with the mental health consequences of family–work trajectories. Kei Nomaguchi and Melissa Milkie (2003) found that entering parenthood affects well-being, but its effects vary by gender and marital status. For married women, those becoming parents were better off than those who remained childless; for unmarried men, those who became fathers over the five-year time frame were more depressed than nonfathers.

School Contexts

Schools are a second major agent of socialization. Although technically designed to impart knowledge about many subjects, the classroom is also a place to learn norms of behavior and to (re)produce workers of various types. Schools are also a place where inequalities are reproduced, and children learn their social standing (Harvey 2023). In schools, children are placed in large, homogeneous classrooms in which peer influences dominate the social context. Sociologists have studied the socialization processes that occur in schools, including learning the official curriculum, the learning goals imposed by the state, and the absorbing of the unofficial curriculum. The unofficial curriculum, which is imparted through teachers and peers in school settings, includes the teaching of values and beliefs from the larger culture (Brint, Contreras, and Matthews 2001; Weisz and Kanpol 1990).

Classroom Structure and Socialization Processes

Much like the family group structures, the classroom represents a group, albeit a larger one, from which children learn about the world. Because one or two adults typically attend to classes of 20 or 30 children, classroom settings are less intimate and provide children less exposure to adult behavior than home settings. Classrooms are also unique in that they contain children of the same age group and are typically divided relatively equally by gender, at least in Western nations (Gecas 1992). Hence, classrooms have less direct adult–child interaction than home environments and more competition for attention and resources among children.

Classrooms are also bureaucratically structured in a way that limits child–adult bonds (children leave a teacher after the successful completion of one school year) and emphasizes rationalization and competition among similar age groups (Gecas 1992). Harry Gracey (1972) argues that, starting at a very young age, children begin the process of learning two curriculums in schools: the official curriculum that includes reading, writing, and arithmetic and the enacted curriculum that includes teaching children how to interact in a bureaucratic world. In this sense, kindergarten becomes a "boot camp" in which children first face the facts of a bureaucratic world with a rigid set of rules and an inflexible schedule. In a more contemporary example, Matt Aronson and Steve Bialostok (2016) propose that modern teachers emphasize the expression of self-awareness through dialogue and expression of thought that they argue are necessary for workers in Western, knowledge-based economies. It is still the case that the ways schools are conducted reflect the needs of the economy, albeit a much different economy than for children growing up in the 1970s.

Some research shows that larger schools lead students to be less attached to their schools than do smaller schools. Students in larger schools are also less likely to bond with their teachers and less likely to participate in extracurricular activities (Crosnoe, Johnson, and Elder 2004). However, there is no single model of school organization and culture that applies to all educational settings, especially in the U.S. school system, which is decentralized (Hedges and Schneider 2005). The culture of any given school can be considered negotiated—an ongoing interaction among educational leaders (Hallett 2007). Students clearly play a role in this relationship, making staff rethink policies and procedures that they wish to implement.

And yet even staff may feel the influence of events in the larger culture that push them in particular policy directions. Following the horrific tragedy at Sandy Hook elementary school in Newtown, Connecticut, in 2012, where a 20-year-old man murdered 20 young children and six staff, many schools across the United States experienced a "culture shift." Safety and security became increasingly paramount, leading to changes in everyday procedures. Thus, the creation of school culture includes many layers of social dynamics ranging from a national-level development of educational goals and standards (e.g., the No Child Left Behind policy) and a "climate of fear" to the negotiated order found within each classroom. Notably in other Western societies, the culture of fear in schools is likely to be lesser given that school shootings are not a part of the fabric of their societies. In the book *Lesson Plans*, Judson Everitt (2017) reviews the processes by which teachers learn how to be teachers (being socialized themselves!), adapting educational policies to the lesson plans they will need to use to manage the day-to-day lives of a diverse classroom of learners. The classroom becomes the space between the larger institution of education and individual students' lives.

Pygmalion Effect and Children's Social Statuses

Teachers' interactions with children affect the values and beliefs of children in much the same way as parents' interactions do. However, teachers do not share the same relationships with their students as do parents. For instance, if you are reading this book as part of a class, your parents probably care more about your grade in the class than does your professor. The social distance among teachers and students can open the door to subtle forms of bias, some negative and some positive.

In a classic study, *Pygmalion in the Classroom*, researchers Robert Rosenthal and Lenore Jacobson (1968) gave a group of elementary students an intelligence test at the beginning of the school year. They then randomly selected a small percentage of the students and told teachers that these were the students who should be expected to "bloom" intellectually over the coming year. The researchers' statements were not true, but the teachers believed that the randomly selected students possessed great potential. Rosenthal and Jacobson then retested the students at the end of the year. They found that those students who were randomly deemed to be "bloomers" at the beginning of the year showed a 12-point average improvement in their intelligence test scores compared to an 8-point average improvement among students who had not been labeled. Thus, teacher expectations can influence students' intellectual development, a dynamic that is often called the **Pygmalion effect**.

The ramifications of the Pygmalion study can be applied to processes that occur in relation to other types of labels and categorizations of students. Students labeled as "slow learners" at a young age may be influenced by expectations in the classroom that limit their academic responsibilities or generally expect less from them. When parents of school-aged children have been incarcerated, they become less involved with the school system, creating a "system avoidance" (Haskins and Jacobson 2017), which ultimately disadvantages their children. Children from racialized minority and other less-advantaged groups may find additional hurdles to their intellectual development because of potentially biased interactions with teachers and other important cultural gatekeepers (Alexander, Entwisle, and Thompson 1987; Condron 2009; Cooper and Allen 1998; Crosnoe 2009). The Wisconsin Model of Status Attainment, reviewed in Chapter 4, shows the roles of adults, including teachers, in the maintenance of inequality in society. Jessica McCrory Calarco's (2014) ethnographic study of classroom behaviors found that teachers' responses to students varied between middle- and working-class students in a way that perpetuated inequalities. These types of studies show the subtle ways that classroom interactions can perpetuate existing social systems.

Being a member of a minority group may influence classroom processes in other ways. According to the United States Census Bureau in 2023, 19 percent of Americans were Hispanic, 14 percent were African American, and six percent were of Asian descent. Thus, a fully integrated classroom of 20 students in a community reflecting the racial makeup of the United States might have about four Hispanics, three African Americans, and one Asian American. Although classrooms may be homogeneous in terms of age, the minority members of the classroom may feel strain in the face of their differences from majority members. In other words, these students stand out from the rest of the class. Morris Rosenberg (see Elliott 2001; Rosenberg 1986) called this feeling

Box 6.3 Jobs in Socialization

There are many roles in society that directly relate to the idea of socialization. Teaching is probably the most directly related to the concept, a career for which you may need a bachelor's degree in education. There are also jobs in the arena of human resources in which you help socialize new employees in a particular field or into a large organization. You can do some of this work with a background in social psychology, but you will likely need some additional training or you may want to consider degrees more specific to those fields. You definitely want to do some internships to build your resume with related work experience.

1. **Early Start Home Visitor**, LifeWorks Community Action (New York). Duties: Home Visitor supports families who are not in a class setting to move toward school readiness. The Home Visitor works with families to assess and identify barriers that impede school readiness and strengths that can encourage school readiness. The position is mobile and requires staff to complete home visits as described. Qualifications: A Minimum of a home-based CDA credential or comparable credential, or equivalent coursework with 12 early childhood education credits as part of an associate's or bachelor's degree. Must be skilled in communicating and motivating people. Computer skills and knowledge of Windows and other platforms, and familiarity with mobile devices, online training platforms, and software applications helpful.
2. **Child Care Program Manager** (Ohio) Right at School. Duties: Drive to inspire a love for learning and ability to engage children in learning activities in fun and interactive ways. Qualifications: Two years of direct experience working with children under 13, one year of supervisory experience, minimum 18 college credits in early childhood education, elementary education, or a related field.

It is clear that these jobs require some additional training and experience than what you would normally find solely from an undergraduate social science major. That is where minors and certificates become important. Also, doing some work in the summers or doing an internship would help immensely to demonstrate that you have experience in the field. If you do it long enough, you may find that you will be offered some management experience as well!

contextual dissonance. Minority students feel many of the same peer pressures found in more homogeneous classrooms but also may feel that they stand apart from other students. Rosenberg's research shows that contextual dissonance, whether based on class, racial category, or ability, may reduce students' senses of self-esteem.

Peer Culture

Most of our discussion of socialization agents has emphasized the passive nature of child development: children learn social expectations by modeling and "taking in" family and teacher behavior. School adds the influence of peers to socialization processes, but most research continues to emphasize children as recipients of some formal developmental goals. Some research examines how children actively participate in the socialization process (Corsaro 2005; Jencks 1996; Keel 2016). Much of this work has emphasized children's peer cultures.

Peer-Group Structures

An important difference between school and peer-group cultures is the voluntary nature of peer-group affiliation. Children have more flexibility in a peer-group context than they do inside the classroom. They may also choose to structure their relationships to include like-minded others. In addition, children can choose to leave the group, unlike their family and school groups (Corsaro 2005; Gecas 1992; Jencks 1996). In some sense, peer groups serve to teach children how to think more independently from institutional and adult constraints. Much of our adult life is spent navigating formal and informal contexts, including work, school, family, and friends. The increasing influence of peer groups into the teen years prepares children to manage complex role relationships without much guidance from their immediate families.

In one sense, children's peer culture is largely egalitarian because it is free of institutional restraints. However, research shows that children learn to stratify at young ages—and children are active participants in stratification processes (Callejas and Shepard 2020). Patricia Adler and Peter Adler (Adler 1996; Adler and Adler 1998) conducted an extensive study of elementary schoolchildren to understand children's hierarchies, using both interview data and personal observations. Their research showed that children form friendship cliques that represent their relative status in children's culture, largely derived from the larger adult culture. In that era in the late twentieth century in the United States, the cliques were divided into four major groups:

1. The popular clique.
2. The wannabes.
3. Middle friendship circles.
4. Social isolates.

The **popular clique** includes children with active social lives and the largest number of friends. They also have the most control over their peers' culture. That is, the kids among the popular crowd had more say in the activities and the definition of *cool* than children in other cliques. It is estimated that the popular clique represents about a third of children (Adler and Adler 1998).

The **wannabes** represent children that want to be popular but do not quite get accepted into this group. Although they are occasionally accepted into the popular clique's activities, they never sustain that status in the group. This group represents about 10% of children. The **middle friendship circles**, in contrast, represent about half of children. This group forms smaller circles of friends and is less hierarchical than the two previous groups. They do not seek popularity but obtain social comfort from their small circles of friends.

The final group, the **social isolates**, represents a relatively small percentage of children. This group has trouble establishing any relationships with kids in the other cliques. These children may have behavioral problems or simply have trouble relating to other children. Adler and Adler (1998) observed that many of these children turned to each other as a source of comfort, although this method was not always successful because many isolates want to avoid the stigma associated with being an isolate (Kless 1992). Many of them simply spent time alone, drifting around the playgrounds, watching the other children play. Social experiences at school in the elementary years may be different across time and place, of course.

Peer hierarchies are important to children and adolescents as they use them to decide how to act, much like adult status hierarchies. Lower-status peers look toward high-status peers as references for their senses of self. Higher-status peers have more influence on the thoughts and behaviors of lower-status peers than the converse (Harding 2009; Vargas 2011).

Peer-Group Socialization Processes

Viktor Gecas (1992) proposed that peer-group socialization includes three areas of child development:

1. Development and validation of the self.
2. Development of competence in the presentation of self.
3. Acquisition of knowledge not provided by parents or schools.

Peers provide additional information from which to evaluate our senses of worth. This process can occur through informal interactions, such as the remarks and reactions our friends make about our behaviors. Because peer associations are more voluntary than family and school contexts, rewards and punishments offered by peers can have a particularly powerful effect on individual self-evaluations.

Children must also learn subtle aspects of social life. They must learn how to interact in different social contexts. A small part of this "act" is related to manners of behavior, such as the appropriate fork to use at the dinner table. It also includes appropriate greetings and salutations and things to do to avoid causing a fight. Although some of these things are learned at home, many of them fall in the purview of peer relationships. Peer groups provide knowledge unique to a given age group or generation. In other words, parental norms may not be appropriate for same-aged peer groups. Examples of conflict between family and peer-group norms are numerous. Think about a time when you wanted to wear a particular piece of clothing or jewelry when you were living with your parents. Your choices may have been driven by the latest fashion or fad. You may find it particularly "cool," but your parents see it as questionable for any number of reasons, reflecting the values and tastes they derived from growing up in a different peer culture with different tastes. Ultimately, the conflict will continue until either the parents decide to relent or the child defers to their parents' wishes.

Peers also help us develop knowledge about the world that we tend not to get from traditional sources. Parents and teachers may share some rudimentary information about the process of having sex and its consequences, however, these sources of information do not always review the more subtle aspects of sexual behavior, such that what "turns on" the other person, what activities are deemed "normal," and so on. Individuals may feel more comfortable discussing such topics with their peers or finding information from the media than by consulting their parents or teachers. Peer discussions and interactions also give people an opportunity to think and decide about such things in a less stressful environment but also create different sets of pressures on youth. Gareth Davey and Xiang Zhao (2020), for instance, found that peer influences were particularly strong in the decision to become a smoker among youth in China. Their desire to avoid shame in the group was a driving force to start their journey as a user.

Kathleen Bogle (2008) investigated the culture of "hooking up" on college campuses. Hooking up refers to sexual activities that occur outside of committed relationships. Interviewing 76 men and women on college campuses, she provides a detailed review of the practice, discussing how it develops among college students but then tends to end after students graduate. The role of peers in college becomes most pronounced in this practice because it develops and is taught among peers, not from any other agent of socialization. The structure of college life makes peer influence especially prominent, with dense living arrangements mixed with little authoritative oversight.

Other Socializing Agents: The Role of Media and Technology

There are other agents of socialization in your life that we have not discussed. You may have been influenced by a small-town community, a religious organization, or some other group unique to your life. The media is a particularly prominent agent in the Western world and is a growing influence on the rest of the world. Americans spend at least 15 hours a week on average watching shows on television or through other media; about three hours per day by one estimate in 2022 (Robinson and Godbey 1997; Stoll 2022). Children's viewing of television and use of electronic media have increased in recent years too (Brown and Marin 2009; Laricchia 2023). Other media include video games, YouTube, TikTok, X (formerly known as Twitter), and other online platforms and computer applications (Apps). A major way that agents of socialization affect us is merely through observation and adaptation: we watch other people do things and adopt those behaviors over time. It can also include attitudes and even emotions (e.g., the appropriate response to a social script). In this way, watching people on television or other media may provide role models for our own thoughts, feelings, and behavior. It also provides scripts we can use during interactions with other people (see Chapter 2 on social scripts). One of the most studied topics in this area is the role of media violence on violent behavior. Hundreds of assess the relationship between watching media images and subsequent aggressive behavior (Comstock 2008). Most of this research shows that there is at least a correlation between watching violent programming and aggressive behavior. Some researchers question whether this cross-sectional correlational research—research in which viewing behavior is shown to vary with aggressive behavior at one time period—adequately captures whether there are long-range effects of television violence on aggressive behavior (Brown and Marin 2009; Grimes and Bergen 2008; Wilson 2008).

Other similar research indicates that media can affect almost anything that we do, both in negative and positive ways. Studies show, for instance, that negative stereotypes exist in television and video games, among other sources of media (Dill and Thill 2007; Mastro, Behm-Morawitz, and Kopacz 2008; Saeed 2007). However, despite these negative stereotypes, in a Brazilian study of television viewing, heavy television watchers reported holding more liberal attitudes toward Blacks and were more supportive of interracial marriage than those who watched less television (Leslie 1995). One of the most important influences of the media is as a pervasive presence throughout society in helping to define what is "normal" (Milkie 1999; Raisborough 2011). Hence, whatever your values and beliefs, those things are programmed into the media, which subsequently affects people's thoughts, feelings, and behaviors.

The role of media in the socialization process is more active in the modern world as media and technology change. Video games, for instance, place individuals inside a digital environment where real people compete and interact with artificial intelligence (AI) as well as other people. Robots are being developed to help in many functions ranging from teaching tai chi, a form of Chinese martial art, to caring for babies (Cometa 2022; Cuthbertson 2022). Despite these technological advancements, most of these efforts involve intensive human programming and interaction, which brings in many of the same biases and foibles found in purely human socialization.

The future of online socialization will likely include hybrid models. For instance, in a study of transnational families, those in which family members are in more than one country, technology was used to connect families in a way not available until recently. As a result, technology becomes prioritized and young people often have to teach their parents how to use it, showing the agentic behaviors of both parents and their children (Francisco-Menchavez 2018). In another example, Casey Scheibling (2020) analyzed 201 blog posts from 40 dad bloggers to examine how men write about fatherhood, finding that the platform gave men the opportunity to shape and reinforce the meanings of fatherhood above and beyond what they would have experienced through day-to-day interactions with other fathers. These and other studies show that socialization is a process, but the content and methods of transmitting culture can vary from place to place and change over time with outcomes that reflect the humans that created it.

Section Summary

This section applied the social structure and personality perspective to answer two questions: "What are the elements of life-course sociology?" and "What are agents of socialization, and how do they affect our lives?" The life-course perspective incorporates the ideas of historical times, timing of transitions, linked lives, and human agency to explain individual development. Specifically, it examines how historical conditions affect our selves, the relationships we have with significant others, and our ability to make decisions about our trajectories. Agents of socialization include the family, schools, and peers. These and other agents of socialization play important roles in the socialization process because they give the individual different contexts for learning about society.

A Take-Away Message

This section provides tips for changing your life course as well as your children's lives. While we may not have control over the historical times we live in, we can control the conditions under which we manage them. Through lives linked with others, we are more or less affected by events. Parents become the "linked lives" for children, helping them manage the stresses of society and making choices that ideally influence their lives in the most positive way, given the (often limited) possibilities. Professionally, you should consider the socialization processes that are affecting you now and how you are influencing the people around you. Having this knowledge will make you a better manager and peer, and help you to guide colleagues. You also may consider the most effective ways of learning how to interact more effectively on the job by observing and adapting the best behaviors of your peers.

GROUP PROCESSING AND SOCIALIZATION

> *I took the GREs [Graduate Record Exam] twice, but I can't seem to get the score I want. What is my problem? Why is it that people around me seem to be doing so well but I am not? Maybe I have a learning disability. I don't know.*
>
> —Rich, senior sociology major

The answer to Rich's question about his "low" score may seem pretty straightforward—the test probably reflects his actual abilities. He took the test twice, verifying its findings. But these test scores are relative in two ways. First, Rich's score is relative to those of other people who took the test. Compared to the highest score, his score may seem low; however, a large number of people likely scored lower than Rich, and of course only a small percentage of the people in North America or around the world take the test at all. Only the relatively privileged few, university graduates who plan to go on to graduate school, will take this exam. In addition, aptitude tests may reflect cultural biases that make it difficult to assess "real" ability. Work in the group processes perspective tries to assess how these biases can be manifested in group contexts.

Finding Socialization in Group Processes

Most theories in the group processes tradition are tested through experiments. We discussed the experimental method in Chapter 3. In a typical experiment, two groups of people experience conditions that are identical except for one element that is varied by the researchers. Experimentalists assign groups to different levels of an independent variable before measuring a dependent variable. For example, a researcher interested in the effects of violent television (the independent variable) on aggressive behavior (the dependent variable) might randomly assign one group to watch television with violence and another to watch television without violence and then measure levels of aggression in the two groups.

Although the described study represents a socialization experience, sociologists are typically interested in more long-term socialization experiences that can last over periods of up to several years. For that reason, experiments usually are not well suited to examining socialization processes. How could we use socialization as an independent variable in an experiment? Because socialization is a lifelong process, whereas the typical experiment lasts no longer than an hour or two, researchers could not give one group a particular socialization experience and another group a different one. Time, money, and a number of other factors make it impossible to give people a meaningful socialization experience in a laboratory.

One way around the problem of socializing people in an experiment lies in the fact that people from different groups experience different socialization processes. So, experimental researchers might assign people to groups based on their socialization experiences. For example, male, female, and other gender participants could be assigned to different experimental groups. Doing that, however, would take away the major strength of experiments—random assignment. We can't randomly assign people's gender in an experiment. Without random assignment, we could not know that any differences between genders in the study were due to socialization and not something else, such as biological differences.

Although socialization is not well suited to experimental investigations, experimental work in the group processes tradition has nonetheless contributed to our understanding of socialization processes.

Recall the discussion of status characteristics theory from Chapter 4. Status characteristics theory describes the process through which the characteristics that people possess lead to inequalities in groups. According to the theory, and supported by countless studies, people (often unconsciously) develop expectations for the performances of people in groups based on their characteristics. People expected to perform better talk more in the group, are evaluated more highly, and have more influence over group decisions.

Status characteristics theory helps us understand how the contributions of women and minority group members become devalued in our society, and it is probably the most successful theory in the group processes tradition. Importantly, however, status characteristics theory has no propositions and makes no predictions about race, gender, or any other characteristics. In other words, status characteristics theory does not propose that women will tend to talk less and have less influence in groups than men. Instead, status characteristics theory lays out the process that will occur *if* something is acting as a status characteristic in a group.

One way to think about this is that the events explained by status characteristics theory begin after people have been socialized. Suppose, for example, that people in our society have been socialized to value the contributions of men more than the contributions of women. Gender, in other words, is a status characteristic. Status characteristics theory then explains how gender will affect what happens when people interact in task groups. Again, the theory doesn't tell us what characteristics are status characteristics—it tells us what will happen *if* something is a status characteristic.

Whenever people get together in a group, they do so in the context of the larger society of which they are a part. For example, we would expect the dominant norms and values of the United States to guide the behaviors of people working in a task group within the United States. Status characteristics theory defines **referential beliefs** as beliefs held in common by people about the usual relationships between status characteristics and reward levels. The source of referential beliefs is the larger society within which a group operates, and the way that we all come to have common referential beliefs is through socialization processes.

Research in status characteristics theory can tell us about socialization processes by telling us about the referential beliefs that guide people in groups. If a particular characteristic is consistently found to act as a status characteristic, for example, then we will have evidence that people hold referential beliefs associated with the characteristic. Moreover, we will have insight into how people are socialized to view the characteristic.

In the case of gender, overwhelming evidence from research in status characteristics theory indicates that the contributions of women are devalued in our society relative to the contributions of men (e.g., Hopcroft, Funk, and Clay-Warner 1998; Lovaglia et al. 2017; Tak, Correll, and Soule 2019; Troyer 2001; Wagner and Berger 1997). In other words, performances by women are rated lower than the same performances by men. There is also evidence that these gender differences appear to be becoming less pronounced (e.g., Foschi and Lapointe 2002). Through all of these experimental studies, we can see that people in our society are socialized to value contributions from women less than contributions from men, but also that this tendency may be moving in the direction of a society in which both men and women receive proper recognition for their performances.

Assessing the Effects of Socialization

Group processes experiments also have the capacity to explain the consequences of socialization processes. One area in which they have contributed is in understanding the consequences of gender socialization. Despite many changes in recent decades in the roles of men and women in American society, gender segregation in the workforce has remained resistant to change. Although there has been a major movement of women into the workforce, and there have been major changes in the types of jobs available (e.g., there has been a dramatic increase in service-related jobs), men and women continue to segregate into different types of occupations. This segregation involves men tending to select into more highly socially valued occupations than women, so much so that the gender segregation in occupations might explain the majority of the gender gap in pay (Peterson and Morgan 1995).

Shelley Correll (2004) sought to experimentally investigate how gender differences in career choices emerge. Most explanations of the differences focus on how various factors contribute to make the demand for men greater, and for women lower, in desirable occupations. Whereas James Lee's (1998) study focuses on how gender identity is linked to future interest in a math or science career, Correll's goal was to address how men and women's attitudes matter—how they develop preferences or aspirations for different types of work. Correll developed a theory in an attempt to explain how the culture in which people live can act to constrain the career paths they see as possible or appropriate, and thus shape the aspirations they develop for different careers. Correll first assumed that people must believe they have the skills necessary for a given career if they are to develop preferences for that career. Second, stereotypes in a society lead to different expectations about the extent to which people from different groups possess different types of skills. Third, people assess their own performances with these stereotypes in mind.

Consider the overrepresentation of men relative to women in careers in math, science, and engineering. According to Correll's theory, people will generally consider careers in these areas only if they believe that they have the necessary skills for the careers. Girls in American society now outperform boys on average at every level of school on almost all measures. So why might young women be less likely than young men to believe they have the requisite skills for careers in math, science, and engineering, and subsequently be less likely to select majors in college that lead to careers in those areas?

According to Correll's theory, the answer may lie in stereotypes about gender that exist in our culture. Research finds that students, parents, and teachers associate mathematical ability, but not verbal skills, with masculinity. Although girls tend to perform as well as boys in math skills, perhaps girls and boys assess their own performances in different ways. In particular, perhaps internalized gender stereotypes in our culture lead boys to interpret their performances as indicating that they have the requisite skills for careers in mathematics, whereas girls would interpret the same performances as indicating that they do not have the necessary skills to pursue a career in mathematics.

To test this explanation, Correll conducted an experiment with college students as participants. One way she could have carried out her experiment would be to give men and women math tests as well as information about their performances. She could have randomly told some men and some women that they performed well on the test and some men and women that they performed poorly. She could have then measured the extent to which the participants felt they had the skills for a career requiring mathematics. If men receiving high scores indicated a higher aptitude for mathematics than women receiving high scores, it would provide some support for Correll's theory. This approach, however, would present at least two problems. First, the participants in Correll's study had certainly taken many math tests in their lives, and they would probably have a good idea after a math test whether they performed well or poorly. Thus, many people, such as people who aced the test but were randomly assigned to receive a low score, likely wouldn't believe the feedback indicating they did well or poorly on the test. Second, college students generally have a sense of whether they are or are not good at math. For this reason, when Correll asked people after they received feedback on the test whether they had the skills for a career in math, she wouldn't know if they were responding based on the test score or their general beliefs about their math ability. Random assignment would typically take care of this issue by making people who think they are good or bad at math be equally likely to get good or bad feedback, but Correll was interested in making comparisons between women and men. Experimenters can't randomly assign participants to different categories of gender, and men and women on average have different perceptions of how good they are at math. Thus, if men and women with similar test scores gave differing career aspirations, Correll couldn't know whether it was because of gender differences in reactions to the scores or because the men and women entered the study with different perceptions of their own math abilities.

To get around these issues, Correll used for her study a fake ability that she led participants to believe was real. Further, rather than telling participants that their own performances were good or bad, she simply gave them their percentage of answers correct along with information about whether men or women usually did better on the type of task. Correll told participants that in her study they were completing a test of "Contrast Sensitivity Ability." Half of the participants in the study were told that research has found that men on average perform better than women on tests of contrast sensitivity. The other half of participants were told that there is no gender difference in scores on tests of contrast sensitivity. Depending on the condition, participants were told either that the experimenters were interested in determining why men and women perform differently or that they were interested in determining why men and women don't perform differently.

Participants in the study then completed a task that they believed measured contrast sensitivity ability. It involved guessing whether each of a series of rectangles had a greater shaded or nonshaded portion. Every rectangle was in fact roughly half shaded and half nonshaded. The participants went through two series of 20 rectangles. After they were finished with each round, participants received their scores for the round. They were all told that they guessed 13 out of 20 correct on the first round and 12 out of 20 correct on the second round.

After participants received their scores, they were asked a number of questions about their performances. When participants believed that men and women perform about the same on contrast sensitivity tests, men and women in the study evaluated their performances about the same. When participants believed that men tend to do better on the tasks, in contrast, men rated their performances significantly higher than did women.

Remember, all participants received the same scores. Nevertheless, men rated their performances higher than did women when participants believed that men were better than women at the task. Because dominant beliefs in our culture link mathematical ability with masculinity, this finding might explain why young men are more likely than young women to select into majors and careers that involve math ability even if they perform no better than women on tests of math ability.

Correll's study produced further evidence that this might be the case. In one question, she asked participants how high a score they would have needed on the test to definitely believe that they possessed high levels of contrast sensitivity ability. When participants did not believe that men and women scored differently on average on tests of contrast sensitivity ability, they answered about the same to this question. Both men and women said that they would need to score about 83% correct to believe that they were high in contrast sensitivity ability. When participants believed that men were higher in contrast sensitivity ability, however, scores differed by gender. Women on average said that they would need to score 89% correct to definitely believe they were high in contrast sensitivity ability. Men, in contrast, said on average that they would need to score only 79% correct to definitely believe they were high in the ability.

Finally, Correll asked participants a series of questions about their aspirations relevant to contrast sensitivity ability. She asked participants how likely they would be to apply to graduate programs requiring high levels of contrast sensitivity ability, apply for jobs requiring high contrast sensitivity ability, and take courses designed for persons high in contrast sensitivity ability. When participants believed that there are no gender differences in contrast sensitivity ability, men were no more likely than women to indicate a high likelihood to enroll in courses or programs requiring high-contrast sensitivity ability or to apply for jobs requiring the ability. When participants believed that men were better in contrast sensitivity ability, in contrast, men became much more likely than women to indicate these aspirations.

Although Correll's experiment could not allow her to assign participants to different socialization experiences, it did show how gender socialization in the form of learning dominant cultural beliefs about gender can act to channel men and women into different educational tracks and occupations. Her findings show that when there are cultural beliefs about how people perform on tasks, people use those beliefs to evaluate their own performances and to develop career aspirations. In this way, the study provides important experimental evidence on the consequences of socialization processes.

In another experimental study that produced results that might reflect differences in gender socialization, Ridgeway and colleagues (2009) gave participants a test of something they called "personal response style." Instructions told participants that there are two types of personal response styles, one called S2 and one called Q2, and that about half of the people in the world fall into each category. After being told they were S2s or Q2s, participants learned that they would be working on a task with a partner in the other category of personal response style (e.g., participants who were told they were S2s learned they were working with a partner who was a Q2).

Personal response style was an attribute made up by the researchers for the purpose of the study, and there is in fact no such thing as S2s and Q2s on response style. But the researchers gave instructions that led participants to believe that either S2s or Q2s were better at the task they would complete with the partner. During the study, participants had opportunities to be influenced by their partners, and at the end of the study, they answered a number of questions about their partners.

What Ridgeway and colleagues found is that people developed beliefs about partners that were consistent with what they were told about S2s and Q2s. In other words, people who had S2 partners and were told S2s were good at the task held high beliefs in the competence of their partners. But the research found an interesting gender effect. Although both men and women held the status beliefs that advantaged S2s or Q2s, only men acted on the status beliefs by deferring more or less to partners in the group task based on whether the partner was an S2 or Q2. Women, even though they held the status beliefs, were less likely to treat people in discriminatory ways based on whether they were S2s or Q2s. Ridgeway and colleagues concluded that the most likely explanation for the gender difference was that women were reluctant to violate gender expectations that they treat other people nicely. In other words, the result that men but not women acted on new status information may have reflected differences in gender socialization between women and men.

Another area in which group processes experiments have contributed to understanding the consequences of socialization is in the examination of group differences in tests of mental ability. As a college student in the United States, you would have almost certainly confronted the important role that standardized tests play in our society. For one thing, scores on standardized tests such as the SAT or ACT probably may have influenced the colleges to which you considered applying and maybe the ones to which you were admitted.

An important issue is whether standardized tests accurately measure ability. Studies find that African Americans score lower on average than Whites on standard ability tests such as intelligence quotient (IQ) tests or the SAT. On tests of IQ, the average difference between Whites and African Americans is somewhere around 10 to 12 IQ points (Herrnstein and Murray 1994). Social scientists are left with the task of determining why Whites tend to score higher.

Michael Lovaglia and his colleagues (Lovaglia et al. 1998) proposed that status characteristics theory might contribute to explaining the gap in test scores between African Americans and White Americans. If you recall the discussion of status characteristics theory from Chapter 4, the theory applies to groups formed for the purpose of completing a task, not to individual performances on tests. Lovaglia and his colleagues extended the theory by proposing that status processes affect individual performances when those performances are likely to affect the status of the individual in the future.

Research in status characteristics theory has shown that race operates as a status characteristic in American society, with the contributions of Whites valued more than the contributions of other group members (Cohen and Roper 1972; Webster and Driskell 1978; Manago, Sell, and Goar 2019). In other words, people in the United States hold referential beliefs that link European Americans to high status, and people (perhaps unconsciously) expect higher performances from European Americans.

Lovaglia and his colleagues (1998) used this information to develop a theory to explain the race difference in standardized test scores. First, Whites are higher in status than African Americans. Second, standardized tests have implications for the future status of people who take them. Third, people are rewarded for performing at levels comparable with their status and punished for performances that contradict their status positions. The Pygmalion study discussed earlier in this chapter, for example, found that intellectual ability was punished when it violated expectations. Lovaglia and colleagues proposed that these factors may combine to lead to lower scores on standardized tests for African American test takers.

The next step was for Lovaglia and his colleagues to test their theory. One way to do it would be to take samples of White and Black students similar in grade point average (GPA), socioeconomic status, and other factors. The researchers could then tell the White test takers that they are expected to do very well and the African American test takers that they are expected to do less well. The researchers could then have participants take a standardized test and measure whether scores differed between the two groups. The problem with this design is that it runs into the problem of random assignment. If there were differences in test scores between the two groups, how would we know that it was due to the status created by the researchers and not to something else that varies across racialized groups, such as differences in socialization experiences? Because it would not allow for random assignment, there is no way to include race as an independent variable in an experimental study without producing results that are difficult to interpret.

Lovaglia and his colleagues solved this problem by creating a new status characteristic and then randomly assigning participants to conditions based on that characteristic. When participants arrived for the study, they were asked if they were left-handed or right-handed. The researchers then placed a bright wristband on the wrist of the preferred hand. Half of the participants in the study were placed in a high-status condition and half in a low-status condition. If a participant was right-handed and in a high-status condition, she was told that right-handedness was associated with a number of positive personal traits (e.g., rationality and organized thinking) and that left-handedness was associated with a number of negative traits (e.g., impulsiveness and inattention). Right-handed low-status participants were told a number of positive traits for left-handers (e.g., creativity) and negative traits for right-handers (e.g., rigid thinking).

In these ways, the researchers created a status characteristic in the laboratory. As with race, people expected higher performances for members in one category of the characteristic than from members in another category. Further linking their created status characteristic with experiences based on race, the researchers told participants in the two groups that they could expect different rewards based on their performances: High-status participants were told that they would receive greater rewards for good performances than would low-status participants. Because most people in society do not actually expect more or less competent performances from left- or right-handed people, the researchers were able to randomly assign people to status conditions. They would not have been able to do this if they had looked directly at race.

After learning that they were either high or low in status based on their handedness, participants took a standard test of mental ability. Lovaglia and his colleagues found that participants in the high-status condition, on average, scored significantly higher on the IQ test than did participants in the low-status condition. The difference they found was almost as large as the average difference in scores between Whites and African Americans.

The research of Lovaglia and his colleagues indicates that socialization processes significantly affect how people perform on tests, over and above their individual ability. Remarkably, the study carried out by Lovaglia and his colleagues created status differences in about 15 minutes of computerized instructions. This was enough to create significant differences in test scores. Imagine how much greater the effects might be of a lifetime of socialization in a culture that values contributions from some groups more than those from others.

Section Summary

This section addressed the question "How do group processes researchers study socialization?" Group processes researchers often focus on the effects of socialization after it occurs. Specifically, status characteristics theory can tell us about socialization processes by shedding light on the referential beliefs that guide people in groups. If a particular characteristic is consistently found to act as a status characteristic, for example, then we will have evidence for socialization that advantages one category or characteristic over another.

A Take-Away Message

Socialization may typically be conceived of as a long-term process, a learning process that continues for 18 years and, as we learned in this chapter, well into adulthood. Group processes research related to socialization in part demonstrates how we can be socialized into a mindset or behavior in a short period of time. This type of research suggests that we also have the power to socialize other people in a short period of time. What we say and how we say it to other people can reframe how people think about an issue. Professionally, it also means that how we organize and interact in a work group can affect what people get out of those groups. What you do and say can have long- and short-term effects on the individuals in and culture of those groups. So, on the job, choose your words and actions carefully!

BRINGING IT ALL TOGETHER

> *I really like to read biographies. I think that if you REALLY want to learn about someone, you need to study ALL of the factors that affected their lives—historical factors, family, school, and anything else that influenced their lives.*
>
> —Ken, senior history major

In this chapter, we applied the three perspectives in sociological social psychology to understand how society shapes how we are socialized. If we want to know how people came to be the way they are, Ken thinks that biographies are the way to go. But we can go beyond biographies to understand human growth and change over time.

From an interactionist perspective, most children learn to relate by adapting adult roles and practicing them. We also examined socialization processes among children's peer cultures—how children have the ability to adapt and transform adult roles in their interaction with other children. The social structure and personality perspective was applied in the form of life-course sociology and in reviewing the role of agents of socialization (e.g., family and peers) in how we "turn out." Finally, the group processes perspective was used to understand the effects of socialization on group processes—how individuals come to learn social norms and beliefs during group interactions.

SUMMARY

1. Sociologists study socialization processes at every stage of development from childhood to late adulthood. The self develops through a symbolic process. An essential aspect of self-development is the ability to take the role of the other.
2. The sociology of childhood focuses on how children are active participants in creating culture.
3. Life-course sociology is based on the notion that humans adapt to different situations based on their social and historical location relative to different events. Four major themes in life-course sociology are historical context, timing, linked lives, and agency.
4. Sociologists view agents of socialization as mediators of the larger society rather than direct causes of socialization. The family is considered the primary agent of socialization because children are raised from infancy with parents and often siblings. Schools and peers are two other important agents of socialization.
5. The group processes perspective often examines the role of socialization after it has occurred, reviewing, for instance, how expectations about gender or race affect group interactions.

KEY TERMS AND CONCEPTS

Agency: An aspect of life-course sociology referring to our ability to improvise roles, make decisions, and control our destiny.

Agents of socialization: Individuals or groups most influential in the process of teaching children the norms and values of a particular culture.

Birth cohort: A group of people born around the same time period.

Children's cultural routines: A stable set of activities or routines, artifacts, values, and concerns that kids produce and share in interaction with each other.

Contextual dissonance: A feeling that minority members of a group may have because they are different from the majority members.

Game stage: The third stage of self-development in which children are capable of managing several different roles.

Gender socialization: Learning expectations about how to behave related to one's gender.

Generalized other: The attitudes of the whole community or society.

Historical and social context: An aspect of life-course sociology referring to how historic and social context affects development for different birth cohorts.

Idiocultures: A system of knowledge, beliefs, behaviors, and customs shared by an interacting group to which members refer and employ as a basis of further interaction.

Life course: The process of change from infancy to late adulthood resulting from personal and societal events and from transitions into and out of social roles.

Life events: Event that can cause significant changes in the course of our lives.

Life stages: Stages that occur at different ages in each society.

Linked lives: An aspect of life-course sociology referring to our relationships with other people.

Looking-glass self: How the self relies on imagined responses of others in its development.

Middle friendship circles: Smaller circles of friends that are less hierarchical.

Play stage: The second stage of self-development in which children begin to use language to make-believe as they play others' roles.

Popular clique: Children with an active social life and with the largest number of friends.

Preparatory stage: The first stage of self-development in which children simply mimic the attitudes and behaviors of their parents and caretakers.

Pygmalion effect: When children develop according to expectations of a group or society.

Racial socialization: Learning about one's racial and ethnic identity in a given culture.

Referential beliefs: In status characteristics theory, beliefs held in common by people about the usual relationships between particular status characteristics and reward levels.

Social isolates: Children who have trouble establishing relationships with those in other cliques.

Socialization: The process by which individuals acquire thoughts, feelings, and behaviors "appropriate" to their positions in society.

Timing: An aspect of life-course sociology referring to the incidence, duration, and sequence of roles, and to the relevant expectations and beliefs based on age.

Turning point: When the "normal trajectory" of someone's life is altered by a life event or role change.

Wannabes: Children who want to be popular but do not quite get accepted into this group.

DISCUSSION QUESTIONS

1. Have you interacted with a group of young children? Can you see socialization processes such as how they play adult roles?
2. Did a major life event affect your development in some way? How did it affect you? Do you think most people would have reacted to that event in a similar way?
3. Which agent or agents of socialization have had the greatest effect on you? In what ways did it affect you? How do you know?
4. Consider what, if any, online activity you currently participate in. How might the things you do online impact how you think about yourself or other people? If you don't have children, do you think you would teach your children to utilize media differently than you? Why or why not?

PART 3

Areas of Social Life

At this point in our social-psychological journey, we have reviewed the major perspectives and methods in the field and have seen how they apply to stratification processes, self and identity, and socialization. In the next several chapters, we will apply the three faces of sociological social psychology—symbolic interactionism, social structure and personality, and group processes—to understand different areas of social life. We start with the social psychology of deviance by examining the ways that people break the rules of social life. Much of the literature we have reviewed thus far focuses on how individuals develop and follow social conventions. But when do people decide not to follow those rules? Most of the work in this area focuses on understanding crime and delinquency, but it can easily be applied to other forms of deviance such as talking back to an authority figure or violating social norms. We follow this chapter with social-psychological research on mental health and illness, the latter of which is sometimes considered a type of deviance. Deviance broadly includes thoughts, feelings, or behaviors of an individual that significantly differ from the people around them, no matter the cause. We also examine the social psychology of attitudes and behavior in Chapter 9 and emotions in Chapter 10, followed by a review of collective behavior in the last chapter, Chapter 11. These chapters cover a plethora of research specialties in the field of sociological social psychology, but all of them share the application of the essential perspectives and methods reviewed in the first section of this book.

7

The Social Psychology of Deviance

Why do people have to hurt each other anyway? Why do people take things from other people? When you think about it, criminals are a huge burden on society.

—Carlos, senior business major

The term "deviance" typically brings to mind behaviors that people view as immoral or illegal. Social psychologists define the concept more broadly than this and without an attached moral judgment. **Deviance**, in social psychology, refers to thoughts, feelings, or behaviors that depart from accepted practices in a society or group. Many deviant behaviors are of course illegal—murder, for instance. Other deviant behaviors, however, are not illegal—singing along out loud with music from your earbuds while walking on a public street, for example. In some cases, behaviors mandated by laws can themselves be deviant, such as driving at or below the speed limit on some highways. Deviance, then, goes beyond the legal code of a society. In simple terms, it refers to any behavior that violates the norms of a group.

Carlos's statement reflects a resentment of lawbreakers. Many laws represent what sociologists call mores. **Mores** refer to widely held beliefs in society, with many so widely held that they are formalized into law, thereafter invoking both deep sentiments and harsh punishments for breaking them. Mores are derived from **folkways**, which are rules of behavior and custom passed down through a group or society. **Taboos** are violations of behavior prescribed through mores, or, according to William Sumner (1906), things that are simply forbidden to do in society. Most treatments of deviance tend to focus on theories and research associated with criminal behavior. A goal of criminology is to understand the processes that lead people to break laws. That is what Carlos wants to understand at the beginning of this section. However, from an interactionist point of view, the role of deviance in society is a bit more complicated. In fact, interactionists generally view deviance as a normal part of the interaction process. Structural and group-centered views of deviance tend to focus on the social conditions that increase the likelihood of breaking laws or norms. These views come from the larger social science specialty of criminology. We emphasize the broader sense of deviance in everyday life before reviewing traditional theories and research on criminal forms of deviance, answering the following questions:

- How do people define what is normal or deviant?
- How does the construction of deviant labels contribute to the development of deviant lifestyles?
- How do structural conditions influence individuals' decisions to commit deviant acts?
- How do group relationships affect the development of deviance and perceptions of deviance?

INTERACTIONIST APPROACHES TO DEVIANCE

> *At first it felt a little weird. I was always told to stay away from drugs. But I always seemed to find myself hanging out with the "wrong crowd" in high school. I let my hair grow long and smoked a little weed—and I chilled out about getting homework done on time. Homework seemed really overrated and I had much better things to do with my time—like smoking weed. People would call me a "hippie-freak" because I looked like the typical 60s hippie. Maybe I was, I don't know. It bothered me at first, then I got used to it. I guess you can say that I am proud of it really. The 1960s were a time of liberation and change. I am all about that.*
>
> —Steve, sophomore undeclared major

In some sense, deviance is a necessary part of the symbolic interaction process of negotiating social reality. Interactionism assumes that individuals decide to maintain (or break) social norms and standards during every interaction. When you talk with a friend, you will likely look her in the eye and maintain an appropriate and comfortable distance between the two of you. Further, the depth of intimacy in the discussion will correlate with the closeness of your friendship. But how do friendships develop over time? Friends must share more intimate aspects of their lives over time to feel a sense of closeness. Intimacy assumes that one person is willing to share details about themselves with the other. Most relationships start with low levels of intimacy but progress toward more intimate levels through successive self-disclosures of personal information. In the beginning, however, one person must decide to deviate from the norm of acquaintance talk—the relationship cannot progress into something more meaningful unless someone breaks the rules. In this way, individuals must deviate from their previous relationship with the other person to change it. Small deviations in social norms are necessary for the development of relationships. You might have felt some anxiety related to this type of deviance when trying to decide whether to say the words "I love you" to a special romantic partner before they said it to you.

Deviance is traditionally applied to larger breaks with social conventions. The process by which Steve decided to experiment with drugs and change his values and beliefs (as well as the length of his hair) suggests a gradual acceptance of alternative norms. At first, Steve seemed hesitant to be associated with the 1960s hippie movement. Over time, he came to accept the label and the stereotypes associated with it. He actually came to embrace the new title, believing that his new values, although different from those of conventional society, are good and true. In this sense, deviance is also about identity formation, or how people come to see themselves as deviant (Herman-Kinney 2003).

Interactionists view deviance as a manifestation of social interactions, just like any other thought, feeling, or behavior. When an individual decides to deviate from the norms of a group, she will likely incur penalties for making such a decision. If it is a mild infraction—belching in public, for instance—it may receive only a few raised eyebrows or a mild statement such as "Excuse you!" A more serious infraction, such as pushing someone who is in your way, may get a few stern statements like "Hey, watch where you're going!" or some physical response—perhaps someone pushing you back.

The symbolic interaction process allows researchers to study deviance at different levels. Within this tradition, ethnomethodology helps us understand minor forms of deviance in everyday life. Labeling theory is often applied to explain how individuals come to deviate from more consequential norms in society.

Ethnomethodology and the Social Construction of Deviance

We introduced ethnomethodology in Chapter 1 as a theory designed to link individual-level interactions with the broader society. It can be considered an extension of symbolic interactionism that emphasizes how individuals account for what is happening in social interaction. However, ethnomethodologists do not assume that there is shared meaning in a given interaction. Rather, individuals enter and leave interactions with somewhat different interpretations of those interactions. Ethnomethodology emphasizes how individuals construct and defend their views of social reality (Pfohl 1985). Thus, individuals have differing sets of boundaries regarding acceptable and unacceptable behavior. People who can provide better accounts of a situation can convince others of those accounts, thereby controlling the meaning of good and bad, or deviance and conformity, in society.

To maintain efficiency in interaction, individuals index thoughts, feelings, and behaviors from their own perspectives, a process called **indexicality**. The meaning of a given behavior may be defined as deviant to one person but not to another person. For instance, smoking a cigarette at an outdoor party might be considered normal to many people but smoking in an office would be quite abnormal (i.e., deviant) today. In addition, a teenager experimenting with smoking may see it as novel or cool, whereas someone older who is trying to quit may see it as a dangerous and expensive habit.

Reflexivity is the process by which individuals think about a behavior within its social context and give meaning to it. At some point, a person's behavior may come to be labeled as deviant to one or more people in a situation. An individual drinking alcohol during the day in an office environment, for example, may reflect on that behavior. If others view the behavior as deviant (assuming they don't have the power to fire her if having alcohol in the drawer is against the rules), the individual decides whether she concurs with the label. If the label is accepted, the individual may categorize herself accordingly, potentially drinking even more often in public as she comes to think of herself as a "partier," a "rebel," or a "drunk." Alternatively, the individual can feel concerned about being categorized as deviant and decide to stop the behavior.

A product of this interaction process is the documentary interpretation of actions or using evidence of the deviant behavior to infer meaning and motive in the behavior of the deviant person (Pfohl 1985). Because we can't read the minds of other people, we rely on their behaviors as our guide to their motives. People are especially likely to use the documentary interpretation of actions when inferring the motives behind deviant behavior because they do not trust deviants, compared to nondeviants, to give honest accounts of their motivations. We use this process ourselves to help us process our own deviant behaviors. For example, in a study of interviews with 26 midwives, Alicia Suarez and Megan Bolton (2014) found that their subjects would justify or provide an account for doing midwifery in states where it is illegal by condemning the people who made laws making it illegal. They would also often appeal to a higher loyalty or deny that they were doing any harm.

Much of the material in this chapter emphasizes criminal deviance. However, the study of deviance has included an array of human conditions that can be defined as undesirably different but not necessarily illegal, such as shyness (Scott 2007), being overweight (Carr and Friedman 2006), and the act of self-injury (Adler and Adler 2008; Brossard 2018). In these examples, deviance may not be considered criminal, but people's attributes or behaviors lead other people to see them as deviant.

Do you consider yourself deviant? A more appropriate question might be "Do you do things that other people would consider to be deviant?" From a symbolic interactionist perspective, meaning is relative to time and place because individuals are constantly negotiating the meaning of what it is to be deviant. Whether a thought or an act is deemed deviant varies not just among people but also across time and culture. Consider the changing mores surrounding premarital sex in the United States. At one historical juncture, the topic was taboo; now, most young people have had nonmarital sex by the age of 20, and sexual relationships are a normal part of media programming (Michael et al. 1995; Regnerus and Ueker 2011). However, some individuals have become more conservative regarding other sexual behaviors such as marital infidelity, and there is a worldwide trend of increasing regulation of some sexual behaviors such as sexual violence (Frank, Camp, and Boutcher 2005; Newport 2009). Attitudes toward topics such as homosexuality have changed in the United States, from a small majority believing it is morally wrong (53%) in 2001 to 56 percent saying it is morally acceptable in 2011 (Jones 2011). In 2023, 71 percent of Americans said that they believe that gay marriage should be valid (Gallup 2023). However, these findings are not reflective of world opinion on the matter (see Figure 7.1) in the early part of this century, where beliefs about homosexuality were quite mixed.

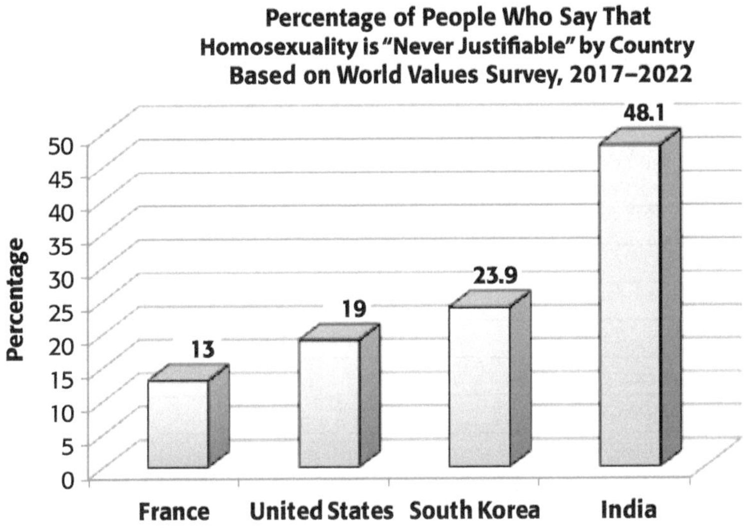

Figure 7.1 Acceptance of Homosexuality around the World: Percent Reporting that it is Never Justified.

Source: World Values Survey (Wave 7, 2017–2022) (www.worldvaluessurvey.org).

How do we learn about what is deviant or not? In one sense, we learn what is deviant like we learn anything else, through the socialization processes outlined in Chapter 6. We enter the world of adults with the assumption that things are the way that they are supposed to be (Martin 2009). However, people have agency and constantly negotiate what is normal and good all of the time. Emily Hofstetter and Jessica Robles (2019) studied the use of deception and manipulation in strategic board game playing interaction. They found that players had to negotiate some moves as more or less acceptable, often utilizing deception strategically in order to succeed in a game. Players had to manage fairness and morality in game playing. This study is a microcosm of our social lives as we manage to make decisions about right and wrong as we seek employment, negotiate the price of a car, or find suitable friends and partners. We decide how to present ourselves and how much information to exchange in order to obtain the things we want from other people.

There are also large-scale societal forces that contribute to the construction of deviance. Paul Knepper (2009) argues that crime has emerged as a transnational problem only in the last two centuries, as technologies and increased trade among nations have contributed to international efforts to define and combat crime—and have given criminals greater access to world markets. Given that deviance can vary by location, it is difficult to enforce rules among people with different definitions of right and wrong. Consider this issue: have you ever used someone else's login information to access online programming such as Netflix or Hulu? Using those services without paying for them is technically illegal, yet many people do it and do not consider it wrong. These

Table 7.1 Americans' Perspectives on the Morality of Different Behaviors*

Type of Behavior	% Believing It to Be Morally Wrong (2010)	% Believing It to Be Morally Wrong (2015)
Married men and women having an affair	92	92
Polygamy, when one husband has more than one wife at the same time	90	84
Cloning humans	88	85
Suicide	77	81
Cloning animals	63	66
Abortion	50	55
Doctor-assisted suicide	46	44
Gay or lesbian relations	43	37
Having a baby outside of marriage	40	39
Sex between an unmarried man and woman	38	32
Buying and wearing clothing made of animal fur	35	39
Medical testing on animals	34	44
Gambling	34	33
Medical research using stem cells obtained from human embryos	32	36
The death penalty	26	40
Divorce	23	29

**Source*: Saad 2010; Newport 2015.

and similar types of deviance have become a global issue (David 2010). The information in Table 7.1 shows the degree to which people in the United States believe that different behaviors are morally wrong with some change between 2010 and 2015, some in each direction of being more or less accepting of behaviors.

Labeling Theory of Deviance

Ethnomethodological perspectives help to elaborate the basic processes by which individuals come to be defined (and define themselves) as deviant in the first place. Labeling theory is more formally applied to the study of these processes from the interactionist perspective. **Labeling theory** proposes that deviance is a consequence of a social process in which a negative characteristic becomes an element of an individual's identity. In short, an individual becomes a deviant through the acceptance of a deviant label, although, in theory, someone can also be labelled with a positive attribute (e.g., being a good person, smart, or hardworking) (Thompson 2014). That label may be the result of interactions with an array of others such as friends or family, or a formal social control agency such as police or doctors. The label may also result from associations made from media portrayals of deviance and conformity (Dotter 2004). Individuals may also self-label based on interactions that indirectly call up a deviant identity (Norris 2011). The labels are especially likely to be applied to those with relatively less power in society, such as those living in poverty. Once the label is applied to us, we then continue to use this identity in interactions, like we would any other aspects of our identities. The result can be a self-fulfilling prophecy in which we act according to our label, ensuring that we live up to the expectations that are set for us. In sum, labeling theory proposes that people who are labeled as deviant become more likely because of the label to commit deviant acts in the future, much as the "drunk" in the preceding example.

The roots of labeling theory stem from symbolic interactionism's focus on the social construction of the self found in the work of George Herbert Mead and Charles Horton Cooley. Cooley's (1922) "looking-glass self" (see Chapter 6) refers to how individuals come to understand their identities based on how they perceive others seeing them. We give meaning to ourselves based on how people react to us and on our assessments of those reactions. If we behave according to social standards of a given group, we may be thought of as "normal" and come to understand ourselves as such. Alternatively, if we act in ways that appear to others to be odd or weird, we may rethink our senses of self to include others' designations of us as deviant.

Photo 7.1 Labeling theory emphasizes the effects of early interactions with law enforcement on the development of deviant identities in adulthood. How might an adolescent come to see herself as a deviant after this type of experience with the police?

Source: boyphare/Shutterstock

Complex identity processes are at work here. Ross Matsueda (1992) examined the formation of reflected appraisals (see Chapter 5) that lead to delinquent behavior. He found that youths develop delinquent identities, in part, based on their parents' appraisals of them as well as their own previous delinquent behavior. Initial delinquent behaviors set in motion a meaning-making set of interactions both externally (what parents think of the child) and internally (youths' reflected appraisals), yielding a delinquent identity based on all three sets of information: their own actions, others' perceptions, and their own perceptions. The influences of reflected appraisals may be pronounced with deviant identities. In a study of criminal and worker identities, for instance, Emily Asencio and Peter Burke (2011) found that reflected appraisals affected the formation of criminal identities but not worker identities. These findings indicate that the effects of reflected appraisals on identities vary by the identities in question. Ultimately, we will act on those identities that we create through interactions with other people, whether they are deviant (i.e., criminal) or not (i.e., worker).

Types of Deviance

The explicit connection of interactionist principles to the study of deviance can be found in the work of Frank Tannenbaum (1938). Tannenbaum conducted some of the earliest research in labeling theory by focusing on the process by which juvenile delinquents are "tagged" as deviants by conventional society, leading these individuals to fall into patterns of deviance. He proposed that the process of defining a person as bad or evil starts with the definition of the individual's acts. First, other people (e.g., friends, family, or authorities) define the individual's act as bad or evil. Second, these people then ascribe the act to the individual (rather than the situation), gradually defining the individual as bad. Finally, a change in self-concept takes place whereby the individual committing the deviant act applies the label of deviance to herself, beginning to think of herself as bad.

Edwin Lemert (1951) extended Tannenbaum's work by proposing that there are two forms of deviance in the labeling process. **Primary deviance** refers to the initial act that causes others to label the individual a deviant. The first arrest of a drug user may lead people to believe a person is a deviant. **Secondary deviance** occurs after an individual accepts the deviant label and continues to commit deviant acts, thus supporting the initial label (see Box 7.1). The logic of this work continues to be relevant. Lonnie Athens' (2017) study of a small group of violent offenders demonstrates the ways the criminals come to terms with their violent pasts and decide whether to continue their violent offenses in the future, considering both their violent identities and possible futures if they decide to try and leave that identity. They face reprisal from their violent peers or rejection from the larger culture. Athens finds that both sets of potential outcomes influence the course of their violent identities.

The acceptance of the deviant label may be the result of many different processes. An individual may accept the label as a means of dealing with the consequences of some deviant behavior. When an individual acts in a deviant manner, others usually label them as deviant. Infractions of social order cause the newly defined deviant to account for their behavior simply to restore order by either accepting the indexing process reviewed

Box 7.1 Lemert's Stages Leading to Secondary Deviance

Lemert (1951) argued that it takes multiple attempts at deviance before it moves from primary to secondary. The following stages show the process by which individuals' interactions with other people may lead them to accept the deviant label. It is not as simple as accepting a label on the completion of a single deviant act.

1. Primary deviance.
2. Social penalties.
3. Further primary deviation.
4. Stronger penalties and rejections.
5. Further deviation.
6. Crisis reached in the tolerance of such deviance acceptable by a community.
7. Strengthening of the deviant conduct as a reaction to penalties.
8. Ultimate acceptance of the deviant social status.

Lemert's work focuses on the continual interaction between the individual and the individual's social environments, characteristic of interactionist approaches to all social development, including deviant behavior and identities. Hence, interaction and meaning-making processes are involved in the development of deviance in the same way as any other identity formation.

here or providing another account or reason for the behavior. Indexing may lead an individual to be categorized as deviant. Social order is then restored by applying new sets of rules and expectations for the newly labeled individual, giving them a new set of behavioral guidelines.

A typical example of this process is the behavior and reactions involved in high school pranks. A group of students may decide to illegally enter a high school quad after hours and proceed to douse the trees with streams of toilet paper for a bit of fun. Upon being caught, the teenagers are told to account for their actions in the face of punishment. Ultimately, all of them will be asked to provide motivations for their behaviors. Accepting the act as part of one's identity (i.e., identifying oneself as a deviant) is only one of the possible ways to account for those acts. The students can alternatively account for their behaviors by arguing that they felt peer pressure to do it or say that they simply "didn't know" it was bad.

Most deviance research focuses on more serious infractions of norms or of the law in which police, the courts, medical doctors, and other agents of social control must adjudicate deviant behavior. **Agents of social control** represent the state's attempts to maintain social order; in other words, to enforce the mores of society. Some laws are accepted more readily than others. Murder is almost universally accepted as a form of deviance to be punished, whereas drinking and drug laws vary more widely by nation. Of course, infractions viewed as more serious are associated with the strongest penalties. It is not surprising that murder and robbery get more attention by agents of social

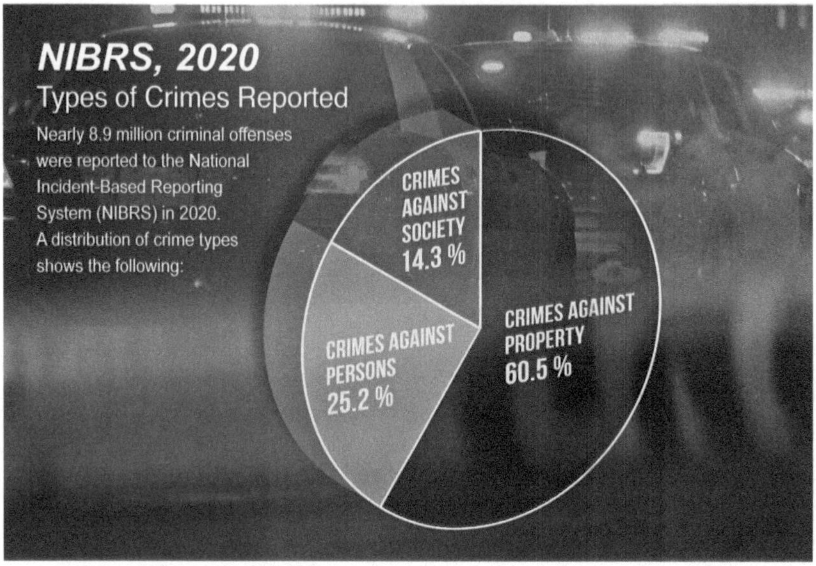

Figure 7.2 Distribution of U.S. crimes.

Source: Federal Bureau of Investigation's National Incident-Based Reporting System (NIBRS) (2020).

control than theft. More people commit less serious offenses compared with the more serious ones (see Figure 7.2). Thus, some of the least perpetrated types of deviance (e.g., murder) are considered the most important types of deviance to control.

Using Lemert's (1951) framework, the role of the larger society is most present during secondary deviance, when an individual comes to identify herself as a deviant. According to labeling theorists, although society does not directly cause primary deviance to occur, it contributes to the labeling process when agents of social control label an act and the person committing the act. A self-fulfilling process develops in which individuals reflect on their deviant behaviors based on the reactions of agents of social control, leading them to commit further deviant acts (i.e., secondary deviance) to support the label.

In one classic example of the labeling process, William Chambliss (1973) followed the lives of two sets of boys in a small Midwestern town; he called them the Saints and the Roughnecks. The Saints were middle-class, college-bound boys, whereas the Roughnecks came from the working class. Both groups participated in a series of delinquent behaviors: drinking, stealing, and vandalism, among other things. However, none of the Saints were ever arrested, but the Roughnecks were often in trouble with law enforcement officers. Chambliss wanted to know why.

Chambliss (1973) found that the Saints, in terms of the absolute number of delinquent acts, were more deviant than the Roughnecks. They engaged in more truancy and drank more regularly than the Roughnecks, and they also committed pranks that put others in potentially dangerous situations. However, the Roughnecks' behavior caused more damage than that of the Saints, and they were more likely to engage in violent behavior. Chambliss concluded that the Roughnecks received a larger portion of law enforcement's (an agent of social control) attention for three reasons. First was differential visibility because of economic standing in the community. Because the Saints had more access to private transportation in the form of cars, they could easily evade detection from police and other enforcers or engage in delinquency away from their hometowns. The Roughnecks had to hang out in public spaces more often, in full view of police. Second, the Saints interacted with authorities differently than the Roughnecks. The Saints would act penitent even when they believed that they had done no wrong (a form of "cultural capital" they acquired in interactions with middle-class people), whereas the Roughnecks would act belligerently to the end. Finally, the agents of social control showed a clear bias for the Saints and against the Roughnecks. Chambliss found that the police interpreted transgressions by the two groups differently: in the eyes of the police, the Saints were simply "sowing wild oats," whereas the economically deprived Roughnecks were "up to no good." Once labeled delinquents, the Roughnecks were much more scrutinized in all their behaviors; as a result, their deviance was more often noticed than that of the Saints.

It could be argued that new media and access to the internet has changed the role of traditional agents of socialization as mediators of crime and deviance in society. Now, people can publish content available to the world almost immediately, thus giving anyone the ability to interpret events, including ones that may be considered deviant (see Schneider 2016). Consider examples of police violence or mass shootings at schools or other public events. Anyone with a phone can use the device to record the event and post it online with their own interpretations of what is going on.

While new technologies may affect who gets to interpret acts as deviant or not, traditional agents of social control are still the primary means of adjudicating people who perpetrate deviant acts through the criminal justice system in the form of prison guards, administrators, and managers of juvenile detention centers. While these types of places serve as a means of social control, to keep order within the institution, they are also involved in resocializing their residents to traditional societal norms, otherwise called treatment (Garot 2010; Price 2005). In an ethnographic study of two drug treatment centers, Darin Weinberg (2005) found that staff defined what he calls "right living" in terms of following the rules of the facilities. In one case, right living meant remaining abstinent, practicing nonviolence, and fulfilling service requirements at the facility. In the other case, rules for right living were much less structured. The expectations for acting normal were defined differently across the two settings, leading to different sets of moral expectations among patrons when they leave those facilities. The goal in both settings is to resocialize individuals toward new ways of thinking about themselves in the world.

Deviant Subcultures

In his seminal work *Outsiders: Studies in the Sociology of Deviance*, prominent labeling theorist Howard Becker (1973) extended the basic premises of labeling theory by elaborating (1) the processes through which primary deviance leads to secondary deviance

Box 7.2 Becoming a Marijuana User

Howard Becker (1953) was famous for his analysis of how individuals come to use mind-altering drugs and how they interpret those experiences. Becker was writing at a time when other researchers, such as the famous psychologist Timothy Leary, were studying drugs as a way of "consciousness raising." Meanwhile, government officials warned of the negative side effects of these drugs. Although drug use may include a physiological and chemical reaction in the body, Becker proposed that subjective reactions to drugs can be studied only through observation and interviews. Drug reactions can be subjective because individuals can focus on any one of a number of physiological effects and interpret those effects differently (e.g., as good or bad).

Becker's observation of drug users showed that reactions to drug use depended on the group being studied. When a new user was in the presence of experienced users, she could rely on them to help her focus on more positive aspects of the experience. Alternatively, a non-user may highlight the more disconcerting aspects of the drug experience simply out of inexperience with the drug. The drug culture provides the user with the tools necessary to interpret and potentially enjoy the drug experience. The result is a negative or positive association with the experience. Becker's work shows that social interpretations are an important part of deviant experiences. This seminal work is still used today to help scholars understand "becoming" identities. For instance, Gareth Davey and Xiang Zhao (2020) used Becker's framework to study how Chinese adolescents started to become tobacco smokers. Notably, the teenagers stress the importance of peers in their "becoming" process.

and (2) the importance of deviant subcultures in maintaining the deviant self-image. His study followed the development of cannabis laws and the recreational use of drugs (see Box 7.2). He also used participant observation of Chicago musicians to illustrate the social life of deviant subcultures. In his book, **outsiders** refer to people labeled as deviants who accept the deviant labels. Outsiders accept their deviant labels and see themselves outside conventional society.

Becker (1973) described a three-stage process by which individuals become outsiders:

1. An individual commits a deviant act (primary deviance).
2. The person is caught doing the act by someone else and begins to accept and act on the deviant status (secondary deviance). The deviance becomes a part of her master status, one that affects all other aspects of her life—the life of an outsider.
3. The deviant joins a deviant subculture, thereby solidifying her deviant status.

In this final stage, the individual comes to live a deviant lifestyle. A considerable amount of research has been conducted to understand these subcultures. In *Codes of the Underworld: How Criminals Communicate*, Diego Gambetta (2009) outlines the norms that exist among criminals. The challenge for criminals, he finds, is that they must find a way to be accepted and trusted as a fellow criminal despite the fact that being a criminal makes one, by definition, untrustworthy. Gambetta finds that criminals must find ways to prove their loyalty to other criminals. They may submit to tests such as committing a crime, or they may share incriminating information about themselves with other criminals, thereby demonstrating that they trust them. Over time, criminals develop "criminal résumés" that establish hierarchies, with those who perpetrate more crimes having a higher status than those people who commit fewer or less severe crimes. Other deviant subcultures also establish sets of norms regarding their behaviors. Andrea Beckmann (2009) studied individuals engaging in bondage, sadomasochism, and other sexual forms of deviance and found that participants were always consenting adults following rules of behavior to ensure their safety. Alice Goffman (2014) demonstrated the ways that whole communities can be part of the process as individuals on parole or with previous criminal records live in fear of being arrested, leading them to always feel "on the run," working with close friends and family to maintain their freedom from

Howard Becker*

Howard Becker was born in Chicago, Illinois, in 1928. He attended the University of Chicago, where he obtained his college education, including a PhD in sociology in 1951. He went on to teach in sociology departments at Northwestern University, the University of Washington, and the University of California, Santa Barbara.

While at the University of Chicago, Becker worked as a professional jazz pianist. This work ultimately led him to research jazz musicians as a professional group, summarized in the book *Outsiders: Studies in the Sociology of Deviance* (Becker 1973), in which he reviews labeling theory. This work serves as a foundation for symbolic interactionist approaches toward deviance. He continues to influence the field of sociological social psychology through his field research over the decades, with works such as *Boys in White: Student Culture in Medical School* (Becker 1961) and *Art Worlds* (1984, reissued at its twenty-fifth anniversary in Becker 2008) still prominent. He served as the president of the Society for the Study of Symbolic Interaction between 1977 and 1978 and received the Cooley-Mead Award in 1985.

*Information for this biography was obtained through personal correspondence with Dr. Becker.

Other resources: *Zur Aktualitat von Howard S. Becker: Einfuhrung in sein Werk* by Dagmar Danko. Wiesbaden: VS Springer, 2015; Muller, Thaddeus. 2014. "Chicago, Jazz and Marijuana: Howard Becker on Outsiders." *Symbolic Interaction* 37: 576–594; Sanders, Clinton. 2013. "Learning from Experience: Recollections of Working with Howard S. Becker." *Symbolic Interaction* 36: 216–28.

the law—but also in fear and suspicion of the people around them who may inform on them for any number of reasons. Thus, this subculture includes a complex set of social relationships that make it difficult to change deviant identities.

Stigma, Passing, and Covering

Symbolic interactionists believe that deviance can take many forms. Erving Goffman (1963) defined **stigma** as "an attribute that is deeply discrediting" in interaction (3). Specifically, stigma can take three forms:

1. Physical disabilities or "abominations of the body."
2. Being part of a devalued social group, such as a racialized or religious minority.
3. Something viewed culturally as a character flaw, including mental disorders, addictions, or a criminal record.

Studies of stigma have included things such as gambling addictions (Wagner et al., 2017), chronic illnesses (Charmaz 2020)—even low-status college majors (Lewis 2017)! Stigma can be socially transmitted to the people surrounding the stigmatized person. In an ethnography of a support group of prisoners' wives in an Israeli prison, for instance, Avihu Shoshana (2020) found that wives felt a sense of stigma being married to an inmate and some of this sense of stigma ironically came from the therapeutic sessions designed to help its members deal with the issues associated with being married to a prisoner.

The first form of stigma in Goffman's list is most noticeable and most difficult to cover up. The last form of stigma may be the least noticeable. In Goffman's work, he tried to find ways in which individuals attempt to manage stigma. He found that individuals often try to pass and cover their deviance to interact in everyday life. **Passing** refers to ways in which people make efforts to manage the information about an undisclosed stigma such as having a criminal record. People with the first form of deviance—physical abominations—probably find it difficult to "pass" because these deviations are usually readily apparent to others. However, those with criminal records can more easily hide information about their history from others, passing in most situations as citizens who have not served time in prison. **Covering** includes ways of downplaying a stigma during interaction to reduce tension for "normal" people. Those with physical limitations such as blindness cannot easily pass as sighted, but they can cover their stigma. Lived examples of passing and covering can include how families of prisoners try to conceal their spouses' status or how sex workers try to hide their identities in this role; even being a certain body type or hair color can be thought of as a stigma (Hannem and Bruckert 2012; Heckert and Best 1997; see also Lichtenstein 2012). Vanessa Panfil (2017) demonstrates the ways that gay male gang members work to display masculine traits and hide their sexuality to portray a tough image. Whether individuals see themselves as deviant may not change their recognition that society sees them as such, leading them to find ways to conceal elements of their social lives.

The internet has become a tool for helping identify people with some stigmas. Sex offenders in the United States must register with the government. Now, maps of sex offenders in almost any part of the United States are easily available online (see Figure 7.3

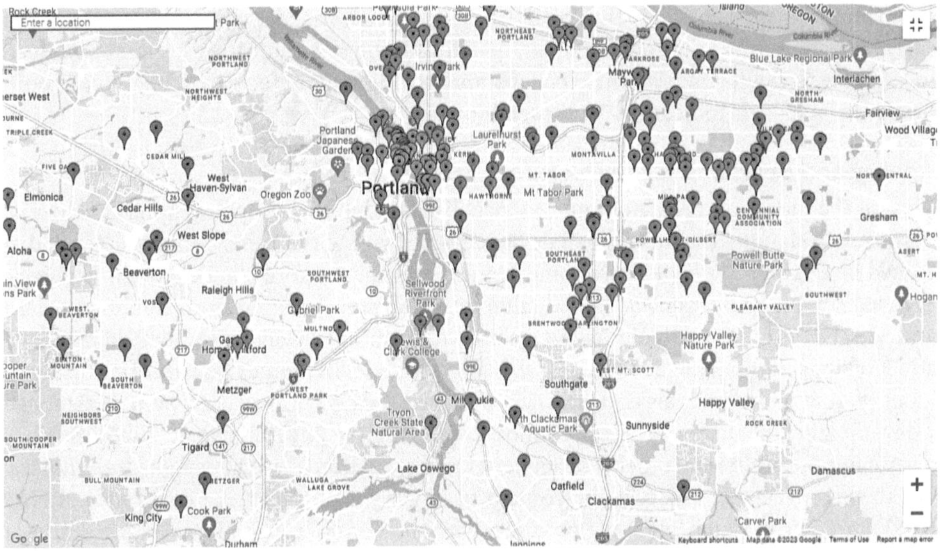

Figure 7.3 A Map of Sex Offenders in Portland, Oregon.

Source: Oregon State Police Sex Offender Registry.

for an example in Portland, Oregon). People sometimes use these maps to help identify more-or-less safe neighborhoods in which to live. Information about each offender is made available, including a picture so that they can be identified when seen. Sex offenders are fully aware of their stigma in society and find multiple ways of accounting for their behaviors (Rickard 2016). Stigma can also be used as a tool against opponents, by associating common stigmas with one's enemies (e.g., posting that your opponent is a racist or dishonest in a comment section of a YouTube video) (Silva and Flynn 2020).

Stigma management strategies can extend beyond just passing and covering. In one study, Lacey Ritter and Koji Ueno (2017) studied stigma management among Humans vs. Zombie gamers in a university setting. They found that gamers used several strategies to manage the stigma they perceived from other students on campus. Gamers would use "othering" (see Chapter 4), disassociating themselves with stereotypical players, to make themselves look or feel better. In other cases, they would challenge player stereotypes (e.g., focusing on its similarities with sports). Ultimately, some participants simply embraced their stigma, choosing to make the stigma a positive attribute or a way to build cohesion in the group, an attribute they share in common.

When individuals choose to accept their stigmas, it may produce a self-fulfilling prophecy. Edwin Schur (1971) proposed that this process may lead to a retrospective interpretation of the person's life to find support for the deviant label. **Retrospective interpretations** refer to reinterpretations of past behaviors in light of the person's new role as a deviant. People, including the deviants themselves, begin to reanalyze past behaviors in light of their new status. The courts can contribute to this process by examining past behaviors to help assess current motives. Once a person is accused of a crime, for example, past behaviors that at the time seemed innocent may be reevaluated as early signs of future criminal behavior. Much like the self-indication process reviewed in Chapter 5, the deviant identity is constantly being negotiated and renegotiated both internally (i.e., self-indication) and socially.

Agency and Emotions in the Deviance Process

Most of the theory and research on deviance discussed in this chapter emphasize the role of society in shaping the meaning of deviance—and giving that label to people. As we discussed in Chapter 2, people have some agency, some element of choice in their behavior. Perhaps some people want to live an alternative lifestyle ranging from holding deviant attitudes, to alternative living arrangements, to criminal behavior (Matsueda, Kreager, and Huizinga 2006; Pape 2005). Also, the very act of deviance may be part of a purposive identity; that is, individuals choose to act in deviant ways because they want to establish a deviant label for themselves (see Halnon 2006; Hughey 2012; Renshaw 2006). But it is always important to remember that agency is contextualized—we may make free choices, but those choices are made in the context of larger social forces. A person may choose to commit a crime such as taking products without paying from a grocery store, but that choice may be influenced by the individual's living conditions, such as poverty (Heimer and Kruttschnitt 2005). In this example, a person may not normally choose to steal but hunger may have a strong influence on their decision-making process.

Agency allows individuals to use retrospective recall in all sorts of ways. In a study of staff and participants at a high-income treatment facility for youth addicts, Jessica Pfaffendorf (2019) found that, "they engage in a stratification project that restores hierarchies where they occupy dominant positions in various social contexts…" (131). In other words, they did not necessarily just accept their stigma or fight it but actively used it as part of a narrative process to restore their status in society. The author concludes that her subjects believe that their stigmatized experiences led them to believe that they "are able to subtly distinguish themselves as more mature, better suited for leadership positions, more adept at performing meaningful work" (125). Stigma, in this case, was used to create a better sense of self.

Emotions are important in the deviance process. In one study, emotions such as anger and depression were found to be a major part of the way delinquents came to view themselves as adults, and they affected later deviant behavior (Giordano, Schroeder, and Cernkovich 2007). Delinquents might consciously choose to commit deviant acts, but their emotional senses of self are equally powerful in their criminal careers because they may serve as the driving force in their decision-making processes.

Delabeling: Leaving the Deviant Identity

How do deviants change their identities once they have been labeled deviant? In addition to some of the programs reviewed earlier in this section that help individuals find ways to drop their deviant identities, they can also try to delabel themselves. In a study of 28 criminal offenders, Alex Harris (2011) found that the offenders would try to distance themselves from past deviant acts to help construct a future "clean" identity. This kind of dialogue, akin to the self-indication process reviewed in Chapter 5, served as a source of motivation to change. However, this research and other studies show that the desire to change is only one part of the change process: internal conflicts, situational constraints, and structural forces produce stresses on the individual that make it very difficult to overcome deviant lifestyles, even among those people who truly want to change (Garot 2010; Howard 2008; Presser 2008). It has generally been believed that taking on adult roles would help individuals separate themselves from their delinquent pasts. At least one study shows that this process is complicated. Michael Massoglia and Christopher Uggen (2010) demonstrate that individuals who continue to commit crime as they age are less likely to see themselves as becoming adults while, conversely, those who choose to desist are more likely to see themselves as adults. The authors conclude that society has come to attach delinquency to adolescence and desistance to adulthood.

Section Summary

This section applied the interactionist perspective to answer the questions "How do we define what is normal or deviant?" and "How does the construction of deviant labels contribute to the development of deviant lifestyles?" First, we applied ethnomethodology to understand the processes of indexicality and reflexivity in making decisions about what thoughts, feelings, and behaviors are deemed normal or undesirably different. Labeling theory extends this perspective of deviance by examining how being labeled deviant leads to subsequent deviant behavior through the development of a self-fulfilling prophecy in which primary acts of deviance produce secondary acts of deviance under certain conditions. Emotions can serve to motivate or prevent people from committing deviant acts.

A Take-Away Message

The symbolic interactionist approach is not only useful for understanding how individuals take on deviant identities, but also helpful in understanding how individuals construct what is "normal." From this perspective, our day-to-day interactions help to reestablish norms and values in society while giving us opportunities for social change, to utilize our agency to find alternative ways to view behaviors that would otherwise be considered deviant. Professionally, social workers and law enforcement personnel regularly use elements of labeling theory in a positive way to help them work with clients to overcome their problems in life. Perhaps you can use this knowledge to deconstruct labels or thwart the labeling process at an early stage. It can also help you develop plans to help other people contemplate their own senses of self and how to change those identities if that is the desired outcome.

SOCIAL STRUCTURE AND DEVIANT BEHAVIOR

My great-grandfather used to tell me a story about growing up in communist Poland. He said that the people there would simply take things from the local construction sites to work on their own homes.

> *People made so little money, it was just "understood" that people would take things to get by. They never called it stealing. In fact, they considered "state" property to be the people's property since it was a communist country at the time. They did it just to get by. It really wasn't stealing according to my great-grandpa.*
>
> —Jim, senior criminal justice major

From a macrosociological perspective, crime is not simply an individual decision. Deviant behavior may often be a choice, but those choices are made in the context of a larger set of factors. Our choices are constrained by the information and resources we have available to cope with our situations. In addition, larger societal forces create limitations on how we can achieve legitimate goals. Many people may want an expensive car but must limit their desires based on what they can afford at any given time. Some people are able to obtain such things quite readily from privileged class positions, whereas others must wait to receive enough income from work or other sources to acquire them. And they may never be able to. Those with fewer resources in an unequal society may become frustrated by not being able to obtain a desired good. Yet, people can be creative in attaining their goals, such as by looking for a higher-paying or additional job or finding a fantastic deal on a nice, older-model car through friends of friends. People could also simply take a vehicle without paying for it. However, the latter alternative is not sanctioned by the state, and the vast majority of us are unlikely to do this. Hence, structural conditions such as economic status influence and constrain our options, tie us to different social networks, and perhaps influence our decisions about how to obtain "the good life."

Jim described a situation in which alternative sets of norms developed in communist Poland. Poland was a communist regime from 1945 to 1989. Communist governments of the Eastern Bloc (as the Soviet Union and its satellite states were called) produced a society in which individuals had very little wealth and the state maintained almost complete control of the economy. At times, this led to shortages in many areas of life. Jim's great-grandfather described the way that citizens began to cope with shortages in building supplies by obtaining them from local construction sites. To obtain needed items, they defined the act of taking property as normal. They later justified their acts based on the limitations induced by a communist economy. Jim's great-grandfather described the way that citizens began to cope with shortages in building supplies by obtaining them from local construction sites. To obtain needed items, they defined the act of taking property as normal. They later justified their acts based on the limitations induced by a communist economy.

For Jim's great-grandfather, sociohistorical conditions influenced the types and levels of deviance and the justification for "stealing." Another macro event, the COVID-19 pandemic and associated disruptions, created a lot of stress on people. During the pandemic and subsequent economic downturns that developed in the 2020s, there were reports of many people taking food from grocery stores because they couldn't afford inflated prices or were frustrated by corporate wealth that had forced so few staff to provide services, like checking out customers. Some people were angry with how essential workers were treated and acted out against corporations. Social media may spread these behaviors as well. Structural theories of deviance tend to focus on the social-structural conditions that affect deviance levels. These theories either emphasize the social conditions that make deviance more likely to occur or the role of individuals' immediate environments that influence their decisions to take on a deviant career.

Anomie and Social Strain

Émile Durkheim is a major figure within the macrosociological perspective called functionalism, which describes society as a system of self-regulating parts held together via social bonds. Durkheim proposed that individuals can lose their senses of place in society, especially in times of great social change, when norms and values become less clear. Under these conditions, individuals may develop a sense of **anomie**, or "normlessness," where there is little consensus about what is right and what is wrong. Without a clear sense of right and wrong, individuals lack the guidance to make clear decisions.

The concept of anomie was applied to the study of deviance by the sociologist Robert Merton. Merton (1968) proposed that deviance is a natural outcome of social conditions in which socially acceptable goals cannot be obtained through legitimate means, serving as the basis of **strain theory**. The story of Jim's great-grandfather shows the Polish people in a situation in which they could not legitimately obtain the items they needed, pushing them to resort to alternative methods. The important thing to remember is that there is an implicit assumption that when people follow the rules of society, they should be able to obtain societal goals.

Although Jim's case may be useful to understand the theft of needed goods, how do we explain the stealing of other items, such as cars or televisions? Strain theory simply argues that these are "legitimate" things to desire in our society; they are socially acceptable, thereby making these items legitimate goals for most people. But what about those people who cannot obtain their goals through conventional means? Should they limit their desires to obtainable goals such as the use of public transportation or ridesharing, and older technologies? Statistics show that most lower-income people do choose this avenue, thus avoiding crime. However, people with lower incomes see the same advertisements as their middle- and upper-class peers. Their limited access to education and their lower-paying jobs, however, stifle their abilities to get these things.

Merton (1968) developed a typology to outline the relationship between society's goals and individual deviance (see Table 7.2). Under this typology, individuals in society fit into one of five categories. **Conformists** represent the comparison group, people who try to obtain the goals of society through accepted means. Going to college or finding a good job that pays well are common ways for Westerners to be conformists. **Innovators** share the goals of society with conformists, but they employ illegitimate means to obtain those goals. For example, if you were an innovator, you may want a nice car or the latest model phone. If you do not have the money to obtain that goal, you may rely on alternative means. For instance, you may decide to steal the car, cheat on your taxes to get enough money to put a down payment on the car, or sell drugs to make money.

Table 7.2 Merton's Typology of Deviance

	Adoption of Culturally Approved Means	Acceptance of Culturally Approved Goals
A. Conformists	+	+
B. Innovators	–	+
C. Ritualists	+	–
D. Retreatists	–	–
E. Rebels	+ or –	+ or –

Ritualists are people who change their attitudes toward success in their lives. They give up trying to achieve wealth and prestige but continue to accept culturally accepted norms of behavior. A ritualist lives with the philosophy "Don't aim high, and you won't be disappointed." Merton associated this pattern with lower-middle-class families emphasizing the importance of social control and accepting one's place in the world, whereas poorer and richer families may be more likely to encourage breaking rules in one way or another. Hence, ritualists do not break laws, but they also recognize that they cannot obtain some of the things valued in society. They are ritualistic because they continue to live traditional lives, perhaps working a low-paying job and taking care of their families, but give up trying to achieve wealth and other societal goals. Alternatively, **retreatists** accept neither the goals of the larger society nor the means to achieve those goals. Essentially, retreatists give up on the American dream and lifestyle. In the movie *The Mosquito Coast* (1986), Harrison Ford plays a character who gets fed up with the middle-class American lifestyle and takes his family to Central America to set himself free. He accepts neither America's goals (e.g., nice house and car) nor the way that Americans go about achieving those goals (e.g., a professional job). He simply tries to opt out of the system. Some retreatists may become drifters—people who wander from place to place with no regular employment.

Finally, **rebellion** occurs when individuals seek to challenge either the traditional goals or the accepted means of achieving those goals. In short, rebels try to change society in some way. The 1960s were associated with a lot of rethinking of middle-class values and goals. Are a big house and fancy car really that important? Maybe we should focus on relationships more than our material well-being. Alternatively, rebels may try to change the ways people obtain some of the traditional goals. Can we find a way to obtain a nice house and car without working 60-plus hours a week? The rebel challenges us to rethink our goals and values.

Strain theory has been revised over the years to include other forms of strains that may lead to deviance. Robert Agnew (1985; 2001), for instance, proposed that strain may result from the blockage of pain-avoidance behavior. Individuals seek to obtain rewards from society but also want to avoid punishment. Deviance may reflect strains at both ends of the spectrum. Specifically, frustration may result from not being able to obtain our goals (rewards) or from trying to escape pain (punishment). If our ability to avoid pain is blocked, Agnew argued, individuals will use deviance to either escape the source of pain or remove the source of aversion.

This revised version of strain theory extends the concept of strain to include a range of social conditions. For instance, in a study of Chinese middle and high school students, researchers examined how strains at home and school (e.g., negative relations with family, friends, and teachers) affected rates of delinquency in the form of violence and property crimes (Bao, Haas, and Pi 2004). They found negative relations with family and friends to be associated with delinquent behavior, partly because these strains led to negative emotions such as anger or resentment, ultimately leading to delinquency. Deviance has also been shown to result from other strains such as racial discrimination (Burt, Simons, and Gibbons 2012; Eitle 2002; Simons, Chen, Steward, and Brody 2003) and negative life events (Sharp et al. 2001). Strains are associated with increases in both traditional (e.g., calling names or use of force) and nontraditional forms of bullying (e.g., cyberbullying) (Patchin and Hinduja 2011).

These findings indicate that reductions in strains may result in lower levels of deviant behavior, and other research indicates that this is true (Eitle 2010). However, the nature of stressful events is complicated by two factors. First, some stressful events are out of the individual's control, such as community conditions. Many people cannot afford to leave neighborhoods with fewer resources. Second, perceptions of stressful events affect how we react to them; not every negative event yields negative emotional or behavioral outcomes, a topic covered in the next chapter. One study found perceptions of strains to be more associated with deviant behavior than objective strains (Froggio and Agnew 2007).

Social and Self-Control Theories

Another structural approach to the study of deviance is social control theory developed by Travis Hirschi (1969). Unlike other theories of deviance that emphasize conditions that cause deviant behavior, Hirschi tried to understand why people choose *not* to commit criminal acts. Under Merton's typology, one might expect most of us to be innovators because we cannot obtain many societal goals. We may be able to legitimately obtain a car but not necessarily the car we want. Hirschi wanted to know why individuals do not choose illegitimate means to attain such goals. If you really want a Corvette and do not have a job that pays enough to buy it, why not just find a way to steal one? Most people do not make that choice. Why not?

Clearly, fear of criminal prosecutions stops many people from attempting to take things that do not belong to them. But other factors may limit our willingness to obtain things illegally. What would your mother think of you if you got caught? What if the neighbors found out about your transgression? What about your religious leader? According to **social control theory**, deviance results when individuals' bonds with conventional society are weakened in some way. In other words, strong social ties tend to breed conformity in groups. When those ties are weakened, people feel free to deviate from norms because they have little concern with how other people will respond to their offenses. This theory also relies on the principle of anomie—that deviance will increase if people feel little connection with society.

Social control theory is based on the principles of the social structure and personality perspective, particularly the proximity principle (see Chapter 2). The proximity principle states that individuals are affected by social structure through their immediate social environments. We feel the effects of society through our friends and family, work, and social lives. Social control theory extends this idea by stating that when the bonds between the individual and their immediate social environment (i.e., friends and family) are not well established, they are less motivated to live by the rules.

Social control theory proposes four ways that individuals are bonded to society: through attachment, commitment, involvement, and belief. **Attachment** refers to emotional bonds with other people. Strong attachments to friends and family help individuals internalize the norms and values of the larger society. They also provide an incentive to follow the rules; knowing that your delinquent behavior may offend someone close to you can make you think twice about committing a crime. **Commitment** is the rational component of conformity, which is the decision to follow the rules (Hirschi 1969). Much like Merton's strain theory, social control theory proposes that people may choose to accept societal goals and means to obtain them or not. If people do decide to accept them, they may become less likely to break the law because the consequences of law breaking (such as jail time) can interfere with the ability to obtain many of society's accepted goals (such as a home life with a partner and children). In addition, she may lose her investment (e.g., time spent on education) in the system. **Involvement** refers to people's participation in acceptable social activities, such as clubs, churches, and other organizations. Being involved in these activities limits people's ability to commit crime and provides additional attachments to people. The final component of social control theory is belief. **Belief** refers to people's respect for law and order in society.

Social control theory is based on the logic that people more vested in society have more to gain from the social system than people who have little connection with society (see Box 7.3 on conformity). If you view society as something of value, then you are less likely to act out against it. Laws represent collective beliefs. Breaking laws is of less consequence if you do not believe them to be part of your identity. Similarly, if you are not concerned with what other people think about your behavior, then there is less reason to inhibit it. In short, our emotional connections with other people help defer gratification and control our impulses for the short-term rewards of crime.

The basic premises of social control theory were tested in Hirschi's (1969) famous book *Causes of Delinquency*. Hirschi used self-reported delinquent behavior in a youth survey conducted in 1965. His data showed that the number of self-reported delinquent acts went down as communication levels increased between fathers and sons. Also, students who were more concerned with their teachers' opinions were significantly less likely to commit delinquent acts than students who did not care much what their teachers thought of them. Students who were more involved in school also reported lower levels of delinquency, supporting the idea that involvement in legitimate activities is associated with less deviance. Finally, Hirschi studied commitment by examining subjects' educational aspirations (their desire to go on to college) and found that as educational aspirations increased, levels of delinquency went down.

Research has challenged some of Hirschi's initial findings. David Greenberg (1999) reanalyzed Hirschi's data using modern statistical techniques. He found that many of the initial findings were accurate, but the strength of those findings was

Box 7.3 Studies in Conformity

Psychological social psychologists are also interested in the social conditions that influence conformity within groups. In a series of studies by Solomon Asch, participants were asked to match the length of a line to three other ones. Each participant was placed last in a series of seven or more other people who were confederates instructed to choose the wrong line. A third or more of the participants would choose a line that was clearly a different size than the original one, conforming to the confederates' incorrect choices. Asch found that the conformists would either question their own judgment of the line or simply "go along to get along" with the group.

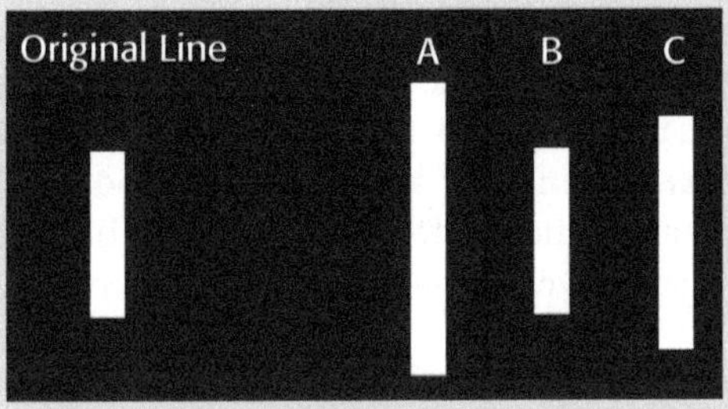

Conformity is a natural process in social life, and this example underscores how hard it is to deviate from the norms and values of other people. If six people before you said that line C was the closest in length to the original line, which line would you choose? These types of studies help us to see the power that other people have in our decision making—both consciously and unconsciously. These processes lead us to "go along to get along."

substantially lower than Hirschi had assumed. He also found some evidence supporting structural strain theory; greater educational strain, when educational aspirations could not be achieved through legitimate means, was associated with higher delinquency rates. In fact, Greenberg stated that the findings supporting strain theory are as strong as the findings supporting social control theory.

Other research continues to support some of the basic elements of social control theory. Robert Sampson and John Laub (Laub and Sampson 1993; 2003; Sampson and Laub, 1990; see also Schulz 2006), for instance, combined the life course perspective (see Chapter 6) and social control theory to examine the lives of two groups of youths (ages 10 to 17) growing up in Boston based on a famous series of studies by Eleanor and Sheldon Glueck (1950; 1968). In Sampson and Laub's work, they examined the Gluecks' data from 500 youths who had no prior record of delinquency, and another 500 youths were sampled from two correctional facilities. Sampson and Laub used the data to examine the role of adult social bonds in moderating effects of past deviant behavior on adult criminal behavior. Their findings showed that the delinquent sample was more likely to lead a life of crime in adulthood than the youths in the nondelinquent sample. However, delinquents who developed strong ties to work and family were less likely to develop deviant careers than those with fewer ties, even after controlling for important background factors. The researchers argued that social bonds can influence levels of criminality, even for people brought up in harsh social environments that limit their abilities to lead more traditional lives.

Not all social ties are good. Having strong connections with family may inhibit criminal behavior, but strong social ties to other criminals (some of whom could be family!) are likely to lead you the other way. This logic can apply to other types of social ties, not just criminal ones. Derek Kreager (2007) studied the relationship between participation in interscholastic sports and male violence. He found that participation in sports, in general, did not inhibit male violence. In fact, he found a strong relationship between participation in contact sports (e.g., football and wrestling) and violence; also, males whose friends play football are more likely to fight than other males. Hence, not all social ties keep us out of trouble—and some may actually make us more likely to get into trouble!

Both good and bad relationships exist in almost every neighborhood. Social control theory can be extended to include such neighborhood conditions. In a study of neighborhoods in Denver and Chicago, Delbert Elliott and his colleagues (2006) found that youth growing up in relatively advantaged neighborhoods were more successful in avoiding problem behavior than those growing up in more disadvantaged neighborhoods. Different neighborhoods provide differential access to social networks and institutional resources with which to manage troubled lives. These conditions intersect with our immediate social surroundings, notably our family lives. A stable family life appears to have a positive effect on youth regardless of neighborhood conditions (Elliott et al. 2006; Simons, Simons, and Wallace 2004).

Self-control theory is an extension of social control theory that assumes that the root cause of criminal behavior is lack of self-control, or an individual's ability to delay gratification; those who engage in criminal behavior cannot restrain their desire for things (stealing), or they act on their anger (violence). It is sometimes called a general theory of crime because it applies to all types of deviant behaviors (Goode 2011); it is sociological in nature because lack of self-control is a result of certain forms of socialization or available structural resources. Some research supports the claims of self-control theory, under some conditions. For instance, Michael Cretacci (2008) found that self-control was associated with property and drug crimes but not violent ones. In another study, Matt DeLisi and Michael Vaugh (2007) found low self-control to be a better predictor of career criminality than race, gender, and economic status.

Social Disorganization versus Genetics

Theorists and researchers have examined different levels of analysis to explain deviant behavior. On one hand, **social disorganization theory** is based on the idea that deviant behavior results from poor community conditions. Specifically, individuals living in places with high residential mobility, low economic status, ethnic heterogeneity, and family disruption are more likely to commit crime because those places lack the social cohesion that helps people avoid deviant behavior (Shaw and McKay 1942). Strong communities provide a sense of empathy that deters people from wanting to perpetrate crime on their fellow citizens and gives them a strong sense of conscience. In short, people are more likely to commit criminal acts against others when they have the opportunities and lack restrictions to do so. In a study of over 10,000 residents in Great Britain living in 238 localities, researchers found that community disorganization and family disruption affected levels of mugging, robbery, and stranger violence (Sampson and Groves 1989). In addition, communities characterized as having fewer local friendship networks and less organizational social participation had higher crime rates, while those communities with more local friendship networks had less crime. A sense of chaos brought about by poor living conditions (a.k.a. broken windows theory) and prevalence of crime creates a self-generating sense of fear that may actually cause more crime than would be found in more stable neighborhoods (Wilson and Kelling 1982). This sense of disorder is reflected in the number of mass shootings in the United States over the last decade (see Figure 7.4 on school shootings), leading some sociologists to conclude that the whole United States continues to move toward

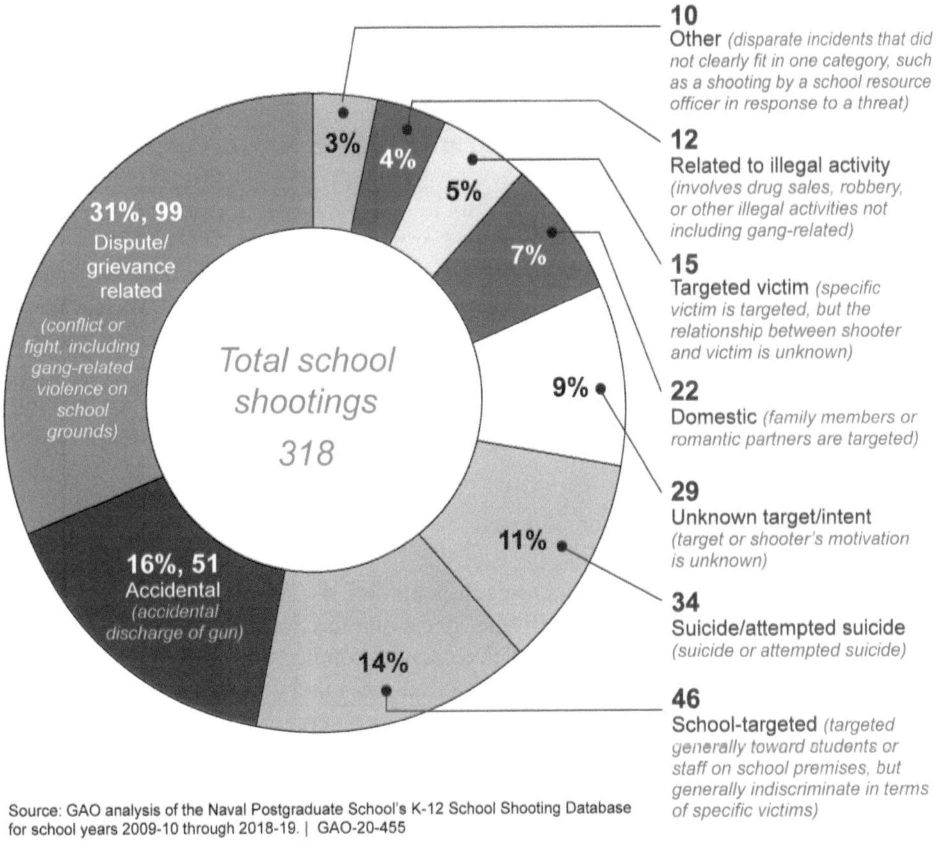

Figure 7.4 Characteristics of school shootings in the United States, 2009–2019.

Source: U.S. GAO

Photo 7.2 Which theories best describe why burglary is one of the most common forms of crime?

Source: Audio und werbung/Shutterstock

a state of disorganization (Derber 2014). The importance of social disorganization theory is that it is able to establish direct links between community life and individual behavior. In this case, deviance is reflected in the organization (or disorganization) of society.

In another line of theory and research, sociologists have been exploring the role of genetics in predicting criminal behavior. Are some people born to be bad? One estimate is that as much as 50 percent of antisocial behavior can be attributed to genetic causes (Moffitt and Caspi 2007). But research indicates that the effects of our genetics are conditioned by our social environment. That is, positive interactions with family, school, and peers (see "Agents of Socialization" in Chapter 6) reduce the delinquency-increasing effects of genes (Guo, Roettger, and Cai 2008). Conversely, weaker social control from family, schools, and peers amplifies the influence of genes on behavior.

Section Summary

A social structure and personality approach is applied to answer the question "What structural conditions influence individuals' decisions to commit deviant acts?" Social strain and social control theories assume that societal conditions provide the context for committing deviance, mostly in the form of delinquency and crime. Social strain theory, for instance, argues that society provides both the goals and the means to obtain those goals. If people lack the ability to achieve societal goals through legitimate means, they may turn to illegitimate means to obtain them. Social control theory incorporates the role of social bonds in the decision to commit deviance; individuals with stronger connections to society are less likely to commit deviant acts than people with fewer bonds. Although genes may play a role in the deviance process, it is also clear that social conditions interact with genes to produce deviant actions.

Box 7.4 Crimes and Misdemeanors on Campus

College campuses bring together large numbers of people from a variety of backgrounds. Sometimes, members of these communities commit deviant acts. University campuses are also sites of particular types of deviant behaviors such as binge drinking and date rape, among others. But college campuses can include a larger swath of crime. Consider the number of employees it takes to run a campus, ranging from professors, deans, and presidents to custodial staff. Many of these people manage large budgets and handle expensive equipment like in any other organization. Hence, college campuses are a microcosm of society with crimes against the person (i.e., violent crimes, including assault and rape), property crimes (e.g., burglary), and white-collar crimes (e.g., embezzlement) (Hickson and Roebuck 2009). One study employed social disorganization theory, with the idea that poor living conditions affect crime levels, to explain college student deviance (Barton, Jensen, and Kaufman 2010). Crime on campus is such an issue that the Clery Act was passed in 1998, requiring institutions of higher education to report crimes on campus as a means of raising awareness among students, faculty, and staff (Jacobsen 2017). College campuses may represent a microcosm of the larger society in many ways, including deviant behaviors.

A Take-Away Message

There are a lot of crime shows in the media. The theories reviewed in this section are certainly applicable to explaining the behaviors of the criminals on those programs. Some criminals are portrayed as being victims of their poor living conditions (strain and social disorganization theories), while others emphasize poor parenting or relationships (social control theory). What theories may help explain why university students commit crimes on campus (see Box 7.4)? As a citizen of a certain country who votes, you will be asked to make decisions on how much of the government's time and money should be spent on law enforcement—your decisions may be influenced by what you believe to be the primary cause of crime. Professionally, if you work in the criminal justice system, you should pause and consider the fact that all of the theories in this chapter have been shown to explain at least some criminal behaviors, indicating that many factors affect why people commit crime. This knowledge may help inform your decisions "in the field," the courtroom, or other parts of the criminal justice system.

GROUP RELATIONSHIPS AND DEVIANCE

I will never forget the email I got from this student, trying to extol the virtues of polygamy. He sent me information about a website for some sort of online magazine. I went to the site and noticed that the articles revolved around this idea that Americans are too uptight about sex and

> *should open their worlds to accepting multiple spouses and partners. I really don't have much of a problem with that except that I started noticing that all of the authors of these articles were men! I think it may take some time for this set of values to catch on with other groups in society!*
>
> —Daniel, family studies instructor

The beginning of this text was dedicated to the social construction of society and the subsequent adoption of societal norms and values by individuals. Although criminologists tend to view deviance as a problem that needs to be addressed, interactionists are more likely to view rule production and subsequent breaking as parts of a larger process. By extension, the fundamental processes involved in the creation of deviance occur in group contexts. However, groups may vary in acceptable rules and standards, even in the same society. Some Americans are part of conservative religious organizations, whereas others attend more liberal-minded congregations or none at all. The groups we spend time with provide the context for deciding what is right and wrong. Some people may appear to be deviating from societal norms simply because they are following the norms of their peers. Their peers, however, may have different norms and values than the larger society. Ironically, then, conforming to our peer groups' norms may lead to deviance from the larger society.

Daniel's example focuses on a movement to normalize polygamy in the United States. The United States—like many nations in the world—has a norm of pair bonding in which two people form some sort of union, often for the purposes of raising children. Polygamy is legal in several countries as well. This group wishes to change American norms to include polygamy. However, Daniel notices that the authors of the website are decidedly male. The authors seem to suggest that people should be open to multiple partners. As a result, Daniel begins to doubt whether the motives of the group are representative of women's views on the matter. Regardless, although the pro-polygamists' perspectives deviate from the larger culture, they are clearly supported by other group members. These alternative norms are "right" and "good" to these men.

The idea that people can simply choose a deviant pathway such as polygamy in a similar way that most of us choose among traditional roads is similar to interactionist approaches to deviance. However, it adds the idea of behaviorist theories in psychology that emphasize the role of operant conditioning and imitation. In behavioral psychology's approach, people learn behaviors based on the rewards and punishments associated with them (i.e., people will learn to continue behaviors that are rewarded and discontinue behaviors that are punished). **Differential association theory** states that deviance is learned through interactions with others. Individuals who associate with deviant people are more likely to learn deviant behavior than those who do not spend time with deviant others. In other words, we learn deviance in the same way that we learn what is considered normal and good—through family, friends, and schooling.

The Principles of Differential Association Theory

Differential association theory was developed by Edwin H. Sutherland and colleagues. Sutherland's goal was to introduce a theory that would explain the social causes of deviance. The theory is based on nine principles (Sutherland and Cressey 1999, pp. 241–242):

1. Criminal behavior is learned.
2. It is learned in interaction with other persons in a process of communication.
3. The principle part of the learning of criminal behavior occurs within intimate personal groups.
4. When criminal behavior is learned, the learning includes techniques of committing the crime as well as motives, drives, rationalizations, and attitudes.
5. The specific direction of motives and drives is learned from definitions of the legal codes as favorable or unfavorable.
6. A person begins delinquent behavior because of an excess of definitions favorable to violation of the law over definitions unfavorable to violation of the law.
7. Differential associations may vary in frequency, duration, priority, and intensity.
8. The process of learning criminal behavior by association with criminal and anticriminal patterns involves all the mechanisms that are involved in any other learning.
9. Although criminal behavior is an expression of general needs and values, it is not explained by those general needs and values, because noncriminal behavior is an expression of the same needs and values.

The key component of differential association theory is that learning occurs in groups. Other group members provide both the motives and the knowledge necessary to commit crime (principle #4). The context of the group is also important: people learn criminal behavior from others to whom they feel close (principle #3). In addition, people learn criminal attitudes and behaviors like any other attitudes and behaviors, through communication and exchange of meaning (principle #2).

The latter principles emphasize the decision-making processes that occur in groups. We may learn how to deviate from a group but choose to do otherwise. Why would one choose to deviate from society? Sutherland proposed that individuals balance the costs and benefits of deviant behavior like any other decisions (principles #6 and #8). If we believe that deviance provides a better alternative than other options, we will choose to be deviant.

Think about a situation in which a low-income man is trying to get to a job interview not accessible by public transportation. He has a car but almost no gas. The interview could mean the difference between a stable income or just barely getting by in life. His friends share a story in which they pumped gas and then left without paying, providing him basic techniques for stealing gas that limit the possibility of being caught (e.g., covering the license plate). Although that behavior may produce an arrest, he also knows how to minimize this risk. Further, the loss of this interview may make life seem almost as unbearable as prison. The costs of not acting on the advice of his peers may outweigh the risk of going to prison.

The deviant's decision to commit the act is like any other cost–benefit analysis, but it is still a decision. However, that decision employs the use of advice and input from friends, family, and acquaintances (see Box 7.5 on white-collar crime). Association with deviant others provides both the information and the motives to commit deviant acts.

Box 7.5 White-Collar Crime and the Dark Web

Differential association theory is useful to understanding how people can rationalize almost any form of deviant behavior. The differences between the Saints and the Roughnecks described earlier in this chapter suggest a bias against lower-status perpetrators. Upper-middle- and upper-class offenders show up as perpetrators in different types of crimes, usually associated with less stigma than working-class crimes. Typical examples of middle- and upper-class **white-collar crimes** include embezzlement, cheating, and laundering money, among others. These are crimes that are associated with higher-status individuals in the course of their work (Sutherland 1940). Similarly, doping—using illegal drugs to boost athletic performance—is another way that high-status individuals participate in deviant behavior (Brissonneau and Montez de Oca 2018).

White-collar crime may sometimes appear to be less serious than other forms of deviance such as rape or murder, but it has huge negative effects on society, as government, private industry, and individual citizens lose millions of dollars as a result of fraud and other such crimes. In Donald Cressey's (1971) social-psychological study of embezzlement behavior, he found that perpetrators try to find ways to justify their crimes to make them appear less serious. Rather than accepting the behavior as deviant, embezzlers talk about their behavior in legitimate terms such as "borrowing" rather than "taking" other people's money. These findings can apply to similar forms of deviance among the middle and upper classes. In a large-scale study of cheating behavior among college students, for example, over two-thirds indicated that they had cheated at some time as an undergraduate student (McCabe 1992). Most of the cheaters defended their cheating by denial of responsibility (e.g., an unfair workload), 61%; condemnation of the teacher or assignment, 28%; an appeal to higher authorities (e.g., peer pressure), 7%; and denial of injury (e.g., cheating was harmless), 4%. Therefore, social conditions influence interpretations of white-collar deviance.

Much of modern white-collar crimes such as embezzlement, can occur readily because of easier access to computer systems compared to past decades. People can "hack" into systems to transfer funds, for instance. But there is a whole part of the World Wide Web that provides a venue for any number of crimes. The Dark Web relies on the traditional internet but utilizes special software and configurations to access it. It also helps keep access anonymous, so people cannot be easily traced. The Dark Web allows for the sale of illegal items (especially drugs) and child pornography, malicious programming, and white-collar crimes such as fraud (Ward 2014). Deviance online can also include more mundane behaviors. Hence, online communities expand traditional ideas of deviance and provide new tools for people to act in deviate ways.

Edwin Sutherland and Donald Cressey (1999) described two boys: one was a sociable, active, athletic boy, and the other boy had "psychopathic" tendencies. They suggested that if the former begins spending time with delinquent boys, he will become a delinquent. Alternatively, in the latter case, if the boy with psychopathic tendencies stays isolated and introverted, he is less likely to become delinquent than he otherwise would because he lacks the interaction with delinquent others. Thus, people's social surroundings influence the direction and outcomes of their dispositions.

Differential Association, Gender, and the Culture of Honor

Research testing differential association theory is generally conducted by examining deviants' relationships with other people. Studies may ask individuals to indicate the types of people they spend the most time with, assessing the deviance of their peers. Research generally supports the idea that people who spend more time with deviants are more likely to support and conduct deviant behavior themselves (Church, Wharton, and Taylor 2009). For instance, in a study of French boys and girls, Clayton Hartjen and S. Priyadarsini (2003) found measures of differential association strongly related to delinquency for both boys and girls. However, other research shows that the role of differential association may be stronger among boys than girls (Piquero et al. 2005). That is, delinquent peer associations seem to be better predictors of delinquency among boys than girls. It is difficult to understand this relationship, but it is important because gender is one of the strongest independent predictors of delinquency, with males being more likely than females to engage in most forms of deviance, although that gap has narrowed in the United States in recent decades.

Differential association can also be used to explain why certain regions of the country tend to have higher rates of violence than other areas. Psychologist Richard Nisbett (1993; Nisbett, Polly, and Lang 1995) completed an extensive study of violence in the southern United States. Southerners are statistically more likely to commit violent crimes than people in any other region of the United States. Nisbett showed that although Southerners generally do not endorse violence any more than Northerners, they are significantly more likely to support certain types of violence—in cases of self-defense and in response to insults—than Northerners. Therefore, under some conditions, there is a culture of honor in the South, a place in which violence is more acceptable as a matter of honor. Being raised in such a culture increases the likelihood of using violence as a response to provocation—one carries some sense of legitimation.

Nisbett (1993) traced the South's culture of honor to its early herding economy. He argued that herding is a more fragile industry than farming because of the amount of time and money put into each animal being raised. Although the loss of a few plants would not reduce the overall value of a yield of corn, the loss of even one animal represents many years of feeding and maintenance. The image of the tough cattle herder may simply reflect individuals' focus on keeping a tight rein on expensive property. Being portrayed as weak may give potential thieves the idea that a person is unable to protect her herd. To reduce the possibility of theft, many herders may have adopted a policy of hyper vigilance toward outsiders, thus leading to a culture of honor.

There are several problems in trying to study violence rates across geographic regions. The prevalence of many crimes is associated with poverty, racialized minorities, and warm weather, all of which are more central in the southern United States. Nesbitt focused on crimes perpetrated by Whites only, comparing rates of crime relative to city size, among other factors. He found homicide rates in more rural areas of the South, where a culture of honor is more likely to exist, to be higher than in urbanized areas, where it is less likely to exist. Further, he found that areas categorized as having a history of herding had significantly higher rates of violence than those areas deemed farming communities. These higher rates of violence are found in herding communities around the world. Nesbitt's findings hold after controlling for a host of other factors generally associated with violent behavior. In this case, the culture of honor helps show the importance that group norms and values may play in our decisions to commit deviant acts.

Studying Deviance in a Lab

In Chapter 6, we said that experimental work in the group processes tradition typically does not address socialization because socialization cannot be manipulated in a laboratory. Experimentalists face similar issues when answering questions about deviance. As you learned while reading the earlier sections of this chapter, most social psychological theory and research on deviance represent efforts to understand criminal behavior. Criminal behavior, like socialization, is difficult to measure in a laboratory setting. Nevertheless, as with socialization, group processes researchers have furthered our understanding of criminal behavior in experimental studies by testing theories of basic social processes that have relevance to crime in the real world.

An important issue in criminology that has received a great deal of empirical and theoretical attention is the role that deterrence factors play in making crime more or less likely. In particular, scholars hold that variations in the certainty and severity of sanctions influence how likely individuals are to commit crimes. *Certainty* refers to how likely people believe it is that they will be caught if they engage in a criminal act. *Severity* refers to how severe they believe the punishment will be in the event that they are caught.

Suppose that a person is faced with the opportunity to commit a serious crime, for instance, embezzling from a bank. If they are almost sure they will be caught (certainty is high), and if they know they will face serious sanctions if they are caught (severity is high), then they will probably be unlikely to attempt the theft. On the other hand, if they are confident that they will get away with the crime (certainty is low), and that sanctions will be low if they are caught (severity is low), they may be more likely to attempt the crime. In these ways, it seems reasonable that certainty and severity influence the likelihoods that individuals will commit crimes.

A problem with this approach is that it is too simplistic. Would you consider theft from a bank? Our guess is that you wouldn't, even if you were nearly certain you wouldn't be caught, that your punishment would be light even if you were apprehended. Most people do not seriously consider committing crimes even when certainty and severity are low.

Box 7.6 Jobs in Deviance

The most commonly found jobs related to deviance center on law enforcement and the courts, those organizations designed to help process or stop criminal deviance from occurring in society. However, if you consider all of the ways we have discussed deviance, you will also see that there is a way to participate in the construction of deviance (e.g., becoming a lawmaker or politician involved in creating or removing laws). If you are looking into work in traditional organizations, you can also work in fields that help people who are victims of crime or manage their deviant labels.

1. **Victim Services Advocate**, Henry County (Georgia). Duties: Provides assistance to victims of crimes: contacts victim by phone, letter, and/or field visits; completes intake forms; determines and evaluates victim experiences and needs; makes referrals and recommendations regarding counseling, safety needs and concerns, housing, food and other needs; explains and provides information and assistance regarding criminal justice processes, what to expect in their particular cases, victim's rights, victim notification policies and procedures. Qualifications: Bachelor's Degree in Social Work, Psychology, or related field required; supplemented by one year of experience in social work, counseling, law enforcement or related field; or any equivalent combination of education, training, and experience which provides the requisite knowledge, skills, and abilities for this job.
2. **US Probation Officer**, (Montana). Duties: Conduct investigations, prepare reports, and make recommendations to the court. Interview offenders/defendants and their families and collect background data from various sources. Interpret and apply policies, procedures, and statutes; *Federal Rules of Criminal Procedures*; and U.S. sentencing guidelines, monographs, and relevant case law, as applicable. Qualifications: Minimum required qualifications for CL-23: Bachelor's degree in a related field of study. Related field of study is a completed degree from an accredited college or university in an area such as criminal justice, criminology, psychology, sociology, human relations, or business or public administration.

There are many opportunities to work in the field of deviance and social control, most of these positions are about the control-side of things. Police officers, security guards and prison guards do not typically require a college degree, but anyone interested in this work will eventually need one if they want to get promoted to higher ranks. Jobs typically associated with the reform-side of the justice system, such as probation officers or victims advocates, do require higher education. In many cases, advanced degrees will eventually be necessary to progress in those fields. Like most jobs, internships (paid or unpaid) and any work-related experience increases your chances of obtaining these positions!

Certainty and severity are features of a situation that sometimes affect likelihoods of criminal acts. Features of individuals also affect their likelihoods to commit crime. For example, people who are low in self-control tend to be more impulsive, self-centered, and incautious than others. Research finds that people low in self-control are more drawn to the excitement and immediate gratification that come from committing criminal acts and also that they are more likely than others to engage in noncriminal but deviant behaviors such as drinking excessively or gambling.

Perhaps deterrence (i.e., certainty and severity of punishment) works differently for individuals high and low in self-control. This is an issue that researchers have addressed. As discussed earlier in this chapter, some researchers (e.g., Gottfredson and Hirschi 1990) propose that because individuals low in self-control are by definition incautious and more likely to take risks, they do not stop to consider situational factors. These scholars thus propose that deterrence factors (such as certainty and severity) will have a smaller effect on individuals low in self-control than on individuals high in self-control. Others argue the opposite. They propose that people high in self-control are the ones who generally don't even consider committing crimes, and situational factors can't influence the likelihood of crime unless the crime is at least considered an option. Thus, they propose that deterrence has the biggest effect on individuals low in self-control.

Think about trying to determine which explanation is more accurate in specifying the relationship between deterrence and self-control, or even just determining the extent to which deterrence factors affect likelihood of crime. It would be hard to do, and research using various approaches has produced conflicting results on the role that deterrence factors play in affecting crime.

One approach to testing deterrence models has been to examine, at one point in time, people's perceptions of certainty and severity of sanctions, along with their own reports of their past involvement in criminal activities. These are called cross-sectional studies. This approach has produced valuable results, but it also has some serious methodological limitations. The most important limitation is that it effectively changes the causal order that the deterrence model proposes. According to the deterrence model, people develop impressions of punishment certainty and severity, and these perceptions then affect their behaviors. Cross-sectional studies, however, ask people to state their perceptions of certainty and severity and then report crimes they have committed in the past. People's perceptions of certainty and severity change over time, and we can't know from these cross-sectional studies whether deterrence factors as perceived at the actual time of the crime (or non-crime) affected whether people committed the crime.

Another approach that in some ways has been more fruitful is the use of longitudinal studies. In these studies, people are usually asked their perceptions of certainty and severity as well as the criminal behaviors they engaged in during the previous year. Then, the same individuals are asked the same questions twelve months later. These studies allow researchers to determine whether perceptions of certainty and severity measured at the first time seemed to affect likelihood of criminal behavior as indicated at the second time measurement.

The longitudinal studies have produced important results, but they are confronted with the same major problem that faces cross-sectional studies: people's perceptions of certainty and severity are not stable over time. In other words, even if we have the causal order right and know people's perceptions of certainty and severity six months before they committed a crime, those perceptions are likely not the same as the ones the people held the moment before committing the crime. In other words, perceptions of certainty and severity change between measurement in the first survey and committing the crime six months later.

The most useful approaches to measuring deterrence effects, and ultimately the relationship between deterrence and self-control, will be to measure perceptions of certainty and severity immediately before individuals decide whether or not to commit criminal acts. This, of course, poses its own problems. How can we know when people are about to decide whether or not they will commit criminal acts? How do we ask them at that point their perceptions of certainty and severity? How could we know that the act of questioning them didn't affect their eventual decisions about whether to commit the crime?

Experimental approaches have the ability to overcome many of these issues through their unique ability to resolve issues of causality (as discussed in Chapter 3). Although field experiments (e.g., experiments carried out in natural settings) have a long history in criminology research (an example is given in this section), experiments in laboratory settings are rare in criminology. This, however, is beginning to change. (See Horne and Lovaglia [2008] for several examples of laboratory experiments in criminology.)

William Kalkhoff and Robb Willer (2008) conducted a laboratory experiment on deterrence and self-control that was designed to overcome limitations that face cross-sectional and longitudinal approaches to studying deterrence. Their goal was to test theories proposing that deterrence matters more for individuals high in self-control versus theories proposing that deterrence matters more for individuals low in self-control.

Deterrence factors are attributes of a situation that can be manipulated by experimenters. Self-control, in contrast, is an individual attribute such as extraversion that cannot be varied experimentally. Kalkhoff and Willer (2008) thus designed an experiment that allowed them to vary levels of deterrence and then measure the effects of deterrence across different levels of self-control. The independent variables in Kalkhoff and Willer's study were thus deterrence and self-control. The dependent variable was likelihood to commit a criminal or deviant act.

To approximate a criminal act in a laboratory experiment, Kalkhoff and Willer gave college student participants in their study the opportunity to cheat on a task to produce an outcome that they thought would earn them more money. Participants in the study were told that they would be completing a task during the study and that their pay for the study would depend on how well they did. When explaining the task to participants, the researcher showed them (supposedly accidentally, but actually on purpose) a way to cheat on the task and get a better score. The task was computer based, and when the researcher hit the control key on the keyboard, it displayed the correct answer to the task item. The researcher acted surprised and told participants to not use the control key during the study.

Kalkhoff and Willer thus had a dependent variable—whether participants used the control key to cheat. One of their independent variables was self-control. Before beginning the task, participants completed a questionnaire that gave the researchers a score for the participant on self-control. Kalkhoff and Willer were thus able to identify whether each participant was either high or low in self-control.

The second independent variable in the study was deterrence. Recall that deterrence has two main elements: certainty and severity. Research has found certainty to have a stronger deterrence effect than severity, and for this reason Kalkhoff and Willer chose to vary certainty between their experimental conditions. They kept severity at the same high level for all participants, with instructions telling all participants that laboratory misconduct (such as vandalism or cheating) would be taken seriously, would result in academic advisors being contacted, and could in extreme cases result in expulsion from the university. In other words, all participants believed that they faced severe sanctions if they cheated and were caught.

To vary certainty, Kalkhoff and Willer randomly assigned all participants to one of two certainty conditions—one of high certainty or one of low certainty. In the high-certainty condition, a video camera was placed directly behind participants in a way that would allow research assistants to closely monitor their behavior. In the low-certainty condition, a video camera was in the room, but it was clear to participants that they could cheat without it being seen by the camera.

Kalkhoff and Willer then measured how deterrence and self-control affected likelihood to cheat. They sought to distinguish between theories proposing that deterrence matters most for persons high in self-control (because those low in self-control don't stop to consider implications) and those proposing that it matters most for persons low in self-control (because those high in self-control don't even consider criminal acts).

Kalkhoff and Willer found that deterrence had a strong effect on cheating. Moreover, they found its effect to be particularly strong for persons low in self-control. Whereas persons high in self-control were unlikely to cheat irrespective of the certainty of sanctions, participants low in self-control became more likely to cheat when certainty of sanctions was low. Kalkhoff and Willer's experimental test supported theories proposing that sanctions matter most for persons low in self-control.

A reasonable response to Kalkhoff and Willer's study would be to wonder what it can tell us about people making decisions about engaging in real criminal activities. The answer is that it can tell us nothing about these cases, at least not directly. Kalkhoff and Willer's study demonstrates a process that is consistent with criminological theory. There may be factors that affect real criminal decisions that modify the processes as they played out in Kalkhoff and Willer's study. What their study provides is compelling evidence that deterrence affects the decisions of those low in self-control. It provides the impetus for more research, perhaps using other methods, to either determine that the processes operate the same way for persons making decisions about real crimes or that certain factors lead the processes to work differently when individuals make choices to commit or not commit actual crimes.

Section Summary

This section applied the group processes perspective to answer the question "How do group relationships influence the development of deviance and perceptions of deviance?" Here, groups provide the context for decision making about deviant behaviors, both our own and other people's behavior. Differential association theory assumes that we learn deviant behavior like any other behavior—from other people. Group processes can also influence the conditions in which we decide to commit deviant acts.

A Take-Away Message

Two of the biggest predictors of deviant behavior are age and gender. In fact, most young males in the United States will commit some criminal act—mostly misdemeanors like vandalism—by the age of 24. What does that say about deviance? Before you answer, consider your past: have you ever committed an illegal act, say beyond going over the speed limit? If you are male, there is a very good chance that the answer is "yes," especially related to initiating a fight, vandalism, or possession of illegal drugs. But you should also consider the context of those decisions to commit the deviant act or acts. There is a very good chance that you did those acts when you were with friends. Members of a group help you discern the risks and consequences of acting in a deviant manner or not. This dialogue may include an internal debate about what your family may think if they found out about it, too. Even if you have never perpetrated a crime, you may have been a victim of one (see Box 7.7 about the study of crime victims). Furthermore, if you ever work in the law enforcement field, you will likely work with people who have deviant careers. You should consider their social contexts, the ways in which their peers are influencing the individuals' decision-making processes. Knowing this kind of information may help you devise a better way of helping these individuals choose alternatives to their deviant careers.

BRINGING IT ALL TOGETHER

> *Crime, to me, is the number one problem in our country today. It seems like we keep putting more police on the street and developing programs to "fix" the problem, but we never seem to get rid of it. How can social psychology fix the problem?*
>
> —Carol, senior accounting major

Although crime is a form of deviance and people like Carol would like to see less crime, social psychologists do not assume that all deviance is bad. At the beginning of this chapter, we defined deviance as any behavior that departs from accepted practices in a society or group. Because accepted practices may vary in time and space, the nature of deviance changes too. From an interactionist perspective, we create deviance and then

Box 7.7 Victimology: The Victim Role

Most of the material in this chapter has tried to answer the question "Why do people commit deviant acts?" Another side of scholarship in criminology assesses the victims of crime. In some cases, there are no clear victims—many nonviolent crimes, for instance, do not produce injury physically or otherwise. Of course, some forms of deviance discussed in this chapter are not crimes, so they do not yield victims either. All crimes against persons produce victims, and property crimes yield victims in the sense that it costs someone the time and money associated with recovering or replacing an item or money that was stolen.

A number of researchers have begun to study the nature of being a victim and how victims react to crime, a field called victimology that started in the 1940s (O'Connell 2008). Modern scholars focus on topics like bullying (Berry 2016), sexual victimization (Javaid 2018), and cyber victimization (Felmlee and Faris 2016). In the last example, the authors found, for instance, that online attacks were more common between current and former friends and dating partners than strangers, similar to what we know about traditional forms of interpersonal violence. From an interactionist perspective, the victim role is constructed through interaction with other people, much like being labeled a criminal (Heru 2001; Leisenring 2006). Creating the victim role helps others know how to relate to the victim, and it provides a script to manage the stress of being a victim. It also helps the victim make sense of their experiences. Impression management is part of this process. Victims are expected to accept the victim role and may suffer consequences if they do not. For instance, in a study of prisoners going up for parole, Martin Silverstein (2006) observed that female drug traffickers increased their chances of parole if they presented themselves as victims of male drug dealers, while males did not benefit from portraying themselves as victims.

Are certain types of people more likely to be victims than others? Ironically, victims most often have the same demographic characteristics as perpetrators: they are most often young and male, have a delinquent past, and associate with delinquent peers (Beaver et al. 2011). We also tend to overestimate the likelihood of being a victim (Quillian and Pager 2010). Thus, much like other social roles and statuses, the causes and outcomes of victimhood are quite complex!

label some people as deviant. From this point of view, deviance is maintained through social interactions in and around the court system. "Fixing" the problems of deviance and crime requires a change in how we relate to deviant people. Structural approaches found in social strain and control theories would suggest that large-scale changes in society, such as reducing economic inequalities, are required if we want to eliminate some forms of deviance or crime. Finally, from a group processes perspective—differential association theory, specifically—we need to change the people with whom someone affiliates to change that person's delinquent behavior. All these perspectives help to show the complex nature of deviance and how it is manifested in society.

SUMMARY

1. From a social-psychological perspective, deviance is a necessary part of the symbolic interaction process of negotiating social reality. Interactionism assumes that individuals decide to maintain (or break) social norms and standards during every interaction. Deviance allows for change in relationships and society as a whole.
2. Ethnomethodological perspectives of deviance emphasize how individuals construct and defend their views of social reality, the "real" boundaries of social life. People who can provide better accounts can convince others of those accounts, thus controlling the meaning of good and bad—deviance and conformity—in society.
3. Labeling theory is a major interactionist perspective of deviance. It is based on the notion that deviance is a consequence of a social process in which a negative characteristic becomes an element of an individual's identity.
4. Strain and social control theories apply macrosociological perspectives of deviant behavior, arguing that deviance results from a larger set of societal conditions. Societal norms create limitations to how we can achieve legitimate goals in life. They also provide goals that are unattainable for some people. Self-control theory assumes that the root cause of criminal behavior is lack of ability to delay gratification
5. Groups provide both the motives and the knowledge necessary to commit crime. Differential association theory states that deviance is learned through interaction with others. This theory may help explain how and why people rationalize deviant behavior, especially in white-collar crimes committed by middle- and upper-class people.

KEY TERMS AND CONCEPTS

Agents of social control: The state's attempts to maintain social order through police, courts, and other representatives of the state.

Anomie: A sense of "normlessness," where there is little consensus about what is right and what is wrong.

Attachment: A component of social control theory referring to emotional bonds with other people in society.

Belief: A component of social control theory referring to people's respect for law and order.

Commitment: A component of social control theory referring to an individual's desire to obtain societal goals through legitimate means.

Conformists: People who try to obtain the goals of society through accepted means.

Covering: Keeping a known stigma from creating tensions in interaction by downplaying it.

Deviance: Any behavior that departs from accepted practices in a society or group.

Differential association theory: A theory that deviance is learned through interaction with others.

Folkways: Less serious rules of behavior in a group or society.

Indexicality: The process by which individuals index thoughts, feelings, and behaviors from their own perspective.

Innovators: People who share the goals of society with conformists but employ illegitimate means to obtain those goals.

Involvement: A component of social control theory referring to people's participation in acceptable social activities, such as clubs, churches, and other organizations.

Labeling theory: A theory arguing that deviance is a consequence of a social process in which a negative characteristic becomes an element of an individual's identity.

Mores: Widely held values and beliefs in a society.

Outsiders: People labeled as deviants who accept the deviant labels.

Passing: Attempts to hide an undisclosed stigma by concealing information about it.

Primary deviance: The initial deviant act that causes other people to label the individual a deviant.

Rebellion: When individuals seek to challenge either the traditional goals or the accepted means of achieving those goals.

Reflexivity: The process by which individuals think about a behavior within its social context and give meaning to it.

Retreatists: People who accept neither the goals of the larger society nor the means to achieve those goals.

Retrospective interpretations: Reinterpretations of past behaviors in light of the person's new role as a deviant.

Ritualists: People who approve of the ways that others should live their lives but give up trying to obtain societal goals.

Secondary deviance: Additional deviant acts that support the initial deviant label.

Self-control theory: An extension of social control theory that assumes that the root cause of criminal behavior is lack of self-control or ability to delay gratification.

Social control theory: A theory that deviance results when individuals' bonds with conventional society are weakened in some way.

Social disorganization theory: A criminological theory based on the idea that communities characterized as having more disorder decrease social control, thereby increasing deviance.

Stigma: An attribute that is deeply discrediting.

Strain theory: A theory that argues that people choose to commit deviance as a natural outcome of social conditions in which socially acceptable goals cannot be obtained through legitimate means.

Taboos: Violations of behavior prescribed through mores.

White-collar crimes: Crimes typically associated with middle- and upper-class individuals, such as embezzlement, cheating, and laundering money.

DISCUSSION QUESTIONS

1. Think about forms of deviance that do not fit into the frame of crime and delinquency. How might an individual incorporate deviance as part of their identity to produce social change?
2. Have you ever been considered a deviant? If so, how do the deviance theories from this chapter apply to your situation?
3. How do you think your attitudes toward deviance and deviant behavior relate to your position or location in society?

8

Mental Health and Illness

My first semester of college was rough. I mean, I was always feeling lonely. I would just sit in my room, maybe check Instagram or something, but I would never study. My grades were terrible, and it only made me feel worse. My roommate kept bugging me—wanting me to go to a club meeting with her. I really did not want to go but she guilted me into it. So I went. I did not think much of it at first, but it got me out talking to people who I really connected with. After a couple of days, I found myself going to class again. Then, I joined another group at a church here. I started to study some more and my grades went up. It is funny how just one club meeting seemed to change so many other parts of my life!

—Sandy, sophomore political science major

Sandy's experience is similar to what a lot of students go through in their first year of college. Most students feel a little anxious and awkward as they begin to experience a new way of life. There is often a large workload from courses and jobs with more pressure than students had in high school. Students also no longer have their routines from high school. Most important, many college students are separated from the people with whom they used to interact in person on a regular basis in their hometowns. This separation cuts off some social support mechanisms—people we turn to for help to get things done and for emotional support, as well as those we talk with to verify our views of the world. When these supports become different—perhaps online rather than in person—we may lose a major source of emotional connection. Most of us gradually find new sources of local support. But some become lonely or anxious enough that it impairs their daily functioning.

Many people believe that mental illness is an individual problem, reflecting internal dilemmas and issues. The sociological view of mental health and illness lies in contrast to this perspective and provides an alternative to solely biological and psychological models of mental illness. In short, sociologists propose that some of the fundamental causes of psychological problems are social. The **sociology of mental health** is the study of the social arrangements that affect mental illness and its consequences (Aneshensel and Phelan 1999).

Sigmund Freud and other psychoanalytic psychologists have emphasized internal (often unconscious) processes, typically stemming from childhood relationships, as the cause of mental illness. Biologists and neurologists examine the role of physiological aspects of mental illness. Although sociologists do not discount biology and psychology in trying to understand mental illness, they believe that a social lens is critical to gaining the whole picture of mental illness. Consider this fact: in one study, rates of loneliness among adolescence doubled around the globe between 2012 and 2018 (Twenge et al. 2021). If causes of well-being are based only on internal or biological factors, what could cause such a momentous change in young people around the world at the same time?

The three areas of sociological social psychology each make unique contributions to the study of mental health and illness: symbolic interaction to the construction of mental illness, social structure and personality to the causation of mental illness, and group processes to some consequences of mental illness labels. Symbolic interactionists focus on how meanings of mental illness change over time and across cultures. Essentially, these scholars assume that meanings about mental illness, like any other entity, are created through interactions within particular cultures—and, as cultures differ, so do ways people understand and treat mental illness. Social structure and personality researchers examine the social statuses and conditions that affect depression, anxiety, substance abuse, and the like. Group processes scholars help us understand how the label of being mentally ill can be stigmatized and may affect interactions among people. Once you read these sociological perspectives on mental health and illness, you may rethink what it means to have psychological problems.

We will address the following questions in this chapter:

- What does it mean to be mentally healthy? How do we construct meanings of mental illness?
- How does mental health influence one's sense of identity and interactions with others?
- What are the structural conditions in society that contribute to distress? What resources can buffer stress, and how?
- How does a mental illness diagnosis become a status characteristic?

THE SOCIAL CONSTRUCTION OF MENTAL HEALTH

In second grade, my uncle Trent was a little wild. His second-grade teacher actually tied him to a chair with a rope in order to keep him calm and focused on his work. Uncle Trent claims it was just a strict school that kept him from expressing his free-spirited ways. But he was thought of as a bad kid for quite a while. I got to thinking that my neighbor Nick, who is now in first grade and also can be wild, would never be tied to a chair. It's just not allowed anymore. Instead, his teacher suggested he be evaluated for attention deficit hyperactivity disorder (ADHD) and maybe even medicated.

—Simone, junior sociology major

In this vignette, Simone begins to question what it means to be "mentally ill." Her young neighbor displays the same kind of behavior as did her uncle, but the two were treated very differently by adults. In an earlier era, her uncle was considered bad, but her neighbor is considered "ill." How can we make sense of this? Perhaps these maladies have always been around but were unnamed until scientists labeled them as such. Alternatively, societies may construct new illnesses and then label people who have traits thought to reflect those labels.

In Simone's case, an older family member had trouble managing behavior in the classroom and was labeled as deviant and then treated as such. Her neighbor today is treated like a "sick" person who needs treatment more than punishment. This example reflects a philosophical debate regarding the line between criminal and medical deviance. Are people different because they choose to act differently within the structures of their social situation, or do behavioral differences reflect physiological problems that need treatment, like any malady? Interactionists examine the ways deviance is constructed and how mental illness is treated when it is identified as a malady.

Defining Mental Illness

An interesting feature of mental conditions with which people can be diagnosed is that many of these categories are relatively new. ADHD was not known by the general population when Simone's Uncle Trent was a boy—the label did not exist. Moreover, it remains essentially nonexistent in many countries around the world today, showing how cultural boundaries are critical in how we understand and treat emotional and behavioral problems.

Societies have always had some people who act somewhat different or seemingly strange, exhibiting an array of "symptoms" that do not necessarily make sense to others. Several sociologists focus on the socially constructed nature of what we call "mental illness." They emphasize historical changes that have led to a redefinition of mental illness or current-day examples of how groups work together to create new labels for mental illnesses.

Madness and Civilization

Michel Foucault (1965) was a French social philosopher who studied the meaning of mental illness through history. He examined the ways that Western society viewed the role of madness from the Middle Ages to the present, emphasizing the seventeenth, eighteenth, and nineteenth centuries. He said that 1656 was an important year in the history of mental illness because that is the year that the "Hôpital General" opened in Paris, marking the start of the "great confinement" in which the insane and other deviants were housed together and separated from the rest of society. The "mad" were set aside from the masses, much like lepers had been in past generations. For the first time in the West, madness formally became something to keep away from society for its protection.

The Hôpital General and other places of confinement housed people who deviated from social norms and laws, some with mental illnesses and some without. Criminals were kept with people who, by today's standards, would be considered sick and in need of medical attention. Hence, deviance was the primary distinction between residents and nonresidents of the Hôpital General. The meaning of being sick changed dramatically after the Middle Ages. Foucault (1965) attributed this change to several societal-level changes in Europe during this period. He argued that the increased focus on reason that accompanied the Enlightenment made unreason unfathomable. In addition, new economic developments led to new attitudes toward the vagabond and the idle. Being idle was a scourge to society, something that must be hidden away from the marketplace.

Ideas about madness continued to change over time as reform movements emerged to improve houses of confinement such as the Hôpital General. Foucault (1965) argued that "unreasonable" people in society began to be more accepted, just as the physical sciences were beginning to assert that the universe does not necessarily operate under easily identifiable rules, laws, and principles. Therefore, separating "unreasonable" people made less sense to state leaders and intellectuals in later eras. In addition, economic conditions changed in a way that made the insane more useful. Developing economies included jobs that required cheap labor, thus giving stigmatized mental patients something to do once released from confinement.

The reform movements of the eighteenth and nineteenth centuries also led to the separation of criminals from the insane. Those defined as insane started receiving medical treatment instead of punishment. Although both groups were still considered deviant, only the prisoners continued to be confined en masse. The mentally ill started receiving treatment for their maladies. Some would remain in asylums, but many of them were set free—restrained only by therapy and social stigma, a concept reviewed later in this section. However, both groups were treated as undesirably different from the rest of society.

Current scholars continue to utilize a mix of the symbolic interaction and conflict (see Chapter 1) perspectives to examine the role of psychiatry as a form of social control agents who have the power to define what is normal and are given permission to implement treatments to adjust unacceptable thoughts, feelings, and behavior (Cohen 2016a; Szasz 1968, Szasz 1974, Szasz 2003). Alain Ehrenberg (2010) argues that the meaning of depression has changed over the years in North America from a mood disorder or some sort of prolonged sadness to an ailment that impedes individuals' abilities to carry out their everyday routines. A goal, then, for modern treatment of depression is to restore individuals' pace of life. Allan Horwitz and Jerome Wakefield (2007) also propose that the need for a simple, rational, and acceptable assessment of depression among people in the psychiatric field over the last 30 years moved the field toward a diagnostic model that blurs the line between normal sadness and depression—many people are being treated for clinical depression who would otherwise be deemed "sad" in other societies or at different times in history. These analyses highlight the ways that the meaning of an illness involves input from multiple people and groups and that it can change over time.

The Medicalization of Deviance

Another approach to the study of mental health and illness falls under the category of the **medicalization of deviance**, referring to ways in which social problems—including mental health problems—have come under the boundaries of medicine (Conrad and Potter 2000). Historically, there have been three forces driving what aspects of social life become medicalized (Conrad 2005):

1. The power and authority of the medical profession.
2. Activities of social movements and interest groups.
3. Directed organizational or professional activities.

First, doctors serve as gatekeepers in the medical industry, with the power to label something under the purview of medical science. Labeling is the first step in developing treatment for a disease or medical problem. It also makes a problem more than just a social issue. Labeling by a medical doctor highlights potential biological aspects of the problem and suggests medical solutions to resolve the difficulty. The year 1955 was a critical year in the mental health field with the introduction of Thorazine to treat psychiatric patients. It was the same year that Miltown, the first minor tranquilizer, was released. This drug was widely promoted by psychiatrists as a way to help people with

Photo 8.1 Drug advertisements present a biological explanation of mental illnesses; do you believe that most mental illnesses have biological explanations? Why or why not?

Source: Diomedes Cordero Acevedo/Shutterstock

anxiety and related psychological symptoms. By 1956, as many as one in 20 Americans had tried the drug (Tone 2009). The development of this consumer market for psychotropic drugs led to large-scale competition among manufacturers to sell their products, just like for other types of products.

Another factor in the medicalization of mental health is the development of groups who seek to define problems as medical to legitimize their problems or seek treatments for them. These groups can initiate social movements with the purpose of medicalizing an issue (Conrad 2005). A classic example of this process is the role of organizations in medicalizing posttraumatic stress disorder (PTSD). Since the inception of war, soldiers have suffered mental health problems as a result of their exposure to combat; in earlier eras, they were labeled "shell-shocked" (World War I) or "battle fatigued" (World War II). No combat disorder, however, was included in the first (APA 1952) edition of the *Diagnostic and Statistical Manual* (*DSM-I*) by the American Psychiatric Association (APA), the primary guidebook for diagnosing mental health disorders (see Box 8.1). Rather, this condition was viewed as a reaction to stressors that were temporary in nature (Scott 1990). The second edition of the *DSM* appeared in 1968 (APA 1968), also with no reference to soldiers' problems. Things changed as the United States moved into the final stages of the Vietnam War. Although there was no formal plan to add a category for PTSD to the third edition of the *DSM*, several psychiatrists, social workers, and lawyers pushed the APA to add the category. These efforts led to the creation of a working group that gathered data in support of the development of a category of disorder related to traumatic stress—one that could apply to people exposed to combat or other major stresses. The 1980 *DSM-III* (APA 1980) was released with a category of "posttraumatic stress disorder" among its listing of over 200 other disorders.

Box 8.1 The Diagnostic and Statistical Manual

Most psychological and psychiatric treatment of mental illnesses is guided by *The Diagnostic and Statistical Manual* (*DSM*). First developed in the 1950s, the *DSM* has gone through several revisions. With each revision, new information is added to the manual, and some diagnoses change. The *DSM* serves several purposes (Schnittker 2020). The *DSM* has historically had multiple categories of behaviors such as clinical disorders like depression or anxiety, and developmental and personality disorders such as antisocial disorder and developmental delays. More recent editions take a more holistic approach to diagnosing disorders, recognizing how different conditions relate to each other and how they vary over individuals' lifespan. The current edition of the *DSM* was initiated in 2019 and published in 2022 as the *DSM-5TR*. It involved more than 200 experts in its creation and continues to be a repository for hundreds of mental disorders. It has been criticized for treating mental illnesses as if they are physical illnesses. However, the *DSM* is the primary codification of the medicalization of certain life problems and conditions.

Modern interest groups influencing the medicalization process tend to be more economic than social in nature (Conrad 2005). These include health insurance companies, the pharmaceutical industry, and consumers. Insurance companies commonly limit the types of treatments for which they will pay. For instance, the use of medicines to treat mental illness has increased in recent decades (Frank, Conti, and Goldman 2005). The role of pharmaceutical companies in this process has expanded as they determine the direction of research, emphasizing some treatments more than others, and appealing directly to consumers to buy their products. For instance, pharmaceutical advertisers spend as much money marketing directly to consumers today as they spend marketing to doctors, and spending on television advertising of pharmaceuticals increased sixfold between 1996 and 2000 alone. Indeed, some scholars propose we are in an era of "pharmaceuticalization" as much as medicalization (Abraham 2010).

The growth of professional and health services organizations has contributed to an effort to codify and design specific treatments for mental diseases (Horwitz 2002). If psychologists and psychiatrists were to compete with "real" medical doctors, they would need to treat "real" diseases and report "real" outcomes. We can see a broken arm through certain devices such as X-rays and determine whether that arm has been healed after treatment. The same thing is not true for mental illnesses. The move for more precision in the mental health industry is shown by the increasing specificity in its labeling. For example, the number of disorders listed in the *DSM* more than doubled between the third and fourth editions, a span of 14 years. As mental illness has become medicalized, it has shifted public conceptions. For example, people today are more likely than people in the past to view mental illness as a disease rather than a personal failing under the control of the individual. People have also come to see a broader proportion of psychiatric disorders as diseases than they did a few decades ago. At the same time, negative stereotypes about mental illness remained strong through the twentieth century. For example, a nationally representative sample of Americans in 1996 was significantly more likely to describe mentally ill persons as violent than was a similar sample in 1950 (Phelan et al. 2000; see also American Psychiatric Association 2024 and DeAngelis 2022).

The role of the individual in the medicalization process can be seen in the "self-help" movement in which individuals seek personal development and therapeutic relief of their anxieties. Eva Illouz (2008) traces the roots of the self-help movement to the popular appeal of Sigmund Freud in the nineteenth and twentieth centuries, especially among the middle and upper classes. Illouz's work examines the intersection of the growth of Freudian psychology with the growth of individualism and Western rationality in which people put themselves at the center of a narrative in which suffering helps define the self and a therapeutic culture encourages individuals to find their own solutions to suffering. One can see irony at play here: individuals feel compelled to find solutions to their own problem but then turn to companies for psychiatric drugs and therapies as a means of healing themselves. In this sense, individuals feel that they have a sense of control over their well-being but are relying on a medical system and for-profit companies who promote drugs as the solution to their difficulties.

Photo 8.2 A woman and a trained mental health counselor at a "Friendship Bench," a program to provide mental health support given shortages in psychiatrists and psychologists in Zimbabwe. Do you think such a program would be accepted in other parts of the world?

Source: Costa Juta/ CC BY-SA 4.0

Mental Health and Selfhood

One of the more famous sociologists to study deviance and mental health was Erving Goffman. Goffman became prominent for his study of impression management (see Chapter 5), stigma (see Chapter 7), and other topics. Much of his work focuses on how individuals maintain a healthy image of themselves over time and in interactions with other people. If roles give us direction for our thoughts, feelings, and behaviors, then disobeying these guidelines may be defined as defiance, at best, or irrationality at worst. Hence, Goffman's conception of deviance incorporates everything from criminal behavior (see Chapter 7) to physical deformities and mental health problems. Goffman (1961, p. 81) once wrote, "To be awkward or unkempt, to talk or move wrongly, is to be a dangerous giant, a destroyer of worlds. As every psychotic and comic ought to know, any accurately improper move can poke through the thin sleeve of immediate reality."

Stigma and Mental Illness

In the last chapter, we defined stigma as an attribute that is deeply discrediting. Stigma may include attributes associated with mental illness (Goffman 1963). Much like other forms of stigma, people labeled with mental illness can react by using techniques in interaction such as trying to appear "normal" to other people (covering) or trying to

Box 8.2 Parson's Sick Role

Talcott Parsons (1951) applied elements of role theory (see Chapter 2) to explain the importance of role expectations in "being sick." He proposed that there are social expectations for sick people above and beyond the physical ramifications of the ailment itself. Specifically, he said that sick people have certain rights and responsibilities. Their rights include being exempt from normal social life (e.g., missing work) and the right to be taken care of by other people. However, sick people have a responsibility to try to get well by seeking out professional help to treat their malady. Ignoring these expectations may lead to rebukes from friends and family, like any other role violation. Parson's analysis of the sick role was one of the first attempts to apply sociological perspectives to health and illness. Can you see how this work applies to people with mental illnesses?

conceal an illness (passing as normal) (see Chapter 7). Using this schema, emotional disorders may be more easily concealed, whereas others, such as physical disability, may have physical manifestations that make it difficult to hide the illness (see Box 8.2).

Passing and covering are ways in which individuals manage their self-concepts in public venues. In a study of people diagnosed with dementia and their caregivers, James Fletcher (2020) found that his subjects preferred to conceal their diagnosis, although their tactics changed over time as their disease worsened. This study helps to show how people use agency to manage how they present themselves, incorporating their disease into their impression management tactics. Some diagnoses are more difficult to manage in interaction than others. Thomas Shriver and Dennis Waskul (2006) conducted an ethnography and extensive interviews with over 50 victims of Gulf War illness. This illness produces myriad symptoms, so much so that medical professionals have had a difficult time defining and treating it. The authors found that many of these victims could not pass or cover easily because the symptoms often had physical manifestations. One veteran reported:

> *Three months after I got back from the War it [a rash] started around my neck in red blotches. Since then I go to the hospital and they give me pills. . . . Now it's around my neck, covers down my chest, and around my side to my back. (Shriver and Waskul 2006, p. 476)*

The stigma of having an undefined illness led many of the veterans to doubt their own credibility and redefine their illness in order to manage their relationships with other people. Some of them retreated into their homes or bedrooms. Others became involved with support groups to relieve the stresses associated with the stigmatization they encountered. Finally, some of these veterans came to simply accept that they have a contested illness that may never be properly diagnosed or treated—and that they will forever be stigmatized.

Mental illnesses can sometimes be concealed quite well because they usually have few or no physical manifestations. However, it also makes it difficult to determine how "well" an individual is. Patients with broken legs can say that they are healed when they are able to use their legs without pain. If individuals are hiding their illnesses, which may be especially common for certain problems such as depression or bulimia, then getting help and recovering may be especially hard.

Kroska and Harkness (2008) carried out a study to investigate the complex ways in which persons cope with mental illness diagnoses. They focused on three coping strategies—attempting to conceal the diagnoses, withdrawing from interaction with others, and attempting to educate others about the illness. They found that the more those with mental illness diagnoses perceive mental illness to be stigmatized, the more likely they are to engage in these coping strategies. Also, different mental illness diagnoses appear to lead to different coping strategies. For example, Kroska and Harkness's study indicated that persons with schizophrenia, which may be difficult to "cover," are more likely to seek to educate others, compared to persons with major depression, who will be more likely to attempt to conceal their treatment histories.

The result of stigma is quite clear: it makes it difficult to have positive relationships with other people and can have long-term effects on people's lives (McLeod and Fettes 2007; Santuzzi, Metzger, and Ruscher 2006; Shriver and Waskul 2006). People who are stigmatized have to carefully negotiate social relationships, and being stigmatized as a youth can influence later adult life (Carr and Friedman 2006).

The Career of the Mental Patient

Psychiatric hospitals and prisons serve as the last resort for people who will not or cannot conform to the standards of conduct in society. Erving Goffman (1961) described the ways in which individuals adapt to their captivity in his book *Asylums: Essays on the Social Situation of Mental Patients*. He described mental institutions as **total institutions**, places where individuals are required to isolate themselves from the rest of society. Other total institutions can include monasteries, prisons, youth detention centers, and boarding schools. The goal of the asylum, according to Goffman, is to force the patient to adjust her sense of self to the rules and regulations of the institution. He noted that asylum inmates were subjected to a series of humiliations and debasements to induce this change.

A change that society expects to occur in psychiatric hospitals is associated with the presentation of self. When individuals are not capable of maintaining appropriate behaviors, their behaviors must be adjusted to meet societal standards. But Goffman's (1961) research also shows that individuals resist changes to the self when they become institutionalized. During their confinement, patients find small ways to rebel against the system. A patient may try to steal some extra food or sneak something from the outside world into the hospital. Patients also try to develop senses of individuality by designating different spaces as "out-of-bounds" to others, thereby giving them small senses of control over their lives.

Goffman (1961) also described the different ways that patients manage to cope with their confinement. Some patients, for instance, adapt to the institution by **conversion**, living up to the expectations of the staff and doctors. Alternatively, patients may try **intransigence**, rebelling against the staff expectations. In between these two extremes are forms of **withdrawal**, curtailing interaction with others at the asylum, or **colonization**, when patients use experiences of life from the outside world to show that the asylum is a desirable place to live. Goffman's work on asylums shows that individuals do not conform to any single set of behaviors or attitudes toward the system. Some patients try to accept their transformations of the self to being "normal," whereas others fight to maintain independent senses of self.

Nen Crewe (2009) provides a comparable picture of life in a total institution in his study of an English prison. He found that some prisoners retreat from prison life by isolating themselves from their peers, akin to Goffman's observation of withdrawal. He also concludes that some prisoners choose to rebel against the prison rules (intransigence), while others conform to them (colonization). He also found, however, that many inmates put on a front that they are conforming but really just want to get out of prison. This work demonstrates some level of consistency in the ways in which individuals cope with life inside different types of total institutions.

Erving Goffman*

Erving Goffman was born June 11, 1922, in Mannville, Alberta, Canada. Goffman received his BA degree at the University of Toronto in 1945 and his PhD at the University of Chicago in 1953.

Goffman's main areas of theory and research related to total institutions, stigma, and the dramaturgical model, which he explains by comparing life to a play. An individual performs "roles" in different life situations and within certain institutions. He discusses this idea in his book *The Presentation of Self in Everyday Life* (Goffman 1959).

Goffman carried out extensive research on people placed unwillingly in institutions such as prisons and mental wards, leading to his work *Asylums: Essays on the Social Situation of Mental Patients and Other Inmates* (Goffman 1961), which was researched and written during his first teaching job at the University of California, Berkeley.

In 1968, after 10 years at Berkeley, Goffman became a professor at the University of Pennsylvania, where he began to research interpersonal relations in public, gender dynamics, and various forms of talking. He became the president of the American Sociological Association in 1981, serving until his death on November 19, 1982. He received the Cooley-Mead Award in 1979.

*Information for this biography came from Lemert and Branaman (1997).

Patients are active participants in the diagnosis process; they utilize their agency with more or less engagement at different points (Peräkylä et al., 2022). Like any other social interaction, healthcare providers and patients exchange meanings in conversation which creates bonds between them (Skatvedt 2017). E. Summerson Carr's (2011) ethnography *Scripting Addiction* assesses interactions between therapists and clients at an outpatient drug treatment program. Though this was not a total institution, Carr found that clients and therapists developed roles and scripts in a way similar to what happens in total institutions. Only by accepting the addicted script—by accepting their addiction and using key words such as "honesty" and "openness"—could the clients have therapists begin to believe in their recovery. Like Goffman, Carr found that some clients had agency by retaining some sense of symbolic control over their situations. Notably, some of the clients learned to "flip the script"—using their front stages to perform like a client in recovery. Flipping the script and other such interactions reflect the concept of intransigence reviewed by Goffman in his analysis of total institutions.

Thus, having the status of "mentally ill" significantly affects an individual's life in community settings and institutions. An important insight from group process and symbolic-interactionist researcher is how a label can change how people are viewed by others. Even if two people are behaving identically, the one with a stigmatized status will likely be treated more negatively than the one without such a label. Being aware of this can help us question our assumptions when we have opportunities to deal with people who are labeled with various disorders.

Modified Labeling Theory

Labeling theory was introduced in Chapter 7 to help explain social causes of criminal deviance. If mental health problems are viewed as a form of deviance, labeling theory can also be applied to study mental illnesses. Labeling theory emphasizes that different agents of social control segregate and label criminal and ill groups. Foucault outlined the break between these two groups in France when the police, prisons, and courts began managing criminal deviance, whereas doctors and mental health practitioners managed the mentally ill. The system of defining what is normal and obtaining conformity may vary across cultures (Loe and Cuttino 2008; Scheff 1999; Scott 2007). Each group has its own point at which deviance arouses enough indignation that perpetrators are segregated and labeled based on their deviance.

Modified labeling theory proposes that even if mental illness is only partly socially constructed, the consequence of being labeled as such can produce pathological symptoms (Link 1987; Link et al. 1989; Mustillo, Budd, and Hendrix 2013). Individuals with mental illness diagnoses may come to accept the negative stereotypes about people with mental illness (e.g., as incompetent or dangerous), yielding negative feelings about themselves, as well as fear and expectations of being disvalued, which lead many of them to hide their illness or withdraw from social contacts. These behaviors ultimately lead to poorer mental health (Kroska and Harkness 2008; Link et al. 1989). The negative effects of perceived stigma can include lower self-esteem, income, and life satisfaction, along with increased psychological distress (Link 1987; Link et al. 1989;

Markowitz, Angell, and Greenberg 2011; Mustillo, Budd, and Hendrix 2013; Rosenfield 1997). While medical professionals are the primary means of labeling mental illness, the stigma of mental illness exists within the larger culture, long before someone is diagnosed with an illness. Hence, modified labeling theory involves multiple layers of labeling and stereotyping that can exacerbate an initial diagnosis.

In the case of children's behavioral problems, an important study points to a negative stigma regarding ADHD diagnoses. A study by Owens and Jackson (2017) showed that over children's young life course, children with mild behavioral issues who were diagnosed with ADHD in early childhood, whether medicated or not, were worse off in terms of reading and math scores years later. They were worse off than children with "matched" mild behavioral issues as reported by teachers and parents who were *not* diagnosed. The authors argue that the children themselves, as well as those around them, may have lower expectations for success.

There are many ways to manage the stigma of mental illness. One way is to simply try to resist taking on the label in the first place (Thoits 2011). Jenna Howard (Howard 2008; see also Howard 2006) analyzed the personal narratives of 40 people she deemed "de-labelers"—people who were labeled mentally ill but later began to separate themselves from the label. She found people with more social and fiscal capital found it easier to de-label than those people with fewer resources. Social capital in the form of relationships gave de-labelers alternative identities to focus on outside of the illness identity. These findings indicate that some people may want to disassociate with their illness labels but require more than therapy; they need a host of other resources to complete the de-labeling process.

Section Summary

This section applied the interactionist perspective to respond to the questions "What does it mean to be mentally healthy or ill?" and "How do we construct the meaning of mental illness?" We examined how the meaning of certain behaviors has changed over time in the Western world, moving from a form of deviance akin to criminality, to a form of malady that should be treated with medicine. People with mental ailments may be stigmatized, making their treatment more difficult as they manage the stigma of mental illness. Modified labeling theory helps explain how individuals and groups contribute to the social construction of some mental illnesses.

A Take-Away Message

The names and meanings we give to how people feel and behave are social constructions. What counts as a mental problem or illness has changed significantly over time. Indeed, a lot of what people take for granted today as being a medical problem located in the brain or body (e.g., depression or anxiety, ADHD, or defiant "disorders") have social causes that are often ignored in this era of defining people's experiences as "illnesses." The symbolic interactionist perspective also points to pharmaceuticals and other industries influencing how we conceive of and treat everyday problems of living.

The growth of the self-help industry in the United States is unique in the world today—perhaps in the history of the world. We can use the information in this section to help us better assess our own mental health. How much of my concern for my own well-being comes from a therapeutic culture that tells me that I should be relieved of any suffering? How might a therapeutic culture detract from people who are truly suffering? Regardless of what we believe about the role of self-help and pharmaceutical industries in society, they have a big effect on the way people approach the field of mental health. If you decide to work in the field of mental health, you will need to consider the large amount of information patients come in with when they are seeking treatment—it will likely weigh heavily on your interactions with them!

SOCIAL CAUSES OF STRESS

> *I saw a woman on a bus that makes a stop at the university. She had two little kids with her; one had a disability. She was wearing a wrinkled janitor's uniform, so she must have been dropping them off at childcare somewhere before she went to work. I felt so sad for her and wanted to help. It was very clear from the way she looked that she was depressed. The older kid kept talking to her, but it was like she did not hear him. Obviously life was overwhelming to her.*
>
> —Don, sophomore marketing major

Although specific individuals feel the mental bruises and jolts associated with daily life in different ways, sociologists focus on social patterns in mental health. Those using the social structure and personality approach have identified several patterns related to stress. First, social statuses are strongly related to experiencing stressors, with people of lower-social-class status experiencing the most stressors and most mental health problems. There are also other patterns by ethnicity, gender, and age, but economic status is critical. Don notices a lower-income woman who appears to have many chronic strains in her life—the lack of private transportation, a young child's extensive demands that are associated with his special needs, a difficult low-status and low-paying job, and so on. These conditions appear to Don to manifest themselves in the health and well-being of the mother on the bus.

There are regularities in the outcomes people experience when they are exposed to terrible events or chronic strains that arise in their roles. The **stress process model** helps us understand the connections among stressful events and strains, the resources people have to deal with problems, and the outcomes they experience.

The basic components of the stress process model include stressors, outcomes (distress), moderators, mediators, and social and economic characteristics of individuals (Pearlin 1999; Pearlin et al. 1981) (see Figure 8.1). Distress can be expressed in a number of ways. People may show signs of depression or anxiety, or they may act out their distress through alcoholism or antisocial behavior (see, Aneshensel, Rutter, and Lachenbruch 1991; Serido, Almeida, and Wethington 2004; Turner and Kopiec 2006; Turner, Taylor, and Van Gundy 2004; Umberson, Wortman, and Kessler 1992).

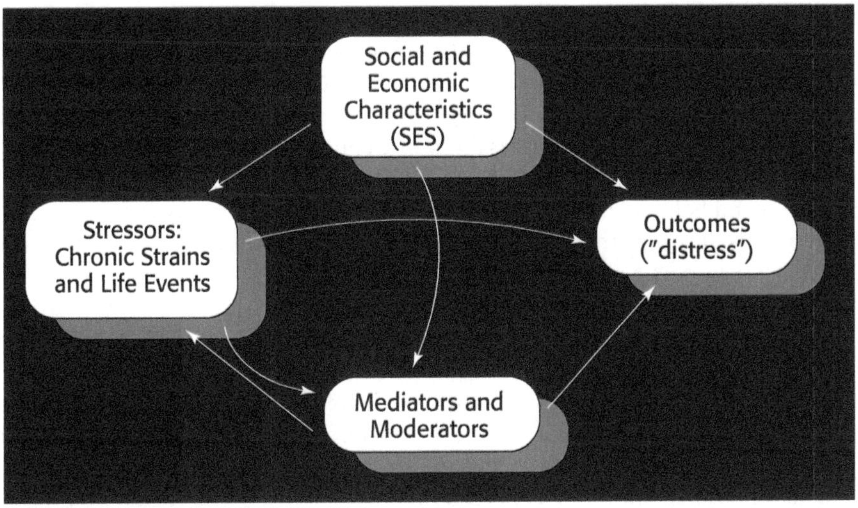

Figure 8.1 The Stress Process Model.

Source: Adapted from Pearlin et al. 1981.

The stress process model emphasizes the social structural conditions by which individuals manifest mental health problems. Hence, from a social structural and personality perspective, mental health is produced, in part, by social conditions. Social conditions influence both the problems people have and their access to resources necessary to manage those problems. In the example of the janitor on the bus, Don understood her problems as social in nature: the expectations to be a good mother, the poor working conditions she might experience each day, the resources available to cope with stress, and the opportunity for stress relief are found in the prevailing social conditions surrounding her.

Stressors and Outcomes

All of us deal with stress every day. Some stress is moderate but long-lasting while other forms of stress are short-lived and can be quite painful. We experience stress in all sorts of ways as we ponder our lives, think about things that we have lost, or question the decisions that we have made (Scott 2019). We have conflict with others and feel concerns about daily living. Stressors can be categorized in at least two forms: negative life events and chronic strain that tax our capacities. **Negative life events** include any events deemed unwanted or stressful to an individual. Exposure to negative life events can lead to distress (Aneshensel 1992; Lantz et al. 2005; Pearlin et al. 1981). Negative life events can include things such as the death of a loved one, marital or relationship separations, becoming unemployed, or exposure to traumatic events like combat or natural disasters (Adams and Anderson 2019; Gotlib and Wheaton 1997; MacLean 2010; Meadows, McLanahan, and Brooks-Gunn 2008;

Rohall, Hamilton, Segal, and Segal 2002). **Chronic strains** include strains within our social roles that may cause mental health problems over time by the accumulation of small amounts of stress rather than a single event. Chronic stressors or daily hassles may have even more influence on individuals compared with events that occur only infrequently. They may include stressful work conditions, financial strain, bad relationships, family problems, or poor living conditions (Milkie, Bierman, and Schieman 2008; Offera and Schneiderb 2011; Pines et al. 2011). Another way that a stressor can affect people is through the creation of other conditions (called "secondary stressors" because they occur after the initial ones) that strain people's lives. For example, Shirin Montazer and colleagues (2022) found that distress levels went up during the COVID-19 pandemic among parents, as compared to nonparents, in part because of a parallel increase in family-to-work conflict and guilt. In other words, the pandemic caused family issues which, in turn, increased distress. What kind of stressors do you think college students experience the most? Most of the stressors that college students are exposed to are an accumulation of different strains (e.g., adjustment problems, roommate situations, financial concerns, and/or managing the demands of school) (Jackson and Finney 2002; Rohall, Ender, and Matthews 2006). Like all people, they also have stresses that come from other aspects of life (see Figure 8.2). Some students do experience the death of a loved one or loss of a job, but these are less likely to occur than in other groups simply because of students' age and length of time in school (4 to 5 years). The stressors they do experience may be manifested in excessive drinking or clinical depression, both considered mental health problems.

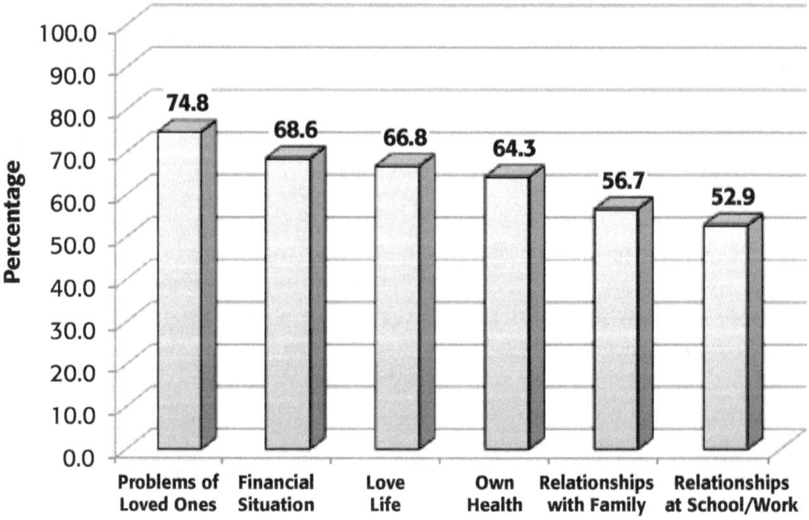

Figure 8.2 Common Stressors among College Students.

Source: Karyotaki et al. 2020.

In the stress process, stressors can affect us in our immediate surroundings, but they can also exist in our mind, akin to the concept of cognitive sociology introduced in Chapter 2. In this case, we know that people can anticipate stressors which may cause some distress, above-and-beyond the effects of life events or chronic strains (Thomeer, LeBlanc, and Bowen 2018). Stress can also be induced by ruminating over things like failure to achieve expected outcomes (Sendroiu, Upenieks, and Schafer 2021). In a sense, your mind is constantly processing external and internal stimuli. How do people react to these external and internal stresses? What conditions determine the degree to which they affect us?

Outcomes of the stress process can include any number of experiences, notably anxiety and depression, but they can also include aggression or substance abuse. Most measures of depression and other mental health problems rely on the person's ability to indicate her emotional state. For instance, the Center for Epidemiological Studies measures depression by asking how often the person has experienced feelings, such as "I did not feel like eating," "I felt lonely," or "I felt depressed," in the last week or month (see Table 8.1). An important aspect of this measure is that it includes a series of possible symptoms—or thoughts and behaviors associated with feeling depressed. A simpler one-item assessment would not be very robust because it includes only one dimension of the problem. For instance, one person may not know how to define *depressed* and rely on a guess about its meaning. Another person may have a more technical definition of the word *depression*, leading to a more accurate answer to the question. Multi-item scales help thwart problems in measuring distress.

Mediating and Moderating Resources

Although many studies have found a direct relationship between stressors and mental health outcomes, the relationship is typically modest (Cockerham 2003; Turner and Roszell 1994). As a result, researchers have tried to determine how and why people differentially respond to the same stressors. According to the stress process model, people have different capacities or resources with which to manage stressful events; thus, variations in resources might explain differences in how people react to stressors (Aneshensel 1992; Pearlin 1989; Pearlin et al. 1981).

Personal and Social Resources

Resources employed to manage stressors can take two forms. **Personal resources** include elements of self-concept that may be beneficial in managing events. People who feel that they have greater control over what happens to them (mastery) tend to deal with life's problems better than those who feel little sense of control (Bierman and Kelty 2014; Glavin and Schieman 2014; Harrod 2013; Turner and Roszell 1994). It may be that those with high levels of mastery feel they are able to manage problems, but it may also be that they are able to avoid problems or stressors more easily. Similarly, people with more positive self-images (self-esteem) seem to be able to cope with stressful events better than those with low self-esteem. Perhaps those with higher senses of self-esteem do not see negative events in terms of their self-worth; thus, they are less concerned about the long-term consequences of events to the self (Pearlin and Schooler 1978; Turner and Roszell 1994).

People also turn to their friends and family for help during difficult times. Access to people to whom you can turn in a time of need is called **social support or social resources**. Social supports can take a variety of forms, such as companions with whom to share your troubles and frustrations. Positive social support is generally associated with lower levels of distress (Meadows 2007; Mossakowski and Zhang 2014). Access to other people, groups, or organizations in dealing with difficult situations has also been found to reduce the distress associated with stressful events (Cockerham 2003; Pearlin 1989). In some cases, perceived support—perceptions of received support irrespective of actual support—has been found to have the same (or stronger) effects as actual support (Sarason, Pierce, and Sarason 1994). Quality of social networks is important too. Having closer relationships with other people is more impactful as a coping resource than weaker ties to networks of friends and family (Lee, Stahl, and Bayer 2020). These findings make sense given the nature of many stressful events. If someone becomes distressed from losing a job, then feeling that others are available to provide money, tips for finding a new job, and comfort may relieve some of the concerns associated with job loss even if she never finds it necessary to call upon that help.

Personal and social resources are **moderators** in the stress process because they affect the direction or strength of the relationship between a stressor and mental health (Baron and Kenny 1986; Pearlin et al. 1989). Imagine a situation in which two people lose their jobs. One person is confident that she can find another job, whereas the other person has no such feelings of mastery. Both may develop a sense of anxiety over the news, but the job loss's effect on distress is going to be more negative for the second

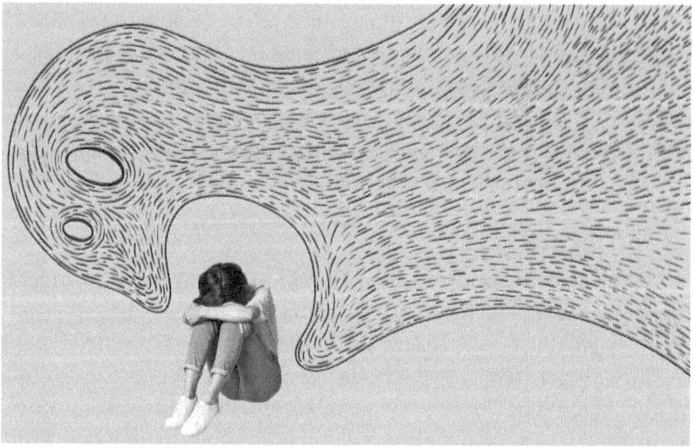

Photo 8.4 Depression is one of the most common mental illnesses. What are some ways that social forces influence your mental health?

Source: Roman Samborskyi/Shutterstock

person. In this case, the sense of mastery moderates the relationship between job loss and mental health. Similarly, having access to more people to turn to may affect your sense of distress; this is important because while social support helps everyone manage stressful events, not everyone has the same levels of support (Sloan, Newhouse, and Thompson 2013).

Social or personal resources can also act as *mediators*. A **mediator** is a variable that can explain the relationship between the stressor and outcome (Baron and Kenny 1986). That is, a mediator connects the stressor to the outcome, or acts as the mechanism by which the stressor "works." One way to think about this is that the stressor causes a change in the mediating variable, then the mediator affects the outcome variable. For instance, losing a job can be linked to mental health through loss of mastery: the loss of a job erodes a sense of control, which, in turn, creates distress. Thus, becoming unemployed can affect mental health through the loss of mastery. Mastery and other personal and social resources, then, can act as either moderators or mediators in the stress process.

Gender and Social Support

Social resources can influence individuals by providing more access to instrumental support (which is concrete support such as money, meals, or job opportunities) and emotional support in times of need (Pearlin 1989). However, social support is not distributed evenly across the population (Turner and Marino 1994). Men and women may have different network sizes with varying density of support, reflecting their structural differences in men's and women's lives, with men's networks relatively more often associated with employment and women's networks often associated with family; both men and women benefit from positive relationships (Moore 1990; Pugliesi and Shook 1998; Umberson et al. 1996). A meta-analysis of social networking sites suggests that women both seek and give more social support online than men (Tifferet 2020). Other research indicates that support differences reflect socialization patterns such that boys and girls are taught to seek different levels and types of support from other people. In one study, researchers found that levels of femininity and masculinity were associated with seeking and receiving emotional support. Specifically, being more feminine—among both males and females—was associated with seeking and receiving emotional support, whereas masculinity was associated with seeking instrumental support (Reevy and Maslach 2001).

Social and Economic Characteristics: The Epidemiology of Mental Health

One component of the stress process model involves individuals' social and economic characteristics, especially social class, race and ethnicity, gender, and age. The **epidemiology of mental health** emphasizes the distribution of mental health conditions, with different social statuses associated with different levels and types of mental health problems. Research in this area is important because it highlights the effects of societal positions on health and well-being. For example, women report higher levels of depression and anxiety than do men, whereas men on average have more substance abuse problems

Box 8.3 Social Media in the Stress Process

The Stress Process helps to incorporate any aspects of social life into categories. Is the online world a stressor or a resource? The question cannot be ignored given that over half of the planet has a social media account (Kemp 2023). In one meta-analysis—a study that examines findings from multiple studies—analyzing 62 studies of media use and depression, Simone Cunningham and colleagues (2021) found a significant but weak positive relationship between time using social networking sites and depression, as well as links between intensity of use and problematic or compulsive usage and depression. Another study that looked at Facebook use alone showed, "the rollout of Facebook at a college had a negative impact on student mental health. It also increased the likelihood with which students reported experiencing impairments to academic performance due to poor mental health. Additional evidence on mechanisms suggests the results are due to Facebook fostering unfavorable social comparisons" (Braghieri, Levy and Makarin, 2022, p. 360). To demonstrate the causal ordering of things (see Chapter 3 on research methods), Melissa Hunt and her colleagues (Hunt et al. 2018) conducted an experiment in which they assigned 142 college students randomly to a group with limited media use of platforms popular at that time (specifically Facebook, Instagram, and Snapchat) or one with no media restrictions for three weeks. They found a causal link between media use and depression and loneliness—more consumption of media was associated with more depression and loneliness. However, Shelia Cotten (2022), a prolific scholar of media and well-being, cautions us to consider that social media can serve as an important source of social support, especially among populations with limited access to traditional social ties like the elderly or during times in which people's face-to-face interactions are restricted in some way, like a global pandemic. Bu Zhong and colleagues (2021) confirmed this perspective. Using data collected in Wuhan, China, where the virus is believed to have originated, the researchers found that social media generally served as a source of information and social support, but excessive use of media led to distress. Ultimately, studies may seem conflicting because media can serve any number of roles in the stress process depending on its use and the background characteristics of the people using it.

than women (Aneshensel, Rutter, and Lachenbruch 1991; Mirowsky and Ross 1995; Turner, Wheaton, and Lloyd 1995). Other important characteristics associated with different mental health outcomes are marital status and social class, with married people reporting lower levels of distress than singles (Turner et al. 1995) and people of lower socioeconomic status (SES) reporting higher levels of distress than those of higher SES, largely because they experience more strains and negative life events (Aneshensel 1992; Aneshensel and Sucoff 1996).

Social statuses are associated with different levels of distress, and they also interact with stressors to produce different outcomes. Race and gender can moderate how stressors affect mental health. Milkie, Bierman, and Schieman (2008) found that adult children's negative treatment toward elderly parents affected mothers' and African Americans' mental health more than fathers' and White parents' mental health. The authors proposed that because the parent role was likely especially important for these groups that were on average less able to have other prominent roles, such as in the workplace or community in an earlier era, the hurts of this relationship were felt more deeply. A major challenge in studying effects of social structure on individuals is that the relationships can be complex and change over time. Research on the epidemiology of mental health tries to unravel this complexity.

Class, Race, and Mental Health

The prevalence of mental health disorders is inversely related to economic status: as levels of education and income go up, the prevalence of disorders goes down. Also, perceived status in the community is also related to well-being (Andersson 2018). This finding is generally true of most types of disorders, including affective disorders such as depression, as well as schizophrenia and personality disorders. In a classic study, Robert Faris and H. Warren Dunham (1960, originally 1939) used Chicago city maps to trace the addresses of over 30,000 people who had received treatment from psychiatric hospitals. They found that a significant number of schizophrenic patients lived in poor areas of the city. This was one of the first studies to show a relationship between class position and well-being. In fact, Bruce Link and Jo Phelan (1995) propose that social statuses like SES are not simply risk factors but also fundamental causes of well-being because they affect many physical and mental health outcomes through many different mechanisms.

Recent studies support Faris and Dunham's (1960) findings. For instance, when measuring class in terms of education, Robins, Locke, and Regier (1991) found that high school graduates were significantly less likely to be diagnosed with a disorder than people without a high school degree (30% to 36%). Similarly, almost half (47%) of people on welfare or receiving disability payments had a disorder at some point, and a third (31%) had active symptoms. Men working in unskilled jobs also had more disorders than those in higher status jobs.

The relationship between class and disorder is relevant when comparing the prevalence of disorder among racial groups, because income is unevenly distributed across them. Research shows that African Americans have higher rates of mental illness than Whites or Latino Americans, though the relationship is complex (Keyes 2009; Robins et al. 1991; Misra et al. 2022; Williams, Takeuchi, and Adair 1992; Wu et al. 2003). African Americans and other minorities may experience more distress than Whites in part because of the stresses associated with racism, as well as due to the higher concentration of Blacks in poverty; that is, race differences reflect class differences (Cockerham 1990; Perry, Pullen, and Oser 2012). Reported stressors are typically higher among African Americans compared to Whites, even controlling for income and other factors (George and Lynch 2003; Kessler and Neighbors 1986; Ulbrich, Warheit, and Zimmerman 1989). However, African Americans may deal more effectively with stressors than do Whites (Keyes 2009). Being emotionally flexible, learning resilience from earlier

Table 8.1 Center for Epidemiologic Studies Depression (CES-D) Scale

Instructions: Using the scale below, please circle the number before each statement that best describes how often you felt or behaved this way *during the past week*:				
	Rarely or None of the Time (Less Than 1 Day)	Some or a Little of the Time	Occasionally or a Moderate Amount of Time	Most or All of the Time
During the past week:				
1. I was bothered by things that usually don't bother me.	0	1	2	3
2. I did not feel like eating; my appetite was poor.	0	1	2	3
3. I felt that I could not shake off the blues, even with help from my family or friends.	0	1	2	3
4. I felt that I was just as good as other people.	0	1	2	3
5. I had trouble keeping my mind on what I was doing.	0	1	2	3
6. I felt depressed.	0	1	2	3
7. I felt that everything I did was an effort.	0	1	2	3
8. I felt hopeful about the future.	0	1	2	3
9. I thought my life had been a failure.	0	1	2	3
10. I felt fearful.	0	1	2	3
11. My sleep was restless.	0	1	2	3
12. I was happy.	0	1	2	3
13. I talked less than usual.	0	1	2	3
14. I felt lonely.	0	1	2	3
15. People were unfriendly.	0	1	2	3
16. I enjoyed life.	0	1	2	3
17. I had crying spells.	0	1	2	3
18. I felt sad.	0	1	2	3
19. I felt that people dislike me.	0	1	2	3
20. I could not get going.	0	1	2	3

Scoring: Items are summed after reverse-scoring items 4, 8, 12, and 16. Total CES-D scores range from 0 to 60, with higher scores reflecting higher levels of depression.

Source: Adapted from Radloff (Radloff 1977).

adversity, or getting support from religious groups may deflect stressors for African Americans (DeAngelis, Upeniek, and Louie 2023). In one study, Michael Hughes and colleagues (2015) found that African Americans who identity more and have a more positive evaluation of their racial group report less depression than those who do not. This finding is important because it helps explain the role of cohesion and morale among groups in the stress process.

Discrimination of any kind—racial or otherwise—is associated with distress (Barr 2008; Chou and Feagin 2008; Jefferson 2011; Mossakowski and Zhang 2014; Schafer and Ferraro 2011). Jay Turner and William Avison (2003) found that when discrimination is included in studies of stressors, we see bigger differences in levels of distress between African Americans and Whites, indicating the importance of including this key form of strain in the study of racial differences. Moreover, they found that daily discrimination and major lifetime discrimination, such as in promotions, in housing, and by police, each influenced distress. Anastasia Yuan (2007) found that perceived age discrimination was also associated with distress levels. These findings indicate that people who receive or perceive discrimination in their day-to-day lives must manage these events as a chronic strain above and beyond other stressors that come along.

Racial stereotypes may also contribute to the disproportionate diagnoses of certain mental illnesses among African American patients. Marti Loring and Brian Powell (1988) conducted a study in which 290 psychiatrists were given two case studies to diagnose. The authors manipulated the race (African American or White) and gender of the described (fictional) patient. The researchers found similar diagnoses among psychiatrists when the gender and race of the patient were absent from the records and when the race and gender of the psychiatrist and patient coincided with one another. White and African American (both male and female) psychiatrists, however, were more likely to diagnose African American male subjects with aggressive disorders compared with other groups (given the same description), underscoring the pervasiveness of cultural stereotypes. More recent research shows that African Americans are less likely to be diagnosed with bipolar disorder and more likely to be diagnosed with schizophrenia than Whites (Neighbors et al. 2003). However, the research found no racial differences in diagnoses of depression, the most common disorder.

Gender, Family, and Well-Being

Marital status is another characteristic associated with mental health and well-being. Married people are generally happier, healthier, and financially better off than single, divorced, and widowed people (Diener et al. 2000; Kim and McKenry 2003; Simon 2002; Waite and Gallagher 2000). Married people on average report higher levels of life satisfaction, lower levels of distress, and better physical health than their single counterparts. Married people report better sex lives, too.

The positive effects of marriage on health and well-being may reflect access to social support or the committed nature of marital relationships. For instance, cohabiting is associated with higher levels of well-being than being single—reflecting access to regular social support. However, being married continues to have a stronger effect on well-being than being single or cohabiting, and the positive effects of marriage continue after controlling for relationship quality (Dush and Amato 2005; Kim and McKenry 2003; Meadows, McLanahan, and Brooks-Gunn 2008; Williams, Sassier, and Nicholson 2008). Some evidence indicates that differences in well-being between those who are married and those who cohabitate without being married lie in differences between these groups in coping resources (Marcussen 2005). In other words, married persons tend to have more resources in their relationships with their partners that help them cope with stress than do persons who cohabitate, and this helps to explain the differences in well-being between those who are married and those who cohabitate. However, these patterns may not be static. Hui Liu and Debra Umberson (2008), using data from the National Health Interview Survey—a longitudinal assessment of health among U.S. residents—found that self-rated health among single, never-married people has improved in recent decades and that the gap between single and married people has converged, at least for men.

As we discussed in this chapter, there are also gender differences in mental health. Studies consistently show that women report higher levels of depression and other emotional disorders than men (Hopcroft and Bradley 2007; Keyes and Goodman 2006). However, men are more likely than women to exhibit behavioral problems such as alcoholism, drug addiction, and aggression.

Why do we observe this difference in expression of distress? Perhaps women are taught to release their stress emotionally, whereas men are taught to resist being openly emotional and encouraged to act on their emotions. Women may also be more open to sharing their emotional problems with researchers or professionals than are men. Hence, women may be more likely to admit to, and seek treatment for, affective disorders than men. Also, Loring and Powell's (1988) research mentioned in this chapter found that male clinicians at one point in time tended to overestimate the prevalence of depression in women. Though there are differences in expression, many scholars argue that the reason that women have more overall distress is structural. John Mirowsky and Catherine Ross (1995) found that although women are more expressive than men, this difference did not explain the differences in distress levels between men and women. Women reported higher levels of most emotions, including sadness, anxiety, and anger, the latter an emotion traditionally associated with men. Mirowsky and Ross, along with Simon (2020) argue that women's less powerful positions in society produce more stressors, leading to more distress.

Community and Neighborhood Contexts

A significant amount of research attempts to link the social-structural conditions of communities to health outcomes. Some of this work emphasizes cultural differences between regions, including consistent patterns of macrosocial life that affect individuals. Several studies examine the effects of neighborhood conditions on their residents, such as Elijah Anderson's (1999) research of Philadelphia's inner-city life in which minority residents must live in harsh social and physical environments and develop interactional strategies to manage those stresses. Communities and neighborhoods represent a set of environmental and social conditions that affect most or all of their residents (McLeod and Lively 2003).

Rural and urban communities represent different worlds and expectations for individuals. Rural areas may have less stimulation and a slower pace of life than urban environments, whereas urban areas may have more activities but more stressful living conditions.

Research assessing differences in mental health between urban or rural contexts has not been consistent. There is some evidence that there is a **malaise** or psychological state of unhappiness associated with living conditions in especially rural or very urbanized areas (Fischer 1973). The rural malaise may reflect the lack of stimulation associated with a repetitive or routine lifestyle found in many rural places, whereas urban malaise tends to be restricted to central areas of larger cities generally associated with poor living conditions.

How do economic conditions affect mental health? First, difficult macrolevel economic conditions can create strains on individuals through their own employment (e.g., losing a job or not making enough money). Those strains may also inhibit social supports available to individuals (Voydanoff 2007). Neighborhood conditions also have effects on individuals' lives. Aneshensel and Sucoff (1996) found that people in poorer neighborhoods report higher levels of distress, probably because there are more "ambient hazards" in their living areas. Ambient hazards represent chronic strains in the form of exposure to crime, poor living conditions, and lack of services. Thus, dire economic conditions associated with some areas within urban regions may affect mental health by producing different numbers and kinds of stressful conditions.

The places we live can influence our well-being through the availability of work. Losing a job and living in an area with high unemployment is associated with higher distress than being unemployed and living in a more economically vibrant area (Dooley, Catalano, and Rook 1988; Dooley, Catalano, and Wilson 1994). The shift for some workers to remote work following the COVID-19 pandemic is a fruitful area of inquiry in the 2020s, as for some more advantaged workers their jobs may become somewhat less tied to a specific place.

Community contexts also influence access to the social resources necessary to manage stressful life events. People in rural areas tend to live farther apart from one another than in urban areas, possibly making face-to-face contact with friends and family more difficult. Hence, access to in-person social networks may be more limited. In one study, Paul Amato (1993) found that urbanites both find more help from, and give more help to, friends than people living in more rural areas. Urbanites also report expecting more help from friends than people in more rural areas because they live farther from their families than rural people; hence, they are more likely to turn to friends for help. A well-integrated community can be a major influence on mental health (Maimon and Kuhl 2008).

It is important to note that all of the processes that fall into the stress process act under larger social systems. Jason Schnittker (2021) argues that we are living in an "age of anxiety" which has both direct effects on our mental health and works indirectly through the components of the stress process. The idea that individual-level processes occur under a larger set of social dynamics has been included in some

Box 8.4 Jobs in Social Psychology: Mental Health

Mental health careers are typically associated with graduate training in psychology, counseling, and social work. There are many other ways you can work for organizations associated with mental health and well-being since there is a need for support staff who manage facilities and assist counselors. Here are two examples of ways to work in this field without a graduate degree.

1. **Psychology Technician, Department of Defense, Military Treatment Facilities under DHA.** Duties: Perform intake for behavioral health patients to determine the mental, emotional, or behavioral needs. Obtain a thorough clinical history through interviews and medical records. Perform group and individual counseling and education. Assist in developing a treatment plan based on interviews, observations, records, and test results. Experience: One year of specialized experience which includes performing intake for behavioral health clients, educating and/or counseling behavioral health clients, and maintaining client records or a half year (i.e., 9 semester hours) of graduate level education in a field directly related to the work of the position, such as Psychology, Human Services, Child & Family Welfare, Counseling, Behavioral Science, Human Development, Social Work, or Sociology or a combination of experience and education.
2. **Treatment Counselor-Substance Abuse (Licensed Chemical Dependency Counselor or LCDC).** CoreCivic (El Paso, TX). Duties: Interviews and assesses prospective program participants; facilitates individual and group treatment interventions; uses standardized offender assessment information in developing treatment plans or specific programs. Experience: Graduate from an accredited college or university with a bachelor's degree in psychology, counseling, social work, or a closely related field; TX LCDC or LCDC Intern license required.*

*Each state has a different set of requirements to be a substance abuse counselor, but a common rule is that level III counselors require a bachelor's degree with several addiction-related courses and many hours of internship or work hours related to substance abuse (e.g., working at a clinic or internships). Because each state is different, you will need to do some research. In Texas, for instance, it includes: (a) at least 135 clock hours (nine semester hours) of the education specific to substance use disorders and their treatment and another 135 clock hours may be specific or related to chemical dependency counseling. Related education hours may include courses in psychology, sociology, counseling, mental health, behavioral science, psychiatric nursing, ethics, and rehabilitation counseling.

versions of the stress process (see Turner 2010). Schnittker demonstrates age and cohort differences in anxiety levels and associates those changes with changes in families, religious participation, and social environments. Hence, society provides the context of stressful events, the types and levels of stressors, as well as being influential in terms of the types and levels of support required to manage those stresses. (See Box 8.4 for ideas for how to work in the mental health field after completing your undergraduate degree.)

Section Summary

In this section, we applied the social structure and personality perspective to answer the question "What are the structural conditions that contribute to distress?" We applied the stress process model to assess how social conditions such as negative life events and chronic strains affect people, often leading to mental health difficulties such as depression and anxiety. We also examined how social and personal resources protect people from the effects of negative events; for instance, a higher sense of mastery and access to social support help to reduce the effects of negative life events and strains on distress. Finally, we examined how exposure to events and access to resources vary by social and economic statuses and community context.

A Take-Away Message

Whereas the previous section of this chapter emphasized the social construction of mental health, which assesses how cultures make meaning surrounding deviance based on labels of "illness," this section, utilizing the social structure and personality perspective, shows a very different way of understanding the influences of society. It examines the everyday social roles and conditions that impact well-being. You can look at the social conditions around you to understand your mental health more readily. You may not be able to control the community you live in, but you are able to develop access to social networks that will help you become more resilient to anxiety, depression, and other disorders. In addition, you should consider the mental benefits of taking one job versus another. Will the job you secure give you the appropriate income and a supportive environment in which to work, potentially keeping financial and workplace stressors at bay? Given your relatively high level of education, especially if you complete a bachelor's degree, you may be less likely to experience many kinds of stressors compared with those with fewer educational credentials.

MENTAL HEALTH IN GROUP PROCESSES

> *I was diagnosed with bipolar depression when I was 14. I remember it pretty clearly because it had a big impact on my relationships with my friends. Some of my friends' parents did not like them hanging out with me. I think that they thought that bipolar was contagious or something. Anyway, I just noticed the parents would talk to me differently than before. It made them nervous somehow.*
>
> —John, freshman biology major

One of the ways that mental disorders differ from physical disorders is that they are more often difficult to notice in a public venue. Erving Goffman's (1963) work on stigma addresses this issue by indicating that people with mental illnesses are sometimes better able to pass as "normal" than are people with disabilities that confine them to wheelchairs. However, when a mental disorder is known to other people, it may serve as a status characteristic affecting interactions in ways similar to other attributes we possess.

John's story tells about being diagnosed with bipolar disorder. He noticed that people around him started treating him differently as a result of his diagnosis. He lost some friends because parents were not comfortable with his condition. He was deemed different even though there were no physical indications of his stigma. People were not sure how to relate to him anymore, perhaps because they were nervous or uncomfortable.

According to the group processes perspective, people set up different expectations of individuals' performance depending on their status characteristics. This idea is the basis of expectation states theory (see Chapter 4). Diffuse status characteristics influence other people's expectations of how well we can perform in a wide variety of social situations.

David Wagner (1993), a scholar who works in the group processes perspective, addressed whether mental illness likely acts as a diffuse status characteristic. He proposed that three properties are required for a mental condition to be considered a diffuse status characteristic. First, the illness must be considered something that is unwanted or less desirable than other states. Like other characteristics, it has to be something that can be ranked as better or as worse than something else. The fact that mental illness is labeled an "illness" suggests that it is a condition that people are trying to relieve or separate from themselves. Experts are paid to help in these efforts, further classifying individuals as sick or well, and in better or worse conditions.

Second, mental illness must also be associated with other characteristics that are tied to the illness. Mentally ill people, for example, tend to be considered less stable, more aggressive, or more unpredictable than "normal" people. Hence, the mentally ill label is negative in and of itself, and it is also associated with other negative attributes. Finally, there must be general expectations associated with a person's ability to perform in a group. There must be an expectation that the mentally ill are less capable than "normal" people.

These expectations can affect group transactions in similar ways as do other status characteristics. Individuals who are mentally ill may be less likely to contribute to a group task because they believe that they are less capable than other group members. Other group members may devalue the contributions made by the mentally ill individual because of the individual's status in the group and the negative assumptions associated with mental illness (Wagner 1993). The result of this process is that individuals labeled as mentally ill will likely have less influence on their social worlds than those who are not labeled as such, partly because of the limitations placed on them by other group members and partly from their own beliefs in their limitations. Having less status in social situations may then perpetuate the original status-organizing processes that lead to negative expectations associated with the stereotype.

Research by Lucas and Phelan (2012) supported Wagner's argument. They found that mental illness labels decreased the influence that persons had over college students on a group task. They also found that college students became more likely to avoid future encounters with a partner if the partner had been diagnosed with a mental illness. Thus, Lucas and Phelan's (2012) research indicates that mental illness does act as a status characteristic in group interactions and additionally that it leads to the social rejection that characterizes stigmatization. Research by Manago and Mize (2022) also found that mental illness labels decrease status, but only in the context of the label being associated with deviant behavior in the group.

Social Support in Groups

Mental health acts as a status characteristic in groups but current research also indicates that stress processes change as a result of group processes. The effect of social supports, for instance, changes based on the type of social support available in a particular group. Consider that some groups involve strangers while others involve close relationships. Each type of group can have different effects on how people are able to manage personal stresses. In one study, Jun Zhao and colleagues (2020) examined the role of social support among female and male friendship groups. They found that Taiwanese high-school-aged girls tended to withdrawal as a result of depressive symptoms, which further exacerbated their personal problems. Boys, on the other hand, were less likely to withdrawal from their peer groups, but at a cost to their friends: depression from one member appears to have spread to their peers, increasing the average depression levels in the group. Thus, social interaction can be a conduit for positive social support, but at least in certain cases, it can also have a neutral or potentially even a negative effect on the larger group's well-being.

Section Summary

This section addressed the question "How does mental health influence sense of identity and interactions with other people?" Traditional research in group processes does not address mental health per se, but groups play a major role in definitions of, and reactions to, people with mental health problems. Mental health conditions may be status characteristics that individuals in groups use as a basis of further interaction.

A Take-Away Message

Mental health and illness statuses are relevant within groups. At the beginning of this chapter, we examined the ways in which individuals and institutions in society contribute to the construction of diagnoses. In this section, we see that mental health can also serve as a status characteristic, much like race or gender. It affects others' reaction to us, and it can become part of our identities.

BRINGING IT ALL TOGETHER

When my son was diagnosed with depression, at first I did not buy it—I really think many diagnoses are made too quickly, and people are overmedicated. But with all the problems going on at my son's school and with his friends, he just never got his homework done and he seemed so listless. I was at my wit's end and I decided to give the drugs a chance. I remember one day, after being on the antidepressant for a number of weeks, he told me that he could literally feel how the drug had lightened his outlook and enabled him to get his school work

> *done. He seemed so much better. I realize he may have gotten better if his school situation could have changed. But I don't know, maybe there is something going on there.*
>
> —Beth, nontraditional student

This chapter addressed the social conditions that affect mental health and well-being. Symbolic interactionists tend to focus on how people construct mental illness, whereas researchers using the social structure and personality perspective study how social conditions cause distress, and how this these conditions disproportionately pile up on those in less advantaged social positions. Group processes scholars emphasize consequences of mental illness, such as how it acts as a status characteristic that may influence group dynamics.

Although we focused on the social conditions that influence mental health and well-being, sociologists do not discount biological roots to mental disorders. In the preceding vignette, Beth is skeptical of mental health diagnoses and treatment at first, but starts to rethink her position when her son starts taking an antidepressant drug for his difficulties. These perspectives—the social and biological causes of mental illness—are not exclusive. Indeed, social conditions may influence genetic expression. Bernice Pescosolido and her colleagues (2008), for instance, found that the effects of genetic predisposition toward alcoholism were greater among men than women, among people with less family support compared to those with more family support, and among people who grow up in poverty. The researchers concluded, "Social experiences, both positive and negative, affect whether and how genotypes translate into behavioral phenotypes. Specifically, a history of deprivation during childhood may trigger the genetic tendency" (Pescosolido et al. 2008, p. 192). Hence, social stressors, such as role strains and overloads, can interact with biological factors such as genetic predispositions toward certain disorders to create distress. Moreover, both the likelihood and experience of taking a drug for emotional or behavioral problems are influenced by social conditions such as the prominence of pharmaceuticals being seen and promoted as "solutions" in the culture. Ultimately, biological factors may be important, but social factors create distress in patterned ways across social groups, and they influence treatments in ways that are fascinating—and critical—to examine.

SUMMARY

1. The history of madness and civilization shows that the meaning and treatment of mental illness have changed dramatically over the centuries. In Europe, into the seventeenth century, mental illness was considered similar to other forms of deviance such as criminality.
2. Mental illness may serve as a source of identity that impacts interactions with other people in the form of stigma. Patients housed in institutions may try to cope in many different ways, including conversion, intransigence, and forms of withdrawal and colonization.

3. Sociologists view many manifestations of mental illness to be the result of social conditions that tax individuals' capacity to manage their lives. The stress process model helps us understand the relationship of negative life events and chronic strains with our mental health and well-being. It also focuses on the resources we use to manage those stressors.
4. Social and economic characteristics are associated with different levels of distress, with social class status a critical factor in the stress process. Other important social characteristics that are implicated in the experience of stressors, the level of resources, and the expressions of distress include gender, age, and race and ethnicity.
5. According to the group processes perspective, people have different expectations for individuals' performance depending on their status characteristics. Mental illness may be considered a diffuse status characteristic that influences members' expectations of the mentally ill in a group setting as well as the contributions made by those members.

KEY TERMS AND CONCEPTS

Chronic strains: Day-to-day role or other strains that may cause mental health problems over time by the accumulation of demands.

Colonization: A way in which patients manage institutionalization by showing that their institution is a desirable place to live.

Conversion: A way in which patients manage institutionalization by living up to the expectations of the staff and doctors.

Epidemiology of mental health: The study of the distribution of mental disorders and distress across social groups.

Intransigence: A way in which patients manage institutionalization by rebelling against staff expectations.

Mediators: Part of the stress process referring to resources that act as mechanisms through which stressors relate to outcomes.

Medicalization of deviance: Ways in which social problems—including mental health—have come under medical boundaries.

Moderators: Part of the stress process that includes the personal and social resources that affect the direction or strength of the relationship between a stressor and mental health.

Modified labeling theory: The consequence of accepting a label as mentally ill, which ultimately may produce pathological symptoms.

Negative life events: Part of the stress process referring to any event deemed unwanted or stressful and taxing to an individual.

Personal resources: Part of the stress process referring to elements of our self-concept that may be beneficial in managing events and strains.

Social support or social resources: Access to friends and family available to help during stressful or difficult times.

Sociology of mental health: The study of the social arrangements that create distress and mental illness, as well as the consequences of those problems and labels.

Stress process: A model that outlines the relationships among social statuses, stressful experiences (stressors), the resources people bring to deal with problems, and the outcomes (distress) they experience.

Total institutions: Places where individuals are isolated from the rest of society.

Withdrawal: A way of managing life in an institution involving the curtailing of interaction with others.

DISCUSSION QUESTIONS

1. Have you ever been diagnosed with a cognitive, emotional, or behavioral disorder? If so, how did other people react to your condition? Do you know someone who has been diagnosed with a mental health condition? How did your relationship change, if at all, with this person once you learned of the diagnosis?
2. If certain mental illnesses are affected by social conditions, such as workplaces, neighborhoods, or educational systems that are stressful, how might we change social policies to reduce mental disorders?
3. There is great debate about the institutionalization of people with severe mental illnesses. Do you think people with such problems should be institutionalized? Why or why not?

9

Social Attitudes

My dad was always very clear when we were young. All people of all races and religions are to be treated with respect and are considered equal. I really thought that was an important part of the way he was raising us. Then my younger sister started dating someone of a different religion. He did not exactly freak out, nor did he forbid the relationship, but you just knew that all his negative comments were only because of this kid's religion. My dad couldn't stand it and seemed very stressed out for seven months until they broke up.

—Bea, senior physical education major

An **attitude** is a positive or negative evaluation of an object, person, group, or idea. Although political scientists, psychologists, and sociologists all study attitudes, they approach the field in different ways. Political scientists often study attitudes by measuring people's evaluations of government policies or politicians. Psychologists tend to focus on the nature and formation of attitudes. Sociologists examine how people's positions in society affect attitude formation, often emphasizing the roles of social class, race, gender, and/or generation in how people develop and maintain attitudes about the world around them (Schuman 1995).

The social psychological study of attitudes focuses on how social forces affect individuals' attitudes and how these attitudes in turn relate to behavior. One of the interesting things that you will learn in this chapter is that people's attitudes are not necessarily linked with parallel behaviors. Bea's experience with her father shows just that. Although attitudes are sometimes correlated with behaviors, the relationship is complex. First, the relationship between attitudes and behavior is often quite weak. Second, general attitudes do not necessarily lead to specific behaviors—you may have a positive attitude about the importance of exercise but find that you never set aside time to work out. Finally, people can change certain attitudes somewhat readily, thus making the relationship between attitudes and behavior difficult to study.

In Chapter 5 we reviewed self-attitude, or sense of self, a main focus of symbolic interactionism. In this chapter, after discussing how attitudes are conceptualized, we will emphasize three areas of study within sociological social psychology. First, we will examine how attitudes are constructed from an interactionist perspective. Second, we will examine how attitudes vary by social location. Finally, we will discuss the group processes perspective on attitudes, particularly related to attitudes toward other people in groups. Specifically, this chapter will address the following questions:

- What is the nature of an attitude? How do researchers study attitudes and behaviors?
- How do people construct attitudes?
- How do attitudes vary across social groups? Do attitudes change over time?
- How do attitudes toward other people form in group contexts?

THE NATURE AND CONSTRUCTION OF ATTITUDES

I never really thought much about weed until I came to college. I had seen all of the advertisements about how bad drugs are, but then my friends kept telling me it was OK. Of course, they were all doing it. I gave it a shot. It wasn't so bad. I guess I would be for legalizing it in more places.

—Darrell, junior economics major

The interactionist perspective views attitudes like any other aspect of social life: they are regularly being constructed based on interactions between people. Direct experience with specific people or objects may have as strong or stronger effects on attitude development than preexisting values and beliefs (Maio et al. 2003). These findings probably reflect the fact that values and beliefs are largely derived from indirect experience, whereas direct exposure to a person or an object provides tangible information from which to form attitudes (see the discussion of the social contact hypothesis in the "Changing Prejudicial Attitudes" section of this chapter).

Darrell's experience with cannabis reflects these research findings: despite all the antidrug campaigns, he tries weed and decides that it is not so bad after all. Of course, his friends have a lot to do with his attitude change, providing arguments in support of the drug. The positive experience he derives from using the drug probably influences his opinion on the matter, too. The goal of this section is to review the basic components of attitudes, the major interactionist perspectives on attitude construction, and the relationship between attitudes and behavior (see Box 9.2 on how people merge new experiences with existing attitudes).

Dimensions of Attitudes

We have defined attitudes as positive or negative evaluations of an object, person, group, or idea. Some attitudes can change quite readily. However, other attitudes are consistent over time and can have strong effects on our behavior. **Values and beliefs** refer to strongly held, relatively stable sets of attitudes. Values may be learned through socialization in families and school, as well as in society at large.

Attitudes are composed of several dimensions. First, there are "thinking" and "feeling" components of attitudes toward any object. The cognitive or "thinking" aspect of an attitude is formally called an **opinion**. This distinction between thinking and feeling is important because people can think about a person or object in one way but then *feel* different about that same object. You may have cognitions or beliefs that gender fluidity is fine, but still feel uneasy among a group of transgender people. Therefore, if you simply ask someone for an opinion, you may not get a true sense of that person's attitude because you will capture only one aspect of it. One way to capture the feeling component of an attitude is with a "feeling thermometer" in which people are asked how hot or cold they feel toward an issue, person, policy, or group of people (see Figure 9.1). In a questionnaire, a respondent may be asked to look at a picture of a thermometer and give a temperature rating of a person or an object. Nevertheless, most public opinion polls focus on cognitions about particular topics.

In addition to having thinking and feeling components, attitudes can be measured in terms of direction and strength:

- Direction—whether attitudes toward an object are negative or positive.
- Strength—the level of positive or negative response to that object.

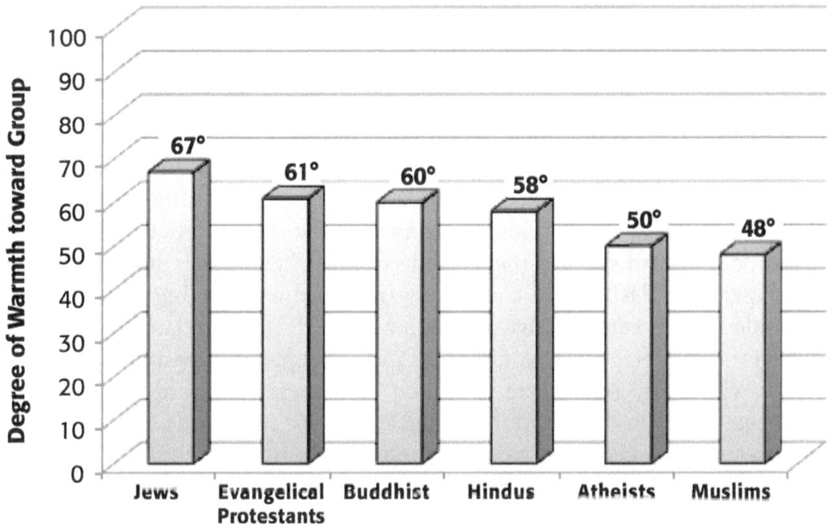

Figure 9.1 Temperature Ratings of Different Religious Groups in the United States based on a "Feeling Thermometer" (Ranging from 0 to 100, 100 Being More Positive).

Source: Pew Research Center 2017.

Current perspectives on attitudes incorporate the idea that there are situations in which attitudes do not exist or in which someone has mixed feelings about an object. So, it is possible to have a **nonattitude** toward an object when you do not care much about it. For instance, you may have no opinion about a political issue because you do not have enough information to form a view. Some research also shows that people will give you an attitude or opinion of an issue even when they have limited or no information about the topic (Converse and Presser 1986; Fletcher and Chalmers 1991; Schuman and Presser 1980). Alternatively, people may have both negative and positive attitudes toward an issue; they may dislike some aspects of the death penalty, for instance, but approve of other aspects of it. Such complexities make it difficult to use opinion polling to precisely define what a person thinks about a topic or an issue. One or two questions on a poll are often not enough to capture the full breadth of a person's attitudes.

Linking Attitudes and Behavior

One of the reasons people study attitudes is to predict their behaviors. How is knowing something about someone's attitude useful in predicting that person's behavior? (See Box 9.1 on the Theory of Planned Behavior in psychology and Box 9.3 on the study of time use.) One of the earliest uses of public opinion surveys was to predict how people would vote. Polls successfully predicted that Franklin Roosevelt would beat Alfred Landon in the 1936 presidential race (Sudman, Bradburn, and Schwarz 1996), and then became increasingly used for predicting election results. However, pollsters failed to predict Harry Truman's victory over Thomas Dewey in 1948, causing many to question the ability to use polling to predict how people will act in the voting booths. Polls in 2016 overwhelmingly, and incorrectly, showed that Hillary Clinton was likely to beat Donald Trump.

One way that researchers try to assess the relationship of attitudes with behaviors is through statistical correlation. A correlation of 0 means that attitudes and behavior are completely unrelated, whereas a correlation of 1 means that attitudes and behavior are perfectly correlated (they vary together perfectly). The relationship between attitudes and behavior is typically small, with an average correlation of about 0.38 (Kraus 1995). Thus, if attitudes toward keeping the workplace "green" through reducing, reusing, and recycling paper and plastic were completely unrelated to recycling behavior, the correlation would be 0. If very positive attitudes were perfectly correlated to very frequent green behaviors, the correlation would be 1. And, if people with positive attitudes about keeping the workplace green were *less* likely to recycle than others, the correlation would be negative. Even if we find that a particular type of attitude is highly correlated with its corresponding behavior, we cannot assume the attitude causes the behavior. It could be that behaving in particular ways shapes people's attitudes. In the recycling example, if people are forced to recycle due to new rules, laws, or shortages, it is possible that their attitudes about recycling will become more favorable.

The weak relationship between attitudes and behavior—and between attitudes and other attitudes—may somewhat reflect poor measurement of attitudes and/or behaviors (Raden 1985; Schuman 1995). Several conditions increase the likelihood that

Box 9.1 Ajzen's Theory of Planned Behavior

A prominent theory linking attitudes and behavior comes from two psychologists, Icek Ajzen and Martin Fishbein. They tried to understand how attitudes interact with people's larger sets of beliefs and social norms in decision-making processes. They proposed that one of the reasons we do not find large correlations between attitudes and behavior is that we must incorporate social norms into our predictive models. In addition, attitudes predict only our intention to act toward an object rather than the actual behavior. For instance, you may dislike someone (attitude) and plan to cause them harm (intention), but that does not necessarily mean that you will actually harm them (behavior).

The model presented here is one of its most recent versions. It includes individuals' attitudes toward a behavior but also includes the idea that people consider the likelihood of their actions having the intended effect (perceived behavioral control) before acting. Using the previous example, the intention to harm someone may be curbed if you believe that you are not capable of producing harm to the other person.

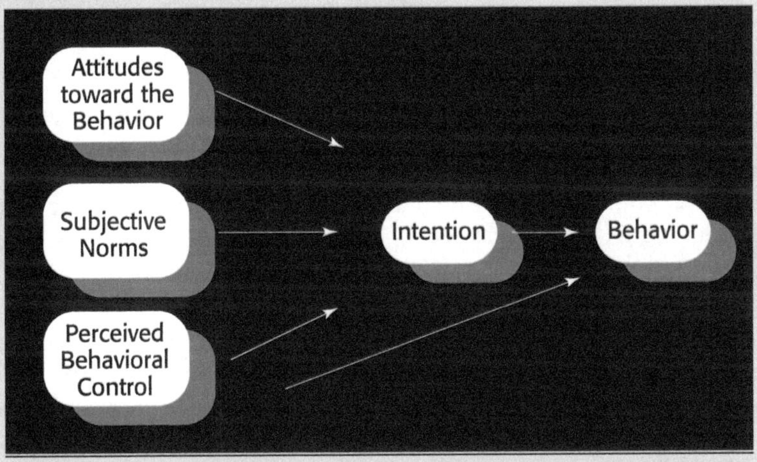

Source: Based on Icek Ajzen's website, www.people.umass.edu/~aizen. See also Ajzen (1991).

The theory of planned behavior (also known as the theory of reasoned action) also incorporates our beliefs about what other people would think about the behavior under the heading "subjective norms." If we believe that other people will support the behavior, we are more likely to act on an attitude than we would if they do not support it. Hence, this model recognizes the importance of social relationships in deciding whether to act on an attitude, helping to explain why some attitudes lead people to act in some cases but not in others.

Box 9.2 The Weighted Average Model in Psychology

The weighted average model assumes that we process information such as attitudes in the same way as adding new numbers to a pool of existing numbers, with new numbers getting averaged into the existing set of numbers. Hence, if you have a negative opinion about someone and learn that they did something nice, you will not immediately develop a favorable opinion of them. Instead, you will average the new positive information with the existing data that say that they are not a good person. Your new image of the person may be less negative but will still be negative overall.

The model does not assume that all information is equally assessed. Some information will have more power over your assessment than other information. We bias information about a person or an object based on the person who is giving us the new information as well as the nature of the data. For instance, you will probably weight information from trustworthy sources, such as family and friends, more than information from strangers or acquaintances. Further, we tend to weight early information (e.g., first impressions) more than subsequent information. This dynamic is called the primacy effect. However, some research shows that a recency effect can also occur when the most recent information is weighted more than other information. The recency effect is particularly likely when much time has passed since the first impression.

The weighted average model incorporates interactionist conceptions of the relationship between agency and interaction—that people take information about the world and process it before making any conclusions. That is, people are not simply empty vessels being manipulated by outside forces, but are active participants in attitudinal processes.

researchers will find relationships between attitudes and behaviors or between attitudes and other attitudes. First, researchers need to be specific about the attitudes and behaviors in question. Asking respondents about abortion generally, for example, will elicit different responses than when asking about abortion in which the life of the mother is at risk. In addition, general attitudes are often called on when people are unaware of the specificities associated with a particular issue. For instance, if you want to ask people their opinions toward building a nuclear power plant in their town, they may have little knowledge of the costs and benefits, leaving them to rely on more general attitudes toward nuclear power to make their decisions. Hence, most people will provide an opinion on a topic when asked, but some people are more informed about the topic than others, making their responses more reliable and consistent over time.

Prejudicial Attitudes

One major application of symbolic interactionism to the study of attitudes and behaviors is in the study of **prejudice**, an attitude of dislike or active hostility toward a

Box 9.3 Jobs in Social Psychology: Attitudes

Social psychologists regularly study people's attitudes, using some of the same techniques reviewed in Chapter 3. While some of this work requires advanced, graduate-level training, you can also become employed as an attitude researcher with an undergraduate degree. As reviewed in this chapter, the study of attitudes is used in work related to diversity, understanding the causes of prejudice and working to end those prejudices. Here are two examples of positions related to attitudes.

1. **Research Assistant (Science & Society)**, Pew Research Center, Washington, DC. Duties: Studies attitudes about the impact of scientific research and innovation on society and how those views tie to behaviors. Responsibilities include fact-checking, proofreading, and background research to support the design and data collection of new research projects, statistical analysis, producing charts and tables, writing and editing research reports. Experience: Bachelor's degree with a concentration in a social science field, experience with MS Word, Excel, and PowerPoint, SPSS or other statistical software.
2. **Diversity Specialist (Training & Education)**, Augusta University, Georgia. Duties: Promotes initiatives and supports departments, students, and leadership bodies that serve the strategic goals of the university including, but not limited to, campus engagement, campus culture and climate, student outreach and support, and diversity planning. Responsible for coordinating student engagement with the division and developing programming and outreach initiatives that respond to student need and cultural support, particularly during moments of student crisis and unrest. Experience: Bachelor's degree from an accredited institution of higher education; three (3) years of related experience. Master's degree preferred.

particular group in society. One of the earliest major writers on American racial prejudice was W. E. B. Du Bois. Du Bois, one of the pioneering figures in the field of sociology, made observations of the prejudice of Whites toward African Americans in both the United States and Europe. In a work originally published in 1920, he wrote,

> *The discovery of whiteness among the world's peoples is a very modern thing—nineteenth and twentieth century matter, indeed. The ancient world would have laughed at such distinction. . . . Today we have changed all that, and the world in a sudden, emotional conversion has discovered that it is white and by that token, wonderful! This assumption that of all hues of God whiteness alone is inherently and obviously better than brownness or tan leads to curious acts. (Du Bois 2003, originally 1920, p. 44)*

Du Bois considered the subtle and not-so-subtle ways that prejudice manifests itself in society, through both words and deeds. In the same article about Whites, he wrote:

> *[W]hite faces . . . I see again and again, often and still more often, a writing of human hatred, a deep and passionate hatred, vast by the vagueness of its expression . . . I have seen a man—an educated gentleman—grow livid with anger because a little, silent, black woman is sitting by herself in a Pullman car. I have seen a great grown man curse a little child, who had wandered into the wrong waiting room. (Du Bois 2003, originally 1920, pp. 46–47)*

Although many Western cultures have changed to some degree since Du Bois's observations, prejudice is still common, and researchers continue to study prejudicial attitudes, examining how and why they develop and how they relate to specific behaviors.

Unconscious Racism

Earlier in this chapter, we distinguished between cognitive and emotional dimensions of attitudes, whereby the cognitive dimension is the individual's opinion. Conscious racism can be measured by asking people if they dislike a particular group or if they believe themselves to be superior to one group or another. Many researchers today are finding unique ways to assess **unconscious racism**, or bias against a group without being aware of it.

Researchers employ unique techniques to study unconscious racism among individuals with tests such as the Implicit Association Test (IAT) (Tetlock and Mitchell 2008). Participants taking the IAT are asked to categorize a series of items that appear on a computer screen. These studies show that people most often pair concepts in ways that link more positive attributes with Whites than with Blacks, leading researchers to believe that they are learned associations. We also know that IAT scores are positively associated with conscious racial beliefs (Dambrun, Villate, and Richetin 2008). However, there is some debate about the veracity of such tests (Quillian 2008). We cannot say, for certain, if a person is racist when they respond to a test in a certain way because we can only infer that they have racist tendencies from the results. In addition, these tests may not be able to predict prejudicial behavior in realistic settings, like on the job (Tetlock and Mitchell 2008). What do you think? Try it out for yourself! You can take implicit association testing online to assess your views of different groups of people at https://implicit.harvard.edu/implicit.

Public opinion polls show that most Americans and Europeans are not consciously racist, or if they are, they don't acknowledge it when asked their attitudes. When asked whether any form of racial inequality is acceptable, they generally respond no. Yet we know that there are continued inequalities in society based on race, and perceptions of racism vary by race. In the United States, for instance, 78 percent of African Americans but only 51 percent of Whites believe that racism is widespread (Jones 2008). Other studies show that racism exists in society, even if people do not consider themselves

Photo 9.1 Prejudicial attitudes are reflected in many ways in society, some more clearly than others. What are some signs of racial prejudice that still exist today?

to be racists. Critics cite the devastating effects of Hurricane Katrina on New Orleans's majority black population in 2005, questioning whether the slow movement of government resources toward victims would have occurred if they were predominately White and middle class (Brunsma, Overfelt, and Picou 2007). National leaders publicly denied any conscious decisions based on the race and class of the victims, who were predominately low-income African Americans. Could unconscious racism have contributed to the slow response to help these victims?

What evidence of unconscious racism exists? First, we will review two classic studies of prejudice that reveal the complex relationship between conscious racism, unconscious racism, and behaviors. We will then examine more contemporary attempts to study unconscious prejudice.

One way to assess prejudicial attitudes is by examining social distance. **Social distance** refers to how close we desire to be to other people. Emory Bogardus (1882–1973) developed an instrument called the Social Distance Scale in the 1920s to assess individuals' senses of social distance to people of particular ethnic and racial groups. The statements included the following activities:

1. Would marry.
2. Would have as close friends.
3. Would have as neighbor.
4. Would have as co-worker.

5. Would have as speaking acquaintances only.
6. Would have as visitors only to my nation.
7. Would bar from my country.

The most positive score for attitudes toward people from a particular group would be a 1 (would marry), and the most negative score would be a 7 (would bar from my country). The average score for each group represents the average social distance people feel toward those groups.

Findings from 40 years of research in the United States through the middle of the twentieth century showed that college and university students felt "closest" to "Canadians," "Americans," and "English" (see Table 9.1) (Owen, Eisner, and McFaul 1981). Groups with the worst scores included Asians and Blacks. The worst scores rarely exceeded 4 (remember that higher scores reflect greater social distance), suggesting that respondents stated that they felt OK with having Asian or Black co-workers or acquaintances but not necessarily neighbors, intimate friends, or family members.

In more recent applications of the scale, Vincent Parrillo and Christopher Donoghue (2005; 2013) found some similarities and differences regarding levels of social distance in a national study of college students conducted in 2001, with an overall score of 1.45 among 30 groups in 2005 and 1.68 in 2011. As with the earlier studies, European Americans received the most positive scores. However, African Americans were in the top five of groups with the lowest social distance in the data collected in 2011. The most negative scores continue to be Arabs and Muslims. Consistent with earlier findings, women appear to be more tolerant than men, and the authors point out that people generally feel closer to people like themselves, who share similar racial and cultural backgrounds.

The Social Distance Scale has been adapted to study racial and ethnic attitudes in places such as Canada (Weinfurt and Moghaddam 2001), the Czech Republic (Rysavy 2003), and Ukraine (Panina 2004). Much of the previously cited works focus on responses of White college students. Seventy percent of Parrillo and Donoghue's (2005) sample, for instance, were White, and only 10 percent were African American. Findings vary depending on the race of the respondents. In a study that included perspectives from African Americans and Latinos in a suburban North Carolina suburb, for instance, Nancy Randall and Spencer Delbridge (2005) found that African Americans expressed a greater social distance than Whites toward Mexicans; the sentiment was reciprocated, as Mexicans showed greater social distance than Whites did toward African Americans. Hence, the nature of the sample can have a large impact on overall sense of social distance toward any single group.

Findings from studies using the Social Distance Scale indicate that most people are open to some racial and ethnic diversity—they certainly report being open to having people from other ethnic backgrounds in their country. However, neighborhoods in the United States and other countries continue to be segregated, and research finds racial

Table 9.1 Research Using the Bogardus Social Distance Scale

	>1926		1946		>1956		>1966		2001*		2011	
Rank	Group	Score	Group	Score	Group	Score	Group	Score	Group	Score	Group	Score
1	English	1.06	Americans	1.04	Americans	1.08	Americans	1.07	Americans	1.07	Americans	1.15
2	Americans	1.10	Canadians	1.11	Canadians	1.16	English	1.14	Italians	1.15	Italians	1.32
3	Canadians	1.13	English	1.13	English	1.23	Canadians	1.15	Canadians	1.20	Canadians	1.35
4	Scots	1.13	Irish	1.24	French	1.47	French	1.36	British	1.23	British	1.36
5	Irish	1.30	Scots	1.26	Irish	1.56	Irish	1.40	Irish	1.23	African Americans	1.42
26	African Americans[1]	3.28	Japanese Am	2.90	Japanese	2.70	Turks	2.48	Indians (India)	1.60	Koreans	1.87
27	Turks	3.30	Koreans	3.05	African Americans[1]	2.74	Koreans	2.51	Haitians	1.63	Indians (India)	1.89
28	Chinese	3.36	Indians, Asia	3.43	Mexicans	2.79	Mexicans	2.56	Vietnamese	1.69	Haitians	1.91
29	Koreans	3.60	African Americans[1]	3.60	Indians, Asia	2.80	African Americans[1]	2.56	Muslims	1.88	Arabs	2.16
30	Indians, Asia	3.91	Japanese	3.61	Koreans	2.83	Indians, Asia	2.62	Arabs	1.94	Muslims	2.23

[1]Updated language to reflect current standards

Sources: Adapted from Owen et al. 1981 and Parillo and Donoghue 2013.

biases are associated with segregation (Sharkey 2008). For instance, one study showed that both the size of an immigrant population and its rate of increase are associated with outmigration of native-born White and African American populations from certain areas (Crowder, Hall, and Tolney 2011). In another study from the early twenty-first century, researchers found that the racial composition of a neighborhood influenced how it was rated. Whites preferred all-White neighborhoods, while African Americans found racially mixed neighborhoods most appealing (Krysan et al. 2009). Thus, what we say about race is not necessarily what we do; we may claim to be open to racial diversity but not act in a way that reflects these sentiments.

An important classic study shows that we do not necessarily act on racist or ethnocentric beliefs either. That is, just because you feel prejudice toward an individual—or people from a particular race, class, or gender—does not mean that you will necessarily act on those attitudes. Richard LaPiere (1934) spent two years traveling extensively with a Chinese couple in the United States, staying at various hotels and eating at local restaurants. His work was being conducted during a time in the United States when racial segregation was still considered acceptable by many people. He wanted to know if people's attitudes toward different races coincided with their treatment of people of those races. To study this relationship, he conducted a survey of racial attitudes from the owners of the establishments he had visited during his travels with the couple as well as some restaurants and hotels he did not visit over that period of time.

LaPiere's (primary survey question was "Will you accept members of the Chinese race as guests in your establishment?" He then compared the survey responses to their actual experiences at those establishments. One hundred and twenty-eight hotels and restaurants that had been visited responded to the survey. Of those that responded, 92% indicated that they would *not* give service to Chinese people. Only one of the respondents said that they would provide service to this group. The rest were undecided. However, their actual experiences differed markedly from the attitudes expressed in the survey. Of the 251 hotel and restaurant visits (both accompanied and unaccompanied by the author), the Chinese couple was refused service at only one hotel. In fact, almost 40% of the responses to the couple were coded as being "very much better than [the] investigator would expect to have received [himself]" (LaPiere 1934, p. 235). A simple summary of his findings can be found in Table 9.2.

LaPiere's (study was one of the first to show that attitudinal research is limited in its ability to predict individuals' behaviors. According to LaPiere, attitudes exist as symbolic representations in the minds of individuals. What individuals do with those symbolic representations is highly dependent on the social conditions surrounding those individuals, especially when confronted with real people and tangible physical conditions.

Unconscious racism appears in everyday interactions as well. Tanya Stivers and Asifa Majid (2007) studied pediatric physicians' interactions with children and their parents. They found that doctors were less likely to ask African American and Latino children questions about their health. It appears that the physicians might have

Table 9.2 Summary of LaPiere's Attitude–Behavior Experiment

	Responses to Survey about Service to Chinese People*	Actual Experience with Service at the Same Hotels and Restaurants
Would not provide service to Chinese patrons, or Undecided	127	1
Would provide service to Chinese patrons	1	250

*Based on responses to the question "Will you accept members of the Chinese race as guests in your establishment?" Only 128 hotels and restaurants visited responded to the survey.
Source: Adapted from LaPiere (1934).

trusted White children to be more competent in responding to their questions. In another study, Devah Pager and Lincoln Quillian (2005) compared employers' self-reports about their willingness to hire Black and White ex-offenders and their actual hiring behavior in a creative field experiment. Although there were no differences in employers' statements about hiring ex-offenders of either race, the study showed that White (pseudo) ex-offender candidates were more likely to actually get callbacks from employers than Black (pseudo) ex-offenders who presented the exact same résumés. The results indicate that employers consciously or unconsciously acted against their stated attitudes.

The role of prejudice encompasses more than interactions between individuals. Norman Denzin (2007) proposed that racism is entrenched in our cultural heritage and in our interpretations of history, among other things. In his historical analysis of the Lewis and Clark expedition (1804–1806) to the West at the request of Thomas Jefferson, he finds the story laden with racism and ethnocentrism. Contemporary historical interpretations of the story focus on the struggles that Lewis and Clark overcame, their positive interactions with Native Americans, and their great discoveries. Denzin points out that slavery and racism were alive and well at the time of the journey, and these men were not immune to these biases as they interacted with Native Americans. Examples of racial prejudice and discrimination toward Native Americans abound. However, he says, we have reconstructed the memory of the journey to fit the norms and standards of our times. From an interactionist perspective, personal and collective memories of interactions or events are reinterpreted to help maintain a positive self-attitude or to match the current standards of our society.

The connection between unconscious racism and conscious choices is not well established. From a symbolic interaction perspective, many situational conditions may intervene between the unconscious mind and social reality—much like LaPiere showed that conscious racism does not always lead to discrimination. In addition to laws limiting discrimination in the workplace, people must manage cultural norms against discrimination in their day-to-day lives. Mica Pollock (2004) conducted an ethnographic study of race interactions in a California high school. She found that people publicly discussed race freely under some conditions and not others. When it was a sensitive issue, race talk occurred only behind the scenes. Kristin Myers (2005) conducted a systematic observation of how people talk about race in their day-to-day lives. She found not only that talk of race was commonly used in everyday life but also that people relied heavily on racial stereotypes in their interactions. In Chapter 5, we reviewed Monica McDermott's (2006) study which showed that race relations vary by context: working-class Whites, she found, were much more likely to express prejudice against African Americans when African Americans were not present. It is clear from these studies that the norms governing racial attitudes and behaviors are highly structured to include people's conscious and unconscious biases, situational dynamics, information from the larger culture (e.g., stereotypes), and sets of norms governing the appropriate contexts to share thoughts regarding race.

In the book *White Fragility*, Robin Diangelo (2018) argues that racism is a system in which a society's racial prejudice is supported by legal authority. Under this framework, individuals' biases became reified into a system of inequality that includes laws and everyday practices that ultimately lead to the same outcomes. Racial groups live and interact separately from each other, and anti-Black and institutional racism means Whites on average do better in the economy. **Institutional Racism** is a form of structural racism in which racialized minority groups are not provided the same services or opportunities as majority groups. Under this framework, simply changing attitudes about race will not fix issues of inequality. This is one way in which a society can have "racism without racists"—people who see themselves as egalitarian, regardless of political ideology, yet racist differences still exist (Bonilla-Silva 2022). This disjuncture between individuals' beliefs about themselves and the systems in which they are living can cause individuals to be defensive and feel a sense of guilt when topics of race come up. It also allows individuals to let systems of inequality continue because individuals believe that they are not complicit with it.

Subtle Sexism

As with race, prejudice against women can be conscious or unconscious. Few people admit to being consciously sexist or prejudiced against women. However, researchers observe **subtle sexism**, or unequal treatment of women that goes unnoticed by the person engaging in it (Swim and Cohen 1997). Manifestations of subtle sexism abound. Martha Foschi and her colleagues (Foschi et al. 1994) conducted an experiment in which 85 college students in Canada were asked to review job applications of men and women applying for an engineering position. When men had better records, study participants chose them for the job and gave them higher competency ratings more often compared with women when their records were better. These differences held true only for the male study participants; gender of the applicant did not on average affect female participants' assessments. Recent studies also show that women experience discrimination in "male jobs," such as electricians, when identical information about backgrounds is provided. In one study in Australia, researchers conducted a large-scale experiment with created job applications submitted with men's names versus women's with otherwise identical applications (Adamovic and Leibbrandt 2023). Applications that had men's names received more callbacks than those with women's names in male-dominated occupations, whereas men received fewer callbacks from actual recruiters within occupations that were women-dominated, such as caterer or receptionist (notably lower paying positions). The gender of the CEO or the recruiter did not seem to make a difference, showing the large-scale gendered stereotypes that are entrenched and may influence who is deemed appropriate for particular jobs.

There are other ways to assess subtle sexism in everyday life. Using masculine pronouns in different texts may be considered a male-biased element of Western culture whereby texts tend to utilize "he" in reference to characters in passage rather than "she" or "he or she" (Madson and Shoda 2006). You will notice in this book that we use female pronouns frequently throughout the text in part to call attention to the pervasiveness of "he"-ness, and to counter gender bias in books. Sexist cultural beliefs can also affect men's and women's career aspirations. In one study, Shelley Correll (2004) informed undergraduate students that men were better at a particular task and then asked them to complete that task. She found that the men in the experiment assessed their abilities higher than the women even though their scores were the same. Further, men also reported higher aspirations to do jobs related to that task. How might this study apply to the "real world"? Perhaps men and women come to believe that they are better or worse at particular professions because of subtle gender beliefs in the culture that disadvantage women. As a result, women may self-select out of good jobs when they have the same skills. In this case, they may not truly believe that they are less competent, but they are utilizing cultural stereotypes, not objective facts regarding their abilities, in making their assessments.

Theory of Group Position

How does prejudice form? Herbert Blumer (1958) proposed that prejudice is largely a group phenomenon rather than an individual attribute because it defines a group characteristic: one's race. According to the **theory of group position**, prejudicial attitudes reflect and are formed to maintain a group's relative position in society. Specifically, among the dominant group, themes of group superiority (toward one's own group) and inferiority (toward the minority group) help to sustain one's higher status in society. These two factors influence the development of the feeling of entitlement among dominant groups, in which they believe that they deserve their positions and fear the lower-status group.

Although Blumer's work was focused on African American and White relationships in the United States, it can also be applied to other ethnic groups and in other places (Williams and Correa 2003). Race serves as a source of identity relevant to other groups in societies who compete for limited resources. Greater competition among groups increases hostility among them as each vies for relative position (Bobo and Hutchings 1996). Prejudicial attitudes are linked to groups that are seen as a threat to the economic and cultural interests of another group, potentially leading to the development of negative attitudes toward those groups (Perry 2007). For example, residents of a small town may develop negative attitudes toward new immigrants because they are seen as taking away jobs from people already living in the community. This is often despite evidence that immigration has contributed to American economic growth (Lazear and Marron 2007).

Changing Prejudicial Attitudes

Regardless of how prejudice is produced, how do we fix the problem? One of the most cited theories about improving relationships between groups is the social contact hypothesis. Gordon Allport (1897–1967) proposed that groups can be taught to have better attitudes toward each other but only under specific conditions. Simply putting them together in a room will not do it. First, the members of each group must have equal status, such as similar age or educational level, whatever is relevant for the groups involved. Second, they must have some kind of shared goal to complete together, something that they can accomplish as a team. Third, there must be interaction among group members. Finally, there must be some outside authority supporting and guiding the process.

Sociological research generally supports the contact hypothesis if most or all of these factors are in place (e.g., Burke et al. 2017; Caspi 1984; Lee, Farrell, and Link 2004; Sigelman and Welch 1993; Tropp, Okamoto, Marrow, and Jones-Correa 2018; Verkuyten, Thijs, and Bekhuis 2010). Research has been done in the context of university campus contacts, showing that beliefs about meritocracy and racial inequality change through interaction with different-race dorm roommates (Mijs 2023). In an international example, a study of immigration in Germany by Urlich Wagner and colleagues (Wagner et al. 2020) examined the prevalence of hate crimes in 402 districts based on the proportion of foreigners and refugees in the district, controlling for economic and other factors. The researchers found that, "even after controlling for all possible confounds, a larger proportion of foreigners in a district was associated with a lower prevalence of hate crimes" (200). They did not find that the proportion of refugees had any effect, probably because they had not been in the districts long enough to create significant contact opportunities. Similarly, Christopher Ellison and collaborators (Ellison, Shin, and Leal 2011) found that having close contact with Latinos was associated with Whites having more favorable or empathetic attitudes toward Latinos. Those Whites with closer Latino ties had less restrictive views about immigration than did others.

There is one important element that is often missing from the contact hypothesis: the presence of an outside authority to ensure that the social processes lead to positive outcomes. In many peace negotiations among nations, for instance, a third nation may represent that authority. In everyday life, Kouri (2003) proposes that pro-diversity social norms and cultural values may serve a similar function in breaking down barriers between different ethnic and racial groups. People's dispositions, prior prejudices, can affect whether they even engage in intergroup friendships (Stark 2015). Content and context of interactions may also be important. Henriette Esholdt (2019), for instance, studied the positive role that ethnic humor played in diffusing tensions among majority Danes and minority immigrants in everyday work settings.

There is no guarantee that frequency of contact will lead to positive outcomes, even under the best of conditions (Hein and Moore 2009). In a study of Muslims and Christians in Indonesia, Agnieszka Kanas and colleagues (Agnieszka, Scheepers, and Sterkens 2015) found that perceived *quality* of contacts was more important to attitudes toward the outgroup than *quantity* of contacts. In another study, researchers showed that imagining intergroup contact prior to the actual contact promoted favorable intergroup attitudes (Choma, Charlesford, and Hodson 2014). Hence, organizations and institutions can produce beneficial outcomes by developing policies and programs that encourage positive interactions among people of diverse backgrounds.

Prosocial Attitudes and Behaviors

Reading many textbooks in sociology and psychology (including this one), an outside observer might start thinking that humans harbor mainly negative attitudes (e.g., prejudice) and behaviors (e.g., criminal acts). A number of psychologists and sociologists are also dedicated to the study of positive attitudes and behaviors, often under the heading of prosocial behavior and/or altruism. **Prosocial behavior** includes any behavior that benefits another person, while **altruism** refers to prosocial behavior that is motivated by concern for the other person. Traditional research on prosocial behavior shows that it starts when children are able to take the role of the other and develop some level of moral reasoning. Having a positive mood and living in a rural area have consistently been associated with greater prosocial behavior (Eisenberg 1991). In one study, Brent Simpson and Robb Willer (2008) extended a typical social exchange theory approach to studying prosocial behavior. Will people help others when it is at a cost to themselves? If so, it breaks the basic exchange principle of reciprocity—people expect about as much in a social relationship as they give to it. People may expect a generalized exchange or indirect reciprocity, that they will receive benefits for helping over time (see Chapter 4 for a review of exchange theory). In their experiment, Simpson and Willer found that "egoists" (people who seek immediate acknowledgment when doing prosocial behavior) tended to act prosocially only in public, where their acts would be noticed, while "altruists" acted prosocially both in public situations and in private ones in which they could not receive credit for their positive behaviors.

Are there other ways to address prejudicial attitudes in society without having to create situations in which different groups interact with one another? A common way for Western, industrialized countries to address this issue in the workplace is through diversity training. Typically, these types of training are in classroom-like settings where participants learn about the genesis of prejudice and the ways that it may manifest at work. Are programs like these effective? In a meta-analysis of 260 studies from 234 research articles, Katerina Bezrukova and colleagues (Bezrukova et al. 2016) (see also, Dobbin and Kalev 2016) looked at the role of diversity training programs on participants' attitudes and cognitive learning. Their analysis of multiple studies showed that, as a whole, diversity training did produce positive impacts on attitudes. Longer training did better than shorter training, perhaps because it permits more contact among participants, reflecting elements of the contact hypothesis

Section Summary

This section addressed the questions "What is the nature of an attitude?" "How do researchers study attitudes and behaviors?" and "How do people construct attitudes?"

Here, we reviewed the cognitive and emotional dimensions of attitudes. Specifically, we analyzed the development of prejudicial attitudes and behavior, assessing the role of group position in developing negative attitudes toward minority groups. We also examined how prejudicial attitudes do not always lead to prejudicial behaviors and the role of unconscious prejudices in our lives. Finally, changing prejudicial attitudes may require work at every level of society to be effective.

A Take-Away Message

Attitudes are complex. They include multiple dimensions. So, if you want to figure out the minds of the people around you, you are going to have to consider those dimensions. Consider the fact that we may not be aware of our own prejudices in everyday life. We focused on the issues of racial and gender prejudice in this section of the chapter, but we can apply the same logic to other types of prejudices that we carry, such as toward people who are of different religions than we are, or those across a variety of queer identities. Perhaps we can take a lesson from the contact hypothesis and make extra efforts to spend time with people who are different from us. This logic is especially appropriate in the workplace, where we are directed toward a group goal—to get the job done! By working with people from different backgrounds to complete our work, we can create a sense of unity while peeling away the conscious and unconscious biases that we have accumulated over time.

SOCIAL STRUCTURE, ATTITUDES, AND BEHAVIOR

> *I really don't think I have "values" per se. I take things as they come. I guess you could say that I am a "renaissance" man in that I am well educated and base my decisions on what is rational. I see my religious friends making bad decisions based on a bunch of unfounded beliefs and values that they memorize from their parents and churches or temples. I am beyond all of that. . . . Maybe that is why I am a science major.*
>
> —Mike, junior biology major

Most of us think that we develop our attitudes and values using rational decision-making processes. Mike certainly believes that this is the case. He thinks that he is "above" religious and family influences on his decision-making processes, relying more on rationality than systems of beliefs represented in religious doctrines. However, his decisions may actually be based on North American cultural views of rationality and science. He probably spends a lot of time with groups that espouse his values. Although he does not filter ideas through a religious doctrine, he may be filtering them through a science-based paradigm popular in Western cultures. Like many of us, Mike may not be aware of the norms and values that govern his decision-making processes. In this section, we will review structural conditions that influence attitudes, including the roles of agents of socialization and social positions based on race, gender, and age.

Attitudes and Agents of Socialization

From a structural point of view, individuals rely on their primary agents of socialization (e.g., family, school, and peers) for initial sets of values and beliefs that govern attitude processes. Life experiences allow people to form new attitudes using information gained from direct experience. If your parents are prejudiced in some way, your direct experience with different groups may alter the socialization you receive from your parents. Thus, we are neither exact repositories of attitudes learned from our friends or families, nor do we simply take on new attitudes without considering past experiences. Rather, early socialization experiences serve as an anchor for the development of new attitudes over time that incorporate new perspectives into old ones (see Box 9.2 on the weighted average model). Thus, the values and attitudes of our parents have strong but not absolute influences on our values and attitudes later in life. Figure 9.2 demonstrates that there is a 70% overlap between teens' political ideologies (conservative, liberal, or moderate) and their parents' ideologies. But there is not a perfect correspondence between our beliefs and those of our parents, indicating that attitudinal change is somewhat common across the life course.

Box 9.4 Studying Behavior: How People Use Their Time

In some ways, our behaviors can reflect our attitudes: perhaps we take part in a clean-up of a local waterway or attend a rally because we care about climate change. If we are passionate about animal rights, we will take the time to sign an online petition linked to protecting animals. However, we also know that attitudes do not necessarily correlate highly with behavior. **Time use research** is conducted to determine exactly what people do on a day-to-day basis. In part, time is heavily structured based on social statuses, such as being a parent or a student, and characteristics such as age and gender. But also, particularly if we examine leisure or housework, studying the time use of a population is a way to really know what people value, regardless of what they say. Do people value physical activity? One way to tell is if time in exercising or walking or riding bikes trends upward, for example. Still sociologists would want to ask questions such as what social factors (say of urban environments—walkability and bike paths for example) encourage more time in one activity versus another.

Time use researchers examine productive and free time, as well as personal care time. Productive time refers to paid work, housework and child care, and traveling associated with productive work (i.e., commuting to work). Free time refers to leisure activities such as reading, sports, watching television, using social media, and other activities that we do for our own pleasure. Researchers have tried to assess individuals' use of time by asking them how much time they spend in various activities each day or week, either with the use of surveys or with time diaries. The diary method has people indicate what they did and how much time

(continued)

they spent doing each activity in sequence, typically beginning in the early morning and continuing over a 24-hour period.

John Robinson and Geoffrey Godbey's (1997) study of time illuminates how Americans use their time and compares these findings with other countries. Their research shows that the average American spends over 120 hours a week on productive activities, including work, family care, and personal care (including sleep). The rest of their time is "free time"—time spent on activities such as watching television or socializing, two of the most popular uses of free time (see Table 9.3 below for a current review of how Americans use their time). Across different countries, researchers can measure gender equity, work time, commutes, and more, and can see trends over the decades in how time is used. Twenge and colleagues (Twenge et al. 2019) propose that teenagers are more prone to loneliness because they have less in-person time with friends than youth of prior generations, despite a decline in paid work and stability in homework and extracurricular time.

Table 9.3 Average Hours Per Day Spent in Selected Activities

Activity	Total Hours per Week
Personal care, including sleep	9.84
Eating and drinking	1.20
Household activities	1.92
Purchasing goods and services	0.66
Caring for and helping household members	0.50
Caring for and helping nonhousehold members	0.17
Working and work-related activities	3.56
Educational activities	0.39
Organizational, civic, and religious activities	0.24
Leisure and sports	5.15
Telephone calls, mail, and email	0.16
Other activities, not elsewhere classified	0.21

Source: United States Bureau of Statistics, 2023.

Families transmit attitudes in at least two ways. First, families generally produce children with a similar social status to themselves. For example, middle-class families reproduce their class status because their children also typically end up middle class through a variety of mechanisms. Because status is associated with attitude similarity, the children will be like their parents through ending up in similar social positions. Second, families socialize or teach their children their values and beliefs (Glass, Bengsten, and Dunham 1986), either explicitly or more subtly. Some parents impart their values more effectively than others. In one longitudinal study of parents and children,

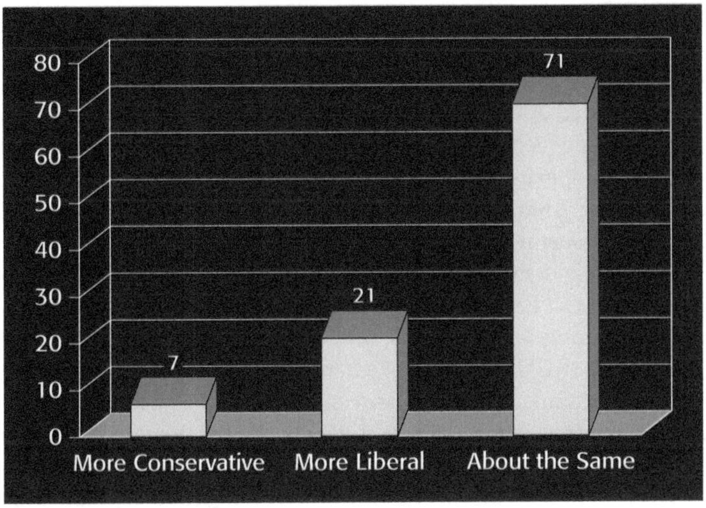

Figure 9.2 Passing on Values and Attitudes. Based on the questions: "Thinking about social and political issues, how do your views compare to those of your parents? Are your views more conservative, more liberal, or about the same?"

Source: Adapted from Lyons (2005).

researchers found that parent–adolescent attitudes were most similar in families in which adolescents were involved in decision making and had warm relationships with their parents (Brody, Moore, and Glei 1994). Hence, attitude similarity remained strongest among warm, loving families.

Families transmit not only attitudes but also behaviors. In a study of student activism during the Persian Gulf War, Duncan and Stewart (1995) found that students' reports of their parents' activities during the Vietnam War were strongly related to their children's activist behaviors during the Persian Gulf War. They also found that parents' behavior indirectly affected students' activism through the development of attitudes toward war, ultimately affecting the likelihood of activism more generally.

Social Status, Identity, and Attitudes

Gendered Attitudes

Few pollsters would conduct a survey or poll without including a series of questions about socioeconomic characteristics of respondents, such as age, race and ethnicity, education level, income, and gender. Social structure and personality researchers are also interested in whether social statuses affect attitudes. And they do. For instance, about 36% of Americans identify themselves as "very conservative" or "conservative," 24% say they are "liberal" or "very liberal," and 37% say they are "moderate" on social issues (Saad 2022). Therefore, on average, Americans' political attitudes can be defined as moderate to conservative. However, these values vary by region and social location.

For instance, in the United States, people living on the West Coast or in the Northeast are more likely to lean toward more liberal (Jones 2009). Married people tend to be more conservative than singles, and young adults tend to be more liberal than older adults (Jones 2003; Saad 2009).

The relationship between gender and attitudes depends on the topic. Women, for instance, were less supportive of invading Iraq with US ground troops than were men (Moore 2002). Similarly, Smith (1984) found women to be less supportive of the use of force or violence in an array of law enforcement situations. When it comes to politics, majorities of women and men believe that women can perform as well as men, but women are much more likely to believe that women would work better under pressure, be better at making compromises, and create a more respectful tone in politics (Horowitz and Goddard 2023). However, there are not a lot of differences in men's and women's attitudes on some topics (Hughes and Tuch 2003). Therefore, gender may be more relevant for understanding some attitudes than others.

What might explain differences in men's and women's attitudes toward some issues and not others? Psychotherapist John Gray (1992) wrote a popular book years ago about marital communication titled *Men Are from Mars, Women Are from Venus*. This book, which is still selling many copies decades later, encapsulated a psychological perspective that men and women are genetically different from one another, leading them to different thinking processes. Under this schema, women are inherently disposed toward things like empathy and caring, which helps explain why women are less supportive of the death penalty than men, for example, whereas men are oriented toward an ethic of justice. Critics of this perspective note that men and women are socialized toward these gender roles (see Gilligan 1982). More importantly, sex category, masculinity and femininity, and gender are different concepts (see Chapter 4). In a study of attitudes toward volunteer behavior, researchers found that those who scored higher in femininity reported higher scores on a measure of caring than those people ranked higher in masculinity, regardless of gender (Karniol, Grosz, and Schoor 2003). Findings such as these may help to explain differences in attitudes as they relate to cultural beliefs about men's and women's role expectations in society—differences in attitudes among men and women may reflect the cultural expectations of the roles associated with their sex categories.

Race, Ethnicity, and Attitudes

Racial or ethnic statuses also influence attitudes. Polls and studies regularly show that African Americans and Whites disagree on average on many social issues. For example, African Americans tend to be more supportive of public policies related to civil rights (Wolf 1998), including some civil liberties related to gay rights (Lewis 2003; Wolf 1998), affirmative action policies (Bobo 1998), and are also less likely to support the death penalty than Whites (Unnever and Cullen 2007). Matthew Hunt (2007) studied data from the General Social Survey (see Chapter 3) collected between 1977 and 2004. Overall, he found a decline in the support of the purely racist belief that the disadvantaged social positions of African Americans are due to innate inferiority. He also found that Whites were most likely to attribute inequality between groups to a lack of motivation or willpower (50%) and lack of chance for education (43%). Among African Americans, 61% attributed inequalities to discrimination, with only 41% of Latinos and 31% of Whites agreeing. Finally, Hunt concludes that there has been a growing similarity in beliefs about discrimination among all racial groups, as African Americans and Latinos in 2004 were less likely to endorse a discrimination-based explanation than in the past.

These differences in values and beliefs among racial groups may reflect structural positions of African Americans in US society who share a history of discrimination and lack of entitlements (Wolf 1998) or may reflect different cultural identities and beliefs, an issue that will be addressed in more detail under the rubric of social identity theory later in this chapter. In any case, race and ethnic status continue to predict differences in many social values.

The Social and Media Context of Attitudes

Because individuals have multiple statuses, understanding attitudes requires examining people's multiple characteristics and social contexts. For instance, both men and Whites in the United States have generally supported the use of the death penalty more than women and African Americans (Carroll 2004). More recent research shows that Asians and Whites have a closer view of the death penalty than African Americans and Hispanics (Pew Research Center 2021, see Figure 9.3). While the internet has given people access to a world of information, most of that information must be mediated in one way or another. Hence, we form our opinions, in part, based on how those media sources

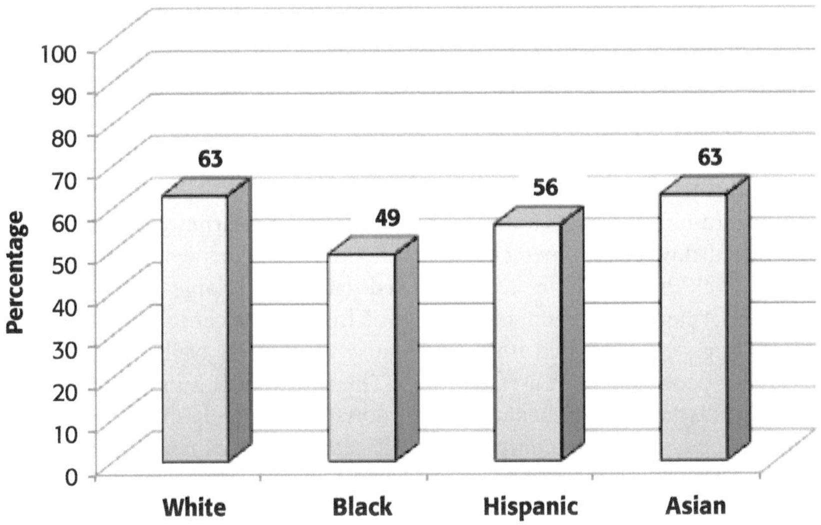

Figure 9.3 Percentage Favoring the Death Penalty by Race. Based on the question: "Are you in favor of the death penalty for a person convicted of murder?"

Source: Pew Research Center 2021.

convey it to us in what David Altheide (2016) calls the "Media Syndrome." Much like Marshall McLuhan's (2005, originally 1967) work about media reviewed in Chapter 2, Altheide goes on to provide 12 case studies of the ways that popular opinions of events such as the First Persian Gulf War were influenced by media representations. In some sense, you could say that our personal attitudes are the sum total of our social roles, groups, and the media that we consume.

Do some of our roles and group memberships have bigger effects on our attitude formation than others? One way to study these relationships is to examine multiple affiliations at the same time. In a study of support for the Iraq War, for instance, David Rohall and his colleagues (Rohall et al. 2006) found that military academy and Reserve Officers Training Corps students were significantly more supportive of the war than civilian students. Traditionally, these differences have been explained by arguing that military personnel are socialized to be more accepting of war than their civilian counterparts, creating a culture of war. However, almost half of the effects of military affiliation on attitudes toward war were explained by the disproportionate number of males who were in the military—men (both military and civilian) are generally more supportive of this war than women. In this case, gender had a greater effect on attitudes toward war than did military affiliation.

The relationship between group affiliations and attitudes becomes even more complex when we consider the context of community. In one study, Scott Schieman and Leonard Pearlin (2006) studied effects of community-level disadvantage, measured using census indicators such as the number of households below the poverty line and individuals receiving public assistance, as well as subjective perceptions of neighborhood problems, and the degree to which older adult respondents believed their neighborhoods to be noisy and run down. People living in poor neighborhoods (measured by census conditions) believed their neighborhoods were more disordered. But Schieman and Pearlin also found that this relationship was strongest among people who feel relatively advantaged, people who themselves believed that they were better off financially than their neighbors. Here, we see how personal biography intersects with neighborhood conditions to affect perceptions.

In another study, researchers found that perceptions of discrimination among African Americans went down as the percentage of African Americans went up in a neighborhood (Hunt et al. 2007). The researchers used data from a large-scale survey of over 40,000 African American women, measuring the frequency of both lifetime experiences with racism (e.g., being treated unfairly because of race) as well as everyday racism (e.g., receiving poor service in a restaurant). The researchers found that respondents' perceptions of discriminatory behavior went down in relatively mixed neighborhoods and neighborhoods primarily composed of African Americans relative to those neighborhoods in which African Americans were a minority.

Sociological Model of Attitudes and Identity

Earlier in this chapter, we defined values as strongly held, relatively stable sets of attitudes. Jan Stets and Michael Carter (2012) proposed that individuals can incorporate values into their identities, which help to explain how people develop attitudes and behaviors in different situations (see, in contrast, Box 9.5 on psychological perspectives on attitudes). Utilizing principles from identity theory (see Chapter 5), they showed that when individuals value something strongly, they are more likely to act on those

Box 9.5 Balance and Cognitive Dissonance Theories

Psychologists have long been interested in how individuals process information. Attitudes are not developed or changed without using existing cognitive resources to interpret new information. This information may come from interactions with other people or through reading, using social media, or being exposed to material on television or the Internet. How do people manage so many different sources of information? How does this knowledge affect how we act?

Fritz Heider (1896–1988), a psychologist, developed balance theory to explain how individuals manage opinions with the people around them. The basic model consists of three parts: (1) the person, (2) another person, and (3) an attitude object.

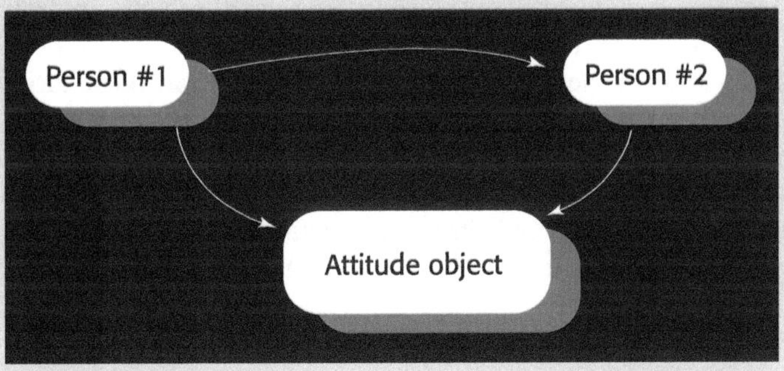

To achieve balance, the attitude of person #1 toward the attitude object must be in sync with her attitude toward the other person and that person's attitude toward the object. A hypothetical example can be assessed—let's say that you are pro-choice and your friend is pro-life. This is considered an imbalanced state because you have a positive relationship with your friend. Ways to resolve this situation include changing your opinion toward abortion, changing your friend's opinion of abortion, or no longer being friends with the person.

Cognitive dissonance theory was developed by Leon Festinger (1919–1989) in the 1950s. The theory extends balance theory by incorporating individuals' behaviors into their attitude processes. Festinger argued that individuals must assess their attitudes relative to their behaviors. If we act in a way that conflicts with

(continued)

our beliefs, this disjunction produces a sense of dissonance, or psychological tension. We can reduce this dissonance by changing our beliefs about the behavior or by changing our behavior. For example, you might consider yourself easygoing and believe this to be a good quality, but find yourself blowing up over what you realize, on reflection, were minor incidents. You would probably feel dissonance over these events. According to cognitive dissonance theory, you would likely reduce the dissonance by either changing your attitudes (deciding you are indeed a little bit reactive) or changing your behavior (blowing up less often).

values. Further, if people define themselves as moral and act immorally in a situation, they were more likely to feel a sense of shame and guilt than if they do not define themselves as moral. Hence, while situational factors may affect how we think and behave, our identities help us make decisions in complex situations involving different attitudinal and behavioral choices; we are motivated to keep our attitudes and behaviors aligned to our values.

In one application of this model, researchers measured participants' "environmental identity," or how they view themselves in relationship to the environment and to environmental attitudes and behavior (Stets and Biga 2003). Many people may have positive attitudes toward the environment but do not act on those attitudes. The researchers found that having a strong environmental identity—one in which people view themselves as someone passionate or very concerned about the natural environment—was associated with reporting pro-environmental behavior such as contributing money to or volunteering for environmental organizations. Moreover, environmental identity was more important than environmental attitudes in predicting environmental behaviors.

Attitudes across the Life Course

Symbolic interactionists show that attitudes can change over time as people interact with different people and that the expression of behaviors related to attitudes is tied to current social contexts. We also know that whole groups of people change over time as they are exposed to similar life events. Large-scale events such as wars, pandemics, social movements, and assassinations provide similar identity-forming contexts among people who experience them at the same time. For instance, we reviewed Glen Elder's study of children of the Great Depression in Chapter 6. This event had long-term effects on some of the children growing up at that time. The amalgamation of such events for a particular group who are exposed to them creates a unique cohort of people. Generational changes due to exposure to unique life events may also account for change in societal values and beliefs over time. If newer cohorts are more liberal, for instance, they make the average American (or Canadian, or whatever group is being examined) more liberal when they replace the earlier, more conservative cohorts. Social structure and personality researchers study cohort replacement by comparing attitudes toward social issues based on the birth cohort, or generation, to which people belong.

Attitude Stability and Change

Americans' attitudes toward social issues have changed in several ways over the years. Duane Alwin (2002, p. 43) cited examples like the fact that 39 percent of Americans said that there should be a law against interracial marriage in 1972 compared to just 12 percent in 2000. Similarly, 48 percent of Americans believed sex before marriage was wrong (Alwin 2002); in 2022 the number was 28 percent (Statistica 2023).

Historical experiences such as the Great Depression, the Great Recession of 2008, or the 2020 global COVID-19 pandemic can affect some groups of people, whereas other groups are left relatively unaffected, as discussed in Chapter 6. Thus, many of the social changes that have occurred in different countries occur unevenly across social groups.

Cohort Differences

In Chapter 6, we examined the effects of generational differences in exposure to life events on our senses of self. According to the interactionist perspective, generations should develop different attitudes based on their different social interactions and experiences over time. More recent cohorts, for example, tend to be ideologically more liberal in terms of their political affiliation than earlier generations (Carlson 2003). However, this study and many others like it simply compare cross-sectional data in which individuals are grouped by age and differences are assumed to be caused by generational factors. This distinction is important because people generally become more conservative as they age; thus, differences in attitudes may be more reflective of the age of respondents than of their generation (Alwin 2002). An excellent way to assess generational change is to compare attitudinal questions by the same age group at different time periods (e.g., 20-year-olds in 2024 compared to 20-year-olds in 1994).

One area of generational research is the study of continuity and change associated with attitudes toward sex and sexual relations. Americans have generally become more liberal in their attitudes toward gender and sexual behavior since the 1970s (Bolzendahl and Myers 2004; Harding and Jencks 2003; Smith 1992). However, many of these changes occurred in the 1960s and the 1980s, showing some leveling off in the 1990s (Hardings and Jencks 2003). Therefore, attitudes vary by generation, but these changes may not be linear or consistent over time. The youngest generation, those 18–29 in 2022, were much more likely than older adults to say that people have not gone far enough in accepting people who are transgender (Parker, Horowitz, and Brown 2022). The Pew Research Center website is an excellent one to bookmark to see trends in all kinds of attitudes of those living in the United States.

Section Summary

This section applied the social structure and personality perspective to answer the questions "How do attitudes vary across social groups?" and "How do attitudes change over time?" We examined how attitudes, values, and beliefs are often passed on from parents to children. We also see that attitudes vary based on group affiliation, with men and women and different racial/ethnic and age groups varying in their beliefs about social issues. Finally, we applied the life course paradigm to understand the ways that attitudes change across generations.

A Take-Away Message

Poll findings are regularly cited in the news. Political observers use polls to show support for policies or their perspectives on a matter. The material reviewed in this section shows that you can make assessments of people's attitudes toward different issues, but it should also be clear that attitudes and attitude change are quite complex. Having this complexity will make you a better consumer of poll information in the media, recognizing that you cannot rely on a single poll or responses to a few questions to fully understand what people really think and feel about an issue. You may also consider that polling is an industry and you can make a career by collecting data on people's opinions! Political groups, marketing firms, and other organizations regularly rely on polls to make decisions. If you have some interest in these matters, you may want to consider taking more classes on attitudes and survey research methods.

GROUP PROCESSES AND ATTITUDES

> *Let's face it, some people have it, some people don't. People either follow you or they don't. Leaders are born, not made.*
>
> —Frank, sophomore English major

The interactionist and social structure and personality perspectives on attitudes place attitude formation and development in the context of statuses and interactions among individuals. Researchers in the group processes perspective continue this line of reasoning by examining how group processes shape attitude formation. Frank clearly believes people are born to be liked or to lead other people. Group processes work shows that interactions in groups affect attitudes toward people inside and outside of the group.

Status Construction Theory

Earlier in this chapter, we introduced the social contact hypothesis. Ridgeway and Balkwell (1997; also see Berger, Ridgeway, and Zelditch 2002) combined elements of the social contact hypothesis and the group processes perspective in the development of status construction theory. The theory is concerned with how attributes that differentiate people in society come to form the basis of status distinctions between groups.

Status construction theory is concerned with how status beliefs form. We have noted that multiple attributes act as status markers in our society, including gender, education, occupation, and race. But how did these attributes come to act as status characteristics? Status construction theory proposes that the ways in which people in different categories on some social difference (e.g., women and men) interact can cause shared status beliefs to form and become widespread in a population. According to the theory, if members of different social groups interact in ways that advantage one group over another—such as one group having more resources than the other—then people will begin to develop beliefs linking higher status to persons advantaged by the interactions. If people repeatedly see these differences in multiple contexts, then the perceived status differences, according to the theory, will become culturally held status beliefs. Additionally, the theory proposes that people will internalize these beliefs and spread them in future interactions. Consider the case of gender: According to the theory, as long as men and women continue to repeatedly interact in settings that tend to favor men (men, for example, are significantly more likely than women to hold top leadership positions in organizations), status beliefs that advantage men over women will continue.

In one experiment, Ridgeway and her colleagues (Ridgeway et al. 1998) had students team up in groups of two, each with a confederate (individuals who participants believed were fellow research subjects but were in fact part of the research team). The researchers studied interaction between two sets of groups: those deemed to have more resources (high-resource group) and those with fewer resources (low-resource group). They also assessed participants' attitudes toward other group members after a series of activities. Research dating to the 1930s has shown that individuals have positive biases toward their own groups and negative biases against people in other groups (see Box 9.6). However, Ridgeway and colleagues found that individuals in both

Box 9.6 The Robbers Cave Experiment in Psychology

In a classic psychological study conducted in the 1950s, Muzafer Sherif and his colleagues (Sherif, 1988, originally 1954) conducted a field experiment with 22 White 11-year-old boys, none of whom knew each other prior to the experiment. The boys were sent to a remote summer camp in Oklahoma at Robbers Cave State Park. The boys were randomly assigned to one of two groups: the Eagles or the Rattlers. Sherif had the groups participate in a series of competitions over a four-day period. He found that prejudicial attitudes started to develop as the competitions continued. These prejudices continued despite the introduction of meetings designed to ease tensions between the groups. It was only when the groups had a "superordinate" goal, a problem that required the groups to work together, that the groups dropped some of their negative attitudes toward one another—supporting Allport's social contact hypothesis reviewed earlier in this chapter.

This study shows the power that groups have in constructing opinions about other people. In particular, we make distinctions between "in-groups" and "out-groups"—people we identify with versus those we do not (see the discussion of social identity theory in Chapter 5). Sherif easily manipulated the boys' attitudes toward members of the outside group by creating tension and conflict between the groups through competition.

Cecilia Ridgeway*

Cecilia L. Ridgeway is the Lucie Stern Professor of Social Sciences in the Sociology Department at Stanford University. She also spent 13 years as a professor at the University of Wisconsin–Milwaukee, and six years at the University of Iowa. She is the former chair of the Stanford Sociology Department as well as the former editor of *Social Psychology Quarterly* (2001–2003). Ridgeway is past president of the Pacific Sociological Association, and she received the Cooley-Mead Award for lifetime achievements in social psychology in 2005 and the Jesse Bernard Award for contributions to gender scholarship in 2009. She was also the President of the American Sociological Association in 2013.

Ridgeway began her academic career at the University of Michigan at age 16 and received her BA in sociology in 1967. She went on from Michigan to receive her MA and PhD from Cornell University in 1969 and 1972, respectively. It was here that she was influenced greatly by William Lambert, who helped her to develop an interest in social psychology.

One of Ridgeway's major accomplishments has been to theorize and conduct empirical research on gender as a social status and to use gender relations as a basis for furthering the ideas and foundations of expectation states theory. Ridgeway has formulated "status construction theory" to help explain how status beliefs develop around attributes such as gender and race. She wrote *Framed by Gender* (2011) and edited the book *Gender, Interaction, and Inequality* (Ridgeway 1992), and she has also been one of the ongoing editors of the *Advances in Group Processes* series.

*Information about this biography was obtained from Edward Lawler's (Lawler, 2006) introduction of the Cooley-Mead Award printed in *Social Psychology Quarterly* and personal correspondence with Dr. Ridgeway.

the low- and high-resource groups developed positive biases toward the high-resource group. People in the high-resource group were judged to be higher in status, more respectable, and more competent than people in the disadvantaged group. These positive attitudes may make it easier for both groups to get some benefits from the other group: dominant groups get compliance from the subordinate group, whereas subordinates receive positive sentiment and some support from the dominant groups. These findings are supported by other laboratory and cross-national studies (Brashears 2008; Oldmeadow, Collett, and Little 2008). For example, Noah Mark and his colleagues (Mark, Smith-Lovin, and Ridgeway 2009) found that once status beliefs are formed, they can be transferred to another person but they can also be lost. Hence, we can create and undo status biases through group interactions.

The applications of status construction theory to day-to-day life are clear. If you have the opportunity to interact with a disadvantaged person, you may treat her differently than someone who shows signs of wealth and prosperity. Moreover, this bias will likely

Photo 9.2 Social psychologists examine the social nature of attitudes: how our attitudes, in part, reflect the information we gain through social interaction. Where do you get most of your information about the world?

Source: Konstantinos Kokkinis/Shutterstock

lead to differential evaluation of people from these groups. Your attitudes toward other people may be constructed from both your direct experiences with people in certain social positions, and the traits, statuses, and resources—such as race, gender, income, or appearance of your interacting partner. Further, if you are a lower-status person, you are likely to share positive biases toward individuals who show signs of being prosperous.

Social Identity Theory and Attitudes

One of the fundamental tenets of social identity theory is that people tend to categorize themselves into groups and use those categorizations as reference points for their attitudes toward members of other groups in society (see Chapter 5). The groups with which we identify are considered to be **in-groups**, whereas the groups with which we do not identify are called **out-groups**. Our in-groups traditionally include people who share similar background characteristics to us, such as race and ethnicity, even if we are not aware of this bias. In a study of Hungarian secondary school students, for instance, Zsófia Boda and colleagues (Boda, Néray, and Snijders 2020) found that students among the majority ethnicity showed greater dislike of students perceived as minority (Roma) students. In addition, threats to groups serve to magnify the effects of group identity. When a group is threatened by another group, the first group will likely form tighter bonds while developing a stronger animosity toward the out-group.

Nationality represents one type of group affiliation. Canadians differentiate themselves from Americans, for example, and Americans differentiate themselves from Canadians. Such group designations often serve as important aspects of our identities (see Chapter 5). Groups also serve as sources of information about other groups. Threats serve to heighten our identity with the in-group—in this case, our national identity.

The terrorist attacks against the United States on September 11, 2001, provided a natural experiment to see how social identity affected Americans' attitudes. Robb Willer (2004) used public opinion data on Americans' attitudes toward President George W. Bush and the number of terror warnings issued by the federal government. He found that government-issued terror warnings led to increases in approval ratings for the president. Attitudes toward the president became more positive as fears of outsiders increased. These findings are attributed to the tendency to view members of our in-group, in this case Americans, more positively when the group is threatened. In this case, the terrorist alerts served as a sign of potential threat against the United States.

In another study employing social identity theory, Shawn Burn and colleagues (Burn, Aboud, and Moyles 2000) analyzed support for feminism among men and women. They found that women who rated high on gender self-esteem (feeling positive about women) were more likely to show support for feminism than those who reported lower group self-esteem. In addition, women were more supportive of feminism than men, suggesting that in-group members (women), especially those who strongly identify with this group, are more supportive of in-group ideologies.

These studies show the importance of group contexts in developing attitudes. These contexts can include gender and ethnic groups, among others. Being a member of a group, particularly if that group identity is salient to you, affects your interpretation of information given to you and your attitudes toward external objects—the people and things around you (Bonilla-Silva, Embrick, 2007; Semyonov, Raijman, and Gorodzeisky 2006; Voci et al. 2008). These biases may go far beyond simply developing positive or negative attitudes toward people from other groups. It can include assessments of other traits. For example, in a study soliciting volunteers from Amazon Mechanical Turk, a crowdsourcing online marketplace, Kimmo Eriksson (2018) found that people affiliated with the Republican party tended to value individualist traits more than people affiliated with the Democratic party who valued communalistic traits. The author also found that, "Republicans were found to judge their own group as especially superior on agentic traits, where Democrats judged their own group as especially superior in communal traits" (181). These findings clearly show that a whole set of attitudes can emanate from the social dynamics of group affiliations.

If group affiliations start a process of attitude formation, a challenge for scholars is to define the symbolic social boundaries by which we create in- and out-groups (Bail 2008). It may start within us as individuals. Psychologists also recognize something called *myside bias*: "when people evaluate evidence . . . in a manner biased toward their own prior opinions and attitudes" (Stanovich, West, and Toplak 2013, 259). Similar biases can be applied to individuals we consider to be important to us (e.g., friends and partners) (see, for example, Flint et al. 2020). Hence, it appears that people tend to form attitudes and opinions starting with their individual biases and extend those biases to our in-group affiliations.

We reviewed the ways that ethnic identities can change over time in Chapter 5. In addition, a group identity may be more or less salient in a group context (e.g., when you are the only one of your race in a particular group). Therefore, which group identities are salient can change over time and across different social settings. In this sense, too, those who become "one of us" changes, as do who we define as "others," or members of the out-group.

Groups can even form in-and out-groups within its own members! In one study, Patrick Casey (2018) used interview data among 23 Muslims living in the United States to study the role of religion in their lives. He found that some members of the group stigmatized other members who were considered more acculturated into American society compared to the others. Thus, evidence indicates that attitudes and opinions can be influenced by group dynamics, both within and between groups.

Section Summary

This section applied theories and research from the group processes perspective to address the question "How do attitudes toward other people form in group contexts?" According to status construction theory, beliefs about individuals in groups form through interaction in group contexts. Individuals bring in expectations of group members based on societal biases that affect future interpretations of performance in the group. Social identity theory helps us to understand how our group identities affect attitudes toward people within our group and toward outsiders. From this perspective, group contexts provide a venue to evaluate our attitudes and behavior toward other people in the world.

A Take-Away Message

Group processes research provides clear evidence of the importance of status in everyday life. Not only do we have status beliefs about race, class, and gender, but we also have a tendency to form status beliefs quickly—and, once made, they change the ways that we relate to each other. The good news is that we have some control over the process. A first step is to try to be constantly aware of how we are picking up biases and to counter them. As a colleague or a boss, you can influence unfair biases by changing the way you talk about someone and her abilities, if you can see these status dynamics developing around you!

BRINGING IT ALL TOGETHER

> *I just don't understand why there is so much hate in the world. We've got people bombing innocent civilians, hate groups killing for no apparent reason. Why can't people get along?*
>
> —Dennis, freshman undeclared major

Dennis has a serious concern. One of the reasons we study attitudes and behaviors is to understand how to make the world a better place. If we can find the root causes of anger and hatred between people, maybe we could stop the violence among them.

In this chapter, we applied the three social psychological perspectives to provide insights into attitude processes more generally and prejudicial attitudes specifically.

Symbolic interactionism helps us understand the nature of attitudes and behavior. We examined the multidimensional nature of attitudes as having both rational and evaluative components, and the social construction of prejudice. Using the social structure and personality perspective, we find that attitudes vary based on our social groups, including our race and ethnicity, gender, and age among other social statuses. Finally, research and theory from the group processes perspective show that beliefs about others are informed by our positions within groups and group memberships in general.

SUMMARY

1. Attitudes incorporate emotional, cognitive, and behavioral dimensions—how we feel, think, and act toward an object. Attitudes are measured in terms of their direction and strength, although people can also have nonattitudes toward objects.
2. The relationship between attitudes and behavior, on average, is relatively small with an average correlation of 0.38. The weak relationship between attitudes and behavior—and between attitudes and other attitudes—may reflect poor measurement of attitudes or the complexities of attitudes themselves.
3. Interactionist perspectives view attitudes like any other aspect of social life: they are constructed based on our interactions with other people. Our group memberships can have a large influence on our attitudes toward people in other groups based on the relative standing of those groups.
4. Some attitudes and opinions have been found to vary based on social statuses. Men and women regularly report different attitudes toward some social issues, as do African Americans and Whites. Many attitudes toward major social issues have changed over the last half century, indicating that newer cohorts have different values compared with earlier generations.
5. A sociological model of attitudes and identity emphasizes the ways that people incorporate values into their identities, which, in turn, explains how people develop attitudes in different situations.
6. Status construction theory posits that individuals develop status value through face-to-face interaction as well as from larger societal prejudices. Social identity theory emphasizes the role of in-groups and out-groups in our attitude development.

KEY TERMS AND CONCEPTS

Altruism: Refers to the motivation to help another person.

Attitude: A positive or negative evaluation of an object, a person or group, or an idea.

In-groups: Groups with whom we identify.

Institutional racism: A form of structural racism in which racialized minority groups lack the same access to services or opportunities afforded other group members in an organization or society.

Nonattitude: When we do not care either way about something.
Opinion: The cognitive or "thinking" aspect of an attitude.
Out-groups: Groups with which we do not identify.
Prejudice: An attitude of dislike or active hostility toward a particular group in society.
Prosocial behavior: Includes any behavior that benefits another person.
Social distance: How close we feel to other groups of people.
Status construction theory: Group processes theory that posits that individuals develop status value in face-to-face interactions with other people.
Subtle sexism: Unequal treatment of women that goes unnoticed.
Theory of group position: Theory that prejudicial attitudes reflect a group's position in society.
Time use research: The study of how people allocate and experience time.
Unconscious racism: Ways in which we may be biased against a group without being aware of it.
Values and beliefs: Strongly held, relatively stable sets of attitudes.

DISCUSSION QUESTIONS

1. Think about some of your values and beliefs. How do you think they would be different if you lived in another place or were of a different gender?
2. Think about your upbringing. What aspects of your life affected the values and beliefs you have today? Your nonattitudes? Although it is not easy to observe about ourselves, can you identify factors that influence your decisions on a day-to-day basis?
3. Can you think of a situation in which you were judged incorrectly in a group setting based on a social characteristic like age, ethnicity, or religion? What caused that misperception?

10

The Sociology of Emotions and Relationships

I always feel embarrassed when I think about it—my grandmother's funeral, that is. I could not stop laughing. She had such a great sense of humor, so I think I was remembering that. I loved my Gram and wanted to show the deepest respect for her, but I just couldn't stop the laughter. She was a funny woman.

—Janet, freshman psychology major

Imagine that one of your professors has scheduled an exam covering difficult course material. The exam will significantly affect your course grade, and you have spent days mastering the material. You are sure that you will ace the test. When the day of the exam arrives, your professor notifies the class that she has decided to drop the test and instead assigns a twenty-page course paper. How do you think you would respond to this? Would you be angry? Would you let go with a stream of obscenities? Do you think you might hit, kick, or break things?

How you answer the preceding questions would likely depend in large part on where you were when you learned the information. If you read the information in an email in your apartment or dorm room, you would probably react differently than if the professor announced it in class. It is more likely, for example, that you would kick over a chair in your dorm room than in your classroom. How we express emotions, then, is affected by social conditions. It is not just our reactions, however, that are affected by the setting. Our emotions themselves can be determined by characteristics of our social environments.

We tend to think of our emotions as things over which we have little control. We do not choose to cry during sad movies or to become angry with annoying family members. Instead, we see emotions as carrying us away. Consider a professional baseball player who charges the pitcher after he is hit by a pitch. On some level, the player knows as soon as he starts running toward the pitcher that he is facing a suspension, a fine, and public condemnation. But he continues nonetheless. His emotions seem innate and hard to control, and his only goal becomes to hurt this other person.

We often think that emotions override rational thought. Indeed, discussions often treat rationality and emotion as though they are opposite ends of some spectrum. Acting emotionally, to some, means abandoning reason. If we look more closely, however, we can see that there is at least some rational calculation involved in even those actions that seem completely driven by emotion. Consider the baseball player who loses control and charges the pitcher. What is the one thing that essentially every baseball player who charges the pitcher does before he takes off to the mound? He puts down his bat. The player seems intent on hurting this other person, but he puts down something that would give him a big advantage in the fight he is about to start! Just as the player knows at some level that charging the mound will lead to trouble, he knows that bringing the bat will lead to *big* trouble—likely the difference between a suspension from his job and both the end of his career and felony assault charges.

The sociology of emotion does not disregard the biology or psychology of emotion. Rather, sociologists are interested in how people interpret their physical sensations, in the social conditions that are likely to produce physiological stimulation, and in how structural conditions influence both of these processes. In short, sociologists want to know how society affects feelings and expressions of emotions.

Although emotions may be to some extent hardwired into our biological systems, our emotions are also affected by social conditions. Under most social conditions, we follow

Photo 10.1 Social interactions are associated with different emotional responses such as crying at a funeral, leading sociologists to study the social conditions that produce particular emotions. Have you ever found yourself feeling emotions that were inappropriate in a given situation (e.g., laughing at a funeral)?

Source: Kzenon/Shutterstock

the rules, laughing when it is appropriate to laugh and crying when we "should" cry. However, there are times when we cannot—or choose not to—follow these rules. Janet's story highlights some of these issues. She questions whether people should naturally feel bad at funerals. What makes a death something to be mourned in the first place? Janet knows that it is inappropriate to laugh at a funeral, yet she finds that it seems impossible to stop herself from doing so. Even though privately she may justify her laughter, the "weight" of emotion norms surrounding death in Western cultures is manifest in Janet's embarrassment.

The **cybernetic approach** to the study of emotion asserts that individuals try to self-regulate emotions by reducing the discrepancy between actual and desired emotions. If individuals feel sad but want to feel happy, they will make some effort to create the desired emotions utilizing their available resources in social contexts (Tamir 2021). Sociologists extend this perspective by arguing that social conditions shape emotions and, in turn, emotions act to maintain social structures (Franks 2003). Like much of sociological social psychology, the approach views social interaction as both shaping and being shaped by society. Although social conditions give rise to different emotions, emotions are also essential to the maintenance of social organization. For example, when nonprofit organizations use emotions to solicit contributions, people become more likely to volunteer and to donate (Paxton, Velasko, and Ressler 2020). This chapter will start by reviewing how sociologists study the upward movement of emotions in the creation of society and the social construction of emotions more generally. It will also review the structured nature of emotions, and how society shapes the scope and expression of emotions. Other important topics will be addressed by answering the following questions:

- What are emotions? What are the components of emotions?
- How do people learn emotions?
- How is identity related to emotions?
- How do symbolic interactionists approach the study of relationships?
- How do our statuses in society affect our uses of emotions?
- How do social structural conditions affect relationships in society?
- What norms govern the use of emotions in different social settings?
- How do group settings affect emotions?
- How do group processes researchers approach the study of emotions and relationships?

CONSTRUCTING EMOTIONS AND RELATIONSHIPS

I always thought that emotions are innate. I read in psychology class that some emotions are "hardwired" in that researchers have found them to exist in all countries in the world today. Doesn't that mean that they exist outside of any influence of culture?

—Francis, sophomore computer science major

Important early sociological writings about emotions came from Charles Horton Cooley, who defined sentiment as a feeling that has been given meaning by society (Stets 2003). In short, sentiments give meaning to stimuli occurring in the body. For example, you may feel pain and decide if it is good or bad, or strong or mild, among other things. Alternatively, you may wonder whether a feeling you have for someone else is love or sexual attraction. Society helps individuals develop meanings for feelings (see Schröder, Hoey, and Rogers 2016). Languages provide dozens of terms that can be applied to a range of feelings.

Francis's beliefs about the biological foundations of emotions are well founded. Many scholars in sociology, psychology, and anthropology propose that some emotions are based on instinct, developed over hundreds of thousands of years of evolution. Fear, for example, may result from human beings' desire to avoid dangerous situations. From a purely social constructionist point of view, even the most basic emotions are learned through social interaction, from our primary agents of socialization and then the larger society (see Chapter 6). What do we fear? We must learn what objects and situations are "dangerous" and which are not. Still other scholars accept that some emotions are instinctual but that they have different meanings and values depending on the culture.

Defining Emotions

We defined sentiment as a feeling that has been given meaning by society. Sociologists sometimes use the terms "sentiment" and "emotion" interchangeably. In contrast, Peggy Thoits (1989) treats emotions and sentiment as distinct, and defines emotions as having four dimensions:

1. Situational cues.
2. Physiological changes.
3. Expressive gestures.
4. An emotion label.

Thus, **emotions** are a compilation of feelings, social conditions, and labels. **Situational cues** tell what emotion is appropriate and when in a given social interaction, ultimately producing changes in people's bodies. **Physiological changes** are those changes in our body that reflect the situation. **Expressive gestures** are usually associated with a particular emotion that "goes" with a particular label. A child given a present at a birthday party is using the cue of the gift to stimulate happiness and excitement. These feelings are expressed with a smile or some other gesture. We give an **emotional label** to feelings, in this case happiness. All these conditions do not have to occur simultaneously for an emotion to exist or be recognized by another person (Turner and Stets 2005). Thoits (1989) uses the examples of being afraid without knowing why and notes that children can get emotional without having the words to express their feelings.

Many other terms are associated with the concept of emotion. **Affect** is an evaluative component of an emotion, whether it is good or bad (Doan 2012; Smith-Lovin 1995), whereas **mood** refers to more diffuse emotional states that last a relatively long period of time. Finally, **feelings** may be referred to as internal states associated with a particular emotion (Stets 2003). As we noted above, **sentiments** are societies' imprint on our feelings, moods, affect, and emotions—the constructed meanings associated with them. For most of this chapter, we will take a broad approach to emotion that incorporates these different elements.

Theodore Kemper (1987) proposed two types of emotions. **Primary emotions** refer to physiologically grounded emotions that we inherit and that resulted from evolutionary processes, including happiness, anger, fear, and sadness (see also Box 10.1). **Secondary emotions** derive from primary emotions when we attach varying meanings to primary emotions. Secondary emotions are most similar to sentiments and are learned through socialization. Guilt, for example, is a response to the arousal of the primary emotion of fear. Sociologists tend to focus on secondary emotions where meaning is derived from social interactions. That is, according to Kemper, society may have more effects on the formation and meaning of secondary emotions than on primary ones. Secondary emotions are sometimes called "social emotions" because they are acquired through agents of socialization. Affection, pride, and conceit may be considered secondary emotions.

Secondary emotions are sometimes conceived of as being combinations of primary emotions (Turner and Stets 2005). For instance, a mixture of fear and anger, both primary emotions, may emote feelings of hate, jealousy, or envy. Similarly, depression and happiness can produce nostalgia or yearning. This typology suggests that social conditions can produce a kaleidoscope of emotional outcomes. It may also explain the experience of having "mixed emotions" with no specific feeling to attach to a situation.

Jacques-Philippe Leyens and his colleagues (Leyens et al. 2000) provide a good way to distinguish primary and secondary emotions. They ask, "Would I apply this emotional term to an animal such as a rabbit or a fish?" (Leyens et al. 2000, p. 189).

Box 10.1 Universal Expression of Emotion

Most sociologists and psychologists believe that there are "primary emotions" that emerged through evolutionary processes and thus can be recognized in every culture around the world. Paul Ekman and his colleagues (see, for example, Ekman 2007) have conducted extensive research on the meaning of facial expressions in cultures as diverse as Sumatra, Japan, Germany, and Greece. The researchers show subjects a series of pictures of people with various facial expressions designed to represent emotions such as anger, disgust, fear, and happiness, among others. The researchers find a tremendous amount of agreement about the meaning of these facial expressions across cultures. In particular, five emotions can be recognized in both literate and nonliterate cultures: anger, fear, happiness, sadness, and disgust. Note that four out of five of these emotions are negative, suggesting that emotions developed for survival purposes, to protect us against danger by preparing for attack (anger or disgust) or fleeing from it (fear).

If not, chances are the emotion in question is a human construct. This distinction can have ramifications for defining what it is to be human. Think about it: if you believe a person is "not even capable of love"—you are saying they are not fully human! **Emotional discrimination** occurs when people attribute secondary (i.e., human) emotions to their in-groups and not to their out-groups (see Chapter 9 on in-groups and out-groups). In other words, we tend to see our own groups as more human than people in out-groups, or those people with whom we do not affiliate. Not only do we discriminate more against out-groups, for example those with a different race or ethnicity than our own, but also we are less likely to help people in out-groups as a result of emotional discrimination (Cuddy, Rock, and Norton 2007; Leyens et al. 2000; Paladino et al. 2002). Thus, emotions help us define what it is to be human, and we use this distinction to discriminate against other groups (see Chapter 9 on unconscious racism).

Emotions and Society

We may think of emotions as deeply personal aspects of life. From a symbolic interactionist point of view, this perspective may be true, but emotions can be socially constructed and also influence society. Consider the conditions under which you feel happiness or sadness—they are sometimes associated with social events such as graduations, weddings, and funerals. Thus, social conditions influence emotional arousal. On the other side of things, emotions are an important part of social change—they help motivate people to participate in acts of social change such as protest movements or supporting social change organizations (Summers-Effler 2010). Emotional expressions among in-group members also help people decide how they should evaluate out-group members.

In Chapter 1, we reviewed three levels of sociological analysis: the micro-, meso-, and macro-levels. On the micro-level, emotions are an important aspect of symbolic exchange processes, even though we may not always be conscious of them (Franks 2003). From this perspective, there are three ways that emotions contribute to social interactions:

1. Emotions can serve as the basis of our thought processes.
2. Emotions can give meaning to different physical and social conditions.
3. Emotions are directly linked to our decision-making processes.

As an illustration of these principles, consider how a sense of embarrassment may influence the way we act in a public setting. Being embarrassed may make us decide to act more reserved so as to not call attention to ourselves. The feelings of embarrassment may be a result of someone insulting us. The feelings help us decide how to act on the insult, perhaps by leaving the group setting or retaliating in some way. In essence, emotional states help us make decisions about the different ways to interact with the people around us.

In a study of emotional management among wheelchair users, Spencer Cahill and Robin Eggleston (1994) found that emotions played an important role in the behaviors of their subjects. Simply deciding whether to venture out in public was associated with mixed feelings of excitement, fear, and embarrassment—the excitement of being in public places, mixed with the fears associated with having a disability within spaces that are sometimes not well designed and the embarrassment of standing out among "stand-up people" (Cahill and Eggleston, 1994, p. 302). The researchers found that wheelchair users, once out in public, regularly managed the challenges of having a disability with different emotions. Humor is an important asset to interactions among wheelchair users and stand-up people, allaying the anxiety resulting from the accidents that inevitably resulted from crowded stores and streets. One informant in their study shared this interaction:

> *I wheeled up to the entrance to a dressing room while my friend held a number of garments. I forgot to set the brakes on my chair, so when I started to raise myself up with my crutches, the chair went rolling backward while I went falling forward onto the floor. My friend stood there with this look of alarm until I started laughing, and then a saleswoman came rushing over: "My goodness, are you all right?" I answered, "Yes, I'm fine" while still laughing. Her facial expression went from alarm to unconcern in a flash, once she realized we were laughing. (Cahill and Eggleston, 1994, p. 303)*

This example shows the importance of emotional displays during everyday interactions—in this case, employing humor to divert other feelings such as embarrassment for the subject and fear and concern from the saleswoman.

Randall Collins's (1981; 2004) **theory of interaction ritual chains** applies a symbolic interaction perspective to analyze the role of emotions in the interaction process. The theory focuses on the **interaction ritual**, the exchange of symbols and emotions between individuals, as the unit of analysis (see also Goffman 1967), emphasizing the situation rather than the individuals. Each person has a chain of previous encounters that they bring to each new interaction. Collins argues that encounters produce **emotional energy**—referring to a heightened sense of excitement produced by a feeling of belonging—within individuals, which serves as the basis of the interactions. Emotional energy is important because it gives people the motivation to carry on the ritual process, to participate in society. Collins describes the role of emotions in the interaction process as "charg[ing] up symbol objects with significance" (Collins 2004, p. 38). In other words, emotions make attitude objects (i.e., people, events, or physical objects) worth talking about or interacting with. This helps explain why people initiate and continue to stay committed to social interactions.

According to Collins's theory, emotions are present in any social interaction. It goes further to state that individuals in social settings seek to develop a common mood, or a generalized feeling. For instance, you may be talking with other students about a professor's assignment. Each student may provide different sentiments on the issue, but according to the theory, members of your group will likely seek a common sentiment toward the teacher. This emotional coordination produces a sense of solidarity, a connection between you and the group. If you leave with a strong sense of solidarity, it will give you higher levels of emotional energy, and you will have confidence in the interaction process, which symbolic interactionist approaches see as the basis of society. Alternatively, you may leave feeling no connection with the other group members, leading you to feel low emotional energy, perhaps manifested by feelings of depression and low self-esteem. Emotional energy is necessary in the development of solidarity. Collins (2008) also shows that violence between people is relatively rare (compared to crimes such as theft or burglary) and most people do not act on their anger or threats. He suggests that the need for social bonds is so strong that we avoid acting out in ways that may break them.

People can utilize agency to start creating community in each and every interaction. However, it can be tough to start this process because of dramaturgical limitations (see Chapter 5). Research shows that people are concerned about what other people may think if they try to create interactions, especially among strangers. One study found that people underestimated the desire for strangers to connect; they also found that all connections, however created, were equally positive among those who initiated contact and recipients of it (Epley and Shroeder 2014). Connecting can literally involve physical contact. In an understudied area, Asta Cekaite and Lorenza Mondada (2021) demonstrate the powerful role of touch as a means of exchanging positive feelings, coordinating action, and creating intimacy.

Jonathan Turner's (2007a) sociological theory of emotions proposes that the micro-level use of emotions during interactions supports the development of meso- and macro-level social structures. From his perspective, emotions have their evolutionary origins in primate behavior where emotions developed as a way to build social bonds. Now humans use emotions to stimulate interaction in groups, similar to Collins's work on emotional energies. Groups, in turn, influence the development and expression of emotions. Also, on the macro-level, cultures serve to contextualize emotional arousal, providing guidelines for the appropriate expression of emotions.

Jonathan Turner and Jan Stets (2006) outline four types of **moral emotions**, those emotions that compel us to follow the rules of society.

1. Self-directed emotions of shame and guilt.
2. Other-directed emotions of contempt, anger, and disgust.
3. Sympathizing and empathizing responses to distress.
4. Emotions associated with praising others for their moral behaviors.

Emotions such as shame help people conform to the rules of society (Scheff 1990). When we decide not to conform, this may produce a bad feeling, making us turn that feeling into pride by "following the rules." If social order exists through the laws and rules a society has created, then emotions such as shame and guilt are important emotions in maintaining that order. We can help ensure that others follow the rules of society through emotions such as contempt and disgust. Have you ever experienced a situation in which you saw someone act inappropriately in public? Perhaps you confronted the person directly, but many times you would simply give them a look that reveals a sense of disgust. Alternatively, we can praise people when they stand up for the ideals of society. When a friend contributes a lot of time and energy toward a charity, we may honor them with kind words. In these ways, emotions serve to maintain the norms of a community.

Socialization of Emotions

Symbolic interactionists view the learning of emotions like any aspect of social life. We develop meaning—whether a cognitive or affective meaning—of an object or person through interactions with other people. We use this meaning to help guide our behavior in day-to-day life. The **sociocentric model of emotional socialization** proposes that the primary means of learning about emotions comes from social instruction, such as family, friends, and schooling (Pollack and Thoits 1989). Agents of socialization interpret and label children's emotions during their interactions, helping them recognize the causes and consequences of their feelings.

In a study of three- to five-year-old children in a therapeutic school, Lauren Pollak and Peggy Thoits (1989) studied at least two dimensions of the emotion learning process. First, instructors tried to identify and explain children's emotions. Typically, instructors would associate an emotion word (e.g., anger or frustration) with a situational cause. The authors provided the following example (Pollack and Thoits 1989, p. 26):

> GIRL [SEVERAL TIMES]: My mom is late.
> STAFF MEMBER: Does that make you mad?
> GIRL: Yes.
> STAFF MEMBER: Sometimes kids get mad when their moms are late to pick them up.

In this example, the child is taught to associate her emotion (anger) with an appropriate cause (being late). In short, the emotion is labeled and connected to a specific cause.

Children are also taught appropriate ways to express emotions. Pollak and Thoits found that songs were often employed to help students make the connection between emotions and expressions, such as "If you're happy and you know it, clap your hands" (Pollak, Thoits, 1989, p. 29). Instructors would rely on statements such as "most children" as a way of letting children know how their behavior fit in the larger context of society. The researchers made it clear that the goal of the staff was not to control students' internal feelings but rather their outward expressions, notably expressions of aggression. They concluded that simply labeling an emotion is not enough to teach children how to develop their emotional lives. Rather, children need a more elaborate socialization process that explicitly links situational conditions, expression of the emotion, and words to identify the feeling.

The meaning of emotions can change over the life course, in both direction and strength (Ross and Mirowsky 2008). Emotions also serve as a means of giving meaning to life events. Peggy Giordano and her colleagues' (Giordano et al. 2007) research on the role of life events, such as marriage, on criminal behavior suggests that emotions are an important dimension of life change. Traditional research emphasizes the cognitive dimensions of such events—a criminal who marries may choose to live a better life for the sake of her spouse, for instance. However, their work suggests that it is a person's emotional attachments to significant others that drive decisions to lead a more conventional life. Potentially positive life transitions without positive emotions, they argue, will not necessarily lead to positive change.

Identities, Interactions, and Emotions

Once learned, emotional expressions act as symbols. We use them in day-to-day interactions as ways of communicating with other people. We may pass someone in the hallway and give a nod and smile, indicating that we mean no harm or wish to make a connection. Emotions also help us better understand ourselves (see Chapter 5). Emotions provide information about how well we are maintaining our self as well as our presentation of that self. In Chapter 7, we defined reflexivity as the process in which an individual reflects back on and gives meaning to an object, including the sense of self. In the case of emotions, Morris Rosenberg (1990) proposes that people use reflexive processes to identify, display, and experience emotions. Thus, individuals try to produce emotional states in themselves and others.

Under the framework of identity theory (see Chapter 5), emotions serve as an indicator of how well we are displaying our identities to the people around us (Stets 2006). If you believe that you are a good student and receive confirmation from your peers or professors, it is likely to produce a positive emotion. Alternatively, if you believe you are a strong student and yet receive negative feedback from your professor, you will likely react with a negative emotion such as anger or shame until you are able to restore your sense of self. You may work harder on your next exam, you may decide to lower your expectations, or you might decide your professor is unfair. In any case, you restore a sense of balance between your sense of self and the verification of an identity. Whichever way you choose to proceed, emotions serve as a driving force behind these dynamics.

The relationship between identities and emotions is more complex than simply examining when identities are confirmed or not. Different types and levels of emotions emerge under different conditions. More intense emotions tend to result when an identity especially important to a person is disconfirmed (Stets 2006). In addition, the types of emotions we experience may vary depending on *who* disconfirms our identity: if we are the cause of disruption—a difference between our sense of self and our behaviors or others' reactions to us—it will likely yield disappointment or embarrassment. But, if other people cause disruption in the identity confirmation process, it will likely produce anger. If our identity is not verified but in a *positive* direction, when people think more highly of us than we do, it tends to produce positive emotions—probably as a result of a boost in our self-esteem. Finally, more salient identities are likely to produce greater emotions in these processes, and higher status individuals are more likely than others to have their identities verified in interactions.

Erving Goffman's work on impression formation (see Chapter 5) relies heavily on the idea that emotions help people develop and maintain self-presentations to others. If we attempt to present a front that includes being intelligent or "cool" and fail in this effort, it will likely be embarrassing for ourselves and the other people (including, perhaps, our friends and family). Thus, emotions serve as signals about our impressions. Emotions also provide motivation to restore our impressions, and sympathy helps others to contribute to this restoration process. Believe it or not, other people usually want to quickly help you to not look so foolish because it is uncomfortable for everyone. Spilling a drink in class will likely be met with help from a number of people to both assist you in cleaning the mess as well as make you feel less awkward about the accident. For example, one of the helpers might make a quick joke about the incident or provide examples when she did something similar in the past.

Louis Zurcher (1982) employed the principles of impression management to study emotional performances of fans, coaches, and players at a college football game. He found that each of these groups followed **emotional scripts**, or expectations about when and how to display certain emotions such as excitement or anger. A winning pass is associated with joy. Crowds are expected to act with applause in this case. In addition, certain emotional cues provoke rapidly changing emotional expressions. That is, under some conditions, individuals must know when to change their emotions rather quickly, to keep pace with the events at a game. **Emotional cues** give people information about when and what emotions are appropriate in a given social setting. A football player, for instance, may raise his arms in the air, trying to arouse the crowd to cheer on the team's players, hence motivating them to play better. Scripts and cues help people guide the development and expression of emotion—in essence, we make rules for emotions in the same way we do for norms and values.

Emotional scripts can be found in almost every aspect of our emotional lives. In a series of in-depth interviews with over 30 people who recently lost a loved one to murder, Sara Goodrum (2008) found that the bereaved expected others to express heartfelt sympathy for their loss. The bereaved were often hurt when they did not receive expected responses. These scripts can also be used to assess other people. In a field study of a drug treatment program, Leslie Paik (2006) found that staff assessed clients' emotional displays as a way of determining whether they were truly recovering. Being able to control rage is a sign of being a recovering addict. The "emotional" recovery process is not immediate but includes inputs from many people (counselors and other recovering addicts) over time so as to learn the appropriate ways to use emotions during everyday interaction. Even the feeling of being surprised requires the use of impression management (Wilkinson and Kitzinger 2006). Professional performers such as actors and musicians use knowledge of emotional scripts to better their performances onstage (Bessett 2006; Orzechowicz 2008).

Breaking a social script can cause embarrassment, but it can also be a source of humor and a way of relieving tension associated with inappropriate behavior. Humor is so interesting because it can evoke a variety of emotions. It is pleasurable because it creates laughter and joy based on the vagaries of social life, but it can also skewer some people in the process, creating embarrassment. Anyone who has been the butt of a joke knows well the ability of humor to sting.

Humor is culture bound. What one culture finds funny may not translate well in another place, usually because different cultures cannot understand the subtle social rules that govern what is "normal." The nature of a joke, then, is social and often involves breaking social norms or failing to maintain the front stage (see Chapter 5) (Paolucci and Richardson 2006). A comedian may cuss a lot or talk about sensitive topics to get her audience primed for the act. She may make fun of things that happen in everyday life or give examples of embarrassing moments. Humor can also be used to ridicule others, such as the sarcasm that late-night talk show hosts sometimes use with their guests (Billig 2005). Finally, humor is also stratified: what is funny differs for men and women and people from different social classes. In a study comparing humor in the United States and the Netherlands, Giselinde Kuipers (2006) found that more educated respondents tended to enjoy traditional (prepared, memorized) jokes less than people with less education. Men preferred traditional jokes more than women. While there is a business to humor in the form of performance art, everyday humor can be like a social glue—it is a means of social interaction between people. We use laughter to manage our impressions and interactions with other people.

From Emotions to Relationships

Emotions can serve to start, maintain, or end relationships. The challenge of studying relationships is that they come in many forms, each with its own set of emotional outcomes. Dating someone elicits feelings of attraction, for example, that are not present in, say, sibling relations, even if relationships with partners and brothers or sisters produce positive feelings. A considerable amount of theory and research on relationships in social psychology revolves how we make friendship choices. The four pillars of attraction to sociological social psychologists are as follows:

1. Proximity.
2. Similarity.
3. Physical attractiveness.
4. Reciprocal liking.

Proximity refers to the physical location of the other person; we tend to be attracted to people to whom we have access and with whom we have regular interactions. The more time we spend with people, the more likely we are to get to know them, helping to explain elements of the Contact Hypothesis reviewed in Chapter 4. In a recent study, Jeffrey Hall (2019) studied people who had moved recently and were asked to identify someone they met since moving. Not surprisingly, people who spent more time together reported closer relationships. Hall found that "[c]asual friends become friends somewhere between 57 hr[s] . . . after 3 weeks and 164 hr[s] . . . over 3 months" (1292). However, the content of the time spent together was important: simply "hanging out" and doing leisure activities was associated with closer relationships compared to doing work- or school-related activities.

We also tend to be attracted to people who have similar attributes and values as our own. **Homophily** refers to the tendency of people to be attracted to others with similar background traits as our own, such as our education level or religion. The internet has changed the ways that people find partners (Rosenfeld and Thomas 2012). That is, dating sites and apps provide a way to help find people who are similar to us, and we evaluate potential partners online more positively if they share our values and beliefs (Huber and Malhotra 2016). People are increasingly using the internet for social interaction more broadly (Figure 10.2). Of course, we are more attracted to people who we find physically attractive and people who we believe like us (Orbuch and Sprecher 2003).

Photo 10.2 The nature of relationships may be changing since the introduction of social media such as Instagram, TikTok, and Snapchat. Does posting or exchanging images on social media give you the same sense of friendship as you receive from people with whom you interact in person every day?

Source: PixieMe/Shutterstock

Symbolic interactionists examine the changing nature of relationships—the social construction of what it means to be a family member, a friend, or a lover, for instance (see Box 10.2 for a discussion of how artificial intelligence can play a role in the future of relationships). Consider the fact that how societies define families can have different levels of meaning ranging from biological (parent and child), to legal (e.g., marriage), to interactional (Brynin and Ermisch 2009). Would any two people cohabiting as romantic partners always form a family? In the United States, the answer would be "no" (see Figure 10.1 as an example of the importance people from different countries give toward family and friends.) However, a cohabiting couple reflects an interactional sense of family in the sense that they do many of the same things as traditional families, such as living together and exchanging intimacies. In the early part of the century, researchers analyzing Americans' definitions of family found that nearly everyone in the United States agrees that a married woman and man constitute a family (with or without children), but fewer view same-sex couples as families. Also, most people also believe that single parents with children constitute a family. However, less than half of Americans believe that unmarried couples living together constitute a family, unless they have children—in which case, the proportion believing it is a family goes just above 50 percent (Powell et al. 2010).

In addition to the social construction of the meaning of relationships within society, symbolic interactionists study the social construction of relationships themselves. For example, how do couples come together and work as a single unit? Each member of a couple brings two sets of values and beliefs (their own and their family background) into a single couple. At first, partners "play act" as a couple until their true beliefs about

Box 10.2 The Future of Artificial Intelligence in Relationships*

Artificial intelligence (AI) has already begun to have a profound impact on how humans interact with each other and the world around us. As AI technology continues to develop and advance, it is likely that it will have an even greater influence on human interactions in the future. One way that AI will influence human interactions is in the realm of communication. With the advent of natural language processing (NLP) technologies, AI will continue to improve in its ability to understand human speech and respond in a more conversational way. This means that chatbots, virtual assistants, and other AI-powered communication tools will become even more common in our daily lives, changing how we communicate with each other. Another way AI will change human interactions is through automation. As AI and robotic technologies become more sophisticated and capable, they may be able to take over many jobs that are currently performed by humans. This could have significant economic and social impacts, as traditional career paths are disrupted and new opportunities emerge.

AI will also affect how people form and maintain relationships. Social media platforms and other digital tools will continue to be an important part of social lives, but AI-powered recommendations and algorithms could help us find and connect with people who share our interests and goals. This could lead to more meaningful and productive relationships, both online and offline. Finally, AI may have a significant effect on how people think about and address societal challenges. AI technologies could help us better understand human behavior and social dynamics, and enable us to develop more effective solutions to complex problems such as climate change, healthcare access, and economic inequality.

In conclusion, AI will undoubtedly have a significant effect on the ways humans interact with each other in the future. While there are concerns about job displacement and privacy, if developed and implemented responsibly, AI has the potential to improve our social, economic, and environmental outcomes, and enable us to lead more fulfilling lives.

*As an example of the potential power of AI, the original version of this essay was written by ChatGPT in 2023 at https://chat.openai.com and edited by one of the human authors.

relationships become clear. When differences in their values and beliefs become clear, they must then decide how committed they are to the relationship—ultimately choosing to negotiate a change in the relationship or to end it (Kaufman 1998, Kaufman 2009). Rituals are created in the family, like they are in the larger culture, giving individuals the ability to communicate meaning and order to the family's members. In this sense, the construction of relationships represents a microcosm of the symbolic processes in society.

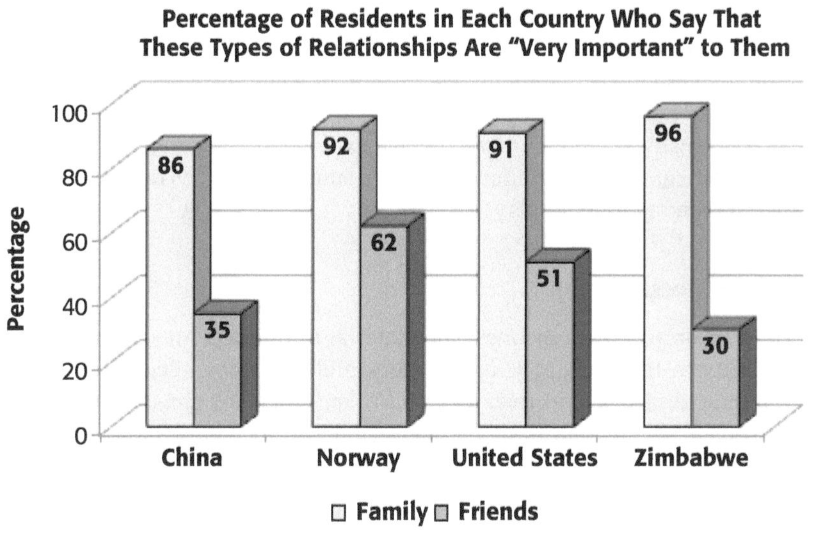

Figure 10.1 The Importance of Different Types of Relationships by Country.

Source: World Values Survey, 2017–2022.

Relationships, Online

The global COVID-19 pandemic that emerged in 2020 led many nations to require people to stay home as a means of limiting the transmission of the virus. People used the internet during this time period as a means of connecting to others who they would otherwise meet face-to-face. Many of the same dynamics reviewed in this chapter (and elsewhere in the book) play out online as well. Consider that you can utilize dramaturgy to express feelings (real or not) as long as other people are able to see your expressions. You can also express your feelings with the tone of your voice. Does the mode of interacting change relationship formation in any way? Maybe. Susan Specher (2021) conducted an experiment in which some unacquainted participants were asked to work on a self-disclosure task in person while others did the same task in separate rooms via computer. She found that dyads that communicated face-to-face reported more liking and closeness, all things considered, than those people who utilized computer-mediated communication.

Section Summary

In this section, we applied the interactionist perspective to address several questions: what are emotions? What are the components of emotions? How do people learn emotions? How is identity related to emotions? How do symbolic interactionists approach the study of relationships? We examined the physiological, social, and behavioral components of emotions. Emotions include sensations as well as emotional states of being or moods. Interactionists believe that emotions are constructed like other aspects of social life, through interaction with other people. In addition, emotions are important in developing and maintaining identities, serving as a cue for when people are playing their roles appropriately, and they help to motivate people to participate in society in the first place. Finally, symbolic interactionists examine the meanings of different types of relationships (e.g., the changing nature of the family) as well as the factors that influence attraction among individuals.

A Take-Away Message

What does it mean to love someone? The material in this section shows that you have the opportunity to think about your emotions and how they affect your life. From a symbolic interactionist perspective, love and other emotions are socially constructed; once constructed, social conditions influence how those emotions play out in interactions. In this sense, the meaning of love changes over time. If you are prepared for those changes, you may have a better handle on how to manage your closest relationships. Professionally, you probably know that emotions can affect the workplace experience in a number of ways. For example, a conflicted-laden workforce may produce less and be less satisfying than one where management cares about their workers. If emotions are socially constructed, then you have some control over creating a positive work environment by creating situations that yield positive feelings and encourage a sense of community.

STRUCTURAL CONDITIONS AFFECTING EMOTIONS AND RELATIONSHIPS

> *I don't know . . . there is just something about the guy. Maybe it was the way that he spoke at the convention. He really cares about people. I mean, a man with all of that experience. He is so smart. Even if he does not win the election, I will support him in whatever he does. He is a great guy.*
>
> —Jason, senior marketing major

The cybernetic approach to emotions proposes that emotions go from being created in microsocial interactions "upward"—that is, to contributing to the construction of society. They also go "downward"; once certain structures in society are created, they can influence the development of emotions in a group or population. Social-structural phenomena that typically influence individuals include norms, statuses, and positions (see Chapter 2). Sociological social psychology focuses on how people's positions in society affect their emotions and the emotions they elicit from other people.

Jason's feelings about a politician show the importance of emotion in maintaining status structures in society. His affection for this leader makes Jason want to follow him, even if he does not win the election. We discussed the importance of class position in developing favorable opinions of powerful people and groups in society in Chapter 9.

Class position plays an important role in how we develop favorable opinions of powerful people and groups in society. Similar research and theory are applied to emotions because attitudes can include feelings about a person or an object.

Power, Status, and Emotions

Randall Collins's (1981; 2004) work on the role of emotions in the development of society shows the importance of emotion for social position. In short, our emotional competence may influence our position in a group. Once that position is established, however, it also contributes to future emotional displays of group members. Theodore Kemper (1991; 2011) proposed that power and status serve as universal emotion elicitors. In his view, power and status are the primary causes of emotions in our day-to-day lives.

Kemper's theory is called the **power–status approach** to emotions. Kemper (1991) proposed that "a very large class of human emotions results from real, anticipated, imagined, or recollection of outcomes of social relations" (Kemper 1991, p. 333). Power is defined as the ability to obtain what you want from other people despite resistance, whereas status refers to a position in a group based on respect or esteem. Although other aspects of our lives are important to the development and expression of emotion, Kemper proposed that power and status are the most important structural determinants of our emotional lives.

The power–status approach assumes three agents in any given interaction: (1) self, (2) other, and (3) third parties or circumstances such as God, fate, or other forces. In the model, a loss of status should generally yield negative emotions, such as shame, while gains in status should produce feelings of pride. The effects of the loss or gain of status of others depend on our relationship with them: if you like others, their status gain will yield positive feelings such as happiness and their loss of status will make you feel unhappy. A third agent also influences your emotional reaction to status gain or loss. If your friend loses her job by your actions, you are likely to feel shame; if her status loss is due to an outside force, it will likely make you feel unhappy.

Consider a situation in which you are working with a good friend. If she gets a promotion, how might that make you feel? According to the power–status approach, you will likely feel a sense of happiness. But what if you are working with someone you dislike? Their promotion will likely make you feel angry. Additionally, if you are responsible for getting your friend demoted, it would make you feel a sense of shame. However, you would simply feel unhappy if the loss of the position had nothing to do with you. The power–status approach helps us understand the complex ways in which changing positions in society are associated with different emotional outcomes.

Status may also affect how people express all sorts of emotions in day-to-day interactions. Higher status and more powerful people in society should experience and express different emotions compared with lower status and less powerful people. Research indicates that high-power individuals express more anger and contempt, whereas submissive individuals express more fear and surprise—and other people expect those groups to elicit such emotions (Mondillon et al. 2005). Emotions also have important consequences for status hierarchies. In one study, Alison Bianchi and Donna Lancianese (2007) showed how positive emotions can work to dampen the effects of status hierarchies in groups. In their study, participants had the opportunity to give gifts to fellow study participants. Bianchi and Lancianese found that these gift-giving processes produced positive emotions among participants. They also found that status hierarchies based on status characteristics, while still forming, did not reach the same magnitude of difference as when gifts were not exchanged. Thus, positive emotions between group members can work to make status differences between them less pronounced.

In terms of gender, there is some evidence that boys and girls are socialized to express different types of emotion, with boys punished and girls encouraged to express feelings of sadness and fear (Garside and Klimes-Dougan 2002). Research also shows that women are more likely than men to be diagnosed with emotional disorders such as depression (Aneshensel, Rutter, and Lachenbruch 1991; Mirowsky and Ross 1995; Turner, Wheaton, and Lloyd 1995). But other research shows very little difference in the types and intensity of emotion expressed by men and women. Robin Simon and Leda Nath (2004), for instance, found no difference in the frequency with which men and women report anger or shame, though they did find that women report more sadness than men. The disparities in these findings may simply reflect the specific types of emotions being studied (with women reporting more of some emotions than men but not others). Other research (Simon and Lively 2010) indicates that women report more intense and persistent anger than men, but women have a tendency to suppress it while men are more likely to express their anger.

Feeling Rules and Norms

Power and status are only two ways in which societal conditions affect day-to-day lives. Like other aspects of social lives, there are norms or expectations about how to feel in different situations. Arlie Russell Hochschild (1983) called the norms that govern our emotional lives "feeling rules." **Feeling rules** tell us how we should feel in different social interactions. Feeling rules are different than behavioral rules in that they are rarely explicitly specified. We may say that some behaviors, such as robbery or murder, are inappropriate for people to do and thus codify these behavioral boundaries into a law. The same is not done in the arena of emotions.

Although social groups do not codify rules regarding emotional expectations, Hochschild (1983) proposed that we can discover these rules in a variety of ways. Much like the breaching experiments discussed in Chapter 2, the best way to know when feeling rules exist is to attempt to break those rules. We may receive "rule reminders" from friends and family when we do not "feel" appropriately. For instance, if you act depressed at your college graduation, someone might say, "You should be happy today! Most people feel a sense of pride when they accomplish something like this." This reminds you that you are not feeling what most people are expected to feel in similar situations. Another way that people give rule reminders is to assume how you are feeling in a particular situation. You may be at a school volleyball game that is going particularly well for your team when a friend from another school approaches you and says, "You must be totally excited for your team!" Many women are told when they give birth to a baby, "This is so wonderful!" and "You must be so happy!" Yet new motherhood can be a time of fear and anxiety, exhaustion, and generally negative emotions. Although the comments are well meaning and certainly make sense when we consider them within the context of North American culture, where motherhood is highly valued, they may fuel new mothers' anxieties that they don't feel the "right" emotions of joy and excitement.

Emotion Work

Hochschild (1983) proposed that certain jobs in our economy require **emotion work**, the self-generation of prescribed emotions to meet the demands of a job. Emotion work is particularly prevalent in service jobs such as flight attendants, nurses, retail sales, and other professions in which workers are expected to feel and display certain emotions toward their clients or customers. For instance, nurses are expected to feel sympathy toward their patients, and attendants are expected to act positively toward customers. Feeling rules associated with emotion work often conflict with people's actual feelings, producing a sense of strain, especially if workers blame themselves for the emotional deviance.

The commodification of emotions is associated with a concept called **McDonaldization**. This is the idea that service work is hyperrational, to the extent that assembly-line techniques are part of interpersonal work (Ritzer 1993). Workers at a fast-food restaurant, for instance, must follow prescribed formulas for producing and delivering food to customers. Unlike traditional factory work, in which individuals interact with machines to produce outcomes, service work requires that the same production logic be used in face-to-face interactions with other human beings, mechanizing the interaction process through rules and regulations (e.g., workers in a fast food restaurant being required to say "my pleasure" whenever thanked by a customer).

Although all jobs probably require some sort of emotion work, modern Western economies rely heavily on service work, which involves interaction among people rather than producing goods in factories. Consider a marketing expert. She must deal with clients (being confident and positive) while submitting proposals and results to her boss (while being compliant) and colleagues (while being friendly and helpful). Emotion work is essential to achieving success in the modern professional world, leading some psychologists such as Daniel Goleman to argue that **emotional intelligence**, or our ability to control and employ emotions in our social environments, is as important as intellectual abilities on the job (Goleman 1997). While a product of the field of psychology, the idea of emotional intelligence resonates with the principles of symbolic interaction and the meaning-making processes reviewed in Chapter 2. Individuals use emotions to define situations and situations can generate any number of emotions. People have agency and can choose to accept or reject the emotions that may be typically associated with a particular situation (e.g., happiness at a holiday party or anger at having to work extra hours) (Perinbanayagam 2016). As a tool, emotional intelligence can allow us to choose to accept or reject a negative look from a co-worker, among other things. Goleman later added the concept of social intelligence (2006) as a way of demonstrating that some people are better able to navigate their social worlds than others.

Box 10.3 Making Emotion Work

Emotions are an immense part of people's work lives. Whether it is managing your emotions as you deal with organizational dilemmas and hardships or managing stressful situations, your emotional intelligence will make huge difference in how you are able to cope with day-to-day situations on the job. Hence, workers benefit from knowing something about emotions and emotion work. Here are some examples of a couple of jobs in which it is especially important to understand the processes reviewed in this book.

1. **Human Resources Generalist**, Flathead Valley Community College, Kalispell, MT. Duties: Works collaboratively with employees, students, and the public by providing leadership and guidance in employee and labor relations, payroll, classification, and benefits administration. Partners with employees, students, and the public as their primary human resource contact at the college. Coordinates employee onboarding. Experience: An equitable combination of four years of higher education and/or related work experience; knowledge of principles, practices, and standards of human resource administration; and the ability to work effectively with people from a variety of culturally diverse backgrounds.
2. **Human Services Caseworker**, State of Illinois, Department of Human Services. Duties: Receives and assists customers to provide public assistance services available through Department of Human Services (DHS) programs to all eligible customers timely and accurately. Serves as part of a public assistance delivery network to verify clients are receiving appropriate services and support, as well as achieving welfare-to-work goals and other Welfare Reform goals and DHS initiatives. Experience: A bachelor's degree in psychology, sociology/anthropology, social welfare, or a closely related field; requires one year of professional casework or crisis intervention experience in a social service agency or successful completion of an agency-sponsored training program.

Any job that requires working with people will likely be challenging. This kind of work often requires that we understand our limits and can set boundaries to protect our own emotional well-being.

He argues that all of us can learn how to improve our emotional intelligence, a skill that can help people in Western economies dominated by providing services to people rather than manufacturing or other labor that does not require a lot of human interaction.

Emotions can also lead to the blurring of lines between people's economic and personal lives (Zelizer 2005). How much should someone be compensated for the loss of a loved one that resulted from negligence? How much should someone get from a divorce settlement? Is it based on how much we put into it or how much we cared? How much do we pay people who care for our children? Your answers to these questions involve putting economic value to emotions such as love, and often involved in care work, which modern Western culture assumes should be free flowing and priceless. Yet these kinds of questions have to be answered every day as people enter court to determine insurance claims, finalize divorces, or make childcare decisions.

Emotion work has been studied in a variety of work contexts, including exotic dancing, sales, victim advocacy, clubs, homeschooling, and others (Barton 2006; Godwyn 2006; Kolb 2014; Lois 2006; Smith 2008; Thomas 2015). John Pruit (2019), for example, studied the work lives of teachers at a Montessori preschool. He demonstrates that teachers are supposed to display a sense of care most times and be a positive role model for children. The result is that they must find ways to manage negative emotions as they come along during the day. These displays become part of the learning and socialization processes as teachers become emotional role models, helping students learn how to manage their emotions in public.

The routinization of people's emotional lives is juxtaposed with **edgework**, which is thrill-seeking behavior designed to produce intense emotions. Edgework is behavior that pushes us to the edge of our physical or mental abilities, such as skydiving. Given that edgework activities can easily produce serious injury or death, why do people do these things? Stephen Lyng (1990; 2004) proposed that such activities give people a relief from the routine of society. Edgework can occur as hobbies such as mountain climbing or motorcycle riding, but it can also be part of certain jobs. In an ethnographic study of rescue volunteers, Jennifer Lois (2003) found that workers had to learn how to act with humility even though their jobs gave them hero status due to saving people's lives. She also found that edgework required ways of releasing tensions—with some workers turning to alcohol or withdrawing from the group because of the intense emotions produced on the job. Edgework may also help to explain everyday risks people may choose to take as well as the emotional side of deviance and delinquency (Lyng 2004; Turner 2007).

The Socioemotional Economy

Candace Clark (1987) extended the concept of feeling rules by proposing that there is a socioemotional economy governed by feeling rules. The **socioemotional economy** is a system for regulating emotional resources among people. This economy links individuals into larger networks of people. Sympathy may seem to be a natural process, but Clark's research highlights the amazing social fabric underlying the exchange of sympathy among people. She proposed that sympathy, like many emotions, requires at least two people, a sympathizer and a sympathizee—someone to give the sympathy and someone to receive it.

Clark found that there are different expectations for the sympathizer and the sympathizee, depending on the social situation. There are two basic principles of sympathy etiquette. First, you give sympathy only when it is appropriate; the person must be worthy of sympathy, and you must be the appropriate person to provide sympathy. For instance, if you work at a local grocery store, it may not be appropriate to send flowers to the company's chief executive officer after hearing of the death of her husband. Second, sympathy should be reciprocated. If someone is nice to you during a difficult time, you are expected to reciprocate that sympathy to her if the appropriate situation arises.

Clark's research established four rules of sympathy etiquette:

1. Do not make false claims to sympathy.
2. Do not claim too much sympathy.
3. Claim some sympathy.
4. Reciprocate to others for the gift of sympathy.

The first rule of sympathy makes sense: do not try to claim sympathy when you do not deserve it. Perhaps you work with someone who is always complaining about a problem, but you later learn that she is being dishonest about the problem, even fabricating it, perhaps to get attention. This type of behavior empties her **sympathy account**—or an amount of sympathy that a person can expect from other people.

Similar to the first rule, the second rule states that a person should not claim too much sympathy. In the previous example, even if your co- worker had been honest about all her problems, she may run the risk of using up all of the sympathy credits stored in her account. People may decide to ignore the co-worker over time, at best, or make fun of her, at worst.

The third sympathy rule assumes that people should accept some sympathy. If a colleague displays sympathy for some loss you have had, you should admit to the loss and accept her sympathy, perhaps by providing some gratitude for her expression of sympathy. Also, you will be expected to return the sympathy to that person in the future, initiating the fourth rule, that sympathy needs to be reciprocated. Some people may try to avoid sympathy from friends and colleagues because they are concerned about having to repay others for their kindness.

Emotion Culture

Emotion culture refers to a society's expectation about how to experience different emotions (see Stearns and Stearns 1986). It represents the fact that individuals learn to experience feelings similarly to other things. Lyn Lofland (1985) studied the cultural conception of grief, arguing that the intensity and duration of grief in a society depends on the following:

1. How much particular relationships are invested with significance.
2. The mortality rates of the group.
3. To what degree feelings are controlled.
4. To what degree individuals are physically isolated from others.

These factors are predicted to interrelate differently in each society over time. For example, some cultures may have high mortality rates, making people invest less emotional energy in a child (because they fear imminent loss). In contrast, in contemporary Canada and the United States, which have relatively low infant mortality rates and few children per family compared with the past, children are viewed as emotionally priceless (Zelizer 1985).

Sociologists have also tried to understand the cultural context of emotions. Ann Swidler (2001), for instance, studied how Americans conceive of love and relationships. To Swidler, culture is like a "toolkit" that people use to help decide how to act.

For example, people use their cultures to define love and what it means to be in a good relationship. Swidler's research showed that Americans continue to hold two conflicting views of love, one that focuses on the mythic aspects of love found in novels and movies and another view of love that emphasizes the realistic aspects of relationships. Love is also seen as something voluntary—a matter of individual choice. She found that Americans use the mythic view of love to initiate and end relationships, such as deciding when to marry and when to divorce someone. However, people use the realistic view of love to maintain committed relationships on a day-to-day basis. That is, if we want to marry someone, we might focus on the great feelings that are produced in the presence of the other person. Similarly, we may say that those feelings have disappeared as we explain to our friends the reasons for a divorce.

Community and Relationships

Emotions may be associated with intimate relationships, but sociological social psychologists also examine meso- and macro-level conditions that create emotional responses. Have you entered a room and felt like something was "off"? You may have worked in an organization that just "felt right" for you at the time. People often try to create a certain "mood" for a party or other social event. Such atmospheres can be thought of as the shared ways of feeling created through a mix of physical elements (e.g., room layout), sounds, and interactions among people. However produced, it is often the sense or feel of a group or situation that gives it meaning and stays in our memory (e.g., was it a good party?) (Sumartojo and Pink 2019).

On the macro level, community conditions affect the nature of relationships in society. The concept of community is difficult to define (Hill 2010). Traditional sociology has differentiated between two types of community relationships: **gemeinschaft** and **gesellschaft**. The classic German sociologist Ferdinand Tonnies (1957, originally 1887) applied gemeinschaft to societies in which relationships are based on family and kinship; they are more cohesive and share a strong sense of identity. Conversely, he proposed that relationships in most modern societies are based on self-interest, a concept he called gesellschaft. Gemeinschaft is often associated with a more communal spirit with close-knit relationships, while gesellschaft is associated with an emotionally cold world, one in which people are surrounded by strangers.

If modern society is based on self-interest, what are the means by which people relate to one another? In Georg Simmel's (Simmel 1978, originally 1900) famous work, *The Philosophy of Money*, he proposed that money has become a means by which individuals in society relate. Money carries with it a trust in social institutions in that it has no inherent value except the value given to it by society. We use it in almost every aspect of life. Money is bound in modern relationships, including friends (e.g., buying gifts or lunch) as well as family members (paying tuition for college, for instance) (Zelizer 2011). The influence of money on Western culture has led many analysts to agree that interactions themselves have been commodified, reflecting the concept of McDonaldization reviewed earlier in the chapter. People become consumers rather than producers of products and are reduced to selling themselves to find work (Bauman 2007).

The nature of community life has been especially scrutinized in the United States since the 1970s as a smaller percentage of people in recent generations are getting involved in committed organizational life such as being involved in churches, clubs, or voluntary groups (Anderson, Curtis, and Grabb 2006; Putnam 2000). These findings reflect a gesellschaft society, one based on self-interest. The effect of this transformation toward a self-interested society has led some sociologists to be concerned about a decline in personal relationships. Self realization becomes the measure of a relationship as individuals come into groups only to be "alone together" (Amato 2007; Brynin and Ermisch 2009; Illouz 2007). Some research does show that access to strong friendships and committed relationships have been in decline, but other research suggests that friendship networks have remained stable over time (McPherson, Lynn Smith-Lovin, and Brashears 2006; Scheff 2011; Wang and Wellman 2010). Still other research shows that individuals are still engaged in community life but in less formal, committed ways than in the past (Musick and Wilson 2008).

Put together, it is clear that transformations in modern society have changed the nature of the ways that we relate to each other, but it is not clear whether these changes are good or bad. We know that neighborhoods, organizations, and associations bridge individuals and society, building senses of well-being and trust on the individual level (Kusenbach 2006; Paxton 2007; Small 2009). These groups provide a source of interaction and sense of similarity—they are also a source for both fiscal and social capital. Perhaps the online world can serve a similar role in society as have traditional organizations or neighborhoods. Through the internet, people can maintain connections to people with whom they have no physical interaction, and those connections are almost instantaneous. The online world has become a place for connecting with others through social media, dating apps, gaming, and chat rooms, among other forums. Is this medium good or bad for social relationships? In one sense, being online gives us more control over the presentation of self through social media (see Chapter 5): we can even create avatars to control how we present ourselves to other people (Hillis 2009). Online communities can also serve to prompt face-to-face relationships (Chayko 2008). Much like when groups of people gathered for a light evening of cards decades ago, many people in the modern world continue to enjoy gaming environments as a place to express ephemeral roles, ones that are different from everyday life and reflects one's position in a particular group or situation (Perinbanayagam 2014; Zurcher 1970). A similar logic applies to online gaming such as Fortnite or League of Legends (Madigan 2016). In any case, it is an opportunity to turn off a front-stage performance and create a different one. In some sense, it is a way that society provides a place to be different. However, the same dilemmas found in physical communities exist in online environments. Participants in online dating, for instance, often view their relationship searches as a "market" like any other product, and individuals do misrepresent themselves to potential intimates (Hancock and Toma 2009; Heino, Ellison, and Gibbs 2010; Barraket and Henry-Waring 2008). Hence, it appears that being online, like other aspects of social life, can serve as a way to both build and hinder relationships.

Growing share of Americans say they use YouTube; Facebook remains one of the most widely used online platforms among U.S. adults

% of U.S. adults who say they ever use ...

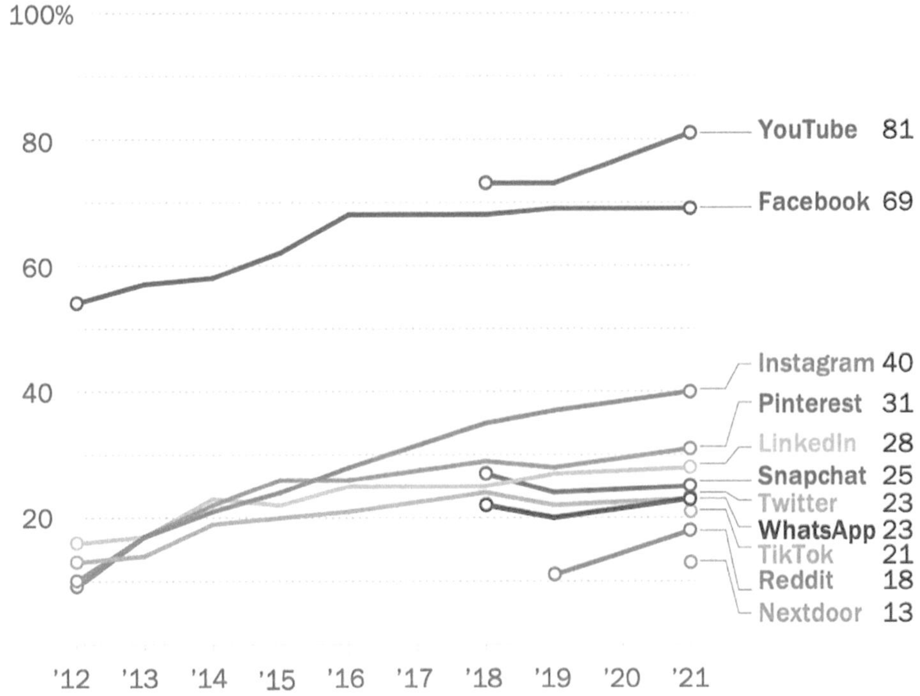

Note: Respondents who did not give an answer are not shown. Pre-2018 telephone poll data is not available for YouTube, Snapchat and WhatsApp; pre-2019 telephone poll data is not available for Reddit. Pre-2021 telephone poll data is not available for TikTok. Trend data is not available for Nextdoor.
Source: Survey of U.S. adults conducted Jan. 25-Feb. 8, 2021.
"Social Media Use in 2021"

PEW RESEARCH CENTER

Figure 10.2 Percent of People who Utilize Popular Online Sites.

Source: Auxier and Anderson (2021).

If video games can replace in-person games as a means of sustaining friendships, can we create gemeinschaft online? Can Instagram posts replace a neighborly exchange? Are online chatrooms the same as an evening meal together? Modern manifestations of community has been called **networked individualism**. It refers to "the ways in which people connect, communicate, and exchange information" using computers, mobile devices and other technologies (Rainie and Wellman 2014, p. 7). It is less about being embedded in groups than individuals who are connected. Such networks give individuals the ability to connect to a large number of people in a way that was not possible in the past. The individual is the center of this universe. While the internet provides a venue to find large numbers of like-minded others, levels of loneliness among youth have grown globally and is associated with smartphone access and internet use (Su and He 2024; Twenge et al. 2021). Taylor Dotson (2017) argues that there are different types of community, and the internet can only provide a type of community, it is not a direct replacement of traditional forms of interaction. It is clear that technology will continue to serve the purpose of connecting people, but it can never totally replace in-person interaction.

Section Summary

This section applied the social structure and personality perspective to answer the questions "do power and status affect the experience and use of emotions?" "What norms govern the use of emotions in different social settings?" and "How do social structural conditions affect relationships in society?" First, emotions are affected by positions in society in that people with higher positions may be more likely to express different types of emotions than people in lower positions. Second, there are a number of feeling rules and norms about the appropriate expression of emotion, such as those linked to gender or occupation. Finally, structural conditions such as the changing nature of society or increases in the use of the internet have changed the ways that people relate to one another by providing new ways to interact with one another. Thus, the social structure and personality perspective emphasizes how society structures the types of emotions that individuals express at any given time and the ways that we relate to one another.

A Take-Away Message

Have you ever experienced a situation in which you had to "fake" an emotion? It may have been a work or school setting in which you had to make a presentation about a project you cared little about. You may have had to smile as a cashier when you felt tired or stressed. Emotion rules help us to know how to display emotions under different conditions. It is the essence of emotional intelligence, which can help you at all levels of work. Managers need this skill when dealing with employees. Professionals must know how to manage emotions in tough situations like tight deadlines or working with difficult customers or co-workers. Knowing the sociology of emotional work may help you appreciate emotional dilemmas and concerns. Knowing how to manage your emotions the "appropriate" ways to respond to customers, colleagues, and management can help meet your needs in any given situation and ease tensions that arise on a day-to-day basis.

GROUP PROCESSES AND EMOTIONS

> *Man, that really made me mad. I worked my tail off on that group paper but only got a B. That's just not fair; I worked harder than the others, and they got Bs too!*
>
> —Justine, junior physics major

The group processes perspective seeks to study the development of emotion in group contexts. Like symbolic interactionism, group processes theory and research views emotions as stemming from interactions among individuals. Group processes scholars also incorporate the importance of statuses and norms in the development and expression of emotions. Some of the earliest work on group processes found that group interaction requires some level of socioemotional leadership to achieve its goals (Bales 1965).

In Justine's case, a sense of unfairness produces feelings of anger. Her desire for parity is an essential component of the exchange processes reviewed in previous chapters. We are not only motivated to maintain a balance between what we contribute to a group and what we get out of it, but a host of emotions are also associated with these processes. Group processes work on emotions tries to uncover the conditions under which different emotions are produced during interactions among people.

Feelings and Social Exchange

Imagine a situation in which you competed in a race only to lose narrowly to another runner. At first you congratulate the runner and then go on to receive the second-place award. However, you later find out that the winner cheated. How do you think that this news would make you feel? You would most likely see the loss as unfair, perhaps generating a sense of disgust and anger. If you cannot change the ruling of the race, that may also introduce a sense of frustration.

We reviewed social exchange theory in Chapter 4. One of the primary principles of social exchange theory is that individuals expect reciprocity in their interaction with other people. If we help other people, we expect about the same level of help from them some time in the future (Simpson et al. 2018). Researchers using social exchange theory study the effects of exchange processes on individuals' emotions (Whitham 2021). For example, exchange researchers want to know people's emotional reactions when they get too much or too little out of a series of exchanges. They also try to determine how the rules of the exchange, the procedure by which rewards are given in a group, influence people's emotional reactions to an interaction. In other words, it is not only who wins the game but also how the game is played.

A basic proposition of exchange theory is that emotions are affected by what people get out of their social interactions (Molm 1991) (see Box 10.3). In general, we are more satisfied when we get more than when we get less. Trying to predict the emotions people will feel based on the rewards they get, however, becomes more complex than simply saying that those who get more will feel more positive emotions. Imagine going to court for a speeding ticket and learning that the fine has been dropped. Now imagine working eight hours one day at a job, only to have your boss tell you at the end of the day that he has decided not to pay you for your time. Your reaction to an outcome of "nothing" in

Box 10.3 Aggression and Love in Psychology

Two traditional areas of research in psychological social psychology are love and aggression. One popular psychology theory argues that love has several different forms. Robert Sternberg developed the Triangular Theory of Love. This theory proposes that love has three basic components that can be combined to form eight types of love. The three basic components of love are intimacy (emotional closeness), passion (physical arousal), and commitment (the promise to maintain the relationship). Nonlove is when all three of these factors are not present in a relationship. This model is important because it can be applied to many different types of relationships, including family, friends, and lovers.

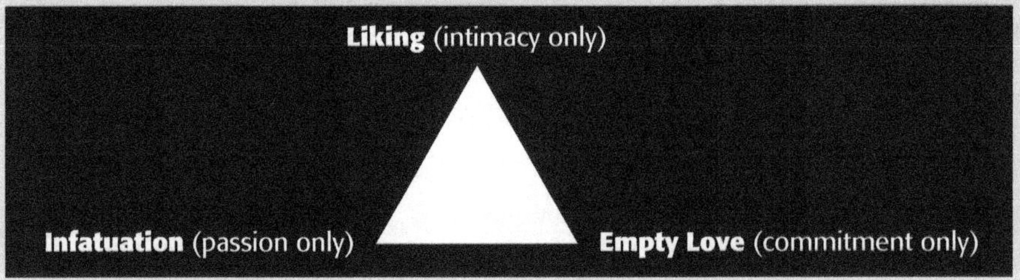

Aggression refers to the intentional harm of one person by another. One traditional explanation of aggression is the frustration–aggression hypothesis that argues that all aggression results from frustration linked to the blocking of a goal. Imagine you are driving to work and someone cuts you off, thus blocking your goal of getting to work safely and on time. This will likely cause a sense of frustration, leading you to act aggressively to resolve this emotion. This aggression may also be displaced on an individual other than the one who obstructed your plans.

These theories of love and aggression emphasize individual processes. They also assume a universal quality that can be applied to love and aggression in different cultures and at different times. Sociologists emphasize aspects of love and aggression that are beyond the individual. For example, interactionists would point to the fluid nature of emotions as they are constructed over time and place. Hence, the meaning of love varies across place and time.

those two situations would likely be very different—happy in the first situation, furious in the second. Social exchange theory proposes that our emotions are based on what we actually get in a situation as compared to some comparison referent. That comparison might be what we expected to get, what we think we should get, or what other people in similar situations have gotten. These comparisons are linked to matters of fairness and justice (Jasso 1980).

The **affect theory of social exchange** proposes that exchange relationships produce emotions that are used as an internal source of rewards and punishments for developing cohesion among individuals or between individuals and the group as a whole (Lawler 2001; Lawler, Thye, and Yoon 2008). Emotions serve as the basis of microsocial orders. When exchanges are successful, they produce positive feelings such as joy and pride, while less successful exchanges produce negative feelings such as anger or shame. The subsequent section examines ways in which emotions play a part in social exchange processes.

Justice and Emotion

Social exchange research often occurs in settings in which members of a group contribute to a group effort and are rewarded for their efforts. For instance, you may be asked to solve problems for your group. If you are particularly good at solving those problems, you might think you should be rewarded more than someone who has produced less for the group. Traditionally, exchange theorists propose that any imbalanced exchange should produce a negative emotion. Getting less reward for your work than you deserve may be met with anger, whereas getting more than you deserve may produce a sense of guilt.

The equity theory of emotion is based on the principle that individuals feel negative emotions when they perceive inequity in relationships—anger, for instance, if they get less than they deserve and guilt if they get more than they deserve (Turner and Stets 2005). There are at least two ways in which the fairness of exchange processes may affect emotions. Belief about the fairness of what people get is called **distributive justice**. If you believe that the amount of money you and your co-workers make is fair, then you feel that there is distributive justice. All things being equal, research shows that people expect to be compensated at the same rate as other people doing similar types and levels of work (Schneider and Valet 2017; Narisada 2020). However, people are also concerned about the procedures used to decide the distribution of goods. You may think that the outcomes are fair but that the procedures used to decide the outcomes are suspect. Belief about the fairness of the methods used to make distributions is called **procedural justice**.

In terms of distributive justice, research shows that people generally experience negative emotions when they get less than they think they deserve out of an exchange (Smith-Lovin 1995). Guilt is generally expected when people get more out of an exchange than they think they deserve, but research in this area has been inconsistent, sometimes showing guilt and sometimes not (Hegtvedt and Killian 1999; Homans 1974). In some cases, people may feel a positive emotion as a result of getting more out of an interaction than they think they deserve (Hegtvedt 1990; Smith-Lovin 1995).

In other cases, people feel guilty when they get more than their contributions merit. Finally, perceived fairness regarding procedural justice generally produces positive feelings about negotiations and helps relieve negative emotions about the outcomes of the exchanges between people (Hegtvedt and Killian 1999).

Can we apply these principles to our day-to-day lives? Consider a family in which some people believe that they are doing more work around the house than other members of the family. How do you think those people will feel? In a study of household labor, Kathryn Lively and her colleagues (Lively et al. 2010) studied the relationship between perceived equity in household chores and negative emotions such as anger, sadness, and shame. They found that individuals either under- or over-benefitting regarding household labor reported more negative emotions than people who perceived an equitable arrangement of chores, reflecting a sense of distributive justice.

Lynn Smith-Lovin*

Lynn Smith-Lovin received the Cooley Mead award in 2006 for her accomplishments as a sociological social psychologist. Smith-Lovin is the Robert L. Wilson Professor of Arts and Sciences at Duke University. Some of her best-known research has been on linking identities, emotions, and social action. She has been at the forefront of the development and application of affect control theory.

Lynn Smith-Lovin received her bachelor's and master's degrees in journalism at the University of North Carolina at Chapel Hill. She actually began to take sociology and psychology courses just for fun and ended up studying sociology with David Heise whose courses first drew her interest. There she quickly became a part of Heise's research team and began her journey to help explore and define affect control theory. She subsequently earned her PhD in sociology at the University of North Carolina.

Smith-Lovin's first job as an assistant professor was at the University of South Carolina, where she worked with John Skvoretz to collect and analyze a dataset of small group interactions that has become very widely used. In the late 1980s, Smith-Lovin moved to Cornell University. From there she relocated to the University of Arizona, where she teamed up with a former graduate school colleague, Linda Molm, to co-edit *Social Psychology Quarterly*.

Smith-Lovin has published more than 75 research articles to date, many in sociology's top journals. She has shaped and helped define the core of the sociology of emotions. She has been contributing to the intellectual and professional field of sociology for over a quarter of a century and has made a lasting impact on it.

*Information about this biography was obtained from Dr. Dawn Robinson's (Robinson 2007) introduction of the Cooley-Mead Award printed in *Social Psychology Quarterly* and personal correspondence with Dr. Smith-Lovin.

Status and Emotion

Earlier in this chapter, we discussed the importance of power and status for emotions. People who gain status develop a sense of pride, whereas losing status creates shame. Status characteristics theory (a theory in the expectation states program; see Chapter 4) focuses on the role of status in group relationships. Exchange processes represent a fundamental way in which individuals interact with one another, and people's statuses in groups influence those exchange processes in important ways.

The discussion of status characteristics theory in Chapter 4 made clear that group interactions go differently for high-status group members than for low-status group members. Individuals with high status in groups talk more, have their performances evaluated more highly, are asked more for their input, and have more influence over group decisions. In short, high status comes with perks. One outcome of this is that high-status group members experience more positive emotions. Michael Lovaglia and Jeffrey Houser (1996) carried out a study in which they randomly assigned some people to high-status positions by giving them titles. They found that participants who received the high-status titles enjoyed future interactions more than those who did not receive the titles. Other research (e.g., Kemper 1991; Lucas 1999; Stets and Asencio 2008) supports this basic finding: high-status group members experience more positive emotion than do low-status group members and have more control over emotional experiences in a group.

High- and low-status group members differ not only in their emotional experiences but also in their emotional expressions. Although group members of all statuses experience emotions, these emotions can be either suppressed or expressed. High-status group members, compared to low-status members, are freer to openly express their negative emotions (Ridgeway and Johnson 1990). In this way, social structure constrains the expression of emotion, with low-status group members facing pressure to not display the negative emotions they are more likely to feel. What do low-status people get in these types of interactions? Why don't they just leave them? Exchange theory and research suggests that high status members of groups may give things like respect to low status members in exchange for low-status members' deference to high status members (Ridgeway and Nakagawa 2017). Such exchanges of feelings are essential to the maintenance of relationships with varying levels of status among its members.

Power and Emotion

As we discussed, emotion is affected by what we get from our social interactions. In general, people who receive more feel more positive emotion than people who receive less (see Box 10.4 on Positive Psychology). Power is the ability to get what we want, even if other people want to stop us from getting it. As a result, we should expect power to affect emotional reactions.

Power comes from a different source than does status. Status in a group is based on esteem or respect. For example, you will likely defer to a doctor on medical matters because you respect her judgment. People with power might be respected, but they can get what they want even when they are not. Suppose that your boss tells you to do something. You may not like your boss, and you may not want to comply with her request, but if you don't do it, she has the power to fire you or otherwise create difficult work conditions for you.

Power in exchange comes from being structurally positioned to essentially demand compliance from other people. Edward Lawler and his colleagues (Lawler 2001; Lawyer, Thye, and Yoon 2000; Lawler and Yoon 1993) have developed a program of theory and research on the emotions that result from exchange relationships. They proposed that people feel positive emotion in exchange relationships when they feel a sense of control in those relationships.

Imagine that three students—Jorge, Susan, and Michael—are all in the same difficult class. The students sometimes share notes and discuss the class. However, of the three, only Susan has a clear understanding of the material. As a result, Jorge and Michael depend on her more than she does on either of them, and Susan will likely feel a greater sense of control. The work of Lawler and his colleagues indicates that she will experience more positive emotions in the interactions than will Jorge and Michael.

A question that is of fundamental interest to group processes scholars and to sociologists more generally is, "What binds people to their social relationships?" If we can understand what keeps people in their exchange relationships with others, then we will have solved a basic problem of social order: We will better understand why societies and the groups in them form and remain stable.

The work of Lawler and his colleagues shows that positive emotions bind people to their social relationships. In other words, when people feel positive emotions in their relationships with other people, they become committed to those relationships. Moreover, Lawler and colleagues have shown that relationships characterized by equal power are especially likely to engender positive emotion and commitment. Imagine what would likely happen in the study group example—Susan knows the material much better than Jorge or Michael. If the students are only tied to each other based on being in the same class, would you expect their study relationship to continue throughout the semester? Probably not. Susan would likely resent giving more than her fair share to the group, and Jorge and Michael might feel guilty about not contributing.

Now imagine a group of three students who both have a pretty good understanding of the course material. These students meet regularly to discuss the course, share notes, and so on. Would you expect the students to continue meeting throughout the semester? Probably. The students have equal power, and they derive equal benefits from the relationship. According to Lawler and his colleagues, they would likely feel positive emotion and develop a sense of commitment to the relationship.

Social Exchange Theory of Intimate Relationships

We have reviewed many ways in which exchange processes enter into relationships of every kind: perceptions of inequality occur on the job as well as in the home. Group processes researchers have also applied social exchange theory to study attraction processes. Here, attraction is based on principles of exchange: what people want from another person (e.g., companionship, money, personality, or looks) and what they have to exchange for those things. One common stereotype is a young beautiful woman dating

Box 10.4 Positive Psychology: The Science of Happiness

Work on emotion by psychologists has tended to focus on solving problems linked to negative emotions such as depression and anxiety. However, some psychologists focus on the opposite end of the spectrum. Instead of researching what makes people depressed, they systematically examine what makes people happy. Dr. Martin Seligman at the University of Pennsylvania is considered the father of this field, opening the Positive Psychology Center there. This research shows that most people are generally happy and that happiness levels fluctuate during different activities and at different times of the day (Layard 2005; Seligman 2002). Happiness also seems to be related to activity on the left-side of the brain and it is related to our genes: identical twins have more similar levels of happiness than nonidentical twins. Richard Layard (2005) indicates the "big seven" factors affecting happiness are family relationships, financial situation, work, community and friends, health, personal freedom, and personal values.

Research shows that social statuses such as being married, and employed, and being healthy appear to be associated with happiness and these relationships appear to be quite robust (Graham 2009). Sociologists tend to emphasize societal trends and conditions that affect happiness. Jason Schnittker (Schnittker 2008), for instance, studied this paradox: real incomes have gone up in US society over the last 30 years, but happiness levels have remained stagnant or have gone down. His research shows that one of the major contributors to the loss of happiness is the decline in marriage and marital satisfaction in the last 30 years. Yang Yang (2008) also found that happiness levels tend to increase as we age. In fact, differences in happiness by gender, race, and education decrease with age. Some cohorts are happier than others. Yang found that the baby-boom generation was less happy than others born before or after this time period, perhaps because the large size of this cohort increased competition in the labor market, creating more strains to achieve expected economic success among its members. That said, a national poll shows that the majority (73%) of Gen Z, those people born between 1997 and 2012, report being very or somewhat happy (Clifton and Hrynowski 2024).

It is also important to know that happiness is not necessarily always the best thing for you. Michael Hughes (2006) provides some evidence that humans need a mix of positive emotions (including happiness) along with a sense of meaning and purpose to produce enhanced quality of life. Although many things we do in life are challenging, such as caring for a young child or a person with a disability, and these experiences at times may not yield a great deal of happiness, they do give us a sense of meaning and purpose in life. Conversely, several activities associated with short-term positive emotions like drug and alcohol use have been shown to have negative long-term consequences for well-being. In short, true "happiness" is more than simply feeling good all of the time!

an older man. What might they have to exchange? Of course, we know that the woman has her youth and beauty, but the man is typically more financially secure. In this case, perhaps he exchanges his wealth for access to her youth and beauty.

What about situations when people leave relationships that appear to benefit them? Exchange theory could explain that with the satiation principle, in which people may devalue what they receive in an exchange over time (see Chapter 2). In addition, we must consider the alternatives to the object of our desire: can another person provide more than my current partner? This idea is referred to as the comparison level of alternatives:

A (Attraction) = CL (Comparison Level) − CLa (Comparison Level of Alternatives)

According to this approach, you enter a new relationship when you believe that what you get from that relationship is more than what you receive from other available alternative relationships. But what if your selection was limited by some factor—perhaps to the eligible population on a small rural campus? If you then leave for another, larger school in a big city, you will probably find that you have many more alternatives to choose from. From an exchange perspective, you will likely leave the initial relationship when you find someone with more (or different things) to offer you!

According to exchange theory, we will tend to leave relationships that do not benefit us in some way. A key question then remains: why do people stay in bad relationships? In this case, the outcomes of the relationship are negative. Here again, we can apply the idea of alternative comparisons. Your desire to stay in a bad relationship will be weighed against your opportunities in other relationships. Someone might stay in a relationship in which she is treated poorly if she perceives that all of her other possible relationships will have similar or worse disparities.

Exchange theory can also be applied to understand relationships in society more broadly. A major concern among modern scholars is the nature of trust. As we discussed earlier in the chapter, the nature of social life has changed dramatically as we have moved from a society based on gemeinschaft to one based more on geselleschaft. How are independent agents going to establish the kind of trust necessary for important, long-term, committed relationships if the relationships are based on self interest? In this case, it would be to our advantage to take advantage of others in every case. Edward Lawler and his colleagues (Lawler et al. 2009; see also Thye, Lawler, and Yoon 2011) propose that exchange network properties can be designed to promote collectively oriented behavior, despite the self-interest of individual members. Linda Molm and her colleagues (Molm et al. 2012) indicate that developing reciprocal exchanges is critical for groups—regardless of type—to establish trust among group members. A history of reciprocal exchange—one in which individuals give benefits to each other over time without obligations to do so—appears to build bonds of trust among individuals. Exchanging birthday and holiday gifts with friends and acquaintances, and alternating inviting each other to parties at your homes, represent the types of reciprocal exchanges that build trust and commitment in relationships.

This type of work is important to many interactions among people in the modern world. Consider online interactions, many of which are not close ties. How can you trust individuals on websites such as Amazon or Facebook Marketplace to pay for items or send good items through the mail? In this venue, trust is established based on past relationships—individuals are often rated on whether they have upheld their agreements in the past (Cook et al. 2009). Given the global dimensions of many modern relationships, often using the internet, scholars have begun to explore interpersonal ways to create cooperation without the use of trust (Molm, Hardin and Levi, 2006) or to find more micro-level systems for creating trust. Creating an environment in which people believe that others are trustworthy and performing prosocial behaviors helps to promote cooperative behaviors in groups (Cohen and Isaac 2020; Doyle 2021; Kong and Yao 2021). These types of studies help to demonstrate the ways that individuals in work and other groups can participate in the creation of trust even if the larger culture is not conducive to establishing trusting relationships.

The economic approach to families overlaps with social exchange theory to help explain why we have children and how many. In one sense, children cost more than they provide: they are unable to provide work or income for many years. Why do parents invest in them? According to economist Gary Becker (1991; see also Foster 1993), families invest in their children in order to gain benefits in one way or another. As income goes up, families can afford to have more children and to invest more in each child, usually in the form of education. However, the more you spend on quantity, the less you have to spend on quality. Hence, from this perspective, families must choose between the two, which may explain why some people choose to have fewer children. This variation of social exchange principles suggests that all human interactions, even in families, have a utility motive.

Section Summary

Group processes research was used in this section to answer the questions "How do group settings affect emotions?" and "How do group processes researchers approach the study of relationships?" Group contexts are important to understanding emotions in two ways. First, the principles of social exchange theory suggest that individuals in groups seek justice and fairness. If people do not perceive justice, especially if they feel under-rewarded, negative emotions result. Second, our positions in groups can affect our emotions. Higher status people, for instance, experience more positive emotions because of the rewards that accompany high status. Positive emotions also help to sustain group interactions. Exchange principles are also important to relationship development because they help explain the conditions under which people choose to enter some relationships and not others.

A Take-Away Message

Fairness matters. As children, we may tell our parents that they are not being fair. Perhaps your sibling got more dessert than you did. You may have responded by saying to your parents, "That's not fair—she got more than I did!" Research and theory in the group processes perspective suggest that we carry that attention to fairness into adulthood. We may not say anything, but we feel it and it may influence our interactions with other people. Perhaps we should not be afraid to tell people when we believe that something is not fair. At least in personal relationships, it may help resolve some tension. You may also consider these dynamics before you enter into a relationship with someone, to ensure that there is fairness from the start. On the job, much of office politics revolve around perceptions of fairness. Perhaps someone got a promotion that other people did not consider "fair." As a manager, you would have to consider not only what you consider to be fair but also what others would perceive as fair. By doing so, you may not only reduce negative emotions but potentially increase a sense of cohesion in your work group.

BRINGING IT ALL TOGETHER

> *Without love, you really wouldn't have anything when you think about it. Your friends and family would mean nothing to you and you'd have no reason not to hurt someone else. Even your job would become a bore without some love for it, or at least for your co-workers.*
>
> —Janelle, sophomore anthropology major

We have applied three sociological social psychology theoretical perspectives to understand the role of emotions in society. Emotions can be barriers within and across civil societies—more specifically, as fuel for feuds and disputes among people. However, we have also seen the important role that emotions can play in the development of society. Janelle's analysis of love reflects the positive effect of emotions in our lives—giving people and activities purpose and meaning. A considerable amount of work using the symbolic interactionist perspective focuses on the social construction of emotional states. From this perspective, emotions serve to help construct and maintain society by providing cues for how to behave during interactions and as a motivation to participate in social life.

The social structure and personality perspective shows that emotions are not necessarily irrational. Research and theory from this perspective emphasizes the ways that emotional outcomes are structured by social arrangements with positions and social norms governing types and degrees of emotional expression. Finally, the group processes perspective studies emotions in group contexts, showing how emotions both reflect group position and affect relationships between group members. Together, these perspectives tie individuals' emotional expressions to larger social conditions.

SUMMARY

1. Sociological perspectives on emotion emphasize the cybernetic approach to the study of emotion—that emotions radiate upward from individual-level interactions to maintain social structures as well as downward in the form of social structure helping to shape our emotions.

2. Symbolic interactionists believe we learn emotions like we learn about other aspects of social life, through interaction with other people. The sociocentric model of emotional socialization argues that the primary means of learning about emotions comes from social instruction, whereas affect control theory argues that people use emotions as signals as to how well they are performing their role in a given situation.
3. The four pillars of attraction are proximity, similarity, physical attractiveness, and reciprocal liking.
4. People use emotional scripts and cues to help use and manage emotions in day-to-day life. The theory of interaction ritual chains emphasizes the role of emotions in maintaining macrosociological social institutions.
5. The power–status approach to emotions says that emotions result from real, anticipated, imagined, or recollected outcomes of social interactions. The gain and loss of power and status are primary ways in which our position affects our emotional life.
6. The norms that govern our emotional lives are called "feeling rules." We may receive "rule reminders" from friends and family when we do not "feel" appropriately. Emotion work refers to the generation of prescribed emotion to meet the demands of a job. The commodification of emotions is associated with the concept of "McDonaldization."
7. The nature of community life (e.g., the nature of gemeinschaft vs. gesellschaft) influences the nature of relationships developed in society by focusing on self-interest and rational approaches to intimate relationships.
8. The socioemotional economy is a system for regulating emotional resources among people that link individuals into larger networks of people. Sympathy is an important example of this economy. Emotion culture refers to a society's expectation about how to experience different emotions.
9. Exchange theory of emotions is based on the idea that people feel positive emotion in exchange relationships when they feel a sense of control in those relationships.
10. Exchange has also been used to understand attraction processes: what people want from another person (e.g., companionship, money, personality, or looks) and what they have to exchange for those things.

KEY TERMS AND CONCEPTS

Affect: An evaluative component of an emotion.

Affect theory of social exchange: Exchange-based theory in which exchange relationships are thought to produce emotions that are used as internal sources of rewards and punishments for developing cohesion among individuals and groups.

Cybernetic approach: The study of emotion that assumes that social conditions shape our emotions; and in turn, our emotions act to maintain social structures.

Distributive justice: In exchange theory, it is the beliefs about the fairness of what people get.

Edgework: Thrill-seeking behaviors designed to produce intense emotions.

Emotion culture: A society's expectation about how to experience different emotions.

Emotion work: The generation of prescribed emotion in order to meet the demands of a job.
Emotional cues: Information about when and what emotions are appropriate in a given social setting.
Emotional discrimination: Attributing secondary (i.e., human) emotions to our in-groups and not to our out-groups.
Emotional energy: A heightened sense of excitement produced by a feeling of belonging in society.
Emotional intelligence: Our ability to control and employ emotions in our social environments.
Emotional label: Element of emotion referring to the terms we use to label our feelings.
Emotional scripts: Expectations about when and how to act excited, angry, sad, and so on.
Emotions: Feelings that incorporate situational cues, physiological changes, expressive gestures, and an emotion label.
Ephemeral role: A role that is different from everyday life and reflects one's position in a particular group or situation.
Equity theory of emotion: Theory based on the principle that individuals feel negative emotions when they perceive inequity in exchange relationships.
Evaluation: Element of affect control theory referring to how a person's sentiment toward an object is good or bad.
Expressive gestures: Element of an emotion referring to the indications we give of the emotion we are experiencing.
Feeling rules: Rules that tell us how we should feel in different social interactions.
Feelings: Internal states associated with a particular emotion.
Gemeinschaft: Societies in which relationships are based on family and kinship.
Gesellschaft: Societies in which relationships are based on self-interest.
Homophily: The tendency to be attracted to people from the same ethnic or social class background.
Interaction ritual: The exchange of symbols and emotion between individuals essential to maintaining society.
McDonaldization: The process of hyperrationality of the service workforce, or applying assembly-line techniques to interpersonal work.
Mood: A diffuse emotional state that lasts a relatively long period of time.
Moral emotions: Those emotions that compel us to follow the rules of society.
Networked individualism: A new social operating system in which people relate in less hierarchical networks of interaction using technology.
Physiological changes: Element of emotion referring to the changes in our body that reflect the emotion in a given situation.
Potency: Element of affect control theory referring to how a person's sentiment toward an object is powerful or powerless.
Power–status approach: The study of emotions based on the idea that human emotions result from real, anticipated, imagined, or recollected outcomes of social relations.
Primary emotions: Physiologically grounded emotions that we inherit through evolutionary processes, including anger, fear, or sadness.

Procedural justice: In exchange theory, it is the beliefs about the fairness of the methods used to make distributions.

Secondary emotions: Emotions that derive from primary emotions when we attach varying meanings to primary emotions.

Sentiment: A feeling that has been given meaning by society.

Situational cues: Element of emotion that tells when and what emotion is appropriate in a given social interaction.

Sociocentric model of emotional socialization: Theory that argues that the primary means of learning about emotions comes from social instruction, primarily through family, friends, and schooling.

Socioemotional economy: A system for regulating emotional resources among people.

Sympathy account: The amount of sympathy that a person can expect from other people.

Theory of interaction ritual chains: Theory that emphasizes the role of emotions in maintaining macrosociological institutions.

DISCUSSION QUESTIONS

1. How many different words can you come up with to describe the emotions of love, frustration, or anger? That is, how many different dimensions of a "feeling" can you come up with?
2. Think of a social situation in which an emotion was present (e.g., a sports event, party, or funeral). How do you think other people would have reacted if you acted with no emotion? Why?
3. To what degree do you think that emotions are innate versus learned? Why?
4. Do you think you could develop and sustain a strong personal relationship completely online, with no physical interaction? Why or why not?
5. Consider some of the intimate relationships you have been in. Can you apply the principles of attraction reviewed earlier in the chapter to explain why you entered a recent relationship? How might exchange principles explain why you left (or someday might leave) it?
6. Discuss some of the ways you have felt when someone treated you unfairly. What were some of things you did, if anything, to manage your feelings?

11

Collective Behavior

I was terrified entering the grocery store. The whole town was on lockdown because of COVID and I had this one chance to go and get my food. Just as I left my car, I realized that I did not have a mask. Holding the phone tightly against my face, I tried to enter the store, grab my food, and use the self-checkout before anyone would notice. Everyone noticed. The looks they gave me, even though I really could just see their eyes, met every expectation I had that they would call me out. And someone did, "What are you doing in here without a mask!" a woman angrily shouted at me. I was petrified! I just dropped everything and ran out of the store in tears.

—Danielle, senior education major

In crowds and other collectives of people, we sometimes act differently than we otherwise would. Danielle's story reflects the experiences of many people early in the COVID-19 epidemic. People in many nations were ordered to stay home and the few times they could go out was to obtain essential things like food. Were the people in the store really overcome with anger or fear toward the lone person without a mask? Even if they were not, Danielle believed that they were going to do something to her, and those beliefs affected her in a direct way. She will certainly never forget this experience!

Sociologists have studied crowd behaviors in many different forms including celebrations, ceremonies, riots, fads, disasters, demonstrations, and social movements. We can also think about mob behaviors as part of crowd actions. Scholars studying collective behaviors assess collective ways of thinking and feeling as well as social movements, which are political actions in which individuals come together to change the world in some way. This chapter will provide an overview of social psychological theories and research on collective behavior. Earlier in the book we defined collective behavior as action or behavior of people in groups or crowds, usually as a reaction to an event or to express a common sentiment (Rohlinger and Snow 2003). This behavior typically includes situations in which individuals act differently in group contexts or when numbers of people become fixated on an object or idea for a period of time.

The term collective behavior came into use in the 1920s, when Samuel Henry Prince (1920) discussed "collective behavior" in his study of the great Halifax, Nova Scotia, explosion of 1917. The first introductory sociology text ever published, Robert Park and Ernest Burgess's *Introduction to the Science of Sociology* (1921), also included a chapter on collective behavior. Although crowds are viewed by sociologists as a form of collective behavior, one of the earliest books written about crowds, Charles Mackay's *Memoirs of Extraordinary Popular Delusions and the Madness of Crowds* (1852), never used the term collective behavior. Likewise, Gustave LeBon, who is often credited as the pioneer of "collective behavior," never used the term when he wrote his book *The Crowd* (1960, originally 1895). The early work of Mackay and LeBon focused on crowd excitement and included discussions of the fickleness, sentimentality, mania, and amorality of crowds. This treatment of crowds as irrational entities came to dominate most of the first century of sociological writing about crowds and collective behavior.

In 1968, Carl Couch challenged views of crowds as irrational when he proposed crowds are no more or no less bizarre than other social systems (Couch 1968). Evidence to support his view soon came. Researchers working through the newly established Disaster Research Center at Ohio State University began to regularly find that survivors of disasters could care for themselves and others and restore order to their communities rather quickly; they did not stampede from danger or become helpless because of emotional shock, as earlier stereotypes suggested.

In the 1970s, Clark McPhail led teams of observers to demonstrations, civil disorders, sporting events, and shopping malls to systematically observe crowds. McPhail's teams utilized multimedia data collection techniques. They first used notepads and check sheets for recording data manually, and later augmented these with film and video cameras. Simultaneous observations were made at several locations in or near crowds. After studying and comparing data from hundreds of events, McPhail concluded that much of what had been previously written about crowds and collective behavior was not accurate (Miller 2000). To distinguish his work from earlier treatments, he began to refer to crowds as gatherings and to write about collective action within gatherings. By the 1980s, sociologists generally began to use the term **collective action** to reflect the seemingly purposive nature of people's behavior when they collectively celebrate, mourn, worship, protest, compete in athletics, or confront disasters.

Another major concept in the literature on collective behavior and action is "social movements." Herbert Blumer (1972) defined **social movements** as collective action designed to produce new social orders. Collective action can sometimes turn into social movements, which incorporate large-scale goals and plans that often exceed the temporary nature of most other forms of collective behavior or action. This chapter will review theories and research related to the concepts of collective behavior, collective action, and social movements (see Box 11.1 for a discussion of the ways that the COVID-19 pandemic reflected dimensions of collective behavior). Specifically, we will address the following questions:

- Do people act differently in large groups than when they are alone? How do crowds contribute to the development of mass hysteria?
- What theories explain individuals' behavior in large groups?
- What structural conditions affect crowd behaviors?
- What are the phases of collective action found in large social movements? What kinds of behavior occur during a period of collective action?
- How do group and individual motivations interact in social movements?

CONSTRUCTING COLLECTIVE BEHAVIOR

> *It will be remarked that among the special characteristics of crowds there are several—such as impulsiveness, irritability, incapacity to reason, the absence of judgment, and of the critical spirit, the exaggeration of the sentiments, and others besides are almost always observed in beings belonging to inferior forms of evolution—in women, savages, and children, for instance.*
>
> —Gustave LeBon (1960, originally 1895, p. 36)

Photo 11.1 Along with a focus on protests and riots, researchers investigate other types of collective action such as flash mobs, in which participants learn about when and where to show up via social media. Have you ever seen or been part of a flash mob?

Source: Evgeny Krasilnikov/Shutterstock

Box 11.1 The COVID-19 Pandemic as Collective Behavior

The COVID-19 pandemic became a major issue around the world starting in March of 2020. Many stores were shut down and people were advised to stay home. But the measures taken in North America may be comparatively mild compared to China, where citizens had been directed to stay home long before that date. Can we apply concepts associated with collective behavior to the study of the impacts of the pandemic? This pandemic was a global phenomenon. While not every country "locked down" like the United States, Canada, and China, many of them did, reflecting the concept of collective action. (Note that World War I and World War II did not involve every country, but they are still referred to as "world" wars.). It is clear that many people acted in a state of panic, uncertain of the effects of the virus. Stories of people being hypervigilant about cleaning and wearing masks abounded. Some people left packages unopened for days or weeks over concerns that they may get the virus by touching them. There are elements of social movements present during COVID-19 times, such as the "antivaccination" movement, that existed before this pandemic (see Reich 2016). While most of these attitudes and behaviors are no longer covered in popular media, governments continue to invest time and resources in getting people vaccinated against COVID and preparing for another outbreak while other groups try to defy government edicts with a lasting distrust of large pharmaceutical companies. Do you remember where you were during the height of the pandemic? How did you react, if at all? How might your thoughts, feelings, and behavior be reflected in the concepts reviewed in this chapter?

The French Revolution (1789–1794) is associated with some of the ghastliest behaviors by groups in the history of humankind. Mobs of French citizens would go through the streets of Paris, collecting people to be killed in the name of the Revolution. A state of paranoia existed in France at the time. Although Gustave LeBon lived after the French Revolution, he sought to understand why such "cultured" people could become like dogs, killing their victims in packs. The French went from being seen among the most "civilized" people in the world to individuals willing to commit the most barbaric acts when in crowds.

Since LeBon's writings, social scientists have tried to understand the social conditions that produce such changes in individuals. Some contemporary perspectives stem from LeBon's early work, emphasizing the emotional changes in people that result from being in a crowd. Other scholars emphasize the rational aspects of crowd behavior.

Mass Hysteria Theory

Everyday life is composed of a wide variety of collective events, such as high school basketball games, that are characterized by the joined expression of intense feeling. Early writers such as Mackay (1852) found such "crowd madness" a worthy subject for pioneering work. LeBon was struck by the more spectacular, emotion-laden events that were part of revolutions that overthrew the monarchies of Europe. The concern for collectively experienced and expressed emotion is the basis of the earliest general theory in the field of collective behavior.

LeBon probed the workings of crowds, representative forms of government, and social movements throughout his academic career. In bold terms, LeBon wrote that all crowds exert an inherently negative influence on people. This thinking is the basis of **mass hysteria theory** (also called **contagion theory**), in which individuals in crowds lose the ability to think and act rationally. LeBon describes groups' influence on their members as a rapidly transmitted, **contagious mental unity**, a sense of a shared emotional bond that emerges whenever people interact in a group—be it a revolutionary street crowd or a parliament—making individuals act more on animalist emotions than reason. For LeBon, contagious mental unity, or when people are overcome with a shared emotion in a crowd, was the root cause of the horrors he witnessed during the Paris riots of 1871.

Like other writers of his time, LeBon adopted terminology drawn from Darwin's essays on biological evolution and spoke in degrading, misogynistic ways that would not be accepted now. LeBon stated that the contagious mental unity of crowds reduces the mental capacity of enlightened and cultured people to the level of "those inferior forms of evolution," such as "women, savages, and children." The three main ingredients of contagion theory are as follows:

1. *Intensity of behavior*: situations in crowds in which people quickly lose their inhibitions to act, and the tempo of their behavior increases.
2. *Homogeneity of mood and action*: people in crowds exhibit a shared willingness to follow suggestions, as in a hypnotic trance.
3. *Irrational behavior*: when people within crowds act without reason, they are incapable of respect for social standards, conventions, and institutions.

With these three ingredients, the crowd is unable to sustain focus and moves rapidly from one object or idea to another. Increased intensity is accompanied by homogeneity of mood and action in which people exhibit a shared willingness to follow suggestions, which LeBon described as similar to a hypnotic trance. Finally, the result of these processes, according to mass hysteria theory, is that this contagious mental unity overcomes individuals' rational capabilities. People in the crowd do not consider consequences of their actions; perceptions are distorted, and feelings of power emerge that become the basis of attacks on authorities or unfortunate victims. Mass hysteria theory proposes that without critical ability and powers of reflection, people within crowds are incapable of respect for social standards, conventions, and institutions—irrational behavior, when people act without reason, is characteristic of the crowd.

Although LeBon described the effects of contagious mental unity, he did not explain how this mental unity emerges in crowds. For this reason, the famous sociologist Robert K. Merton (1960) characterized LeBon as a problem finder rather than a problem solver. Sigmund Freud, a contemporary and critic of LeBon, attempted to explain contagious mental unity as the result of crowd members' unconscious love of the crowd leader. This psychoanalytic explanation, set forth in *Group Psychology and the Analysis of the Ego* (Freud 1945, originally 1921), has had little influence within the field of collective behavior, but there have been other attempts to account for contagious mental unity.

The idea of contagion and mass hysteria do not have to involve large-scale violent events. They can apply to other situations as well. For example, one of the earliest studies examined peoples' reaction to the *War of the Worlds* radio broadcast that aired on October 30, 1938, in which radio broadcasters portrayed an invasion of Earth by Martians (Cantril 1940, 1966). The broadcast was designed to sound realistic, using real places and street names. Media accounts of the broadcast suggested that residents fled New York en masse to escape the alien invasion. Careful study of public reaction, however, showed very little mass hysteria among city residents. Virtually all the listeners who became frightened by the broadcast tuned in about 12 minutes into the broadcast, when the studio actors enacted a realistic-sounding news report from where the spaceship supposedly landed. But only a small group of residents became panic-stricken by the event. Even those who fled the city primarily got in their cars and went to the homes of friends and family. In other words, accounts of mass hysteria in reaction to the broadcast were exaggerated. On a more mundane level, Jeffrey Stokes (2017) applied the logic of contagion to explain how husbands and wives come to assess marital quality, showing that "for both husbands and wives, baseline marital quality was significantly related with one's own and one's partner's marital quality four years later" (215). That is, one spouses' baseline marital quality ratings impacted the other spouses' marital quality ratings four years later. Similar findings have been found via networks of friends and family with other emotions and states like happiness, loneliness, and depression (see Christakis and Fowler 2013). It may not be mass hysteria as conceived by LeBon, but it does suggest that emotional contagion appears in everyday life and there is no reason to believe that it cannot happen in large crowds taking the form or riots and protests.

Herbert Blumer and Circular Reaction

In 1934, 39 years after *The Crowd* was published, symbolic interactionist Herbert Blumer wrote an essay titled "Outline of Collective Behavior" (Blumer 1972). He shared LeBon's belief that people are affected by crowds—crowds can create emotional reactions that dispose people to act differently than when they are alone—but Blumer's "Outline" is not as value laden as LeBon's *The Crowd*. For example, Blumer did not describe contagious mental unity as similar to the mental processes of "inferior forms of evolution." Unlike *The Crowd*, Blumer's "Outline" is a more objective classification and analysis of crowd-related phenomena. More so than LeBon, Blumer attempted to describe social-psychological mechanisms through which mental unity develops. Blumer also classified different types of crowds. In some sense, any human gathering can set the stage for collective activities as individuals become charged with emotional energies (see Chapter 10). Alice Goffman (2018) proposed that interactions among individuals in groups can lead to personal change, based on learning new ideas to incorporate into personal goals and plans that had never been considered before. It would make sense that those same energies can be used to motivate individuals in such groups into collective action.

On the macro-level, remarkable events, such as the destruction of the World Trade Center and Pentagon on September 11, 2001, create tensions that dispose individuals to gather together. Full of energy from both the event and emotion simply from being around each other, people anxiously move about in a seemingly aimless and random fashion. Blumer (1972) called such apprehensive behavior **milling**. He pointed out that milling is not a feature of all crowds, and that milling can vary in intensity.

According to Blumer, intense milling can transform human interaction in a fundamental way. He stated that there is ordinarily a largely covert, **interpretive phase** to human interaction; that is, people respond to one another by interpreting the other's gestures and remarks, rehearsing or visualizing a possible response, and then responding. This phase of interaction acts as a buffer that lengthens the time between stimulus and response, thus allowing people to differentiate themselves from others by composing their own responses rather than mirroring other's action in a simple stimulus–response fashion. Finally, it is within the interpretive phase of interaction that rationality resides, where outcomes or consequences of action are envisioned, and where alternative lines of action are compared.

Under conditions of intense milling, the interpretive phase of the act is disrupted; in some situations, such as a crowded gymnasium during a sports game, it may become so noisy that people cannot "hear themselves think." As the interpretive phase of interaction deteriorates, the buffer effect is lost, and behavior becomes intense and rapid, differentiation becomes more difficult, and people act alike—unanimity in mood and action prevails. Finally, with the interpretive phase of interaction gone, people become suggestible and irrational. Blumer described this state as **circular reaction** and called it a natural mechanism of collective behavior.

To LeBon, crowds are inclined toward destruction and foolishness. Blumer (1972) presented a more elaborate classification of crowds based on focus and internal cohesiveness. **Acting crowds** develop a focus, or goal, and act with unity to achieve the goal. An example of the acting crowd is a throng of townspeople who assemble a brass band and hastily build a speaker's platform in anticipation of a surprise visit from their governor. An **expressive crowd** lacks a goal and is primarily just a setting for tension release, often through rhythmical action such as applause, dancing, or singing. An audience offering a standing ovation at the end of a concert or theatre production, for example, is an expressive crowd.

Blumer stated that aggregates of people dispersed over large geographic areas can, under conditions of social unrest, assume some of the characteristics of compact acting and expressive crowds. A **public** is an aggregate of people, often from the same social class, who are concerned with a specific issue. A public discusses ways to address the issue, such as a community deciding on a school bond referendum. A **mass** is composed of anonymous individuals from many social strata; it is loosely organized and does not engage in discussion or interaction. Blumer cited the California Gold Rush of 1849 and other human migrations as examples of mass behavior.

Blumer (1972) emphasized how collective behavior evolves into new forms of group and institutional conduct. Within crowds, publics, and masses appear new expectations, values, conceptions of rights and obligations, tastes, and moods on which new social systems are founded. For LeBon, crowds bring about the downfall of civilizations; for Blumer, crowds play an important part in the development of new forms of social life.

Linking Social and Collective Identities

One underlying assumption of the crowd transformation perspective is that there is some sort of connection between group members that makes people in a crowd less individualistic than in other social settings. This sense of "oneness" is important to understanding why people join and continue to participate in collective activity (Rohlinger and Snow 2003). Although we no longer speak of "contagious mental unity," the basic idea continues to be an important aspect of research in collective behavior. **Collective identity** refers to individuals' sense of connection with a larger community or group (Polletta and Jasper 2001). Collective identity provides boundaries for its social movement members, a shared sense of purpose that motivates individual members to work for the movement (Stryker, Owens, and White 2000). During a year-long ethnography in Chicago and Hong Kong of the Falun Gong, a Chinese religious movement that has global reach, Cheris Shun-ching Chan (2013) demonstrated the importance of ideology and "doing ideology" in sustaining the movement: "The collective gatherings of the FLG followers were essential to sustaining individual followers' faith, as they provided a platform for engaging in discursive practices to enact and reproduce their ideological commitment" (14). In this sense, when members of a movement incorporate the movement into their identities, it yields the same kind of dynamics as predicted by identity and social identity theories (see Chapter 5) (Stryker 2000). For example, individuals' level of participation in a social movement will depend, in part, on how salient the movement is to their identities. If a movement is particularly important to you, you are more likely to participate in its activities and contribute your time and money. However, this dynamic is complicated by the fact that most of us are members of different groups and roles that may impinge on our desire to support one particular movement. For instance, you may really want to help the poor, but your school, work, and home commitments make it hard for you to act on your desire to help. You may even join a service organization designed to bring food to people living in poverty within your community but miss meetings or rarely volunteer to do service for the group because it conflicts with your work obligations or responsibilities at home. Such complexities may leave you feeling conflicted because you are unable to live up to the demands of your various identities. You truly want to help those with fewer resources through this group, but you also want to be a good student, worker, and family member. Multiple roles and group memberships may help to explain why some members are more involved than others, even if the movement is equally important to all of them.

Collective identity affects every stage of collective behavior. First, movements may emerge because individuals from varying backgrounds develop a sense of connection resulting from shared frustration over an issue (Ghaziani and Baldassarri 2011; Lindsay 2008; Polletta and Jasper 2001; Reger, Myers, and Einwohner 2008). For instance, you may have a strong concern over environmental or gay-rights issues, drawing you to affiliate with people who have similar convictions. Movements that center around specific issues rather than class-based political mobilizations (e.g., workers' rights) have been dubbed **new social movements** (see Lee 2007). Our senses of collective identity may also help in maintaining commitment to such causes. Members of a movement may use this sense of connection—this collective identity—to motivate others to join the cause. It may also serve to motivate current members to become more active in the movement. A member may share her experience helping to change policy, giving people a sense of hope in achieving their goals. Emotional bonds among members may serve a similar role in the formation and maintenance of social movements, inspiring members to continue their work in the movements (Parker and Hackett 2012). William Roy (2010) argues that folk music, which is often associated with protest movements of the 1960s, serves as a source of solidarity among members of a movement and an agent of social change—an emotional call to social change.

Collective identities also help movement leaders make choices regarding the direction and goals of a movement (Polletta and Jasper 2001). Collective identities help define who we are. A pacifist group, for example, will likely choose a nonviolent sit-in as a protest rather than aggressive tactics to maintain congruence between their goals and methods. Finally, identities play a role in the outcomes of social movements, either as a part of the movement itself (e.g., self-help movements) or as a way of transforming the culture, giving greater legitimacy to the movement or the activists' senses of self over time. Hence, collective identities can serve to transform a group's members and the larger culture.

Rational Choice in Collective Behavior: Emergent Norm Theory

One challenge of studying collective behavior is that both highly charged, emotional behavior as well as calm, rational behavior can occur in groups. Blumer (1972) tried to address this combination in his theory of circular reaction in which heightened emotions result from lack of communication among group members. More recently, researchers have focused on the rational side of behavior in large groups—the decisions people make during panics and other such events (Mawson 2007). These researchers tend to call this behavior "collective action" rather than collective behavior (Miller 2000). The idea is that people in groups are purposive in their decisions and actions in everyday life, including larger group events. Groups do not usually transform into mobs, and people continue to have a sense of agency during such events (McPhail 2006). The same can be said of social movements (Youngblood 2016). Several theories and research studies have addressed this topic.

In their book, *Collective Behavior*, Ralph Turner and Lewis Killian (1972) proposed that groups constrain their members more than producing some sort of contagious emotional reaction. In short, the **emergent norm theory** of collective behavior focuses on how individuals come to accept the constraints imposed by a group. These norms are conveyed using techniques that include gestures and verbal statements. This perspective also assumes that individuals enter groups with unique attitudes and perspectives, a feature of the crowd called **differential expression**. Because of this, people in a crowd might not act in unison.

Individuals may change their attitudes as members of a group over time, but this process is relatively rational compared to the contagion models discussed earlier in this chapter. Most group interactions are rational simply because cultures have learned ways to manage those events. Funerals, weddings, and other such events have prescribed roles and norms that govern how people should act in those situations. However, some groups may face situations in which there are no norms to guide individual behavior. Protests and rallies often lack clear guidelines for how members should act. In these cases, behavior may seem irrational because the group has not had the time to develop norms for its members. However, rationality is the norm; that is, groups move toward rationality when possible and tend to fall into irrationality only under conditions that limit the ability of group members to communicate behavioral guidelines.

In one application of emergent norm theory, researchers interviewed over 400 people who worked in New York's World Trade Center after the 1993 bombing there to assess evacuation behaviors (Aguirre, Wenger, and Vigo 1998). The explosion occurred around noon on February 26, killing six people. Thousands of people from the two 110-story buildings had to be evacuated amid fire and smoke-filled stairways. Electrical power was lost, leaving elevators, lighting, and public address systems inoperable. The researchers studied the milling behavior of evacuees, assessing the effects of group size and social relationships on their evacuation patterns. They found that most people were in groups, and about half of those groups had 20 or more people. A considerable amount of milling occurred in these groups, which involved largely rational behavior such as seeking information about the event and advice about what to do. Most found the people around them to be helpful during the event. Less than 10% of the workers fled the scene without engaging in confirmatory behavior. Amazingly, even under quite threatening conditions, the symbolic interaction (i.e., meaning-making) processes among co-workers were used to help shape appropriate evacuation procedures.

Turner and Killian (1972) also described different types of crowd participants. People bring different backgrounds and resources to an event that may affect their responses. These types include the following:

1. **Ego-involved participant**: a person who participates in a crowd activity because of a strong personal commitment to the issue with which the group is involved.
2. **Concerned participant**: a crowd participant motivated by concern over a group's goal or issue who does not incorporate the issue into her identity.
3. **Insecure participant**: a participant looking for direction from the group.
4. **Curiosity seeker**: a crowd participant motivated by curiosity about the group or event.

Consider the men who went to the Million Man March a generation ago in 1995, or all of the people who went to the 2013 mass protest in New York City over the killing

Photo 11.2 In 2018, hundreds of thousands of people gathered in Washington, DC, during a March for Our Lives rally.

Source: Joseph Sohm/Shutterstock

of Trayvon Martin, which is associated with the beginnings of the Black Lives Matter movement. Some of these people may have been there because the movements represented an important part of who they were. African American identity was an important aspect of their lives, shaping their thoughts and opinions about the world. There may also have been participants who shared the leaders' concerns over issues facing African American people but who did not incorporate the movement into their own senses of self. A third group included people who were looking for a sense of identity in the march; by participating in it, they hoped to gain a better sense of who they were as African American men and fathers (in the case of the Million Man March) or as those concerned with black lives, including African Americans and those of other racialized groups (in the case of Trayvon Martin). The people can be referred to as insecure participants. Finally, the curiosity seekers simply wanted to know what the march was all about and what the leaders had to say.

Turner and Killian's (1972) work on types of crowd participants can be referred to as a "dispositional approach" to the study of collective behavior because it emphasizes that individuals may be more or less susceptible to crowd influences, depending on their relationship to the crowd or social movement (Rohlinger and Snow 2003). People more connected to a movement may be more influenced by crowd behavior than those who are simply there out of curiosity. Also, experiences with the movement itself can change people's identities in the group. For example, a person might join the movement out of curiosity, but through interactions with other members become more motivated by the cause, becoming a concerned or even ego-involved participant (Munson 2008; see also Johnson 2021). What type of person comes to a protest rally in the modern world? According to research by Neal Caren and his colleagues (Caren et al. 2011), more people are involved in protest activity in the twenty-first century than prior to the 1960s, and the typical participant in current protests they studied was a liberal, well educated, a union member, and living on the West or East Coast. More recent research shows that the average protester is younger (18–29) (41%), urban or suburban (83%), and leans toward the US Democratic party (79%) (Barroso and Minkin 2020).

Value-Added Theory

Another major theoretical perspective in the study of collective behavior is **value-added theory**, associated with Neil Smelser (Miller 2000). From this perspective, there are different types of collective behavior and several social-structural determinants of collective behavior. Hence, to fully understand the causes of a particular event or events, according to value-added theory, we need to distinguish the type of collective behavior in question and the social conditions surrounding it.

Ralph Turner*

Ralph Turner was Professor Emeritus of Sociology at the University of California, Los Angeles. He attended Pasadena Junior College, University of Southern California (BA and MA), University of Wisconsin, and the University of Chicago, where he received a PhD in sociology in 1948. He was president of the American Sociological Association, vice president of the International Sociological Association, president of the Sociological Research Association, president of the Society for the Study of Symbolic Interaction, president of the Pacific Sociological Association, and editor of *Sociometry* (which became *Social Psychology Quarterly*) and *Annual Review of Sociology*. His books include *Collective Behavior* (1957, 1972, 1987: with L. Killian), *The Social Context of Ambition* (1964), *Robert Park on Social Control and Collective Behavior* (1967), *Family Interaction* (1970), and *Waiting for Disaster: Earthquake Watch in California* (1986; with J. Nigg and D. Paz). He coedited with Morris Rosenberg *Social Psychology: Sociological Perspectives* (1981, 1990)—the book that inspired the development of this textbook. In the years prior to his death in 2014, his research interests included the theory of social roles (especially dynamic processes and the relationship between role and person and the social self), collective behavior including social movements and response to disasters and threats of disaster, and the history of sociology.

*Information about this biography was obtained from personal correspondence with Dr. Turner in the early 2010s.

Types of Collective Behavior

Value-added theory describes five types of collective behavior: the panic, the craze, the hostile outburst, the norm-oriented social movement, and the value-oriented social movement. One of the reasons why it is difficult to predict behaviors in a crowd setting is that the people may be gathered for different reasons, producing different kinds of outcomes. People in these different types of groupings have different goals and expectations.

Value-added theory's five different types of crowd settings are as follows:

1. **Panic**: when large numbers of people are overwhelmed with a common fear.
2. **Craze**: when large numbers of people become obsessed with a product, behavior, or idea.
3. **Hostile outbursts**: any type of mass violence or killings.
4. **Norm-oriented social movements**: movements to change the way things are regulated in society.
5. **Value-oriented social movements**: attempts to change the social order of society.

A panic refers to a situation in which large numbers of people are overwhelmed with a common fear. The 1929 stock market crash is often used as an example of a wide-scale panic. A craze simply refers to when large numbers of people become obsessed with something, such as the purchase of a product (e.g., a certain app) or an activity (e.g., a popular dance). In current times, social media platforms such as on TikTok can quickly lead to crazes for certain products or pushes to engage in certain unusual pranks or behaviors. For example, the New York Times reported on social media influences on some groups of teenage boys who have become crazed over high-end fragrances (Holtermann 2024). Hostile outbursts include any type of mass violence or killings, such as the Rwandan genocide in the 1990s. Norm-oriented social movements include movements to change the way things are regulated in society, such as the temperance movement in the United States before the 1920s. Finally, value-oriented social movements include attempts to change the social order of society—replacing a religious government with a secular democracy, for instance.

From the value-added approach, the role of emotion in collective behavior partly depends on the type of group behavior being considered. We would expect the most rational behavior to occur in social movements (both norm and value oriented) because they require some level of coordination and communication to succeed. Alternatively, panics, by definition, are based on emotion. Therefore, we would predict more emotional behavior in those cases than during social movements.

Determinants of Collective Behavior

According to value-added theory, there are five determinants of collective behavior.

1. There must be structural conduciveness—a society must be in a condition amenable to the formation of movements.
2. There must be some level of structural strain in society over some issue or problem—the driving force of a collective behavior that provides a motivation to reduce strain.

3. There must be a generalized belief—a shared view of the problem and how to resolve the tension.
4. There must be some sort of mobilization for action—individuals' reaction to an immediate threat.
5. There must be action of social control in terms of how authorities react to the behavior, which determines how an event will be manifested in society.

Specifically, the social control agents in society—such as the government and police—can relieve or instigate fears and anxieties by modifying any of the previous components. For instance, the government may issue a statement to tell citizens not to panic, and even precisely how to behave, during a crisis event.

According to value-added theory, each determinant of collective behavior must be present for collective action to take place. For instance, the stock market crash of 1929 could not occur in a small hunting-and-gathering society without an advanced economy (structural conduciveness). Nor could it occur in a society that had not inflated the stock market in a way that required a large-scale shift to correct itself (structural strain). Investors shared the same idea about how to fix the problem: get out of the market before losing all their investments (generalized belief). In the case of the stock market crash, investors reacted to the lack of information available to make investment decisions (mobilization for action), causing them to fear for their financial lives. Finally, the inaction of financial and government leaders to the crisis left people to act on their worst fears (action of social control). The compilation of these determinants led to wide-scale panic, producing a massive financial downturn.

Characteristics of the targets of social movements may also influence the development and nature of a particular social movement. One study found that increases in the size of collective groups were associated with increased violence against the state but not other targets (Martin, McCarthy, and McPhail 2009). Different targets represent different vulnerabilities, hence their ability to respond to pressure. Social movement organizations must consider the nature of their target (i.e., state, business, or social norms) when developing strategies for social change (Walker, Martin, and McCarthy 2008).

Perception Control Theory

Another rational choice approach to collective behavior is perception control theory. **Perception control theory** is based on the premise that people must be able to monitor and interpret one another's behavior in order for collective action to occur. In short, people adjust their actions to make them congruent with what is expected of them. According to McPhail (1994), there are three sources of perception control input:

1. *Independent instructions*: individual decisions.
2. *Interdependent instruction*: assumes that individuals work together to make decisions.
3. *Organizational instruction*: information provided by a movement's leadership or some other outside force.

Each form of instruction occurs naturally in different types and stages of collective behavior. The latter form of instruction is probably most necessary in larger demonstrations, where coordination is more difficult to maintain than in smaller groups. Interdependent instruction is important amid the crowd members themselves, as they turn to each other for assistance and cooperation during an event. This perspective is supported by the finding that most violence and looting in riots occur sporadically and in small groups rather than by the entire larger group (McPhail 1994). Perception control theory extends rational views of collective behavior by narrowing the range of interaction among people, helping to explain the ways people try to maintain order in groups. As in Blumer's theory of circular reaction, however, these communication lines, regardless of their form, often break down, leading to confusion, perhaps explaining both rational (when communication lines are intact) and irrational (when they break down) behaviors.

Section Summary

This section applied the interactionist perspective to address the questions "Do people act differently in large groups than when they are alone?" "How do crowds contribute to the development of mass hysteria?" and "What theories explain individuals' rational behavior in large groups?" Traditional interactionist approaches to the study of collective behavior focus on the ways that groups produce hysteria among their members, a result of the normlessness that often comes from the lack of communication among group members during collective events. However, groups also form new norms to manage such events and avoid hysteria. Hence, collective events can produce both rational and irrational behaviors, depending on the type of group and the participants involved in a given collective event.

A Take-Away Message

Despite popular perceptions, few demonstrations lead to violence, and members of demonstrations are usually acting based on particular goals and interests. In terms of your professional and personal development, you may consider getting involved in organized groups involved in social change. Knowing the factors that influence behavior in collective groups may give you an advantage in those agencies. If you do a simple online search, you will find hundreds of social change organizations—some have only volunteer staff, while others have large organizations with paid workers. If there is something you care about, there are bound to be groups formed around that issue.

THE STRUCTURE OF CROWDS AND SOCIAL MOVEMENTS

> *I guess you can say that I am a committed activist. I think if people want to change things, they just need to get up and start doing it. If more people did that, we would have a better world. First, you have to change yourself, then you change the system. If you get people together, you can get the whole society to change.*
>
> —Dustin, senior history major

Dustin's perspective emphasizes the importance of the individual in the transformation of society; he believes that if individuals want to change the world, they just need to get up and do it. This process starts from a personal change and then includes getting other people together to assert changes in society. In contrast to Dustin's perspective, a more structural position would argue that society includes strains such as poverty that lead people to want change. But some people have more access to the resources necessary to change society (e.g., money to advertise or access to elites who have more control over resources), and there are other groups who have alternative agendas for society. Society, in other words, provides strains, resources, and limitations that help or limit individuals' abilities to change the system through social movements (Snow, Soule, and Cress 2005). We will examine two structural perspectives on social movements, followed by an examination of research on protest behaviors.

Social Structure and Social Movements

Most of our discussion in this chapter has emphasized collective behavior and action. The study of social movements incorporates elements of these concepts but also examines the social-structural conditions that may lead people into social movements. Interactionist perspectives of social movements do not preclude the importance of structural conditions in explaining behavior and outcomes of those movements; rather they see structure as a source of interaction. That is, social-structural conditions provide a reason to initiate social movements as well as the context in which individuals make decisions during such movements (Snow 2003). In addition, charismatic leadership may help to provoke individuals to participate in movements that they otherwise would not (Andreas 2007).

What are the structural conditions that lead people to initiate social movements? According to **resource mobilization theory**, movements are a product of the interaction between the social conditions that lead people to want change and resources available to make those changes (Zald and Ash 1964; Snow 2003). Some of these movements may be spontaneous, but many of them reflect organizational efforts—usually nonprofit organizations—to produce progressive social change (Chetkovich and Kunreuther 2006). These types of movements tend to reflect reactions to inequality in societies, such as the Black Lives Matter movement or collective social action based on the desire to obtain better living conditions. They may also reflect responses to social change. Nella Van Dyke and Sarah Soule (2002), for example, studied the growth of the patriot and militia movement in the 1990s, showing a relationship between the decline of manufacturing jobs and family farms associated with the mobilization of these groups. In these cases, mobilization of the movements was considered a response to a threat produced by structural changes in society.

Resource mobilization theory emphasizes how groups (rather than individuals) interact to produce social movements. Individuals may formalize groups to bring about social change. These groups are referred to as **social movement organizations**. Once formed, they must negotiate for social change given resources available to them—and other social movement organizations seeking the same set of limited resources.

In support of the theory, research shows that environmental social movement organizations (McLaughlin and Marwan 2000) and the feminist movement (Soule et al. 1999) tended to prosper during periods of economic prosperity.

Another approach that examines group-level interactions in the development of social movements is the political process or "opportunity" theory. **Political process theory** examines the interaction of competing interests and opportunity structures in groups' decisions and ability to produce social change (Gamson 1990; Lipsky 1968). A group may want to produce changes in society and have the resources to help make those changes but must compete with other groups with different interests. They must also compete with dominant cultural beliefs that limit the movement's ability to gain support (Woehrle, Coy, and Maney 2008). Alternatively, some groups may seek and obtain social change with few resources and still be effective. Under this schema, researchers must recognize that there are multiple factors that may influence the development or decline in social movements in addition to fiscal resources (Jenkins, Jacobs, and Agnone 2003).

Political and economic resources can work in concert with the development of social movement activity. For instance, Wesley Longhofer and Evan Schofer (2010) found that involvement in environmental associations increased in more educated and democratic societies around the world, implying the need for both resources and political opportunities for change. In addition, among industrialized Western nations, the availability of funds from philanthropic foundations increased the numbers of environmental associations as did the passage of favorable environmental legislation.

Behavior during Collective Events

Collective behavior is sometimes associated with situations in which large groups of people act irrationally in the face of danger, such as when people trapped in a burning building push and shove each other as they make their way out, potentially slowing their exit and injuring people in their path who would have otherwise escaped easily. These forms of collective behavior are the ones you see the most prominently highlighted in the media. But, as discussed earlier in this chapter, some aspects of collective behavior and social movements can be predictable and even rational. Research over the decades has given us an idea about the size, scope, and behaviors occurring in modern social movements. Here, we examine patterns of behavior within social movements—how many people show up to specific events, what they do while they are there, and social conditions that influence behavior at events.

Phases of Collective Behavior

Social movement gatherings can be divided into phases (McPhail and Tucker 2003):

1. **Assembling phase**: a time when people come together into the same place at the same time.
2. **Gathering phase**: behaviors occurring during an event.
3. **Dispersal phase**: behaviors leading to the end of a social movement gathering.

The processes and behaviors in each of these phases have been studied extensively. The first phase focuses on the conditions that lead people to enter social movements. The dispersal phase emphasizes the behaviors occurring when people leave a movement. Finally, there is research into what happens during collective behavior. What exactly do people in a crowd of 500,000 do?

The assembling phase refers to the factors that bring people together into the same place at the same time. Research shows that most people learn about events linked to social movements from their friends, family, and acquaintances, now occurring often through social media (McPhail and Tucker 2003). In fact, the best predictor of participating in a protest is simply being asked to attend the event (Schussman and Soule 2005). Our friends or family members inform us about where to meet, when to be there, and what is going on. We learn what to expect when we arrive. Not everyone who is informed about a gathering shows up. Generally, people who have no other obligations and have easy access to the site of the meeting are more likely to participate because there are fewer competing demands or limitations to their participation. Therefore, images of students at a protest reflect people who likely have flexible schedules. Those working 9:00 a.m. to 5:00 p.m. are not likely to have the flexibility to easily leave their jobs to participate in a social movement at midday or to travel across the country to a particular meeting site.

Imagine being in the middle of Washington, DC, at the height of the 1960s protests. There are thousands of people around you. Most of the protests occur in the summer months when people have more time off from work, and the weather is more hospitable for traveling. But it is also very humid and hot. You need access to facilities, water, and food. As you look around, you don't know many people. In addition, you can barely hear any speakers. March leaders may not have detailed guides about what to do at each step of the movement. You rely on information from the people around you to get by. Today, the use of phones allows for information to be relayed to large crowds that was not available for the last 100 years of such movements.

After many decades of research watching and recording large public demonstrations, researchers have found that simple behaviors make up most of these types of events. The first important structural condition of such large gatherings is that they are usually composed of small clusters of friends and family (McPhail 2008; McPhail and McCarthy 2004). Once in the crowd, individuals tend to form lines to access various services or events, such as the purchase of food and water or waiting for the use of bathrooms. Other behaviors include the development of an arc or ring around performers or speakers as well as the use of noises and gestures to evaluate such performances, usually in the form of cheers or jeers. Symbols are also important to such gatherings; giving people a message about the meaning of the gathering can provide a sense of solidarity among its members. Individuals tend to walk and look in the same direction, not at one another. This stage is similar to the milling process we reviewed earlier in this chapter.

There are many different forms of collective action, and there are different ways in which people leave gatherings. The end of a protest march is going to produce a different behavior than a crowd trying to leave a burning building. A **routine dispersal** is one in which participants leave a gathering in a rational, orderly fashion (Miller 2000).

Box 11.2 Hurricane Katrina

Hurricane Katrina occurred in 2005. It formed in the Bahamas and moved its way to New Orleans and other nearby places. Ultimately, it resulted in billions of dollars in damage and killed over 1,800 people. About half of the New Orleans population left for other regions in the United States after the hurricane, many permanently. This natural disaster led many researchers to study the social forces linked to the event. For example, scholars have argued that the tragedy revealed prejudice and discrimination against the poor and racialized minorities because they were disproportionately affected by the hurricane and the government was slow to respond to their needs (Brunsma, Overfelt, and Picou 2007; Hartman and Squires 2006; Potter 2007). In addition, conflicts arose as groups competed for limited resources in New Orleans. And, the social structural conditions prior to the storm set the stage for a poor dispersal: the high levels of poverty among residents in New Orleans meant they would not have the resources with which to weather the storm.

The vast majority of gatherings end with a routine dispersal, partly because most gatherings are peaceful. **Coerced dispersals** include situations in which a third party attempts to break up a group. This type of dispersal is often associated with police trying to end riots or break up protests.

Emergency dispersals are those that occur during emergency situations such as fires or explosions. Research shows that even in these situations, people rarely act without reason; individuals do develop fear and anxiety, but it rarely leads to incapacitation or extreme behavior (McPhail and Tucker 2003). When such behaviors occur, they tend to be a result of the inability to see exits or limited access to them as masses of people attempt to leave through one exit point. Governments require that businesses limit the number of people allowed in their buildings to avoid problems should a fire or other emergency require quick evacuation of the premises.

Here we see that there are certain patterns of crowd behavior, in the form of dispersal behaviors. In some cases, social conditions induce more emotional and random acts (e.g., emergency dispersals) than others. For the most part, collective events largely produce routine, rational behavior—at least in the form of dispersal patterns (see Box 11.2).

Size and Media Coverage of Protests

Another aspect of collective behavior that has been studied extensively is the size and scope of different social movements over time. As the capital of the United States, Washington, DC, has been a center of American protest movements. Protests and marches occur in other cities, but Washington, DC, gives protestors access to lawmakers and political leaders, providing a unique venue for social movements. Researchers over the last decades have tried to assess the size and scope of these movements. However, the controversies over the actual number of participants at the Million Man March led to the prohibition of the United States Park Police from providing attendance estimates of any such gathering.

The "gold standard" for estimating the size of a crowd or gathering is based on a simple formula that includes the percentage of a site occupied by people, the square footage of the site, and crowd density (McPhail and McCarthy 2004). An average of one person per five square feet is often used to estimate crowd sizes. To get a sense of proportion, there is about one person for two square feet in a crowded elevator. The density of the crowd varies by people's positions, with people in the front and center closer to one another than people in back and to the sides. The ratio of people to square feet continues to decrease as you move to the margins of the group. Taking these differences into account is important in accurately assessing the size of crowds.

Differences in estimating crowd sizes can be large. Clark McPhail and John McCarthy (2004), for instance, used a formulaic approach to estimate the number of participants at the protests against the Iraq War in Washington, DC, in 2003. They used the dimensions of the area while accounting for differences in crowd density and estimated that 50,000 people showed up at the rally compared to the 500,000 people estimated by the protest organizers!

Despite the controversies over counting large-scale protests, most protests and marches are relatively small in nature. About a third of the demonstrations in Washington, DC, are small pickets and vigils followed by another third representing larger marches and rallies (McPhail and Tucker 2003). Very few marches go over 100,000 participants, and most do not involve civil disobedience. There is a divergence between the types of gatherings that actually occur and what is reported in the news. McCarthy and colleagues (McCarthy et al. 1996) compared the percentage of protests given permits in Washington, DC, and those reported by any media source in 1981 and 1991. They show that only about 7% of protests actually get reported. Further, smaller protests are least likely to be reported, even though they represent the majority. Hence, there is a bias in the types of protests covered, leading to a skewed understanding of the size and scope of protests in the United States.

Two examples of large-scale social movements include the Arab Spring movements in the Middle East and the #MeToo movement in the United States. The Arab Spring movement was associated with large-scale protests in many countries, including Egypt, Tunisia, Libya, Syria, and Yemen. This movement is believed to have led the Egyptian president, Hosni Mubarak, to resign from his office in 2011 after 30 years of rule. The #MeToo movement is associated with sexual assault survivor Tarana Burke who coined the term in 2006. The hashtag #MeToo went viral in 2017 when actress Alyssa Milano used the phrase on Twitter (now X) to share her experience of sexual abuse. These movements have largely been peaceful in nature but have received a tremendous amount of media attention because of their size and scope.

Other factors can influence news coverage of social movements. Kenneth Andrews and Neal Caren (2010) studied news coverage of 187 environmental groups in 11 different daily newspapers and found that groups that are volunteer led and focus on novel issues do not tend to get much attention. Another study showed that disruption in the form of violent protests, strikes, or boycotts is associated with greater media coverage, in addition to the size of the movement (Amenta et al. 2009). The same study reported

Photo 11.3 The Occupy Frankfurt Movement followed the Occupy Wall Street Movement that started in the United States in 2011. What would motivate you to show up at a protest like the Occupy Wall Street protests?

Source: Patrick Poendl/Shutterstock

that labor groups, civil rights groups (particularly African American ones), and veterans' groups received the most media coverage in the *New York Times* over the last century, followed by feminist, supremacist, and environmental groups.

Collective Memory

Most of this chapter addresses collective behavior, but this behavior is often provoked or followed by shared emotions and beliefs. The basic premise behind much of the early literature on collective behavior is that emotions are a driving force in the event—people are swept away by their emotions. **Collective memory** refers to a shared belief about a person, an event or interaction, or an object. Collective memories are both products of social interaction and a continuing process in that they are used in everyday interaction (Fine and Beim 2007). We write history books, collecting memories of events (memory as a product), and we use memories to make decisions during our interactions with other people. Like collective behaviors, collective memories can involve entire societies, but they can also influence groups in society differently. Bin Xu (2019), for instance, found that class position shaped the autobiographical memories of people who experienced China's "zhiqing" or "sent-down youth" generation in which 17 million youths were moved from their city homes to the countryside in the 1960s and 1970s to address unemployment and develop rural areas. The study found that people coded as the "faithful red"—strong supporters of the dominant communist party—had more positive memories than people who were less tied to the party. This study demonstrates that collective memories can include subgroups of people in any given society.

Memories can drive some decision making during collective action. Such memories may induce fear and panic about the worst-case scenario during an event. For instance, people in a crowded bar that has just caught fire may consider the worst-case scenario associated with a recently publicized event that began in a similar way, with little knowledge of what is really going on in their own situation. In this sense, collective memory can take the form of probabilistic thinking (Clarke 2006). Such memories interact with social conditions and people's own sense of agency, making predictions of behavior in groups quite difficult.

Some social psychologists study how people develop collective memories in a similar manner as collective behavior, by examining (1) the conditions that produce spontaneous thoughts or feelings at the same time, (2) how conditions coalesce to bring people to believe something is true, (3) what an event means to a people, and (4) how people categorize those memories with other historical events (Fine 2007; Fine and Biem 2007; Teeger and Vinitzky-Seroussi 2007). The use of storytelling in the social construction of collective memories is important (Seeger and Sellnow 2016). Mallary Allen (2015), for instance, demonstrates that both the pro-choice and pro-life social movements use stories to support their perspectives. Analyzing stories posted from sites for women who have had an abortion, ImNotSorry.net (pro-choice) and SilentNoMoreAwareness.org (pro-life), she found that pro-choice stories centered around the idea that their pregnancies were unintended and how the abortion led to empowering outcomes. Pro-life stories focused less on what led to the abortion and more on themes such as regret and atonement, emphasizing how women came to terms with their decision afterward. In both cases, real stories of abortion intersect with the rhetoric of movement leaders, sometimes reflecting movement values and sometimes not.

In some cases, groups and individuals actively campaign to create and sustain a collective memory (Fine 2001; Fine and Beim 2007; Yeh 2015). The media can also play a part in this process. Clifford Bob (2005) studied how some oppressed groups in the world are able to gain positive media attention while others are not. He used two case studies, the Ogoni people of the Niger Delta region in Nigeria and the Zapatista struggle in Chiapas, Mexico. These movements relied on the cultural capital of its leaders combined with the use of multiple media sources (e.g., email and the internet) to help frame these struggles for the larger public. They can also take place in art. Norman Denzin (2011) compared paintings of the Battle of the Little Big Horn by White and Native American artists, showing the ways that George Custer, who commanded U.S. government troops in a battle against native Americans in 1876, was depicted in these two groups. White artists traditionally focused on Custer and his heroism while many Native American artists deemphasized his role or dropped him from the battle altogether.

However formed, collective memories exist both in our attitudes and in their links to places such as historical buildings or monuments (Drozdzewski, De Nardi, and Waterton 2016). People change their collective beliefs about history, and they then sometimes seek to remove public manifestations of previous beliefs. With outcries against the police and other institutions after the death of George Floyd in 2020 and similar events in the United States, for instance, many monuments to historical figures who had links to slavery or racial oppression were taken down by crowds. Many universities also renamed buildings that had names of such historical figures.

The other side of collective memory is collective forgetting (Schwartz 2009). Just as some aspects of social life become part of our collective memory, there are a number of events and people that get left out of our collective thoughts. We can also have a collective imagination in which people form similar beliefs about the future of events or things (Borer 2010). The **sociology of the future** studies how people come to believe their future should be and how they come to choose the best path to achieve those goals (Beckert 2016). It includes an analysis of the ways that different societies try to predict the future. Some countries today put time and money into statistical predictions (e.g., economists predicting good or bad markets) while ancient societies are associated with the use of oracles and soothsayers. In any case, individuals in society use these devices to predict the future and plan accordingly.

Collective memories are essential for societies or groups to initiate social change or bolster existing social movements. The use of stories and rhetoric gives social, political, and media leaders the ability to appeal to people's sense of solidarity as well as their fears and vulnerabilities (Clarke 2006; Polletta 2006). Framing social events to produce fears for personal well-being can mobilize people to act in ways that they otherwise would not. Shoon Lio and colleagues (Lio et al. 2008) applied this logic to help explain how leaders of the gun rights and English-only movements were able to mobilize support in the United States. Analyzing documents such as speeches, testimonies, and letters from two prominent organizations linked to these movements showed how the leaders framed the debates in ways that induced feelings of fear if their movements did not succeed. Another study showed that those who remembered the American civil rights movement as an especially important event had more liberal views on race than those who framed the civil rights movement in other ways (Griffin and Bollen 2009).

A similar process occurs as we collectively ponder the future of society. Joel Best (2018) argues that different groups in society employ language related to fears of the future to activate people into voting, donations, and activism, among other things. Whether it be about fears of the impacts of climate change or immigration, it creates a type of emotion that can be harnessed by the people drawing on those fears. The key is that they rely on conjuring a collective sense of the future, one that has not been realized, yet impacts us nonetheless. Not all collective futures are about fears; they can include an idealist sense of the future as well serving the same purpose of inspiring people to act in the present time. Together, collective memory, forgetting, and imagination help us to understand the psychological dimensions of collective behavior.

Section Summary

In this section, we focused on theory and research using a social structure and personality perspective to address the following questions: What structural conditions affect crowd behavior? What are the phases of collective behavior found in large social movements? What kinds of behaviors actually occur during a period of collective behavior? Here, we see that groups enter and act in some social movement events like they do in any other social act, seeking to address wants and needs of individuals and the collective. Structural conditions produce strains that lead people to work together for change and resources necessary to carry out desired changes. Although some group members may act irrationally, movements as a whole generally result from the desire to obtain rational outcomes. Further, most collective events are quite small, and they tend to follow rational patterns with specific phases of assembling and dispersal. Collective memory is an extension of the concept of collective behavior, referring to shared beliefs about a person, an event or interaction, or an object, and they can help to initiate social change or bolster existing social movements.

A Take-Away Message

It is clear that if you want to change the world, you are going to have to gather some resources. That means finding money. In some cases, it is about finding a wealthy person or organization willing to fund your work. In addition, you will have to be astutely political, selling the issue to people both to gain supporters and to get fiscal support. Some of these factors are relevant to the growth of any organization you work for, in the sense that marketing is essential for growth.

GROUP PROCESSES AND COLLECTIVE BEHAVIOR

> *I sometimes feel that big business is working together to destroy the little guy. I am worried that there is a conspiracy in which the rich work together against the average Joe.*
>
> —Ricardo, first-year sociology major

Some research in sociology's group processes tradition focuses on collective action in terms of how it relates to structural power. In previous chapters, we defined power as a position in a structure that allows actors to get what they want even when others resist. Whether or not Ricardo's concerns about big business are realistic, social science research indicates conditions under which coalitions might form. For example, suppose that some company, CompuGiant, specializes in selling a certain type of computer used in small businesses—we will call it the SBPro. CompuGiant is the only company in the world that sells this type of computer. Furthermore, suppose that there are three manufacturers that make SBPros—MomAndPopSB, MiniSBSupply, and SmallPlayerSB. We could represent the relationship between these companies in a diagram that looks like that in Figure 11.1.

Box 11.3 Becoming a Social Activist

While many social movements rely on volunteers, there is paid work for all sorts of social changes. Whatever your beliefs, there are likely organizations dedicated to a cause of your choosing. If not, you can always create one! Like any business, it takes a lot of hard work and capital. If you are looking for a path to start your activism, here are some examples of paid work in the field.

1. **Community Organizer**, ACLU of Arizona, Phoenix, AZ. Duties: Recruiting and training volunteers, mobilizing people in the community who share values with the ACLU-AZ; develop and execute advocacy campaigns to influence decision-makers and community leaders to adopt policy changes that contribute to Arizonans civil rights. Qualifications: Experience in community/field organizing and leadership development, working directly with volunteers, a membership base, community leaders, or directly impacted people; exceptional interpersonal, communication, and facilitation.
2. **Digital Organizer**, Make the Road New York, New York, NY. Duties: The Digital Organizer will lead the digital campaign to create a permanent fund for workers excluded from state and federal unemployment relief and as well as work on other organizing priorities for the organization. This position is ideal for an ambitious go-getter with a deep commitment to social justice, interest or experience in media work, and strong persuasive writing and communication skills. Qualifications: Possess a commitment to collective action and community organizing; experience working in a multicultural and multiethnic work environment; one year of experience using social media platforms (X, Facebook, and Instagram) to advance social justice campaigns; strong writing, editing, communications and presentation skills.
3. **Student Trainee (Office Support)**, The Office of Housing and Urban Development (HUD), Washington, DC. The Office of Housing and Urban Development is committed to building and preserving healthy neighborhoods and communities through homeownership, rental housing, and healthcare opportunities. Duties: Receive visitors and phone calls, respond to inquiries, compose routine correspondence, such as replies to requests for general information, or completion of standard form letters, arrange conferences and meetings, which include scheduling space, preparation of materials, notification of participants, greeting and signing in guests, etc. Qualifications: Current students in an accredited high school, college (including 4-year colleges/universities, community colleges, and junior colleges).

The great thing about these types of jobs is that you can start volunteering to gain experience almost any time. These organizations rely on lots of volunteers but many of them have a paid staff as well. Volunteering will help you understand the "business" of social change and provide a network of resources for finding paid work in the field or starting your own nonprofit organization.

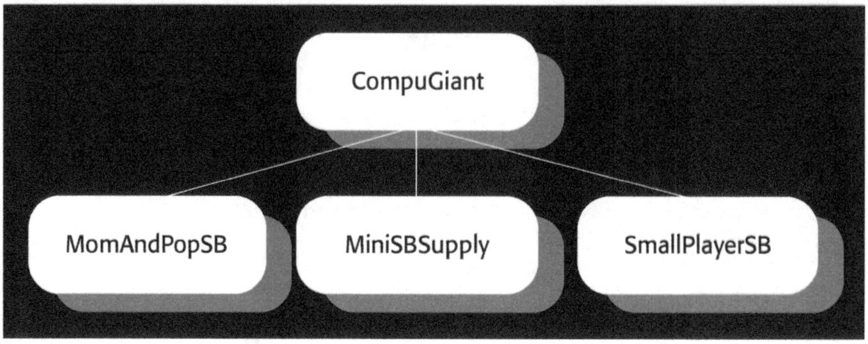

Figure 11.1 Model of Power Distribution.

Suppose that each SBPro costs the manufacturers $1,000 to make. Also suppose that CompuGiant sells the SBPros for $3,000 each. It is not difficult to guess who will have the power in this situation. CompuGiant will be able to set the prices at which it buys the SBPros. As long as CompuGiant offers each supplier at least $1,000 per unit, the suppliers will be forced to sell their products. One or more of the manufacturers might resist at first, but as soon as one starts accepting the low price, the others will be forced to go along or face going out of business—they don't have any options other than CompuGiant.

In the long run, we would expect the manufacturers in this situation to operate at a level making just enough money to stay in business, whereas CompuGiant would make large profits as long as demand for the SBPros remained high. In this situation, CompuGiant is in a structurally powerful position. It can get what it wants (cheap computers) even when others (the manufacturers) resist.

Multiple social situations share characteristics with the example of companies involved in the manufacturing and sale of SBPros. People regularly interact in contexts in which some individuals have more power than others. The famous philosopher Bertrand Russell (1872–1970), in fact, called power the fundamental concept of the social sciences (Russell 1938). Collective action, however, has the ability to mitigate power differences that are based in structural positions.

A **coalition** is an alliance of actors (e.g., people and organizations) formed for the purpose of achieving some goal. In the SBPro example, the manufacturers might be motivated to band together and form a coalition in an effort to take CompuGiant's power away. Although it would be considered collusion and be illegal, the three manufacturers could collectively decide that none of them will sell their computers to CompuGiant for less than $2,500, and they will share their profits with each other. As a result, we can draw a new diagram of the relationships between the companies to look like Figure 11.2.

In this scenario, CompuGiant's structural power has been taken away. By trading as a group, the three manufacturers have created a situation in which CompuGiant has no alternatives but to trade with the coalition. Research in the group processes tradition indicates that people will be likely to form coalitions when they are faced with large

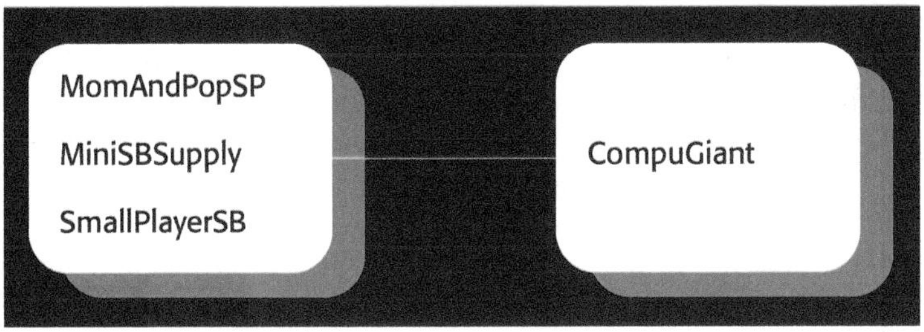

Figure 11.2 Model of Coalition.

power disparities, and also that these coalitions can be successful. Coalitions, however, have their limitations. The biggest of these is the free-rider problem (Simpson and Macy 2004).

The **free-rider problem** occurs when some actors can reap the benefits of a group effort without incurring the costs (Sell 1997). The way many podcasts work is an example of a free-rider problem. Podcasts are sometimes supported by donations, but everyone, not just those who donate, can get the benefits of the podcasts. As a result, there is an incentive to free-ride—to listen to the podcasts but to not contribute. This becomes a problem because if too many people free-ride, podcasts could be unsupported and have to end their runs.

The free-rider problem is an example of a social dilemma. A **social dilemma** is a situation whereby if every person (or company) acts in their own best interests, the results will be bad for the group. For example, think about major traffic delays caused by people who slow down to look at an accident that is off the road. These delays could be avoided if everyone would just continue driving and not slow down to look. Moreover, if you asked people stuck in traffic jams if they would be willing to give up being able to look at the accident to avoid a long traffic jam, we suspect that virtually everyone would say yes.

Now suppose that you are stuck in a traffic jam because of people ahead of you rubbernecking at an accident off the road. You have traveled less than a mile in the last 30 minutes. You now reach the front of the line where the accident is off the road. Would you maintain your slow speed for a few extra seconds to look? The best answer for the group is that you should speed up quickly at this point. Your most self-interested decision, however, would probably be to look at the accident. You already waited through the line, and you are about to accelerate away whether or not you delay a few more seconds. In this situation, everyone acting in their own self-interest leads to an outcome that is bad for the group.

Again, coalitions face the social dilemma that is known as the free-rider problem. Some people can get the benefits of coalitions without incurring the costs. In the preceding example, suppose that MomAndPopSB proposes a coalition to MiniSBSupply and SmallPlayerSB whereby they will share their profits and sell each unit for no less than $2,500. If MiniSBSupply agrees to the coalition, then SmallPlayerSB's best individual option becomes to free-ride. SmallPlayerSB can take advantage of the coalition formed by the other two manufacturers and agree to sell CompuGiant computers for $2,400, undercutting the coalition and guaranteeing itself large profits.

Most coalition situations involve many more participants than the three in our example. Many, in fact, involve hundreds or thousands of companies or people. One thing true of virtually all coalitions, however, is the possibility for free riders. If too many people free ride, a coalition will not be successful. One factor that makes free riding less likely is that those who free ride face social sanctions, while those who are generous are rewarded by the group. Robb Willer (2009) carried out a series of studies in which participants were given amounts of money that they could keep for themselves or contribute to the good of the entire group. Willer found that more generous group members later received more cooperation, gifts, and respect from fellow group members, as well as wielding more influence over them. In other words, giving to the group conferred status to people. Willer also found that people who were granted high status for giving, compared to those who did not get status benefits from giving, later gave more to the group and viewed the group more positively. In our culture, then, it appears that one way we address the free-rider problem is by granting high status to those who contribute generously to the public good. And, it appears that groups that are more differentiated by status lead to more contributions to public goods as low-status group members will tend to match contributions from higher-status members (Simpson, Willer, and Ridgeway 2012). However, solutions to the free-rider problem may be culturally dependent—what works in one culture may not work in others (Berigan and Irwin 2011).

These dynamics are important to social movements and collective behavior more generally because they help explain behavior both within and among groups—and they help to explain how and why people get involved in social movements (Piliavin 2009). Many group members act based on motives other than a group's goals, making it harder for a group to achieve its ends. In addition, motivations in such groups become confounded as people participate for both social and personal gain, making it difficult to predict how people will behave under the same conditions.

Social change organizations have become so common in Western society that they actively participate in coalition formation. Typically, these coalitions target states, focusing on changing laws, but more recent activism includes efforts toward direct change in organizational practices of specific companies. For instance, environmental groups may target large companies to encourage them to develop "greener" policies (Vasi and King 2012). Labor unions are increasingly turning toward outside groups to help revitalize their position in society (Dixon and Martin 2012). By changing tactics and better utilizing coalitions, individuals and groups in society have found new ways to initiate social change.

Technology and the Future of Social Change

The imagery of protest movements in the United States and Europe in the 1960s promotes the idea that it was a unique time for social unrest. But data suggests otherwise. In the United States, data from large-scale surveys show a growing interest in participating in social movements of all types. In 1965, only about 10 percent of Americans said "yes" to question if they felt the urge to protest. This number increased to 36 percent in 2018 and 39 percent in 2022 (see Table 2). Abortion, issues associated with police brutality (e.g., Black Lives Matter), and women's rights (e.g., the "Me Too" movement) top the list of issues motiving Americans to participate in a movement (Table 11.1), The online world provides new ways to protest, making it much easier to gather on short notice. You can use platforms such as TikTok or Instagram to notify people about the time and location of an event, and you can also use Zoom to hold a virtual protest! The principle is the same: Get people to show up at the same time online to hear speeches and share their frustrations on the same issue. They can use the chat features of these platforms to ask questions or for words of encouragement for the speakers or other protesters.

The growth in the abilities and use of artificial intelligence (AI) opens the door to its use of initiating and supporting such movements. It is also being used to track protest behaviors (Sen and Bennett 2022). While images of university students standing in protest still persist in the modern world, the future of social activism will likely include global campaigns connected through the internet, and AI will be used in some way to bolster the movements in coordination with live participants.

Section Summary

This section answered the question "How do group and individual motivations interact in social movements?" Here we emphasize the importance of coalitions during collective behaviors and social movements. Individuals and groups bargain to gain control or access to resources. This process can instigate a series of dilemmas where individuals and groups must choose between their own welfare and that of the larger entity. Together, these concepts help us understand the complex interaction within and between

Table 11.1 Issues that Produce the Urge to Demonstrate in the United States.

	2018	2022
Abortion/Pro-Life/Planned Parenthood	6	31
Law Enforcement/Police Brutality/Black Lives Matter	6	22
Women's Rights/"Me Too" Movement	17	19
Civil Rights/Equal Rights/Human Rights	8	11
Government/Political Issues	5	10
Gun Control/Second Amendment	13	8
LGBTQ+ Rights	2	5
Voting Rights	–	5
Health Issues	2	4
Environmental Issues	8	3

Source: Adapted from Gallup Polls accessed from https://news.gallup.com/poll/395561/abortion-issue-top-factor-urging-americans-protest.aspx.

groups during a social movement. Ultimately, group dynamics can influence the outcomes of social movements above, and technology is providing new ways to initiate social movements.

A Take-Away Message

One of the biggest problems with starting a club on campus is getting members and volunteers. Many people may agree on the goals of the club, in principle, but are not willing to help with any activities. Typically, the top 10 percent of a voluntary organization's membership represents the "true believers" who do most of the organization's work. Your work life probably reflects similar problems where some people do more work than others. Understanding the conditions under which to limit the free-rider problem can help in any situation where you rely on other people to get a job done—whether it is a corporate office or a social change organization.

BRINGING IT ALL TOGETHER

> *I live in the Maryland suburbs of Washington, DC. I remember the first time I went to a rally on the mall in DC. I am not sure why I was there except my buddy wanted me to go and I agreed with what his group was trying to do. It was energizing to be around so many people. But I was afraid to ask anybody what we were supposed to be doing because that seemed a little weird. I stood around for a while but even though there were thousands of people, there was a LOT of space around me. I tried to listen to the speaker but I just couldn't hear him. I was hoping to get more out of it.*
>
> —Jackson, senior sociology major

Jackson's experience is probably not uncommon. He went to a rally but felt a little let down. Despite all the people around him, he did not feel as though he accomplished much, though he did experience heightened emotional energy. But the event followed a pretty routine pattern. What would have happened if something had provoked the crowd a bit, perhaps instigated by police action? The initial emotions may have turned the crowd in another direction.

We have applied three perspectives to understand social movements and collective behaviors. From an interactionist perspective, large-group environments make it difficult to develop and follow norms, though most people eventually do. Social structure and personality researchers emphasize how positions and resources affect participation in and outcomes of social movements. Finally, group processes research and theory help us to understand the role of group dynamics, especially the development of coalitions, in understanding why groups behave the way that they do during a social movement. Together, these perspectives provide a context for understanding some obvious and other quite surprising aspects of collective behavior and social movements.

SUMMARY

1. Traditional theories of collective behavior, collective action, and social movements emphasize the ways in which crowds transform the individuals acting in them, turning them into irrational beings. Rational choice perspectives on collective action emphasize the idea that people in groups are purposive in their decisions and actions in everyday life, including at group events.
2. Structural perspectives of social movements emphasize societal conditions that influence the development and success of movements, especially constraints associated with time and money.
3. Research on protests in the United States over the last decades has shown that most protests and marches are small in nature. Very few marches contain over 100,000 participants, and very few involve civil disobedience. However, the largest protests receive much more media attention.
4. Sociological social psychologists also study how we develop collective memories, examining the conditions that produce spontaneous thoughts or feelings at the same time; how conditions coalesce to bring us to believe something is true; what an event means to a people; and how we categorize those memories with other historical events.
5. Research evidence in the group processes tradition indicates that people will be likely to form coalitions when they are faced with large power disparities. The free-rider problem and social dilemmas are typical problems found in behavior within and between groups.

KEY TERMS AND CONCEPTS

Acting crowds: Groups of people with a focus, or goal, who act with unity to achieve the goal.

Circular reaction: Process by which people become more and more suggestible and irrational after interactions become interrupted.

Coalition: An alliance of actors formed for the purpose of achieving some goal.

Coerced dispersals: Situations in which a third-party attempts to break up a group.

Collective action: The purposive nature of people's behavior when they collectively celebrate, mourn, worship, protest, compete in athletics, or confront disasters.

Collective identity: An individual's sense of connection with a larger community or group.

Collective memory: A shared belief about a person, an event or interaction, or object.

Concerned participant: According to emergent norm theory, there are people who are not directly involved with a group's goal but participate out of concern over an issue.

Contagion theory: *See* mass hysteria theory.

Contagious mental unity: A sense of shared emotional bond that emerges whenever people interact in a group.

Craze: When large numbers of people become obsessed with something like the purchase of a product or an activity.

Curiosity seeker: According to emergent norm theory, it is the type of person who participates in the group out of curiosity.

Differential expression: Aspect of emergent norm theory that argues that individuals enter groups with different attitudes and perspectives.

Ego-involved participant: According to emergent norm theory, it is the type of person who feels a strong personal commitment to the issue that the group is involved with.

Emergency dispersals: Crowd dispersals that occur during emergency situations such as fires or explosions.

Emergent norm theory: Theory of collective behavior focusing on how individuals come to accept the constraints imposed by a group.

Expressive crowd: Crowd that lacks a goal and is primarily a setting for emotional release, which often occurs through rhythmical action such as applause, dancing, or singing.

Free-rider problem: When some actors can reap the benefits of a group effort without incurring the costs.

Hostile outbursts: Any type of mass violence or killings.

Insecure participant: According to emergent norm theory, it is the person participating in a crowd merely for the sense of connection with the group.

Interpretive phase: Part of the circular reaction process in which people respond to one another by interpreting the other's gestures and remarks, rehearsing or visualizing a possible response, and then conveying a response.

Mass: Anonymous individuals from many social strata that are loosely organized.

Mass hysteria theory (or contagion theory): Theory based on the idea that individuals in crowds lose their ability to think and act rationally.

Milling: Part of the circular reaction process in which individuals at an event anxiously move about in a seemingly aimless and random fashion.

New social movements: Those movements that center on specific issues rather than class-based political mobilizations.

Norm-oriented social movements: Movements to change the way things are regulated by society.

Panic: A situation in which large numbers of people are overwhelmed with a common fear.

Perception control theory: Theory based on the premise that people must be able to monitor and interpret one another's behavior for collective action to occur.

Political process theory: Examines the interaction of competing interests and opportunity structures in a group's ability to produce social change.

Public: An aggregate of people who are concerned with a specific issue.

Resource mobilization theory: Theory of collective action that views social movements as a product of the interaction between the social conditions that lead people to want change and resources available to make those changes.

Routine dispersal: A dispersal in which participants leave a gathering in a rational, orderly fashion.

Social dilemma: A situation whereby if every person acts in his or her own best interests, the results will be bad for the group.

Social movement organizations: When individuals formally organize into groups to bring about social change.
Social movements: Collective action designed to produce a new social order.
Sociology of the future: The study of how people come to believe their future should be.
Value-added theory: Theory based on the notion that to fully understand the causes of collective events, you need to distinguish the type of collective behavior in question and the social conditions surrounding it.
Value-oriented social movements: Attempts to change the social order.

DISCUSSION QUESTIONS

1. Think about any large group gathering such as a sporting event that you have been to. Did you feel any sense of arousal from or cohesion with the group? Consider whether the team was winning or losing. Did that change the way you felt?
2. This chapter presented many theories and perspectives on how people act in large groups. Which theories did you find more useful in explaining collective behavior? Why?
3. Have you been involved in a social movement? Trace some of the factors that led to your involvement.
4. How can the group processes research presented at the end of the chapter (e.g., coalitions and dilemmas in groups) help us understand larger collective behavior phenomenon?

REFERENCES

Abraham, John. 2010. "Pharmaceuticalization of Society in Context: Theoretical, Empirical and Health Dimensions". *Sociology* 44: 603–622.

Adamopoulou, Eleni and Lefteris Moussiades. 2020. "Chatbots: History, Technology, and Applications." *Machine Learning with Applications* 2:1–18.

Adamovic, Mladen and Andreas Leibbrandt. 2023. "A Large-Scale Field Experiment on Occupational Gender Segregation and Hiring Discrimination." *Industrial Relations: A Journal of Economy and Society* 62:34–59.

Adams, Terri M. and Leigh R. Anderson. 2019. *Policing in Natural Disasters: Stress, Resilience, and the Challenges of Emergency Management*. Philadelphia, Rome, Tokyo: Temple University Press.

Adler, Patricia A. 1996. "Preadolescent Clique Stratification and the Hierarchy of Identity." *Sociological Inquiry* 2:111–142.

Adler, Patricia A. and Peter Adler. 1982. "Criminal Commitment among Drug Dealers." *Deviant Behavior* 3:117–135.

———. 1994. "Social Reproduction and the Corporate Other: The Institutionalization of Afterschool Activities." *The Sociological Quarterly* 35:309–328.

———. 1998. *Peer Power: Preadolescent Culture and Identity Formation*. New Brunswick, NJ: Rutgers University Press.

———. 1999. "The Ethnographers' Ball Revisited." *Journal of Contemporary Ethnography* 28:442–450.

———. 2003. "The Promise and Pitfalls of Going into the Field." *Contexts* 2:41–47.

———. 2008. "The Cyber Worlds of Self-Injurers: Deviant Communities, Relationships, and Selves." *Symbolic Interaction* 31:33–56.

Agnew, Robert. 1985. "A Revised Strain Theory of Delinquency." *Social Forces* 64:151–167.

———. 2001. "Building on the Foundation of General Strain Theory: Specifying the Types of Strain Most Likely to Lead to Crime and Delinquency." *Journal of Research in Crime and Delinquency* 38:319–361.

Aguirre, B. E., Dennis Wenger, and Gabriela Vigo. 1998. "A Test of the Emergent Norm Theory of Collective Behavior." *Sociological Forum* 13:301 320.

Ajzen, Icek. 1991. "The Theory of Planned Behavior." *Organizational Behavior and Human Decision Processes* 50:179–211.

Aldredge, Marcus. 2006. "Negotiating and Practicing Performance: An Ethnographic Study of a Musical Open Mic in Brooklyn, New York." *Symbolic Interaction* 29:109–117.

Alexander, Karl L., Doris R. Entwisle, and Maxine S. Thompson. 1987. "School Performance, Status Relations, and the Structure of Sentiment: Bringing the Teacher Back In." *American Sociological Review* 52:665–682.

Alger, Janet M. and Steven F. Alger. 2003. *Cat Culture: The Social World of a Cat Shelter*. Philadelphia, PA: Temple University Press.

Allen, Mallary. 2015. "Narrative Diversity and Sympathetic Abortion: What Online Storytelling Reveals About the Prescribed Norms of the Mainstream Movements." *Symbolic Interaction* 38:42–63.

Allison, Scott T., A. Neville Uhles, Arlene G. Asuncion, James K. Beggan, and Diane M. Mackie. 2006. "Self-Serving Biases in Trait Judgments about the Self." *Current Research in Social Psychology* 11:1–13.

Altheide, David L. 2016. *The Media Syndrome*. New York: Routledge.

Alwin, Duane F. 2002. "Generations X, Y and Z: Are They Changing America?" *Contexts* 1:42–51.

———. 2007. *Margins of Error: A Study of Reliability in Survey Measurement*. Hoboken, NJ: Wiley-Interscience.

Amato, Paul R. 1993. "Urban-Rural Differences in Helping Friends and Family Members." *Social Psychology Quarterly* 56:249–262.

———. 2007. *Alone Together: How Marriage in America Is Changing*. Cambridge, MA: Harvard University Press.

Amato, Paul R. and Jacob E. Cheadle. 2008. "Parental Divorce, Marital Conflict and Children's Behavior Problems: A Comparison of Adopted and Biological Children." *Social Forces* 86:1139–1161.

Amenta, Edwin, Neal Caren, Joy Sheera Olasky, and James E. Stobaugh. 2009. "All the Movements Fit to Print: Who, What, When, Where, and Why SMO Families Appeared in the *New York Times* in the Twentieth Century." *American Sociological Review* 74:636–656.

American Psychiatric Association. 2024. "Stigma, Prejudice and Discrimination Against People with Mental Illness." Report accessed on June 27, 2024 at www.psychiatry.org/patients-families/stigma-and-discrimination.

Anderson, Elijah. 1999. *Code of the Streets: Decency, Violence, and the Moral Life of the Inner City*. New York: W. W. Norton.

Anderson, Leon. 2008. "Analytic Autoethnography." *Journal of Contemporary Ethnography* 35:373–395.

Anderson, Robert, James Curtis, and Edward Grabb. 2006. "Trends in Civic Association Activity in Four Democracies: The Special Case of Women in the United States." *American Sociological Review* 71:376–400.

Andersson, Matthew A. 2018. "Modern Social Hierarchies and the Spaces between: How are Subjective Status Inconsistencies Linked to Mental Health." *Social Psychology Quarterly* 81:48–70.

Andreas, Joel. 2007. "The Structure of Charismatic Mobilization: A Case Study of Rebellion during the Chinese Cultural Revolution." *American Sociological Review* 72:434–452.

Andrews, Kenneth T., Matthew Baggetta, Chaeyoon Lim, Marshall Ganz, and Hahrie Han. 2010. "Leadership, Membership, and Voice: Civic Associations That Work." *American Journal of Sociology* 115: 1191–1242.

Andrews, Kenneth T. and Neal Caren. 2010. "Making the News: Movement Organizations, Media Attention, and the Public Agenda." *American Sociological Review* 75:841–866.

Aneshensel, Carol S. 1992. "Social Stress: Theory and Research." *Journal of Health and Social Behavior* 18:15–38.

Aneshensel, Carol S. and J. C. Phelan (eds.). 1999. *Handbook of the Sociology of Mental Health*. New York: Kluwer.

Aneshensel, Carol S., Carolyn M. Rutter, and Peter A. Lachenbruch. 1991. "Social Structure, Stress, and Mental Health." *American Sociological Review* 56:166–178.

Aneshensel, Carol S. and Clea A. Sucoff. 1996. "The Neighborhood Context of Adolescent Mental Health." *Journal of Health and Social Behavior* 37:293–310.

Armstrong, Elizabeth A., Laura T. Hamilton, Elizabeth M. Armstrong, and J. Lotus Seeley. 2014. "'Good Girls': Gender, Social Class, and Slut Discourse on Campus." *Social Psychology Quarterly* 77:100–122.

Aron, Raymond. 1965. *Main Currents in Sociological Thought I*, trans. R. Howard and H. Weaver. New York: Doubleday.

Aronson, Matt and Steve Bialostok. 2016. "'Do Some Wondering': Children and their Self-Understanding Selves in Early Elementary Classrooms." *Symbolic Interaction* 39:229–251.

Asencio, Emily K. 2013. "Self-Esteem, Reflected Appraisals, and Self-Views: Examining Criminal and Worker Identities." *Social Psychology Quarterly* 76:291–313.

Asencio, Emily K. and Peter J. Burke. 2011. "Does Incarceration Change the Criminal Identity? A Synthesis of Labeling and Identity Theory Perspectives on Identity Change." *Sociological Perspectives* 54:163–182.

Athens, Lonnie. 2009. "The Roots of "Radical Interactionism." *Journal for the Theory of Social Behaviour* 39:387–414.

Athens, Lonnie. 2015. *Review of Domination and Subjugation in Everyday Life*. London: Transaction Publishers.

Athens, Lonnie. 2017. "Applying Violentization: From Theory to Praxis," *Victims and Offenders* 12:497–522.

Auxier, Brooke and Monica Anderson. 2021. "Social Media Use in 2021." *Pew Research Center*, www.pewresearch.org/internet/2021/04/07/social-media-use-in-2021.

Axinn, William and Lisa D. Pearce. 2006. *Mixed Methods Data Collection Strategies*. New York: Cambridge University Press.

Babbie, Earl. 2002. *The Basics of Social Research*. Belmont, CA: Wadsworth.

Bail, Christopher A. 2008. "The Configuration of Symbolic Boundaries against Immigrants in Europe." *American Sociological Review* 73:37–59.

Bakker, Dieko M. and Jacob Dijkstra. 2021. "Comparing the Slider Measure of Social Value Orientation with Its Main Alternatives." *Social Psychology Quarterly* 84.

Baldwin, John D. 1986. *George Herbert Mead: A Unifying Theory for Sociology*. Newbury Park, CA: Sage.

Bales, Robert. 1965. "The Equilibrium Problem in Small Groups." Pp. 424–456 in *Small Groups: Studies in Social Interaction*, edited by P. Hare, E. F. Borgotta, and R. F. Bales. New York: Knopf.

Balz, Dan, Scott Clement, and Emily Gaskin. 2022. "Republicans and Democrats Divided over Jan. 6 Insurrection and Trump's Culpability, Post-UMD Poll Finds." *Washington Post*, www.washingtonpost.com/politics/2022/01/01/post-poll-january-6.

Bandura, Albert. 1977. "Self Efficacy towards a Unifying Theory of Behavioral Change." *Psychological Review* 84:191–215.

———. 1997. *Self Efficacy: The Exercise of Control*. New York: W. H. Freeman Company.

Banks, Patricia Ann. 2010. *Represent: Art and Identity among the Black Upper-Middle Class*. New York: Routledge.

Bao, Wan-Ning, Ain Haas, and Yijun Pi. 2004. "Life Strain, Negative Emotions, and Delinquency: An Empirical Test of General Strain Theory in the People's Republic of China." *International Journal of Offender Therapy and Comparative Criminology* 48:281–297.

Barber, Kristen. 2008. "The Well-Coiffed Man: Class, Race, and Heterosexual Masculinity in the Hair Salon." *Gender & Society* 22:455–476.

Barraket, Jo and Henry-Waring, Millsom S. 2008. "Getting it on(line): Sociological Perspectives on E-Dating." *Journal of Sociology* 44:149.

Barnum, Christopher and Barry Markovsky. 2007. "Group Membership and Social Influence." *Current Research in Social Psychology* 13:1–18.

Baron, Reuben M. and David A. Kenny. 1986. "The Moderator–Mediator Variable Distinction in Social Psychological Research: Conceptual, Strategic, and Statistical Considerations." *Journal of Personality and Social Psychology* 51:1173–1182.

Barr, Donald A. 2008. *Health Disparaties in the United States: Social Class, Race, Ethnicity, and Health*. Baltimore, MD: Johns Hopkins University Press.

Barroso, Amanda and Rachel Minkin. 2020. "Recent Protest Attendees are More Racially and Ethnically Diverse, Younger than Americans Overall." *Pew Research Center*, www.pewresearch.org/short-reads/2020/06/24/recent-protest-attendees-are-more-racially-and-ethnically-diverse-younger-than-americans-overall.

Barton, Michael S., Bonnie Lynne Jensen, and Joanne Kaufman. 2010. "Social Disorganization Theory and the College Campus." *Journal of Criminal Justice* 38: 245–254.

Bateman, Amanda. 2016. *Conversation Analysis and Early Childhood Education: The Co-Production of Knowledge and Relationships*. London and New York: Routledge.

Bauman, Zygmunt. 2007. *Consuming Life*. Cambridge, UK: Polity Press.

Beaver, Kevin M., Christina Mancini, Matt Delisi, and Michael G.Vaughn. 2011. "Resiliency to Victimization: The Role of Genetic Factors." *Journal of Interpersonal Violence* 26:874–898.

Becker, Howard S. 1953. "Becoming a Marijuana User." *American Journal of Sociology* 59:235–242.

———. 1963. *Outsiders: Studies in the Sociology of Deviance*. New York: Free Press.

Becker, Howard S. 2014. *What About Mozart? What about Murder?* Chicago: Chicago University Press.

Becker, Howard S. 2017. *Evidence* Chicago: Chicago University Press.

Beckert, Jens. 2016. *Imagined Futures: Fictional Expectations and Capitalist Dynamics*. Cambridge, MA: Harvard University Press.

Beckmann, Andrea. 2009. *The Social Construction of Sexuality and Perversion: Deconstructing Sadomasochism*. New York: Palgrave Macmillan.

Bennett, Tony, Mike Savage, Elizabeth Silva, Alan Warde, Modesto Gayo-Cal, and David Wright. 2009. *Culture, Class, Distinction*. New York: Routledge.

Berger, Joseph, Bernard P. Cohen, and Morris Zelditch, Jr. 1966. "Status Characteristics and Expectation States." Pp. 29–46 in *Sociological Theories in Progress*, vol. 1, edited by J. Berger, M. Zelditch, Jr., and B. Anderson. Boston: Houghton Mifflin.

———. 1972. "Status Characteristics and Social Interaction." *American Sociological Review* 37:241–255.

Berger, Joseph, Cecilia L. Ridgeway, and Morris Zelditch. 2002. "Construction of Status and Referential Structures." *Sociological Theory* 20:157–179.

Berger, Joseph, Susan J. Rosenholtz, and Morris Zelditch, Jr. 1980. "Status Organizing Processes." *Annual Review of Sociology* 6:479–508.

Berger, Joseph, David G. Wagner, and Morris Zelditch, Jr. 1985. "Expectations States Theory: Review and Assessment." Pp. 1–72 in *Status, Rewards, and Influence: How Expectations Organize Behavior*, edited by J. Berger and M. Zelditch. San Francisco: Jossey-Bass.

Berger, Joseph, Murray Webster, Jr., Cecilia Ridgeway, and Susan J. Rosenholtz. 1993. "Status Cues, Expectations, and Behavior." Pp. 1–22 in *Social Psychology of Groups*, edited by E. Lawler and B. Markovsky. Greenwich, CT: JAI Press.

Berger, Peter. 1973. *Invitation to Sociology: A Humanistic Approach*. Woodstock, NY: Overlook Press.

Berger, Peter L. and Thomas Luckmann. 1967. *The Social Construction of Reality: A Treatise on the Sociology of Knowledge*. Garden City, NY: Doubleday.

Berger, Ronald J. and Richard Quinney. 2004. *Storytelling Sociology: Narrative as Social Inquiry*. Boulder, CO: Lynne Rienner Publishers.

Bergman Blix, Stina. 2022. "Making Independent Decisions Together: Rational Emotions in Legal Adjudication." *Symbolic Interaction* 45:50–71.

Berigan, Nick and Kyle Irwin. 2011. "Culture, Cooperation, and the General Welfare." *Social Psychology Quarterly* 74: 341–360.

Berry, Keith. 2016. *Bullied: Tales of Torment, Identity, and Youth*. New York and London: Routledge.

Bessett, Danielle. 2006. "Don't Step on My Groove: Gender and the Social Experience of Rock." *Symbolic Interaction* 29:49–62.

Best, Joel. 2018. *American Nightmares: Social Problems in an Anxious World*. Oakland, CA: University of California Press.

Bezrukova, Katerina, Chester S. Spell, Jamie L. Perry, and Karen A. Jehn. 2016.

"A Meta-Analytical Integration of over 40 Years of Research on Diversity Training Evaluation." *Psychological Bulletin* 142:1227–1274.

Bianchi, Alison J. and Donna A. Lancianese. 2007. "Accentuate the Positive: Positive Sentiments and Status in Task Groups." *Social Psychology Quarterly* 70:7–26.

Bianchi, Suzanne, John P. Robinson, and Melissa A. Milkie. 2006. *Changing Rhythms of American Family Life.* New York: Russell Sage Foundation.

Biddle, B. J. 1986. "Recent Developments in Role Theory." *Annual Review of Sociology* 12:67–92.

Bierman, Alex and Ryan Kelty. 2014. "The Threat of War and Psychological Distress among Civilians Working in Iraq and Afghanistan." *Social Psychology Quarterly* 77:27–53.

Billig, Michael. 2005. *Laughter and Ridicule: Towards a Social Critique of Humour*. Thousand Oaks, CA: Sage.

Blair-Loy, Mary. 2009. "Work without End? Scheduling Flexibility and Work-to-Family Conflict among Stockbrokers." *Work and Occupations* 36:279–317.

Blank, Rebecca M., Marilyn Dabady, and Constance F. Citro (eds.). 2004. *Panel on Methods for Assessing Discrimination of the National Research Council.* Washington, DC: National Academies Press.

Blau, Francine and Lawrence M. Kahn. 2000. "Gender Differences in Pay." *Journal of Economic Perspectives* 14:75–99.

Blau, Peter M. 1964. *Exchange and Power in Social Life.* New York: John Wiley & Sons.

Blau, Peter M. and Otis Dudley Duncan. 1967. *The American Occupational Structure*. New York: Wiley.

Blok, Anders, Maria D. Lindstrom, Marie L. Meilvang, and Inge K. Pederson. 2019. "Ecologies of Boundaries: Modes of Boundary Work in Professional Proto-Jurisdictions." *Symbolic Interaction* 42:588–617.

Blumer, Herbert. 1958. "Race Prejudice as a Sense of Group Position." *Pacific Sociological Review* 58:3–7.

———. 1969. *Symbolic Interactionism: Perspective and Method.* Berkeley: University of California Press.

———. 1972. "Outline of Collective Behavior." Pp. 22–45 in *Readings in Collective Behavior*, edited by R. R. Evans. Chicago: Rand McNally.

Bob, Clifford. 2005. *The Marketing of Rebellion: Insurgents, Media, and International Activism.* Cambridge, UK: Cambridge University Press.

Bobo, Lawrence. 1998. "Race, Interest, and Beliefs about Affirmative Action." *American Behavioral Scientist* 41: 985–1003.

Bobo, Lawrence and Vincent Hutchings. 1996. "Perceptions of Racial Group Competition: Extending Blumer's Theory of Group Position to a Multiracial Social Context." *American Sociological Review* 61:951–972.

Boda, Zsófia, Bálint Néray, and Tom A.B. Snijders. 2020. "The Dynamics of Interethnic Friendships and Negative Ties in Secondary School : The Role of Peer-Perceived Ethnicity." *Social Psychology Quarterly* 83:342–362.

Bogle, Kathleen A. 2008. *Hooking Up: Sex, Dating, and* Relationships *on Campus*. New York: New York University Press.

Bolzendahl, Catherine I. and Daniel J. Myers. 2004. "Feminist Attitudes and Support for Gender Equality: Opinion Change in Women and Men, 1974–1998." *Social Forces* 83:759–789.

Bonacich, Phillip. 1998. "A Behavioral Foundation for a Structural Theory of Power in Exchange Networks." *Social Psychology Quarterly* 61:185–198.

Bonilla-Silva, Eduardo. 2022. *Racism Without Racists: Color-Blind Racism and the Persistence of Racial Inequality in America*. Lanham: Rowman & Littlefield.

Bonilla-Silva, Eduardo and David G. Embrick. 2007. "'Every Place Has a Ghetto ...': The Significance of Whites' Social and Residential Segregation." *Symbolic Interaction* 30:323–345.

Boocock, Sarane Spence and Kimberly Ann Scott. 2005. *Kids in Context: The Sociological Study of Children and Childhoods*. Lanham, MD: Rowman & Littlefield.

Borer, Michael Ian. 2010. "From Collective Memory to Collective Imagination: Time, Place, and Urban Redevelopment." *Symbolic Interaction* 33:96–114.

Bogardus, Emory S. 1958. "Racial Distance Changes in the United States during the Past Thirty Years." *Sociology and Social Research* 43:127–135.

Borgatta, Edgar F. and Robert F. Bales. 1953. "Interaction of Individuals in Reconstituted Groups." *Sociometry* 14: 302–320.

Borgatta, Edgar F., Robert F. Bales, and Arthur S. Couch. 1954. "Some Findings Relevant to the Great Man Theory of Leadership." *American Sociological Review* 19:755–759.

Borgerson, Janet and Jonathan Schroeder. 2017. *Designed for Hi-Fi Living*. Cambridge, MA: MIT Press.

Bourdieu, Pierre. 1984. *Distinction: A Social Critique of the Judgment of Taste*, trans. Richard Nice. Cambridge, MA: Harvard University Press.

Boyle, Kaitlin M. and Ashleigh E. McKinzie. 2015. "Resolving Negative Affect and Restoring Meaning: Responses to Deflection Produced by Unwanted Sexual Experiences." *Social Psychology Quarterly* 78:151–172.

Braghieri, Luca, Ro'ee Levy, and Alexey Makarin. 2022. "Social Media and Mental Health." *American Economic Review* 112:3660–93.

Brand, Jennie E. and Yu Xie. 2010. "Who Benefits Most from College? Evidence for Negative Selection in Heterogeneous Economic Returns to Higher Education." *American Sociological Review* 75:273–302.

Brashears, Matthew E. 2008. "Sex, Society, and Association: A Cross-National Examination of Status Construction Theory." *Social Psychology Quarterly* 71: 72–85.

Brennan, Geoffrey, Lina Eriksson, Robert E. Goodin, and Nicholas Southwood. 2013. *Explaining Norms*. Oxford: Oxford University Press.

Brint, Steven, Mary F. Contreras, and Michael T. Matthews. 2001. "Socialization Messages in Primary Schools: An Organizational Analysis." *Sociology of Education* 74:157–180.

Briscoe, Forrest and Catherine C. Kellogg. 2011. "The Initial Assignment Effect: Local Employer Practices and Positive Career Outcomes for Work-Family Program Users." *American Sociological Review* 76: 291–319.

Brissonneau, Christophe and Jeffrey Montez de Oca (Eds). 2018. *Doping in Elite Sports: Voices of French Sportspeople and Their Doctors*. New York: Routledge.

Brockmeier, Jens and Donal Carbaugh (eds.). 2001. *Narrative and Identity: Studies in Autobiography, Self and Culture*. Amsterdam: John Benjamin Publishing Company.

Brody, Gene H., Kris Moore, and Dana Glei. 1994. "Family Processes during Adolescence as Predictors of Parent–Young Adult Attitude Similarity." *Family Relations* 43:369–373.

Brossard, Baptiste. 2018. *Why Do We Hurt Ourselves? Understanding Self-Harm in Social Life*. Indianapolis: Indiana University Press.

Brown, Brett and Pilar Marin. 2009. *Child Trends Research Briefs*. National Health and Information Center. http://www.childtrends. org/Files/Child_Trends-2009_05_26_RB_ AdolElecMedia.pdf

Brown, Tony N. and Chase L. Lesane-Brown. 2006. "Race Socialization Messages across Historical Time." *Social Psychology Quarterly* 69:201–211.

Brunsma, David L., David Overfelt, and J. Steven Picou, 2007. *The Sociology of Katrina: Perspectives on a Modern Catastrophe*. Lanham, MD: Rowman & Littlefield.

Brynin, Malcom and John Ermisch (eds.). 2009. *Changing Relationships*. New York: Routledge.

Budig, Michelle J. and Melissa Hodges. 2010. "Differences in Disadvantage: Variation in the Motherhood Penalty across White Women's Earnings Distribution." *American Sociological Review* 75: 705–728.

Burke, Peter J. 1997. "An Identity Model of Network Exchange." *Social Psychology Quarterly* 62:134–150.

———. 2003. *Advances in Identity Theory and Research*. New York: Kluwer Academic/ Plenum.

———. 2004. "Identities, Events, and Moods." *Advances in Group Processes* 21: 25–49.

———. 2006. "Identity Change." *Social Psychology Quarterly* 69:81–96.

Burke, Sara E., John F. Dovidio, Sylvia P. Perry, Diana J. Burgess, Rachel R. Hardeman, Sean M. Phelan, et al. 2017. "Informal Training Experiences and Explicit Bias against African Americans among Medical Students." *Social Psychology Quarterly* 80:65–84.

Burke, Peter J. and Jan E. Stets. 1999. "Trust and Commitment through Self-Verification." *Social Psychology Quarterly* 62:347–366.

———. 2009. *Identity Theory*. New York: Oxford University Press.

Burke, Peter J., Jan E. Stets, and Christine Cerven. 2007. "Gender, Legitimation, and Identity Verification in Groups." *Social Psychology Quarterly* 70: 27–42.

Burn, Shawn Meghan, Roger Aboud, and Carey Moyles. 2000. "The Relationship between Gender Social Identity and Support for Feminism." *Sex Roles* 42: 1081–1089.

Burnett, Judith. 2010. *Generations: The Time Machine in Theory and Practice*. Surrey, UK: Ashgate.

Burt, Callie Harbin, Ronald L. Simons, and Frederick X. Gibbons. 2012. "Racial Discrimination, Ethnic-Racial Socialization, and Crime: A Micro-Sociological Model of Risk and Resilience." *American Sociological Review* 77:648–677.

Buyukozturk, Bertan. 2022. "Reproducing the Gaming Gender Hierarchy." *Symbolic Interaction* 45:27–49.

Cahill, Spencer E. 2003. "Childhood." Pp. 857– 874 in *Handbook of Symbolic Interactionism*, edited by L. T. Reynolds and N. J. Herman-Kinney. Lanham, MD: Rowman & Littlefield.

Cahill, Spencer E., William Distler, Cynthia Lachowetz, Andrea Meaney, Robyn Tarallo, and Teena Willard. 1985. "Meanwhile Backstage: Public Bathrooms and the Interaction Order." *Urban Life* 14:33–58.

Cahill, Spencer E. and Robin Eggleston. 1994. "Managing Emotions in Public: The Case of Wheelchair Users." *Social Psychology Quarterly* 57:300–312.

Cahill, Spencer E., Gary Alan Fine, and Linda Grant. 1995. "Dimensions of Qualitative Research." Pp. 605–629 in *Sociological Perspectives on Social Psychology*, edited by K. S. Cook, G. A. Fine, and J. S. H. House. Boston: Allyn & Bacon.

Calarco, McCrory Jessica. 2011. "'I Need Help!' Social Class and Children's Help-Seeking in Elementary School." *American Sociological Review* 76:862–882.

———. 2014. "The Inconsistent Curriculum: Cultural Tool Kits and Student Interpretations of Ambiguous Expectations." *Social Psychology Quarterly* 77: 185–209.

Callejas, Laura M. and Hana Shepherd. 2020. "Conflict as a Social Status Mobility Mechanism in Schools: A Network Approach." *Social Psychology Quarterly* 83:319–341.

Calvey, David. *Covert Research: The Art, Politics, and Ethics of Undercover Fieldwork*. Los Angeles: Sage.

Campana, Kathryn L., Sandra Henderson, Arnold L. Stolberg, and Lisa Schum. 2008. "Paired Maternal and Paternal Parenting Styles, Child Custody and Children's Emotional Adjustment to Divorce." *Journal of Divorce and Remarriage* 48:1–20.

Campero, Santiago, and Roberto M. Fernandez. 2019. "Gender Composition of Labor Queues and Gender Disparities in Hiring." *Social Forces* 97:1487–516.

Cantril, Hadley. 1940. *The Invasion from Mars*. New York: Harper & Row.

———. 1966. *The Invasion from Mars: A Study in the Psychology of Panic*. New York: Harper & Row.

Caplan, Leslie J. and Carmi Schooler. 2007. "Socioeconomic Status and Financial Coping Strategies: The Mediating Role of Perceived Control." *Social Psychology Quarterly* 70:43–58.

Caputo, Richard K. 2003. "The Effects of Socioeconomic Status, Perceived Discrimination and Mastery on Health Status in a Youth Cohort." *Social Work in Health Care* 37:17–42.

Caren, Neal, Andrew Raj Ghoshal, and Vanesa Ribas. 2011. "A Social Movement Generation: Cohort and Period Trends in

Protest Attendance and Petition Signing." *American Sociological Review* 76:125–151.

Carli, Linda L. 1991. "Gender, Status, and Influence." Pp. 89–114 in *Advances in Group Processes: Theory and Research*, edited by E. J. Lawler, B. Markovsky, C. Ridgeway, and H. A. Walker, Greenwich, CT: JAI Press.

Carlson, Darren K. 2003. "Ideological Crossroads: Gen X Marks the Spot." Gallup poll. Washington, DC: Gallup Organization.

Carr, Deborah and Michael A. Friedman. 2006. "Body Weight and the Quality of Interpersonal Relationships." *Social Psychology Quarterly* 69:127–149.

Carr, E. Summerson. 2011. *Scripting Addiction: The Politics of Therapeutic Talk and American Sobriety.* Princeton, NJ: Princeton University Press.

Carr, Nicholas. 2010. *The Shallows: What the Internet Is Doing to Our Brains*. New York: W.W. Norton.

Carroll, Joseph. 2004. "Who Supports the Death Penalty?" Gallup poll. Washington, DC: Gallup Organization.

Casey, Patrick Michael. 2018. "Stigmatized Identities: Too Muslim to Be American, Too American to be Muslim." *Symbolic Interaction* 41:100–119.

Caspi, Avshalom. 1984. "Contact Hypothesis and Inter-Age Attitudes: A Field Study of Cross-Age Contact." *Social Psychology Quarterly* 47:74–80.

Cassidy, Clare and Karen Trew. 2001. "Assessing Identity Change: A Longitudinal Study of the Transition from School to College." *Group Processes & Intergroup Relations* 4:49–60.

Cast, Alicia D. 2003a. "Identities and Behavior." Pp. 41–53 in *Advances in Identity Theory and Research*, edited by P. J. Burke, T. J. Owens, R. Serpe, and P. A. Thoits. New York: Kluwer Academic/Plenum.

———. 2003b. "Power and the Ability to Define the Situation." *Social Psychology Quarterly* 66:185–201.

Cast, Alicia D. and Allison M. Cantwell. 2007. "Identity Change in Newly Married Couples: Effects of Positive and Negative Feedback." *Social Psychology Quarterly* 70:172–185.

Cekaite, Asta and Lorenza Mondado. 2021. *Touch in Social Interaction: Touch, Language, and Body*. New York: Routledge.

Chambliss, William J. 1973. "Race, Sex, and Gangs: The Saints and the Roughnecks." *Trans-Action* 11:24–31.

Chan, Tak Wing (ed.). 2010. *Social Status and Cultural Consumption*. New York: Cambridge University Press.

Chandra, Anita, Steven C. Martino, Rebecca L. Collins, Marc N. Elliott, Sandra H. Berry, David E. Kanouse, and Angela Miu. 2008. "Does Watching Sex on Television Predict Teen Pregnancy? Findings from a National Longitudinal Survey of Youth." *Pediatrics* 122:1047–1054.

Charles, Maria and Karen Bradley. 2009. "Indulging Our Gendered Selves? Sex Segregation by Field of Study in 44 Countries." *American Journal of Sociology* 114: 924–976.

Charmaz, Kathy. 2020. "Experiencing Stigma and Exclusion: The Influence of Neoliberal Perspectives, Practices, and Policies on Living with Chronic Illness and Disability." *Symbolic Interaction* 43: 21–45.

Chayko, Mary. 2008. *Portable Communities: The Social Dynamics of Online and Mobile Connectedness*. Albany, NY: SUNY Press.

Chayko, Mary. 2017. *Superconnected: The Internet, Digital Media, & Techno-Social Life*. Los Angeles: Sage.

Chen, Feinian, Yang Yang, and Guangya Liu. 2010. "Social Change and Socioeconomic Disparities in Health over the Life Course in China: A Cohort Analysis." *American Sociological Review* 75:126–150.

Cheris, Shun-ching Chan. 2013. "Doing Ideology Amid a Crisis: Collective Actions and Discourses of the Chinese Falun Gong Movement." *Social Psychology Quarterly* 76:1–24.

Chetkovich, Carol and Frances Kunreuther. 2006. *From the Ground Up: Grassroots Organizations Making Social Change*. Ithaca, NY: Cornell University Press.

Cheung, Siu-Kau and Stephen Y. K. Sun. 2000. "Effects of Self-Efficacy and Social Support on the Mental Health Conditions of Mutual-Aid Organization Members." *Social Behavior and Personality* 28:413–422.

Choma, Becky L., Jaysan J. Charlesford, and Gordon Hodson. 2014. "Reducing Prejudice with (Elaborated) Imagined and Physical Intergroup Contact Interventions." *Current Research in Social Psychology* 22:1–7.

Choo, Hae Yeon and Myra Ferree. 2010. "Practicing Intersectionality in Sociological Research: A Critical Analysis of Inclusions, Interactions, and Institutions in the Study of Inequalities." *Sociological Theory* 28:129–149.

Chou, Rosalind S. and Joe Feagin. 2008. *The Myths of the Model Minority: Asian Americans Facing Racism*. Boulder, CO: Paradigm Publishers.

Choudhry, Sultana. 2010. *Multifaceted Identities of Interethnic Young People: Chameleon Identities*. Burlington, VT: Ashgate.

Christakis Nicholas A., and James H. Fowler. 2013. "Social Contagion Theory: Examining Dynamic Social Networks and Human Behavior." *Statistics in Medicine* 32:556–77.

Christie-Mizell, C. Andre and Rebecca J. Erickson. 2007. "Mothers and Mastery: The Consequences of Perceived Neighborhood Disorder." *Social Psychology Quarterly* 70:340–365.

Church, Wesley R. Tracy Wharton, and Julie K. Taylor. 2009. "An Examination of Differential Association and Social Control Theory: Family Systems and Delinquency." *Youth Violence and Juvenile Justice* 7:3–15.

Clark, Candace. 1987. "Sympathy Biography and Sympathy Margin." *American Journal of Sociology* 93:290–321.

Clark, Kenneth B. 1963. *Prejudice and Your Child.* Middleton, CT: Wesleyan University Press.

Clarke, Lee. 2006. *Worst Cases: Terror and Catastrophe in the Popular Imagination*. Chicago: University of Chicago Press.

Clausen, John A. 1998. "Life Reviews and Life Stories." Pp. 189–212 in *Methods of Life Course Research: Qualitative and Quantitative Approaches*, edited by J. Giele and G. H. Elder, Jr. Newbury Park, CA: Sage.

Clay, Cassandra M., Michael A. Ellis, Margaret L. Griffin, Maryann Amodeo, and Irene R. Fassler 2007. "Black Women and White Women: Do Perceptions of Childhood Family Environment Differ?" *Family Process* 46:243–256.

Clifton, Jon and Zach Hrynowski. 2024. "How Happy Is Gen Z? New Report Shows School and Work are Keys to Contentment." *The Gallup Organization*. Washington, DC.

Cline, Krista Marie Clark. 2010. "Psychological Effects of Dog Ownership: Role Strain, Role Enhancement, and Depression." *Journal of Social Psychology* 150:117–131.

Cockerham, William C. 1990. "A Test of the Relationship between Race, Socioeconomic Status, and Psychological Distress." *Social Science and Medicine* 31: 1321–1326.

———. 2003. *Sociology of Mental Disorder*. Upper Saddle River, NJ: Prentice Hall.

Cohen, Marc A. and Mathew S. Isaac. 2020. "Trust Does Beget Trustworthiness and Also Begets Trust in Others." *Social Psychology Quarterly* 84:189–201.

Cohen, Bruce M.Z. 2016a. *Psychiatric Hegemony: The Marxist Theory of Mental Illness*. London: Palgrave Macmillan.

Cohen, Ira J. 2016b. *Solitary Action: Acting on Our Own in Everyday Life*. New York: Oxford University Press.

Cohen, Elizabeth G. and S. Roper. 1972. "Modification of Interracial Interaction Disability: Application of Status Characteristics Theory." *American Sociological Review* 37:643–655.

Cohen, Philip N. and Matt L. Huffman. 2007. "Working for the Woman? Female Managers and the Gender Wage Gap." *American Sociological Review* 72: 681–704.

Cohen, Bruce M.Z. 2016a. *Psychiatric Hegemony: The Marxist Theory of Mental Illness*. London: Palgrave Macmillan.

Cohen, Ira J. 2016b. *Solitary Action: Acting on Our Own in Everyday Life*. New York: Oxford University Press.

Coleman, James S. 1988. "Social Capital in the Creation of Human Capital." *American Journal of Sociology* 94:S95–S120.

Collett, Jessica L., Kelci Vercel, and Olevia Boykin. 2015. "Using Identity Processes to Understand Persistent Inequality in Parenting." *Social Psychology Quarterly* 78:345–364.

Collins, Patricia Hill. 1990. *Black Feminist Thought: Knowledge, Consciousness, and the Politics of Empowerment*. New York: Routledge.

———. 1995. "Symposium: On West and Fenstermaker's Doing Difference." *Gender and Society* 9:491–494.

Collins, Randall. 1981. "On the Microfoundations of Macrosociology." *American Journal of Sociology* 86:984–1014.

———. 1985. *Three Sociological Traditions*. New York: Oxford University Press.

———. 2004. *Interaction Ritual Chains*. Princeton, NJ: Princeton University Press.

———. 2008. *Violence: A Micro-Sociological Theory*. Princeton, NJ: Princeton University Press.

———. 2019. *Intersectionality as Critical Social Theory*. Durham, North Carolina: Duke University Press.

———. 2020. *Charisma: Micro-Sociology of Power and Influence*. New York: Routledge.

Cometa, Michelle. "Faculty Researchers Develop Humanoid Robotic System to Teach Tai Chi." *RIT*. www.rit.edu/news/faculty-researchers-develop-humanoid-robotic-system-teach-tai-chi.

Comstock, George. 2008. "A Sociological Perspective on Television Violence and Aggression." *American Behavioral Scientist* 51:1184–1211.

Condron, Dennis J. 2009. "Social Class, School and Non-School Environments, and Black/ White Inequalities in Children's Learning." *American Sociological Review* 74:683–708.

Conley, Dalton. 2009. *Elsewhere, U.S.A.: How We Got from the Company Man, Family Dinners, and the Affluent Society to the Home Office, BlackBerry Moms, and Economic Anxiety*. New York: Pantheon Press.

Conrad, Peter. 2005. "The Shifting Engines of Medicalization." *Journal of Health and Social Behavior* 46:3–14.

Conrad, Peter and Deborah Potter. 2000. "From Hyperactive Children to ADHD Adults: Observations on the Expansion of Medical Categories." *Social Problems* 47: 559–582.

Converse, Jean M. and Stanely Presser. 1986. *Survey Questions: Handcrafting the Standardized Questionnaire*, vol. 7, edited by M. S. Lewis-Beck. Newbury Park, CA: Sage.

Conway, B. and B. Spruyt. 2018. Catholic Commitment around the Globe: A 52-Country Analysis. *Journal for the Scientific Study of Religion*, 57(2):276–299.

Cook, Karen S., Richard M. Emerson, Mary R. Gillmore, and Toshio Yamagishi. 1983. "The Distribution of Power in Exchange Networks: Theory and Experimental Results." *American Journal of Sociology* 89:275–305.

Cook, Karen S., Chris Snijders, Vincent Buskens, and Coye Chesire (eds.). 2009. *eTrust: Forming Relationships in the Online World*. New York: Russell Sage Foundation.

Cook, Karen S. and Toshio Yamagishi. 1992. "Power in Exchange Networks: A Power-Dependence Formulation." *Social Networks* 14:245–265.

Cooley, Charles Horton. 1909. *Social Organization: A Study of the Larger Social Mind*. New York: Charles Scribner's Sons.

———. 1922. *Human Nature and the Social Order*. New York: Charles Scribner's Sons.

Cooper, Erica and Mike Allan. 1998. "A Meta-Analytic Examination of the Impact of Student Race on Classroom Interaction." *Communication Research Reports* 15:151–161.

Correll, Shelley J. 2004. "Constraints into Preference: Gender, Status, and Emerging Career Aspirations." *American Sociological Review* 69:93–113.

Corsaro, William. A. 1992. "Interpretive Reproduction in Children's Peer Cultures." *Social Psychology Quarterly* 55:160–177.

———. 1994. "Introduction of Glen H. Elder, Jr. for the Cooley-Mead Award." *Social Psychology Quarterly* 57:1–3.

———. 2005. *The Sociology of Childhood*. Thousand Oaks, CA: Pine Forge Press.

———. 2020. "Big Ideas from Little People: What Research with Children Contributes to Social Psychology." *Social Psychology Quarterly* 83:5–25.

Corsaro, William A. and Donna Eder. 1995. "Development and Socialization of Children and Adolescents." Pp. 421–451 in *Sociological Perspectives on Social Psychology*, edited by K. S. Cook, G. A. Fine, and J. S. House. Boston: Allyn and Bacon.

Corsaro, William A. and Laura Fingerson. 2003. "Development and Socialization in Childhood." Pp. 125–156 in *Handbook of Social Psychology*, edited by J. Delamater. New York: Kluwer Academic/Plenum.

Cotten, Shelia. 2022. "Is Technology Use Leading to the Demise of Our Mental Health and Well-Being?" Footnotes 50: 1–4. www.asanet.org/footnotes-article/technology-use-leading-demise-our-mental-health-and-well-being.

Couch, Carl J. 1968. "Collective Behavior: An Examination of Some Stereotypes." *Social Problems* 15:310–322.

Couldry, Nick and Adreas Hepp. 2016. *The Mediated Construction of Reality*. Cambridge, MA: Polity Press.

Cousineau, Matthew J. "A Blumerian Approach to Storytelling." *Symbolic Interaction* 43: 721–738.

Crenshaw, Kimberlé Williams. 1991. "Mapping the Margins: Intersectionality, Identity Politics, and Violence against Women of Color." *Stanford Law Review* 43(6):1241–129.

Cressey, Donald R. 1971. *Other People's Money: A Study in the Social Psychology of Embezzlement*. Belmont, CA: Wadsworth Publishing Company.

Cretacci, Michael A. 2008. "A General Test of Self-Control Theory: Has Its Importance Been Exaggerated?" *International Journal of Offender Therapy and Comparative Criminology* 52:538–553.

Crewe, Ben. 2009. *The Prisoner Society: Power, Adaptation, and Social Life in an English Prison*. New York: Oxford University Press.

Crocker, Jennifer and Lora E. Park. 2003. "Seeking Self-Esteem: Construction, Maintenance, and Protection of Self-Worth." Pp. 291–313 in *Handbook of Self and Identity*, edited by M. R. Leary and J. P. Tangney. New York: Guilford Press.

Crosnoe, Robert. 2009. "Low-Income Students and the Socioeconomic Composition of Public High Schools." *American Sociological Review* 74:709–730.

Crosnoe, Robert and Glen H. Elder, Jr. 2004. "From Childhood to the Later Years: Pathways of Human Development." *Research on Aging* 26:623–654.

Crosnoe, Robert, Monica Kirkpatrick Johnson, and Glen H. Elder, Jr. 2004. "School Size and the Interpersonal Side of Education: An Examination of Race/Ethnicity and Organizational Context." *Social Science Quarterly* 85:1259–1274.

Crowder, Kyle, Matthew Hall, and Steward Tolney. 2011. "Neighborhood Immigration and Native Out-Migration." *American Sociological Review* 76:25–47.

Crystal, David. 2008. *Txtng: The Gr8 Db8*. Oxford, UK: Oxford University Press.

Cuddy, Amy J. C., Mindi S. Rock, and Michael I. Norton. 2007. "Aid in the Aftermath of Hurricane Katrina: Inferences of Secondary Emotions and Intergroup Helping." *Group Processes and Intergroup Relations* 10:107–118.

Cunningham, Mick. 2001. "Parental Influences on the Gendered Division of Housework." *American Sociological Review* 66: 184–203.

Cunningham, Simone, Chloe C. Hudson, and Kate Harkness. 2021. "Social Media and Depression Symptoms: a Meta-Analysis." Research on Child and Adolescent Psychopathology 49:241–253.

Cuthbertson, Anthony. "Chinese Scientists Build Robot Nanny to Care for Babies in Artificial Womb." Independent. www.independent.co.uk/tech/robot-nanny-china-population-b2004342.html. Cuthbertsonsadf.

Dalsgard, Anne Line, Martin Frederiksen, Susanne Hojlund, and Lotte Meinert (Eds) (2014). Ethnographies of Youth and Temporality: Time Objectified. Philadlphia, PA: Temple University Press.

Dambrun, Michael, Magali Villate, and Juliette Richetin. 2008. "Implicit Racial Attitudes and Their Relationships with Explicit Personal and Cultural Beliefs: What Personalized and Traditional IAT's Measure." *Current Research in Social Psychology* 13:16.

Danigelis, Nicholas L., Melissa Hardy, and Stephen J. Cutler. 2007. "Population Aging, Intracohort Aging and Sociopolitical Attitudes." *American Sociological Review* 72:812–830.

Davey, Gareth and Xiang Zhao (2020). "Turning Points to Becoming a Tobacco Smoker: Smoking Initiation and Identity Change among Chinese Youth." *Symbolic Interaction* 43:308–331.

David, Matthew. 2010. *Peer to Peer and the Music Industry: The Criminalization of Sharing*. Thousand Oaks, CA: Sage.

Davis, Jenny L. 2014. "Triangulating the Self: Identity Processes in a Connected Era." *Symbolic Interaction* 37:500–523.

Davis, Joanna R. 2006. "Growing Up Punk: Negotiating Aging Identity in a Local Music Scene." *Symbolic Interaction* 29:63–69.

Davis, Jenny L., Tony P. Love, and Phoenicia Fares. 2019. "Collective Social Identity: Synthesizing Identity Theory and Social Identity Theory Using Digital Data." *Social Psychology Quarterly* 82: 254–273.

de Koster, Willem. 2010. "Contesting Community Online: Virtual Imagery among Dutch Orthodox Protestant Homosexuals." *Symbolic Interaction* 33:552–577.

De Soucey, Michaela. 2010. "Gastronationalism." *American Sociological Review* 75: 432–455.

de Rond, Mark. 2017. *Doctors at War: Life and Death in a Field Hospital*. Ithaca, NY: Cornell University Press.

DeAngelis, Tori. 2022. "Mental Illness and Violence: Debunking Myths, Addressing Realities." *Monitor on Psychology* 52. www.apa.org/monitor/2021/04/ce-mental-illness.

DeAngelis, Reed, Laura Upeniek and Patricia Louie. 2023. "Religious Involvement and Allostatic Resilience: Findings from a Community Study of Black and White Americans." *Journal of Racial and Ethnic Health Disparities* 11:137–149.

Deaux, Kay and Daniela Martin. 2003. "Interpersonal Networks and Social Categories: Specifying Levels of Context in Identity Processes." *Social Psychology Quarterly* 66:101–117.

Debies-Carl, Jeffrey S., and Christopher M. Huggins. 2009. "'City Air Makes Free': A Multi-Level, Cross-National Analysis of Self-Efficacy." *Social Psychology Quarterly* 72:343–364.

DeGloma, Thomas. 2007. "The Social Logic of 'False Memories': Symbolic

Awakenings and Symbolic Worlds in Survivor and Retractor Narratives." *Symbolic Interaction* 30:543–565.

———. 2014. *Seeing the Light: The Social Logic of Personal Discovery*. Chicago: University of Chicago Press.

DeLisi, Matt and Michael Vaughn. 2007. "The Gottfredson–Hirschi Critiques Revisited: Reconciling Self-Control Theory, Criminal Careers, and Career Criminals." *International Journal of Offender Therapy and Comparative Criminology* 52: 520–537.

Deluca, Stefanie and James E. Rosenbaum. 2001. "Individual Agency and the Life Course: Do Low-SES Students Get Less Long-Term Payoff for Their School Efforts?" *Sociological Focus* 34:357–376.

Demo, David H. 1992. "Parent–Child Relations: Assessing Recent Changes." *Journal of Marriage and the Family* 54:104–117.

Denzin, Norman K. 1971. "Childhood as a Conversation of Gestures." *Sociological Symposium* 7:23–35.

———. 1977. *Childhood Socialization: Studies in the Development of Language, Social Behavior, and Identity*. San Francisco: Jossey-Bass.

______. 2007. "Memory: Lewis and Clark in Yellowstone, circa 2004." *Symbolic Interaction* 30:297–321.

Denzin, Norman K. 2011. Custer on Canvas: Native Americans Memory, Museums and Violence in the New West. Walnut Creek, CA: Left Coast Press.

Derber, Charles. 2014. Wilding of America, 6th Edition. New York: Worth.

DiAngelo, Robin. 2018. White Fragility. Boston: Beacon Press.

Diekmann, Andreas and Kurt Schmidheiny. 2004. "Do Parents of Girls Have a Higher Risk of Divorce? An Eighteen-Country Study." *Journal of Marriage and Family* 66:651–660.

Diener, Ed, Carol L. Gohm, Eunkook Suh, and Shigehiro Oishi. 2000. "Similarity of the Relations between Marital Status and Subjective Well-Being across Cultures." *Journal of Cross-Cultural Psychology* 31: 419–436.

Dill, Karen E. and Kathryn P. Thill. 2007. "Video Game Characters and the Socialization of Gender Roles: Young People's Perceptions Mirror Sexist Media Depictions." *Sex Roles* 57:851–864.

Dixon, David J. and Greg L. Robinson-Riegler. 2008. "The Effects of Language Priming and Unique vs. Collective Self-Priming on Independent and Interdependent Self-Construal among Chinese University Students Currently Studying English." *Current Research in Social Psychology*, 14:122–133.

Dixon, Mark and Andrew W. Martin. 2012. "We Can't Win This on Our Own: Unions, Firms, and Mobilization of External Allies in Labor Disputes." *American Sociological Review* 77:946–969.

Doan, Long. 2012. "A Social Model of Persistent Mood States." *Social Psychology Quarterly* 75:198–218.

Doan, Long, Lisa R. Miller, and Annalise Loehr. 2015. "The Power of Love: The Role of Emotional Attributions and Standards in Heterosexuals' Attitudes toward Lesbian and Gay Couples." *Social Forces* 94:401–425.

Dobbin, Frank and Alexandra Kalev. 2016. "Why Diversity Programs Fail: And

What Works Better." *Harvard Business Review* July-August: 52–59.

Dodoo, F. Nii-Amoo, and Baffour K. Takyi. 2002. "Africans in the Diaspora: Black-White Earnings Differences among America's Africans." *Ethnic and Racial Studies* 25:913–941.

Dooley, David, Ralph Catalano, and Karen S. Rook. 1988. "Personal and Aggregate Unemployment and Psychological Symptoms." *Journal of Social Issues* 44: 107–123.

Dooley, David, Ralph Catalano, and Georjeanna Wilson. 1994. "Depression and Unemployment: Panel Findings from the Epidemiologic Catchment Area Study." *American Journal of Community Psychology* 22:745–765.

Dotson, Taylor. 2017. *Technically Together: Reconstructing Community in a Networked World*. Cambridge, MA: MIT Press.

Dotter, Daniel L. 2004. *Creating Deviance: An Interactionist Approach*. Walnut Creek, CA: AltaMira Press.

Dow, Dawn Marie. 2016. "The Deadly Challenges of Raising African American Boys: Navigating the Controlling Image of the 'Thug.'" Gender & Society 30:161–188.

Doyle, Joshua. 2021. "The Effect of Cultural Trust on Cooperation in Two Behavioral Experiments." Social Psychology Quarterly 84:246–266.

Doyle, Jamie Mihoko and Grace Kao. 2007. "Are Racial Identities of Multiracials Stable? Changing Self-Identification among Single and Multiple Race Individuals." *Social Psychology Quarterly* 70:405–423.

Drozdzewski, Danielle, Sarah De Nardi, and Emma Waterton. 2016. *Memory, Place, and Identity: Commemoration and Remembrance of War and Conflict*. New York: Routledge.

Du Bois, W. E. B. 2003. "The Souls of White Folk." *National Review* 55:44–58.

Due, Brian L. 2021. "Distributed Perception: Co-Operation between Sense-Able, Actionable, and Accountable Semiotic Agents." *Symbolic Interaction* 44: 134–162.

Duncan, Lauren E. and Abigail J. Stewart. 1995. "Still Bringing the Vietnam War Home: Sources of Contemporary Student Activism." *Personality and Social Psychology Bulletin* 21:914–924.

Durkheim, Emile. 1951. *Suicide: A Study in Sociology*. New York: Free Press.

Dush, Claire M. Kamp and Paul R. Amato. 2005. "Consequences of Relationship Status and Quality for Subjective Well-Being." *Journal of Social and Personal Relationships* 22:607–627.

Edgley, Charles. 2013. *Drama of Social Life: A Dramaturgical Handbook*. Abingdon, Oxon and New York: Ashgate.

Ehrenberg, Alain. 2010. *The Weariness of the Self: Diagnosing the History of Depression in the Contemporary Age*. Montreal, CA: McGuill Queen's University Press.

Eisenberg, Nancy. 1991. "Meta-Analytic Contributions to the Literature on Prosocial Behavior." *Personality and Social Psychology Bulletin* 17:273–282.

Eitle, David J. 2002. "Exploring a Source of Deviance-Producing Strain for Females: Perceived Discrimination and General Strain Theory." *Journal of Criminal Justice* 30:429–442.

———. 2010. "General Strain Theory, Persistence, and Desistence among Young

Adult Males." *Journal of Criminal Justice* 38:1113–1121.

Ekman, Paul. 2007. *Emotions Revealed, Second Edition: Recognizing Faces and Feelings to Improve Communication and Emotional Life.* New York: Holt.

Elder, Glen H., Jr. 1987. "War Mobilization and the Life Course: A Cohort of World War II Veterans." *Sociological Forum* 2:449–472.

———. 1994. "Time, Human Agency, and Social Change: Perspectives on the Life Course." *Social Psychology Quarterly* 57:4–15.

———. 1999. *Children of the Great Depression*. Boulder, CO: Westview Press.

Elder, Glen H., Jr. and Rand D. Conger. 2000. *Children of the Land: Adversity and Success in Rural America*. Chicago: University of Chicago Press.

Eliason, Scott R., Jeylan T. Mortimer, and Mike Vuolo. 2015. "The Transition to Adulthood: Life Course Structures and Subjective Perceptions." *Social Psychology Quarterly* 78:205–227.

Elliott, Delbert S., Scott Menard, Bruce Rankin, Amanda Elliott, David Huizinga, and William Julius Wilson. 2006. *Good Kids from Bad Neighborhoods: Successful Development in Social Context.* New York: Cambridge University Press.

Elliott, Gregory C. 1986. "Self-Esteem and Self-Consistency: A Theoretical and Empirical Link between Two Primary Motivations." *Social Psychology Quarterly* 49:207–218.

———. 2001. "The Self as a Social Product and a Social Force: Morris Rosenberg and the Elaboration of a Deceptively Simple Effect." Pp. 10–28 in *Extending Self-Esteem Theory and Research: Sociological and Psychological Currents*, edited by T. J. Owens, S. Stryker, and N. Goodman. Cambridge, MA: Cambridge University Press.

Elliott, Gregory C., Melissa F. Colangelo, and Richard J. Gelles. 2005. "Mattering and Suicide Ideation: Establishing and Elaborating a Relationship." *Social Psychology Quarterly* 68:223–238.

Elliott, Gregory C., Suzanne Kao, and Ann-Marie Grant. 2004. "Mattering: Empirical Validation of a Social-Psychological Concept." *Self and Identity* 3:339–354.

Ellis, Carolyn. 1999. "Keynote Addresses from the First Annual Advances in Qualitative Methods Conference." *Qualitative Health Research* 9:669–683.

———. 2004. *The Ethnographic I: A Methodological Novel about Autoethnography*. Newbury, CA: AltaMira Press.

Ellison, Christopher G., Heeju Shin, and David L. Leal. 2011. "The Contact Hypothesis and Attitudes toward Latinos in the United States." *Social Science Quarterly* 92:938–958.

Emerson, Richard M. 1992. "Social Exchange Theory." Pp. 30–65 in *Social Psychology: Sociological Perspectives*, edited by M. Rosenberg and R. H. Turner. New Brunswick, NJ: Transaction Publishers.

Epley, Nicholas and Juliana Schroeder. 2014. "Mistakenly seeking solitude." Journal of Experimental Psychology 143: 1980–1999.

Epstein, Cynthia Fuchs. 2007. "Great Divides: The Cultural, Cognitive, and Social Basis of the Global Subordination of Women." *American Sociological Review* 72:1–22.

Eriksson, Kimmo. 2018. "Republicans Value Agency, Democrats Value Communion." *Social Psychology Quarterly* 81: 173–184.

Esholdt, Henriette Frees. 2019. "Virgins, Terrorists, and Ten Children: Immigrants' Humerous Play with Ethnic Stereotypes in Bonding Danes in the Workplace." *Symbolic Interaction* 42:691–716.

Everitt, Judson G. 2013. "Inhabitants Moving In: Prospective Sense-Making and the Reproduction of Inhabited Institutions in Teacher Education." *Symbolic Interaction* 36:177–196.

Everitt, Judson G. 2017. *Lesson Plans*. New Brunswick, NJ: Rutgers University Press.

Falci, Christina D. 2011. "Self-Esteem and Mastery Trajectories in High School by Social Class and Gender." *Social Science Research* 40:586–601.

Farberman, Harvey A. 2019. *Essays in Interactionist Sociology*. Boston, MA: Archway Publishing.

Faris, Robert E. and H. Warren Dunham. 1960. *Mental Disorders in Urban Areas: An Ecological Study of Schizophrenia and Other Psychoses*. New York: Hafner Publishing Co.

Felmlee, Diane and Robert Faris. "Toxic Ties: Networks of Friendship, Dating and Cyber Victimization." *Social Psychology Quarterly* 79:243–262.

Ferguson, Kathy E. 1980. *Self, Society, and Womankind: The Dialectic of Liberation*. Westport, CT: Greenwood Press.

Fernandez, Roberto M. and Isabel Fernandez-Mateo. 2006. "Networks, Race, and Hiring." *American Sociological Review* 71:42–71.

Fields, Corey D. 2014. "Not Your Grandma's Knitting: The Role of Identity Processes in the Transformation of Cultural Practices." *Social Psychology Quarterly* 77:150–165.

Fine, Gary Alan. 1979. "Small Groups and Culture Creation: The Idioculture of Little League Baseball Teams." *American Sociological Review* 44:733–745.

———. 2001. *Difficult Reputations: Collective Memories of the Evil, Inept, and Controversial*. Chicago: University of Chicago Press.

———. 2004. *Everyday Genius: Self-Taught Art and the Culture of Authenticity*. Chicago: University of Chicago Press.

———. 2007. "The Construction of Historical Equivalence: Weighing the Red and Brown Scares." *Symbolic Interaction* 30:27–40.

———. 2014. "The Hinge: Civil Society, Group Culture, and the Interaction Order." *Social Psychology Quarterly* 77: 27–53.

Fine, Gary Alan and Aaron Beim. 2007. "Introduction: Interactionist Approaches to Collective Memory." *Symbolic Interaction* 30:1–5.

Fine, Gary Alan and Tim Hallett. 2023. *Group Life: An Invitation to Local Sociology*. Cambridge and Hoboken, NJ: Polity.

Fischer, Claude S. 1973. "Urban Malaise." *Social Forces* 52:221–235.

Fisek, M. Hamit, Joseph Berger, and Robert Z. Norman. 2005. "Status Cues and the Formation of Expectations." *Social Science Research* 34:80–102.

Fisk, Susan R. 2018. "Who's on Top? Gender Differences in Risk-Taking Produce

Unequal Outcomes for High-Ability Women and Men." *Social Psychology Quarterly* 81:185–206.

Fisk, Susan R. and Jon Overton. 2019. "Who Wants to Lead? Anticipated Gender Discrimination Reduces Women's Leadership Ambitions." *Social Psychology Quarterly* 82:319–332.

Fletcher, James Rupert. 2020. "Distributed Selves: Shifting Inequalities of Impression Management in Couples' Living with Dementia." *Symbolic Interaction* 43:405–427.

Fletcher, Joseph F. and Marie-Christine Chalmers. 1991. "Attitudes of Canadians toward Affirmative Action: Opposition, Value Pluralism, and Nonattitudes." *Political Behavior* 13:67–95.

Flint, Daniel, Antonio Pagan, Tom Cook, Michael Bailey, and Max Butterfield. 2020. "Situation Attribution Mediates Intention to Overlook Negative Signals Among Romantic Interests." *Current Research in Social Psychology* 28:1–12. https://crisp.org.uiowa.edu/sites/crisp.org.uiowa.edu/files/2020-04/crisp_28_3_flint.pdf.

Flores, David. 2016. "From Prowar Soldier to Antiwar Activist: Change and Continuity in the Narratives of Political Conversion among Iraq War Veterans." *Symbolic Interaction* 39:196–212.

Fomby, Paula and Andrew J. Cherlin. 2007. "Family Instability and Child Well-Being." *American Sociological Review* 72: 181–204.

Foschi, Martha. 1996. "Double Standards in the Evaluation of Men and Women." *Social Psychology Quarterly* 59:237–254.

———. 2000. "Double Standards for Competence: Theory and Research." *Annual Review of Sociology* 26:21–42.

Foschi, Martha, Larissa Lai, and Kirsten Sigerson. 1994. "Gender and Double Standards in the Assessment of Job Applicants." *Social Psychology Quarterly* 57: 326–339.

Foschi, Martha and Vanessa Lapointe. 2002. "On Conditional Hypotheses and Gender as a Status Characteristic." *Social Psychology Quarterly* 65:146–162.

Foster, E. Michael. 1993. "Foster, How Should Sociologists Treat Becker's 'Treatise on the Family?'" *Sociological Forum* 8:317–329

Foucault, Michel. 1965. *Madness and Civilization: A History of Insanity in the Age of Reason*, trans. R. Howard. New York: Vintage Books.

Francisco-Menchavez, Valerie. 2018. *The Labor of Care: Filipina Migrants and Transnational Families in the Digital Age.* Urbana, IL: University of Illinois Press.

Frank, David John, Bayliss J. Camp, and Steven A. Boutcher. 2010. "Worldwide Trends in the Criminal Regulation of Sex, 1945 to 2005." *American Sociological Review* 75:867–893.

Frank, Richard G., Rena M. Conti, and Howard H. Goldman. 2005. "Mental Health Policy and Psychotropic Drugs." The Milbank Quarterly 83:271–98.

Franks, David D. 2003. "Emotions." Pp. 787–809 in *Handbook of Symbolic Interactionism*, edited by L. T. Reynolds and N. J. Herman-Kinney. Lanham, MD: Rowman & Littlefield.

Freeland, Robert E. and Catherine E. Harnois. 2020. "Bridging the Gender Wage Gap: Gendered Cultural Sentiments, Sex Segregation, and Occupation-Level Wages." *Social Psychology Quarterly* 83:129–151.

Freese, Jeremy, Brian Powell, and Lala C. Steelman. 1999. "Rebel without a Cause or Effect: Birth Order and Social Attitudes." *American Sociological Review* 64:207–231.

Freud, Sigmund. 1945. *Group Psychology and the Analysis of the Ego*. London: Hogarth.

Friedman, Asia M. 2012. "Believing Not Seeing: A Blind Phenomenology of Sexed Bodies." *Symbolic Interaction* 35:284–300.

Froggio, Giacinto and Robert Agnew. 2007. "The Relationship between Crime and 'Objective' versus 'Subjective' Strains." *Journal of Criminal Justice* 35:81–87.

Gabb, Jacqui. 2010. *Researching Intimacy in Families*. Basingstoke, UK: Palgrave Macmillan.

Gallup. 2023. "LGBTQ+ Rights. Report from the Gallup Organization." https://news.gallup.com/poll/1651/gay-lesbian-rights.aspx.

Gambetta, Diego. 2009. *Codes of the Underworld: How Criminals Communicate*. Princeton, NJ: Princeton University Press.

Gamson, William. 1990. *The Strategy of Social Protest*. Homewood, IL: Dorsey.

Garfinkel, Harold. 1967. *Studies in Ethnomethodology*. Cambridge, MA: Polity Press.

Garner, Betsie and David Grazian. 2016. "Naturalizing Gender through Childhood Socialization Messages in a Zoo." *Social Psychology Quarterly* 79: 181–198.

Garot, Robert. 2010. *Who You Claim: Performing Gang Identity in School and on the Streets*. New York: New York University Press.

Garside, Rula Bayrakdar and Bonnie Klimes-Dougan. 2002. "Socialization of Discrete Negative Emotions: Gender Differences and Links with Psychological Distress." *Sex Roles* 47:115–128.

Gartner, Scott Sigmund. 2008. "Ties to the Dead: Connections to Iraq War and 9/11 Casualties and Disapproval of the President." *American Sociological Review* 73:690–695.

Gawley, Tim. 2008. "University Administrators as Information Tacticians: Understanding Transparency as Selective Concealment and Instrumental Disclosure." *Symbolic Interaction* 31:181–204.

Gaztambide-Fernandez, Ruben A. 2009. *The Best of the Best: Becoming Elite at an American Boarding School*. Cambridge, MA: Harvard University Press.

Gecas, Viktor. 1982. "The Self-Concept." *Annual Review of Sociology* 8:1–33.

———. 1989. "The Social Psychology of Self-Efficacy." *Annual Review of Sociology* 15:291–316.

———. 1990. "Morris Rosenberg: 1989 Cooley-Mead Award Recipient." *Social Psychology Quarterly* 53:1–2.

——. 1992. "Contexts of Socialization." Pp. 165–199 in *Social Psychology: Sociological Perspectives*, edited by M. Rosenberg and R. H. Turner. New Brunswick, NJ: Transaction Publishers.

———. 2001. "The Self as Social Force." Pp. 85–100 in *Extending Self-Esteem Theory and Research: Sociological and Psychological Currents*, edited by T. J. Owens, S. Stryker, and N. Goodman. Cambridge, MA: Cambridge University Press.

George, Linda K. and Scott M. Lynch. 2003. "Race Differences in Depressive Symptoms: A Dynamic Perspective on Stress Exposure and Vulnerability." *Journal of Health and Social Behavior* 44:353–369.

Gerber, Theodore P. and Olga Mayorova. 2010. "Getting Personal: Networks and Stratification in the Russian Labor Market, 1985–2001." *American Journal of Sociology* 116:855–908.

Gergen, Kenneth J. 2000. *The Saturated Self: Dilemmas of Identity in Contemporary Life*. New York: Basic Books.

Gergen, Kenneth J. and Mary M. Gergen. 1997, "Narratives of the Self." Pp. 161–184 in *Memory, Identity, Community*, edited by Lewis P. Hinchman and Sandra K. Hinchman. Albany, NY: SUNY Press.

Gerhards, Jurgen and Silke Hans. 2009. "From Hasan to Herbert: Name-Giving Patterns of Immigrant Parents between Acculturation and Ethnic Maintenance." *American Journal of Sociology* 114: 1102–1128.

Ghaziani, Amin and Delia Baldassarri. 2011. "Cultural Anchors and the Organization of Differences: A Multi-Method Analysis of LGBT Marches on Washington." *American Sociological Review* 76:179–206.

Gibson, Barry and Jan Hartman. 2013. *Rediscovering Grounded Theory*. London: Sage.

Gilleard, Chris and Paul Higgs. 2005. *Contexts of Aging: Class, Cohort and Community*. Malden, MA: Polity Press.

Gilligan, Carol. 1982. *In a Different Voice: Psychological Theory and Women's Development*. Cambridge, MA: Harvard University Press.

Giordano, Peggy C., Ryan D. Schroeder, and Stephen A. Cernkovich. 2007. "Emotions and Crime over the Life Course: A Neo-Meadian Perspective on Criminal Continuity and Change." *American Journal of Sociology* 112:1603–1661.

Glass, Jennifer, Vern L. Bengtson, and Charlotte Chorn Dunham. 1986. "Attitude Similarity in Three-Generation Families: Socialization, Status Inheritance, or Reciprocal Influence?" *American Sociological Review* 51:685–698.

Glavin, Paul and Scott Schieman. 2014. "Control in the Face of Uncertainty: Is Job Security a Challenge to the Mental Health Benefits of Control Beliefs?" *Social Psychology Quarterly* 77:319–343.

Glueck, Sheldon and Eleanor Glueck. 1950. *Unraveling Juvenile Delinquency*. New York: Commonwealth Fund.

———. 1968. *Delinquents and Nondelinquents in Perspective*. Cambridge, MA: Harvard University Press.

Godwyn, Mary. 2006. "Using Emotional Labor to Create and Maintain Relationships in Service Interactions." *Symbolic Interactions* 29:487–506.

Goffman, Alice. 2014. *On the Run: Fugitive Life in an American City*. Chicago: Chicago University Press.

Goffman, Alice. 2018. "Go to More Parties? Social Occasions as Home to Unexpected Turning Points in Life Trajectories." *Social Psychology Quarterly* 82:51–74.

Goffman, Erving. 1959. *The Presentation of Self in Everyday Life*. Garden City, NY: Doubleday.

———. 1961. *Asylums*. New York: Anchor.

———. 1963. *Stigma: Notes on the Management of Spoiled Identity*. Englewood Cliffs, NJ: Prentice Hall.

———. 1967. *Interaction Ritual Essays in Face to Face Behavior*. Chicago: Aldine.

———. 1974. *Frame Analysis: An Essay on the Organization of Experience*. Cambridge, MA: Harvard University Press.

Goleman, Daniel. 1997. *Emotional Intelligence*. New York: Bantam.

Goleman, Daniel. 2006. Social intelligence: The new science of human relationships. New York: Bantam Books.

Goode, Erich. 2011. *Deviant Behavior*, 9th ed. Upper Saddle River, NJ: Pearson.

Goodrum, Sarah. 2008. "When the Management of Grief Becomes Everyday Life: The Aftermath of Murder." *Symbolic Interaction* 31:422–442.

Goodwin, Marjorie and Asta Cekaite. 2018. *Embodying Family Choreography*. London and New York: Routledge.

Gordon, Hava Rachel. 2010. *We Fight to Win: Inequality and the Politics of Youth Activism*. New Brunswick, NJ: Rutgers University Press.

Gotlib, Ian H. and Blair Wheaton. 1997. *Stress and Adversity over the Life Course: Trajectories and Turning Points*. Cambridge, MA: Cambridge University Press.

Gottfredson, Michael R. and Travis Hirschi 1990. *A General Theory of Crime*. Palo Alto, CA: Stanford University Press.

Gottschalk, Simon. 2010. "The Presentation of Avatars in Second Life: Self and Interaction in Social Virtual Spaces." *Symbolic Interaction* 33:501–525.

Gottschalk, Simon. 2018. *The Terminal Self: Everyday Life in Hypermodern Times*. London: Routledge.

Govorushko, Sergey. 2018. *Human-Insect Interactions*. Boca Raton, FL: CRC Press.

Grace, Sherry L. and Kenneth L. Cramer. 2002. "Sense of Self in the New Millennium: Male and Female Student Responses to the TST." *Social Behavior and Personality* 30:271–280.

Gracey, Harry. 1972. *Curriculum or Craftmanship: Elementary School Teachers in a Bureaucratic System*. Chicago: University of Chicago Press.

Graham, Carol. 2009. *Happiness around the World: The Paradox of Happy Peasants and Miserable Millionares*. Oxford, UK: Oxford University Press.

Granberg, Ellen. 2006. "'Is That All There Is?' Possible Selves, Self-Change, and Weight Loss." *Social Psychology Quarterly* 69:109–126.

Granovetter, Mark S. 1973. "The Strength of Weak Ties." *American Journal of Sociology* 78:1360–1380.

———. 1995. *Getting a Job: A Study in Contacts and Careers*. Chicago: Chicago University Press.

Gray, John. 1992. *Men Are from Mars, Women Are from Venus: A Practical Guide for Improving Communication and Getting What You Want in Your Relationships*. New York: HarperCollins.

Greenberg, David F. 1999. "The Weak Strength of Social Control Theory." *Crime and Delinquency* 45:66–81.

Griffin, Larry J. and Kenneth A. Bollen. 2009. "What Do These Memories Do: Civil Rights Remembrance and Racial Attitudes." *American Sociological Review* 74: 594–614.

Grigsby, Mary. 2009. *College Life through the Eyes of Students*. Albany, NY: State University of New York Press.

Grimes, Tom and Lori Bergen. 2008. "The Epistemological Argument against a Casual Relationship between Media Violence and Sociopathic Behavior among Psychologically Well Viewers." *American Behavioral Scientist* 51:1137–1154.

Grodsky, Eric and Devah Pager. 2001. "The Structure of Disadvantage: Individual Occupational Determinants of the Black-White Wage Gap." *American Sociological Review* 66:542–567.

Grow, André, Károly Takács, and Judi Pál. 2016. "Status Characteristics and Ability Attributions in Hungarian School Classes: An Exponential Random Graph Approach." *Social Psychology Quarterly* 79:156–167.

Guhin, Jeffrey, Jessica McCrory Calarco, and Cynthia Miller-Idriss. 2021. "Whatever Happened to Socialization?" *Annual Review of Sociology* 47:109–129.

Guo, Guang, Michael E. Roettger, and Tianji Cai. 2008. "The Integration of Genetic Propensities into Social-Control Models of Delinquency and Violence among Male Youths." *American Sociological Review* 73:543–568.

Guo, Guang and Elizabeth Stearns. 2002. "The Social Influences on the Realization of Genetic Potential for Intellectual Development." *Social Forces* 80:881–910.

Hackstaff, Karla B., Feiwel Kupferberg, and Catherine Negroni. 2012. *Biography and Turning Points in Europe and America*. Great Britain: The Policy Press.

Hahl, Oliver, Ezra W. Zuckerman, and Minjae Kim. 2017. "Why Elites Love Authentic Lowbrow Culture: Overcoming High-Status Denigration with Outsider Art." *American Sociological Review* 82:828–856.

Hall, Jeffrey A. 2019. "How Many Hours Does it Take to Make a Friend?" *Journal of Social and Personal Relationships* 36:1278–1296.

Hallett, Tim. 2007. "Between Deference and Distinction: Interaction Ritual through Symbolic Power in an Educational Institution." *Social Psychology Quarterly* 70:148–171.

Hallett, Tim and Emily Meanwell. 2016. "Accountability as an Inhabited Institution: Contested Meanings and the Symbolic Politics of Reform." *Symbolic Interaction* 39:374–396.

Hallsten, Martin. 2010. "The Structure of Educational Decision Making and Consequences for Inequality: A Swedish Test Case." *American Journal of Sociology* 116: 806–854.

Halnon, Karen Bettez. 2006. "Heavy Metal Carnival and Disalienation: The Politics of Grotesque Realism." *Symbolic Interaction* 29:33–48.

Hamermesh, Daniel S. 2011. *Beauty Pays: Why Attractive People Are More Successful*. Princeton, NJ: Princeton University Press.

Monk, Jr., Ellis P. 2015. "The Cost of Color: Skin Color, Discrimination, and Health among African-Americans." *American Journal of Sociology* 121:396–444.

Hancock, Jeffrey T. and Catalina L. Toma. 2009. "Putting the Best Foot Forward: The Accuracy of Online Dating." *Journal of Communication* 59:367–386.

Handel, Gerald, Spencer E. Cahill, and Frederick Elkin. 2007. *Children and*

Society: The Sociology of Children and Childhood Sociology. Los Angeles: Roxbury.

Hannem, Stacey and Chris Bruckert (Eds). 2012. *Stigma Revisited: Implications of the Mark*. Ottawa, ON: University of Ottawa Press.

Harding, David J. 2009. "Violence, Older Peers, and the Socialization of Adolescent Boys in Disadvantaged Neighborhoods." *American Sociological Review* 74: 445–464.

Harding, David J. and Christopher Jencks. 2003. "Changing Attitudes toward Premarital Sex: Cohort, Period, and Aging Effects." *Public Opinion Quarterly* 67: 211–226.

Harris, Alexes. 2011. "Constructing Clean Dreams: Accounts, Future Selves, and Social and Structural Support as Desistance Work." *Symbolic Interaction* 34: 63–85.

Harrod, Michael M. 2013. "Further Examining the Buffering Effect of Self-Esteem and Mastery on Emotions." *Current Research in Social Psychology* 21:42–51.

Hartjen, Clayton A. and S. Priyadarsini. 2003. "Gender, Peers, and Delinquency: A Study of Boys and Girls in Rural France." *Youth & Society* 34:387–414.

Hartman, Chester and Gregory D. Squires. 2006. *There Is No Such Thing as a Natural Disaster: Race, Class, and Hurricane Katrina*. New York: Routledge.

Harvey, Peter Francis. 2023. ""Everyone Thinks They're Special": How Schools Teach Children Their Social Station." *American Sociological Review* 88: 493–521.

Haskins, Anna R., and Wade C. Jacobsen. 2017. "Schools as surveilling institutions? Paternal incarceration, system avoidance, and parental involvement in schooling." *American Sociological Review* 82: 657–684.

Hausmann, Amy Jonason and Erika Summers-Effler. 2011. "Interaction Ritual Theory and Structural Symbolic Interactionism." *Symbolic Interaction* 34:319–329.

Heath, Andrew C., K. Berg, Lindon Eaves, M. H. Solaas, L. A. Corey, J. Sundet, P. Magnus, and W. E. Nance. 1985. "Education Policy and the Heritability of Educational Attainment." *Nature* 314: 734–736.

Heath, Shirley Brice. 1983. *Ways with Words: Language, Life, and Work in Communities and Classrooms*. New York: Cambridge University Press.

Heckert, Druann Maria and Amy Best. 1997. "Ugly Duckling to Swan: Labeling Theory and the Stigmatization of Red." *Symbolic Interaction* 20:365–384.

Hedges, Larry V. and Barbara Schneider (eds.). 2005. *The Social Organization of Schooling*. New York: Russell Sage Foundation.

Hegtvedt, Karen A. 1990. "The Effects of Relationship Structure on Emotional Responses to Inequity." *Social Psychology Quarterly* 53:214–228.

Hegtvedt, Karen A. and Caitlin Killian. 1999. "Fairness and Emotions: Reactions to the Process and Outcomes of Negotiations." *Social Forces* 78:269–303.

Hegtvedt, Karen A., Cathryn Johnson, Ryan Gibson, Kate Hawks, and Jennifer L. Hayward. 2022. "Power and Procedure: Gaining Legitimacy in the Workplace." *Social Forces 101*:176–201.

Heilman, Madeline E., Aaron S. Wallen, Daniella Fuchs, and Melinda Tamkins. 2004. "Penalties for Success: Reactions to Women Who Succeed at Male Gender-Typed Tasks." *Journal of Applied Psychology* 89:416–427.

Heimer, Karen and Candace Kruttschnitt. 2005. *Gender and Crime: Patterns of Victimization and Offending*. New York: New York University Press.

Hein, Jeremy and Christopher D. Moore. 2009. "Race Relations Stories: How Southeast Asian Refugees Interpret the Ancestral Narration of Black and White Peers." *Social Psychology Quarterly*, 72:9–23.

Heino, Rebecca D., Nicole B. Ellison, and Jennifer Gibbs. 2010. "Relationshopping: Investigating the Market Metaphor in Online Dating." *Journal of Social and Personal Relationships* 27:427–447.

Heise, David R. 1985. "Affect Control Theory: Respecification, Estimation, and Tests of the Formal Model." *Journal of Mathematical Sociology* 11:191–222.

———. 1999. "Controlling Affective Experience Interpersonally." *Social Psychology Quarterly* 62:1–16.

———. 2002. "Understanding Social Interaction with Affect Control Theory." Pp. 17–40 in *New Directions in Sociological Theory*, edited by J. Berger and M. Zelditch. Boulder, CO: Rowman & Littlefield.

———. 2007. *Expressive Order*. New York: Springer.

Heise, David and Steven J. Lerner. 2006. "Affect Control in International Interactions." *Social Forces* 85:993–1010.

Heisig, Jan Paul. 2011. "Who Does More Housework: Rich or Poor? A Comparison of 33 Countries." *American Sociological Review* 76:74–99.

Herman-Kinney, Nancy J. 2003. "Deviance." Pp. 695–720 in *Handbook of Symbolic Interactionism*, edited by L. T. Reynolds and N. J. Herman-Kinney. Lanham, MD: Rowman & Littlefield.

Herrnstein, R. J. and Charles Murray. 1994. *The Bell Curve: Intelligence and Class Structure in American Life*. New York: Free Press.

Hertz, Rosanna. 2006. *Single by Chance, Mothers by Choice: How Women Are Choosing Parenthood without Marriage and Creating the New American Family*. New York: Oxford University Press.

Heru, Alison M. 2001. "The Linkages between Gender and Victimhood." *International Journal of Social Psychiatry* 47:10–20.

Hewitt, John P. 2003a. *Self and Society: A Symbolic Interactionist Perspective*. Boston: Allyn and Bacon.

———. 2003b. "Symbols, Objects, and Meanings." Pp. 307–348 in *Handbook of Symbolic Interactionism*, edited by L. T. Reynolds and N. J. Herman-Kinney. Lanham, MD: Rowman & Littlefield.

Hicks, Allison M. 2008. "Role Fusion: The Occupational Socialization of Prison Chaplains." *Symbolic Interaction* 70:7–26.

Hickson, Mark and Julian Roebuck. 2009. *Deviance and Crime in Colleges and Universities: What Goes on in the Halls of Ivy*. Springfield, IL: Charles C. Thomas.

Highfield, Tim. 2016. *Social Media and Everyday Politics*. Cambridge: Polity Press.

Hill, Patricia. 2010. "The New Politics of Community." *American Sociological Review* 75:7–30.

Hillis, Ken. 2009. *Online a Lot of the Time: Ritual, Fetish, Sign*. Durham, NC: Duke University Press.

Hirschi, Travis. 1969. *Causes of Delinquency*. Berkeley, CA: University of California Press.

Hochschild, Arlie Russell. 1983. *The Managed Heart: Commercialization of Human Feelings*. Berkeley, CA: University of California Press.

Hodges, Jessica, Bailey Dodd, and Jana Hackathorn. 2021. "Parental Rejection and Peer Acceptance: The Mediating Role of Cognitive Bias." *Current Research in Social Psychology* 30:21–30.

Hofstetter, Emily and Jessica Robles. 2020. "Manipulation in Board Game Interactions: Being a Sporting Player." *Symbolic Interaction* 42:301–320.

Hogg, Michael A. and Cecilia Ridgeway. 2003. "Social Identity: Sociological and Social Psychological Perspectives." *Social Psychology Quarterly* 66:97–100.

Hogg, Michael A., Deborah J. Terry, and Katherine M. White. 1995. "A Tale of Two Theories: A Critical Comparison of Identity Theory with Social Identity Theory." *Social Psychology Quarterly* 58:255–269.

Hollander, Jocelyn A. and Hava R. Gordon. 2006. "The Process of Social Construction in Talk." *Symbolic Interaction* 29: 181–212.

Hollander, Jocelyn A. and Judith A. Howard. 2000. "Social Psychological Theories on Social Inequalities." *Social Psychology Quarterly* 63:338–351.

Holstein, James A. and Jaber F. Gubrium. 2003. "The Life Course." Pp. 835–855 in *Handbook of Symbolic Interactionism*, edited by L. T. Reynolds and N. J. Herman-Kinney. Lanham, MD: Rowman & Littlefield.

Homans, George Caspar. 1946. "The Small Warship." *American Sociological Review* 11:294–300.

———. 1974. *Social Behavior: Its Elementary Forms*. New York: Harcourt, Brace, Jovanovich.

Hopcroft, Cathryn, Stephanie J. Funk, and Jody Clay-Warner. 1998. "Organizational Contexts and Conversation Patterns." *Social Psychology Quarterly* 61:361–371.

Hopcroft, Rosemary L. and Dana Burr Bradley. 2007. "The Sex Difference in Depression across 29 Countries." *Social Forces* 85:1483–1507.

Horne, Christine. 2009. *The Rewards of Punishment: A Relational Theory of Norm Enforcement*. Stanford, CA: Stanford University Press.

Horne, Christine, Naa Dodua Dodoo and F. Nii-Amoo Dodoo. 2018. "The Conditionality of Norms: The Case of Bridewealth." *Social Psychology Quarterly* 81:319–339.

Horne, Christine and Michael J. Lovaglia (eds.). 2008. *Experiments in Criminology and Law: A Research Revolution*. New York: Rowman & Littlefield.

Horowitz, Juliana and Isabel Goddard. 2023. *Women and Political Leadership Ahead of the 2024 Election*. Pew Research Center Report. www.pewresearch.org/social-trends/wp-content/uploads/sites/3/2023/09/ST_2023.09.27_Women-Leaders-Politics_Report.pdf

Horwitz, Allan V. 2002. *Creating Mental Illness*. Chicago: University of Chicago Press.

Horwitz, Allan V., Tami M. Videon, Mark F. Schmitz, and Diane Davis. 2003. "Rethinking Twins and Environments: Possible Social Sources of Assumed Genetic Influences in Twin Research." *Journal of Health and Social Behavior* 44:1–129.

Horwitz, Allan V. and Jerome C. Wakefield. 2007. *The Loss of Sadness: How Psychiatry Transformed Normal Sorrow into Depressive Disorder*. New York: Oxford University Press.

House, James S. 1977. "The Three Faces of Social Psychology." *Sociometry* 40: 161–177.

———. 1992. "Social Structure and Personality." Pp. 525–561 in *Social Psychology: Sociological Perspectives*, edited by M. Rosenberg and R. H. Turner. New Brunswick, NJ: Transaction Publishers.

Howard, Jenna. 2006. "Expecting and Accepting: The Temporal Ambiguity of Recovery Identities." *Social Psychology Quarterly* 69:307–324.

———. 2008. "Negotiating an Exit: Existential, Interactional, and Cultural Obstacles to Disorder Disidentification." *Social Psychology Quarterly* 71:177–192.

Huber, Gregory A. and Neil Malhotra. 2016. "Political Homophily in Social Relationships: Evidence from Online Dating Behavior". *The Journal of Politics* 79:269–283.

Hughes, Diane. 2003. "Correlates of African American and Latino Parents' Messages to Children about Ethnicity and Race: A Comparative Study of Racial Socialization." *American Journal of Community Psychology* 31:15–33.

Hughes, Diane and Deborah Johnson. 2001. "Correlates in Children's Experiences of Parents' Racial Socialization Behaviors." *Journal of Marriage and the Family* 63:981–995.

Hughes, Diane and Steven A. Tuch. 2003. "Gender Differences in Whites' Racial Attitudes; Are Women's Attitudes Really More Favorable?" *Social Psychology Quarterly* 66(4):384–401.

Hughes, Michael. 2006. "Affect, Meaning and Quality of Life." *Social Forces* 85:611–629.

Hughes, Michael, K. Jill Kiecolt, Verna M. Keith, and David H. Demo. 2015. "Racial Identity and Well-Being among African Americans." *Social Psychology Quarterly* 78:25–48.

Hughey, Matthew W. 2012. "Stigma Allure and White Antiracist Identity Management." *Social Psychology Quarterly* 75: 219–241.

Humphries, Laud. 1970. *Tearoom Trade: Impersonal Sex in Public Places*. Chicago: Aldine.

Humphries, Lee. 2018. *The Qualified Self: Social Media and the Accounting of Everyday Life*. MIT Press.

Hunt, Matthew O. 2007. "African American, Hispanic, and White Beliefs about Black/White Inequality, 1977–2004." *American Sociological Review* 72:390–415.

Hunt, Elle. 2016. "Tay, Microsoft's AI Chatbot, Gets a Crash Course in Racism from Twitter. *The Guardian*. www.theguardian.com/technology/2016/mar/24/tay-microsofts-ai-chatbot-gets-a-crash-course-in-racism-from-twitter.

Hunt, Matthew O., Lauren A. Wise, Marie-Calude Jipguep, Yvette C. Coziea, and Lynn Rosenberg. 2007. "Neighborhood

Racial Composition and Perceptions of Racial Discrimination: Evidence from the Black Women's Health Study." *Social Psychology Quarterly* 70:272–280.

Hunt, Melissa G., Rachel Marx, Courtney Lipson, and Jordyn Young. 2021. "No More FOMO: Limiting Social Media Decreases Loneliness and Depression." *Journal of Social and Clinical Psychology* 37:751–768.

Hurh, Won Moo. 2003. *Personality in Culture and Society*. Dubuque, IA: Kendall/ Hunt.

Hysom, Stuart J. 2009. "Status Valued Goal Objects and Performance Expectations." *Social Forces* 87:1623–1648.

Ictech, Brad. 2019. "Smartphones and Face-to-Face Interaction: Digital Cross-Talk During Encounters in Everday Life." *Symbolic Interaction* 42:27–45.

Illouz, Eva. 2007. *Cold Intimacies: The Making of Emotional Capitalism*. Cambridge, UK: Polity Press.

———. 2008. *Saving the Modern Soul: Therapy, Emotions, and the Culture of Self-Help*. Berkeley, CA: University of California Press.

Ivie, Rachel L., Cynthia Gimbel, and Glen H. Elder, Jr. 1991. "Military Experience and Attitudes in Later Life Contextual Influences across Forty Years." *Journal of Political and Military Sociology* 19:101–117.

Jackson, Pamela Braboy and Montenique Finney. 2002. "Negative Life Events and Psychological Distress among Young Adults." *Social Psychology Quarterly* 65:186–201.

Jackson, Pamela Braboy and Sonia P. Lassiter. 2001. "Self Esteem and Race." Pp. 223–254 in *Extending Self-Esteem Theory and Research: Sociological and Psychological Currents*, edited by T. J. Owens, S. Stryker, and N. Goodman. Cambridge, MA: Cambridge University Press.

Jacobsen, Shannon K. 2017. "Examining Crime on Campus: The Influence of Institutional Factors on Reports of Crime at Colleges and Universities". Journal of Criminal Justice Education 28:1–21.

Jary, David and Julia Jary. 1991. *The Harper-Collins Dictionary of Sociology*. New York: HarperPerennial.

Jasso, Guillermina. 1980. "A New Theory of Distributive Justice." *American Sociological Review* 45:3–32.

Jasso, Guillermina and Murray Webster, Jr. 1999. "Assessing the Gender Gap in Just Earnings and Its Underlying Mechanisms." *Social Psychology Quarterly* 62: 367–380.

Javaid, Aliraza. 2018. Male Rape, Masculinities, and Sexualities: Understanding, Policing, and Overcoming Male Sexual Victimisation. London: Palgrave Macmillan.

Jefferson, Stephen. 2011. "The Role of Shame as a Mediator between Anti-Black Racial Identity Attitudes and Negative Affect in a Sample of African American College Students." *Current Research in Social Psychology* 16:1–11.

Jencks, Chris. 1996. *Childhood*. London: Taylor & Francis.

Jenkins, J. Craig, David Jacobs, and Jon Agnone. 2003. "Political Opportunities and African American Protest." *American Journal of Sociology* 109:277–303.

Jennings, Elyse A., William G. Axinn, and Dirgha J. Ghimire. 2012. "The Effect of Parents' Attitudes on Sons' Marriage Timing." *American Sociological Review* 77:923–945.

Jerolmack, Colin. 2005. "Our Animals, Our Selves? Chipping away the Human–Animal Divide." *Sociological Forum* 20: 651–660.

———. 2009. "Humans, Animals, and Play: Theorizing *Interaction* When Intersubjectivity Is Problematic." *Sociological Theory* 27:371–389.

Johannessen, Lars. 2019. "Negotiated Discretion: Redressing the Neglect of Negotiation in "Street-Level Bureaucracy."*Thematic Issue: Interaction and Organizations* 42: 513–538.

Johns, Mark D. 2010. "Inter-net, Interaction." *Symbolic Interaction* 33:499–500.

Johnson, Cathryn, Timothy J. Dowd, and Cecilia L. Ridgeway. 2006. "Legitimacy as a Social Process." *Annual Review of Sociology* 32:53–78.

Johnson, J. L. "'Meet Them Where They Are': Attentional Processes in Social Movement Listening." *Symbolic Interaction* 44:728–747.

Johnson, J. L. and Amy L. Best. 2012. "Radical Normals: The Moral Career of Straight Parents as Public Advocates for Their Gay Children." *Symbolic Interaction* 35:321–339.

Johnson, Monica Kirkpatrick, Justin Allen Berg, and Toni Sirotzki. 2007. "Differentiation in Self-Perceived Adulthood: Extending the Confluence Model of Subjective Age Identity." *Social Psychology Quarterly* 70:243–261.

Johnson, Monica Kirkpatrick, Rayna Amber Sage, and Jeylan T. Mortimer. 2012. "Work Values, Early Career Difficulties, and the U.S. Recession." *American Sociological Review* 75:242–267.

Jones, Jeffrey M. 2003. "Large Marriage Gap Evident on Moral Issues." Gallup poll. Washington, DC: Gallup Organization.

———. 2008. "Majority of Americans Say Racism against Blacks Widespread." Gallup poll. Washington, DC: Gallup Organization.

———. 2009. "Political Party Affiliation: 30 States Blue, 4 Red in '09 So Far." Gallup poll. Washington, DC: Gallup Organization.

———. 2011. "Support for Legal Gay Relations Hit New High." Gallup poll. Washington, DC: Gallup Organization.

Jones, Nikki. 2009. "'I Was Aggressive for the Streets, Pretty for the Pictures': Gender, Difference, and the Inner-City Girl." *Gender & Society* 23:89–93.

Joyce, Joyce A. 2007. *Women, Marriage, and Wealth: The Impact of Marital Status on the Economic Well-Being of Women through the Life Course*. New York: Gordian Knot Books.

Juette, Melvin and Ronald J. Berger. 2008. *Wheelchair Warrior: Gangs, Disability, and Basketball*. Philadelphia, PA: Temple University Press.

Jurik, Nancy C. and Cynthia Siemsen. 2009. "'Doing Gender' as Canon or Agenda: A Symposium on West and Zimmerman." *Gender & Society* 23:72–75.

Kalev, Alexandra. 2009. "Cracking the Glass Cages? Restructuring and Ascriptive Inequality at Work." *American Journal of Sociology* 114:1591–1643.

Kalkhoff, William, and Christopher Barnum. 2000. "The Effects of Status-Organizing and Social Identity Processes on Patterns of Social Influence." *Social Psychology Quarterly* 63:95–115.

Kalkhoff, William and Robb Willer. 2008. "Deterring Deviance: Rationality and Self-Control." Pp. 39–62 in *Experiments in Criminology and Law: A Research Revolution*, edited by Christine Horne and Michael J. Lovaglia. New York: Rowman & Littlefield.

Kalkhoff, William, David Melamed, Josh Pollock, Brennan Miller, Jon Overton, and Matthew Pfeiffer. 2020. "Cracking the Black Box: Capturing the Role of Expectation States in Status Processes." *Social Psychology Quarterly* 83:26–48.

Kalton, Graham. 1983. *Introduction to Survey Sampling*, vol. 35, edited by M. S. Lewis-Beck. Newbury Park, CA: Sage.

Kanas, Agnieszka, Peer Scheepers, and Carl Sterkens . 2015. "Interreligious Contact, Perceived Group Threat, and Perceived Discrimination: Predicting Negative Attitudes among Religious Minorities and Majorities in Indonesia". *Social Psychology Quarterly* 78:102–126.

Kane, Emily W. 2006. "'No Way My Boys Are Going to Be Like That!' Parents' Responses to Children's Gender Nonconformity." *Gender & Society* 20:149–176.

———. 2009. "'I Wanted a Soul Mate': Gendered Anticipation and Frameworks of Accountability in Parents' Preferences for Sons and Daughters." *Symbolic Interaction* 32:372–389.

Karniol, Rachel, Efrat Grosz, and Irit Schorr. 2003. "Caring, Gender Role Orientation, and Volunteering." *Sex Roles* 49:11–19.

Karyotaki, Eirini, Pim Cuijpers, Yesica Albor, Jordi Alonso, Randy P. Auerbach, Jason Bantjes, et al. 2020. "Sources of Stress and Their Associations With Mental Disorders Among College Students: Results of the World Health Organization World Mental Health Surveys International College Student Initiative." *Frontiers in Psychology* 11:1–11.

Katovich, Michael A. 2017. *Carl J. Couch and the Iowa School: In His Own Words and in Reflection (Volume 49 Series of Studies in Symbolic Interaction)*. Bingley, West Yorkshire, England: Emerald Publishing.

Kaufmann, Jean-Claude. 1998. *Dirty Linen: Couples as Seen through Their Laundry*, trans. Helen Afrey. London: Middlesex University Press.

———. 2009. *Gripes: The Little Quarrels of Couples*, trans. Helen Morrison. Cambridge, UK: Polity Press.

Keel, Sara. 2016. *Socialization: Parent-Child Interaction in Everyday Life*. Abingdon: Routledge.

Kehily, Mary Jane (ed.). 2004. *An Introduction to Childhood Studies*. Maidenhead, UK: Open University Press.

Kelland, Kate. 2007. "World's Cities Step Up Pace of Life in Fast Lane." *Reuters*, www.reuters.com/article/idUSKUA248545.

Kelley, Jonathan and Nan Dirk De Graaf. 1997. "National Context, Parental Socialization, and Religious Belief: Results from 15 Nations." *American Sociological Review* 62:639–659.

Kemmelmeier, Markus and Belinda Yan-Ming Cheng. 2004. "Language and Self-Construal Priming: A Replication and Extension in a Hong Kong Sample." *Journal of Cross-Cultural Psychology* 35:705–712.

Kemp, Simon. 2023. "The Changing World of Digital 2023." *We Are Social.*

https://wearesocial.com/us/blog/2023/01/the-changing-world-of-digital-in-2023.

Kemper, Theodore D. 1987. "How Many Emotions Are There? Wedding the Social and Autonomic Components." *American Journal of Sociology* 93:263–289.

———. 1991. "Predicting Emotions from Social Relations." *Social Psychology Quarterly* 54:330–342.

———. 2011. *Status, Power and Ritual Interaction: A Relational Reading of Durkheim, Goffman, and Collins*. Farnham, Surrey: Ashgate.

Kerckhoff, Alan C. 1995. "Social Stratification and Mobility Processes: Interaction between Individuals and Social Structures." Pp. 476– 496 in *Sociological Perspectives on Social Psychology*, edited by K. S. Cook, G. A. Fine, and J. S. House. Boston: Allyn & Bacon.

Kessler, Ronald C. and Harold W. Neighbors. 1986. "A New Perspective on the Relationships among Race, Social Class, and Psychological Distress." *Journal of Health and Social Behavior* 27:107–115.

Keyes, Corey L. M. 2009. "The Black-White Paradox in Health: Flourishing in the Face of Social Inequality and Discrimination." *Journal of Personality* 77: 1677–1706.

Keyes, Corey L. M. and Sherryl H. Goodman. 2006. *Women and Depression: A Handbook for the Social, Behavioral, and Biomedical Sciences*. New York: Cambridge University Press.

Khanna, Nikki and Cathryn Johnson. 2010. "Passing as Black: Racial Identity Work among Biracial Americans." *Social Psychology Quarterly* 73:380–397.

Kim, Hyoun K. and Patrick C. McKenry. 2003. "The Relationship between Marriage and Psychological Well-Being: A Longitudinal Analysis." *Journal of Family Issues* 23:885–911.

Kim, Hyun Sik. 2011. "Consequences of Parental Divorce for Child Development." *American Sociological Review* 76:487–511.

Kless, Steven J. 1992. "The Attainment of Peer Status: Gender and Power Relationships in the Elementary School." *Sociological Studies of Child Development* 5:115–148.

Kmec, Julie A. and Lindsey B. Trimble. 2009. "Does It Pay to Have a Network Contact? Social Network Ties, Workplace Racial Context, and Pay Outcomes." *Social Science Research* 28: 266–278.

Knepper, Paul. 2009. *The Invention of International Crime: A Global Issue in the Making, 1881– 1914*. Basingstoke, UK: Palgrave Macmillan.

Koenig, Christopher J. 2011. "Patient Resistance as Agency in Treatment Decisions." *Social Science & Medicine* 72: 1105–1114.

Kohn, Melvin L. 1969. *Class and Conformity: A Study in Values*. Homewood, IL: Dorsey.

———. 2005. *Change and Stability: A Cross-National Analysis of Social Structure and Personality*. Boulder, CO: Paradigm Publishers.

Kohn, Melvin L. and Carmi Schooler. 1983. *Work and Personality: An Inquiry into the Impact of Social Stratification*. Norwood, NJ: Greenwood.

Kolb, Kenneth H. 2014. *Moral Wages: The Emotional Dilemmas of Victim Advocacy and Counseling*. Berkley, CA: University of California Press.

Konecki, Krysztof T. 2018. "Classic Grounded Theory—The Latest Version: Interpretation of Classic Grounded Theory as Meta-Theory for Research." Symbolic Interaction 41:547–564.

Kong, Dejun Tony and Jingjing Yao. 2021. "Words beyond the Partial Deed: Prosocial Framing of a Partial-Trust Act Promots Reciprocation between Strangers." *Social Psychology Quarterly* 84:267–280.

Kosinski, Micahel, Yilun Wang, Himabindu Lakkaraju, and Jure Leskovec. 2016. "Mining Big Data to Extract Patterns and Predict Real-Life Outcomes." *Psychological Methods* 21:493–506.

Koskinen, Emmi, Melisa Stevanovic, and Anssi Peräkylä. 2021. "The Recognition and Interactional Management of Face Threats: Comparing Neurotypical Participants and Participants with Asperger's Syndrome." *Social Psychology Quarterly* 84:132–154.

Kouri, Kristyan M. 2003. "Black/White Interracial Couples and the Beliefs That Help Them to Bridge the Racial Divide." Pp. 355–372 in *New Faces in a Changing America*, edited by H. Debose and L. Winters. Thousand Oaks, CA Sage.

Kraus, Stephen J. 1995. "Attitudes and the Prediction of Behavior: A Meta-Analysis of the Empirical Literature." *Personality and Social Psychology Bulletin* 21:58–76.

Kreager, Derek A. 2007. "Unnecessary Roughness? School Sports, Peer Networks, and Male Adolescent Violence." *American Sociological Review* 72:705–724.

Kroska, Amy and Sarah K. Harkness. 2008. "Exploring the Role of Diagnosis in the Modified Labeling Theory of Mental Illness." *Social Psychology Quarterly* 71:193–208.

———. 2011. "Coping with the Stigma of Mental Illness: Empirically-Grounded Hypotheses from Computer Simulations." *Social Forces* 89:1315–1340.

Kroska, Amy and Trent C. Cason. 2019. "The Gender Gap in Business Leadership: Exploring an Affect Control Theory Explanation." *Social Psychology Quarterly* 82:75–97.

Krysan, Maria, Mick P. Couper, Reynolds Farley, and Tyrone A. Forman. 2009. "Does Race Matter in Neighborhood Preferences? Results from a Video Experiment." *American Journal of Sociology* 115:527–559.

Kuhn, Manford H. and Thomas S. McPartland. 1954. "An Empirical Investigation of Self-Attitudes." *American Sociological Review* 19:69–85.

Kuipers, Giselinde. 2006. *Good Humor, Bad Taste: A Sociology of the Joke*. New York: Mouton de Gruyter.

Kusenbach, Margarethe. 2006. "Patterns of Neighboring: Practicing Community in the Parochial Realm." *Symbolic Interaction* 29:279–306.

Lantz, Paula M., James S. House, Richard P. Mero, and David R. Williams. 2005. "Stress, Life Events, and Socioeconomic Disparities in Health: Results from the Americans' Changing Lives Study." *Journal of Health and Social Behavior* 46:274–288.

LaPiere, Richard T. 1934. "Attitudes vs. Action." *Social Forces* 13:230–237.

Lareau, Annette. 2003. *Unequal Childhoods: Class, Race, and Family Life*.

Berkeley, CA: University of California Press.

Laub, John H., Daniel S. Nagin, and Robert J. Sampson. 1998. "Trajectories of Change in Criminal Offending: Good Marriages and the Desistance Process." *American Sociological Review* 63:225–238.

Laub, John H. and Robert J. Sampson. 1993. "Turning Points in the Life Course: Why Change Matters to the Study of Crime." *Criminology* 31:301–325.

———. 2003. *Shared Beginnings, Divergent Lives: Delinquent Boys to Age 70*. Cambridge, MA: Harvard University Press.

Laurent-Simpson, Andrea. 2017. "Phil's Calling Grandma …": The Role of External Support in Human–Companion Animal Identity Pairings." Symbolic Interaction 40:212–228.

Lawler, Edward J. 2001. "An Affect Theory of Social Exchange." *American Journal of Sociology* 107:321–352.

———. 2006. "Introduction of Cecilia Ridgeway: Recipient of the 2005 Cooley-Mead Award." *Social Psychology Quarterly* 69:1–4.

Lawler, Edward J., Shane R. Thye, and Jeongkoo Yoon. 2000. "Emotion and Group Cohesion in Productive Exchange." *American Journal of Sociology* 16:616–657.

———. 2008. "Social Exchange and Micro Social Order." *American Sociological Review* 73:519–542.

———. 2009. *Social Commitments in a Depersonalized World*. New York: Russell Sage Foundation.

Lawler, Edward J. and Jeongkoo Yoon. 1993. "Power and the Emergence of Commitment Behavior in Negotiated Exchange." *American Sociological Review* 58:465–481.

Layard, Richard. 2005. *Happiness: Lessons from a New Science*. London: Penguin.

Lazear, Edward P. and Donald B. Marron. 2007. *Immigration's Economic Impact. White House Report*. https://georgewbush-whitehouse.archives.gov/cea/cea_immigration_062007.html.

LeBon, Gustave. 1960. *The Crowd*. New York: Viking Press.

Lee, Barrett A., Chad R. Farrell, and Bruce G. Link. 2004. "Revisiting the Contact Hypothesis: The Case of Public Exposure to Homelessness." *American Sociological Review* 69:40–63.

Lee, James D. 1998. "Which Kids Can 'Become' Scientists? Effects of Gender, Self-Concepts, and Perceptions of Scientists." *Social Psychology Quarterly* 61:199–219.

Lee, Jooyoung. 2009. "Escaping Embarrassment: Face-work in the Rap Cipher." *Social Psychology Quarterly* 72: 306–324.

Lee, Su H. 2007. *Debating New Social Movements: Culture, Identity, and Social Fragmentation*. Lanham, MD: University Press of America.

Lee, David S., Jonathan L. Stahl, and Joseph B. Bayer. 2020. "Social Resources as Cognitive Structures: Thinking about a Dense Support Network Increases Perceived Support." *Social Psychology Quarterly* 83:405–422.

Leibow, Elliot. 1967. *Tally's Corner: A Study of Negro Street Corner Men*. Boston: Little, Brown and Company.

Leisenring, Amy. 2006. "Confronting 'Victim' Discourses: The Identity Work of Battered Women." *Symbolic Interaction* 29:307–330.

Lemert, Charles and Ann Branaman (eds.). 1997. *The Goffman Reader*. Oxford, UK: Wiley-Blackwell.

Lemert, Edwin M. 1951. *Social Pathology: A Systematic Approach to the Theory of Sociopathic Behavior*. New York: McGraw-Hill.

Lengermann, Patricia and Gillian Niebrugge. 2007. "Moments in the Methodology of Meso History. *The American Sociologist* 38:340–351.

Leslie, Michael. 1995. "Television and the Cultivation of Modern Racism: The Case of Brazil." *Journal of Afro-Latin American Studies and Literatures* 3:191–208.

Levine, Robert V. and Ara Norenzayan. 1999. "The Pace of Life in 31 Countries." *Journal of Cross-Cultural Psychology* 30: 178–205.

Lewandowski, Gary W. and Samantha Harrington. 2006. "The Influence of Phonetic Abbreviations on the Evaluations of Student Performance." *Current Research in Social Psychology* 11:1–12.

Lewis, Clara. 2017. "Crisis Rhetoric, Stigma Play: The Contested Status of Humanities Majors on an Elite University Campus." *Symbolic Interaction* 40:378–395.

Lewis, Gregory B. 2003. "Black-White Differences in Attitudes toward Homosexuality and Gay Rights." *Public Opinion Quarterly* 67:59–78.

Leyens, Jacques-Philippe, Paola M. Paladino, Ramon Rodriquez-Torres, Jeroen Vaes, Stephanie Demoulin, Armando Rodriguez-Perez, and Ruth Gaunt. 2000. "The Emotional Side of Prejudice: The Attribution of Secondary Emotions to Ingroups and Outgroups." *Personality and Social Psychology Review* 4:186–197.

Liberman, Kenneth. 2013. *More Studies in Ethnomethodology*. Albany, New York: State University of New York Press.

Lichtenstein, Bronwen. 2012. *Social Stigmas & Sexual Epidemics: Dangerous Dynamics*. Boulder, CO: First Forum Press.

Liebler, Carolyn A. and Gary D. Sandefur. 2002. "Gender Differences in the Exchange of Social Support with Friends, Neighbors, and Co-Workers at Midlife." *Social Science Research* 31:364–391.

Lim, Chaeyoon and Carol Ann MacGregor. 2012. "Religion and Volunteering in Context: Disentangling the Contextual Effects of Religion and Voluntary Behavior." *American Sociological Review* 77:747–779.

Lin, Tony Zhiyang and Xiaoli Tian. 2019. "Audience Design and Context Discrepancy: How Online Debates Lead to Opinion Polarization." *Symbolic Interaction* 42:70–97.

Linderoth, Jonas. 2012. "The Effort of Being in a Fictional World: Upkeying and Laminated Frames in MMORGPSs." *Symbolic Interaction* 35:474–492.

Lindsay, D. Michael. 2008. "Evangelicals in the Power Elite: Elite Cohesion Advancing a Movement." *American Sociological Review* 73:60–82.

Link, Bruce G. 1987. "Understanding Labeling Effects in the Area of Mental Disorders: An Assessment of the Effects of Expectations of Rejection." *American Sociological Review* 52:96–112.

Link, Bruce G., Francis G. Cullen, Elmer Struening, Patrick E. Shrout, and Bruce P. Dohrenwend. 1989. "A Modified Labeling

Theory Approach to Mental Disorders: An Empirical Assessment." *American Sociological Review* 54:400–423.

Link, Bruce G. and Jo Phelan. 1995. "Social Conditions as Fundamental Causes of Disease." *Journal of Health and Social Behavior* 35:80–94.

Lio, Shoon, Scott Melzer, and Ellen Reese. 2008. "Constructing Threat and Appropriating 'Civil Rights': Rhetorical Strategies of Gun Rights and English Only Leaders." *Symbolic Interaction* 31:5–31.

Lipsky, Michael. 1968. "Protest as Political Resource." *American Political Science Review* 62:1144–1158.

Liu, Hui and Debra J. Umberson. 2008. "The Times They Are a Changin': Marital Status and Health Differentials from 1972 to 2003." *Journal of Health and Social Behavior* 49:239–253.

Lively, Kathryn J. and David R. Heise. 2004. "Sociological Realms of Emotional Experience." *American Journal of Sociology* 109:1109–1136.

Lively, Kathryn, Carr Lala Steelman, and Brian Powell. 2010. "Equity, Emotions, and Household Division of Labor Response." *Social Psychology Quarterly* 73:358–379.

Livingston, Eric. 2008. *Ethnographies of Reason*. Burlington, VT: Ashgate.

Livingston, Gretchen. 2018. "Stay-at-Home Moms and Dads Account for about One-in-Five U.S. Parents." *Pew Research Center*. www.pewresearch.org/fact-tank/2018/09/24/stay-at-home-moms-and-dads-account-for-about-one-in-five-u-s-parents.

Loe, Meika and Leigh Cuttino. 2008. "Grappling with the Medicated Self: The Case of ADHD College Students." *Symbolic Interaction* 31:303–323.

Lofland, Lyn H. 1985. "The Social Shaping of Emotion: The Case of Grief." *Symbolic Interaction* 8:171–190.

———. 1992. "Collective Behavior: The Elementary Forms." Pp. 411–446 in *Social Psychology: Sociological Perspectives*, edited by M. Rosenberg and R. H. Turner. New Brunswick, NJ: Transaction Publishers.

Lois, Jennifer. 2003. *Heroic Efforts: The Emotional Culture of Search and Rescue Volunteers*. New York: New York University Press.

———. 2006. "Role Strain, Emotion Management, and Burnout: Homeschooling Mothers' Adjustment to the Teacher Role." *Symbolic Interaction* 29:507–530.

Longhofer, Wesley and Evan Schofer. 2010. "National and Global Origins of Environmental Association." *American Sociological Review* 75:505–533.

Lorek, Melanie. 2018. "'It Did Not Affect Me': The (IR)Relevance of the German Reunification in Autobiographical Narratives of East Germans." *Symbolic Interaction* 41:210–226.

Loring, Marti and Brian Powell. 1988. "Gender, Race, and DSM-III: A Study of the Objectivity of Psychiatric Diagnostic Behavior." *Journal of Health and Social Behavior* 29:1–22.

Louie, Patricia, Laura Upenieks, Christy L. Erving, and Courtney S. Thomas Tobin. "Do Racial Differences in Coping Resources Explain the Black–White Paradox in Mental Health? A Test of Multiple Mechanisms." *Journal of Health and Social Behavior* 63, no. 1 (2022): 55–70.

Loseke, Donileen. 2019. *Narrative Productions of Meanings*. Lanham, MD: Lexington Books.

Lovaglia, Michael J. 1995. "Power and Status: Exchange, Attribution, and Expectation States." *Small Group Research* 26: 400–426.

Lovaglia, Michael J. and Jeffrey A. Houser. 1996. "Emotional Reactions and Status in Groups." *American Sociological Review* 61:867–883.

Lovaglia, Michael J., Jeffrey W. Lucas, Jeffrey A. Houser, Shane R. Thye, and Barry Markovsky. 1998. "Status Processes and Mental Ability Test Scores." *American Journal of Sociology* 68:464–480.

Lovaglia, Michael J., Shane D. Soboroff, Christopher P. Kelley, Christabel L. Rogalin, and Jeffrey W. Lucas. 2017. "The status value of age and gender: Modeling combined effects of diffuse status characteristics." Pp. 81–101 in *Advances in Group Processes*. Emerald Publishing Limited.

Lucas, Jeffrey W. 1999. "Behavioral and Emotional Outcomes of Leadership in Task Groups." *Social Forces* 78:747–778.

———. 2003. "Status Processes and the Institutionalization of Women as Leaders." *American Sociological Review* 68:464–480.

Lucas, Jeffrey W. and Jo C. Phelan. 2012. "Stigma and Status: The Interrelation of Two Theoretical Perspectives." *Social Psychology Quarterly*, 75:310–333

Lucas, Jeffrey W., Kristin Kerns-D'Amore, Michael J. Lovaglia, Shane D. Soboroff, and Jasmón Bailey. 2022. "The Legitimacy of Power in Status-Differentiated Groups." In *Advances in Group Processes*, 75–96. Bingley, United Kingdom: Emerald Publishing Limited.

Lupton, Deborah. 2015. *Digital Sociology*. New York: Routledge.

Lyman, Stanford M. and Arthur J. Vidich. 1988. *Social Order and the Public Philosophy: An Analysis and Interpretation of the Work of Herbert Blumer*. Fayetteville, AR: University of Arkansas Press.

Lyness, Karen S., Janet C. Gornick, Pamela Stone, and Angela R. Grotto. 2012. "It's All about Control: Worker Control over Schedule and Hours in Cross-National Context." *American Sociological Review* 77:1023–1049.

Lyng, Stephen. 1990. "Edgework: A Social Psychological Analysis of Voluntary Risk Taking." *American Journal of Sociology* 95:851–886.

——— (ed.). 2004. *Edgework: The Sociology of Risk-Taking*. New York: Routledge.

Lynn, Freda B., Mark H. Walker, and Colin Peterson. 2016. "Is Popular More Likeable? Choice Status by Intrinsic Appeal in an Experimental Music Market." *Social Psychology Quarterly* 79:168–180.

Lyons, Linda. 2005. "Teens Stay True to Parents' Political Perspectives." Gallup poll. Washington, DC: Gallup Organization.

Mackay, Charles. 1852. *Memoirs of Extraordinary Popular Delusions and the Madness of Crowds*. London: Office of the National Illustrated Library.

Mackie, Marlene. 1983. "The Domestication of Self: Gender Comparisons of Self-Imagery and Self-Esteem." *Social Psychology Quarterly* 46:343–350.

MacKinnon, Neil J. and David R. Heise. 2010. *Self, Identity, and Social Institutions*. New York: Palgrave Macmillan.

Maclean, Alair. 2010. "The Things They Carry: Combat, Disability, and Unemployment among U.S. Men." *American Sociological Review* 75:563–585.

MacLeod, Jay. 1993. *Ain't No Makin' It: Aspirations & Attainment in a Low-Income Neighborhood*. Boulder, CO: Westview Press.

Madden, Mary and Kathryn Zickuhr. 2011. *65% of Online Adults Use Social Networking Sites*. Pew Research Center report. http://pewinternet. org/reports/2011 /social-networking-sites.aspx

Madigan, Jamie. 2016. *Getting Gamers: The Psychology of Video Games and Their Impact on the People Who Play Them*. Lanham, MD: Rowman & Littlefield.

Madson, Laura and Jennifer Shoda. 2006. "Alternating between Masculine and Feminine Pronouns: Does Essay Topic Affect Readers' Perceptions?" *Sex Roles* 54:275–285.

Maimon, David and Danielle C. Kuhl. 2008. "Social Control and Youth Suicidality: Situating Durkheim's Ideas in a Multilevel Framework." *American Sociological Review* 73:921–943.

Maio, Gregory R., James M. Olson, Mark M. Bernard, and Michelle A. Luke. 2003. "Ideologies, Values, Attitudes, and Behavior." Pp. 283–308 in *Handbook of Social Psychology*, edited by J. Delamater. New York: Kluwer Academic/Plenum.

Maliepaard, Mieke and Karen Phalet. 2012. "Social Integration and Religious Identity Expression among Dutch Muslims." *Social Psychology Quarterly* 75: 131–148.

Maloney, Emily. 2020. "The Social Psychology of Occupational Status Groups: Relationality in the Structure of Deference." *Social Psychology Quarterly* 83: 463–475.

Manago, Bianca, Jane Sell, and Carla Goar. 2019. "Groups, Inequality, and Synergy." *Social Forces* 97:1365–88.

Manago, Bianca and Trenton D. Mize. 2022. "The Status and Stigma Consequences of Mental Illness Labels, Deviant Behavior, and Fear." *Social Science Research* 105:102690.

Marcussen, Kristen. 2005. "Explaining Differences in Mental Health between Married and Cohabiting Individuals." *Social Psychology Quarterly* 68:239–257.

Mark, Noah P., Lynn Smith-Lovin, and, Cecilia L. Ridgeway. 2009. "Why Do Nominal Characteristics Acquire Status Value? A Minimal Explanation for Status Construction." *American Journal of Sociology*, 115:832–862.

Markovsky, Barry. 1985. "Toward a Multilevel Distributive Justice Theory." *American Sociological Review* 50:822–839.

Markovsky, Barry, David Willer, and Travis Patton. 1988. "Power Relations in Exchange Networks." *American Sociological Review* 53:220–336.

Markowitz, Fred E., Beth Angell, and Jan S. Greenberg. 2011. "Stigma, Reflected Appraisals, and Recovery Outcomes in Mental Illness." *Social Psychology Quarterly* 74:144–165.

Martin, Andrew, John D. McCarthy, and Clark McPhail. 2009. "Why Targets Matter: Toward a More Inclusive Model of Collective Violence" *American Sociological Review* 74:821–841.

Martin, Daniel D. 2010. "Identity Management of the Dead: Contests in the

Construction of Murdered Children." *Symbolic Interaction* 33:18–40.

Martin, Karin A. 2009. "Normalizing Heterosexuality: Mothers' Assumptions, Talk, and Strategies with Young Children." *American Sociological Review* 74:190–207.

Massoglia, Michael and Christopher Uggen. 2010. "Settling Down and Aging Out: Toward an Interactionist Theory of Desistance and the Transition to Adulthood." *American Journal of Sociology* 116:543–582.

Mastro, Dana E., Elizabeth Behm-Morawitz, and Maria A. Kopacz. 2008. "Exposure to Television Portrayals of Latinos: The Implications of Aversive Racism and Social Identity Theory." *Human Communications Research* 34:1–27.

Mathews, Gordon, Linessa Dan Lin, and Yang Yang. 2017. *The World in Guangzhou*. Chicago: University of Chicago Press.

Matsueda, Ross L. 1992. "Reflected Appraisals, Parental Labeling, and Delinquency: Specifying a Symbolic Interactionist Theory." *American Journal of Sociology* 97:1577–1611.

Matsueda, Ross L., Derek A. Kreager, and David Huizinga. 2006. "Deterring Delinquents: A Rational Choice Model of Theft and Violence." *American Sociological Review* 71:95–122.

Mawson, Anthony R. 2007. *Mass Panic and Social Attachment: The Dynamics of Human Behavior*. Aldershot, UK: Ashgate.

May, Reuben A. 2001. "'The Sid Cartwright Incident and More': An African American Male's Interpretive Narrative of Interracial Encounters at the University of Chicago." *Symbolic Interaction* 24: 75–100.

Maynes, Mary Jo, Jennifer L. Pierce, and Barbara Laslett. 2008. *Telling Stories: The Use of Personal Narratives in the Social Sciences and History*. Ithaca, NY: Cornell University Press.

McCabe, Donald L. 1992. "The Influence of Situational Ethics on Cheating among College Students." *Sociological Inquiry* 62: 365–374.

McCabe, Kristen M. 1997. "Sex Differences in the Long Term Effects of Divorce on Children: Depression and Heterosexual Relationship Difficulties in the Young Adult Years." *Journal of Divorce and Remarriage* 27:123–135.

McCall, George J. 2003. "The Me and the Not-Me: Positive and Negative Poles of Identity." Pp. 11–26 in *Advances in Identity Theory and Research*, edited by P. J. Burke, T. J. Owens, R. Serpe, and P. A. Thoits. New York: Kluwer Academic/Plenum.

McCarthy, E. Doyle. *Emotional Lives: Dramas of Identity in an Age of Mass Media*. Cambridge: Cambridge University Press

McCarthy, John D., Clark McPhail, and Jackie Smith. 1996. "Images of Protest: Dimensions of Selection Bias in Media Coverage of Washington Demonstrations, 1982–1991." *American Sociological Review* 61:478–499.

McDermott, Monica. 2006. *Working-Class White: The Making and Unmaking of Race Relations*. Berkeley: University of California Press.

McFarland, Daniel A. and Reuben J. Thomas. 2006. "Bowling Young: How Youth Voluntary Associations Influence Adult Political Participation." *American Sociological Review* 71:401–425.

McKinnon, Jessie D. and Claudette E. Bennett. 2005. "We the People: Blacks in the United States." Census 2000 Special Reports. Washington, DC: U.S. Census Bureau.

McKinzie, Ashleigh E. 2017. "Scared to Death: Reflections on Panic and Anxiety in the Field." *Symbolic Interaction* 40: 483–497.

McLaughlin, Paul and Khawaja Marwan. 2000. "The Organizational Dynamics of the U.S. Environmental Movement: Legitimation, Resource Mobilization, and Political Opportunity." *Rural Sociology* 65:422–439.

McLeod, Jane D. and Danielle L. Fettes. 2007. "Trajectories of Failure: The Educational Careers of Children with Mental Health Problems." *American Journal of Sociology* 113:653–701.

McLeod, Jane D. and Katherine J. Lively. 2003. "Social Structure and Personality." Pp. 77–102 in *Handbook of Social Psychology*, edited by J. D. DeLamater. New York: Kluwer Academic/ Plenum.

McLuhan, Marshall and Quentin Fiore. 1967. *The Medium Is the Massage*. New York: Random House.

McPerson, Miller, Lynn Smith-Lovin, and Matthew E. Brashears. 2006. "Social Isolation in America: Changes of Core Discussion Networks over Two Decades." *American Sociological Review* 71:353–375.

McPhail, Clark. 1994. "The Dark Side of Purpose: Individual and Collective Violence in Riots." *The Sociological Quarterly* 35:1–32.

______. 2006. "The Crowd and Collective Behavior: Bringing Symbolic Interaction Back In." *Symbolic Interaction* 29: 433–464.

______. 2008. "Gatherings as Patchworks." *Social Psychology Quarterly* 71: 1–5.

McPhail, Clark and John McCarthy. 2004. "Who Counts and How: Estimating the Size of Protests." *Contexts* 3:12–18.

McPhail, Clark and Charles W. Tucker. 2003. "Collective Behavior." Pp. 721–742 in *Handbook of Symbolic Interactionism*, edited by L. T. Reynolds and N. J. Herman-Kinney. Lanham, MD: Rowman & Littlefield.

McPherson, Miller, Lynn Smith-Lovin, and Matthew E. Brashears. 2006. "Social Isolation in America: Changes in the Core Discussion Networks over Two Decades." *American Sociological Review* 71:353–375.

McVeigh, Ryan. 2020. "The Body in Mind: Mead's Embodied Cognition." *Symbolic Interaction* 43:493–513.

Mead, George Herbert. 1934. *Mind, Self, and Society from the Standpoint of a Social Behavioralist*. Chicago: Chicago University Press.

Meadows, Sarah O. 2007. "Evidence of Parallel Pathways: Gender Similarity in the Impact of Social Support on Adolescent Depression and Delinquency." *Social Forces* 85:1143–1167.

Meadows, Sarah O., Sara S. McLanahan, and Jeanne Brooks-Gunn. 2008. "Stability and Change in Family Structure and Maternal Health Trajectories." *American Sociological Review* 73:314–334.

Meanwell, Emily. 2013. "Profaning the Past to Salvage the Present: The Symbolically Reconstructed Pasts of Homeless Shelter Residents." *Symbolic Interaction* 36: 439–56.

Meeker, Barbara Foley and Robert K. Leik. 1995. "Experimentation in Sociological Social Psychology." Pp. 630–649 in *Sociological Perspectives on Social Psychology*, edited by K. S. Cook, G. A. Fine, and J. S. H. House. Boston: Allyn & Bacon.

Melamed, David, Christopher W. Munn, Leanne Barry, Bradley Montgomery, and Oneya F. Okuwobi. 2019. "Status Characteristics, Implicit Bias, and the Production of Racial Inequality." *American Sociological Review* 84: 1013–1036.

Melamed, David, Oneya Okuwobi, and Leanne Barry. 2023. "How Do Nominal Characteristics Lose Status Value? Asymmetry in Status Deconstruction." *Social Psychology Quarterly* 01902725231162351.

Menchik, Daniel A. and Xiaoli Tian. 2008. "Putting Social Context into Text: The Semiotics of E-mail Interactions." *American Journal of Sociology* 114:332–370.

Merolla, David M., Richard T. Serpe, Sheldon Stryker, and P. Wesley Schultz. 2012. "Structural Precursors to Identity Processes: The Role of Proximate Social Structures." *Social Psychology Quarterly* 75:149–172.

Merrill, Bryce. 2010. "Music to Remember Me By: Technologies of Memory in Home Recording." *Symbolic Interaction* 33:456–474.

Merton, Robert K. 1960. *The Ambivalences of LeBon's* The Crowd*: Introduction to the Compass Edition of* The Crowd. New York: Viking Press.

———. 1968. *Social Theory and Social Structure*. New York: Free Press.

———. 1995. "The Thomas Theorem and the Matthew Effect." *Social Forces* 74:379–422.

Michael, Robert T., Edward O. Laumann, John H. Gagnon, and Gina Bari Kolata. 1995. *Sex in America: A Definitive Survey*. Clayton, Australia: Warner Books.

Mijs, Jonathan J.B. 2023. "Learning About Inequality in Unequal America: How Heterogeneity in College Shapes Students' Beliefs About Meritocracy and Racial Discrimination." *Research in Social Stratification and Mobility* 85.

Mik-Myer, Nanna and Mark Haugaard. 2021. "Performance of Agency in Real Life-Encounters: Unequal Power and Structural Constraint into Collaboration." Symbolic Interaction 44:504–532.

Milkie, Melissa A. 1999. "Social Comparisons, Reflected Appraisals, and Mass Media: The Impact of Pervasive Beauty Ideals on Black and White Girls' Self-Concepts." *Social Psychology Quarterly* 62:190–210.

Milkie, Melissa A., Alex Bierman, and Scott Schieman. 2008. "How Adult Children Influence Older Parents' Mental Health: Integrating Stress-Process and Life-Course Perspectives." *Social Psychology Quarterly* 71:86–105.

Milkie, Melissa A. Catharine H. Warner, and Rashawn Ray. 2014. "Current Theorizing and New Direction in the Social Psychology of Social Class Inequalities." In *Handbook of the Social Psychology of Inequality*, edited by Jane McLeod, Edward Lawler and Michael Schwalbe. New York: Springer.

Milkie, Melissa A., Robin W. Simon, and Brian Powell. 1997. "Through the Eyes of Children: Youth's Perceptions and Evaluations of Maternal and Paternal Roles." *Social Psychology Quarterly* 60: 218–237.

Miller, Dan E. 2011. "Toward a Theory of Interaction: The Iowa School." *Symbolic Interaction* 34:340–348.

Miller, David L. 2000. *Introduction to Collective Behavior and Collective Action*. Prospect Heights, IL: Waveland.

Miller, Brennan J., Will Kalkhoff, Joshua Pollock, and Matthew A. Pfeiffer. 2019. "Persistent Identity Threats: Emotional and Neurological Responses." *Social Psychology Quarterly* 82:98–111.

Mills, C. Wright. 1959. *The Sociological Imagination*. London: Oxford University Press.

———. 2002. *White Collar: The American Middle Classes*. Oxford, UK: Oxford University Press.

Miner, Horace. 1956. "Body Ritual among the Nacirema." *American Anthropologist* 58:503–507.

Mirowsky, John and Catherine E. Ross. 1995. "Sex Differences in Distress: Real or Artifact?" *American Sociological Review* 60:449–468.

———. 2007. "Life Course Trajectories of Perceived Control and Their Relationships to Education." *American Journal of Sociology* 112:1339–1382.

Misra, Supriya, Onisha S. Etkins, Lawrence H. Yang, and David R. Williams. 2022. "Structural Racism and Inequities in Incidence, Course of Illness, and Treatment of Psychotic Disorders Among Black Americans". *American Journal of Public Health* 112: 624–632.

Moffitt, Terrie and Avshalom Caspi. 2007. "Evidence from Behavioral Genetics for Environmental Contributions to Antisocial Conduct." Pp. 108–152 in *The Explanation of Crime: Context, Mechanisms, and Development*, edited by Per-Olof H. Wikström and Robert J. Sampson. Cambridge, UK: Cambridge University Press.

Molder, Hedwig te and Jonathon Potter. 2005. *Conversation and Cognition*. Cambridge, UK: Cambridge University Press.

Molinsky, Andrew. 2005. "Language Fluency and the Evaluation of Cultural Faux Pas: Russians Interviewing for Jobs in the United States." *Social Psychology Quarterly* 68:103–120.

Molm, Linda D. 1991. "Affect and Social Exchange: Satisfaction in Power-Dependence Relations." *American Sociological Review* 56:475–493.

———. 2010. "The Structure of Reciprocity." *Social Psychology Quarterly* 73: 119–131.

Molm, Linda, Russell Hardin, and Margaret Levi. 2006. "Cooperation Without Trust?" *Administrative Science Quarterly* 51:305–307.

Molm, Linda D. and Karen S. Cook. 1995. "Social Exchange and Exchange Networks." Pp. 209– 235 in *Sociological Perspectives in Social Psychology*, edited by K. S. Cook, G. A. Fine, and J. S. House. Boston: Allyn & Bacon.

Molm, Linda D., Monica M. Whitham, and David Melamed. 2012. "Forms of Exchange and Integrative Bonds: Effects of History and Embeddedness." *American Sociological Review* 77:141–165.

Molm, Linda D., David Melamed, and Monica M. Whitham. 2013. "Behavioral Consequences of Embeddedness: Effects of Underlying Forms of Exchange." *Social Psychology Quarterly* 76:73–97.

Mondillon, Laurie, Paula M. Niedenthal, Markus Brauer, Anette Rohmann, Nathalie Dalle, and Yukiko Uchida. 2005. "Beliefs about Power and Its Relation to Emotional Experience: A Comparison of Japan, France, Germany, and the United States." *Personality and Social Psychology Bulletin* 31:1112–1122.

Monk, Ellis, Jr. 2015. "The Cost of Color: Skin Color, Discrimination, and Health among African-Americans." *American Journal of Sociology* 121:396–444.

Montazer, Shirin, Krista M. Brumley, Laura Pineault, Katheryn Maguire, and Boris Baltes. 2022. "COVID-19 Onset, Parental Status, and Psychological Distress among Full-Time Employed Heterosexual Adults in Dual-earning Relationships: The Explanatory Role of Work-family Conflict and Guilt." *Society and Mental Health* 12:119–136.

Moore, David W. 2002. "Gender Gap Varies on Support for War." Gallup poll. Washington, DC: Gallup Organization.

Moore, Gwen. 1990. "Structural Determinants of Men's and Women's Personal Networks." *American Sociological Review* 55:726–735.

Morgan, S. Philip. 2003. "Is Low Fertility a Twenty-First-Century Demographic Crisis?" *Demography* 40:589–603.

Mortimer, Jeylan T. and Roberta G. Simmons. 1978. "Adult Socialization." *Annual Review of Sociology* 4:421–454.

Mortimer, Jeylan, Lei Zhang, Chen-Yu Wu, Jeanette Hussemann, Monica Kirkpatrick Johnson. 2017. "Familial Transmission of Educational Plans and the Academic Self-Concept: A Three Generation Longitudinal Study." Social Psychology Quarterly 80:85–107.

Mossakowski, Krysia N. and Wei Zhang. 2014 "Does Social Support Buffer the Stress of Discrimination and Reduce Psychological Distress among Asian Americans?" *Social Psychology Quarterly* 77: 273–295.

Mullaney, Jamie L. 2020. "A Year Then Forever: Personal Resolution Making and the Temporal Bridge of the Near Future." Symbolic Interaction 43:332–355.

Munson, Ziad W. 2008. *The Making of Pro-Life Activists: How Social Change Movement Mobilization Works*. Chicago: University of Chicago Press.

Musick, Marc A. and John Wilson. 2008. *Volunteers: A Social Profile*. Bloomington, IN: Indiana University Press.

Musolf, Gil Richard. 2003a. *Structure and Agency in Everyday Life*. Lanham, MD: Rowman & Littlefield.

———. 2003b. "The Chicago School." Pp. 91–118 in *Handbook of Symbolic Interactionism*, edited by L. T. Reynolds and N. J. Herman-Kinney. Lanham, MD: Rowman & Littlefield.

Mustillo, Sarah A., Kristen Budd, and Kimber Hendrix. 2013. "Obesity, Labeling, and Psychological Distress in Late-Childhood and Adolescent Black and White Girls: The Distal Effects of Stigma. *Social Psychology Quarterly* 76:268–289.

Myers, Kristen A. 2005. *Racetalk: Hiding in Plain Sight*. Lanham, MD: Rowman & Littlefield Publishers.

Nagel, Joanne. 1995. "American Indian Ethnic Renewal: Politics and the Resurgence of Identity." *American Sociological Review* 60:947–965.

Narisada, Atsushi. 2020. "Job Pressure, the Work-Family Interface, and the Sense of Distributive Justice: An Elaboration of the Work-Related Inputs among Twenty-First Century Workers." Social Psychology Quarterly 83:107–128.

Nash, Jeffrey E. 2000. "Racism in the Ivory City: The Natural History of a Research Project." *Symbolic Interaction* 23: 147–168.

Nath, Leda E. 2007. "Expectation States: Are Formal Words Status Cues for Competence?" *Current Research in Social Psychology* 13:1–14.

Neighbors, Harold W., Steven J. Trierweiler, Briggett C. Ford, and Jordana R. Muroff. 2003. "Racial Differences in DSM Diagnosis Using a Semi-Structured Instrument: The Importance of Clinical Judgment in the Diagnosis of African Americans." *Journal of Health and Social Behavior* 44:237–256.

Nelson, Steven M. 2006. "Redefining a Bizarre Situation: Relative Concept Stability in Affect Control Theory." *Social Psychology Quarterly* 69:215–234.

Neuman, W. Lawrence. 2004. *Basics of Social Research: Qualitative and Quantitative Approaches*. Boston: Pearson.

Newport, Frank. 2009. "Extramarital Affairs, Like Sanford's, Morally Taboo." Gallup poll. Washington, DC: Gallup Organization.

———. 2015. "Americans Continue to Shift Left on Key Moral Issues." *The Gallup Organization*. Washington, DC.

Nielson, Francois. 2006. "Achievement and Ascription in Educational Attainment: Genetic and Environmental Influences on Adolescent Schooling." *Social Forces* 85: 193–216.

Nippert-Eng, Christena. 2010. *Islands of Privacy*. Chicago: University of Chicago Press.

Nisbett, Richard E. 1993. "Violence and U.S. Regional Culture." *American Psychologist* 48:441–449.

Nisbett, Richard E., Gregory Polly, and Sylvia Lang. 1995. "Homicide and U.S. Regional Culture." Pp. 135–151 in *Interpersonal Violent Behaviors: Social and Cultural Aspects*, edited by R. B. Ruback and N. A. Weiner. New York: Springer.

Nolan, Patrick and Gerhard Lenski. 2004. *Human Societies: An Introduction to Macrosociology*. New York: Paradigm.

Nomaguchi, Kei M. and Melissa A. Milkie. 2003. "Costs and Rewards of Children: The Effects of Becoming a Parent on Adults' Lives." *Journal of Marriage and the Family* 65:356–374.

Nomaguchi, Kei M. and Melissa A. Milkie. 2020. "Parenthood and Well Being: A Decade in Review." *Journal of Marriage and Family* 82:198–223.

Norris, Dawn R. 2011. "Interactions That Trigger Self-Labeling: The Case of Older Undergraduates." *Symbolic Interaction* 34: 173–197.

O'Brien, John. 2011. "Spoiled Group Identities and Backstage Work: A Theory of Stigma Management Rehearsals." *Social Psychology Quarterly* 74:291–309.

———. 2017. *Keeping It Halal: The Everyday Lives of Muslim American Teenage Boys*. Princeton , NJ: Princeton University Press.

O'Connell, Michael. 2008. "Victimology: A Social Science in Waiting?" *International Review of Victimology* 15:91–104.

Offera, Shira and Barbara Schneiderb. 2011. "Revisiting the Gender Gap in Time-Use Patterns Multitasking and Well-Being among Mothers and Fathers in Dual-Earner Families." *American Sociological Review* 76:809–833.

Oldmeadow, Julian A., Gemma Collett, and Christine Little. 2008. "Bridging the Gap: The Role of Shared Group Membership in Status Generalization." *Current Research in Social Psychology* 13: 199–218.

Oldmeadow, Julian A., Michael J. Platow, Margaret Foddy, and Donna Anderson. 2003. "Self-Categorization, Status, and Social Influence." *Social Psychology Quarterly* 66:138–153.

Olsen, Karen M. and Svenn-Age Dahl. 2007. "Health Differences between European Countries." *Social Science & Medicine* 64:1665–1678.

Olson, Karin. 2016. *Essentials of Qualitative Interviewing*. New York: Routledge.

Orbuch, Terri L. and Susan Sprecher. 2003. "Attraction and Interpersonal Relationships." Pp. 339–362 in *Handbook of Social Psychology*, edited by J. D. DeLamater. New York: Kluwer Academic/Plenum.

Orne, Jason. 2017. *Boystown: Sex and Community in Chicago*. Chicago: University of Chicago Press.

Ortiz-Ospina, Esteban. 2020. Who Do We Spend Time with across Our Lifetime? Paper accessed on November 6, 2023 at https://ourworldindata.org/time-with-others-lifetime.

Orzechowicz, David. 2008. "Privileged Emotion Managers: The Case of Actors." *Social Psychology Quarterly* 71: 143–156.

Osgood, Charles H. 1962. "Studies of the Generality of Affective Meaning Systems." *American Psychologist* 17:10–28.

Overton, Jon. 2021. "When Does Status Transfer between People? A Crowdsourced Experiment on the Scope of Status by Association." *Social Psychology Quarterly* 84:309–330.

Owen, Carolyn A., Howard C. Eisner, and Thomas R. McFaul. 1981. "A Half-Century of Social Distance Research: National Replication of the Bogardus Studies." *Sociology and Social Research* 66:80–98.

Owens, Jayanti and Heidi Jackson. 2017. "Attention-Deficit/Hyperactivity Disorder Severity, Diagnosis, & Later Academic Achievement in a National Sample". *Social Science Research* 61: 251–265.

Owens, Timothy J. and Sheldon Stryker. 2001. "The Future of Self-Esteem Research: An Introduction." Pp. 1–9 in *Extending Self-Esteem Theory and Research: Sociological and Psychological Currents*, edited by T. J. Owens, S. Stryker, and N. Goodman. Cambridge, MA: Cambridge University Press.

Padavic, Irene and Barbara F. Reskin. 2002. *Women and Men at Work*, 2nd ed.. Thousand Oaks, CA: Pine Forge Press.

Pager, Devah and Lincoln Quillian. 2005. "Walking the Talk? What Employers Say versus What They Do." *American Sociological Review* 70:355–380.

Paik, Leslie. 2006. "Are You Truly a Recovering Dope Fiend? Local Interpretive Practices at a Therapeutic Community Drug Treatment Program." *Symbolic Interaction* 29:213–234.

Paladino, Maria-Paola, Jacques-Philippe Leyens, Ramon Rodriguez, Armando

Rodriguez, Ruth Gaunt, and Stephanie Demoulin. 2002. "Differential Association of Uniquely and Non Uniquely Human Emotions with the Ingroup and the Outgroup." *Group Processes and Intergroup Relations* 5:105–117.

Pampel, Fred C. 2001. *The Institutional Context of Population Change: Patterns of Fertility and Mortality across High-Income Nations*. Chicago: University of Chicago Press.

Panfil, Vanessa R. 2017. *The Gang's All Queer: The Lives of Gay Gang Members*. New York: New York University Press.

Panina, Natalia. 2004. "On the Measurement of Social Distance in the Research of Ethnic Toleration in Ukraine." *Studia Socjologiczne* 4:135–159.

Paolucci, Paul and Margaret Richardson. 2006. "Sociology of Humor and a Critical Dramaturgy." *Symbolic Interaction* 29: 331–348.

Pape, Robert A. 2005. *Dying to Win: The Strategic Logic of Suicide Terrorism*. New York: Random House.

Park, Robert E. and Ernest W. Burgess. 1921. *Introduction to the Science of Sociology*. Chicago: University of Chicago Press.

Parker, John N. and Edward J. Hackett. 2012. "Hot Spots and Hot Moments in Scientific Collaborations and Social Movements." *American Sociological Review* 77:21–44.

Parker, Kim, Juliana Horowitz, Anna Brown, and Tanya Arditi. 2022. Americans Complex Views on Gender Identity and Transgender Issues. Pew Research Center Report. Accessed from www.pewresearch.org/social-trends/wp-content/uploads/sites/3/2022/06/PSDT_06.28.22_GenderID_fullreport.pdf.

Parrillo, Vincent N. and Christopher Donoghue. 2005. "Updating the Bogardus Social Distance Studies: A New National Survey." *Social Science Journal* 42: 257–271.

Parrillo, Vincent N. and Christopher Donoghue. 2013. "The National Social Distance Scale: Ten Years Later." *Sociological Forum* 28:597–615.

Parsons, Talcott. 1951. *The Social System*. Glencoe, IL: Free Press.

Pascoe, C. J. 2007. *Dude You're a Fag: Masculinity and Sexuality in High School*. Berkeley: University of California Press.

Patchin, Justin W. and Sameer Hinduja. 2011. "Traditional and Nontraditional Bullying among Youth: A Test of General Strain Theory." *Youth & Society* 43: 727–751.

Paules, Greta Foff. 1991. *Dishing It Out: Power and Resistance among Waitresses in a New Jersey Restaurant*. Philadelphia: Temple University Press.

Paxton, Pamela. 2007. "Association Memberships and Generalized Trust: A Multilevel Model across 31 Countries." *Social Forces* 86:47–76.

Paxton, Pamela, Kristopher Velasco, and Robert W. Ressler. 2020. "Does Use of Emotion Increase Donations and Volunteers for Nonprofits?" *American Sociological Review* 85:1051–1083.

Pearlin, Leonard I. 1989. "The Sociological Study of Stress." *Journal of Health and Social Behavior* 30:240–256.

———. 1999. "The Stress Process Revisited: Reflections on Concepts and

Their Interrelationships." Pp. 395–415 in *Handbook of the Sociology of Mental Health*, edited by Carol S. Aneshensel and Jo C. Phelan. New York: Plenum.

Pearlin, Leonard I. and Allen J. LeBlanc. 2001. "Bereavement and the Loss of Mattering." Pp. 285–300 in *Extending Self-Esteem Theory and Research*, edited by N. Goodman, T. Owens, and S. Stryker. Cambridge, UK: Oxford University Press.

Pearlin, Leonard I., Elizabeth G. Menaghan, Morton A. Lieberman, and Joseph T. Mullan. 1981. "The Stress Process." *Journal of Health and Social Behavior* 22:337–356.

Pearlin, Leonard I. and Carmi Schooler. 1978. "The Structure of Coping." *Journal of Health and Social Behavior* 19:2–21.

Peng, Yusheng. 2010. "When Formal Laws and Informal Norms Collide: Lineage Networks versus Birth Control Policy in China." *American Journal of Sociology* 116:770–805.

Peräkylä, Anssi, Liisa Voutilainen, Maarit Lehtinen and Mariel Wuolio. 2022. "From Engagement to Disengagement in the a Psychiatric Assessment Process." *Symbolic Interaction* 45:257–296.

Percheski, Christine. 2008. "Opting Out? Differences in Professional Women's Employment Rates from 1960 to 2005." *American Sociological Review* 73:497–517.

Perinbanayagam, Robert. 2012. *Identity's Moments: The Self in Action and Interaction*. Lanham, MD: Lexington Books.

———. 2014. *Varieties of the Gaming Experience*. Piscataway, NJ: Transaction Publishers.

———. 2016. *The Rhetoric of Emotions: A Dramatist Exploration*. London and New York: Routledge.

Perry, Brea L., Erin L. Pullen, and Carrie B. Oser. 2012. "Too Much of a Good Thing? Psychosocial Resources, Gendered Racism, and Suicidal Ideation among Low Socioeconomic Status African American Women." *Social Psychology Quarterly* 75: 334–359.

Perry, Pamela. 2007. "White Universal Identity as a 'Sense of Group Position.'" *Symbolic Interaction* 30:375–393.

Pescosolido, Bernice A., Brea L. Perry, J. Scott Long, Jack K. Martin, John I. Nurnberger, Jr., and Victor Hesselbrock. 2008. "Under the Influence of Genetics: How Transdisciplinarity Leads Us to Rethink Social Pathways to Illness." *American Journal of Sociology* 114:171–201.

Peterson, Jean Treloggen. 1993. "Generalized Extended Family Exchange: A Case from the Philippines." *Journal of Marriage and the Family* 55:570–584.

Peterson, Trond and Laurie A. Morgan. 1995. "Separate and Unequal: Occupation-Establishment Sex Segregation and the Gender Wage Gap." *American Journal of Sociology* 101:329–365.

Petts, Richard J. 2009. "Family and Religious Characteristics' Influence on Delinquency Trajectories from Adolescence to Young Adulthood." *American Sociological Review* 74:465–483.

Pew Research Center. 2012. *American Exceptionalism Subsides: The American– Western European Values Gap*. Pew Research Center report. http://www.pewglobal. org/2011/11/17/the-american-western-european-values-gap/?src=prc-headline

Pew Research Center. 2015. "Parenting in America: The American Family Today." www.pewresearch.org/social-trends/2015/12/17/1-the-american-family-today.

Pew Research Center. 2017. "Americans Express Increasingly Warm Feelings Toward Religious Groups." www.pewresearch.org/religion/wp-content/uploads/sites/7/2017/02/Feeling-thermometer-report-FOR-WEB.pdf

Pew Research Center. 2021. "Most Americans Favor the Death Penalty Despite Concerns About Its Administration." www.pewresearch.org/politics/2021/06/02/most-americans-favor-the-death-penalty-despite-concerns-about-its-administration.

Pew Research Center. 2024. "Mobile Fact Sheet." www.pewresearch.org/internet/fact-sheet/mobile.

Pfaffendorf, Jessica. 2019. "Wayward Elites: From Social Reproduction to Social Restoration in a Therapeutic Boarding School." *Social Psychology Quarterly* 82: 113–133.

Pfeffer, Jeffrey. 1993. *Managing with Power: Politics and Influence in Organizations.* Cambridge, MA: Harvard Business School.

Pfohl, Stephen J. 1985. *Images of Deviance and Social Control: A Sociological History.* New York: McGraw-Hill.

Phelan, Jo C., Bruce G. Link, Ann Stueve, and Bernice A. Pescosolido. 2000. "Public Conceptions of Mental Illness in 1950 and 1996: What Is Mental Illness and Is It to Be Feared?" *Journal of Health and Social Behavior* 41:188–207.

Piliavin, Jane Allyn. 2009. "Altruism and Helping: The Evolution of a Field: The 2008 Cooley-Mead Presentation." *Social Psychology Quarterly* 72:209–225.

Pines, Ayala Malach, Margaret B. Neal, Leslie B. Hammer, and Tamar Icekson. 2011. "Job Burnout and Couple Burnout in Dual-Earner Couples in the Sandwiched Generation" *Social Psychology Quarterly* 74:361–386.

Pink, Sarah and Jennie Morgan. 2013. "Short-Term Ethnography: Intense Routes to Knowing." *Symbolic Interaction* 36: 351–361.

Piquero, Nicole Leeper, Angela R. Gover, John M. Macdonald, and Alex R. Piquero. 2005. "The Influence of Delinquent Peers on Delinquency: Does Gender Matter?" *Youth & Society* 36:251–275.

Pollack, Lauren Harte and Peggy A. Thoits. 1989. "Processes in Emotional Socialization." *Social Psychology Quarterly* 52:22–34.

Polletta, Francesca. 2006. *It Was Like a Fever: Storytelling in Protest and Politics.* Chicago: University of Chicago Press.

Polletta, Francesca and James M. Jasper. 2001. "Collective Identity and Social Movements." *Annual Review of Sociology* 27:283–305.

Pollock, Mica. 2004. *Colormute: Race Talk Dilemmas in an American School.* Princeton, NJ: Princeton University Press.

Porter, Judith R. and Robert E. Washington. 1993. "Minority Identity and Self-Esteem." *Annual Review of Sociology* 19: 139–161.

Potter, Hillary (ed.). 2007. *Racing the Storm: Racial Implications and Lessons Learned from Hurricane Katrina.* Lanham, MD: Lexington Books.

Potter, J. 2015. *Crisis at Work: Identity and the End of the Career.* London: Macmillan.

Poulson, Stephen C., Timothy J. Carter, and Daniel M. Crowley. 2017. "Cooperative

Accounts: Avoiding Conflict and Repairing Social Relations." *Symbolic Interaction* 41:143–164.

Powell, Brian, Catherine Bolzendahl, Claudia Geist, and Lala Carr Steelman. 2010. *Counted Out: Same-Sex Relations and Americans' Definitions of Family*. New York: Russell Sage Foundation.

Powell, Brian and Douglas B. Downey. 1997. "Living in Single-Parent Households: An Investigation of the Same-Sex Hypothesis." *American Sociological Review* 62: 521–539.

Prager, Jeffrey. 2006. "Beneath the Surface of the Self: Psychoanalysis and the Unseen Known." *American Journal of Sociology* 112:276–290.

Presser, Lois. 2008. *Been a Heavy Lifter: Stories of Violent Men*. Urbana, IL: University of Illinois Press.

Price, Paul-Jahi Christopher. 2005. *Social Control at Opportunity Boys' Home: How Staff Control Juvenile Inmates*. New York: University Press of America.

Price, Taylor. 2020. "Cognition in Situations." *Symbolic Interaction* 43: 692–720.

Prince, Samuel Henry. 1920. *Catastrophe and Social Change*. New York: Columbia University Press.

Pruit, John C. 2019. *Between Teaching and Caring in the Preschool: Talk, Interaction, and the Preschool Teacher Identity*. Lanham, MD: Lexington Books.

Prissé, Benjamin, and Diego Jorrat. 2022. "Lab vs Online Experiments: No Differences." *Journal of Behavioral and Experimental Economics* 100:1–8.

Puddephatt, Antony J., William Shaffir, and Steven W. Kleinknecht (eds.). 2009. *Ethnographies Revisited: Constructing Theory in the Field*. New York: Routledge.

Pugh, Allison. 2009. *Longing and Belonging: Parents, Children, and Consumer Culture*. Berkeley, CA: University of California Press.

Pugh, Meredith D. and Ralph Wahrman. 1983. "Neutralizing Sexism in Mixed-Sex Groups: Do Women Have to Be Better than Men?" *American Journal of Sociology* 88:746–762.

Pugliesi, Karen and Scott L. Shook. 1998. "Gender, Ethnicity, and Network Characteristics: Variation in Social Support Resources." *Sex Roles* 38:215–238.

Putnam, Robert D. 2000. *Bowling Alone: The Collapse and Revival of American Community*. New York: Simon & Schuster.

Quillian, Lincoln. 2008. "Does Unconscious Racism Exist?" *Social Psychology Quarterly* 71:6–11.

Quillian, Lincoln and Devah Pager. 2010. "Estimating Risk: Two on Race." *Social Psychology Quarterly* 73:79–104.

Raden, David. 1985. "Strength-Related Attitude Dimensions." *Social Psychology Quarterly* 48:312–330.

Radloff, Lenore S. 1977. "The CES-D Scale: A Self-Report Depression Scale for Research in the General Population." *Applied Psychological Measurement* 1: 385–401.

Rainie, Lee and Barry Wellman. 2014. *Networked: The New Social Operating System*. Cambridge, MA and London: The MIT Press.

Raisborough, Jayne. 2011. *Lifestyle Media and the Formation of the Self*. Hampshire, UK: Palgrave Macmillan.

Randall, Nancy Horak and Spencer Delbridge. 2005. "Social Distance in an Ethnically Fluid Community." *Sociological Spectrum* 25: 103–122.

Rane, Thomas R. and Brent A. McBride. 2000. "Identity Theory as a Guide to Understanding Fathers' Involvement with Their Children." *Journal of Family Issues* 21:347–366.

Rashotte, Lisa Slattery. 2002. "What Does That Smile Mean? The Meaning of Nonverbal Behaviors in Social Interaction." *Social Psychology Quarterly* 65:92–102.

Raudenbush, Danielle T. 2012. "Race and Interactions on Public Transportation: Social Cohesion and the Production of Common Norms and the Collective Black Identity." *Symbolic Interaction* 35: 456–473.

Raudenbush, Stephen W. and Anthony S. Bryk. 2002. *Hierarchical Linear Models: Applications and Data Analysis Methods*. Thousand Oaks, CA: Sage.

Rawls, Anne Warfield and Waverly Duck. 2020. *Tacit Racism*. Chicago: Chicago University.

Ray, Victor. 2019. "A Theory of Racialized Organizations." *American Sociological Review* 84:26–53.

Raymond, Chase Wesley and Anne Elizabeth Clark White. 2017. "Time Reference in the Service of Social Action." Social *Psychology Quarterly* 80:109–131.

Read, Jen'nan Ghazal and Sharon Oselin. 2008. "Gender and the Education–Employment Paradox in Ethnic and Religious Contexts: The Case of Arab Americans." *American Sociological Review* 73: 296–313.

Ream, Robert Ketner. 2005. *Uprooting Children: Mobility, Social Capital, and Mexican American Underachievement*. New York: LFB Scholarly Publishing.

Reay, Diane, Miriam E. David, and Stephen Ball. 2005. *Degrees of Choice: Social Class, Race, and Gender in Higher Education*. North Sterling, VA: Trentham Books.

Reevy, Gretchen M. and Christina Maslach. 2001. "Use of Social Support: Gender and Personality Differences." *Sex Roles* 44: 437–459.

Reger, Jo, Daniel J. Myers, and Rachel L. Einwohner (eds.). 2008. *Identity Work in Social Movements*. Minneapolis, MN: University of Minnesota Press.

Regnerus, Mark and Jeremy Uecker. 2011. *Premarital Sex in America: How Young Americans Meet, Mate, and Think about Marrying*. New York: Oxford University Press.

Reich, Jennifer A. 2010. "Children's Challenges to Efforts to Save Them: Competing Knowledges in the Child Welfare System." *Symbolic Interaction* 33: 412–434.

Reich, Jennifer A. 2016. *Calling the Shots: Why Parents Reject Vaccines*. New York: NYU Press.

Renshaw, Scott W. 2006. "Postmodern Swing Dance and Secondary Adjustment: Identity as Process." *Symbolic Interaction* 29:83–94.

Reynolds, John R., Stephanie Woodham Burge, Cheryl L. Robbins, Emily M. Boyd, and Brandy Harris. 2007. "Mastery and the Fulfillment of Occupational Expectations in Midlife." *Social Psychology Quarterly* 70:366–383.

Reynolds, Larry T. 2003. "Intellectual Precursors." Pp. 39–58 in *Handbook of Symbolic Interactionism*, edited by L. T. Reynolds and N. J. Herman-Kinney. Lanham, MD: Rowman & Littlefield.

Reynolds, Larry T. and Nancy J. Herman-Kinney (eds.). 2003. *Handbook of Symbolic Interactionism*. Lanham, MD: Rowman & Littlefield.

Rickard, Diana. 2016. *Sex Offenders, Stigma, and Social Control*. New Brunswick, NJ: Rutgers University Press.

Ridgeway, Cecilia L. 1982. "Status in Groups: The Importance of Motivation." *American Sociological Review* 47:76–88.

———. 2001. "Gender, Status, and Leadership." *Journal of Social Issues* 57: 637–655.

Ridgeway, Cecilia L. and James W. Balkwell. 1997. "Group Processes and the Diffusion of Status Beliefs." *Social Psychology Quarterly* 60:14–31.

Ridgeway, Cecilia L. and Joseph Berger. 1986. "Expectations, Legitimation, and Dominance Behavior in Task Groups." *American Sociological Review* 51:603–617.

Ridgeway, Cecilia L. and David Diekema. 1989. "Dominance and Collective Hierarchy Formation in Male and Female Task Groups." *American Sociological Review* 54:79–93.

Ridgeway, Cecilia L. and Cathryn Johnson. 1990. "What Is the Relationship between Socioemotional Behavior and Status in Task Groups?" *American Journal of Sociology* 95:1189–1212.

Ridgeway, Cecilia L., Kathy J. Kuipers, Elizabeth Heger Boyle, and Dawn T. Robinson. 1998. "How Do Status Beliefs Develop? The Role of Resources and Interactional Experience." *American Sociological Review* 63:331–350.

Ridgeway, Cecilia L., Yan E. Li, Kristan G. Erickson, Kristen Backor, and Justine E. Tinkler. 2009. "How Easily Does a Social Difference Become a Status Distinction? Gender Matters." *American Sociological Review* 74:44–62.

Ridgeway, Cecilia L. and Sandra Nakagawa. 2017. "Is Deference the Price of Being Seen as Reasonable? How Status Hierarchies Incentivize Acceptance of Low Status." *Social Psychology Quarterly* 80:132–152.

Ridolfo, Heather, Amy Baxter, and Jeffrey W. Lucas. 2010. "Social Influences on Paranormal Belief: Popular versus Scientific Support." *Current Research in Social Psychology* 15:33–41.

Ridolfo, Heather, Valerie Chepp, and Melissa A. Milkie. 2013. "Race and Girls' Self-Evaluations: How Mothering Matters." *Sex Roles* 68:496–509.

Ritter, Lacey J. and Koji Ueno. 2017. "Construction and Management of Stigma Based on a Voluntary-Achieved Status." *Symbolic Interaction* 40:541–560.

Ritzer, George. 1993. *The McDonaldization of Society: An Investigation into the Changing Character of Contemporary Social Life*. Newbury Park, CA: Pine Forge Press.

———. 1996. *Sociological Theory*. New York: McGraw-Hill.

Rivera, Lauren A. 2012. "Hiring as Cultural Matching: The Case of Elite Professional Service Firms." *American Sociological Review* 77:999–1022.

Rivera, Lauren A., and András Tilcsik. 2019. "Scaling Down Inequality: Rating Scales, Gender Bias, and the Architecture of Evaluation." *American Sociological Review* 84:248–274.

Robins, Lee N., B. Z. Locke, and Darrel A. Regier. 1991. "An Overview of Psychiatric Disorders in America." Pp. 328–366 in *Psychiatric Disorders in America*, edited by L. N. Robins and D. A. Regier. New York: Free Press.

Robinson, Dawn. 2007. "Introduction of Lynn Smith-Lovin: Recipient of the 2006 Cooley-Mead Award." *Social Psychology Quarterly* 70:103–105.

Robinson, John P. and Geoffrey Godbey. 1997. *Time for Life: Surprising Ways Americans Use Their Time*. University Park, PA: Pennsylvania State University Press.

Robison, Jennifer. 2003. "Social Classes in U.S., Britain, and Canada." Gallup poll. Washington, DC: Gallup Organization.

Roehrkasse, Alexander F. 2021. "Race, Poverty, and U.S. Children's Exposure to Neighborhood Incarceration." *Socius* 7. https://doi.org/10.1177/23780231211067871

Rodriquez, Jason. 2009. "Attributions of Agency and the Construction of Moral Order: Dementia, Death, and Dignity in Nursing-Home Care." *Social Psychology Quarterly* 72:165–179.

Roehrkasse, Alexander F. 2021. "Race, Poverty, and U.S. Children's Exposure to Neighborhood Incarceration." *Socius* 7.

Rogalin, Christabel L. and Shirley A. Keeton. 2011. "Does 1 + 1 = 3? Combining Disparate Identity Meanings." *Current Research in Social Psychology* 16:1–11.

Rohall, David E., Morten G. Ender, and Michael D. Matthews. 2006. "The Effects of Military Affiliation, Sex, and Political Ideology on Attitudes toward the Wars in Afghanistan and Iraq." *Armed Forces and Society* 33:59–77.

Rohall, David E., V. Lee Hamilton, David R. Segal, and Mady W. Segal. 2001. "Downsizing the Russian Army: Quality of Life and Mental Health." *Journal of Political and Military Sociology* 29:73–91.

Rohlinger, Deana A. and David A. Snow. 2003. "Social Psychological Perspectives on Crowds and Social Movements." Pp. 503–528 in *Handbook of Symbolic Interactionism*, edited by L. T. Reynolds and N. J. Herman-Kinney. Lanham, MD: Rowman & Littlefield.

Roschelle, Anne R. and Peter Kaufman. 2004. "Fitting In and Fighting Back: Stigma Management Strategies among Homeless Kids." *Symbolic Interaction* 21:23–46.

Rosenberg, Morris. 1986. *Conceiving the Self*. Malabar, FL: Krieger.

———. 1990. "Reflexivity and Emotion." *Social Psychology Quarterly* 53:3–12.

Rosenberg, Morris and B. Claire McCullough. 1981. "Mattering: Inferred Significance and Mental Health among Adolescents." *Research in Community and Mental Health* 2:163–182.

Rosenberg, Morris and Leonard I. Pearlin. 1978. "Social Class and Self-Esteem among Children and Adults." *American Journal of Sociology* 84:53–78.

Rosenberg, Morris, Carmi Schooler, and Carrie Schoenbach. 1989. "Self-Esteem and Adolescent Problems: Modeling Reciprocal Effects." *American Sociological Review* 54:1004–1018.

Rosenfeld, Michael J. 2007. *The Age of Independence: Interracial Unions, Same-Sex*

Unions and the Changing American Family. Cambridge, MA: Harvard University Press.

Rosenfeld, Michael J. and Reuben J. Thomas. 2012. "Searching for a Mate: The Rise of the Internet as a Social Intermediary." *American Sociological Review* 77:523–547.

Rosenfield, Sarah. 1997. "Labeling Mental Illness: The Effects of Received Services and Perceived Stigma on Life Satisfaction." *American Sociological Review* 62: 660–672.

Rosenthal, Robert and Lenore Jacobson. 1968. *Pygmalion in the Classroom: Teacher Expectation and Pupils' Intellectual Development*. New York: Holt, Rinehart and Winston.

Ross, Catherine E. and John Mirowsky. 2008. "Age and the Balance of Emotions." *Social Science and Medicine* 66:2391–2400.

Rossi, Giovanni and Tanya Stivers. 2020. "Category-Sensitive Actions in Interaction." *Social Psychology Quarterly* 84:49–74.

Roy, William G. 2010. *Reds, Whites, and Blues: Social Movements, Folk Music, and Race in the United States*. Princeton, NJ: Princeton University Press.

Russell, Bertrand. 1938. *Power: A New Social Analysis*. New York: W. W. Norton.

Rysavy, Dan. 2003. "Social Distance toward the Roma: The Case of University Students." *Sociologicky Casopis* 39:55–77.

Saad, Lydia. 2009. "'Conservatives' Are Single-Largest Ideological Group." Gallup poll. Washington, DC: Gallup Organization.

———. 2010. "Four Moral Issues Sharply Divide Americans." Gallup poll. Washington, DC: Gallup Organization.

———. 2022. "U.S. Political Ideology Steady; Conservatives, Moderates Tie." *The Gallup Organization*. Washington, DC.

Sacks, Oliver. 1985. *The Man Who Mistook His Wife for a Hat and Other Clinical Tales*. New York: Summit Books.

Saeed, Amir. 2007. "Media, Racism and Islamophobia: The Representation of Islam and Muslims in the Media." *Sociology Compass* 1:443–462.

Sampson, Robert J. and W. Byron Groves. 1989. "Community Structure and Crime: Testing Social-Disorganization Theory." *American Journal of Sociology* 94:774–802.

Sampson, Robert J. and John H. Laub. 1990. "Crime and Deviance over the Life Course: The Salience of Adult Social Bonds." *American Sociological Review* 55:609–627.

———. 1996. "Socioeconomic Achievement in the Life Course of Disadvantaged Men: Military Service as a Turning Point, Circa 1940–1965." *American Sociological Review* 61:347–367.

Santuzzi, Alecia M., Patricia L. Metzger, and Janet B. Ruscher. 2006. "Body Image and Expected Future Interaction." *Current Research in Social Psychology* 11:1–19.

Sarason, I. G., G. R. Pierce, and B. R. Sarason. 1994. "General and Specific Perceptions of Social Support." Pp. 151–177 in *Stress and Mental Health: Contemporary Issues and Prospects for the Future*, edited by W. R. Avison and I. H. Gottlib. Plenum Series on Stress and Coping. New York: Plenum.

Sauder, Michael. 2005. "Symbols and Contexts: An Interactionist Approach to the Study of Social Status." *The Sociological Quarterly* 46:279–298.

Sawyer, R. Keith. 2019. "Dialogic Status in Design Education: Authority and Peer Relations in Environment." *Social Psychology Quarterly* 82: 407–430.

Schafer, Markus H. and Kenneth F. Ferraro. 2011. "The Stigma of Obesity: Does Perceived Weight Discrimination Affect Identity and Physical Health?" *Social Psychology Quarterly* 74:76–97.

Schafer, Markus H. and Laura Upenieks. 2016. "The Age-Graded Nature of Advice: Distributional Patterns and Implications for Life Meaning." *Social Psychology Quarterly* 79:22–43.

Scheff, Thomas J. 1990. *Microsociology: Discourse, Emotion, and Social Structure*. Chicago: University of Chicago Press.

———. 1999. *Being Mentally Ill: A Sociological Theory*. New York: Aldine de Gruyter.

———. 2006. *Goffman Unbound! A New Paradigm for Social Science*. Boulder, CO: Paradigm Publishers.

———. 2011. *What's Love Got to Do with It? Emotions and Relationships in Popular Songs*. Boulder, CO: Paradigm Publishers.

———. 2011. "Goffman on Emotions: The Pride/Shame System." *Symbolic Interaction* 37:108–121.

Scheibling, Casey. 2020. "Doing Fatherhood Online: Men's Parental Identities, Experiences, and Ideologies on Social Media." *Symbolic Interaction* 43:472–492.

Schieman, Scott and Leonard I. Pearlin. 2006. "Neighboring Disadvantage, Social Comparisons, and the Subjective Assessment of Ambient Problems among Older Adults." *Social Psychology Quarterly* 69: 253–269.

Schieman, Scott, Tetyana Pudrovska, and Melissa A. Milkie. 2005. "The Sense of Divine Control and the Self-Concept: A Study of Race Differences in Later Life." *Research on Aging* 27:165–196.

Schieman, Scott and John Taylor. 2001. "Statuses, Roles, and the Sense of Mattering." *Sociological Perspectives* 44:469–484.

Schilke, Oliver, and Gabriel Rossman. 2018. "It's Only Wrong if it's Transactional: Moral Perceptions of Obfuscated Exchange." *American Sociological Review* 83:1079–1107.

Schneider, Christopher J. 2016. *Policing and Social Media: Social Control in an Era of New Media*. Lanheim, MA: Lexington Books.

Schneider, Simone M. and Peter Valet. 2017. "Relative Standards and Distributive Justice: How Social Comparison Orientiations Moderate the Link Between Relative Earnings and Justice Perceptions." *Social Psychology Quarterly* 80:276–287.

Schnittker, Jason. 2008. "Diagnosing Our National Disease: Trends in Income and Happiness, 1973 to 2004." *Social Psychology Quarterly* 71:257–280.

Schnittker, Jason. 2020. *The Diagnostic System: Why the Classification of Psychiatric Disorders Is Necessary, Difficult, and Never Settled*. New York: Columbia University Press.

Jason Schnittker. 2021. *Unnerved: Anxiety, Social Change, and the Transformation of Modern Mental Health*. New York: Columbia University Press.

Schooler, Carmi. 1976. "Serfdom's Legacy: An Ethnic Continuum." *American Journal of Sociology* 81:1265–1286.

Schooler, Carmi, Mesfin Samuel Mulatu, and Gary Oates. 2004. "Occupational Self-Direction, Intellectual Functioning, and Self-Directed Orientation in Older Workers: Findings and Implications for Individuals and Societies." *American Journal of Sociology* 110:161–197.

Schooler, Carmi and Gary Oates. 2001. "Self-Esteem and Work across the Life Course." Pp. 177–197 in *Extending Self-Esteem Theory and Research: Sociological and Psychological Currents*, edited by T. J. Owens, S. Stryker, and N. Goodman. Cambridge, MA: Cambridge University Press.

Schröder, Tobias, Jesse Hoey, and Kimberly B. Rogers. 2016. "Modeling Dynamic Identities and Uncertainty in Social Interactions: Bayesian Affect Control Theory." *American Sociological Review* 81: 828–855.

Schulz, Stefan. 2006. *Beyond Self-Control: Analysis and Critique of Gottfredson and Hirschi's General Theory of Crime*. Berlin: Duncker & Humblot.

Schuman, Howard. 1995. "Attitudes, Beliefs, and Behavior." Pp. 68–89 in *Sociological Perspectives on Social Psychology*, edited by K. S. Cook, G. A. Fine, and J. S. House. Boston: Allyn & Bacon.

———. 2008. *Method and Meaning in Polls and Surveys*. Cambridge, MA: Harvard University Press.

Schuman, Howard and Stanley Presser. 1980. "Public Opinion and Public Ignorance: The Fine Line between Attitudes and Nonattitudes." *American Journal of Sociology* 85:1214–1225.

Schur, Edwin M. 1971. *Labeling Deviant Behavior: Its Sociological Implications*. New York: Harper & Row.

Schussman, Alan and Sarah A. Soule. 2005. "Process and Protest: Accounting for Individual Protest Participation." *Social Forces* 84:1083–1108.

Schwalbe, Michael. 2008. *Rigging the Game: How Inequality Is Reproduced in Everyday Life*. New York: Oxford University Press.

Schwalbe, Michael. 2020. "The Spirit of Blumer's Method as a Guide to Sociological Discovery." *Symbolic Interaction* 43: 597–614.

Schwalbe, Michael L., Sandra Godwin, Daphne Holden, Douglas Schrock, Shealey Thompson, and M. Wolkomir. 2000. "Generic Processes in the Reproduction of Inequality: An Interactionist Analysis." *Social Forces* 79:419–452.

Schwalbe, Michael L. and Clifford L. Staples. 1991. "Gender Differences in Sources of Self-Esteem." *Social Psychology Quarterly* 54:158–168.

Schwartz, Barry. 2009. "Collective Forgetting and the Symbolic Power of Oneness: The Strange Apotheosis of Rosa Parks." *Social Psychology Quarterly* 72:123–142.

Schweingruber, David and Nancy Berns. 2003. "Doing Money Work in a Door-to-Door Sales Organization." *Symbolic Interaction* 26:447–471.

Scott, Susie. 2007. *Shyness and Society: The Illusion of Competence*. New York: Palgrave Macmillan.

———. 2015. *Negotiating Identity: Symbolic Interactionist Approaches to Social Identity*. Malden, MA: Polity Press.

Scott, Susie. 2019. *The Social Life of Nothing: Silence, Invisibility, and Emptiness in Tales of Lost Experiences*. New York: Routledge.

Scott, Susie. 2020. "The Unlived Life Is Worth Examining: Nothings and Nobodies behind the Scenes." *Symbolic Interaction* 43:156–180.

Scott, Susie, Tamsin Hinton-Smith, Vuokko Härmä, and Karl Broome. 2013. Goffman in the Gallery: Interactive Art and Visitor Shyness." *Symbolic Interaction* 36:417–438.

Scott, Wilbur J. 1990. "PTSD in DSM III: A Case in the Politics of Diagnosis and Disease." *Social Problems* 37:294–310.

Scott, Marvin B. and Stanford M. Lyman. 1968. "Accounts." *American Sociological Review* 33:46–62.

Seeger, Matthew W. and Timothy L. Sellnow. 2016. *Narratives of Crisis: Telling Stories of Ruin and Renewal*. Stanford, CA: Stanford University Press.

Seligman, Martin. 2002. *Authentic Happiness*. New York: Free Press.

Sell, Jane. 1997. "Gender, Strategies, and Contributions to Public Goods." *Social Psychology Quarterly* 60:252–265.

Semyonov, Moshe, Rebecca Raijman, and Anastasia Gorodzeisky. 2006. "The Rise of Anti-Foreigner Sentiment in European Societies, 1988–2000." *American Sociological Review* 71:426–449.

Sen, Ari and Dereka K. Bennett. September 2022. "Tracked: How Colleges use AI to Monitor Student Protests." *Dallas Morning News*. https://interactives.dallasnews.com/2022/social-sentinel.

Sendroiu, Ioana, Laura Upenieks, and Markus H. Schafer. 2021. "The Divergent Mental Health Effects of Dashed Expectations and Unfulfilled Aspirations: Evidence from American Lawyers' Careers." *Social Psychology Quarterly* 84:376–397.

Serido, Joyce, David M. Almeida, and Elaine Wethington. 2004. "Chronic Stressors and Daily Hassles: Unique and Interactive Relationships with Psychological Distress." *Journal of Health and Social Behavior* 45:17–33.

Serpe, Richard T. 1987. "Stability and Change in Self: A Structural Symbolic Interactionist Explanation." *Social Psychology Quarterly* 50:44–55.

Serpe, Richard T. and Sheldon Stryker. 1987. "The Construction of Self and the Reconstruction of Social Relationships." *Advances in Group Processes* 4:41–82.

———. 1993. "Prior Social Ties and Movement into New Relationships." *Advances in Group Processes* 10:283–304.

Sewell, William H., Robert M. Hauser, Kristen W. Springer, and Taissa S. Hauser. 2004. "As We Age: A Review of the Wisconsin Longitudinal Study, 1957–2001." *Research in Stratification and Mobility* 20:3–111.

Sgourev, Stoyan and Niek Althuizen. 2017. "Is It a Masterpiece? Social Construction and Objective Constraint in the Evaluation of Excellence." *Social Psychology Quarterly* 80:289–309.

Shackelford, Susan, Wendy Wood, and Stephen Worchel. 1996. "Behavioral Styles and the Influences of Women in Mixed-Sex Groups." *Social Psychology Quarterly* 59:284–293.

Shank, Daniel B., Alexander Burns, Sophia Rodriguez, and Madison Bowen. 2017. "Software Program, Bot, or Artificial Intelligence? Affective Sentiments across General Technology Labels." *Current Research in Social Psychology*. 28:32–41.

Sharkey, Patrick. 2006. "Navigating Dangerous Streets: The Sources and

Consequences of Street Efficacy." *American Sociological Review* 71:826–846.

———. 2008. "The Intergenerational Transmission of Context." *American Journal of Sociology* 113:931–969.

Sharp, Susan F., Toni L. Terling-Watt, Leslie A. Atkins, Jay Trace Gilliam, and Anna Sanders. 2001. "Purging Behavior in a Sample of College Females: A Research Note on General Strain Theory and Female Deviance." *Deviant Behavior* 22:171–188.

Shaw, Clifford and Henry McKay. 1942. *Juvenile Delinquency and Urban Areas*. Chicago: University of Chicago Press.

Sheperd, Hana R. and Nicole Stephens. 2010. "Using Culture to Explain Behavior: An Integrative Cultural Approach." *Social Psychology Quarterly* 73:353–354.

Sherif, Muzafer, O. J. Harvey, B. Jack White, William R. Hood, and Carolyn W. Sherif. 1988. *Intergroup Conflict and Cooperation: The Robbers Cave Experiment*. Middletown, CT: Wesleyan University Press.

Sherman, Rachel. 2007. *Class Acts: Service and Inequality in Luxury Hotels*. Berkeley, CA: University of California Press.

Shornack, Lawrence L. 1986. "Exchange Theory and the Family." *International Social Science Review* 61:51–60.

Shoshana, Avihu. 2020. "Love, Stigma, and Resistance: 'Therapeutic Microaggressions' in a Prisoners' Wives' Support Group." *Symbolic Interaction* 43: 102–125.

Shriver, Thomas E. and Dennis D. Waskul. 2006. "Managing the Uncertainties of Gulf War Illness: The Challenges of Living with Contested Illness." *Symbolic Interaction* 29:465–486.

Sigelman, Lee and Susan Welch. 1993. "The Contact Hypothesis Revisited: Black-White Interaction and Positive Racial Attitudes." *Social Forces* 71:781–795.

Silva, Jennifer. 2012. "Constructing Adulthood in an Age of Uncertainty." *American Sociological Review* 77:505–522

Silva, Eric O. and Matthew B. Flynn. "Liminal Stigma and Disaligning Activity: Online Comments about Trump's Family Separation Policy." *Symbolic Interaction* 43:126–155.

Silver, Laura. 2019. "Where Americns and Europeans Agree—and Differ—in the Values They See as Important. *Pew Research Center*. www.pewresearch.org/short-reads/2019/10/16/where-americans-and-europeans-agree-and-differ-in-the-values-they-see-as-important.

Silverstein, Martin. 2006. "Justice in Genderland: Through a Parole Looking Glass." *Symbolic Interaction* 29:393–410.

Simi, Pete, Kathleen Blee, Matthew DeMichele, and Steven Windisch. 2017. "Addicted to Hate: Identity Residual among Former White Supremacists." *American Sociological Review* 82:1167–1187.

Simmel, Georg. 1950. *The Sociology of Georg Simmel*, trans. K. H. Wolff. Glencoe, IL: Free Press.

———. 1978. *The Philosophy of Money*, trans. Tom Bottomore and David Frisby. London: Routledge.

Simon, Robin W. 2002. "Revisiting the Relationships among Gender, Marital Status, and Mental Health." *American Journal of Sociology* 107:1065–1096.

Simon, Robin W. 2020. "Gender, Emotions, and Mental Health in the United States: Patterns, Explanations, and

New Directions". *Society and Mental Health* 10:97–111.

Simon, Robin W. and Kathryn Lively. 2010. "Sex, Anger and Depression." *Social Forces* 88:1543–1568.

Simon, Robin W. and Leda E. Nath. 2004. "Gender and Emotion in the United States: Do Men and Women Differ in Self-Reports of Feelings and Expressive Behavior?" *American Journal of Sociology* 109: 1137–1176.

Simons, Ronald L., Yi-Fu Chen, Eric A. Stewart, and Gene H. Brody. 2003. "Incidents of Discrimination and Risk for Delinquency: A Longitudinal Test of Strain Theory with an African American Sample." *Justice Quarterly* 20:827–854.

Simons, Ronald L., Leslie Gordon Simons, and Lora Ebert Wallace. 2004. *Families, Delinquency, and Crime: Linking Society's Most Basic Institution to Antisocial Behavior*. Los Angeles, CA: Roxbury.

Simpson, Brent, Ashley Harrell, David Melamed, Nicholas Heiserman, and Daniela V. Negraia. 2018. "The Roots of Reciprocity: Gratitude and Reputation in Generalized Exchange Systems." *American Sociological Review* 83:88–110.

Simpson, Brent and Michael W. Macy. 2004. "Power, Identity, and Collective Action in Social Exchange." *Social Forces* 82:1373–1409.

Simpson, Brent and Robb Willer. 2008. "Altruism and Indirect Reciprocity: The Interaction of Person and Situation in Prosocial Behavior." *Social Psychology Quarterly* 71:37–52.

Simpson, Brent, Robb Willer, and Cecilia L. Ridgeway. 2012. "Status Hierarchies and the Organization of Collective Action." *Sociological Theory* 30: 149–166.

Simpson, Eyler Newton. 1998. "Edward A. Ross and the Social Forces." *Sociological Origins* 1:27–32.

Simpson, Ruth. 2009. *Men in Caring Occupations: Doing Gender Differently*. New York: Palgrave Macmillan.

Skaggs, Rachel. 2019. "Harmonizing Small-Group Cohesion and Status in Creative Collaborations: How Songwriters Facilitate and Manipulate the Cowriting Process." *Social Psychology Quarterly* 82:367–385.

Skatvedt, Astrid. 2017. "The Importance of "Empty Gestures" in Recovery: Being Human Together." *Symbolic Interaction* 40:396–413.

Sloan, Melissa M., Ranae J. Evenson Newhouse, and Ashley B. Thompson. 2013. "Counting on Coworkers: Race, Social Support, and Emotional Experiences on the Job." *Social Psychology Quarterly* 76: 343–372.

Small, Gary W., Michael W. Propper, Eugenia T. Randolph, and Eth Spencer. 1991. "Mass Hysteria among Student Performers: Social Relationship as a Symptom Predictor." *American Journal of Psychiatry* 148:1200–1205.

Small, Mario Luis. 2009. *Unanticipated Gains: The Origins of Network Inequality in Everyday Life*. New York: Oxford University Press.

Smelser, Neil. 2009. *The Odyssey Experience: Physical, Social, Psychological, and Spiritual Journeys*. Berkeley, CA: University of California Press.

Smirnova, Michelle. 2016. "I am a Cheerleader, but Secretly I Deal Drugs" Authenticity through Concealment and Disclosure." *Symbolic Interaction* 39: 26–44.

Smith, R. Tyson. 2008. "Passion Work: The Joint Production of Emotional Labor in Professional Wrestling." *Social Psychology Quarterly* 71:157–176.

Smith, Tom W. 1984. "The Polls: Gender and Attitudes toward Violence." *Public Opinion Quarterly* 48:384–396.

———. 1992. *Attitudes towards Sexual Permissiveness: Trends, Correlations, and Behavioral Connections*. Chicago: National Opinion Research Center.

Smith-Lovin, Lynn. 1992. "Joseph Berger: Recipient of the 1991 Cooley-Mead Award." *Social Psychology Quarterly* 55:1–2.

———. 1995. "The Sociology of Affect and Emotion." Pp. 118–148 in *Sociological Perspectives on Social Psychology*, edited by K. S. Cook, G. A. Fine, and J. S. H. House. Boston: Allyn & Bacon.

———. 1999. "Introduction of David R. Heise: Recipient of the 1998 Cooley-Mead Award." *Social Psychology Quarterly* 62: 1–3.

———. 2007. "The Strength of Weak Identities: Social Structural Resources, Situation, and Emotional Experience." *Social Psychology Quarterly* 70:106–124.

Smith-Lovin, Lynn and Linda D. Molm. 2000. "Introduction to the Millennium Special Issue on the State of Sociological Social Psychology." *Social Psychology Quarterly* 63:281–283.

Snow, David A. 2003. "Social Movements." Pp. 811–833 in *Handbook of Symbolic Interactionism*, edited by L. T. Reynolds and N. J. Herman-Kinney. Lanham, MD: Rowman & Littlefield.

Snow, David A. and Cynthia L. Phillips. 1982. "The Changing Self-Orientations of College Students: From Institutions to Impulse." *Social Science Quarterly* 63: 462–476.

Snow, David A., Sarah A. Soule, and Daniel M. Cress. 2005. "Identifying the Precipitants of Homeless Protest across 17 U.S. Cities, 1980– 1990." *Social Forces* 83:1183–1211.

Soule, Sarah A., Doug McAdam, John McCarthy, and Yang Su. 1999. "Protest Events: Cause or Consequence of State Action? The U.S. Women's Movement and Federal Congressional Activities, 1956–1979." *Mobilization* 4:239–255.

Sprecher, Susan. 2021. "Closeness and Other Affiliative Outcomes Generated from the Fast Friends Procedure: A Comparison with a Small-Talk Task and Unstructured Self-Disclosure and the Moderating Role of Mode of Communication." *Journal of Social and Personal Relationships* 38:1452–1471.

Stanovich, Keith E., Richard F. West, and Maggie E. Toplak. 2013. "Myside Bias, Rational Thinking, and Intelligence." *Current Directions in Psychological Science* 22:259–64.

Staples, Brent. 1995. *Parallel Time: Growing Up in Black and White*. New York: Pantheon.

Stark, Laura. 2012. *Behind Closed Doors*. Chicago: University of Chicago Press.

Stark, Tobias H. 2015. "Understanding the Selection Bias: Social Network Processes and the Effect of Prejudice on the Avoidance of Outgroup Friends." *Social Psychology Quarterly* 78:127–50.

Stasio, Valentina Di and Edvard N. Larsen. 2020. "The Racialized and Gendered Workplace: Applying an Intersectional Lens to a Field Experiment on Hiring Discrimination in Five European

Labor Markets." *Social Psychology Quarterly* 83:229–250.

Statham, Anne and Katherine Rhoades. 2001. "Gender and Self-Esteem." Pp. 255–284 in *Extending Self-Esteem Theory and Research: Sociological and Psychological Currents*, edited by T. J. Owens, S. Stryker, and N. Goodman. Cambridge, MA: Cambridge University Press.

Statista. 2023. "Opinions on Sex Between an Unmarried Man and Woman in the United States in 2022." www.statista.com/statistics/1367103/us-opinions-on-sex-before-marriage.

Adamovic, Mladen and Andreas Leibbrandt. 2021. "A Large-Scale Field Experiment on Occupational Gender Segregation and Hiring Discrimination." *Industrial Relations* 62:34–59.

Stearns, Carol Zisowitz and Peter N. Stearns. 1986. *Anger: The Struggle for Emotional Control in America's History*. Chicago: University of Chicago Press.

Steele, Claude M. and Joshua Aronson. 1995. "Stereotype Threat and the Intellectual Test Performance of African Americans." *Journal of Personality and Social Psychology* 69:797–811.

Steelman, Lala C., Brian Powell, Regina Werum, and Scott Carter. 2002. "Reconsidering the Effects of Sibling Configuration: Recent Advances and Challenges." *Annual Review of Sociology* 28:243–269.

Stein, Karen. 2011. "Getting Away from It All: The Construction and Management of Temporary Identities on Vacation." *Symbolic Interaction* 34:290–308.

Stern, Daniel N. 2004. *The Present Moment in Psychotherapy and Everyday Life*. New York: W. W. Norton.

Stets, Jan E. 2003. "Emotions and Sentiment." Pp. 309–338 in *Handbook of Social Psychology*, edited by J. Delamater. New York: Kluwer Academic/Plenum.

———. 2005 "Examining Emotions and Identity Theory." *Social Psychology Quarterly* 68:39–74.

———. 2006. "Identity Theory and Emotions." Pp. 203–223 in *Handbook of the Sociology of Emotions*, edited by Jan E. Stets and Jonathan H. Turner. New York: Springer.

———. 2021. "Micro, Meso, and Macro Processes in Identity Change: The 2020 Cooley-Mead Award Address. *Social Psychology Quarterly* 84:286–308.

Stets, Jan E. and Emily K. Asencio. 2008. "Consistency and Enhancement Processes in Understanding Emotions." *Social Forces* 86:1055–1078.

Stets, Jan E. and Chris Biga. 2003. "Bringing Identity Theory into Environmental Sociology." *Sociological Theory* 21: 398–423.

Stets, Jan E. and Peter J. Burke. 1996. "Gender, Control, and Interaction." *Social Psychology Quarterly* 59:193–220.

———. 2005. "New Directions in Identity Control Theory." *Advances in Group Processes* 22:43–64.

———. 2014 "Emotions and Identity Nonverification." *Social Psychology Quarterly* 77:387–410.

Stets, Jan E., Peter J. Burke and Scott V. Savage. 2018. "Exchange, Identity Verification, and Social Bonds." *Social Psychology Quarterly* 81:207–227.

Stets, Jen E. and Michael J. Carter. 2012. "A Theory of the Self for the Sociology of

Morality." *American Sociological Review* 77:120–140.

Stets, Jan E. and Alicia D. Cast. 2007. "Resources and Identity Verification from an Identity Theory Perspective." *Sociological Perspectives* 50:517–543.

Stets, Jan E. and Michael M. Harrod. 2004. "Verification across Multiple Identities: The Role of Status." *Social Psychology Quarterly* 67:155–171.

Stewart, Quincy T. and Jeffrey C. Dixon. 2010. "Is It Race, Immigrant Status, or Both? An Analysis of Wage Disparities among Men in the United States." *International Migration Review* 44:173–201.

Stewart, Simon. 2010. *Culture and the Middle Classes*. Surrey, UK: Ashgate.

Stingl, Alexander I. 2016. *The Digital Coloniality of Power: Epistemic Disobedience in the Social Sciences and the Legitimacy of the Digital Age*. Lanham, MD: Lexington Books.

Stivers, Tanya and Asifa Majid. 2007. "Questioning Children: Interactional Evidence of Implicit Bias in Medical Interviews." *Social Psychology Quarterly* 70:244–441.

Stokes, Jeffrey E. 2017. "Do 'His' and 'Her' Marriages Influence One Another? Contagion in Personal Assessments of Marital Quality among Older Spouses over a Four-Year Span." *Social Psychology Quarterly* 80:204–215.

Stoll, Julia. 2022. "Time Spent Watching Television in the U.S. 2019–2023." *Statista*. www.statista.com/statistics/186833/average-television-use-per-person-in-the-us-since-2002.

Stolte, John F. and Shanon Fender. 2007. "Framing Social Values: An Experimental Study of Culture and Cognition." *Social Psychology Quarterly* 70:59–69.

Strathdee, Robert. 2005. *Social Exclusion and the Remaking of Social Networks*. Burlington, VT: Ashgate.

Struber, Jenny M. 2011. *Inside the College Gates: How Class and Culture Matter in Higher Education*. Lanham, MD: Lexington Books.

Stryker, Sheldon. 1992. "Symbolic Interactionism: Themes and Variations." Pp. 3–29 in *Social Psychology: Sociological Perspectives*, edited by M. Rosenberg and R. H. Turner. New Brunswick, NJ: Transaction Publishers.

———. 2000. "Identity Competition: Key to Differential Social Movement Participation?" Pp. 21–39 in *Self, Identity, and Social Movements*, edited by Sheldon Stryker, Timothy J. Owens, and Robert W. White. Minneapolis, MN: University of Minnesota Press.

———. 2002. *Symbolic Interactionism: A Social Structural Version*. Caldwell, NJ: Blackburn.

Stryker, Sheldon and Peter J. Burke. 2000. "The Past, Present, and Future of an Identity Theory." *Social Psychology Quarterly* 63:284–297.

Stryker, Sheldon, Timothy J. Owens, and Robert W. White. 2000. "Social Psychology and Social Movements: Cloudy Past and Bright Future." Pp. 1–17 in *Self, Identity, and Social Movements*, edited by Sheldon Stryker, Timothy J. Owens, and Robert W. White. Minneapolis, MN: University of Minnesota Press.

Stryker, Sheldon and Richard T. Serpe. 1982. "Commitment, Identity Salience and Role Behavior: A Theory and

Research Example." Pp. 199–218 in *Personality, Roles, and Social Behavior*, edited by W. Ickes and E. S. Knowles. New York: Springer-Verlag.

Stryker, Sheldon and Kevin D. Vryan. 2003. "The Symbolic Interactionist Frame." Pp. 3–28 in *Handbook of Social Psychology*, edited by J. D. DeLamater. New York: Kluwer Academic/ Plenum.

Su, Peng and Mu He. 2024. "The Mediating Role of Loneliness in the Relationship between Smartphone Addiction and Subjective Well Being." *Scientific Reports* 14:4460.

Suarez, Alicia and Megan Bolton. 2018. "Catching Babies in Prohibition States: Midwives' Accounts for an Illegal Profession." *Symbolic Interaction* 41:165–184.

Sudman, Seymour, Norman M. Bradburn, and Norbert Schwarz. 1996. *Thinking about Answers: The Application of Cognitive Processes to Survey Methodology*. San Francisco: Jossey-Bass.

Sumartojo, Shanti and Sarah Pink. *Atmospheres and the Experiential World: Theory and Methods*. New York: Routledge.

Sumerau, J. E. 2017. *Cigarettes & Wine*. Rotterdam, The Netherlands: Sense Publishers.

Sumner, William Graham. 1906. *Folkways: A Study of Mores, Manners, Customs and Morals*. Mineola, NY: Dover Publications.

Summers-Effler, Erika. 2010. *Laughing Saints and Righteous Heroes: Emotional Rhythms in Social Movements*. Chicago: University of Chicago Press.

Sunshine, Jason and Tom Tyler. 2003. "Moral Solidarity, Identification with the Community, and Importance of Procedure Justice: The Police as Prototypical Representatives of a Group's Moral Values." *Social Psychology Quarterly* 66: 153–164.

Sutherland, Edwin H. 1940. "White Collar Criminality." *American Sociological Review* 5:1–12.

Sutherland, Edwin H. and Donald R. Cressey. 1999. "The Theory of Differential Association." Pp. 237–243 in *Theories of Deviance*, edited by S. H. Traub and C. B. Little. Itasca, IL: F. E. Peacock.

Sweeney, Joanne and Marilyn R. Bradbard. 1988. "Mothers' and Fathers' Changing Perceptions of Their Male and Female Infants over the Course of Pregnancy." *Journal of Genetic Psychology* 149:393–404.

Swidler, Ann. 2001. *Talk of Love: How Culture Matters*. Chicago: University of Chicago Press.

Swim, Janet K. and Laurie L. Cohen. 1997. "Overt, Covert, and Subtle Sexism." *Psychology of Women Quarterly* 21:103–118.

Szasz, Thomas S. 1968. "The Myth of Mental Illness." Pp. 222–281 in *The Social Control of Mental Illness*, edited by H. Silverstein. New York: Thomas Y. Crowell.

———. 1974. *The Myth of Mental Illness: Foundations of a Theory of Personal Conduct*. New York: Harper & Row.

———. 2003. "Cleansing the Modern Heart." *Society* 40:52–59.

Tajfel, Henri. 1982. "The Social Psychology of Interracial Relations." *Annual Review of Psychology* 33:1–39.

Tak, Elise, Shelley J. Correll, and Sarah A. Soule. 2019. "Gender Inequality in Product Markets: When and How Status Beliefs Transfer to Products." *Social Forces* 98:548–577.

Tannenbaum, Frank. 1938. *Crime and the Community*. Boston: Ginn and Company.

Tamir, Maya. 2021. "Effortful Emotion Regulation as a Unique Form of Cybernetic Control." *Perspectives on Psychological Science* 16:94–117.

Tavory, Iddo and Ann Swidler. 2009. "Condom Semiotics: Meaning and Condom Use in Rural Malawi." *American Sociological Review* 74:171–189.

Taylor, John and R. Jay Turner. 2001. "A Longitudinal Study of the Role and Significance of Mattering to Others for Depressive Symptoms." *Journal of Health and Social Behavior* 42:310–325.

Taylor, Lisa. 2008. *A Taste for Gardening: Classed and Gendered Practices*. Aldershot, UK: Ashgate.

Teeger, Chana and Vered Vinitzky-Seroussi. 2007. "Controlling for Consensus: Commemorating Apartheid in South Africa." *Symbolic Interaction* 30:57–78.

Tetlock, Philip E. and Gregory Mitchell. 2008. "Calibrating Prejudice in Milliseconds." *Social Psychology Quarterly* 71: 12–16.

Thoits, Peggy A. 1989. "The Sociology of Emotions." *Annual Review of Sociology* 15:317–342.

———. 1991. "On Merging Identity Theory and Stress Research." *Social Psychology Quarterly* 57:101–112.

———. 1995. "Identity-Relevant Events and Psychological Symptoms: A Cautionary Tale." *Journal of Health and Social Behavior* 36:72–82.

———. 2011. "Resisting the Stigma of Mental Illness." *Social Psychology Quarterly* 74:6–28.

———. 2012. "Role-Identity Salience, Purpose and Meaning in Life, and Well-Being among Volunteers." *Social Psychology Quarterly* 75:149–172.

———. 2013. "Volunteer Identity Salience, Role Enactment, and Well-Being: Comparisons of Three Salience Constructs." *Social Psychology Quarterly* 76: 373–398.

Thomas, George M., Henry Walker, and Morris Zelditch. 1986. "Legitimacy and Collective Action." *Social Forces* 65: 378–404.

Thomas, James M. 2015. *Working to Laugh: Assembling Differences in American Stand-Up Comedy Venues*. Boulder, CO: Lexington Books.

Thomas, W. I. 1966. "The Relation of Research to the Social Process." Pp. 289–330 in *W. I. Thomas on Social Organization and Social Personality*, edited by M. Janowitz. Chicago: University of Chicago Press.

Thomas, William I. and Dorothy Swaine Thomas. 1928. *The Child in America: Behavior Problems and Programs*. New York: Knopf.

Thomas, William I. and Florian Znaniecki. 1958. *The Polish Peasant in Europe and America*. New York: Dover.

Thomeer, Mieke Beth, Allen J. LeBlanc, David M. Frost, and Kayla Bowen. 2018. "Anticipatory Minority Stressors among Same-sex Couples: A Relationship Timeline Approach." *Social Psychology Quarterly* 81:126–148.

Thompson, Gregory. 2014. "Labelling in Interactional Practice: Applying Labeling Theory to Interactions and Interactional Analysis to Labeling." *Symbolic Interaction* 37:458–482.

Thorne, Barrie. 1993. *Gender Play: Girls and Boys in School*. New Brunswick, NJ: Rutgers University Press.

Thornton, Arland, William G. Axinn, and Yu Xie. 2007. *Marriage and Cohabitation*. Chicago: University of Chicago Press.

Thye, Shane R. 2000. "A Status Value Theory of Power in Exchange Relations." *American Sociological Review* 65: 477–508.

Thye, Shane R., Edward J. Lawler, and Jeongkoo Yoon. 2011. "The Emergence of Embedded Relations and Group Formation in Networks of Competition." *Social Psychology Quarterly* 74:387–413.

Tian, Xiaoli. 2017. "Embodied versus Disembodied Information: How Online Artifacts Influence Offline Interpersonal Interactions." *Symbolic Interaction* 40: 190–211.

Tifferet, Sigal. 2020. "Gender Differences in Social Support on Social Network Sites: A Meta-Analysis". *Cyberpsychology, Behavior, and Social Networking* 23: 199–209.

Tillmann, Lisa M. 2008. "Father's Blessing: Ethnographic Drama, Poetry, and Prose." *Symbolic Interaction* 631:376–399.

Tone, Andrea. 2009. *The Age of Anxiety: A History of America's Turbulent Affair with Tranquilizers*. New York: Basic Books.

Tonnies, Ferninand. 1957 (originally 1887). *Community and Society*. East Lansing Michigan: Michigan State University Press.

Torkelson, Jason. 2015. "Seeing (Transitions to) Adulthood in Youth (Sub)cultural Studies Through the Eyes of Straightedge Adherents." *Symbolic Interaction* 38:352–370.

Trettevik, Ryan. 2016. "Identities, Goals, and Emotions." Social Psychology Quarterly 79:263–283.

Tropp, Linda R., Dina G. Okamoto, Helen B. Marrow, and Michael Jones-Correa. 2018. "How Contact Experiences Shape Welcoming: Perspectives from U.S.-Born and Immigrant Groups." *Social Psychology Quarterly* 81:23–47.

Troyer, Lisa. 2001. "Effects of Protocol Differences on the Study of Status and Social Influence." *Current Research in Social Psychology* 6:182–204.

Tsushima, Teresa and Peter J. Burke. 1999. "Levels, Agency, and Control in the Parent Identity." *Social Psychology Quarterly* 62:173–189.

Turkle, Sherry. 2011. *Alone Together: Why We Expect More from Technology and Less from Each Other*. New York, NY: Basic Books.

Turner, Heather A. and Kathleen Kopiec. 2006. "Exposure to Interparental Conflict and Psychological Disorder among Young Adults." *Journal of Family Issues* 27:131–158.

Turner, Jonathan H. 2007a. *Human Emotions: A Sociological Theory*. New York: Routledge.

———. 2007b. "Self, Emotions, and Extreme Violence: Extending Symbolic Interactionist Theorizing." *Symbolic Interaction* 30:501–530.

———. 2011. "Extending the Symbolic Interactionist Theory of Interaction Processes: A Conceptual Outline." *Symbolic Interaction* 34:330–339.

Turner, Jonathan H. and Jan E. Stets. 2005. *The Sociology of Emotions*. Cambridge: Cambridge University Press.

———. 2006. "Moral Emotions." Pp. 544–566 in *Handbook of the Sociology of Emotions*, edited by Jan E. Stets and Jonathan H. Turner. New York: Springer.

Turner, Jonathan R. 2010. "Understanding Health Disparities: The Promise of the Stress Process Model." Pp 3–23 in *Advances in the Conceptualization of the Stress Process*. New York: Springer.

Turner, R. Jay and William Avison. 2003. "Variations in Stress Exposure: Implications for the Interpretation of Research on Race, Socioeconomic Status, and Gender." *Journal of Health and Social Behavior* 44:488–505.

Turner, R. Jay, Donald A. Lloyd, and Patricia Roszell. 1999. "Personal Resources and the Social Distribution of Depression." *American Journal of Community Psychology* 27:643–670.

Turner, R. Jay and Franco Marino. 1994. "Social Support and Social Structure: A Descriptive Epidemiology." *Journal of Health and Social Behavior* 35:193–212.

Turner, R. Jay and Patricia Roszell. 1994. "Psychosocial Resources and the Stress Process." Pp. 179–210 in *Stress and Mental Health: Contemporary Issues and Prospects for the Future*, edited by W. R. Avison and I. H. Gottlib. Plenum Series on Stress and Coping. New York: Plenum.

Turner, R. Jay, John Taylor, and Karen Van Gundy. 2004. "Personal Resources and Depression in the Transition to Adulthood: Ethnic Comparisons." *Journal of Health and Social Behavior* 45:34–52.

Turner, R. Jay, Blair Wheaton, and Donald A. Lloyd. 1995. "The Epidemiology of Social Stress." *American Sociological Review* 60:104–125.

Turner, Ralph H. and Lewis M. Killian. 1972. *Collective Behavior*. Englewood Cliffs, NJ: Prentice Hall.

Tuthill, Zelma Oyarvide. 2021. "The Intersection of Sexual and Racial/Ethnic Identity Centrality and Mental Well-Being among Black and Latinx Sexual Minority Adults." Social Psychology Quarterly 84: 331–352.

Twenge, Jean M., Jonathan Haidt, Andrew B. Blake, Cooper McAllister, Hannah Lemon, and Astrid Le Roy. 2021. "Worldwide Increases in Adolescent Loneliness." Journal of Adolescence 93: 257–269.

Twenge, Jean M., Brian H. Spitzberg and W. Keith Campbell. 2019. "Less in-Person Social Interaction with Peers among U.S. Adolescents in the 21st century and Links to Loneliness." *Journal of Social and Personal Relationships* 36: 1892–1913.

Twenge, Jean, Sara Konrath, Joshua Foster, W.Keith Campbell, and Brad J. Bushman. 2008. "Egos Inflating over Time: A Cross-Temporal Meta-Analysis of the Narcissistic Personality Inventory." *Journal of Personality* 76:875–902.

Ulbrich, Patricia M., George J. Warheit, and Rick S. Zimmerman. 1989. "Race, Socioeconomic Status, and Psychological Distress: An Examination of Differential Vulnerability." *Journal of Health and Social Behavior* 30:131–146.

Umberson, Debra, Meichu D. Chen, James S. House, Kristine Hopkins, and Ellen Slaten. 1996. "The Effect of Social Relationships on Psychological Well-Being: Are Men and Women Really So Different?" *American Sociological Review* 61:837–857.

Umberson, Debra, Camille B. Wortman, and Ronald C. Kessler. 1992. "Widowhood and Depression: Explaining Long-Term Gender Differences in Vulnerability." *Journal of Health and Social Behavior* 33: 10–24.

Unnever, James D. and Frances T. Cullen. 2007. "The Racial Divide in Support for the Death Penalty: Does White Racism Matter?" *Social Forces* 85:1281–1301.

Van Ausdale, Debra, and Joe R. Feagin. 2002. *The First R: How Children Learn Race and Racism*. Lanham, MD: Rowman & Littlefield.

van den Brink, Femke, Manja Vollmann, and Shane Weelie. 2020. "Relationships between Transgender Congruence, Gender Identity Rumination, and Self-Esteem in Transgender and Gender-Nonconforming Individuals." *Psychology of Sexual Orientation and Gender Diversity* 7: 230–235.

Van den Hoonaard, Will C. 2011. *The Seduction of Ethics: Transforming the Social Sciences*. Toronto: University of Toronto Press.

Van Dyke, Nella and Sarah A. Soule. 2002. "Structural Social Change and the Mobilizing Effects of Threat: Explaining Levels of Patriot and Militia Organizing in the United States." *Social Problems* 49:497–520.

Vannini, Phillip, Dennis Waskul, and Simon Gottschalk. 2011. *The Senses in Self, Society, and Culture: A Sociology of the Senses*. New York: Taylor and Francis Group.

Vargas, Robert. 2011. "Being in 'Bad' Company: Power Dependence and Status in Adolescent Susceptibility to Peer Influence." *Social Psychology Quarterly* 74:310–332.

Vasi, Ion Bogdan and Brayden G. King. 2012. "Social Movements, Risk Perceptions, and Economic Outcomes: The Effect of Primary and Secondary Stakeholder Activism on Firms' Perceived Environmental Risk and Financial Performance." *American Sociological Review* 77:573–596.

Verkuyten, Maykel, Jochem Thijs, and Hidde Bekhuis. 2010. "Intergroup Contact and Ingroup Reappraisal: Examining the Deprovincialization Thesis." *Social Psychology Quarterly* 73:398–416.

Vincent, James. 2016. "Twitter Taught Microsoft's AI Chatbot to be a Racist Asshole in Less than a Day." *The Verge*. www.theverge.com/2016/3/24/11297050/tay-microsoft-chatbot-racist.

Voci, Alberto, Miles Hewstone, Richard J. Crisp, and Mark Rubin. 2008. "Majority, Minority, and Parity: Effects of Gender and Group Size on Perceived Group Variability." *Social Psychology Quarterly* 71: 114–142.

Voydanoff, Patricia. 2007. *Work, Family, and Community: Exploring Interconnections*. Mahwah, NJ: Lawrence Erlbaum.

Wagner, David G. 1993. "The Labelling of Mental Illness as a Status Organizing Process." Pp. 51–68 in *Social Psychology of Groups: A Reader*, edited by E. J. Lawler and B. Markovsky. Greenwich, CT: JAI Press.

Wagner, David G. and Joseph Berger. 1993. "Status Characteristics Theory: The Growth of a Program." Pp. 23–63 in *Theoretical Research Programs: Studies in Theory Growth*, edited by J. Berger and

M. Zelditch, Jr. Stanford, CA: Stanford University Press.

———. 1997. "Gender and Interpersonal Task Behaviors: Status Expectation Accounts." *Sociological Perspectives* 40:1–32.

Wagner, Jascha, D'Janna Hamilton, Tammy L. Anderson, and Veronica F. Rempusheski, 2017. "Identity Work, Techniques of Neutralization, and Deviance: Exploring the Relationship Among Older Adult Gamblers." *Symbolic Interaction* 40: 352–377.

Wagner, Ulrich, Sarantis Tachtsoglou, Patrick Ferdinand Kotzur, Maria-Therese Friehs, and Uwe Kemmesies. 2020. "Proportion of Foreigners Negatively Predicts the Prevalence of Xenophobic Hate Crimes within German Districts." *Social Psychology Quarterly* 83:195–205.

Waite, Linda J. and Maggie Gallagher. 2000. *The Case for Marriage: Why Married People Are Happier, Healthier, and Better Off Financially*. New York: Doubleday.

Wajcman, Judy. 2015. *Pressed for Time: The Acceleration of Life in Digital Capitalism*. Chicago: University of Chicago Press.

Wajcman, Judy and Nigel Dodd. 2017. *The Sociology of Speed: Digital, Organizational, and Social Temporalities*. Oxford: Oxford University Press.

Walker, Lisa Slattery. 2019. "Controlling Status Effects of Gender." In *Advances in Group Processes*, 47–59. Bingley, United Kingdom: Emerald Publishing Limited.

Walker, Mark H. and Freda B. Lynn. 2013. "The Embedded Self: A Social Networks Approach to Identity Theory." *Social Psychology Quarterly* 76:151–179.

Walker, Edward T., Andrew W. Martin, and John D. McCarthy. 2008. "Confronting the State, the Corporation, and the Academy: The Influence of Institutional Targets on Social Movement Repertoires." *American Journal of Sociology* 114:35–76.

Walker, Henry A., George M. Thomas, and Morris Zelditch, Jr. 1986. "Legitimation, Endorsement, and Stability." *Social Forces* 64:620–643.

Wallace, Lora Ebert and Chason, Holly B. 2007. "Infant Feeding in the Modern World: Medicalization and the Maternal Body." *Sociological Spectrum* 27:405–438.

Walsh, Michael James and Shannon Jay Clark. 2019. "Co-Present Conversation as 'Socialized Trance': Talk, Involvement Obligations, and Smart-Phone Disruption." *Symbolic Interaction* 42:6–26.

Wang, Hua and Barry Wellman. 2010. "Social Connectivity in America: Changes in Adult Friendship Network Size from 2002 to 2007." *American Behavioral Scientist* 53:1148–1169.

Ward, Mark. 2014. "Tor's Visited Hidden Sites Host Child Abuse Images." *BBC News*. www.bbc.com/news/technology-30637010

Warren, John Robert, Robert M. Hauser, and Jennifer T. Sheridan. 2002. "Occupational Stratification across the Life Course: Evidence from the Wisconsin Longitudinal Study." *American Sociological Review* 67:432–455.

Waskul, Dennis D. and Phillip Vannini. 2008. "Smell, Odor, and Somatic Work: Sense-Making and Sensory Management." *Social Psychology Quarterly* 71:53–71.

Waskul, Dennis D. and Phillip Vannini. 2015. *Popular Culture as Everyday Life*. London: Routledge.

Wasserman, Jason Adam and Jeffrey Clair. 2009. *At Home on the Street: People, Poverty and a Hidden Culture of Homelessness*. Boulder, CO: Lynne Rienner Publishers.

Waters, Mary C. 1999. *Black Identities: West Indian Immigrant Dreams and American Realities*. Cambridge, MA: Harvard University Press.

Weber, Max. 1978. *In Economy and Society: An Outline of Interpretive Sociology*, edited by G. Roth and C. Wittich. Berkley, CA: University of California Press.

Webster, Murray, Jr. and James E. Driskell. 1978. "Status Generalization: A Review and Some New Data." *American Sociological Review* 43:220–236.

Webster, Murray, Jr. and Martha Foschi. 1988. *Status Generalization*. Stanford, CA: Stanford University Press.

Webster Jr, Murray, and Lisa Slattery Walker. 2022. "Status and Expectation Processes." In *Unequals: The Power of Status and Expectations in Our Social Lives*. Oxford University Press.

Webster, Murray, Jr. and Joseph M. Whitmeyer. 2002. "Modeling Second-Order Expectations." *Sociological Theory* 20:306–327.

Wei, Junhow. 2016. "I'm the Next American Idol": Cooling Out, Accounts, and Perseverance at Reality Talent Show Auditions." *Symbolic Interaction* 39:3–25.

Weinberg, Darin. 2005. *Of Others Inside: Insanity, Addiction, and Belonging in America*. Philadelphia, PA: Temple University Press.

Weinberg, Thomas S. and Staci Newmahr. 2015. *Selves, Symbols, and Sexualities: An Interactionist Anthology*. Los Angeles: Sage.

Weinfurt, Kevin P. and Fathali M. Moghaddam. 2001. "Culture and Social Distance: A Case Study of Methodological Cautions." *Journal of Social Psychology* 141: 101–110.

Weisz, Eva and Barry Kanpol. 1990. "Classrooms as Socialization Agents: The Three R's and Beyond." *Education* 111: 100–104.

Wen, Ming, Christopher R. Browning, and Kathleen A. Cagney. 2003. "Poverty, Affluence, and Income Inequality: Neighborhood Economic Structure and Its Implications for Health." *Social Science & Medicine* 57:843–860.

West, Candace and Sarah Fenstermaker. 1995. "Doing Difference." *Gender & Society* 9:8–37.

West, Candace and Don H. Zimmerman. 1987. "Doing Gender." *Gender & Society* 1:125–151.

Weston, Kath. 2008. *Traveling Light: On the Road with America's Poor.* Boston: Beacon Press.

Wilson, James Q. and George L. Kelling. 1982. "Broken Windows: The Police and Neighborhood Safety." *The Atlantic*. www.theatlantic.com/magazine/archive/1982/03/broken-windows/304465/ on March 27, 2023.

Whitham, Monica M. 2021. "Generalized Generosity: How the Norm of Generalized Reciprocity Bridges Collective Forms of Social Exchange." *American Sociological Review* 86:503–531.

Whyte, William Foote. 1993, originally 1943. *Street Corner Society: Social Structure of an Italian Slum*. Chicago: University of Chicago Press.

Wilde, Melissa J. 2001. "From Excommunicationto Nullification: Testing and Extending Supply-Side Theories of Religious Marketing with the Case of Catholic Marital Annulments." *Journal for the Scientific Study of Religion* 40:235–249.

Wiley, Norbert. 2016. *Inner Speech and the Dialogical Self*. Philadelphia, PA: Temple University Press.

Wilkinson, Sue and Celia Kitzinger. 2006. "Surprise as an Interactional Achievement: Reaction Tokens in Conversation." *Social Psychology Quarterly* 69: 150–182.

Willer, David G. and Travis Patton. 1987. "The Development of Network Exchange Theory." Pp. 199–242 in *Advances in Group Processes*, vol. 4, edited by E. J. Lawler and B. Markovsky. Greenwich, CT: JAI.

Willer, Robb. 2004. "The Effects of Government-Issued Terror Warnings on Presidential Approval Ratings." *Current Research in Social Psychology* 10:1–12.

———. 2009. "Groups Reward Individual Sacrifice: The Status Solution to the Collective Action Problem." *American Sociological Review* 74:23–43.

Willer, Robb, Ko Kuwabara, and Michael W. Macy. 2009. "The False Enforcement of Unpopular Norms." *American Journal of Sociology* 115:451–490.

Williams, David R., David T. Takeuchi, and Russell K. Adair. 1992. "Socioeconomic Status and Psychiatric Disorder among Blacks and Whites." *Social Forces* 71:179–194.

Williams, Kristi, Sharon Sassier, and Lisa M. Nicholson. 2008. "For Better or for Worse? The Consequences of Marriage and Cohabitation for Single Mothers." *Social Forces* 86:1481–1511.

Williams, Norma and Minerva Correa. 2003. "Race and Ethnic Relations." Pp. 743–760 in *Handbook of Symbolic Interactionism*, edited by L. T. Reynolds and N. J. Herman-Kinney. Lanham, MD: Rowman & Littlefield.

Wilson, Barbara J. 2008. "Media and Children's Aggression, Fear, and Altruism." *The Future of Children* 18:87–118.

Woehrle, Lynne M., Patrick Coy, and Gregory Maney. 2008. *Contesting Patriotism: Culture, Power, and Strategy in the Peace Movement*. Lanham, MD: Rowman & Littlefield.

Wolf, Alan. 1998. *One Nation After All*. New York: Penguin.

Wolfinger, Nicholas H. 2005. *Understanding the Divorce Cycle: The Children of Divorce in Their Own Marriages*. New York: Cambridge University Press.

Wood, Naaman and Susan Ward. 2010. "Stigma, Secrets, and the Human Condition: Seeking to Remedy Alienation in PostSecret's Digitally Mediated Environment." *Symbolic Interaction* 33:578–602.

Wouters, Cas. 2007. *Informalization: Manners and Emotions since 1890*. Thousand Oaks, CA: Sage.

Wright, Terence. 2010. *Visual Impact: Culture and the Meaning of Images*. Oxford, UK: Oxford University Press.

Wu, Zheng, Samuel Noh, Violet Kaspar, and Christoph M. Schimmele. 2003. "Race, Ethnicity, and Depression in Canadian Society." *Journal of Health and Social Behavior* 44:426–444.

Xu, Bin. 2019. "Intragenerational Variations in Autobiographical Memory: China's "Sent-Down Youth" Generation. *Social Psychology Quarterly* 82:134–157.

Yang, Yang. 2008. "Social Inequalities in Happiness in the United States, 1972 to 2004: An Age-Period-Cohort Analysis." *American Sociological Review* 73:204–226.

Yeh, Hsin-Yi. 2015. "Maintaining and Strengthening a Shaky Regime with Mnemonic Work: Inventing a Chinese National Day from 1949 Through 1987." *Symbolic Interaction* 38:22–41.

Yi, Zeng and Wu Deqing. 2000. "Regional Analysis of Divorce in China since 1980." *Demography* 37:215–219.

Yip, Tiffany. 2005. "Sources of Situational Variation in Ethnic Identity and Psychological Well-Being: A Palm Pilot Study of Chinese American Students." *Personality and Social Psychology Bulletin* 31:1603–1616.

Yodanis, Carrie. 2005. "Divorce Culture and Marital Gender Equality: A Cross-National Study." *Gender & Society* 19: 644–659.

Youngblood, Michael. 2016. *Cultivating Community: Interest, Identity, and Ambiguity in an Indian Social Movement*. Pasadena, CA: South Asian Studies Association.

Youngreen, Reef and Christopher D. Moore. 2008. "The Effects of Status Violations on Hierarchy and Influence in Groups." *Small Group Research* 39:569–587.

Yuan, Anastasia S. 2007. "Perceived Age Discrimination and Mental Health." *Social Forces* 86:291–311.

Zald, Mayer N. and Roberta Ash. 1964. "Social Movement Organizations: Growth, Decay, and Change." *Social Forces* 44: 327–341.

Zelditch, Morris, Jr. 2001. "Processes of Legitimation: Recent Developments and New Directions." *Social Psychology Quarterly* 64:4–17.

Zelizer, Viviana. 2005. *The Purchase of Intimacy*. Princeton, NJ: Princeton University Press.

———. 2011. *Economic Lives: How Culture Shapes the Economy*. Princeton, NJ: Princeton University Press.

Zelizer, Viviana and A. Rotman. 1985. *Pricing the Priceless Child: The Changing Social Value of Children*. New York: Basic Books.

Zerubavel, Eviatar. 1997. *Social Mindscapes: An Invitation to Cognitive Sociology*. Chicago: University of Chicago Press.

Zerubavel, Eviatar and Eliot R. Smith. 2010. "Transcending Cognitive Individualism." *Social Psychology Quarterly* 73: 321–325.

Zhao, Jun, Dawn T. Robinson, and Chyi-In Wu. 2020. "Isolation but Diffusion? A Structural Account of Depression Clustering among Adolescents." *Social Psychology Quarterly* 83:363–82.

Zhong, Bu, Yakun Huang, and Quian Liu. 2021. "Mental Health Toll from the Coronavirus: Social Media Usage Reviews Wuhan Residents' Depression and Secondary Trauma in the COVID-19 Outbreak." *Computers in Human Behavior* 114: 1–10.

Zurcher, Louis. 1970. "The 'Friendly' Poker Game: A Study of an Ephemeral Role." *Social Forces* 49:175–186.

Zurcher, Louis. 1977. *The Mutable Self*. Beverly Hills, CA: Sage.

———. 1982. "The Staging of Emotion." *Symbolic Interaction* 5:1–22.

INDEX

Note: Page numbers followed by italicized letters *f* or *t* indicate figures and tables respectively.